Mastering
Twentieth-Century Russian History

Palgrave Master Series

Accounting
Accounting Skills
Advanced English Language
Advanced English Literature
Advanced Pure Mathematics
Arabic
Basic Management
Biology
British Politics
Business Communication
Business Environment
C Programming
C++ Programming
Chemistry
COBOL Programming
Communication
Computing
Counselling Skills
Counselling Theory
Customer Relations
Database Design
Delphi Programming
Desktop Publishing
Economic and Social History
Economics
Electrical Engineering
Electronics
Employee Development
English Grammar
English Language
English Literature
Fashion Buying and Merchandising
  Management
Fashion Styling
French

Geography
German
Global Information Systems
Human Resource Management
Information Technology
Internet
Java
Management Skills
Marketing Management
Mathematics
Microsoft Office
Microsoft Windows, Novell
  NetWare and UNIX
Modern British History
Modern European History
Modern United States History
Modern World History
Networks
Organisational Behaviour
Pascal and Delphi Programming
Philosophy
Physics
Practical Criticism
Psychology
Shakespeare
Social Welfare
Sociology
Spanish
Statistics
Strategic Management
Systems Analysis and Design
Team Leadership
Theology
Twentieth-Century Russian History
Visual Basic
World Religions

www.palgravemasterseries.com

Palgrave Master Series
Series Standing Order ISBN 0–333–69343–4
(outside North America only)

You can receive future titles in this series as they are published by placing a standing order. Please contact your bookseller or, in case of difficulty, write to us at the address below with your name and address, the title of the series and the ISBN quoted above.

Customer Services Department, Macmillan Distribution Ltd.
Houndmills, Basingstoke, Hampshire RG21 6XS, England

Mastering
Twentieth-Century Russian History

Norman Lowe

palgrave

First published 2002 by
PALGRAVE
Houndmills, Basingstoke, Hampshire RG21 6XS and
175 Fifth Avenue, New York, N.Y. 10010
Companies and representatives throughout the world

PALGRAVE is the new global academic imprint of
St. Martin's Press LLC Scholarly and Reference Division and
Palgrave Publishers Ltd (formerly Macmillan Press Ltd).

ISBN 0–333–96307–5

This book is printed on paper suitable for recycling and
made from fully managed and sustained forest sources.

A catalogue record for this book is available
from the British Library.

Library of Congress Cataloging-in-Publication Data

Lowe, Norman.
   Mastering twentieth-century Russian history / Norman Lowe.
      p.   cm.—(Palgrave master series)
   Includes bibliographical references and index.
   ISBN 0–333–96307–5 (pbk.)
   1. Russia—History—20th century—Outlines, syllabi, etc.   2. Soviet
Union—History—Outlines, syllabi, etc.   3. Russia (Federation)—History—1991—
Outlines, syllabi, etc.   I. Title: Mastering 20th century Russian history.   II. Title.
III. Series.

DK246 .L68 2002
947.084—dc21

                                                                        2001059834

10   9   8   7   6   5   4   3   2   1
11   10   09   08   07   06   05   04   03   02

Printed and bound in Great Britain by
Creative Print & Design (Wales), Ebbw Vale

For Nathaniel, Millie and Anna

Mounds of human heads recede into the distance,
I am diminishing there – already I'll not be noticed;
but in warm-hearted books and in children's games
I'll rise from the dead to say that the sun is shining.

Osip Mandelstam, 1936–37

[*Poems from Mandelstam*, translated by R.H. Morrison, Farleigh Dickinson University Press, London and Toronto, 1990]

Contents

List of maps

List of illustrations

◼ ⚈ Preface

It must have been somewhere around 1986 when I first suggested to the editors of the Master Series that a volume on twentieth-century Russian history might be a good idea. Nothing came of it at the time, and as events turned out, they were absolutely right to wait. It is now possible to deal with the whole of the twentieth century, including the collapse of the Soviet Union, which happened so dramatically and unexpectedly in 1991. The ensuing ten years have given historians time to wallow in the newly opened archives and to begin to try and put the Soviet experiment into some sort of perspective. It may be thought that yet another history of modern Russia is hardly necessary, given the large number which have appeared in the last few years, written by leading scholars. Many of these books are specialized and highly detailed, and can therefore be confusing for students beginning a study of Russian history for the first time. It seems to me that there is a need for a book which provides a clear introduction to the complexities of the subject, an overview of the twentieth century in Russia, a summary of the main historiographical debates, and a guide for further study. I hope I have succeeded in producing exactly this. Both in the text and in the documents for discussion, I have also tried to give something of the flavour of what the Russian people and their associated nationalities have experienced and suffered during the twentieth century. The book is aimed principally at Advanced Level students, and undergraduates studying History and Politics; I hope that the general reader interested in this period of Russian history will also find it approachable.

I have not worked in the archives, and therefore I owe a great debt of gratitude to all those scholars over the last twenty years whose researches I have made use of and who are acknowledged in the notes (at the end of each chapter) and in the suggestions for further reading (at the end of the book). I am grateful also to my friends Glyn Jones, formerly of Bede College, Billingham, Michael Hopkinson, formerly Head of History at Harrogate Grammar School, and James Brindle, who read the manuscript and made many helpful and sometimes vital suggestions; to my wife, Jane, who helped to eradicate numerous errors and polish up my English; and to Suzannah Burywood and Philippa Thomas of Palgrave for their patience, encouragement and advice.

■ ⊻   Acknowledgements

The author and publishers would like to thank the following photographic sources: Novosti (London), pp. 2, 14, 15, 315, 354, 380, 467; AGK London, pp. 64, 93, 121, 171, 210, 288, 300, 408.

The author and publishers would like to thank the following for permission to reproduce copyright material:

Extracts from *A People's Tragedy. The Russian Revolution* by Orlando Figes, published by Jonathan Cape (1996), used by permission of the Random House Group Limited.

Extracts from *Stalin: Triumph and Tragedy* by Dmitri Volkogonov, translated by Harold Shukman (2000 edition), reproduced by permission of Phoenix Press.

Extracts from *An Economic History of the USSR 1917–1991* (third revised edition 1992) by Alec Nove reproduced by permission of Penguin Books Limited.

Extracts from *Lenin's Tomb. The Last Days of the Soviet Empire* © 1993 by David Remnick (Penguin, New York). Reprinted by permission of the author.

The verse by Osip Mandelstam on page vi, from *Poems from Mandelstam*, translated by R.H. Morrison, is reprinted by permission of Associated University Presses, Cranbury, New Jersey, USA.

The poem by Osip Mandelstam on page 263, from *Hope Against Hope: A Memoir* (1999 edition) by Nadezhda Mandelstam, translated by Max Hayward, is reprinted by permission of The Harvill Press Ltd.

Every effort has been made to trace all the copyright holders, but if any have been inadvertently overlooked the publishers will be pleased to make the necessary arrangement at the first opportunity.

◼ ◢ Glossary

apparat	The administrative apparatus of the Communist Party
apparatchik	Someone who works in the party administration
artel	A co-operative work group, especially a farm collective
Article 6	The article in the Soviet constitution which gave the Communist Party the right to be the only political party in the USSR
blat	Informal system of favours and connections
Bolsheviks	Meaning 'majority' – the name taken by Lenin and his supporters after the Social Democrat party split in 1903; it eventually became the Communist Party.
bourgeoisie	Term used by the Marxists to describe the capitalist middle classes
CC or CCCP	Central Committee of the Communist Party
Cheka	The secret police set up by Lenin; it kept changing its title, becoming in turn GPU, OGPU, NKVD, MVD and KGB
Comecon	The Council for Mutual Economic Assistance among the eastern bloc countries
Cominform	The Communist Information Bureau for the eastern bloc countries
Comintern	The Communist International, set up in 1919 to further the cause of world revolution. It was dissolved by Stalin in 1943
Commissar	A minister or other high official in the Soviet government
CPSU	The Communist Party of the Soviet Union
dacha	A house in the country
dekulakization	Removal of kulaks to Siberia, the Urals or labour camps during collectivization
Duma	The elected lower house of the Russian parliament 1906–17 and again after December 1993
FRG	Federal Republic of Germany (West Germany)
FYP	Five-Year Plan
GDR	German Democratic Republic (East Germany)
glasnost	Gorbachev's policy of openness or frankness
GOSPLAN	The State Planning Commission – the body which had overall responsibility for the economy, until the USSR ended in 1991
Iskra	Meaning 'spark'; the name of the Social Democrat newspaper founded by Lenin and Martov in 1898
Izvestiya	Meaning literally 'news'; the name of the official newspaper of the Soviet government

Kadets	Constitutional Democrats (the main liberal party up to October 1917)
KGB	Committee of State Security (earlier known as the Cheka), secret police
kolkhoz	Collective farm; it means literally 'collective economy'
kolkhoznik	A male worker on a collective farm
kolkhoznitsa	A female worker on a collective farm
kombedy	Committees of poor peasants
Komsomol	The League of Young Communists
kulak	A wealthy peasant; always used in a critical sense, or as a term of abuse
Mensheviks	Meaning 'minority'; the name taken by the followers of Plekhanov and Martov after the split in the Social Democrat party in 1903
mir	Village community; it also means 'world'
Narkomindel	The People's Commissariat of Foreign Affairs
Narkomprod	The People's Commissariat of Supply
NATO	North Atlantic Treaty Organization
NEP	New Economic Policy
Nepman	A private trader or manufacturer; somebody who did well out of NEP
NKVD	The secret police
Novy Mir	Means 'New World'; a famous literary journal
Octobrists	The liberal–conservative party which supported the Tsar's October Manifesto after 1905
OGPU	The secret police
Okhrana	The Tsarist secret police
Oktyabr	A literary journal
perestroika	Gorbachev's policy of reforming or restructuring
Politburo	The top political committee of the Communist Party, chosen by the party Central Committee. It was the main decision-making body, or cabinet under the Soviet system. From 1952 to 1966 it was known as the Presidium
Pood or **pud**	Measurement of weight equivalent to 36 pounds or 16.38 kg
Pravda	Means literally 'truth'; the official newspaper of the Communist Party
Presidium	Name given to the Politburo between 1952 and 1966
Prodrazverstka	Compulsory delivery of surplus foodstuffs by the peasants to the government
proletariat	Marxist term for the revolutionary working class
Rabkrin	Workers' and Peasants' Inspectorate
RAPP	Association of Proletarian Writers
RSDLP	Russian Social Democrat Labour Party – see SDs
RSFSR	Russian Soviet Federated Socialist Republic
SALT	Strategic Arms Limitation Treaty

SDs	Social Democrats, a Marxist revolutionary party which split into two factions in 1903: Bolsheviks (Majority) and Mensheviks (Minority)
Soviet	Council
sovkhoz	State collective farm
Sovnarkhoz	Council of the National Economy (1957–65) introduced by Khrushchev
Sovnarkom	Council of People's Commissars; in effect the government from 1917 until 1946 when it became the USSR Council of Ministers
SRs	Socialist Revolutionaries, a non-Marxist revolutionary party
uskorenie	Gorbachev's policy of acceleration
USSR	Union of Soviet Socialist Republics
vozhd	Leader
Vperod	Meaning 'forward'; title chosen by Lenin for one of the Bolshevik journals
VSNKh	Supreme Council of the National Economy
War Communism	The economic policy operated by the Soviet government during the Civil War from June 1918 until March 1921, when it was replaced by the NEP
Zemstvo	Elected local government assembly at provincial and district level from 1864 to 1917; dominated by nobility
Znamya	Meaning literally 'banner' or 'flag'; a well-known journal

■ ⌄ Note on dates

Until 1 February 1918 the Russians used the Julian calendar, which during the nineteenth century was twelve days behind the Gregorian calendar used by the rest of Europe, and then thirteen days behind until the end of January 1918, when Russian dating was brought into line with the rest of the world. Thus Lenin was born in April 1870 – on the 10th by the Julian calendar in Russia, but on the 22nd by the Gregorian calendar in Europe. The events which the Russians know as the February revolution, beginning on 23 February 1917 (Julian), began on 8 March as far as the rest of Europe was concerned. When the Bolsheviks took power on 25 October (Julian), it was 7 November in the rest of Europe. In the text the Julian calendar is used for internal events, and the Gregorian calendar for international events such as the First World War, until 1 February 1918.

Chronology of main events

1854–1856	Russian defeat in the Crimean War.
1855–1881	**Reign of Alexander II, the 'Tsar Liberator'.**
1861	Emancipation of the serfs.
1878	Russia suffers diplomatic defeat at the Congress of Berlin.
1881	Assassination of Alexander II by the 'People's Will'.
1881–1894	**Reign of Alexander III.**
1894 (Jan.)	Russia signs alliance with France.
1894	Death of Alexander III.
1894–1917	**Reign of Nicholas II, the last Tsar.**
1890s	Witte and the 'great spurt' in industrialization.

1902
March — Lenin publishes *What Is To Be Done?*

1903
July–August — Social Democrats split into two factions – Bolsheviks and Mensheviks.

1904
February — Russo–Japanese War begins; it ends in 1905 in defeat for Russia.

1905
January — Major strike in St Petersburg, organized by Father Gapon, leads to Bloody Sunday and develops into the 1905 Revolution.
June — Mutiny on the battleship *Potemkin*.
October — St Petersburg Soviet formed. Nicholas signs October Manifesto promising a Duma (parliament) and other reforms.
November — Moscow Soviet formed.
December — Uprising in Moscow suppressed by force.

1906
April — Stolypin becomes Minister of the Interior; opening of the first Duma.
July — Nicholas dissolves first Duma.

August	Stolypin begins his agrarian reforms.

1907

February	Second Duma opens.
June	Nicholas dissolves second Duma and changes the voting rules.
August	Russia signs an agreement with Britain, completing the Triple Entente of Russia, France and Britain.
November	Third Duma opens and stays in session until 1912.

1911

September	Murder of Stolypin.

1912

February	Lena goldminers' strike; troops kill 200 strikers.
April	Strike spreads to St Petersburg; government bans unions, but strikes continue through 1913 and into 1914.
November	Fourth and last Duma opens.

1914–1918	First World War

1914

July	Nicholas orders partial and then full Russian mobilization.
19 July/1 Aug.	Germany declares war on Russia.
August	Russians invade East Prussia but suffer heavy defeats, and Galicia (Austria) where they capture Lemberg (Lwow), the capital.

1915

April	Germans invade Poland.
July/August	Russians withdraw from Poland; Progressive Bloc formed – demands that the Duma be allowed to form a government. Nicholas assumes command of all Russian forces and leaves Petrograd for military HQ.

1916

May/June	Brusilov's offensive begins successfully, but does not change the outcome of the war.
November	Duma reconvenes and Milyukov makes his 'stupidity or treason' speech.
December	Rasputin murdered.

1917

23 February	Demonstrations in Petrograd turn violent, and on 25th Nicholas orders them to be suppressed by force.
26–27 Feb.	Troops mutiny; Petrograd Soviet elected.
2 March	Nicholas II abdicates; Provisional Government formed under Prince Lvov.

3 April	Lenin arrives in Petrograd in 'sealed' train, from exile in Switzerland and soon publishes his *April Theses*.
May	Lvov takes six socialists into his coalition; Kerensky becomes War Minister. Trotsky arrives in Petrograd from New York.
June/July	Kerensky's offensive launched, but soon ends in failure.
3–5 July	The 'July Days' lead to Lvov's resignation and unpopularity for the Bolsheviks. Kerensky becomes prime minister.
24–31 August	The Kornilov Affair discredits the right and helps revive Bolshevik popularity.
25 October	Bolsheviks seize power in Petrograd.
26 October	Lenin forms first Council of People's Commissars (Sovnarkom) and issues its first decrees – on land and peace.
November	Elections for the Constituent Assembly; SRs win most seats.
2 (15) Dec.	Armistice signed with Germany.

1918

5–6 January	Constituent Assembly meets but is closed at gunpoint by Bolsheviks.
12 January	Ukraine declares independence.
1 February	Russia adopts Gregorian calendar, moving into line with the rest of the world.
24 February	Estonia declares independence.
March	Capital moves to Moscow.
3 March	Treaty of Brest–Litovsk signed with Central Powers.
4 March	Trotsky becomes Commissar for War and begins to organize Red Army.
19 March	Left SRs resign from Sovnarkom.
22 April	Transcaucasian Federation proclaims independence.
May	Czechoslovak Legions take control of Trans-Siberian Railway.
26–28 May	Transcaucasian Federation breaks up into independent republics of Georgia, Armenia and Azerbaijan.
11 June	*Kombedy* – committees of poor peasants formed. Abolished in December.
14 June	Bolsheviks expel Mensheviks and Right SRs from the All-Russia Central Executive Committee of Soviets.
6 July	Left SRs murder Mirbach and rebel against the Soviet government.
16–17 July	Nicholas II and family murdered by the Bolsheviks at Yekaterinburg.
2 September	Soviet government launches terror campaign against its enemies.
November	Whites declare Admiral Kolchak 'Supreme Ruler' of Russia.
18 November	Latvia proclaims independence.

1919

March	First Congress of the Communist International (Comintern).
July	Reds take Yekaterinburg; Kolchak driven eastwards.
October	Denikin's Volunteer Force defeated.
Oct.–Nov.	Trotsky leads defence of Petrograd; Iudenich's White forces defeated.

1920

25 April	Polish forces invade Ukraine, beginning Russo–Polish War.
28 April	Red Army captures Baku and brings Azerbaijan back into the Union.
2 December	Armenia becomes a Soviet republic again.

1921

25 February	Red Army occupies Georgia and makes it a Soviet republic.
28 Feb.–18 Mar.	Insurrection of sailors at Kronstadt; eventually suppressed by force.
8–16 March	Tenth Communist Party Congress: defeats Workers' Opposition, bans factions within the party, and decides to introduce the New Economic Policy (NEP).
18 March	Russo–Polish War officially ends with the Treaty of Riga.
June	Third Comintern Congress.
Summer onwards	Serious famine in many parts of Russia.

1922

March	Georgia, Armenia and Azerbaijan form Transcaucasian SSR.
26 March	Lenin has his first stroke.
March–April	Eleventh party Congress; Stalin becomes general secretary of the party.
16 April	Treaty of Rapallo signed with Germany.
Summer	Clampdown on religious, literary and cultural freedom; intellectuals exiled.
December	Lenin begins to dictate his 'Testament'.
December	New constitution formally inaugurates the USSR.

1923

9 March	A further stroke effectively removes Lenin from politics.
Summer onwards	The 'scissors crisis'.

1924

21 January	Death of Lenin; Zinoviev, Kamenev and Stalin unite against Trotsky.
22 May	Leaders decide not to act on Lenin's 'Testament'.

October	Trotsky publishes *Lessons of October*, attacking Kamenev and Zinoviev.
December	Stalin introduces 'socialism in one country', supported by Bukharin.

1925

January	Trotsky forced to resign as Commissar for War.
December	Stalin and Bukharin defeat the 'Left' Opposition at the 14th party congress.

1926

January	Trotsky and Zinoviev form United Opposition.
April	Treaty of Berlin signed with Germany.
July/October	Zinoviev, Trotsky and Kamenev removed from Politburo.

1927

April	Chiang Kai-Shek launches his anti-communist campaign in Shanghai.
May	Britain breaks off diplomatic relations with USSR; 'war scare' begins.
September	Problems as peasants reduce grain sales to the government.
November	Trotsky and Zinoviev expelled from the Communist Party.

1928

January	Trotsky exiled to Alma-Ata in Kazakhstan.
January	Stalin visits Siberia to investigate the problems with grain supplies; begins to favour compulsory collectivization.
March	Beginning of the 'Cultural Revolution'.
May	Shakhty trials begin.
July	Bukharin and the 'Right' oppose Stalin's collectivization policy.
October	First Five-Year Plan for industry begins officially.

1929

9–10 February	Bukharin and the 'Right' Opposition condemned by the Politburo.
November	Bukharin removed from the Politburo.
21 December	Stalin's 50th birthday; usually taken as the beginning of the 'Stalin Cult'.
27 December	Stalin calls for the speeding up of collectivization and dekulakization.

1930

July	Litvinov becomes commissar for foreign affairs; favours collective security.
November	Ordzhonikidze takes over as director of industrialization.

1931

June	Stalin ends the 'Cultural Revolution' and begins so-called 'Great Retreat'.
September	Japanese forces occupy the whole of Manchuria and declare it independent.

1932

April	RAPP and other workers' cultural associations dissolved.
Autumn onwards	Severe famine in Ukraine and other areas, lasting through most of 1933.
October	Opposition to Stalin develops – the Ryutin Affair.
November	Stalin's wife, Nadezhda Alliluyeva, commits suicide.
December	First Five-Year Plan declared completed.

1933

January	Second Five-Year Plan begins.
January	Hitler comes to power in Germany.
November	USA formally recognizes the USSR and diplomatic relations begin.

1934

18 September	USSR enters League of Nations.
1 December	Kirov assassinated in Leningrad; the Purges begin.

1935

1 January	End of food rationing which had been in operation since 1930.
15–16 Jan.	Kamenev and Zinoviev on trial; Kamenev given 10 years, Zinoviev 5.
2 May	USSR signs Treaty of Mutual Assistance with France.
July/August	The Comintern drops its 'world revolution' programme and adopts 'Popular Front' line and collective security.
August	Beginning of Stakhanovite campaign.
2 November	Stalin makes his 'life has become more joyous' speech.

1936

January	Stalin launches attack on Shostakovich's opera, *Lady Macbeth of Mtsensk*.
July	Spanish Civil War begins.
19–24 August	'Show trial' of Kamenev and Zinoviev, who are both found guilty and shot.
5 December	Stalin's new USSR constitution comes into operation.

1937

18 February	Ordzhonikidze commits suicide.

May–June	Army purges – Tukhachevsky and many other commanders executed.

1938

13 March	Russian language made compulsory in all schools in the USSR.
2–13 March	'Show-trial' of Bukharin and other 'Rightists' who are all found guilty. Bukharin and 18 others executed.
30 September	Munich agreement signed; Stalin feels betrayed by Britain and France.

1939

3 May	Molotov replaces Litvinov as commissar for foreign affairs.
May–August	Soviet and Japanese troops clash.
23 August	Nazi–Soviet Non-Aggression Pact signed; secret protocols added later.
1 September	Germans invade Poland, beginning Second World War, which lasts until 1945.
17 September	Soviet forces occupy eastern Poland, as agreed in the secret protocols.
30 November	War breaks out with Finland and lasts until 12 March 1940.

1940

April	NKVD murder 15,000 Polish officers at Katyn.
August	Latvia, Lithuania and Estonia brought into USSR, as agreed in the protocols.
20 August	Trotsky assassinated in Mexico.

1941

22 June	**Germans invade the USSR; the Great Patriotic War begins.**
28 June	Minsk falls to the Germans.
8 September	The 900-day siege of Leningrad begins.
18 September	Kiev captured by the Germans.
September	Germans massacre 34,000 Jews at Babi Yar, near Kiev.
30 September	The battle for Moscow begins.
7 December	Japanese attack Pearl Harbor, bringing the USA into the war.

1942

May–July	Germans advance eastwards and reach Stalingrad.
17 July–2 Feb. 1943	Battle of Stalingrad; German Sixth Army forced to surrender. First great Russian victory.
28 July	Stalin issues his 'Not one more step back' order.

1943

23 May	Stalin agrees to dissolve the Comintern.

5 July–23 Aug.	The great tank battle of Kursk; another Russian victory.
September	Stalin softens up on religion and allows the election of a new Patriarch.
28 November	Teheran Conference begins.
Nov.–Dec.	Mass deportations of non-Russian groups begin, lasting until the following May; including Kalmyks, Chechens and Crimean Tatars.

1944

27 January	Siege of Leningrad ends.
May	Crimea finally cleared of German troops.
6 June	The Second Front begins at last; Americans and British land in Normandy.
3 July	Minsk liberated.
Aug.–October	Warsaw uprising crushed by the Germans.

1945

4–11 February	Stalin, Roosevelt and Churchill meet at the Yalta Conference.
April–May	Soviet campaign to capture Berlin ends in triumph on 8 May.
8–9 May	End of Second World War in Europe.
May–June	Britain forcibly repatriates 50,000 Cossacks; many commit suicide rather than return to the USSR.
17 July–2 Aug.	Potsdam Conference.
6 August	USA drops first atomic bomb on Hiroshima.
8 August	USSR declares war on Japan and attacks Japanese forces in Manchuria.
2 September	Japanese surrender; Second World War ends.

1946

9 February	George Kennan's 'Long Telegram'. Cold War begins to get under way.
5 March	Churchill's 'Iron Curtain' speech in Fulton, Missouri.
August	Zhdanov begins his attack on writers and other cultural figures.

1947

12 March	Truman Doctrine declared.
5 June	Marshall Plan announced but is rejected by USSR on behalf of the east European states.
September	The USSR sets up the Cominform in response to the Marshall Plan.

1948

February	Communists seize power in Czechoslovakia.

27 March	Breach between the USSR and Yugoslavia.
24 June	Berlin blockade begins; lasts until Stalin admits defeat on 5 May 1949.
July–August	The Leningrad Affair – purge of the party leaders in Leningrad.

1949

April	North Atlantic Treaty Organization (NATO) formed.
1 October	Mao Zedong announces formation of People's Republic of China.

1950

26 June	Korean War begins: communist North Korea invades the south; ends July 1953.
29 August	The USSR successfully explodes its first atomic bomb.

1953

13 January	So-called 'Doctors' Plot' announced.
5 March	Death of Stalin.
June	Rising in East Berlin suppressed by Soviet troops.
26 June	Beria arrested and later executed.
September	Khrushchev becomes first secretary of the Communist Party.

1954

February	Khrushchev's virgin lands scheme introduced.

1955

January	Government accepts Khrushchev's plan to 'increase the area under maize'.
May	USSR signs peace treaty with Austria. Formation of Warsaw Pact announced.
July	Geneva Summit – Khrushchev meets Eisenhower.

1956

February	Khrushchev's 'secret speech' at 20th party Congress begins de-Stalinization.
April	Cominform dissolved.
June–October	Unrest in Poland; Khrushchev flies to Warsaw and a compromise is reached.
23 October	Hungarian revolution begins; suppressed by Soviet forces early in November.

1957

June	Attempt to get rid of Khrushchev fails.

August	USSR produces the inter-continental ballistic missile (ICBM).
4 October	USSR launches *Sputnik*, the first artificial Earth satellite.

1958

October	Pasternak awarded Nobel Literature Prize after publication of *Doctor Zhivago* in Italy.
November	Crisis over Berlin; ends with the building of the Berlin Wall (August 1961).

1959

September	Khrushchev pays his first visit to the USA; has successful talks with Eisenhower at Camp David.

1960

April	USSR's rift with China becomes public knowledge.
1 May	American U-2 spy plane is shot down near Sverdlovsk. Khrushchev walks out of the Paris Summit in protest.
September	Khrushchev attends UN in New York, and bangs his shoe on the table.

1961

12 April	Yuri Gagarin becomes the first man in space.
July	Khrushchev meets Kennedy in Vienna.
October	Stalin's body removed from the mausoleum.

1962

June	Demonstrations in Novocherkassk; 23 people killed as troops restore order.
October	Cuban missiles crisis.

1963

5 August	Nuclear Test Ban Treaty signed.

1964

14 October	Khrushchev removed as first secretary and replaced by Brezhnev.

1965

February	Americans begin bombing of North Vietnam. Kosygin begins his economic reform programme.

1966

February	Trial of Sinyavski and Daniel.

1967	Introduction of the five-day working week and other reforms.

1968 **Jan.–August**	'Prague Spring'; ends when Soviet forces invade and occupy Czechoslovakia. Brezhnev Doctrine announced.

1969 **March**	Fighting breaks out between Soviets and Chinese along Siberian frontier.
October	Solzhenitsyn awarded the Nobel Literature Prize.

1970	
	Sakharov and Chalidze form Human Rights Committee.
12 August	USSR signs Renunciation of Force Treaty with West Germany. Kosygin's economic reforms largely abandoned by the end of this year.

1971 **3 September**	Four Power Agreement signed on the status of Berlin.

1972 **May**	Brezhnev and Nixon sign SALT I in Moscow.

1974 **February**	Solzhenitsyn deported by KGB.

1975 **1 August**	Helsinki agreement on human rights and international co-operation signed.
December	Sakharov awarded the Nobel Peace Prize.

1977 **7 October**	Brezhnev's new constitution for the USSR adopted.

1979 **June**	Brezhnev and Carter sign SALT II in Vienna.
December	Soviet troops move into Afghanistan; so US Senate refuses to ratify SALT II.

1980 **May**	Sakharov exiled to Gorky, a city closed to foreigners.
August	Polish trade union, Solidarity, formed.

1981

13 December   Polish leader, Jaruzelski, suppresses Solidarity and declares martial law.

1982

10 November   Brezhnev dies; Andropov becomes leader.

1983

March   Reagan announces his Strategic Defence Initiative (Star Wars).

1 September   Soviets shoot down a Korean airliner with the loss of 269 lives.

1984

9 February   Andropov dies and is succeeded by Chernenko.

1985

10 March   Chernenko dies; Gorbachev becomes leader.

November   Gorbachev's first meeting with Reagan, in Vienna.

1986

February   Gorbachev announces his policy of *glasnost* (openness).

26 April   Nuclear explosion at Chernobyl in Ukraine.

October   Gorbachev and Reagan's summit meeting in Reykjavik, Iceland.

December   Gorbachev invites Sakharov to return to Moscow from Gorky.

December   Demonstrations in Kazakhstan when Gorbachev appoints a Russian as party leader.

1987

                   Gorbachev tries to intensify his policy of *perestroika* (restructuring).

November   Yeltsin is sacked as Moscow party boss after criticizing Politburo members.

December   Gorbachev and Reagan sign the Intermediate Nuclear Forces (INF) Treaty.

1988

January   Law on State Enterprises comes into operation.

February   Nagorno–Karabakh crisis begins.

13 March   Nina Andreyeva's letter demands return to Stalinism.

April   Geneva agreement ends war in Afghanistan.

1989

April	Government uses troops to suppress demonstrations in Tbilisi, Georgia.
May	Estonia and Lithuania declare sovereignty.
15–18 May	Gorbachev's visit to Beijing; official reconciliation between USSR and China.
25 May	Newly elected Congress of People's Deputies meets.
4 June	Chinese government crushes democracy movement in Tiananmen Square.
July onwards	Striking miners demand independent trade unions and more power to the Soviets.
24 August	Non-communist government comes to power in Poland.
9 November	Berlin Wall demolished.
29 December	Non-communist elected president of Czechoslovakia.

1990

January	Government sends troops to restore order in Azerbaijan.
6 March	Article 6 of constitution cancelled; USSR no longer a one-party state.
March	Non-communist governments elected in Hungary and East Germany.
May	Yeltsin elected Chairman of the Russian Supreme Soviet.
July	Yeltsin resigns from the Communist Party.
August	The '500 Days Programme' for a crash privatization programme drawn up.
3 October	Germany officially reunited.
15 October	Gorbachev awarded Nobel Peace Prize.
20 December	Shevardnadze resigns as foreign minister, warning of threat of dictatorship.

1991

January	Soviet troops fire on demonstrators in Latvia and Lithuania.
12 June	Yeltsin elected president of the Russian Federation.
18–21 August	Attempted coup by communist right-wingers to remove Gorbachev fails.
25 August	Gorbachev resigns as general secretary of the Communist Party.
Autumn	Attempts to preserve the USSR in some form collapse when Ukraine and Belarus decide to become independent states.
November	Yeltsin bans Communist Party in Russia.
25 December	Gorbachev resigns as president of the USSR.
31 December	USSR ceases to exist. Commonwealth of Independent States (CIS) begins.

1992

2 January	Gaidar launches his 'shock therapy' for a rapid shift to a market economy, but it causes inflation, unemployment and shortages.
14 December	Yeltsin replaces Gaidar as prime minister with Chernomyrdin.

1993

25 April	Referendum shows strong support for Yeltsin's policies, in spite of problems.
September	Yeltsin dissolves parliament and produces a new constitution with elections for a state Duma. Parliament resists and members occupy the White House.
3–4 October	Yeltsin orders the army to storm the White House.
December	New constitution approved; in the Duma elections, communists and nationalists do better than radical reformers.

1994

December	Russian troops invade Chechnya which had declared independence.

1995

December	Duma election; communists again do well, but Yeltsin remains president.

1996

June–July	Yeltsin elected for a second term as president, defeating Zyuganov, the communist leader. Cease-fire agreed in Chechnya.

1997

2 April	Russia and Belarus sign treaty of union.
27 May	Yeltsin and NATO leaders sign an act of mutual co-operation and security.

1998

August	Miners strike, as economic crisis continues. Severe financial crisis; rouble devalued. Yeltsin appoints Primakov as prime minister; he begins to stabilize situation.

1999

March	Primakov replaced by Stepashin.
June	Yeltsin protests at NATO bombing of Yugoslavia.

August	Stepashin replaced by Putin.
September	Putin sends forces into Chechnya after terrorist bombs explode in Moscow.
31 December	Yeltsin retires as president; Putin becomes acting president.

2000

March	Putin elected president.

■ Ⅳ ▮ Introduction: Russia in the twentieth century

1.1 An overview of Russian history in the twentieth century

On 6 May 1896, in the Cathedral of the Assumption in Moscow, Nicholas II was crowned Emperor and Autocrat of All Russia; Tsar of Moscow, Kiev, Poland, Siberia; Grand Prince of Lithuania, Podolia and Finland; Prince of Estonia, Livonia and Bulgaria, and of lots of other areas as well. It was a splendid ceremony as befitted the ruler of such vast territories, but unfortunately the coronation was marked by tragedy. Thousands of people had flocked into Moscow to witness the processions and celebrations, and the day after the ceremony there was a huge gathering in the Khodynka Fields hoping to receive the commemorative tankards and other gifts – free beer and sausage – which were traditionally distributed on such occasions. The crowds were tightly packed round the distribution points, and as more people arrived, a rumour went round that there wouldn't be enough for everybody. Those at the back began to push to try and get closer, and things got out of control. Suddenly there was a great surge forward and many in the front ranks were trampled on and crushed. When calm was restored and the crowds dispersed, 1280 bodies were left behind and at least 10,000 people had been injured. Public opinion was outraged when Nicholas allowed the celebrations to go ahead as planned over the next few days; he even went so far as to attend a ball the same evening while the dead were being carried away.

This tragedy was seen by many people as an ill-omen for the future of Nicholas's reign. In fact the next hundred years turned out to be full of trauma for the unfortunate peoples of the Russia empire. By 1905 Russia had suffered military defeat at the hands of Japan, a nation not previously considered to be in the first rank, and was in the throes of a revolution which forced Nicholas to make some half-hearted concessions. In 1914 the Russians became involved in the First World War and found themselves invaded by German forces. As defeat followed defeat, Nicholas II was forced to abdicate (February 1917) and the autocratic monarchy was at an end. Under the Provisional Government it seemed that Russia was to have some form of democracy, but the new rulers were no more successful than the Tsar had been in dealing with the problems facing the country. The situation continued to deteriorate; in October 1917 Lenin and the Bolsheviks seized power and soon took Russia out of the war.

The new government, under the leadership of Lenin, did not at first bring stability: its policies provoked a great deal of opposition leading to a civil war

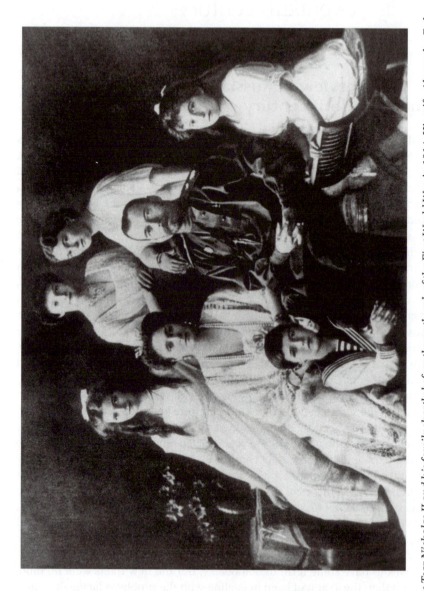

Figure 1.1 The Tsar Nicholas II and his family shortly before the outbreak of the First World War in 1914. His wife, Alexandra Fedorovna, is sitting on his right, and their daughter, Anastasia, on his left. Behind are the other three daughters, Marie, Tatiana and Olga. Sitting in front is the Tsarevich Alexis.

which lasted until 1921. Ordinary people – especially peasants – in most areas of Russia and her empire suffered hardships as both sides seized grain to feed their armies, and both sides committed innumerable atrocities. The Bolsheviks, who now called themselves Communists, won the war, and by the time of Lenin's death in January 1924, most of the elements of the USSR (Union of Soviet Socialist Republics) were in place – central control of the economy and administration and a one-party dictatorship. After the death of Lenin there was a power struggle from which, by 1929, Stalin had emerged as the leader. He remained in power until his death in 1953, and during that quarter of a century nobody was immune from the effects of his drastic policies. Basically these consisted of modernization by force – the Five-Year Plans regimented workers in a vast industrialization campaign and peasants were coerced into joining the collectivization of agriculture. In addition came famine and Stalin's purges and then in 1941 invasion by the Germans. Much of the western part of the empire suffered a brutal enemy occupation; both Moscow and Leningrad escaped capture, but the unfortunate citizens of Leningrad were forced to endure a 900-day siege.

Russian forces played the vital role in the defeat of Germany and succeeded in reaching Berlin in 1945, before the Americans and British. Stalin set about rebuilding Russia, but his methods were just as drastic and extreme as before the war. Tensions between the USSR and its former allies in the West increased and both sides were unwilling to withdraw their troops from Germany. Both suspected each other's motives: when Stalin created a Russian 'outer-empire' by extending Soviet control over the states of eastern Europe, the Cold War was precipitated.

After the death of Stalin in 1953, the next phase was dominated by Nikita Khrushchev. Under his leadership communism became more civilized; he was critical of Stalin's excesses and he tried to modernize and improve the system. However, though they were not without success, his policies did not please everybody. His agricultural reforms were disappointing and Soviet prestige suffered a blow with what seemed like defeat in the Cuban missile crisis of 1962. In 1964 the Central Committee of the party voted Khrushchev into retirement on the grounds of ill health. Leonid Brezhnev eventually emerged as the next leader; he was reluctant to take any initiatives and both industry and agriculture stagnated. When Mikhail Gorbachev became leader in 1985 he was determined to reform and modernize the system, though he wanted Russia to remain communist. At the forefront of his new approach were *glasnost* (openness) and *perestroika* (restructuring). He encouraged criticism of Stalin, claiming that Stalinism was a distortion of true communism and that he intended to return the regime to the true path of Lenin. However, as more and more openness was allowed, criticism of Lenin and the communist party also developed. In the 'outer-empire' communism had been largely abandoned by the end of 1989. Many of Gorbachev's party colleagues were dismayed by this turn of events and tried to remove him from power (August 1991). Thanks to Boris Yeltsin, the *coup* attempt failed and the communist party was discredited. The USSR began to fall apart as the separate Soviet republics chose to go their own ways. On Christmas Day 1991 Gorbachev resigned as President of the USSR, which had ceased to exist.

And so once again Russia was left in chaos: Yeltsin, as President of Russia, announced a de-communization policy and a rapid move to a capitalist market economy. But for over 70 years the people of the USSR had lived under the rule of a highly centralized, one-party dictatorship with a state-controlled command economy. Communism was a complete way of life that could not simply be jettisoned overnight. Yeltsin found that the problems of reforming the economy, the administration and the political system all at the same time were acute. Some progress had been made by 1999 when he resigned because of ill health, to be replaced by Vladimir Putin, but there is still a long way to go, and probably many years, before the transformation will be complete.

1.2   The writing of Russian history

It is not surprising that such a complex and turbulent period of history has given rise to a whole host of differing interpretations. First of all there was the official view of Soviet historians that Lenin and the Bolsheviks, steeped in the 'scientific' theories of revolutionary Marxism (see section 2.3 for details about Marxist theories), played the vital role in bringing down the incompetent regime of Nicholas II. Following this, they 'made' the October revolution by galvanizing the oppressed masses into action. Together they overthrew the Provisional Government, and then the Bolsheviks proceeded to introduce socialism, the 'dictatorship of the proletariat' – a genuine workers' state, which rescued Russia from economic backwardness and political autocracy. The official version of events emphasized the Marxist view that there was nothing accidental about the October revolution: it was inevitable as soon as the working classes became strong enough and organised enough to overthrow the class-based tsarist regime. It was the ultimate climax of the class struggle, the most important event in world history so far, and one which, according to the scientific laws of historical development and progress, was bound to happen. Soviet historians painted as black a picture of the state of Russia under Nicholas II as they possibly could in order to make the Soviet achievement appear all the more impressive. In spite of all the efforts of Russia's defeated classes, who waged a treacherous civil war against the new regime, the workers' state survived. An alternative way of organizing society, in which ordinary people were in control of their own lives, free from the exploitations of capitalism, had been successfully launched. In the Soviet view the workers' utopia continued to function successfully, with a few amendments, under Stalin and Khrushchev and into the 1980s. All Soviet historians had to stick firmly to this interpretation – it was the way in which the communists sought to establish the legitimacy of their regime.

What is regarded as the traditional Western liberal view began to take shape soon after the Second World War, with the beginning of the Cold War. The USSR and communism were seen, particularly in the USA, as a threat to Western civilization, and there was an almost obsessive desire to 'understand the enemy'. Western historians challenged the official Soviet interpretation of events on almost every point. Both sides agreed that the Tsarist system was incompetent and Russia backward, and they acknowledged the crucial role of Lenin and the Bolsheviks in the overthrow of the Provisional Government. But there the agreement ended. Western liberal historians rejected the Marxist theory of the inevitability of the revolution and the whole idea of 'scientific' laws governing history. The idea that the entire course of world history was governed by the class struggle was seen as ridiculous, since there are many other factors at work which help to determine what happens in any situation. Although a revolution was likely, given the combination of circumstances in Russia in the early twentieth century, events could have turned out very differently; for instance, the First World War might not have broken out, Nicholas II might have been an intelligent and talented politician, the leaders of the Provisional Government might have been more politically astute, Lenin and Trotsky could have been prevented from returning to Russia. This traditional Western view paid very little attention to the role of the masses; they were just simple people who knew nothing about politics and had been manipulated by Lenin and the Bolsheviks, who exploited the general chaos. Lenin and his party were strictly disciplined and rigidly organized, and Lenin himself was utterly ruthless and motivated purely by his lust for power. The authoritarian nature of Bolshevism led inexorably to a centralized, one-party state based on violence and terror; Stalinism was simply a continuation of Leninism, and neither of them did a lot to help the Russian people.

There is a third group of historians – radical left-wingers – who are often described as libertarians. They include a few Marxists, non-Marxists, anarchists and some Russian socialist, but anti-Bolshevik writers, who were forced into exile after the Bolsheviks came to power. They disagree on many of the details, but there is some consensus on certain basic points. They argue that the production of wealth breeds economic oppression and humiliation for the workers. This can only be overcome when the workers themselves are able to organize and manage production. In the view of libertarian historians the masses were responsible for both revolutions in Russia in 1917 – there was a genuinely democratic movement in which the Russian people tried to take control over their own lives. Workers' factory committees began to be formed after the February revolution, and *before* the Bolsheviks seized power. The workers took the slogan 'all power to the Soviets' literally and wanted and expected a decentralized government. Then in October the Bolsheviks hi-jacked their revolution and distorted it; control was taken out of the hands of the workers and given to officials appointed by the state. The masses therefore got the very opposite of what they had expected – a centralized dictatorship. It was no more than a change of oppressors; ordinary workers and peasants were just as exploited in the USSR as they had been under Tsarism.

There have been variations on similar themes from individual writers like Leon Trotsky who in 1937 published a book with the significant title *The Revolution Betrayed: What is the Soviet Union and Where is it Going?* His interpretation was that October 1917 was a genuine workers' revolution and that Lenin had been on the right road to socialism; he had never wanted to be a dictator – it was Stalin who had ruined things by introducing the cult of personality and the excessive use of state terror. This debate about Lenin and Stalin has been a recurring theme: supporters of the 'discontinuity' theory – such as Isaac Deutscher and Adam Ulam – believe that Stalin destroyed Leninism by making himself a dictator and introducing a totalitarian state; supporters of 'continuity' argue that Leninism inevitably led on to Stalinism (see section 5.10).

On the other hand a few Western historians took a more sympathetic view of both Lenin and Stalin. E.H. Carr for example, although he did not approve of the use of terror, nevertheless argued that Russia was so backward that authoritarian methods were needed to enable the country to catch up with the West. For him, the great thing about Lenin and Stalin was that their policies were successful. 'The pattern of life of ordinary people changed for the better,' he wrote; 'the Soviet worker, and even the Soviet peasant, of 1967 was a very different person from his father and grandfather in 1917. He could hardly fail to be conscious of what the revolution had done for him; and this outweighed the absence of freedoms which he had never enjoyed or dreamed of. The harshness and cruelty of the regime were real. But so also were its achievements.'[1]

One of the problems for all non-Russian historians trying to write about the Soviet period was that they were hampered by the difficulty of finding reliable documentary evidence and reliable statistics. Stalin made it almost impossible to get at the truth by throwing a wall of secrecy around the activities of the communist party and the government; only approved information was made available and this tended to exaggerate the achievements of his regime. Western historians attempting to work in Soviet libraries and archives were sometimes accused of spying and expelled from the country.

In the mid-1960s the writing of the history of the revolutionary period entered a new phase, sometimes referred to as 'revisionist' history. This happened partly as a result of Khrushchev's determination to let some of the truth come out about the horrors of Stalinism, and partly because of the relaxation of Cold War tensions. The Soviet government began to allow Western historians more access to their archives, though there were still many restrictions, and it was understood that nothing derogatory must be written about Lenin. All this coincided with a further growth of interest in Russian history among American historians. The 'revisionists' did not agree on every detail, but they all had similar attitudes: they were prepared to challenge traditional views and refused to allow themselves to be swayed by the 'anti-left' attitudes of most Western historians; they wanted to investigate the experiences of the mass of ordinary people – their social and economic problems – to which very little attention had been paid by earlier historians. Their conclusions were that social forces had been at least as important as politics in causing the revolutions. The traditional interpretation was that political events in Petrograd, the capital, were the driving force behind both revolutions; the actions of members of the Duma, the Provisional Government, the Petrograd Soviet and the Bolshevik party leaders were all-important, and it seemed, according to this interpretation, that the great mass of ordinary people made little or no contribution. The 'revisionists' revealed that industrial workers, soldiers and peasants had been extremely active, not just in Petrograd, but in Moscow and other regions as well. The October revolution in particular was not simply a political *coup* in the capital, it was a genuine popular uprising which had the backing of ordinary people all over the empire. This interpretation therefore played down the contribution of the Bolsheviks – it was the support of the masses rather than any special organizational genius on the part of Lenin that brought the party to power. At the same time some historians began to look again at the pre-revolutionary period, suggesting that the situation was not as bad as Soviet historians would have it. One of the first to do so was Alexander Gershenkron who, in 1962, concluded that 'it seems plausible to say that Russia on the eve of the [First World] war was well on the way towards a westernization or, perhaps more precisely, a Germanization of its industrial growth.'[2]

Yet another change took place during Gorbachev's *glasnost* (openness) era when people were allowed much greater freedom to speak out about their experiences under Stalin. Russian historians were encouraged to be critical of Stalin; text-books of Soviet history were withdrawn and history examinations cancelled until the rethink was completed. Horrifying details soon emerged about the excesses and atrocities committed during Stalin's collectivization of agriculture and his purges. In 1990 General Dmitri Volkogonov produced a highly critical biography of Stalin which would not have been allowed before Gorbachev's time. But criti-cism also spread to Lenin who came under fire for his ruthlessness during the civil war and his rejection of democracy.

After the collapse of the USSR and the communist party there was a dramatic change in the historiography of the revolution and the Soviet period. Yeltsin threw open all the archives; from 1991 until 1993 Volkogonov was in charge of the declassification of communist party and state documents and he was respon-sible for releasing seventy eight million files. As Sheila Fitzpatrick points out, 'for historians, particularly historians of the Soviet period, this was a bonanza comparable with the opening of Nazi-period records in Germany after the col-lapse of the Third Reich.'[3] Much new information came out, especially about the activities of Lenin and Stalin, the terror and the purges of the 1930s, and about the great famine of 1932–33. Also available were secret police reports and docu-ments belonging to the Central Committee of the Communist Party and the Politburo. There was a flood of books and articles on various aspects of the revolutionary period.

The new freedom for historians had several important results. First of all it led to the complete discrediting of the traditional Soviet account. Volkogonov himself published a devastating biography of Trotsky (1992), and an equally hostile one of Lenin followed in 1994. Correspondingly, Russian writers went into raptures about the Tsarist regime, so much so that Professor Paul Dukes of the University of Aberdeen, who took part in an international historians' conference in Russia in April 1993, had this to say: 'There is some danger at the present time of looking at the Tsarist empire of Nicholas II as a kind of "Merrie Russia", a won-derful dream ruined by the Revolution and the ensuing Soviet nightmare. During one of the recesses of the conference, one of the younger Russian participants expressed his firm belief in the sainthood of Nicholas II and the return of absolutist Tsarism by Divine Right as the only hope for his country's future.'[4]

Another result of the new openness was to provide what seemed to be fresh authenticity to the traditional Western view. If the Soviet interpretation of events had been wrong all along, it suggested that those historians who had been most critical of it – traditional Westerners – might have been right. Richard Pipes, the veteran Professor of History at Harvard University, and a long-time traditionalist, brought out *The Russian Revolution 1899–1919* (1990) and *Russia under the Bolshevik Regime 1919–1924* (1993), in which he completely disregarded the work of the revisionists and restated the traditional Western interpretation. He took a strongly anti-Bolshevik and anti-Lenin view and ignored the revisionists' emphasis on the widespread working-class support for the October revolution. For Pipes, there was nothing inevitable about the revolution, and it was not the product of a genuine mass movement – it was simply an opportunist seizure of power by the Bolsheviks. There never was a workers' state; what Lenin did, motivated purely by his lust for power, was to bring in a totalitarian system, very like the old tsarist autocracy, except that there was a different group of people in control.

It has to be said that most Western historians disagree with the Pipes interpretation of events. Edward Acton, Professor of Modern European History at the University of East Anglia, is completely dismissive: he claims that each one of Pipes's propositions 'flies in the face of the most detailed and meticulous specialist research; the overall picture painted is a mere caricature of the momentous social drama which that research is gradually recovering. It is as if, because the collapse of the USSR took place when the right was riding high in the West, a veil was about to be drawn over the implications of the best work of recent decades in an attempt to ensure that popular understanding of the revolution would be based on old myths resuscitated.'[5] The latest research attaches even more importance to the actions of ordinary people. As Christopher Read puts it in his book *From Tsar to Soviets: The Russian People and their Revolution, 1917–21* (1996), 'in the Russian Empire, the revolution was constantly driven forward by the often spontaneous impulse given to it from the grass roots. In the course of their struggle peasants, workers and, perhaps most important in the short term, soldiers and sailors thought out their programmes and developed tactics to achieve them locally and regionally.'[6]

The research of many historians of the younger generation, including Russians, Americans and Europeans, has taken off in yet new directions. Often described as 'post-modernists', these historians are much less interested in Marxism, in concepts of class and in social concerns than were earlier historians; they tend to focus on areas such as ideas, culture and nationality. Their approach has a tendency to treat all interpretations of the past as determined by the cultural position of the historian in the present. In one sense this brings them into conflict with the revisionists and their interest in the social and economic aspirations of the working class. It is probably on the Stalinist era that their work has had the greatest impact; some of them, for example, seek to emphasize the 'paternalistic' aspects of Stalinism[7] (see section 6.6).

During the last century, so many unexpected events have happened in Russia, so many controversial changes have taken place, and the Russian people have undergone such terrible traumas, that it is no wonder there is such a wide variety of interpretations. But this is what makes Russian history so fascinating, and this book, which makes use of the most recent research by leading scholars of Russian history, is designed to make it as accessible as possible. Each chapter begins with a short summary of events and a brief mention of the main areas of debate, and then goes on to examine what happened and to discuss the different views in detail. I have tried to steer a comprehensible course through the rich but bewildering variety of interpretations and to present a balanced and objective account of what happened and why. At the end of each chapter there is a selection of documentary evidence relating to some of the areas of debate; this can be used as a basis for discussion or simply read for sheer enjoyment!

Notes

1. E.H. Carr, *The Russian Revolution from Lenin to Stalin, 1917–1929*, pp. 188–9.
2. A. Gerschenkron, 'Agrarian Policies and Industrialisation: Russia, 1861–1917', *The Cambridge History of Europe*, vol. 6, part 2, p. 209.
3. Sheila Fitzpatrick (editor), *Stalinism: New Directions*, p. 1.
4. Paul Dukes, 'From Soviet to Russian History', *History Today*, vol. 43, August 1993.
5. Edward Acton, 'The Revolution and its Historians', in Acton, Cherniaev and Rosenberg (editors), *Critical Companion to the Russian Revolution 1914–1921*, p. 13.
6. Christopher Read, *From Tsar to Soviets: The Russian People and their Revolution, 1917–21*, p. 5.
7. See for example Lewis H. Siegelbaum, 'Socialist Paternalism and Soviet rural "notables" in the mid-1930s', in S. Fitzpatrick (editor), *Stalinism: New Directions*, pp. 231–55.

2 Russia before the First World War

Summary of events

The Russian Empire in 1900 covered an enormous area stretching from its frontiers with Germany and Austria–Hungary in the west, across eastern Europe and Asia to the Pacific Coast, a distance of over five thousand miles; from Murmansk in the Arctic north down to the frontier with Turkey the distance is about two thousand miles, making Russia by far the largest state in the world in area. It also had the largest population – estimated at around 132 million. However, this vast empire was not stable: although regarded as one of the great powers, **Russia had not kept up with the world's leading nations – the USA, Germany and Britain – in industrial development, in social progress or in progress towards democracy.**

Since 1613 Russia had been ruled by members of the Romanov dynasty who were absolute autocratic monarchs; there was no elected parliament to act as a check on their exercise of power, there were no legal political parties and there was no long tradition of regional or town local government. A strict press censorship was in operation.

The last three Tsars were:

Alexander II (1855–81)	A man of some vision, he was prepared to contemplate reforms, and was responsible for the emancipation of the serfs in 1861. He was assassinated in 1881.
Alexander III (1881–94)	Turned firmly against all further reform and presided over a period of total reaction.
Nicholas II (1894–1917)	Continued the policy of reaction until the 1905 revolution, when he was forced to make some concessions.

Although both Nicholas and Alexander III realised the need for, and encouraged industrial progress, they were both reluctant to give up any of their power, and were **devoted to preserving the autocracy intact**. They both lacked the vision to cope with the modernization of their vast country.

1904–05 – War with Japan. The government made the mistake of becoming involved in war with Japan, expecting an easy victory. However, it ended in humiliating defeat for Russia.

The 1905 Revolution. There was a long revolutionary tradition in Russia; in spite of political parties being illegal, there were a number of groups which functioned 'underground' – Populists, Socialist Revolutionaries and Marxists. There was unrest among industrial workers and peasants and in 1905, in the middle of the war with Japan, disturbances broke out which soon spread to most parts of the empire, and became serious enough to be called a revolution. Nicholas was forced to issue **the October Manifesto** in which he made some concessions: he allowed an elected national parliament, **the Duma**, and legalized political parties and trade unions. A number of political parties, which had been active in secret, were now able to function openly.

The Duma experiment fails. Although the October Manifesto seemed to promise progress towards democracy, Nicholas himself was determined to ignore the Duma as much as possible, though some of his ministers, notably Petr Stolypin, tried to co-operate with it. Between 1907 and 1917 there were four Dumas, but for a number of reasons, the Tsar and the Duma failed to develop a harmonious relationship.

Economic progress. Great progress was made in industry and agriculture in the years up to 1914, though there is great discussion among historians about exactly how successful these programmes were, and about whether the Tsarist regime was likely to have survived, had it not been for the First World War.

Main areas of debate:

- How active were the masses politically?
- How successful were the modernization programmes in industry and agriculture and could Russia really be regarded as a 'modern' state in 1914?
- Was there a real chance of democracy developing?
- Was revolution already inevitable in 1914 or could Tsarism have survived?

2.1 Russian government and society before 1905

(a) Alexander II (1855–81) and his reforms

During the first half of the nineteenth century there were rigid class divisions: about one per cent of the people were aristocrats or nobles, 90 per cent were peasants, and the remainder consisted of townspeople, industrial workers and middle classes. Until 1861 the majority of peasants were serfs, owned by their aristocratic landlords; they were not allowed to own land; although most were allowed to farm a small area for their own use, this remained the property of the landlord; and they were not allowed to leave their villages. The Tsar Alexander II introduced some important reforms in the hope of revitalizing and stimulating the country and the economy, after Russia's humiliating defeat in the Crimean War (1854–56). However, he did not want to change the basic political framework, which he was determined must remain an autocracy.

The most important reform was the abolition of serfdom in1861 which meant that peasants were now free and were allotted a portion of land taken from their landlord. The state paid landlords compensation for land given to peasants, but peasants were expected to repay the state in instalments – known as redemption payments – over 49 years. The *mir* or village commune held this peasant land in collective ownership, and was responsible for making sure redemption payments were made. In local government new elected provincial and district assemblies known as *zemstva* were introduced in 1864 in the European part of the empire. Each *zemstvo* was allowed to raise local taxes and was given some responsibility for education, health, prisons, transport and roads, credit and insurance, famine relief and general care of the poor. Where appropriate, *zemstva* were expected to encourage industry and new methods of agriculture. The voting system for elections to the district *zemstva* was based on class divisions: nobles, townspeople and peasants each voted for their own representatives in a separate electoral college, which ensured that the nobles always had a majority in every *zemstvo*. Members took their responsibilities seriously and the *zemstva* soon began to employ large numbers of teachers, doctors, nurses and other experts. Cities and large towns were allowed to have elected municipal councils (1874) though again the right to vote depended on a property qualification. Another important reform was the remodelling of the legal system along Western lines, with the introduction of public trial by jury, and elected justices of the peace to deal with minor cases. Universities were given more control over their own affairs, and there was some relaxation of the strict press censorship. The army, which had not distinguished itself during the Crimean War, also underwent some modernization – universal conscription was introduced and attempts were made to build up a more efficient and professional officer corps. In the late 1870s some of Alexander's ministers proposed that he should take steps to set up some sort of mechanism for him to consult representatives of the *zemstva* and the municipal councils.

Tragically the Tsar Liberator, as Alexander became known, was killed by a terrorist bomb in 1881, on the very day that he had apparently decided to accept some of the proposals. His son and successor, Alexander III (1881–94), instead of drawing the conclusion that further reform was needed to make the regime popular, decided that reform had gone too far, and introduced a package of measures known as 'the Reaction' to tighten up government control and put a stop to any further moves towards democracy in both central and local government. The powers of the secret police (the *Okhrana*) were increased, the reformist ministers who had suggested 'consultation' to Alexander II were dismissed and any judges and magistrates who were thought to be too 'reformist' or too liberal were sacked. The *zemstva* lost many of their powers and could be overruled by government officials known as land captains, who were appointed by provincial governors. Land captains were mostly nobles and were given wide powers over the peasants. This repressive policy was continued by Nicholas II until the 1905 revolution.[1]

(b) Society according to the 1897 census

The first census ever held in Russia – in 1897 – gave a total population for the empire of 126 million, of which 92 million lived in the European part. The census also showed that class divisions were still very much alive:

Ruling class (Tsar, court and government)	0.5%
Upper class (nobles, higher clergy, army and navy officers)	12.0%
Middle class (merchants, factory owners, financiers, teachers)	1.5%
Working class (factory workers, miners, small shopkeepers)	4.0%
Peasants	82.0%

It was an overwhelmingly rural society: only 15 per cent of the population lived in cities or large towns; 75 per cent of all working people were employed in agriculture, while only 9 per cent worked in mining and other industries. By 1914 this figure had increased to 10 per cent and the total population had also increased to 155 million of whom 18 per cent now lived in urban areas. The population of the few big cities increased sharply during those 17 years: St Petersburg (the imperial capital) grew from 1.25 million to 2.12 million, Moscow from roughly one million to 1.76 million, Warsaw from 0.68 million to about one million, and both Riga and Kiev from 250,000 to 500,000 each.[2] These figures alone suggest that some substantial industrial expansion must have taken place. It has to be remembered, however, that all Russian statistics are unreliable and have to be taken as approximate; some estimates put the total population of the empire in 1914 as high as 170 million; a margin of error of 15 million tells us a lot about the reliability and efficiency of the Russian bureaucracy during these years.

(c) The elite nobles and the government

The royal family and a relatively small group of noble families who were immensely rich and influential formed an elite class which more or less ran the country. The Romanovs took their advisers from these leading families who also provided top army personnel. They were a closely knit group bound together by intermarriage, political activity, service of the state, and culture. Even at the beginning of the twentieth century the elite still dominated the court and the government. The basic principle on which government was carried out was autocracy – personal rule by the Tsar, who was God's representative on earth, at least as far as the Russian empire was concerned. It was the Tsar's right and his duty to rule the country completely without constraint from laws, ministers, bureaucracy or parliaments – his decision was final on all matters. Both Alexander III and Nicholas II were encouraged to uphold this principle by conservative advisers like Konstantin Pobedonostsev, the man responsible for persuading Alexander III to introduce his anti-reform policy. The elite was therefore split into two camps. On the one hand were the reformists, who deplored the limitations placed on local government bodies and argued that the problems of modern government were far too complex for one man to cope with almost alone. Many of the officials and civil servants in the Ministry of Finance were reformists since they were expected

Figure 2.1   Extremes of wealth and poverty: a dinner party in the palace of Countess Shuvalov, in St Petersburg.

Figure 2.2   Extremes of wealth and poverty: a soup kitchen for the poor and unemployed in St Petersburg.

to transform the country industrially and yet were hampered by all the obstacles in the way of middle class initiatives and enterprise. They thought it was vital to involve the educated public in some way in government, at the very least in a consultative role. Sergei Witte, the successful Transport and Finance Minister in the 1890s (see section 2.5(a)) was convinced that revolution could only be avoided if Russia was transformed into a fully modern society. On the other hand there were the reactionaries, always numerous in the Ministry of the Interior, which was responsible for keeping law and order. Reactionaries believed that a police state was the best way of keeping the country under control, and they were in the ascendancy under Alexander III and Nicholas II right up until 1905. Nearly all Nicholas II's ministers of foreign and internal affairs, even after 1905, came from old elite noble families.

Government was therefore centralized in the person of the Tsar, who acted through his Council of Ministers, the police, the *Okhrana* and his agents. The principle was the same in local government where every attempt was made to curtail the powers of the *zemstva* in favour of the nobles. The Tsar also had other groups of advisers such as the State Council, some of whose members were elected by the *zemstva;* however, the council was always dominated by reactionary nobles. Any suggestions that a national *zemstvo* should be called were dismissed out of hand, and all political parties were banned. This then was what government in Russia amounted to in the years before 1905.

(d) Nobility

These were the traditional landowning class; in 1861 there were about 128,000 noble families who held land. The majority of landowning families were not members of the elite, and had gone through a difficult period after the abolition of serfdom in 1861. They had lost their cheap serf labour and had to pay wages, which left many of them struggling to make their estates viable. Some decided to sell up and move into the city, and by 1905 the number of landowning families had fallen to about 107,000. After the 1905 revolution many more followed suit and joined one or other of the expanding professional groups, such as university lecturers and lawyers, or went into business – industry, commerce and transport. Many put their capital in shares and bonds or invested successfully in urban property. By 1912 the amount of land owned by nobles had fallen to only half the amount owned by them in 1861. Not surprisingly there was resentment among many nobles at the loss of their privileged position. Around the turn of the century they began to turn to politics; they accused the government of favouring industry at their expense and even ventured to demand reform of the autocracy. They became involved in the work of the *zemstva* and used them as a platform from which to publicize their ideas. The more radical of them formed links with the liberal intelligentsia in the cities (see section 2.2(g)), and played an important role in the development of the 1905 revolution.

Not all nobles fell on hard times, however; those with initiative and drive tried to turn their estates into profitable enterprises; they were willing to invest and introduce the latest agricultural methods, and some became successful capitalists, buying up land cheaply from struggling neighbours. One of the best known of these 'farmer' nobles was Prince G.E. Lvov, who was for a short time the first Prime Minister of the Provisional Government after the collapse of the monarchy. They were the sort of liberal aristocrats who were genuinely concerned about the problems and difficulties faced by the peasants and who were anxious to improve their conditions. They could foresee trouble if nothing was done. Unfortunately, the more conservative nobles resented these liberal tendencies and did their best to block attempts at reform.

The nobility also included top members of the government bureaucracy or civil service and army officers. With the great expansion of the bureaucracy and the army in the last quarter of the nineteenth century there was a corresponding increase in the numbers of people from wider social backgrounds receiving noble status. Between 1875 and 1895, for instance, 37,000 people acquired hereditary noble status.[3] Lenin's father, Ilya Nikolaevich Ulyanov, had become a hereditary noble and a state councillor in 1874 on his appointment as Director of Popular Schools in Simbirsk province. The bureaucracy was gradually becoming more professional and after 1905 the political influence of the nobles increased. For the first time they were allowed to form an organisation – the United Nobility; many of its members were elected to the State Council and the State Duma as members of the Octobrist Party (those who accepted the October Manifesto). Unfortunately the reactionary/reformist split continued: reactionary nobles blocked proposals for further reform, especially some of those proposed by Petr Stolypin (see section 2.6(b)), while the reformists became increasingly frustrated with and resentful of the incompetent and anachronistic police state.

(e) Middle classes

This was a tiny group according to the 1897 census and it was still weak even in 1914 after the industrial progress of the previous two decades. It included the leaders and organisers of industry and trade – factory and mine owners, merchants, bankers and financiers. Some industrialists, like the Putilovs, who owned steelworks in St Petersburg, and the Morozovs, who were in textiles and railway building, were extremely wealthy; the Putilovs employed 54,000 workers by 1914. There were tensions within the business community arising from the fact that Russia's industrialization was carried out with state supervision and intervention and with a great deal of foreign investment. Industrialists who won government contracts were resented by those who did not. The younger generation of businessmen, especially in Moscow, were critical of the conservatism of their elders and wanted to get involved in politics to agitate for a more efficient governmental system. And yet at the same time they needed a strong authoritarian state to help them clamp down on labour unrest. In the early years of the century these entrepreneurs were only just beginning to acquire the status of their counterparts in western Europe, and had nothing like their political influence. The government, nervous of any group which might threaten its autocratic control, kept a close eye on the activities of their professional associations for signs of criticism or subversion. Strangely perhaps, industrialists and financiers made very little contact with nobles, either socially or politically. As Peter Gatrell points out, 'close contact between a member of the Russian landed nobility and an industrialist or banker brought shame and even scandal on the former's family.'[4] But if they lacked political influence, many of them made a significant contribution to the cultural life of the country. This was a period of great cultural revival and vitality in which, in some ways, Russia led the rest of Europe (see section 2.1(k)). Many businessmen were patrons of the arts, helping to finance musicians and the theatre, and building up art collections.

Also part of the middle class were the intelligentsia, though even at the time there was a great debate in Russia about exactly what this term meant and who could claim to be a member of the intelligentsia. It was not simply that every educated person was an *intelligent;* it came to be accepted, especially after the 1905 revolution, at least among the intelligentsia themselves, that they were the people who held the key to progress – and that lay in mounting a challenge to the whole basis of autocracy. The intelligentsia included doctors, lawyers, teachers, engineers, managers, writers and artists, and in fact any educated person who felt impatient with the government's policy of reaction, and who were convinced that society and politics must be changed. Many became active in one or other of the secret political groups (see section 2.2). The earliest intellectuals were nobles, but later, as education became more widespread, they were joined by people from a wider social background. They prided themselves on being non-estate and classless.

(f) Working classes

By 1913 this rapidly growing class had reached about 2.4 million workers in large-scale industry, plus another 8.4 million in small-scale enterprises, building, transport, communications and domestic service.[5] Many of the industrial workers were peasants who had moved to take jobs in towns, in metal and textile factories and in the transport system. They tended to retain their links with their rural area and often went back to their village to help with the harvest; many still kept a small plot of land which was looked after by relatives and which would be very useful whenever there was a slump or a strike. Living and working conditions were primitive (see section 2.3(b)) for more details). There was an elite group of skilled workers or master craftsmen who were better paid than ordinary labourers. They sometimes organized themselves into a sort of co-operative called an *artel.* As education spread, more workers became literate and were receptive to revolutionary literature. However, trade unions were illegal in 1900; the only forms of workers' organizations allowed were those sponsored by the authorities and closely supervised by the police. Industrial workers were therefore completely at the mercy of their employers and of economic fluctuations. In the years after 1900 for example, a world trade depression brought unemployment and wage reductions to Russian workers. By 1905 unrest was so great that even their weak trade unions were determined to challenge the government (see section 2.3(a–c)). After the 1905 revolution unions were legalized and quickly spread; they attracted mainly young, skilled workers in small craft-based industries, though they were not so popular among workers in large-scale industry. By January 1907 union membership had reached 250,000, but in June of that year the government again banned unions and other forms of labour organization (see section 2.6(b)). Although later a few trade unions were allowed, the movement remained extremely weak right up to the outbreak of the First World War in 1914. Nevertheless, urban workers were extremely militant and strikes were common, even though they were illegal.

(g) Peasants

At the turn of the century about 82 per cent of the population were classified as belonging to the peasantry. Serfs belonging to private landowners had been given their personal freedom by the Emancipation Edict of 1861, but state-owned serfs had to wait until 1886 before they were allowed full rights. On the whole peasants were disappointed at the results of emancipation and they seemed to be no better off materially. In the fertile Black-Earth area (a huge swathe of land stretching from the border with Romania, through the Ukraine, Central Russia and on to the Ural mountains) peasants actually came out of it with about 25 per cent less land than they had been allowed to farm for their own use before, because the landowners wanted to take as much of this rich land as they could get their hands on. Landlords were able to do this because of a rule that if, after the handing over of the peasant allotments, a landlord would be left with less than half his estate, he could reduce the size of the peasant allotments. It was generally felt that landowners had been left in possession of far too much land, and peasants bitterly resented the redemption payments. They still had to do military service, they were forbidden to leave their village without the permission of the village commune and they were liable to be publicly flogged (this was abolished in 1904).

And yet the picture was not all bad: the peasants had something which was unique to Russia – the village commune or *mir*. These varied in size from as few as half a dozen households to as many as a thousand; at the turn of the century the average was about 54 households and 290 people. Each commune elected elders and a tax collector, and together with the village assembly, they ran the life of the commune. Most of the village land was jointly owned and from time to time the commune would redistribute the land so that everybody got a share of the best and the households stayed relatively equal. At the same time a larger proportion of peasants was able to read: literacy increased from 21 per cent of the total population of the empire in 1897 to 40 per cent in 1914; among the peasants it was especially high in areas closest to big cities – 90 per cent of peasant recruits into the army from St Petersburg and Moscow provinces were literate in 1904. It is no surprise that many revolutionary activists emerged from the ranks of the peasants; in 1917 they were just as ready to take land by force as they had been in 1905–06.

The nature and characteristics of the peasantry have been the subject of some debate, and a number of myths have been perpetuated. Soviet historians divided the peasants into two mutually hostile groups: ordinary and poor peasants on one hand, and better-off peasants, called *kulaks*, who were portrayed as enemies of socialism, on the other. Recent research suggests that this is far too simplistic an interpretation; obviously some peasants would be more successful than others, but there was probably never a clear-cut division between the two classes; and anyway the situation varied from region to region. Another assumption made by many historians was that the peasants were ignorant, had no understanding of politics, had no ideas about how they would like to organize their lives and were only capable of destructive violence. But it is now clear that the peasants did have ideas about what revolution meant: for them it meant land and freedom. The land should belong to those who cultivated it, and freedom meant the right of the peasant commune to run their own affairs free from interference by the government, the nobles and the Church. And thirdly there was the debate about whether the peasant economy was in crisis in the early years of the twentieth century. Some historians argue that the peasants were becoming increasingly impoverished because of the rapidly growing population: one estimate is that there was a 20 per cent increase in the rural population of the empire between 1900 and 1914.[6] The small size of peasant holdings and old-fashioned farming methods – separate strips and wooden ploughs pulled by horses – meant that food production barely kept up with the population increase. In 1891–92 there was a disastrous famine in the middle Volga region in which 400,000 people died.[7] Some more recent revisionist research suggests that there was no real crisis in agriculture, that peasant productivity was improving, that their spending power was increasing and that this was reflected in the rise in government receipts from indirect taxation. Increasing food production was keeping pace with the growing population.[8] The truth no doubt lies somewhere between the two – conditions varied according to area: the most successful peasants were probably those in southern Russia, around the northern shores of the Black Sea; in the Black Earth zone conditions for many peasants were worsening (see section 2.4(b) for more on the state of the peasants).

(h) Nationalities

The Russian empire was a great multi-national conglomeration with many different languages, religions and cultures. At the time of the 1897 census the Russians themselves made up less than half the total population – 55.6 million out of 126 million. The next largest national groups were Ukrainians with 22.4 million and Poles with 7.9 million. Then came White Russians (in Belorussia) with 5.8 million, Kirgiz (4 million), Tatars (3.4 million), Finns (3.1 million) and Germans (1.8 million). Other small groups included Latvians, Bashkirs, Lithuanians, Armenians, Azerbaijanis, Chechens, Romanians, Estonians, Mordvinians, Georgians, Tajiks, Turkmenians, Greeks and Bulgarians. In addition there were about 5 million Jews. The other main religious groups were Orthodox Christians (70 per cent of the population), Roman Catholics (9 per cent) and Muslims (11 per cent). The Tsarist regime had no sympathy with any non-Russians who showed the slightest desire for a separate cultural and political identity. They carried out a strict 'Russification' policy which aimed to turn the non-Russians into 'true Christians, loyal subjects, and good Russians'; their supporters extolled the special virtues of the Slav peoples. After 1881, all non-Russian languages were banned from schools, official documents and street signs. Jews, who were blamed for the murder of Alexander II in 1881, came in for especially harsh treatment: they were not allowed to own land, work in the Civil Service or become army officers. Consequently both Jews and non-Russians played an important

Map 2.1   **Western Russia about 1900.**

role in the anti-tsarist parties which were developing around the turn of the century. The irony was that the majority of the Russians themselves seemed to have very little sense of nationalism or patriotism. The peasants resented any influence from outside the commune and the government did nothing to encourage them out of isolation or to develop a sense of citizenship.

(i) The church

A survey of Russian society would not be complete without mention of the Russian Orthodox Church which played a large part in everybody's life. It is impossible to say what proportion of the Russian people were genuine Christians, but certainly most of them observed the church rituals with its icons, saints' days and processions. The church taught unquestioning loyalty to the Tsar who was presented as the vicar of God; disobedience to him was condemned as a sin. Obviously this was an important prop for the autocracy which rewarded the church by making it the official Russian religion – the Established Church. Roman Catholics, most of whom were in Poland, and Jews were allowed to practise their religions, but only members of the Orthodox Church were considered to be true Russians. Towards the end of the nineteenth century a radical wing developed in the church which ventured to criticise the regime and disapproved of the close connection between church and state. Some priests were elected to the Duma after 1905, but the church leadership remained strongly supportive of the Tsar. The collapse of the monarchy in 1917 was accompanied by a wave of anti-clericalism and the church lost all its lands.

(j) The military

The Russian army was seen as the most important prop of the autocracy; soldiers took an oath of allegiance not to the state, but to the Tsar in person. Gradually, however, during the second half of the nineteenth century and the early years of the twentieth, the army became increasingly demoralized. This was to some extent because of its poor military performances: it suffered defeat in the Crimean War (1854–56), and it made heavy weather of its short, though victorious campaign against Turkey (1877–78). Attempts to modernize the army and make it more professional seemed to meet with little success, and military expenditure was actually reduced so that more could be spent on modernizing industry. There was a further humiliating defeat in the war against Japan (1904–5). Another cause of demoralization was the fact that troops were constantly being used to suppress unrest – between 1883 and 1903 troops were called out to quell disturbances almost 1500 times.

So both officers and men had grounds for complaint; officers felt that the army should not be used for what they saw as 'police work', and they bitterly resented being expected to fight a war 6000 miles away against Japan, without proper training and preparation. The most outspoken criticism of the government came from the younger generation of non-aristocratic officers who were a product of Alexander II's army reforms. By 1905 almost half the officers came from non-noble backgrounds and were mostly in the infantry, whereas the nobles served in Guards regiments, where they were much better paid and enjoyed a glamorous social life. The non-nobles deplored the old-fashioned thinking of the aristocrats at the top who continued to treat the cavalry as the most important branch of the army, instead of concentrating on motorized transport, machine-guns and heavy artillery.

The vast majority of ordinary rank-and-file soldiers were peasants who resented the brutal treatment with which they were expected to cope as a matter of course. According to Orlando Figes, 'soldiers could expect to be punched in the face, hit in the mouth with the butt of a rifle and sometimes even flogged for relatively minor misdemeanours... even whilst off duty the common soldier was deprived of the rights of a normal citizen. He could not go to restaurants or theatres, ride in trams or occupy a seat in a first- or second-class railway carriage.'[9] Already during the 1905 revolution some units mutinied when they were ordered to fire on their fellow peasants. The autocracy was gradually losing control of its most powerful mainstay.[10]

(k) Culture and the arts

Russia was certainly not backward in its contribution towards European culture. The final years of the nineteenth century and the period up to 1917 saw a great cultural revival after a quiet period following the deaths of writers such as Turgenev (1883) and Dostoevsky (1881). Tolstoy bridged the gap between the golden age of Russian literature and the so-called Silver Age: his great novels *War and Peace* and *Anna Karenina* appeared in 1869 and 1876; his later works of fiction such as the short stories *Master and Man* (1895) and *The Death of Ivan Ilich* (1886), and his novel *Resurrection* (1889), were written after Tolstoy had undergone a spiritual crisis, and were concerned with his new moral convictions – belief in God, renunciation of property, condemnation of violence and the abolition of governments and churches. He was especially outraged by the violence used by the regime in 1905. Many of his works were banned by the censor, and he was excommunicated by the Orthodox Church in 1901; but this also made him a cult figure, and his funeral in 1910 turned into a huge anti-government demonstration. Anton Chekhov (1860–1904), whose grandfather had been a serf, had his plays *The Cherry Orchard* and *The Three Sisters* produced at the Moscow Arts Theatre, founded by the great director Stanislavsky in 1898. Later Chekhov became recognized as one of the first leading exponents of the modern short story. The realist works of Maxim Gorky (1868–1936) were concerned with the effects of poverty on people's lives; in the early years of the twentieth century he helped the Bolsheviks with financial contributions. There were wonderful poets too: the symbolist Alexander Blok (1880–1921) and the futurist Vladimir Mayakovsky (1897–1930). There was a special quality about Russian literature; in a country where censorship made it impossible to write directly about politics, novels, poems and literary journals were the alternative way of spreading social and political ideas.

There was a move towards realism in the world of painting, the best known artist being I.Y. Repin (1844–1930); but by the turn of the century there was a reaction against realism and naturalism. Attention was focused on St Petersburg which could claim to be the world centre of progressive art. Probably the best remembered Russian artist from this period is Wassily Kandinsky (1866–1944), the man credited with having produced the first abstract painting. Other modernist Russian artists included Mikhail Vrubel (1856–1910), Mikhail Larionov (1881–1964), and the designer Alexander Benois (1870–1960). *The World of Art Group* was founded in St Petersburg in 1898. Another area in which Russia could claim to be in front of the rest of Europe was ballet – in 1909 Diaghilev founded the Ballets Russes, which boasted stars like Nijinsky and Pavlova. For some of the ballets, Diaghilev used music by the rising young composer Igor Stravinsky (1882–1971) – scores such as *The Firebird* (1910), *Petrushka* (1911) and *The Rite of Spring* which caused a riot at its first performance in Paris in 1913, and which is thought by many experts to be the beginning of the modernist movement in music. Another innovative young composer who was starting to make his mark on the eve of the First World War was Sergei Prokofiev (1891–1953).

Clearly Russian society was full of the greatest contrasts imaginable – from the glittering and cultured aristocratic circles and salons of St Petersburg all the way through to the minimal living conditions of the poorest urban workers and the village peasants. But in all areas of activity there were moves towards modernization, which meant the emergence of new groups and new classes, more widespread education and greater awareness of the shortcomings of the governmental and administrative systems. The one important area which seemed to be set against its own modernization, even after the warnings of 1905, was the ruling elite, and that was to be the source of the most serious tensions in Russian society.

2.2   Revolutionary ideas and parties

There was a long revolutionary tradition in Russia which manifested itself spectacularly from time to time. For example the Decembrists were a group of progressive army officers who, in December 1825, attempted a coup against the Tsar Nicholas I in the hope of bringing about some reform of the autocracy. The coup failed; five of the leaders were hanged and some 200 others were exiled to Siberia. Later they were regarded as heroes and martyrs by the revolutionaries of the early twentieth century. In the early years of Alexander II's reign a group who became known as Nihilists gained a lot of publicity. They advocated the total rejection of all existing institutions and moral values, and the necessity of unrestricted individual freedom, which they saw as the only way to improve the lot of the Russian people. Thanks to the attentions of right-wing journalists, they came to be regarded as something of a lunatic fringe. Even with Alexander's partial relaxation of the strict press censorship, it was still not easy to spread revolutionary ideas. Political parties were still banned and the tsarist secret police were quick to arrest anybody suspected of being involved in a political movement. Any attempts to organize opposition had to be carried out in secret and political pamphlets had to be circulated privately to avoid falling foul of the censor. Russian radical and revolutionary thought was a complex business, and there were several different strands.

(a) Slavophiles and Westerners

In the mid-nineteenth century a great debate developed about what Russia's future should be; the question was: should she follow Britain (and later Germany and the USA) which had industrialized? There were two general theories.

The *Westerners* thought that Russia should try and catch up with the industrial-ized states of the West and forget that in the past she had been more of an Asiatic country than a European one. Russia must take on Western culture, technology and economic ideas – only in that way could she become a great modern power. This had been in the mind of the Tsar Peter the Great (1695–1725) when he built his new capital at St Petersburg, which he called his 'window on the West'.

In opposition to these ideas, the *Slavophiles* believed that on no account should Russia try to copy the West. They were not impressed by the industrial cities of the West which they saw as decadent and degrading to the workers. They felt that Russia should concentrate on developing her own special attributes. Chief among these were the peasants with their village communes – this was the foundation on which the future of Russia must be built.

(b) Populists

One strand of Slavophile thought developed into Populism which attracted the support of many radical intellectuals during the 1860s and through to the early 1880s. Populists *(Narodniki)* were agrarian socialists, opposed to capitalism which was responsible for the industrialization of the West. They believed that capitalist industrialization had destroyed traditional rural communities by for-cing peasants to become industrial labourers, exploited by their capitalist mas-ters. They wanted to preserve the Russian peasants' village commune which, they believed, embodied the principle of equality, and which would become the basis of a future socialist state. Populists disagreed about how this would be achieved – some favoured peaceful methods, others believed that the only way was to overthrow the existing regime, by revolution.

The moderates, who included people like Peter Lavrov, wanted a process of gradual change by evolution. They relied on propaganda to educate the peasants about their role and seemed to think that the necessary changes would eventually happen by a process of irresistible logic, when the peasants were ready. Once the network of communes had been achieved, there would be no need of centralized control; the state would 'wither away'.

The more extreme populists wanted something much more decisive – revolu-tion as soon as possible. Nikolai Chernyshevsky (1828–89) put forward his ideas in the novel *What is to be Done?* (1862) which tells the story of a group of socialist activists whose leader is portrayed as a pure and noble hero: he rejects the usual pleasures of life – even on one occasion sleeping on a bed of nails in order to suppress his sexual urges – so that he can concentrate on the coming revolution. This novel served as an inspiration to many young revolutionaries, including Lenin himself, who called it 'a book that changes one for a whole lifetime'. Sergei Nechaev, the first revolutionary writer to come from a peasant background, published a pamphlet entitled *A Programme of Revolutionary Action* (1868), while Petr Tkachev produced *The Tasks of Revolutionary Propaganda in Russia* (1874). They all agreed that for a revolution to take place, dynamic leadership would be needed. They advocated the creation of a small group of full-time professional revolutionaries who would be totally dedicated and utterly ruthless. They wanted the revolution as soon as possible because the longer it was delayed, the more industrialized Russia would become on Western capitalist lines; this would destroy the peasant commune and their vision of Russia's future along with it. They disagreed with the moderates about the future role of the state – they believed that the state should not wither away; in fact it would be needed all the more, so that the leaders, the elite group who had guided and inspired the peasant revolution, could introduce a full socialist society. Lavrov had serious misgivings about this view: he felt it might easily end in dictatorship, which could be just as bad as tsarism.

This phase of Populist thinking led, in 1873–74, to a mass campaign in which thousands of the intelligentsia and university students went to the villages to spend time with the peasants. The movement had no central organization and there seemed to be several different aims. Some simply wanted to experience life in a commune, some wanted to educate the peasants about their future role in a socialist society, and others hoped to spread revolutionary propaganda and start activist groups. However, there was very little positive response from the peasants: they were suspicious of their unexpected visitors and some even reported them to the police. The authorities were greatly disturbed and arrested hundreds of the *Narodniki*. The failure of the campaign came as a great disappointment to the Populists: clearly the peasants lacked that vital revolutionary potential, and so the moderates were discredited. This caused a swing towards terrorism: a party calling itself 'Land and Freedom' spread propaganda among the intelligentsia, workers and peasants, while at the same time carrying out assassinations of various officials. Later, some of the extremists formed a group called the 'People's Will', and in 1881 their campaign of violence culminated in the assassination of the Tsar Alexander II. This brought the socialist state no nearer; its main effect was to frighten the tsarist regime into a policy of more repression. This phase of revolutionary activity ended with many of the leading figures in jail and many others in exile.

(c) Socialist Revolutionaries (SRs)

Gradually a new generation of activists began to emerge in the late 1880s as successors of the earlier Populists. They were agrarian socialists who believed that after the overthrow of the existing regime, all land should be shared out among the peasants. Like the Populists they hoped that the new Russia would be a mainly agrarian society based on small peasant communes with collective ownership of the land. Some of the SRs favoured terrorism and others wanted factories to be taken into collective ownership as well. SR groups were formed in towns like Saratov on the Volga, and Minsk (Belorussia), while Viktor Chernov set up a terrorist group in Berlin in 1901. An SR central party organization was formed in Geneva in 1902, where it published its own newspaper which circulated throughout Russia. During the 30 years following the failure of the *Narodniki*, the peasants in many regions had become more militant; from 1902 onwards there were a number of peasant revolts. During the 1905 revolution SR agents were busy stirring up the countryside; in July the first meeting of the All-Russian Peasant Union was held just outside Moscow. They drew up a programme which included an elected Constituent Assembly and the seizure of all land belonging to the royal family, the Church and private landowners. It is not clear just how far the peasants themselves were taking the initiative or whether they were being led by the SRs who attended the meeting. What is clear is that by 1905 there were substantial numbers of peasants who were militant enough to act independently, and there was a wave of attacks on the private property of landlords.[11] What also emerges is that there was growing support for the SRs among industrial workers in the towns. One important development that took place in 1905 was the appearance of committees (*soviets*) of elected representatives of workers, soldiers and peasants. Both the *soviets* and the strike committees included Socialist Revolutionaries and members of the other great socialist party of the time – the Social Democrats. After 1905 the government's policy of encouraging peasants to leave the commune and buy land of their own threatened to destroy the whole basis of the SR programme (see section 2.4(a)). Many SRs were in exile, and for the time being there was a decline in support for the party.

(d) Karl Marx and Marxism

The other great Russian socialist party was the Social Democrats who took their ideas originally from the writings of the German philosopher, Karl Marx (1818–83). After the failure of the German revolutions of 1848, Marx settled in London and spent many years writing about politics, economics and society. His two most famous works were *The Communist Manifesto* (1848) and *Capital* (1867). He was not a politician or even an active revolutionary (at least after 1848); he was a historian and political theorist, but his ideas had enormous influence on socialist and left-wing political thought. The main points that he made were:

- History is never static: change is always taking place in every society and the changes are caused by economic factors – by the relationships between the various classes in society.
- The important factor was who controlled the means of production. Whoever they were, these controllers would exploit the rest of the population and would become more or less synonymous with the state. The whole state system would be geared to further and protect their interests.
- However, this situation could not be permanent, because new factors would develop which would enable other classes to challenge the dominant class. There would be a constant class struggle, and eventually a new class would win the struggle and take control from the previous dominant class. The new ruling class would then change the state system to suit their interests.

Marx developed these theories from his study of the history of Western Europe, where, he believed, the sequence of events had followed this pattern. The first dominant class had been the feudal aristocracy who controlled the factors of production – the land and the peasants who farmed it for them. The next stage, which came with the development of a money economy instead of the feudal barter economy, was when the bourgeois capitalists became dominant. They overthrew the autocratic monarchy and set up systems of liberal democracy which safeguarded private property; the prime example of this was the French revolution which began in 1789. Eventually this bourgeois class began to industrialize, thus creating a large class of industrial workers. The time would come when the working class grew so powerful that they would be able to challenge the capitalists and launch a revolution. The proletariat (the skilled working class) would become the new dominant class and would run the government in their interests – it would be a 'dictatorship of the proletariat'. Marx thought this stage would probably be achieved at a time when capitalist governments were preoccupied with some great disaster which would be a by-product of capitalism; this might be a major war in which the capitalist states fought each other for supremacy, or it might be a great economic crisis caused by the nature of capitalism. 'What the bourgeoisie produces, above all,' wrote Marx in *The Communist Manifesto*, 'are its own gravediggers. Its fall and the victory of the proletariat are equally inevitable.'

The final stage of development would be the classless society – a partnership in which everybody contributed what they could. There would be no need for the state which would consequently 'wither away'. The principle would be: 'from each according to his ability, to each according to his need'. Towards the end of his life Marx modified some of his views and conceded that some flexibility was possible, depending on circumstances.

The Communist Manifesto was soon available in Russia in translation, having somehow succeeded in passing the censor, and *Capital* was translated into Russian in 1872. Many Populists found Marx's ideas attractive but they were disturbed by his portrayal of 'bourgeois society' in Western Europe and were determined that such developments in Russia should be avoided at all costs. Marx was impressed by the enthusiasm of the Populists and he admitted that Russia might be a special case: if the revolutionaries acted quickly enough it would perhaps be possible for Russia to combine the two revolutions – the liberal bourgeois overthrow of the feudal monarchy and the workers' overthrow of the bourgeois capitalists – and so by-pass the capitalist stage altogether. The workers' socialist state could then be based on the village commune. However, there was one vital condition that must be fulfilled: the Russian revolution must be the signal for proletarian revolutions in the West; only as part of a wider series of revolutions could the Russian double-revolution have any chance of success.

(e) Social Democrats

After the failure of the Populist movement many young socialists turned against the idea of a society based on the peasant commune and decided that the best way forward was to go along with industrialization and the progress towards the bourgeois capitalist phase. They supported industrialization because it was a necessary stage on the way to socialism. The intelligentsia were fascinated by Marxism because it seemed to offer a solution to the country's basic problems of backwardness and autocracy: Marx's ideas showed that Russia could catch up with the West, could absorb Western culture, and eventually could sweep away the tsarist regime, the great obstacle to progress. The leading figure was Georgi Plekhanov (1856–1918), a former Populist living in exile in Geneva. Calling themselves Marxists, he and his supporters founded the Emancipation of Labour

Group (1883). It was only logical that they saw the urban working class as their main ally, and with the spread of industrialization in the 1890s, they organised study groups to educate workers about politics and particularly Marxism. In 1898 the Russian Social Democrat Labour Party was formed; its first congress was held at Minsk, though the party was illegal. Members moved on from merely holding discussions groups – they became more directly involved in workers' organizations and in strikes, and in 1905 they had an important role to play in the revolution.

Social Democrats had problems deciding exactly what their party programme should be. Their ultimate aim of course was a socialist revolution to overthrow the liberal bourgeois state. However, according to Marx's analysis, Russia was one stage behind Western Europe where the capitalist phase was well advanced. Russia's liberal bourgeois revolution had not yet happened: the Social Democrats were therefore working for the revolution after next, and that could only take place when the industrial working class had grown large enough. This could take years and was discouraging for the Russian Marxists. Nevertheless Plekhanov stuck rigidly to the view that they must keep to Marx's original sequence, and he ignored Marx's later suggestion that both revolutions might be combined.

Another problem was what attitude they should adopt towards the liberals. A group calling themselves the 'legal Marxists' argued that they should concentrate on working with the liberal movement, which was beginning to gather strength at the turn of the century. They seemed prepared to be satisfied with the gains to be made once the liberal revolution was achieved, and their interest in the next revolution seemed to have waned. Capitalism and socialism could be reconciled with each other under a democratic system. This aroused criticism among the rank and file and eventually the 'legal Marxists' left the party and joined the liberal opposition.

Another group calling themselves 'the Economists' argued that the workers should concentrate on economic issues – for example, by working through trade unions to improve conditions for the workers. Both Plekhanov and Lenin rejected this view, protesting that they were not reformers, they were revolutionaries; if workers' conditions and wages improved substantially, they would be less inclined to join revolutionary movements, and the socialist revolution would be less likely. Although these unwelcome views were silenced, the dilemma about trade unions remained: should they be encouraged or not?

(f) Lenin and the split in the Social Democrat Party

One of the outstanding Marxists of the younger generation was Vladimir Ulyanov (1870–1924), who later took the alias Lenin. He came from a highly respectable middle class family in Simbirsk province on the Volga, where his father was Director of Popular Schools. It came as a great shock when in 1887 his older brother Alexander was executed for being involved in a plot to assassinate the Tsar Alexander III. The death of his admired elder brother no doubt moved the young Vladimir to join agrarian socialist groups to find out more about what had inspired Alexander. Soon after this, he read Chernyshevsky's novel *What is to be Done?* which fired his imagination. Later he became deeply impressed by Marx's writings and in 1893 moved from his home city of Simbirsk to St Petersburg, where he became active in politics. The secret police were soon on to him and after fifteen months in jail followed by three years' exile in Siberia, he decided to leave Russia, moving first to Munich and settling eventually in Geneva. In 1900 he and a group of friends began a newspaper, *Iskra* (The Spark), which was smuggled into Russia. In 1902 he published a booklet called *What is to be Done?* He borrowed the title from Chernyshevsky's novel and sent the booklet into Russia under the name N. Lenin, to confuse the censor and the secret police. It was this booklet which first brought him to the notice of the Marxist movement inside Russia, and so most people knew him as Lenin from then on. It contained his views on the organization and role of the Social Democrat Party; these eventually became known as Marxism–Leninism.

Most importantly, it must be a completely new type of party, strictly disciplined and centralized, and led by a small elite group of dedicated, full-time, professional revolutionaries, working in secret. A more widely based party consisting of anybody who felt like joining would not have the necessary impact. These professionals could come from any class in society – intelligentsia, middle or working class; dedication was the vital requirement, not membership of any particular class. Lenin stressed the importance of unity of aims and ideas in order to keep internal party divisions to a minimum. This 'party of a new type' must act as the vanguard of the workers' revolution, to lead the way and show them the need to overthrow the autocracy. Lenin believed that left to themselves, workers could only achieve 'a trade-union consciousness' and not a revolutionary one. They must be shown that working via trade unions to improve workers' conditions was not enough: their revolutionary consciousness must be aroused too. Once this had been achieved, the working classes should lead the other discontented groups in society, including the peasants. When that happened, nothing could save the Tsarist system, and it would be possible to combine the two revolutions and move straight to the dictatorship of the proletariat. These ideas caused quite a stir among Russian Marxists, because although Lenin claimed that they were orthodox Marxism, they bore many similarities to the ideas of the Populists. The emphasis on centralization and tight discipline was reminiscent of the views of Tkachev in his 1874 pamphlet. Many Marxists, including Plekhanov, began to suspect Lenin of developing dictatorial tendencies.

Disagreements came to a head at the second party congress which began in Brussels in 1903. Harassed by the police, the delegates soon moved to London where the conference continued in a Congregational chapel. The basic dispute arose between Lenin and Yuli Martov over the question of who should be allowed to join the party. The differences in their verbal definitions of a party member seem trivial; what the dispute amounted to was that Lenin wanted members who *actively participated* – the full-time professionals, while Martov wanted people who *gave regular assistance* – in other words, a mass membership, who would help whenever they could. Lenin lost this vote but won the next one – over the membership of the board of *Iskra*, the party newspaper. Lenin wanted to reduce the board from six members to three, but was opposed by Martov who saw this as a bid by Lenin to control the party. Lenin and his supporters won the vote and began to call themselves Bolsheviks (Majority), while Martov responded, ill-advisedly, by calling his supporters Mensheviks (Minority), not an auspicious name to choose for a party. Relations between the three-man board – Lenin, Martov and Plekhanov – soon became tense; Lenin resigned and in 1904 founded his own newspaper – *Vperod* (Forward).

When it first happened, the split seemed unlikely to be permanent. The Mensheviks especially tried to heal the rift and both groups continued to work together in the provinces; but as time went on the two sections grew apart and their programmes became distinct.

The Bolsheviks continued to favour a small elite leadership group and gradually recognized Lenin as their leader. Lenin was excited by the events of 1905, realizing that before long the situation might be ripe for full-scale revolution. He did not believe in waiting for the bourgeois revolution, since the liberal and middle class parties in Russia could not be trusted even to get the first revolution started. In *Two Tactics of Social Democracy* written while the events of 1905 were in full swing, he explained that the task was to galvanize the urban workers and the peasants into a sort of one-stage, continuous revolution. He also talked about a 'provisional revolutionary democratic dictatorship of the proletariat and the peasantry.' After 1905 his writings and speeches became increasingly violent – he used phrases such as 'armed insurrection', 'mass terror', 'civil war' and 'the expropriation of gentry land'. His closest supporters saw nothing objectionable about this sort of language. As Robert Service points out, 'Bolsheviks were a ruthless bunch. They expected to make a revolution and to have to fight against counter-revolutionary forces, and did not see why they should eschew the violent methods developed by Robespierre and his confederates in the French Revolution.'[12]

The Mensheviks foolishly continued to use this party label, which gave them the image of a small minority party, even though they were a larger group than the Bolsheviks. They wanted to stick to the orthodox Marxist pattern: they were against the idea of the centralized, disciplined party; they were prepared to wait for the bourgeois revolution to overthrow the autocracy and then to wait until the industrial workers were in a majority over the peasants before launching the proletarian revolution. There was a small group of Mensheviks, including Leon Trotsky (1879–1940), who wanted to force the pace towards revolution. Trotsky was attracted by the idea of a 'continuous' or 'permanent' revolution, but he was not impressed by the Leninist elite leadership group, which he thought might easily lead to a dictatorship. However, in July 1917 Trotsky formally joined the Bolsheviks.

(g) Liberals

The liberals in late nineteenth century Russia were arguably the most important political movement of the time. They were mainly members of the intelligentsia and the rapidly growing professional class of teachers, doctors, lawyers, engineers, managers, writers and students. They were people who were exasperated with government incompetence and corruption and with their own inability to influence national politics. Many of them were members of *zemstva* or were employed by *zemstva* and so had first-hand knowledge of how successful they could be. There was a wide range of opinion among liberals: moderates would be satisfied with an extension of the *zemstvo* principle at national level, so that the Tsar would at least consult with the representatives of his people. When Nicholas II came to the throne in 1894 some liberals expressed the hope that, unlike his father, he would allow public opinion to be expressed and would actually take notice of it; to which suggestion Nicholas is said to have replied that they were 'intoxicated by senseless dreaming.' Other moderates were more interested in social reform – they believed in primary education for everybody and wanted to improve the conditions of the peasants. Radical liberals wanted a constitutional monarchy whose power was limited by an elected parliament.

Although liberals were not thinking in terms of armed uprising like the SRs, Bolsheviks and Mensheviks, they were viewed with just as much suspicion by the Okhrana, the tsarist secret police. After all, these were the people who, in the Marxist analysis of things, would eventually organize the bourgeois revolution. They were unable to operate as a political party inside Russia, and if they seriously wanted to promote their ideas, they had to live abroad. In 1901 the newspaper *Liberation* was launched in Germany by Petr Struve, a former Marxist, who also formed the Union of Liberation in 1903. Struve argued that violent revolution was not the way forward for Russia – the country needed a period of political and social evolution on Western European lines. The Union was by far the most popular of the radical organizations with university students. But it was harassed so much by the police, in spite of its moderate views, that the members became more militant; at a meeting held in St Petersburg in January 1904, they drew up a programme which included a parliament elected by universal suffrage, self-determination for the non-Russians in the empire, and far-reaching social reforms. In the months before the 1905 revolution they were the most open critics of the autocracy with their 'reform banquets' (see section 2.3(b)).

After the October Manifesto (see section 2.3(c)) the moderate liberals were at last able to organize themselves into a political party, becoming known as the Constitutional Democrats (Kadets). They were far from satisfied with the Manifesto's concessions, but were prepared to accept them and to try and use them in order to bring about full democracy. Their programme was to work for a 'rule-of-law state' in the interests of all classes, nationalities and peoples, and to strive 'not only for workers and peasants, but for the welfare and prosperity of all classes, of the entire Russian state.'[13] This rather generalized attitude meant that the Kadets were distancing themselves from any particular social group. This probably turned out to be a serious weakness because it left them without any strong social base: they were now perceived as too bourgeois for the industrial workers and peasants and too radical for the majority of nobles and wealthy industrialists.

2.3   The revolution of 1905

(a) The revolution begins[14]

The series of events known as the 1905 revolution actually began in 1904 and continued on into 1907. By January 1905 feeling against the autocracy had reached unprecedented heights. On Sunday 9 January there was a protest march by St Petersburg workers, organized not by revolutionaries but by Father Gapon, an Orthodox priest. It was a peaceful demonstration which aimed to present a petition to the Tsar at the Winter Palace, to let him know what their grievances were. It was a widely held, though naive view that the Tsar himself was not to blame for the situation – this was the responsibility of officials and nobles who oppressed the workers. If only they could meet the Tsar and let him know their problems, he would put everything right. Gapon had been organizing workers' groups of the type allowed by the government – a sort of tame trade union under police supervision – since 1903, but the authorities were worried that he would be unable to control a large demonstration; on 7 January he was ordered to cancel it. He was determined to go ahead, convinced that the Tsar, the 'Little Father' of his people, would never allow his troops to fire on a peaceful demonstration. However, Nicholas had arranged to be away from St Petersburg that day. As they approached the Winter Palace, the workers, with lots of women and children in the front ranks, were charged by cavalry and then fired on by the infantry. Altogether that day – 'Bloody Sunday' as it became known – about 200 people were killed, including many children and spectators, and around 800 wounded (see Documents B and C).

The shootings aroused a sense of outrage throughout the country; there was a wave of strikes, with workers forming their own committees (*soviets*) for the first time, mutinies in some parts of the army and navy, national uprisings, peasant uprisings and attacks on officials. At times it seemed that the monarchy could not survive, so widespread was the disaffection and the anger of the people, which sprang from so many different grievances.

(b) What were the causes of the 1905 revolution?

There was widespread discontent among industrial workers, a class which had grown rapidly during the industrialization of the 1880s and 1890s. Hours of work were long: factory workers had to do a 12-hour day and were sometimes required to work as long as 16 hours. Working conditions, especially in industries like mining and oil, were dangerous and insurance was non-existent. Wages were low and irregularly paid; although a few trade unions had been legalized, they were kept under close police supervision and strikes were illegal. Most employers refused even to discuss workers' grievances. An economic depression beginning in 1900 caused unemployment and wage reductions. On top of all this, living conditions were primitive; groups of workers had to share accommodation at exorbitant rents or were forced to live in barracks attached to the factories. Many intelligent workers who could read and write were familiar with Marxist pamphlets which had great influence on the militant labour movement.

A number of strikes had already taken place although they were illegal. The first major one was in St Petersburg in 1896 and there was a miners' strike in the Donetz Basin in 1900. Troops were used to deal with a strike at Rostov-on-Don in 1902, and an attempted general strike in St Petersburg in 1903 was foiled by the army. The main organization of these strikes was carried out by the independent labour movement; but there is also evidence that the Social Democrats played an important part by spreading the propaganda which helped to win such wide support for the strikes. Nor were the Social Democrats all members of the intelligentsia – for example, Semeon Kanatchikov, whose father had been a serf, moved into Moscow and became a skilled worker in the machine-making industry; he read Marx, and on the eve of the 1905 revolution, he left his job to become a full-time 'professional revolutionary' in the Bolshevik party.[15] Many working class grievances were reflected in the demands which Gapon's marchers hoped to present to the Tsar: a maximum eight-hour working day, a minimum wage, the abolition of overtime, and factories 'where it is possible to work without risk of death from wind, rain and snow'.

Peasant poverty was a continuing problem. It is true that by 1905 peasants owned 68 per cent of Russia's arable land and that many of them rented extra land from landowners; but the rapid increase in the peasant population meant that it was still a struggle for most peasants to produce enough to feed their families, especially when rents were often unreasonably high. In some fertile areas landowners stopped renting out land and turned their estates into commercial farming enterprises, growing wheat and sugar-beet. They used harvesters and threshing machines, which meant fewer labouring jobs for peasants. This happened in Poltava province, and so it was no coincidence that the first serious outbreak of peasant violence took place there in 1902. Thousands of peasants were forced to leave the countryside to find work in the industrial cities, where they came into contact with many types of political propagandists. They kept their links with the villages, and so it was a two-way process: peasant unrest was brought to the cities, fuelled by political propaganda, and then revolutionary ideas were taken back to the villages.

The intelligentsia, university students and many of the business community resented their lack of political influence. There were no signs that Nicholas II had any vision of the future, and they had to stand by and watch while the archaic and incompetent political system made only a half-hearted attempt to modernize Russia. The irony was that in order to modernize, the regime needed more educated people; but the larger the educated class became, the more numerous and influential the critics of the autocracy became. And most of them were convinced that only by removing the autocracy could real progress be made. Large numbers of the intelligentsia became activists, joining organizations like the liberal Union of Liberation and the Social Democrats. Even Savva Morozov, the wealthy industrialist, contributed to Social Democrat funds.

All classes resented the government's repressive policies and the fact that Russia was a police state. The limits on the powers of the *zemstva* were bitterly resented by the people most closely involved in their work – thought to be around 70,000 of the intelligentsia in 1905. University students were not allowed to form societies or hold political meetings and any political offender could be held indefinitely without trial. In 1901 there was a huge student demonstration in St Petersburg supported by many members of the liberal bourgeoisie. Without warning a detachment of mounted Cossacks charged into the crowd, killing 13 people and injuring hundreds of others. Around 1500 students were arrested and imprisoned. This sort of treatment only served to make students more militant – there was a rush to join the Socialist Revolutionaries who launched a campaign of terror in retaliation, and some joined the Social Democrats. The most popular organization for students was the liberal Union of Liberation.

Russia suffered humiliating defeats in a war with Japan. In January 1904 Russia became involved in the conflict with Japan over control of Manchuria and Korea. The government thought that the Japanese would be no match for their military machine. Having deliberately pursued a provocative expansionist policy in the Far East and refused offers of compromise, the Russians allowed the Japanese to make the first move by attacking their fleet in the harbour at Port Arthur in Manchuria. Japanese troops occupied Korea and besieged Port Arthur. By the end of the year the Russian army had failed to reach Port Arthur, which was on the point of surrendering, and their Baltic fleet was still on its seven-month voyage round the world in a vain attempt to raise the siege. Port Arthur surrendered in January 1905; the Baltic fleet did not arrive until near the end of May, when it was almost completely destroyed by the Japanese in less than two hours. The army was poorly equipped with old-fashioned weaponry, the generals were incompetent and the navy useless. Again, the government was blamed for failing to look after the country's interests.

The revolutionary parties drew strength from these disasters. The Socialist Revolutionaries continued their campaign of terror: several important officials were assassinated, and the climax came with the murder of the Minister of the Interior, Plehve, who was killed by a bomb in July 1904. Marxist propaganda had a part to play in numerous strikes, culminating in a big strike in St Petersburg which began on 3 January 1905. The main opposition centred around the liberals who started a campaign of banquets, a type of public gathering still allowed by the police, at which activists made stirring speeches, which were widely reported, calling for a national *zemstvo* assembly; by November 1905 they were demanding a Constituent Assembly elected by universal suffrage. But Nicholas would make no concessions which might in any way limit his absolute power. 'I will never agree to the representative form of government, because I consider it harmful to the people whom God has entrusted to me,' he told Prince Mirsky, the new Minister of the Interior, who tried to persuade him that if nothing was done, there would soon be revolution.

(c) Events in the revolution

The shooting of peaceful unarmed protestors, including women and children, singing hymns and carrying religious icons and portraits of the Tsar, caused a wave of disgust and revulsion. Some writers see it as a turning-point in the history of Tsarism, because it destroyed the idea that the Tsar really cared about his people, and seemed to support the view of the revolutionaries that the autocracy was to blame for all their sufferings. The prestige of the monarchy among ordinary people fell to its lowest point. Events began to escalate out of control:

- There was an outbreak of strikes throughout the country, with something like half a million workers involved by the end of January.
- In rural areas peasants went on the rampage, looting and burning the houses of the wealthy and seizing pasture land. There were over 3000 such uprisings in 1905. But it wasn't all violence – in many areas peasants, helped by teachers and radical priests, set up unions and co-operatives. Some of the larger

villages ran themselves almost as independent republics with elected 'governments'.

- Some sections of the army and navy mutinied. The most famous incident was the mutiny on board the battleship *Potemkin* at Odessa on the Black Sea. There were also disturbances among troops returning from Manchuria after suffering defeat in the war with Japan.
- Some of the subject nationalities seized the chance to protest and there were huge demonstrations in Poland, Latvia and Finland. In Georgia the Mensheviks in effect ran a separate national state, with the full support of the peasants.
- Beginning in September with a strike of Moscow printers, a massive wave of strikes developed across the country which by mid-October had become virtually a general strike. When railway workers joined in, the whole nation was brought to a standstill, and the movement of troops and supplies was hampered.
- In St Petersburg workers elected a council, the Soviet, to co-ordinate the strikes and formulate their demands. It had 50 members, including seven from each of the socialist parties – Mensheviks, Bolsheviks and Socialist Revolutionaries. Before long it had taken on the characteristics of an alternative form of government which could take over whenever the autocracy should collapse. For a time Trotsky acted as chairman. Other cities soon followed the example of St Petersburg; in practice, as well as organizing the strikes, the Soviets served as emergency municipal governments, keeping law and order and overseeing the distribution of food in areas where the government had lost control (see Document D).
- Nicholas was faced with two options: he could either use troops to crush all opposition, or he could make concessions. All through the summer his instinct told him to use force; by October all his advisers were telling him that to make concessions was the only way. They were not sure whether they could rely on the troops to obey orders to shoot down large numbers of ordinary, innocent people. Count Witte told him that he must allow a democratically elected parliament and full civil rights. After his cousin, the Grand Duke Nicholas, had threatened to shoot himself if he refused, the Tsar finally agreed. The October Manifesto, a document drawn up by Witte, seemed to grant much of what the liberals were asking for: an elected national assembly known as the Duma, which would have the right to approve all laws; freedom of speech, conscience and association (which meant that trade unions and political parties could exist legally); a relaxation of the press censorship and freedom from unwarranted arrest.
- Although the wording of the document was deliberately vague, so that it was full of loopholes, it had the effect that Witte was hoping for – it split the opposition. The minority of right-wing liberals greeted it with enthusiasm and rallied in support of the Manifesto and the Tsar, calling themselves Octobrists. The more radical liberals or Constitutional Democrats (Kadets), withheld approval, hoping for more concessions. However, both groups suspended revolutionary activities and devoted their energies to forming themselves into parties and preparing for the Duma elections. On the other hand the workers and socialist groups became more militant; Lenin returned from Geneva early in November and urged that the pressure must be maintained.

- The Soviet tried to keep the revolution going by calling a general strike in St Petersburg, but by 3 December Witte felt strong enough to have the leaders of the Soviet arrested. News of this provoked the Moscow Social Democrats to launch an uprising which won considerable support among the workers. By 12 December the rebels controlled the main railway stations and large parts of the city. Witte did not hesitate to send troops in, and the rising was crushed by 23 December; over a thousand people were killed.

During 1906 the regime carried out a harsh campaign to punish the revolutionaries; the militants responded by assassinating some 2000 government officials in 1906 alone. Order was eventually restored with great brutality in both town and countryside and the Georgian peasant republic was stamped out. It has been calculated that by April 1906, when the first Duma met, the regime had already executed 15,000 people, shot or wounded at least 20,000 and exiled 45,000.[16] Nevertheless the Octobrists viewed the so-called revolution as a success – worthwhile gains had been made. The other revolutionary groups saw it as a complete failure – nothing less than the overthrow of the monarchy would satisfy them. Although the liberals had not supported the attack on the workers and peasants, from now on the SDs and SRs saw them as weak and unreliable allies.

(d) Why did the autocracy survive?

The various revolutionary groups were not united and were aiming for different things; although they caused chaos and brought the country to a standstill, the movement lacked central direction. The urban and rural revolutions did not occur simultaneously – disturbances in the countryside only gained momentum in the summer of 1905; things calmed down towards the end of the year and then violence reached a new peak in 1906; but by then it was too late – the regime had recovered its strength. Its chances of survival received a boost when Witte succeeded in ending the war with Japan in August 1905. The Treaty of Portsmouth (New Hampshire, USA) gave the Russians a reasonable peace settlement, considering that they had lost the war; it also meant that its troops could be brought home ready for action against the revolutionaries, at least once the railway strike was over. In spite of some sporadic mutinies, the army stayed loyal and obeyed orders, even though the majority were from peasant backgrounds. Most important of all, it was the intervention of Witte, persuading Nicholas to make concessions, that broke the unity of the opposition and allowed the government a breathing space to bring the army into action.

2.4 Russian agriculture in 1914 – how backward was it?

As we saw in section 2.1(g), one of the most serious problems in the Russian empire was the backward state of agriculture and the poverty of most peasants. At the root of the problem lay the rapidly increasing population in rural areas;

some estimates suggest that it grew by 20 per cent – a rise of over 20 million – between 1900 and 1914. The small size of peasant holdings and old-fashioned methods of farming hampered progress. Some advances had been made, but it was still a constant struggle to produce enough food. After the 1905 revolution the government made a determined effort at agrarian reform.

(a) Stolypin and the 'wager on the strong'

Petr Stolypin (1862–1911), Prime Minister from 1906 until he was assassinated in 1911, came to the conclusion that the autocracy's best hope of survival was to win the support of a large proportion of the peasants. This had been conspicuously lacking in 1905. Stolypin's plan was to break up the peasant communes which were an obstacle to efficient farming, and to develop a class of independent, prosperous and go-ahead peasants, the 'strong and sober' peasant households, who would be loyal to the monarchy; this would make revolution less likely and at the same time help to increase food production. He told the Duma: 'the government has placed its wager on the strong and the sturdy, not on the needy and the drunken;' given twenty years of peace, he argued, there would be no prospect of revolution.

He began with an important concession: redemption payments were cancelled. He followed this by doing all he could to encourage peasants to leave their village communes in order to consolidate their strips into one large enclosed farm which was now their own property; they could also buy and sell land, move into a town or migrate to a different rural area. It is estimated that between 1906 and 1915 around 3.5 million people moved to Siberia and bought land, using low-interest loans provided by a government-sponsored Peasant Land Bank. Some ambitious peasants did extremely well and were even able to buy land from struggling noble landlords. These prosperous peasants, labelled as *kulaks* (fists) by Soviet historians, usually employed other peasants as labourers and used the new techniques – crop rotation, chemical fertilizers and modern tools, and bought the latest agricultural machines. The main product was grain – wheat and rye, but in some areas peasants diversified their activities – there was a big increase in potato and sugar beet production and dairy produce became more important. Another sign of progress was the growth in agricultural education: in 1895 for example, only 75 students had degrees in agronomy; by 1912 there were 3922.

However, Stolypin's scheme seems to have had only limited success, and after his death in 1911, the government lost interest. According to Robert Service, by 1916 only a tenth of the households in the European part of Russia had left the commune and successfully set up consolidated farms; in the most fertile areas such as the Ukraine and the Northern Caucasus – the great grain-producing areas – the average farm was only about 15 acres.[17] Many others had formally separated from the *mir* but had been held up by all the legal and practical problems involved. In fact the administrative system in rural areas was inadequate for carrying out such a complex change. At the outbreak of the First World War, *kulaks* were only a tiny proportion – perhaps two per cent of the total population; the vast majority of peasants remained poverty-stricken and resentful. They were reluctant to leave the relative security of the commune, inadequate though it was, to take all the risks involved in independent farming, and more and more of them were becoming landless labourers. What they most coveted was the uncultivated land in the hands of big landlords, the Tsar and the Church, which they felt could be put to much better use. The basic economic questions were: how much grain could the peasants keep or control for themselves, how much could the state and the landlords take from them in rents and taxes, and how much grain did they have left over once the family had been fed?

(b) Agricultural statistics

Russian statistics are notoriously unreliable, and yet it is always tempting to try and see whether or not they bear out general impressions. How far were the Stolypin reforms reflected in the available statistics of output? Several historians have attempted to calculate what really happened. One of the earliest was the Russian Soviet historian Petr Lyashchenko (1949) who argued that between 1900 and 1913 there was quite a rapid increase in agricultural production, because of improved methods and a run of good summers. He calculated that the net income of agriculture increased by 88.6 per cent in that period; however, this is not as impressive as it might seem, since it was a period of rising world agricultural prices. The actual increase in output was more like 35 per cent. Grain exports were 50 per cent higher on average in the years 1911–13 than they were in 1901–05, and Russia was the largest cereal exporter in the world. Most Western historians accept Lyashchenko's statistics as fair and reasonable, since Soviet historians are not noted for exaggerating the achievements of the Tsarist state.

A different sort of calculation was carried out by the French historian P. Bairoch (1965) who compared productivity in millions of calories per male agricultural worker in various countries, in 1860 and 1910. In Russia there was significant growth, but given the length of the period covered – 50 years – it was not all that great:

	1860	1910
USA	22.5	42.0
UK	20.0	23.5
France	14.5	17.0
Spain	11.0	8.5
Germany	10.5	25.0
Sweden	10.5	16.0
Russia	7.5	11.0
Italy	5.0	6.5

The best that can be said for Russia, judging from these statistics, apart from the fact that she moved one place up the league table, overtaking Spain, is that her agricultural output was growing faster than that of either Britain or France.

The great question is: would this modest improvement have been sufficient to feed the population and develop a prosperous and loyal peasantry? Some Western historians believe that it would, and that if it had not been for the tragedy of the First World War, revolution would have been avoided. But it has to be said that the statistics do not completely bear this out. Alec Nove points out that the overall annual growth rate for agriculture in the period 1860–1914 was only 1.7 per cent, which was only a fraction above the rate of population increase. Thus food consumption per head could hardly have increased at all, especially bearing in mind the increased exports, though admittedly the potential was there at least to feed the population.[18]

As to a prosperous and loyal peasantry becoming the rock on which the autocracy could survive, the majority view is that although many peasants *were* doing well, they were not a large enough proportion of the total to be able to save the monarchy. Given the growing population, there simply wasn't sufficient land to enable a large enough proportion of the peasants to set up consolidated farms, even if they had wanted to. The ill-feeling between the gentry and prosperous peasants on one side and poverty-stricken landless labourers on the other produced a potentially dangerous situation in the countryside. The thousands of peasants who were forced off the land and into the towns and cities only added to the discontented mass of industrial workers. There is a great deal of contemporary evidence supporting the picture of an agrarian crisis among poor peasants: reports of reduced numbers of livestock owned by peasants, worsening diet and primitive living conditions. Although redemption payments were abolished after the 1905 revolution, indirect taxes continued to increase, so that by 1911 the total taxation which peasants had to pay was almost as high as it had been 20 years earlier. There were high taxes for instance on oil, which peasants needed for heating and lighting, on sugar, and on tobacco and vodka.

On the other hand, not all historians are convinced by this analysis; revisionist historians have pointed out that much of the contemporary evidence of peasant poverty is anecdotal, that it is confined to a limited area, and that it originated from people who wanted to blacken the tsarist regime. Peter Gatrell shows that new crops, new types of seed, more crop rotations and more fertilizers were being used, resulting in a substantial rise in yields.[19] In 1994 Stephen Hoch published his investigations of population growth and living standards in the countryside; he came to the conclusion that peasant poverty, land-hunger and overpopulation had been exaggerated, and that living standards were clearly rising.[20] In fact it is estimated that by 1916 almost 90 per cent of all sown land in European Russia was being farmed by peasants, that 80 per cent of all farm machinery was owned by peasants, and that 87 per cent of the total value of the empire's agricultural output between 1909 and 1913 was produced by the peasants.[21] There is also evidence of a rise in peasant savings and an increase in the wages of farm labourers. Moreover, statistics suggest that even with rising grain exports, there was still more grain left per head of the population than there had been 20 years earlier; in other words, grain production was outpacing the population growth.

So was there an agrarian crisis or not? It is important not to generalize about the whole empire from what happened in one area. Peter Waldron, one of the most recent writers about the last years of tsarism, points out that there was a wide variation in the conditions of agriculture, depending on the region, and there were variations within each region. It was only to be expected that peasants in the fertile Black-Earth provinces would be more successful than those in less fertile areas. He concludes that 'the peasant economy was a patchwork. Some peasants prospered, while others became more and more impoverished. Overall the Russian agricultural economy avoided crisis in the half-century after emancipation, despite the huge increase in the empire's population, and yet failed to make the spectacular progress anticipated from changes to the framework of rural life.'[22]

2.5 Russian industry in 1914 – how 'modern' was it?

Defeat in the Crimean War (1854–56) showed up Russia's backwardness in every way, not least militarily and economically, and the lack of railways was a serious handicap to the efficient movement of troops and supplies. It was the building of a railway network that gave Russia its first great push towards industrialization. At the end of the Crimean War there were only about 750 miles of track, and most of that was between St Petersburg and Moscow. By 1885 the network had grown to over 16,000 miles of track, by 1900 there were almost 30,000 miles and by 1914 the total was over 45,000 miles. Railway expansion on this scale stimulated the demand for iron, steel, wood, coal and oil, for the manufacture of rails, locomotives, rolling stock and all the other necessary equipment. It was during the 1890s that Russia's industrialization speeded up dramatically in what has been described as the 'great spurt'.

(a) Witte and the 'great spurt'

Count Sergei Witte (1849–1915), along with Petr Stolypin, was among the few really able ministers appointed by Nicholas II. From 1892 until 1903 Witte held leading positions – first as Transport Minister and then as Finance Minister. He believed that if Russia was to keep its place among the world's leading powers, both economically and militarily, it was vital to modernize. He felt this was too important for initiatives to be left to businessmen – the government must play a part. Witte did everything he could to encourage industry and banking; he used government money to subsidize expansion and arranged loans and investments from abroad. One estimate puts foreign investment in Russian industry at 200 million roubles in 1890 and over 900 million in 1900; by that time about 45 per cent of capital in Russian industrial enterprises had been invested by foreigners. He increased exports, limited imports by imposing a tariff, balanced the budget, and put the rouble on the gold standard; this made the rouble exchangeable for gold, kept the Russian currency at a high value, and provided more security for foreign investors. He also put heavy taxes on items of everyday consumption, forcing the peasants to play a large part in financing industrial development; and without the peasants who moved into the towns to provide the new labour force, the 'great spurt' would not have been possible. Foreign experts were invited in to provide the necessary expertise – there were engineers and advisers from Britain, France, Germany, Sweden and Belgium, all bringing their Western ideas and skills.

Much of the investment went into railways – Witte's great brainchild was the Trans-Siberian Railway linking Moscow to Vladivostock, nearly 4000 miles away on the Pacific. Armaments factories were another priority and so was the metallurgy industry. By 1900 there were eight main industrial areas. The St Petersburg region specialized in textiles, iron and steel production and machine building; Moscow produced textiles, iron and steel, and chemicals. In the west, the Polish centres of Warsaw and Lodz produced textiles, coal, iron and chemicals, while the Donbass area of the Ukraine supplied coal, iron ore and chemicals. The Urals produced iron and various minerals, and the Baku region in Transcaucasia had oilfields developed and expanded by Alfred Nobel. Transcaucasia also produced coal and manganese, and finally the area south of Kiev specialized in beet-sugar processing.

The rapid expansion of the Russian economy in the 1890s was to some extent part of a worldwide industrial boom. In 1900 when an international trade recession began, Russia felt the effects, and the growth rate slowed down. The resulting unemployment and wage reductions helped to cause unrest in the industrial towns and cities which contributed towards the 1905 revolution. From 1909 the economy picked up again and industrial production continued to increase until the outbreak of war in 1914.

(b) How healthy was Russian industry in 1914?

This is a question which has caused some debate among historians and economists. As with agriculture, there is a problem with statistics – these tend to be available only for large- and medium-scale industries, and very few exist for small workshops and handicrafts, which still employed about two-thirds of all industrial workers in 1914. This hasn't prevented historians from carrying out various complex calculations which have led them to reach contradictory conclusions; there is, in fact, a pessimistic and an optimistic view of Russian industrial potential.

The pessimistic view which was held by most Soviet historians is based on statistics of production of the leading world powers in 1914, in million tons (electricity in million kilowatts):

	Coal	Iron	Steel	Oil	Electricity (million kW)
Russia	36.2	3.6	4.1	10.3	2.0
USA	455.0	30.0	32.0	34.0	25.8
Britain	292.0	11.0	6.5		4.7
Germany	277.0	14.7	14.0		
Austria–Hungary	47.0	2.0	2.7		

Clearly Russia was lagging well behind her main rivals, apart from Austria–Hungary; oil output was disappointing because in 1900 Russia had been the world's leading oil producer.[23]

But it wasn't only Soviet historians who give this rather discouraging view; the Frenchman Bairoch and the Russian–American economic historian S.N. Prokopovich reached similar conclusions from their calculations. Bairoch showed that Russia had even fallen behind Italy, not in total production, but in production per head of the population, in other words in efficiency. Prokopovich looked at national incomes and came to the conclusion that Russia had the lowest percentage increase and the lowest national income per head of all the main European countries. Raymond Goldsmith, an American economist, concluded that Russia's real income per head had been relatively higher in 1860 than it was in 1913, in comparison with the USA and Japan, although he also calculated that Russia's growth rate of industrial output was higher than that of the USA and Germany at about 5 per cent per annum between 1888 and 1913. However, Russia's starting point was so low that she was still a long way behind. The general conclusion of the pessimists is that given Russia's vast natural resources, she should have been closing the gap much more quickly. In fact Bairoch's figures suggest that the gap in productive capacity was actually widening.

The optimistic view is taken by a number of Western historians, including two British writers, Paul R. Gregory and M.E. Falkus. They both make the point that Bairoch's *per capita* basis was flawed because he included agricultural workers in the general calculation instead of treating them separately. In view of Russia's special circumstances – a much larger proportion of the population engaged in agriculture than anywhere else in Europe, plus the fact that their productivity was low – Bairoch's method of calculation made Russian industrial workers appear far less efficient than they actually were. They believe that if the average growth rates of the period 1890–1913 had continued over the next 50 years, the Russian people would have been leading a reasonably comfortable existence. Alexander Gerschenkron, another Russian–American economist, took a similar view: although he admitted that Russia was still relatively backward 'by any quantitative criterion', he saw many encouraging signs: the increasingly modern attitudes of Russian businessmen, an improvement in the economic conditions of the workforce, and the reduced importance of foreign engineers and managers. He felt that the great industrial expansion in the years 1908–14 was duplicating what had happened in Germany 20 or 30 years earlier. 'One might surmise,' he wrote, 'that in the absence of the war Russia would have continued on the road of progressive westernization.'[24] A French economist, Edmond Thery, writing in 1912, forecast that if Russia could maintain until 1950 the same rate of economic growth which had occurred since 1900, she would have dominated Europe economically, politically and financially.

For a sensible and balanced conclusion it is best to turn to Alec Nove,[25] probably the most outstanding recent British expert on the economy of Russia and the USSR. He came to the conclusion that Russia was making clear industrial progress, but that it was uneven. The newest developments were very advanced indeed, since the Russians were able to take advantage of Western experience and go straight for the most up-to-date techniques and equipment in large factories. Most of these were concentrated in the St Petersburg and Moscow areas, and in Poland and the Ukraine. However, most of the industry in the rest of the country consisted of small workshops; on the whole, the further south and east you went, the more primitive the industry became. Nove has some telling statistics: in 1915 about 67 per cent of industrial workers (5.2 million people) worked in these small-scale workshops, but they only produced 33 per cent of total industrial output. This means that their output per head was only a quarter of that produced by workers in large-scale industry.

There were other vital weaknesses too: engineering made only limited progress; this was serious because it meant that a large proportion of industrial equipment, tools and machinery had to be imported, a lot of it from Germany, while much agricultural equipment came from the USA. Worst of all, it meant that when the First World War started, Russia was soon short of armaments. In addition the Russians were still short of capital, which left them dependent on foreign investment. Finally the weakness which even the optimistic Gerschenkron commented on, began to make itself felt again – industrialization was itself a threat to political stability, and without political stability, investment would be discouraged and successful industrial advance could not continue. From 1910 onwards full employment meant that the workers, who were still poorly paid and exploited, were able to pressurize employers more. There was an increase in strikes culminating in August 1912 in the shooting of some miners in the Lena goldfields. This was a dangerous mixture: industrial and social unrest soon turned into political unrest.

2.6   The political system after 1905 – the Duma experiment

(a) Nicholas and the Fundamental Laws

To the outsider the October Manifesto might well have suggested that Russia had set out on the path towards liberalism and democracy; democratic institutions had been set up, and political parties and trade unions were legal. Liberal historians have talked about 'the experiment in democracy' and 'the constitutional experiment' which might have saved the monarchy if only Nicholas and the Dumas could have worked together. But the problem was that the Tsar and his circle had no intention of co-operating with the Duma.[26] His main concern was to see how many of the concessions he could withdraw, how much of his autocratic power he could claw back, without actually provoking another revolution. In the Fundamental Laws announced in April 1906, when the elections for the first Duma were in progress, Nicholas restated that 'supreme autocratic power is vested in the Tsar of all the Russias. It is God's command that his authority should be obeyed.' The word 'constitution' was carefully not mentioned. The Duma (or State Assembly) was to have two houses:

- **The State Council** – this was an upper house; half its members were to be appointed by the Tsar and the rest elected by various privileged groups such as landowners, gentry, industrialists and clergy; all members were responsible only to the Tsar, and the Council had the power of veto over the other house.
- **The State Duma** – this was an elected body with very limited powers. No law could be passed without the approval of the Tsar. Although it was stated that the Duma had to approve the annual budget, in reality all expenditure on the army, navy, imperial court, and questions of state loans and debts, which amounted to almost 40 per cent of the total budget, were exempt from the Duma's scrutiny. The voting system was not the democratic one which liberals

and socialists had hoped for, in which everybody had a direct vote and all votes carried equal weight. Instead it was decided to have a system of indirect votes by estates, in order to reduce the numbers of radical members likely to be elected. The ordinary voter would cast his vote, not directly for members of the Duma, but for members of an electoral college, and it was these who in turn selected the Duma members. There were four electoral colleges: gentry, burghers (town property-owners), peasants and workers. The franchise was fixed so that one gentry vote was the equivalent of three burgher, fifteen peasant and forty-five worker votes.

In addition to all this, the Tsar kept the right to appoint ministers, to declare war and make peace, and to dissolve the Duma whenever he felt like it. When the Duma was not in session the Tsar could issue whatever emergency laws were felt to be necessary (this was Article 87). At least the Duma did have two important rights: in certain circumstances it was allowed to question ministers, and members were allowed free speech. According to American historian Richard Pipes, 'this provided a forum for unrestrained and often intemperate criticism of the regime.' He suggests that this probably contributed more to undermining the prestige of the government in the eyes of the general public than all the revolutionary outrages, because it destroyed the impression, which it struggled very hard to maintain, that it was in complete control of the situation.[27]

(b) Nicholas and the Dumas

There were four Dumas, the first two (April–June 1906 and February–June 1907) both had centre-left majorities and were soon dismissed by Nicholas. The franchise was changed after the second Duma, reducing the representation of the lower classes. Consequently the Dumas were less troublesome; the third (1907–12) lasted for its full term of five years, while the fourth was dissolved after just over four years. The four elections produced the following results, though it has to be remembered that some of the 'parties' were loosely organized groups; for this reason almost every source gives slightly different figures:

Party or group	First Duma 1906	Second Duma 1907	Third Duma 1907–12	Fourth Duma 1912–17
Kadets	182	91	54	53
Trudoviki	136	104	13	10
Octobrists	17	42	154	95
Mensheviks	18	47	–	–
Bolsheviks	–	–	19	15
SRs	–	37	–	–
Non-Russians	60	93	26	22
Progressists	27	28	28	41
Rightists	8	10	147	154
Others	–	50	–	42
	448	502	441	432

Kadets (Constitutional Democrats): the moderate or radical liberals who were bitterly disappointed with the October Manifesto; they wanted genuine universal suffrage and a strict limitation on the powers of the Tsar. They were so successful in 1906 because the SRs and the Social Democrats (Mensheviks and Bolsheviks) largely boycotted the elections. For instance the Kadets won all the seats in St Petersburg and Moscow, thanks to the votes of the workers, some of which would have gone to the Social Democrats if they had put up candidates.

Trudoviki (labour group): a left-wing group, mainly small peasant farmers with some middle class members – lawyers and teachers. Many of them would have stood as Socialist Revolutionaries if the party had fought the election.

Octobrists: these were the conservative or right-of-centre liberals who had welcomed the October Manifesto.

Non-Russians: mainly Poles, with some Lithuanians, Latvians and Ukrainians.

Progressists: an elite group of businessmen who were in favour of moderate reform.

Rightists: not an organized party – they represented a wide range of conservative views.

The First Duma, April–June 1906

The election was a triumph for the Kadets and other left-wing groups which had a clear majority. It was a bitter disappointment for Nicholas and especially for Witte, who had assured the Tsar that the revolutionaries and radicals had no mass support and that the peasants would vote for conservative candidates (see Documents E–H). Witte was now viewed by the court as a dangerous radical and was replaced as chief minister by Ivan Goremykin, an old-fashioned reactionary conservative.

From the beginning the deputies were in a militant mood and made far-reaching demands: an amnesty for political prisoners, abolition of the death penalty, abolition of the upper house, the resignation of Nicholas's ministers, a fully democratic electoral system, a fairer tax system and the right to strike. Most important of all was the question of land reform – the redistribution of surplus gentry land among the peasants. Goremykin rejected all these demands and after ten weeks of bitter argument the Tsar decided to dissolve the Duma. The Tauride Palace, where it met, was surrounded by troops and the deputies were forced to disperse. In protest about 200 Kadets and left-wing deputies crossed the border into Finland and met in the town of Vyborg. From there they issued what they called the *Vyborg Manifesto*, condemning the government's action and calling on people to refuse to pay taxes and to do military service. However, there was very little response from ordinary people; many of the Kadets were arrested and barred from Duma membership. They felt let down by the masses and from then on gradually became less radical. Petr Stolypin was appointed chief minister and he soon introduced a policy of repression to restore order.

The Second Duma, February–June 1907

The main change was that the Kadets lost half their seats, probably because the Social Democrats and the Socialist Revolutionaries decided to take part in the election, and because the Kadets were now seen as ineffectual – not radical enough for workers and peasants but too radical for conservatively-minded liberals. The membership of the Second Duma was more polarized than before; the revolutionary SDs and SRs had 84 seats between them and since the national minorities always voted with the opposition, the left-wing groups still had a small majority. The proceedings were acrimonious and disorderly, and although Stolypin tried to work with the Duma, the majority opposed his agrarian reforms (see section 2.4(a)). When the secret police claimed to have found evidence of an SD plot to assassinate the Tsar, Stolypin took the opportunity to have the Second Duma dissolved. The very next day a new electoral system was announced which drastically reduced the representation of the workers, peasants and national minorities. This was a breach of the Tsar's own Fundamental Laws; it meant that only about one in six men had the vote, and that peasants and workers were more or less excluded. In addition, trade unions were banned again, and anybody who tried to form any kind of workers' organization or call a strike was liable to be arrested.

The Third Duma, 1907–12

As the statistics show, the electoral changes produced a Duma with a large right-wing majority. At first relations between the Duma and the government went smoothly, but in 1909 things began to go wrong for Stolypin. There was opposition to his proposal to build four new battleships; in 1911 when he proposed to extend the *zemstva* to the western areas of the empire, his bill was defeated in the upper house – the State Council. The main reason for this was that his right-wing opponents were becoming jealous of his success: his repressive policies had restored order and his agrarian reforms seemed to be going well. In the eyes of reactionaries, he had outlived his usefulness, and this was the perfect opportunity to get rid of him before he introduced any more drastic reforms. Stolypin threatened to resign unless Nicholas suspended the Duma temporarily and passed the bill as an emergency measure under Article 87 of the Fundamental Laws. The Tsar agreed, but Stolypin's victory did him no good. The Tsar felt humiliated at having to act against his right-wing supporters in the State Council, and the Octobrists were outraged at what they saw as his abuse of Article 87.

It may be that Nicholas would have sacked him quite soon; however, on 1 September 1911, during a performance of Rimsky-Korsakov's opera *The Legend of Tsar Sultan* in Kiev, in the presence of Nicholas and his four daughters, Stolypin was shot by a revolutionary who was also acting as a police informer. He died a few days later in hospital. There were rumours that the secret police, and perhaps even the Tsar himself, had connived at Stolypin's murder, but nothing was ever proved. Some historians have argued that his death removed the monarchy's last chance of survival, but it is clear that Stolypin's days of political influence were numbered anyway. The very people he was trying to save had already fatally undermined him.

The Fourth Duma, 1912–17

After the death of Stolypin the government seemed to abandon all ideas of reform and fell back on a policy of repression and reliance on reactionary support. Even the Fourth Duma with its centre-right majority became increasingly critical of the government; but the government for the most part simply ignored the Duma, and by 1914 its influence was in decline. As Alexander Guchkov, the Octobrist leader, told the party conference in 1913:

'The attempt made by the Russian public, as represented by our party, to effect a peaceful, painless transition from the old condemned system to a new order has failed. Let those in power make no mistake about the temper of the people; never were the Russian people so profoundly revolutionized by the actions of the government, for day by day faith in the government is steadily waning, and with it is waning faith in the possibility of a peaceful issue of the crisis.'

(c) Why did the Duma experiment fail?

It ought to have been possible with a little compromise on both sides to develop a workable conservative–liberal partnership that might even have saved the monarchy. However, Nicholas was obsessed with keeping the autocracy intact, and lacked the imagination or the vision to see the advantages of sharing at least some of his power with the parliament; it would have meant for example that some of the criticism and hostility which fell solely on him would have been directed against the Duma. 'I have no intention,' he remarked, 'of renouncing what was bequeathed to me by my forefathers and which I must hand down unimpaired to my son.' He and most of his ministers refused to admit that there was a mass movement against them: in January 1906 the Foreign Minister, Count Lamsdorf, argued in a secret memorandum that the events of 1905 had been promoted 'by the Jews of all countries; the revolutionary movement is being actively supported and partly directed by the forces of universal Jewry.' Nicholas himself added the comment: 'I share entirely the sentiments herein expressed.'[28] He had no intention of trying to co-operate with the Duma and was always looking for an excuse to get rid of it. Of the second Duma he remarked: 'We must let them do something manifestly stupid or mean, and then – slap – and they are gone!' He was convinced that the Duma would be less able to cope with the complex problems facing the Russian empire than he and his advisers.

On the other hand the Duma members were just as reluctant to compromise. They went on the attack from the first day, and played into the Tsar's hands by demanding too much all at once. Paul Milyukov, leader of the Kadets, demanded that the Tsar should accept their entire programme and call a Constituent Assembly. Mackenzie Wallace, an Englishman who knew Russia well, advised the Kadets to be more patient and take things gradually, allowing democracy to develop step by step over the next eight to ten years. 'In England,' he pointed out, 'it took us a century to arrive at a parliamentary monarchy.' 'Eight to ten years is much too long,' replied the Kadet leader. 'We shall never wait so long as that.'[29] And so within the first few days the Duma became a battleground between the autocracy and the liberals, and all possibility of trust was lost.

2.7 Was the collapse of Tsarism inevitable by 1914?

This is one of those perennially fascinating questions to which it is difficult to provide a definitive answer, but that hasn't prevented historians from speculating endlessly about it. The Soviet view was based on the Marxist theory that the collapse of the tsarist regime would be the inevitable completion of the 'unfinished' revolution of 1905–6. The traditional liberal view was that although the regime had obvious and glaring weaknesses in early 1914, it also had a number of strengths. Things were basically improving, and the monarchy would probably have survived if Russia could have kept out of the First World War. The recent revisionist research challenges both these views.

(a) Strengths of the regime

The government seemed to recover remarkably quickly from the 1905 revolution with most of its powers intact. Thanks to Stolypin's repressive policies, order was restored. One contemporary source estimated that from the time Stolypin became chief minister in 1906 until the end of 1909, almost 4000 people were executed and a further 4000 sentenced to hard labour. Stolypin was unpopular with the masses – the noose was nicknamed 'Stolypin's necktie' – but his measures were effective. The secret police had some remarkable successes infiltrating revolutionary groups: Evno Azef, who until 1908 was leader of the fighting section of the SRs, was at the same time a police agent. Roman Malinovski was a member of the Bolshevik Central Committee and was elected as a Bolshevik deputy in the Duma in 1912; but he was also a police spy; he was the man responsible for Stalin's arrest and exile to Siberia in 1913. Hundreds of radical newspapers were closed down, together with many of the newly legalized trade unions which tried to assert themselves. Leon Trotsky, writing about the years 1907–11, observed that 'factories which two or three years ago would strike unanimously over some single arbitrary police action, today have completely lost their revolutionary colour, and accept the most monstrous crimes of the authorities without resistance. Great defeats discourage people for a long time. The consciously revolutionary elements lose their power over the masses.'[30] So the situation seemed to be under tight control; in August 1907 Stolypin told a French newspaper reporter: 'In Russia there is no revolution whatever.'

Stolypin combined his repression with reforms designed to improve life for the masses. The *zemstva*, encouraged and helped by the government, introduced extensive improvements in public health and a system of health insurance for workers. In 1908 a programme was announced to bring about compulsory universal education within ten years. By 1914 an extra 50,000 primary schools had been opened, mainly organized by the *zemstva*. Most important of all, Stolypin's agrarian reforms seemed to be working well until 1911. Lenin was certainly worried by their success; 'if this should continue for long periods of time,' he wrote in 1908, 'it might force us to renounce any agrarian programme at all.' By 1909 the economy was booming again and there was plenty of evidence to support Gerschenkron's optimistic forecast for future economic development (see section 2.5(b)).

Stability depended on the industrial workers and peasants. Richard Pipes argues that no revolution was possible in Russia as long as the rural areas were quiet and calm. He believes that there were no stirrings in the villages either immediately before the war or in the first two years after it began. True, there were half a million workers on strike in 1912, but they were only a tiny minority compared with the 100 million peasants who quietly got on with their business. Pipes argues that the fact that the workers were on strike was a sign that they were progressing to a more advanced economic and social status, since poorly paid and downtrodden labourers have little stomach for going on strike. The strikes were a symptom of the growing maturity of the Russian industrial worker, and judging by Western experience, this would lead in time to greater social stability. [31]

The opposition parties were less militant: a large section of the Kadets had drifted towards the right, while the Social Democrats' membership was falling and their leaders were in exile, scattered all over Europe. Some of the Bolsheviks' tactics made them unpopular: Lenin was against co-operating with trade unions because he claimed they were not capable of developing a revolutionary consciousness (see section 2.2(f)). The Bolshevik practice of robbing banks to augment funds, and stealing arms and ammunition caused something of a scandal. In fact some Social Democrats, especially Mensheviks, were saying that Lenin was finished – he was a man with no political future.

Finally the monarchy seemed to be strengthening itself by encouraging right-wing groups such as the Russian Monarchist Party, the Russian Assembly and the Union of the Russian People (URP). By far the most influential was the URP which wanted to preserve the full apparatus of the autocracy and full Russian control of the empire. URP members hated all political parties and the intelligentsia because they were thought to stand in the way of 'the direct communion between the Tsar and his people'. The URP blamed Jews, non-Russians, non-Orthodox Christians and Muslims for all the problems facing Russia. Their membership included all sorts of people – such as small craftsmen and shopkeepers – who felt threatened by the recent changes and reforms, and they believed that the Tsar was not being decisive enough in his actions against the revolutionaries. They organized paramilitary groups known as Black Hundreds whose aim was to give revolutionary terrorists a taste of their own medicine. By the end of 1906 the URP had taken off in a big way with over a thousand branches throughout the country. The government, delighted at this new support, gave the movement financial assistance. Street violence became commonplace; the Black Hundreds beat up students, radicals, Roman Catholics, anyone suspected of having left-wing opinions, and above all Jews.

The treatment meted out to Jews was appalling – pogroms took place all over Russia: 800 Jews were murdered in Odessa, and whenever any terrorist violence occurred it was always the Jews who were blamed. Nicholas himself went along with this attitude, claiming that nine-tenths of the trouble-makers were Jews. The most notorious case took place in Kiev where, in 1911, the body of a 13-year old Orthodox Christian boy was found stabbed to death. Mendel Beiliss, a completely innocent Jewish clerk, was arrested and tried on a charge of ritual murder. Although two policemen had discovered the real murderers, the trial went ahead and the two policemen were sacked. There was a huge outcry and demonstrations in support of Beiliss and the case aroused considerable interest abroad. In the end he was acquitted, but it later emerged that the Tsar and the government had gone to great lengths to secure a conviction, although they knew he was innocent. Defence witnesses were arrested before the trial began and the judge was bribed; and still the jury had the courage to reach a 'not guilty' verdict. The regime was prepared to go to such disreputable lengths, ignoring international condemnation, because they saw it as part of a quite legitimate counter-revolutionary campaign. Although the Beiliss case ended in defeat for the government, the activities of the URP in general gave the impression that the monarchy was rallying itself and fighting back successfully against the forces of revolution.

(b) Weaknesses of the regime

The key to the question of how close the Russian empire was to revolution in 1914 lies in the attitudes of the peasants and urban workers. By 1912 it was clear that the Stolypin agrarian reforms were not working in the way he had hoped (see section 2.4(b)). Though Richard Pipes claims that the villages were quiet immediately before the war, revisionist historians would point out that this does not necessarily mean that the peasants felt no resentment or hostility. Following the Stolypin repression, when villages were burned down and hundreds of peasants hanged after summary trials in field courts, it is not altogether surprising that they were docile. There is ample evidence that peasants still had their minds firmly fixed on two goals: land and freedom. The American historian Leopold Haimson argued that it was those peasants who moved into towns and cities to work in industry who caused the most problems for the regime by fuelling the existing unrest. He calculated that in 1914 about 50 per cent of industrial workers in St Petersburg had moved in from the countryside comparatively recently. Many of them were full of resentment, not only against the landowning gentry, but against those successful peasants who had left the commune.[32] Haimson claimed that these workers were very much attracted to Bolshevik and anarchist ideas with their simple, emotional slogans, and that they found the SRs and Mensheviks too moderate (see Document J).

By 1912 there was growing unrest in industrial towns and cities. Living and working conditions had probably improved marginally since 1905, and a class of better-off, skilled workers had emerged. But it was exactly these people who were susceptible to revolutionary ideas and propaganda and who were likely to become the spearhead of any revolution. The statistics of strikes tell a significant story.

The upsurge in strikes was mainly a response to the regime's handling of a goldminers' strike in the Lena River area near Yakutsk in Siberia. In February 1912 about five thousand goldminers went on strike for purely economic reasons. They felt themselves to be unreasonably exploited, having to work extremely

Year	Strikes	Workers involved	Politically motivated
1910	222	46,000	8
1911	466	105,000	24
1912	2032	725,491	1300
1913 (first 8 months)	1671	figure not available	761
1914 (first 7 months)	3466	over one million	2500

Statistics from Lionel Kochan, *Russia in Revolution*, pp. 154–5.

long hours, sometimes from 5 am until 7 pm; wages were poor and paid on the truck system. They asked for a maximum eight-hour day and higher wages to be paid in cash; they made no political demands. After a month no agreement had been reached and the government decided to use troops to force the miners back to work; clashes developed and about 200 workers were killed and hundreds of others wounded. There was uproar when news of the Lena massacre reached St Petersburg; by the end of April half a million workers came out on strike in sympathy, and there was a great international outcry. By its own short-sighted reaction, the regime had unnecessarily provoked a political protest which it followed up by banning the militant unions. This of course only drove them underground again and increased the bitterness. The strike wave continued through 1913 and into 1914. Matters were made worse by an outbreak of plague in the Baku oilfields on the Caspian Sea, where living and working conditions were primitive. In June 1914 there was a general strike in the Baku area; again troops were brought in and again protests spread to St Petersburg. Two workers at the Putilov steelworks were killed by police, and within a few days there was a general strike in the capital. It seemed like a repeat performance of 1905, with the authorities apparently having learned nothing in the meantime. This time, however, there were more far-reaching political demands including a democratic republic.

Another threat to the regime was the revival of the revolutionary movements, especially the Bolsheviks. They did not begin the unrest, but once it began to surface again in 1912 they certainly used all their skills to organize and direct it. The Bolshevik daily newspaper *Pravda* was published openly from 1912 and reached sales of 40,000 a day. A small group of Bolshevik deputies was elected to the Duma in 1912 and in August 1913 the Bolsheviks gained control of the Metalworkers' Union, the biggest one in St Petersburg. By 1914 they had won control of all the major trade unions in St Petersburg and Moscow.

The regime's extreme Russian nationalist and anti-Jewish policy turned out to be counter-productive. Instead of making some concessions to win the support of the non-Russians – for example the Polish language could have been allowed – the government continued its policy of 'Russification' – trying to make the Russian language and the Orthodox religion a unifying basis for the whole empire. All efforts to establish separate national identities were suppressed, causing protests from areas as far apart as Latvia and Georgia. By 1914 all the non-Russians were strongly opposed to the regime, and since they made up over half the total population of the empire, this was a serious threat to stability. One of the main threats to the monarchy was in Poland where Josef Pilsudski and his Left Socialist Party were training troops in Krakow (in the part of Poland controlled by Austria–Hungary) and doing all they could to destabilize the part of Poland ruled by Russia. This included co-operating with the Bolsheviks and with Lenin, who was based in Krakow for a time in 1912 and 1913. The anti-Semitic policy was equally short-sighted – the government persisted in treating Jews as an alien group at a time when many young Jews were growing away from their religious and cultural origins and would have been quite prepared to become 'good Russians', given half a chance. So it was no accident that many of the leading revolutionaries were Jewish or non-Russian.

A serious weakness was the unpopularity of the royal family. Nicholas II was a man of limited vision and narrow intellect who found it difficult to contemplate any sort of change. True, his most recent biographer, Dominic Lieven, attempts to defend him, describing him as intelligent and flexible, but his actions speak for themselves. The more pressure built up for liberal reform, the more he fell back on repression; he chose extreme reactionaries for his advisers and withdrew his support from the only two politicians – Witte and Stolypin – who might have been able to save the monarchy. He failed to grasp the possibilities opened up by the creation of the Duma; he did everything in his power to sideline even the third and fourth Dumas which had right-wing majorities, instead of trying to enlist their support. By 1914 even the Octobrists were despairing of him; some of them were now opposed to any suggestion of reconciliation with the regime (see Documents I and K).

The family was further discredited by its association with Grigori Rasputin,[33] a peasant 'holy man' from Siberia who made himself indispensable to the Empress Alexandra by his ability to help the unfortunate heir to the throne, Alexei (aged 10 in 1914), who suffered from haemophilia inherited from his mother's family. On occasion Rasputin was able, apparently by using a combination of prayer and hypnosis, to stop the internal bleeding when Alexei suffered a haemorrhage. A long-running scandal developed as rumours of Rasputin's disreputable behaviour spread. He was said to be a drunkard, a lecher who had endless affairs with court ladies, including the Empress, and it was reported that he had an aristocratic homosexual lover. It was also rumoured that he had an unhealthy influence on government policy and could get ministers appointed and sacked. No doubt much of this was exaggerated, but what mattered was that people believed the rumours; and they brought respect for the monarchy to an all-time low. When the Duma requested that Rasputin should be sent away from the court, Nicholas refused, arguing that it was a family matter.

To be fair to Nicholas, it wasn't his fault that he inherited such a complex set of problems – a huge empire in the throes of industrialization and modernization, with an inadequate administrative system, and a population of peasants, workers and an intelligentsia who felt alienated from the ruling elite. The international situation was not promising: the Russian Empire felt threatened by its neighbours – Germany, Austria–Hungary and Japan – and its armed forces, though large, were not well-equipped. This was a set of circumstances which would have severely stretched whatever government happened to be in power. Even so, different policy decisions could have been made; a more imaginative, less naive Tsar might have followed different advice and avoided Nicholas's worst mistakes. The danger was that after 20 years of rule by Nicholas and his advisers, all the basic problems and tensions in the empire were still there.

(c) The verdict?

Judging by the evidence of the urban unrest and strikes, the revival of Bolshevik activity, the unpopularity of the Tsar and his failure to learn any lessons from the experiences of 1905, it does look as though events were moving towards another upheaval in the summer of 1914, *before* the First World War started. It wasn't only in St Petersburg that disturbances were taking place – there was massive support for change in other cities – Moscow, Kiev, Warsaw, Odessa, Tbilisi (Georgia), Riga (Latvia) and Tallinn (Estonia). The autocracy was simply not equal to dealing with all the complex problems of a huge state in the process of modernization. If the regime continued with its stubborn refusal to address the root causes of the unrest, it is difficult to see how another revolution could have been avoided, even without a war. Whether that would have happened in 1914 or later is impossible to say. One significant point is that the Bolshevik Central Committee called off the St Petersburg strike early in July 1914 because of lack of weapons and 'inadequate party organization'. However, the workers continued the strike for another four days, which suggests that the Bolsheviks had lost control of the movement; in fact, according to a police report, the workers had 'gone berserk'. All this seems to support writers like George Kennan and Leopold Haimson who argued that the regime would have collapsed sooner or later, war or no war. More recently, Sheila Fitzpatrick takes a similar view: 'The autocracy's situation was precarious on the eve of the First World War,' she writes; 'the society was deeply divided, and the political and bureaucratic structure was fragile and overstrained. The regime was so vulnerable to any kind of jolt or setback that it is hard to imagine that it could have survived long, even without the war.'[34] Soviet historians continued to argue to the end that revolution was historically inevitable and that the 'revolutionary upsurge' was reaching a climax in 1914 – in their view the outbreak of war actually delayed the revolution.

Other historians are more cautious. Christopher Read thinks that the overthrow of the monarchy was by no means inevitable and that the situation in the years immediately before 1914 could have continued indefinitely.[35] Robert Service agrees, arguing that although 'the various weaknesses of tsarism were tightly interlinked, leaving the Russian Empire in a condition of general brittleness, ... a sense of proportion has to be maintained; although it was a vulnerable plant, it was not doomed to undergo the root-and-branch revolution of 1917. What made that kind of revolution possible was the protracted, exhausting conflict of the First World War.'[36] Bearing in mind A.J.P. Taylor's famous maxim that nothing is ever inevitable until it has started to happen, perhaps the best conclusion is that revolution was highly likely but not absolutely inevitable. The regime's ability to survive depended in the last resort on whether the army remained loyal; on how long the soldiers would continue to obey orders to shoot striking workers.

Documents

The 1905 Revolution

(A) An Austrian observer talks to a Russian official about the situation in 1904.

'What will be the end, then?'
'The end will be that the terror from above will awaken the terror from below, that peasant revolts will break out and assassination will increase.'
'And is there no possibility of organizing the revolution so that it shall not rage senselessly?'
'Impossible ...'
'There is no one with whom I have spoken who would fail to paint the future of this country in the darkest colours. Can there be no change of the fatal policy which is ruining the country?'
'Not before a great general catastrophe. When we shall be compelled for the first time partly to repudiate our debts – and that may happen sooner than we may now believe – on that day, being no longer able to pay our old debts with new ones – for we shall no longer be able to conceal our internal bankruptcy from foreign countries and from the Emperor – steps will be taken, perhaps ...'
'Is there no mistake possible here in what you are saying?'
'Whoever, like myself, has known the state kitchen for the last twenty-five years has no longer any doubts. The autocracy is not equal to the problems of a great modern power, and it would be against all historical precedent to assume that it would voluntarily yield without external pressure to a constitutional form of government.'
'We must wish then, for Russia's sake, that the catastrophe comes as quickly as possible.'
'I repeat to you that it is perhaps nearer than we all think or are willing to admit. That is the hope; that is our secret consolation ... We are near to collapse, like an athlete with great muscles and perhaps incurable heart weakness. We still maintain ourselves upright by stimulants, by loans, which like all stimulants only help to ruin the system more quickly. With that we are a rich country with all conceivable natural resources, simply ill-governed and prevented from unlocking our resources. But is this the first time that quacks have ruined a Hercules that has fallen into their hands?'

Source: Hugo Ganz, *The Downfall of Russia*, quoted in A. Nove, *An Economic History of the USSR, 1917–1991*, third edition, 1992, pp. 18–19.

(B) Extracts from the Petition of the Workers, Bloody Sunday, 9 January 1905.

Sire: we working men and inhabitants of St Petersburg come to Thee, Sire, to seek for truth and defence. We have become beggars; we have been

(*continued*)

oppressed; we are treated as slaves. The limit of patience has been reached. There has arrived for us that tremendous moment when death is better than the continuation of intolerable tortures. We have left off working and we have declared to the masters that we shall not begin to work until they comply with our demands. We beg but little... The first request was that our masters should discuss our needs with us, but this was refused, on the grounds that by law we have no right to make such a request. They also declared to be illegal our requests to reduce the working hours to eight hours daily, to agree with us about the prices for our work, and to increase the wages of women and general labourers.... Every one of our requests was a crime, and the desire to improve our condition was regarded by them as impertinence.

Sire, here are many thousands of us, but we are human beings in appearance only; there is no human right, not even the right of speaking, thinking, meeting, discussing our needs. Every one of us who dares to raise a voice in defence of working class and popular interests is thrown in gaol or is sent into banishment... We are seeking here the last salvation. Do not refuse assistance to Thy people... order immediately the convocation of representatives of the Russian land from all ranks, including the working people... This is the most capital of our requests.

[Then follows a list of requests for measures to counteract the ignorance and legal oppression, the poverty and the oppression of the Russian people]

Order these requests and Thou wilt make Russia happy and famous and Thou wilt impress thy name in our hearts. If Thou wilt not answer our prayers – we shall die here on this place before Thy palace...

Source: quoted in G.A. Kertesz (ed.), *Documents in the Political History of the European Continent, 1815–1939*, OUP, 1968, p. 297.

(C) Two eyewitness accounts of Bloody Sunday.

The dragoon circled round him [the worker] and, shrieking like a woman, waved his sabre in the air... Swooping down from his dancing horse, he slashed him across the face, cutting him open from the eyes to the chin. I remember the strangely enlarged eyes of the worker and the murderer's face, blushed from the cold and excitement, his teeth clenched in a grin and the hairs of his moustache standing up on his elevated lip. Brandishing his tarnished shaft of steel he let out another shriek and, with a wheeze, spat at the dead man through his teeth. [by Maxim Gorky, a writer and Bolshevik sympathiser].

I observed the faces round me and I detected neither fear nor panic. No, the reverend and almost prayerful expressions were replaced by hostility and even hatred. I saw these looks of hatred and vengeance on literally every face – old and young, men and women. The revolution had been truly born, and it had been born in the very core, in the very bowels of the people. An old man

turned to a young boy and said: 'Remember son, remember and swear to repay the Tsar. You saw how much blood he spilled, did you see? Then swear, son, swear!'
[written by a Bolshevik in the crowd]

Source: quoted in Orlando Figes, *A People's Tragedy, the Russian Revolution 1891–1924*, 1996, pp. 177–8.

(D) The St Petersburg Soviet, October–December 1905; two proclamations.

20 October (following the announcement of the October Manifesto):
In view of the necessity of the working class to organize on the basis of its achieved victories and to arm for a final struggle for a Constituent Assembly on the basis of universal, equal, direct and secret suffrage which is to establish a democratic republic, the Council of Workers' Delegates orders that the political strike be stopped at noon, 21 October. The Council is confident, however, that, should it be required by further developments, the working-men will resume the strike as willingly and devotedly as heretofore.

1 November, call for a general strike in support of the rebellion of sailors at Kronstadt:
The government continues to stride over corpses. It puts on trial before a court-martial the brave Kronstadt soldiers of the army and navy who rose to the defence of their rights and of national freedom. It put the noose of martial law on the neck of oppressed Poland. The Council of Workers' Delegates calls on the revolutionary proletariat of Petersburg to manifest their solidarity with the revolutionary soldiers of Kronstadt and with the revolutionary proletarians of Poland through a general political strike, which has proved to be a formidable power, and through general meetings of protest. Tomorrow, on 2 November, at noon, the working-men of Petersburg will stop work, their slogans being: Down with court-martial! Down with capital punishment! Down with martial law in Poland and all over Russia!

Source: quoted in R. Wolfson, *Years of Change, 1890–1945*, pp. 120–1.

The Duma

(E) Count Kokovtsov, the Minister of Finance describes the opening of the First Duma.

St Georges' Hall, the throne room, presented a queer spectacle at this moment, and I believe its walls had never before witnessed such a scene. The entire right side of the room was filled with uniformed people, members of the State Council and the Tsar's retinue. The left side was crowded with the members

(continued)

of the Duma... the overwhelming majority of which, occupying the first places near the throne, were dressed as if intentionally in workers' blouses and cotton shirts, and behind them was a crowd of peasants in the most varied costumes, some in national dress, and a multitude of representatives of the clergy. The first place among these people's representatives was occupied by a man of tall stature, dressed in a worker's blouse and high, oiled boots, who examined the throne and those about it with a derisive and insolent air. It was the famous F.M. Onipko, who later won great renown by his bold statements in the Duma. While the Tsar read his speech, I could not take my eyes off Onipko, so much contempt and hate did his insolent face show. I was not the only one who was thus impressed. Near me stood P.A. Stolypin, who turned to me and said: 'We both seem to be engrossed in the same spectacle. I even have a feeling that this man might throw a bomb.'

Source: quoted in M. Ferro, *Nicholas II, The Last of the Tsars*, p. 109.

(F) Sergei Kryzhanovski, an official in the Ministry of the Interior, gives his impression of the First Duma.

It was enough to take a look at the motley mob of 'deputies' – and it was my lot to spend among them entire days in the corridors of Taurida Palace – to experience horror at the sight of Russia's first representative body. It was a gathering of savages. It seemed as if the Russian land had sent to St Petersburg everything that was barbarian in it, everything filled with envy and malice. The attempt to found the political system on the will of the people was clearly doomed to failure because in this mass, any consciousness of statehood, let alone of shared statehood, was totally submerged in social hostility and class envy.

Source: quoted in R. Pipes, *The Russian Revolution, 1899–1919*, 1997 edition, pp. 162–3.

(G) Maurice Baring, an English expert in Russian literature, describes his visit to a session of the Duma on 14 May 1906.

I had the good fortune to gain admission to the Duma yesterday afternoon. I think it is the most interesting sight I have ever seen. One saw peasants in their long black coats, some of them wearing military medals and crosses; priests; Tartars; Poles, men in every kind of dress except uniform. When the sitting began I went up to the gallery... The President, C.A. Muromtsev, strikes one as dignity itself. He exercises his functions with perfect serenity and absolute fairness... The speeches were moderate; what struck me most in the speeches I heard was the naturalness of their tone, and the absence of declamatory emphasis. Several of the speeches were eloquent; only one was tedious. Nobody can possibly say the Duma is disorderly; it takes itself with profound seriousness.

Source: quoted in R. Pethybridge, *Witnesses to the Russian Revolution*, 1964, pp. 50–4.

(H) Proclamation by the Tsar to dissolve the First Duma, 21 July 1906.

We summoned the representatives of the nation by Our will to the work of productive legislation. We confidently anticipated benefits for the country and We proposed great reforms in all departments in the national life.

A cruel disappointment has befallen Our expectations. The representatives have strayed into spheres beyond their competence and have been making comments on the imperfections of the Fundamental Laws which can only be modified by Our imperial will. In short, the representatives of the nation have undertaken really illegal acts, such as the appeal by the Duma to the nation. We shall not permit arbitrary or illegal acts, and We shall impose Our imperial will on the disobedient by all the power of the State.

Source: quoted in Wolfson, p. 122.

The situation on the eve of the First World War

(I) Rodzianko, the Octobrist President of the Duma, has an audience with the Tsar in 1913. He complains that, in effect, Russia has no government. Extracts from Rodzianko's Memoirs, published in 1927.

'What do you mean – no government?'
'We are accustomed to think that part of the executive power of the crown is delegated to the ministers and to the nominated members of the council of the empire (state council). These latter execute the will of the government and defend it in the legislative assembly. We, the members of the lower chamber, are accustomed to think so. What do we see? During the last session we debated the bill for the admittance of the Polish language in the schools of the western provinces. It was your imperial majesty's wish that the language should be admitted in order to improve the position of the Poles by comparison with their position in Austria, and so enlist their sympathies on behalf of Russia.'
'Yes,' replied the Tsar, 'that is just what I had in view.'
'So we understood it, and the bill was worked out in the Duma in that sense. Now this bill is being debated in the council of the empire, and its leading principle is defended by a representative of the government. Meanwhile some of the nominated members of the council are absent, others vote against it, and the bill is rejected. Your majesty will agree that the members of the government either do not wish to execute your will, or do not take the trouble to understand

(continued)

it. The population does not know where it is. Each minister has his own opinion. The cabinet for the most part is split into two parties, the state council forms a third, the Duma a fourth, and your own will is unknown to the nation. This cannot go on, your Majesty; this is not a government, it is anarchy.'

Source: M.V. Rodzianko, *The Reign of Rasputin: An Empire's Collapse*, London, 1927, p. 210.

(J) Report on the labour situation by the Ministry of the Interior, October 1913.

Sudden strikes flare up sometimes for the most trivial causes and embracing with extraordinary rapidity wide areas with tens of thousands of workers. But apart from that, the strike movement we are now experiencing has a yet more threatening social significance in that it arouses hostility and bitterness between employer and worker, unites the workers on the basis of an irreconcilable relationship to the existing state and social structure and in this way creates amongst the workers ready cadres to reinforce the revolutionary parties. Under the influence of agitators and the printed organs of the Social-Democratic press, with the moral and material support of different workers' circles, there has recently developed amongst the workers a harmony of action such as indicates their close solidarity and organised nature. The places where strikes take place are put under a boycott, those workers who approach are exposed to bitter persecution and are excluded from work. Orders at strike-bound factories and plants are also placed under a boycott and any factory that might accept them risks a strike amongst its own workers.

Source: quoted in Ferro, p. 160.

(K) Extract from an article by S. Elpatevsky in the journal *Russian Wealth*, January 1914.

The government, after seeking to reach an understanding with the Kadets, then with the Octobrists, has now moved over to the right wing parties, while on the other side of the fence, all expectations within the Duma of any possible legislative work with the government are steadily declining. The crisis has now become so acute that revolution or counter-revolution appear the only way out. Even some of the Octobrists are now being heard to say that there is no longer any sense in trying to safeguard the Duma, while the right wing factions, which for a year now have been loudly warning of 'impending conflict', 'revolution', and 'repetition of 1905', have managed to persuade themselves of the inevitability of a 'catastrophic confrontation'. It is clear that the tensions in national life are rapidly approaching the breaking point.

Source: quoted in Figes, p. 250.

Notes

1. Dominic Lieven, *Nicholas II: Emperor of All the Russias*, and Edvard Radzinsky, *The Last Tsar: The Life and Death of Nicholas II*, London, 1992, are good recent biographies.
2. Theodore Shanin, *Russia as a 'Developing Society'*, vol. 1 of *Russia's Roots of Otherness*, for an excellent survey of Russian society at this time.
3. Dominic Lieven, 'The Aristocracy and the Gentry', in Acton, Cherniaev and Rosenberg (editors), *Critical Companion to the Russian Revolution, 1914–1921*, p. 481.
4. Peter Gatrell, 'Russian Industrialists and Revolution', in Acton, Cherniaev and Rosenberg (editors), *Critical Companion to the Russian Revolution*, p. 574.
5. Robert Service, *A History of Twentieth Century Russia*, p. 7.
6. Alec Nove, *An Economic History of the USSR, 1917–1991*, p.12.
7. Alexander Gerschenkron, 'Agrarian Policies and Industrialization in Russia, 1861–1917', in *Cambridge Economic History of Europe*, vol. 6, part 2, gives a clear statement of this, the traditional view.
8. J.Y. Simms, 'The Crisis in Russian Agriculture at the End of the Nineteenth Century: A Different View', *Slavic Review*, 36, 1977, for one of the earliest statements of the revisionist view. See also Peter Gatrell, *The Tsarist Economy 1815–1917*, p. 34, for a more recent interpretation.
9. Orlando Figes, *A People's Tragedy: the Russian Revolution 1891–1924*, p. 57; Alan Wildman, *The End of the Russian Imperial Army*, vol. 1, pp. 33–5.
10. J. Bushnell, *Mutiny Amid Repression: Russian Soldiers in the Revolution of 1905–1906*, pp. 15–21.
11. Peter Gatrell, 'Peasants and Politics', *Modern History Review*, April 1995, p. 6.
12. Robert Service, *Lenin, A Biography*, p. 171.
13. Quoted in William G. Rosenberg, 'The Constitutional Democrat Party (Kadets)', in Acton, Cherniaev and Rosenberg (editors), p. 256.
14. Abraham Ascher, *The Revolution of 1905: Russia in Disarray* is a good account of the 1905 Revolution.
15. Figes, *A People's Tragedy*, p. 121.
16. *Ibid.*, p. 202.
17. Robert Service, *A History of Twentieth Century Russia*, p. 16.
18. Nove, p. 15.
19. Peter Gatrell, *The Tsarist Economy 1850–1917*, pp. 98–140.
20. Stephen L. Hoch, 'Malthus, Population Trends and Peasant Standard of Living in Late Imperial Russia', *Slavic Review*, 1994, pp. 41–75.
21. Robert Service, *The Russian Revolution, 1900–1927* (1999 edition), pp. 12–13.
22. Peter Waldron, *The End of Imperial Russia, 1855–1917*, p. 61.
23. All the statistics in this section are from Nove, pp. 2–8.
24. Alexander Gerschenkron, p. 207.
25. Nove, pp. 6–7.
26. G.A. Hosking, *The Russian Constitutional Experiment. Government and Duma, 1907–1914*, for a detailed account of the Dumas.
27. Richard Pipes, *The Russian Revolution, 1899–1919*, p. 159.
28. Christopher Read, *From Tsar to Soviets: The Russian People and their Revolution, 1917–21*, pp. 32–3.
29. Marc Ferro, *Nicholas II, the Last of the Tsars*, p. 115.
30. Leon Trotsky, *The History of the Russian Revolution*, p. 57.
31. Pipes, pp. 192–3.
32. L H. Haimson, 'The Problem of Social Stability in Urban Russia, 1905–1917', *Slavic Review*, December 1964, pp. 634–6.
33. Edvard Radzinsky, *Rasputin*, is the most recent biography.
34. Sheila Fitzpatrick, *The Russian Revolution*, p. 38.
35. Read, p. 35.
36. Robert Service, *The Russian Revolution, 1900–1927*, pp. 3–4.

■ ⛝ 3 The First World War and the collapse of Tsarism, 1914–17

Summary of events

Throughout the second half of the nineteenth century Russian interests in foreign affairs had focused on two main areas: the Balkan peninsula stretching down to the Dardanelles – the exit from the Black Sea into the Mediterranean; and the Far East. The interest in the Balkans brought Russia into conflict with Austria–Hungary and Turkey, and in the Far East with Japan, and its policies were not very fruitful:

Military and diplomatic defeats for Russia
- 1854–56   Defeat in the Crimean War
- 1878   Diplomatic defeat at the Congress of Berlin
- 1904–05   Defeat in war with Japan

Europe divides into 'armed camps'
Meanwhile the leading states of Europe were forming themselves into two opposing alliance systems often described as 'armed camps':

- 1882   Triple Alliance completed – includes Germany, Austria–Hungary and Italy
- 1894   Russia and France sign an alliance
- 1902   Britain and Japan sign an agreement
- 1904   Britain and France sign an agreement known as the Entente Cordiale
- 1907   Russia signs an agreement with Britain, completing the Triple Entente

28 June 1914   Assassination of the Archduke Franz Ferdinand in Sarajevo
There were several tense incidents from 1905 onwards, but somehow a major war was avoided. **The event which did eventually lead to war was the assassination of the Archduke Franz Ferdinand** of Austria–Hungary and his wife on 28 June 1914. They were on an official visit to Sarajevo, the capital of Bosnia, when they were both shot dead by a Serbian terrorist. The Austrians blamed the

Serbs and on 28 July declared war on Serbia. After that events moved swiftly and in little more than a week, almost the whole of Europe was at war:

- The following day the Russians, allies of Serbia, ordered a general mobilization of their forces.
- The German government demanded that this should be cancelled (31 July) but the Russians refused to comply, whereupon Germany declared war on Russia (1 August) and on Russia's ally France (3 August).
- Britain came into the war on 4 August after German troops entered Belgium on their way to invade France.
- Austria–Hungary declared war on Russia on 6 August.

1914 The Russians succeeded in mobilizing more quickly than their enemies expected, and launched invasions of both the German territory of East Prussia and the Austrian province of Galicia. Against Austrian forces, the Russians did well, capturing Lemberg (Lwow), the capital of Austrian Galicia. However, the Russian forces were soon struggling against the Germans; they were heavily defeated in two battles in East Prussia: Tannenburg (August) and the Masurian Lakes (September), and were driven out of Germany. Worse was to follow.

1915 The Germans occupied Poland, Lithuania and Latvia, and **Nicholas made the mistake of assuming personal command of all Russian forces,** which took him away from the capital where he was most needed, and made him personally responsible for the army's misfortunes.

1916 At first during 1916 Russian fortunes improved – **General Brusilov launched a successful offensive against the Austrians,** advancing 100 miles and capturing 400,000 prisoners and large amounts of equipment. However, the advantage was thrown away by tactical blunders, and the Germans gradually pushed the Russians back. The strain was beginning to tell on the Russians who continued to suffer defeat whenever they met German troops.

1917 On the home front ministers were sacked and replaced in rapid succession. But it did nothing to improve the situation – there were severe food shortages in the cities and the government seemed to have no idea how to cope with its mounting problems.

The February revolution

- In February there were strikes and demonstrations in Petrograd (St Petersburg), and these soon became violent. Eventually troops disobeyed orders to fire on the crowds and mobs began to seize public buildings. The Duma hurriedly formed a Provisional Committee and soldiers and workers elected representatives to the Petrograd Soviet.
- At first Nicholas was intent on restoring order and still refused to set up a constitutional monarchy. By this time all the leading groups – aristocracy, Duma, industrialists and the army had turned against the Tsar and were convinced

Figure 3.1   The Petrograd Garrison joins forces with the workers during the February revolution – 27 February 1917.

that he must go. Some of his senior generals told him that the only way to save the monarchy was for him to renounce the throne.

- On 2 March 1917, in the imperial train standing in a siding near Pskov, **the Tsar agreed to abdicate** in favour of his brother, the Grand Duke Michael. However, Michael decided not to accept the throne, and the Russian monarchy came to an end. The Provisional Government was formed with Prince Lvov as chairman.

3.1 Russia's foreign relations and the approach of war

(a) Russia feels threatened in Europe

The fact that the Russian empire was the largest country in the world brought with it a special problem – it meant that Russia had the longest frontier in the world to protect (see Map 3.1). In the Far East her neighbours China and Japan were not seen as a problem, since they were considered to be too weak to be a threat. But in Europe there were long borders with Germany, Austria–Hungary and the Ottoman Empire (Turkey). For most of the nineteenth century Russia had enjoyed good relations with Germany and Austria–Hungary, while France and Britain were the powers which threatened Russian interests. However, German foreign policy entered a more aggressive phase in 1890 under her new ruler, the Kaiser Wilhelm II. There were signs that he intended to work closely with Austria–Hungary to extend German influence in south-eastern Europe and the Near East, including the Balkans – areas which were part of the Ottoman Empire. The Turkish government was finding it increasingly difficult to keep control of these provinces in the Balkans, where nationalist independence movements were challenging Turkish rule. Turkey had for a long time been regarded as 'the sick man of Europe' and the other powers were on the look-out for any advantages to be gained if and when the Turkish empire fell apart.

From Russia's point of view, these areas were considered to be within her sphere of influence and it was seen as vital to prevent them falling into the hands of Austria–Hungary and Germany. The Russians had a two-fold interest in the southern Balkans:

- The peoples of this area were largely Slav and Christian, and Russia had traditionally claimed the right to protect them from oppression and persecution by the Muslim Turks.
- Closely connected with this was the question of the Dardanelles – the narrow straits which form the exit from the Black Sea into the Mediterranean (see Map 3.2). Russia was handicapped both militarily and commercially by the fact that many of her ports were ice-bound for several months of the year, while ships could be prevented from sailing to and from her Black Sea ports if

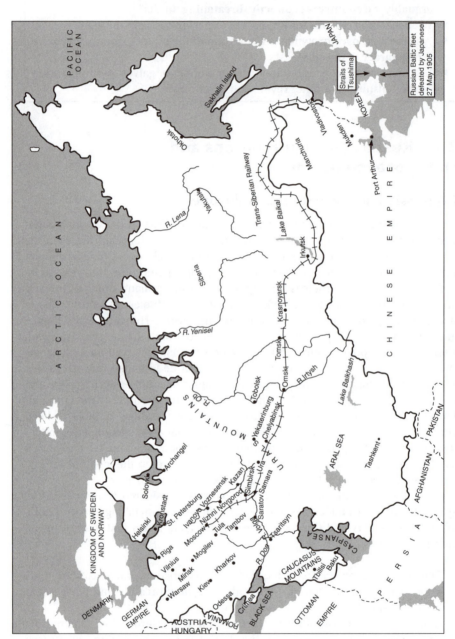

Map 3.1 **The Russian Empire at the time of the Russo–Japanese War, 1904–5.**

a hostile power controlled the Dardanelles. By the early years of the twentieth century almost 50 per cent of Russia's foreign trade passed through the straits. The Germans were talking of building a railway to link Berlin with the Mediterranean and Baghdad. The prospect of a hostile Austria–Hungary, supported by an aggressive Germany, blocking the passage of their merchant and military shipping was enough to throw the Russians into a state of severe anxiety, especially as her relations with the other two great powers – France and Britain – were not altogether healthy (see Document A).

Since 1882 Germany, Austria–Hungary and Italy had been linked together in the Triple Alliance; because of this, Russia felt isolated and under threat. It was for this reason that she began to look towards France as the most likely ally. The French, who were still smarting from their defeat in the recent war with Prussia (1870–71), responded readily and after long negotiations the final agreement was signed in January 1894. It was understood that if France was attacked by Germany, Russia would come to the assistance of France with all available forces. If Russia was attacked by Germany, or by Austria–Hungary supported by Germany, France would use all available forces against Germany. This agreement would remain in force for as long as the Triple Alliance was in existence. The new friendship showed itself in other ways, chiefly in the French willingness to make loans and invest in the developing Russian industry.

Nicholas II still felt insecure as far as Europe was concerned and was alarmed at the cost of trying to keep up with Austria's armaments.[1] This led him to call the first Hague Peace Conference in Holland in 1899, to which 26 states sent representatives. No agreement was reached on disarmament or on compulsory arbitration of disputes but the conference had one great achievement – it set up the International Court of Justice at the Hague, which is still in existence today.

(b) The Russo–Japanese War, 1904–05

This conflict developed from Russia's rivalry with Japan over control of parts of the ailing Chinese empire.[2] The period before the First World War was a time of imperial expansion. The Russians had gradually built up a huge empire, taking over territory in the Ukraine, in Siberia, around the Baltic, in Poland and in Transcaucasia and Central Asia. China, which was militarily weak, seemed the most likely area for the next intervention. Sergei Witte saw China, especially the provinces of Manchuria and Korea, as a lucrative market for exports of Russian manufactured goods, and hoped that the Trans-Siberian Railway (started in 1886) would provide the key to success. In 1896 he persuaded China to allow the railway to pass through Manchuria in order to shorten the route to Vladivostock; this was on condition that Chinese sovereignty over Manchuria was respected. However, the Russians soon broke the agreement by sending troops into Manchuria. The other European powers were interested in China as well: in 1897 the Germans took the Chinese port of Kiaochow, while in 1898 the French secured a base in Kwangchow Bay and the British leased the port of Wei-hai-wei. Anxious not to be outdone, the Russians pressurized the Chinese to lease them the Liaotung Peninsula (1898) where they built the naval base of Port Arthur.

Witte later claimed in his memoirs that his policy was merely economic, and that the war was the fault of Plehve, the Minister of the Interior from 1902 until 1904, who planned it as 'a little victorious war to stem the tide of revolution'. But it is clear from later evidence that the Russian government, Nicholas II and Witte included, had decided by February 1903 that Manchuria would have to be annexed; Russian control was thought to be vital in order to attract the necessary investment to make her economic plans a success.

This was a risky policy which was bound to bring Russia into confrontation with the Japanese, who also had ambitions in Manchuria and Korea. Even so, it need not have led to war; the Japanese were prepared to compromise – they offered to allow Russia a free hand in Manchuria in return for the same freedom in Korea. If Witte had still been in office, it is likely that agreement would have been reached; unfortunately Nicholas had just sacked him (August 1903), and had fallen under the influence of a group of speculators who had business interests in Korea. They persuaded the Tsar to reject the Japanese offer, and from that point war was inevitable. The Japanese, convinced that Russia would not negotiate, openly prepared for war. The Russians, believing that victory was a foregone conclusion, were apparently happy for the Japanese to make the first move, so that they could be blamed for starting the war.

The Japanese duly obliged in January 1904; without a declaration of war, they attacked the Russian fleet at Port Arthur. Several Russian ships were sunk and the rest were blockaded in port. There was an outburst of patriotism, and government propaganda portrayed the Japanese as 'the yellow peril' and 'the Asian hordes' which were threatening the whole of European civilization. Two Russian soldiers, it was said, were worth any three Japanese. With the Russian ships trapped in harbour, the Japanese controlled the sea and this enabled them to land troops in Korea to besiege Port Arthur. A Russian army advancing from Manchuria to relieve Port Arthur was attacked by a smaller Japanese army and forced to retreat to Mukden. Port Arthur fell to the Japanese early in 1905. In February the Russians were forced to withdraw northwards from Mukden, after losing nearly 90,000 troops defending it.

The final humiliation came in May 1905: Russia's Baltic fleet, which had spent over seven months sailing from its base at Kronstadt round to the Far East, was joined by the Black Sea fleet which had sailed by way of the Suez Canal. Together they arrived off the coast of Japan and headed through the Straits of Tsushima on their way to Vladivostock. But the Russian ships were slow and old and when they were attacked by the much faster and more manoeuvrable Japanese, the result was catastrophe. 15 Russian battleships and 54 other ships were sunk and many others were captured; although a few escaped, it was the biggest naval disaster in Russian history.

The Russians were stunned – defeat by a small Asian country had not even been considered a possibility. But the reasons for it were clear: the Russians had completely underestimated the strength of the enemy. They carelessly allowed the Japanese to seize the initiative at the beginning by taking control of the seas, which enabled them to land troops, equipment and supplies without hindrance. The Russians had the disadvantage of having to send reinforcements and supplies thousands of miles from western Russia along the Trans-Siberian Railway, which was not completed – there was a long gap around the southern end of Lake Baikal where there were difficulties with the track sinking in the marshy ground. Although the Russian troops acquitted themselves well, their generals were poorly prepared and showed no imagination; they wasted thousands of lives in pointless charges against fortified artillery positions, and were repeatedly out-manoeuvred by the Japanese. Amazingly, there was no proper General Staff – the war minister was head of the army.

Fortunately for Russia, Japanese losses were also heavy, they had not succeeded in destroying the main Russian armies, and their resources had been strained by the war. Both sides were ready for peace and the USA was prepared to mediate. A peace conference met at Portsmouth, New Hampshire, where Witte, recalled after his earlier sacking, acted as Russia's representative. He negotiated shrewdly, playing on the fact that Japan was equally desperate for peace, and obtained better terms than might have been expected. By the Treaty of Portsmouth (September 1905) Russia gave Japan the southern half of the island of Sakhalin, and this was the only Russian territory lost. It was agreed that Japan should have the Liaotung Peninsula with Port Arthur, and Russia recognized a controlling Japanese interest in Korea. Liaotung and Korea were Chinese territory anyway, and it was also agreed that Manchuria should be restored to China, thus prevent-ing Japan from gaining control. But there was no disguising the fact that Russia's armed forces had been found seriously lacking and that the government was to blame for its carelessness and complacency. It was clear that the army and navy were in need of radical reform and modernization if Russia was to maintain its position as a great power.

(c) Russia, France and Britain – the Triple Entente

The defeat by Japan in the Far East meant that there was no immediate prospect of expansion in that region, and consequently Russian interest turned towards Europe again. Nicholas was interested in an alliance with Germany, whose Kaiser Wilhelm II was his cousin. However, several of his ministers warned Nicholas that this would weaken Russia's relationship with France, and advised him strongly against it, pointing out that France was 'the moneybox'. If friendship with France was so vitally important, it followed that the logical next step was to develop a good working relationship with France's new Entente partner Britain. Thus there occurred a radical change of direction in Russian foreign policy – Russia turned towards the British with whom relations had been strained for many years because of rivalry over Persia and Afghanistan and because Britain suspected Russia of having designs on India; the British seemed to have a horror of the possibility of Russian battleships being able to sail through the straits into the Mediterranean, where British interests might be threatened. Twice in recent history – in the Crimean War (1854–56) and at the Congress of Berlin (1878) – they had gone to great lengths to prevent Russia gaining control of the Dardanelles (see next section). In addition, Russia resented Britain's alliance with Japan, signed in 1902, although the British had given no direct help to the Japanese during the war. Alexander Izvolski, Russia's minister of foreign affairs from 1906 until 1910, was responsible for negotiating an agreement with Britain signed in

August 1907. Persia was divided up into 'spheres of influence' – one for Russia in the north of the country, one for Britain in the south-east, while the central area was to be left neutral; Russia agreed not to interfere in Afghanistan. There was no promise of military assistance, but since Britain had recently signed the Entente with France (1904), the Anglo–Russian agreement produced the Triple Entente and seemed to complete the grouping of Europe into two camps.

It was unfortunate that both Germany and Austria–Hungary viewed the formation of the Triple Entente as a hostile gesture directed against the Triple Alliance (Germany, Austria–Hungary and Italy). Both Russia and Britain protested that this was not so and tried to maintain good relations. But gradually tensions mounted between the two camps. The Germans accused the Entente powers of trying to 'encircle' them; Britain and Germany were engaged in a 'naval race' to see which of them could build most 'Dreadnought' battleships; and Russian and Austrian interests clashed in the Balkans, particularly over the question of Serbia.

(d) Trouble in the Balkans

Russian and Austrian rivalry in the Balkans reached a new climax in 1908, when the Austrians announced the annexation of the Turkish provinces of Bosnia and Herzegovina, sparking off what became known as the Bosnia Crisis (see Map 3.2). It was a complex situation, and this is a good point to look at the background in some detail. The Balkans region had been a source of trouble for much of the nineteenth century. The problem was generally known as *The Eastern Question*; the great question was: as Turkish control of the peoples of the Balkans grew weaker, what was going to happen? Would these peoples – Greeks, Serbs, Croats, Bulgarians and Romanians – be allowed to have their own independent states, or would Russia take control of the area? This was a possibility which the other powers, especially Britain and France, were determined to resist.

In 1828, after helping the Greeks to gain their independence, the Russians defeated the Turks and forced them to sign the Treaty of Adrianople (1829). This gave Russia the mouth of the River Danube, allowed the provinces of Moldavia and Wallachia self-government *under Russian protection*, and guaranteed the passage of Russian merchant ships through the straits.

In 1833 the Russians sent a fleet and 10,000 troops to help the Sultan of Turkey deal with a rebellion in Anatolia, on the Asian side of the straits. There was international consternation as the other European powers feared the Russians would take Constantinople. But Nicholas I was far too shrewd to risk a war with the whole of Europe. After the Turks had signed the Treaty of Unkiar-Skelessi (1833), Russian forces were withdrawn. The agreement was to run for eight years and included promises of mutual assistance as well as a Turkish guarantee to close the straits to all foreign warships. This was a great achievement for the Russians, since it meant that they became special protectors of the 'sick man of Europe' and gave them a permanent excuse to interfere in Turkish affairs.

After their defeat in the Crimean War, the Russians were forced to accept the Treaty of Paris (1856). This stipulated that Russia could not have battleships on the Black Sea, and was a severe blow to any prospect of their controlling the southern Balkans. In 1870, while the rest of Europe was preoccupied with the

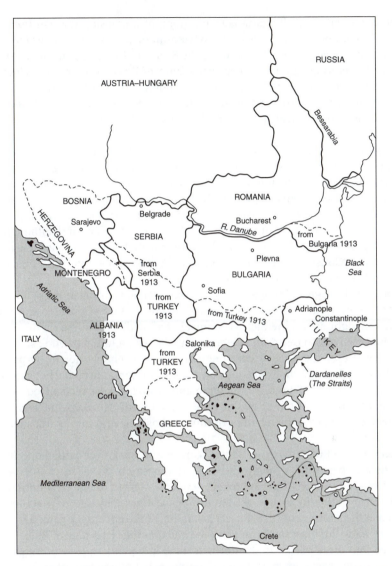

Map 3.2   **The Balkans showing the situation after the Balkan Wars, 1912–13.**

Franco–Prussian War (1870–71), the Russians seized the opportunity to announce that their battleships would sail on the Black Sea, 'for reasons of security and the desire to preserve and strengthen peace.' Since this was supported by Bismarck, the Chancellor of the newly united and victorious Germany, the other powers went along with it too.

By this time there was a strong Panslav movement in Russia; Panslavists believed that it was the duty of the Russians to protect other Slav peoples such as the Serbs and Bulgarians in the Balkans, who were being ruled by non-Slavs. Nikolai Ignatiev, the Russian ambassador in Constantinople from 1864 until 1877, held strong Panslav views, and did not hesitate to stir up nationalist feelings among the Serbs and Bulgarians in the hope of increasing Russian influence. 'Russia must become the master in Constantinople,' he wrote, 'either by a Russian becoming governor of the city and the Straits or by seizing the area. There is no other way to ensure permanent protection of Russian interests.'[3] When the Serbs declared war on Turkey in June 1876, public opinion demanded that Russia should spring to their assistance. The government was not enthusiastic – most of the ministers were not Panslavists, and any Russian military intervention in the Balkans was bound to upset the Austrians, who had their own interests in the region. However, the Serbs soon began to suffer defeats and the pressure of public opinion mounted. The Russians therefore came to an agreement with Austria–Hungary, promising not to capture Constantinople and acknowledging that the western Balkans (especially Bosnia–Herzegovina) were Austria's sphere of influence and the eastern Balkans (especially Bulgaria) were Russia's sphere of influence. In April 1877 Russia declared war on Turkey, and although the campaign was far from easy, the Turks were defeated. The Russians were on the outskirts of Constantinople, but they kept to the agreement and signed the Treaty of San Stefano with the Turks (1878).

This was the high-point of Russia's near-eastern policy – the terms of the treaty were extremely advantageous. A large independent state of Bulgaria was set up stretching right across the Balkan peninsula and with a coastline on the Aegean Sea. Bulgaria was to be administered by Russia 'for an initial period'; she would have the use of the Aegean coastline which would enable her to by-pass the Dardanelles. In addition Russia took territory from Romania giving her control of the Danube mouth. Serbia, Montenegro and Romania were recognized as independent of Turkey, but there was no mention of Bosnia–Herzegovina being given to Austria–Hungary, which had been hinted at as a reward for Austria's remaining neutral.

Sadly for the Russians, the Treaty of San Stefano was never carried out. Britain and Austria protested strongly and moderate opinion prevailed in Russia. Bismarck offered to act as 'honest broker', and it was agreed to hold an international conference in Berlin to renegotiate the peace terms. By the new settlement, signed in the summer of 1878, Russia lost much of the advantage gained from the earlier treaty: the most important change was that the large state of Bulgaria was divided into three parts – in the north, a small independent state of Bulgaria; in the centre, an area known as Eastern Roumelia, belonging to Turkey but having self-government under a Christian governor; and in the south, the area with the Aegean coastline, Macedonia, was to remain part of the Turkish Empire. The Austrians were allowed to occupy and administer Bosnia and Herzegovina, though nominally these provinces still belonged to Turkey.

The Congress of Berlin was a humiliating diplomatic defeat for the Russians; the government of the Tsar Alexander II was severely criticized by the Panslavs for letting down the Slavs of the southern Balkans, and public opinion turned bitterly against Austria–Hungary and Britain. Critics of the Tsar's autocratic rule demanded a more consultative government and a constitution. In the long term the most unfortunate outcome of the Congress was Serbian resentment at the new Austrian influence in Bosnia and Herzegovina. These were provinces on which the newly independent Serbia had designs, and it was this friction between Austria–Hungary and Serbia which was to culminate in the outbreak of the First World War in 1914.

After the Russian defeat in the Far East, her attention turned once again to the Balkans. The Foreign Minister, Alexander Izvolski, was anxious to reassure Austria–Hungary and Germany that the Triple Entente, completed in 1907, was not directed against them. In 1908, following the outbreak of a revolution against the Sultan of Turkey, Izvolski met his Austrian counterpart, Aehrenthal, at Buchlau Castle in Moravia to discuss how this might affect the Balkans. They agreed that both could take advantage of the situation – Austria–Hungary would annexe the Turkish provinces of Bosnia and Herzegovina, with Russian approval; in return Austria–Hungary promised to recognize Russia's right to use the Straits at all times, and to persuade the other European powers to do the same. Aehrenthal went ahead and announced the annexation, which was accepted by the other powers; however, Austria–Hungary did nothing to further Russia's claim to use the Straits at all times, and when the Russians raised the subject, the other powers refused to hear of it.

It turned out to be a diplomatic disaster for Russia: Izvolski had been outmanoeuvred by Aehrenthal, and in fact most of the other Russian ministers were against the agreement, which was seen as a betrayal of the Slavs in Bosnia and Herzegovina. Serbia, which had been hoping to annex the provinces, since many Serbs lived there, was outraged, and appealed to Russia for help. The Russians called for a European conference, expecting French and British support. However, the Germans made it clear that they would support Austria–Hungary in the event of war; Britain and France were lukewarm about becoming involved in a war over the Balkans; in the end caution prevailed, the crisis passed, and Austria–Hungary kept Bosnia and Herzegovina. The Russians had been humiliated: the Serbs had been badly let down, and tsarist Russia, which had proclaimed itself the guardian of all Serbs and other Slavs, had been made to look weak and ineffective. The general public, which was better informed than ever before about foreign affairs, thanks to the Duma and the new freedom enjoyed by newspapers, was highly critical of government incompetence.

Russia's diplomatic defeat stimulated the government into a massive military build-up with extra spending of some 2000 million roubles. The Balkans remained volatile; in a further attempt to limit Austrian influence, the Russians encouraged the formation of an alliance between Serbia and Bulgaria which eventually became the Balkan League (1912). But again the Russian plan backfired: instead of attacking Austria–Hungary, the League declared war on Turkey, starting the First Balkan War (1912). After the League had captured most of Turkey's remaining territory in Europe, a peace conference met in London to share out the spoils. However, Serbia was not satisfied with her gains – she wanted Albania which would give her an outlet to the sea. The Austrians were determined that Serbia should not become any stronger, and with German and British support, they insisted that Albania should become an independent state. The Bulgarians were also dissatisfied with their gains – they wanted Macedonia, but that was given to Serbia. In 1913 Bulgaria began the Second Balkan War by attacking Serbia. Greece, Romania and Turkey rallied to support Serbia; the Bulgarians were defeated and lost most of the territory acquired by the Treaty of

London. Serbia emerged much stronger from these wars, and Austria–Hungary was becoming increasingly worried by this new threat to their empire.

(e) The outbreak of the First World War

Given the volatile nature of the Balkans, it was a provocative move by the Austrians when the Archduke Franz Ferdinand and his wife paid an official visit to Sarajevo, the capital of the recently annexed Bosnia at the end of June 1914. It was obviously calculated to irritate Serbia, and it was a Bosnian Serb nationalist, Gavrilo Princip, who shot them both dead. The Austrians decided to use the murders as a pretext for a 'preventive' war to crush Serbia before it became any more powerful. The Austrians' great fear was that if Serbia seized Bosnia (which contained about three million Serbs), all the other Serbs living inside the Habsburg Empire would want to join Serbia as well. This would encourage other national groups – Czechs, Poles and Italians – to demand independence, and the eventual result would be the collapse of the entire Habsburg Empire. This is why the government in Vienna chose to blame the Serb government for the assassinations and sent an ultimatum demanding the right to send troops to 'police' Serbia. This was clearly unacceptable to the Serbs, and consequently Austria–Hungary, encouraged by Germany, declared war on Serbia.

Russia made the next move, ordering a general mobilization of forces, and soon all the major powers of Europe were involved.[4] Why was Russia so quick to respond with the mobilization order? Earlier in the year Nicholas and many of his ministers had favoured a cautious approach. His military chiefs had told him that the army would not be ready for war until 1917. In February P.N. Durnovo, the Minister of the Interior, warned him that a long war could only result in defeat and revolution. However, it was Nicholas himself who took the decision to mobilize as a matter of prestige – if Russia was to continue to be regarded as a great power, they dare not let Serbia and the Slavs down again and suffer another humiliation as they had done in 1908. Although with hindsight it can be regarded as a rash decision, most of the country seemed to be behind him. Almost all the parties in the Duma were conscious of Russian honour and were expecting some action; public opinion would have been bitterly disappointed if no positive response had been made. And there were other considerations as well: the Russians were worried by the build-up of German economic and cultural influence in Turkey. As well as the Berlin–Baghdad Railway project, there was the appointment of a German general to command the Turkish army at Constantinople and to advise on the reform of the Turkish military organization. All this was taken by the Russians as a deliberate challenge to their hopes of controlling the Straits, and since so much of their trade passed through there, it was a challenge that had to be met. The Russians rightly suspected that Germany had plans to take over some of their western European territories as well, and they feared that Germany was intent on a preventive war before Russian military preparations were completed. The German historian Fritz Fischer showed that both these suspicions were well grounded.[5] And finally there were some ministers who, incredibly after the lessons of the war with Japan, supported Nicholas because they thought that a short victorious war would unite the country and distract attention from all Russia's internal problems.

3.2   The war and its impact on the Tsarist system

(a) The military front and the home front

When the war began there was an immediate outburst of patriotic enthusiasm. There were massive demonstrations of support for the Tsar and the country; students from the university marched on the German embassy in St Petersburg and ransacked it, and the Duma voted war credits almost without question; only the Bolshevik deputies condemned the war and were accordingly arrested. The government changed the name of the capital from St Petersburg, which sounded German, to Petrograd. 'I solemnly swear,' declared the Tsar, 'that I will never make peace so long as one of the enemy is on the soil of the fatherland.' When he appeared on the balcony of the Winter Palace in St Petersburg, the huge crowd went wild with enthusiasm; the whole country was united behind the Tsar. If the war could have been concluded with a swift victory within a few months, like the Prussian defeat of France in 1870–71, the Tsarist regime might well have been strengthened, at least for the time being. Unfortunately, nobody had made plans for a long war; the longer a war lasts, the greater the test for whatever regime happens to be in power; any weaknesses will be mercilessly exposed. Russia had two major weaknesses: an economy which was not as advanced as that of her main enemy, Germany, and an obsolete political system which was incapable of adapting to change.

Although the Russians were always successful on the Austrian fronts, it was a different story against the Germans (Map 3.3). At the Battle of Tannenberg in August 1914 around 70,000 Russian soldiers were killed and almost 100,000, together with 400 guns, were captured; only 10,000 troops escaped; the Russian commander, Samsonov, unable to face the humiliation, shot himself. German troops came to the assistance of the Austrians, and gradually the Russians were pushed back on all fronts (see Documents B and C). By the autumn of 1915 they had lost all the captured Austrian territory in Galicia, the Germans were in control of Poland, and German forces were approaching the great industrial city of Riga on the Baltic. Between 1 May and 1 December 1915 the Russians lost a million men killed and another million taken prisoner. Organization was chaotic; Mikhail Rodzianko, the Chairman of the Duma, found 17,000 wounded soldiers lying unattended at the Warsaw railway station in Petrograd, 'in the cold rain and mud without so much as straw litter.' The enthusiastic support for the government had long since evaporated. The regime's competence was once again seriously in doubt, and it was left to other groups to take necessary initiatives.

Following the lead of the Moscow *zemstvo*, many other *zemstva* and town governments formed themselves into unions to organize the evacuation of the sick and wounded and to provide medical care, hospitals and hospital trains. They eventually united to form *Zemgor* (the Union of *Zemstva* and Municipalities) under the chairmanship of Prince Lvov; they soon extended their activities to

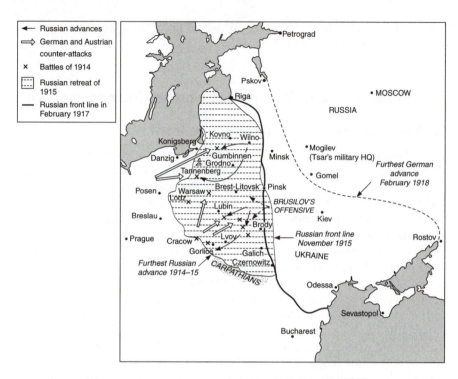

Map 3.3 **Russian operations during the First World War.**

Legend:
← Russian advances
⇒ German and Austrian counter-attacks
× Battles of 1914
▢ Russian retreat of 1915
— Russian front line in February 1917

organizing local industry to provide boots, uniforms, tents, blankets and medical supplies. Another new body was the War Industry Committee chaired by Alexander Guchkov, the Octobrist leader; its function was to supervise the changeover of factories to military production and so increase the output of munitions. In August 1915 the centre parties in the Duma (Kadets, Progressists and Octobrists) formed a Progressive Bloc which had a majority of votes. They hoped to persuade Nicholas to co-operate with the Duma and form what they called 'a government enjoying public confidence' – in other words they wanted him to appoint ministers approved by the Duma. Several of his ministers supported the Progressive Bloc proposals. But once again the Tsar lacked the vision to appreciate the advantages of such a change (see Documents E and F). Instead he adjourned the Duma, sacked the ministers who had ventured to make radical suggestions, and announced that he was taking personal command of the army. From the autumn of 1915 he spent most of his time at army headquarters in Mogilev, leaving the Empress Alexandra and Rasputin to hold the fort in St Petersburg. In fact the Progressive Bloc was an alternative government in waiting and in February 1917 many of its leading members were to form the Provisional Government.

Although casualties had been heavy, the Russian army had not been destroyed; during the winter of 1915–16 there was a lull in the fighting which gave the Russians a chance to train new troops and replenish stocks of arms and ammunition. In the summer of 1916 General Brusilov began an offensive against the Austro–Hungarian forces in Galicia which became the greatest Russian success in the war. Brusilov was a brilliant strategist who quickly learned from earlier failures. The offensive was meticulously planned – the Austrian trenches were carefully mapped, using aerial photography, and the Russians knew exactly where the enemy batteries and machine-guns were situated. Instead of concentrating the attack at one point, the Russians attacked simultaneously at four points spread out along the whole length of the front, so that the Austrians did not know where to expect the main blow. It was a stunning victory – the Austrians lost over half their army in the east either killed or captured, and their morale was destroyed.[6] The Germans withdrew 35 divisions from the western front to send reinforcements to the east, and this enabled the French fortress town of Verdun to survive the German siege.

Brusilov wanted the Russian armies on the north-western front to attack the Germans while the Austrians were still in complete disarray, but the Tsar ignored his repeated requests and instead moved troops from the north to Brusilov's front. However, this only eased pressure on the Germans, enabling them to trans-fer troops to the south to bolster up the Austrians; the Russian offensive gradually came to a halt. Although it was a great victory, it made no difference to the general war situation.

It was on the home front that the signs of strain were most obvious. There were increasing shortages of food, fuel and basic consumer goods; the transport system was in chaos, inflation was rife, and worst of all, there were the continu-ing enormous casualties – there was hardly a family in Russia who had not lost at least one son either killed or taken prisoner. The regime kept on changing its ministers – a practice which became known as 'ministerial leapfrog': between August 1915 and February 1917 no fewer than 36 different ministers held the 13 major posts. When the Duma reconvened in November 1916, the Kadet leader, Paul Milyukov, made a dramatic speech in which he listed his criticisms of the government; after each one he put the question 'Is this stupidity or treason?' (see Document G). The use of the word 'treason' by such a moderate politician (and a professor of history) caused a sensation, especially as the government tried to ban publication of the speech. Milyukov himself later remarked: 'My speech acquired the reputation of a storm-signal for the revolution.' A great political upheaval of some sort was clearly inevitable; the only question was, would it come from above or from below?

(b) Assessment of Russia's performance in the war

Until the mid-1970s the traditional view was that Russia's war effort was a total failure. The economy was too backward to produce arms and ammunition in sufficient quantities to match German production. Russia was crippled by the German blockade of the Baltic and by the Turkish closure of the Dardanelles. No supplies of any sort could get in, and so the Russians slowly ran out of raw mater-ials and equipment. There were severe food shortages caused by a dramatic fall in agricultural production, which was itself caused by millions of peasants being taken away from farming to do military service. Food shortages were especially serious in the large cities. As for the Russian army, that was badly equipped, badly trained and badly led; although it had some successes against Austria–

Hungary, that was only because the Habsburg Empire was even weaker than Russia. As Trotsky put it: 'In the past Russia had only been successful against inwardly decomposing states like Turkey, Poland, Persia ... The disintegrating Habsburg monarchy had long ago hung out a sign for an undertaker.'[7] By the end of 1916 the Russian army had lost its will to fight. By this time too the Russian people were weary of the war and they turned against the Tsar because he wanted to continue the fighting. This was the line of argument consistently followed by Soviet historians who wanted to play down whatever progress had been made under the Tsarist regime in order to exaggerate Stalin's achievement in modernizing Russia.

In the 1970s some of these details were challenged; this does not affect the general conclusion that the Tsarist regime collapsed because it couldn't cope with the war, but it does suggest that Russia's backwardness was not in economic power but in the organization of the ways in which that power was used. Norman Stone was the first historian to show that in fact Russian industry did meet the challenge of war reasonably efficiently. All areas of the economy grew, some of them very fast. Between 1914 and 1917 the output of coal rose by almost 30 per cent and there was a huge expansion of the engineering and chemical industries. By 1916, 78 per cent of machine construction firms were working to supply army requirements, and most factories seem to have adapted their plant successfully to produce arms and ammunition. By September 1916 there had been a 2000 per cent growth in the output of shells and 1000 per cent in artillery and rifles; Russian industry was matching German production of shells for use on the eastern front. The problem was one of transportation and distribution, and there were a large number of bottle-necks which threw the economy into chaos.[8] Another problem was that non-military areas of manufacturing industry were neglected, causing a shortage of household consumer goods and agricultural implements, and this in turn contributed towards inflation. As to the naval blockades cutting off imports, this was not a serious problem by 1916, thanks to the expansion of Russian industry, plus the fact that more supplies were brought in through Murmansk, Archangel and Vladivostock. The real problem turned out to be difficulties in *exporting* Russian grain via the Dardanelles – exports which were vital for a healthy trade balance. By 1917 Russia had a huge trade deficit, causing the government to run short of cash. The regime tried to finance the war effort by the almost unlimited printing of banknotes, but this only escalated the inflation. The side-effect of all this which proved most dangerous for the regime was the fact that the massive expansion of industry brought in hundreds of thousands of new workers from the countryside; for instance the population of St Petersburg grew from 2.2 million in 1914 to 2.5 million in 1917. As inflation soared, real wages dropped alarmingly, and this contributed to the growing disillusion among the workers and led to a wave of strikes towards the end of 1916.

Stone also challenges the view that Russia's military effort was a complete failure. He argues that there was very little to choose in quality between Russian and German ordinary rank-and-file soldiers. General Brusilov showed in his 1916 offensive that when the troops were given good leadership, they were capable of military success. This was one of several occasions during the war when the efforts of the Russian army helped to take pressure off French and British troops fighting on the western front, and it was in this way that the Russians made a vital contribution towards the ultimate allied victory. It was incompetence at the top which reduced Russia's military effectiveness; in March 1916 for example, the War Minister, Polivanov, who was responsible for rebuilding the army after the disasters of 1915, was sacked because the Tsarina Alexandra thought he was too much of a revolutionary; his offence was his willingness to work with Zemgor and the War Industries Committee. The Tsar's tactical blunders threw away the advantages of Brusilov's successful offensive. Stone believes that in spite of all the problems – shortages of war material, the primitiveness of Russia's railway system compared with Germany's, and massive desertion of troops – the majority of Russian forces had not lost their will to fight. The army was not disintegrating and by the beginning of 1917 the front had been stabilized.

Historians have also rejected the claim that there was a dramatic fall in grain output during the war. According to Robert Service, there was no great labour shortage in agriculture because, although over 14 million peasants were taken into the army and navy, this only removed the surplus workers. There were excellent harvests in 1914 and 1915, and the 1916 harvest was only 10 per cent below the average for the five years before 1914. This, together with the reduction in grain exports, meant that there was more wheat in the country during those years than ever before.[9] So why were there food shortages? The reason was again partly transportation problems: the military monopolized the railways in the west to carry troops, ammunition and food to the front, and this caused a shortage of trains for taking grain from the south up to the Moscow and St Petersburg areas. As time went on there was a shortage of spare parts for locomotives and rolling stock which were no longer being imported; by the end of 1916 about a quarter of the trains were out of commission.

Another problem was that peasants were marketing less grain in protest at the low prices being paid by grain dealers who were making huge profits. By 1917 the price of grain had increased to four times the 1914 level, but the peasants themselves received very little in the way of extra profits. Many of them hoped to force dealers to pay a better price by hoarding their grain and others fed more grain to their cattle or made it into vodka. The result – not only was bread in short supply in the towns and cities, it was also expensive, and there were bread queues everywhere. These extreme wartime conditions, as Tsuhoshi Hasegawa points out, were responsible for revitalizing the workers' strike movement; during 1916 the strikes grew in frequency and militancy. Clearly by the end that year, as radical revolutionary groups were able to increase their influence among the workers, things were approaching crisis point. Bread queues were getting longer and workers were going hungry.[10] The failure of the regime lay not in the mobilization of troops or the production of war materials and food, but in the breakdown of administration and distribution – goods, especially food, were simply not being delivered where they were needed.

(c) The revolution of February/March 1917

By the beginning of 1917 all classes in society were disillusioned with the way the government was running the war, and since the Tsar was the leading figure in the government, it meant that everybody was turning against the Tsar. The Duma, whose advice and attempts at compromise he had consistently rejected, was divided: on the one hand Milyukov and the moderates were still hoping for a compromise with the government and were afraid that even a 'limited' revolution would get out of control and sweep away the whole social structure. On the other hand the more radical members such as the socialist Alexander Kerensky, were calling for the overthrow of the regime; they too were worried that if the Duma failed to act soon, the crowds would take matters into their own hands. Others, long since despairing of any sensible compromise with Nicholas and Alexandra, hoped for a coup to replace Nicholas with a more amenable member of the royal family. In December 1916 Alexander Guchkov, the Octobrist leader, and a supporter of the monarchy, was involved in a plan to seize the imperial train with Nicholas on board and force him to abdicate in favour of his son, with Nicholas's brother, the Grand Duke Michael, acting as Regent. Insufficient support caused them to postpone action until March 1917, but by then events had overtaken them.

The middle classes – lecturers, teachers, lawyers, doctors, businessmen and industrialists – were all exasperated by government incompetence and by the Tsar's dismissive treatment of their representatives in the Duma. Industrialists were especially resentful that in spite of all their efforts to produce war materials, administrative failings were bringing Russia to the brink of defeat. The St Petersburg steelworks owner, Putilov, claimed that the entire administrative machine would have to be reformed if Russia was to win the war. As early as June 1915 he told the French ambassador: 'The days of Tsarism are numbered; the revolution is now inevitable. It only awaits its opportunity.'

The nobles had become disaffected for a variety of reasons. Many noble land-owners were in economic difficulties because they could no longer rely on peasants to work on their estates. They were appalled at the wasteful slaughter of their sons in the officer corps. In November 1916 the United Nobility in Petrograd and Moscow passed resolutions supporting the Progressive Bloc. The noble elite in Petrograd had never liked Alexandra because she was German and because she was unwilling to mix in society. As the war dragged on she was suspected of being pro-German and of trying to negotiate a separate peace. The nobles detested her close association with Rasputin and resented the power he seemed to have over her. In December 1916 a small group of nobles led by Prince Yusupov murdered Rasputin, hoping to free the royal family from his influence and force the Tsar to listen to what they called 'the voice of the nation'. However, this made no difference to the conduct of the war, and by January 1917 the Tsar's relatives and other nobles had reached the conclusion that the only way to save the monarchy was to remove Nicholas. They became involved in a plot organised by Prince Lvov to exile Alexandra to the Crimea and to force Nicholas to hand over power to the young Alexei with the Grand Duke Nicholas (a cousin of Alexander III) as Regent. This plan fell through when the Grand Duke turned down the offer on the grounds that ordinary people would not understand what had happened. The fact that the Grand Duke did not inform the Tsar of the plot against him shows how alienated even his own family had become. Many of the top army generals thought of Nicholas as a liability and were considering how best to get rid of him. General Krymov told a secret meeting of Duma members: 'We would welcome the news of a *coup d'état*. A revolution is imminent and we at the front feel it to be so. If you decide on such an extreme step, we will support you. Clearly there is no other way.'

None of these groups actually did anything beyond talking about removing Nicholas. It was the women and the workers of Petrograd and other centres who took the first action. There had already been a wave of strikes in the capital towards the end of 1916 which the government had suppressed. Discontent among the urban workers could only get worse; even a police report in January 1917 shows some sympathy for them and talks of the despair of the workers who are 'reduced to the level of cattle fit only to serve as cannon-fodder' (see Document H). A massive strike and demonstration in Petrograd, on the anniversary of the 1905 Bloody Sunday massacre, passed off peacefully. The real trouble began in the middle of February when stocks of flour and fuel in Petrograd and Moscow fell to their lowest level ever and there were rumours that bread rationing was about to be introduced. It was a colder than average winter and people had to queue for hours on end, even sometimes all night for a single loaf in temperatures well below freezing. The police reports talk of the growing anger and frustration among the women who had to spend so much of their time queuing for food.

On 21 February the Putilov steelworks was forced to close down through lack of fuel, and thousands of workers came out on the streets to demonstrate against the regime. There were speeches, revolutionary songs and anti-tsarist slogans. The following day the weather in Petrograd suddenly turned warmer; the temperature reached 8 degrees centigrade and it stayed mild for a week. Some historians think this had an important effect on the events of the next few days because the warmer weather encouraged more people to come out on the streets, and it was then that the first disorders broke out. 23 February was International Women's Day: there was a demonstration in favour of equality for women and more bread. Thousands of men joined in – some were still laid off from the Putilov works, others were on strike. Over the next few days the demonstrations grew, they were joined by office and shop workers and by students, and they became more violent. Crowds began to attack food shops and on Saturday 25 February red flags appeared; there were clashes with the police and three people were killed. The demonstrators' demands became more political; their banners were now demanding the overthrow of the government: 'Down with the Tsar' and 'Down with the War'.

Until this point General Khabalov, the military commander in Petrograd, had done his best to avoid bloodshed, anxious not to provoke the demonstrators. However, later that day Nicholas, who was at military headquarters at Mogilev, made a fatal mistake – he sent a telegram to Khabalov saying that the unrest in Petrograd could not be tolerated. 'I order you to stop tomorrow the disorders in the capital, which are unacceptable at the difficult time of war with Germany and Austria.' Consequently the next day troops occupied the centre of Petrograd and a curfew was imposed. Still the demonstrators came out; in several parts of the city soldiers fired at them; the worst incident took place in Znamenskaya Square, where a detachment of young trainee soldiers began firing wildly at the crowds, killing at least 50 people.[11] This proved to be the decisive turning point. The regime had failed to realize that the army was as disillusioned as the civilians. It was shortly after this that the troops began to mutiny – about 600 of them at first – and refused to fire on the unarmed crowds. Three days later the entire Petrograd garrison of 170,000 men refused to obey orders, and started shooting their officers and fraternizing with the crowds (see Document K). These troops were a mixture of young peasant conscripts who had not yet seen any real fighting, and soldiers about to be sent back to the front after recovering from wounds. Neither group was reliable and both were sickened at the prospect of having to shoot any more innocent civilians.

Meanwhile Nicholas was still at Mogilev about 600 kilometres south of Petrograd. Rodzianko, the president of the Duma, sent a telegram informing him about the situation and suggesting that 'some person who enjoys the confidence of the country be entrusted at once with the formation of a new government. There must be no delay.' But Nicholas rejected this idea and ordered the Duma to adjourn until April. This was his last chance to work with the Duma to save the monarchy, but once again he failed to understand the situation. Instead he ordered more troops to Petrograd to restore order. The Duma committed its first illegal act by forming a 12-man committee to try and calm the situation itself. Troops supporting the revolution took over the Winter Palace and on 27 February crowds stormed the Peter and Paul fortress and other prisons and freed all the inmates, including the SR and SD leaders who had been arrested in December 1916. The next target was the secret police headquarters which were ransacked and its files and records burnt; then the crowds moved on to loot arsenals, shops and restaurants. By the end of 27 February the regime had lost control of the capital and the next day workers and soldiers elected representatives to the Petrograd soviet. As yet though, the Duma hesitated to announce that it had taken control, since legally the Tsar was still in power. Petrograd now had two potentially rival governments in waiting – the Duma committee and the Soviet – and both of them were meeting in the Tauride Palace, in opposite wings of the building (see Document J).

Nicholas was still unaware of how serious the situation was and of just how quickly events were moving. On 28 February the trains carrying troop reinforcements to restore order in Petrograd were stopped because railway workers had torn up the tracks; when the soldiers learned what had happened in Petrograd, they too mutinied. The imperial train taking the Tsar and his entourage to his residence at Tsarskoe Selo outside the capital was also held up by hostile troops and forced to take a detour to Pskov, where it arrived late in the evening of 1 March. By this time all the elite were ready to sacrifice Nicholas, though they hoped to keep the monarchy, in order to save their own skins. General Ruszky met the Tsar aboard his train and showed him telegrams reporting revolution in Moscow and mutinies in the Baltic fleet and at the Kronstadt naval base. There were telegrams from most of the leading generals urging Nicholas to abdicate 'so as to preserve the country's independence and save the dynasty.' The Tsar always had great respect for the opinions of his generals and this is what finally convinced him that he could not go on. At first Ruszky persuaded him to agree to form a responsible government, but after a telephone call from

Rodzianko explaining that the country was on the verge of anarchy, the Tsar agreed to abdicate in favour of his son Alexei (2 March). When Guchkov and Shulgin, two delegates from the Duma, arrived in Pskov to urge abdication, he had already made up his mind. If he could not rule as an autocratic monarch then he would not rule at all. Soon afterwards Nicholas decided that the boy was not strong enough to take on the role of Tsar and he named his brother the Grand Duke Michael as his successor. Unfortunately nobody had taken the trouble to discover whether or not Michael, who was not the least bit interested in politics, was willing to become the next Tsar. The following day he refused the offer after being told that the Duma could not guarantee his safety. The 300-year-old Romanov monarchy was at an end and Russia became a republic, an outcome which neither the generals nor the Duma politicians had intended. The leaders of the Progressive Bloc formed a temporary government – the Provisional Government – to rule the country until elections for a new Assembly could be held. Nicholas was placed under arrest but allowed to return to his family at Tsarskoe Selo.

(d) Revolution from above or below?

There has been a great deal of discussion among historians about which was the vital element in the overthrow of the Tsarist regime. E.H. Carr, writing back in 1950, offered a wide-ranging explanation which seems to cover all the elements involved. He believed that the February revolution was 'the spontaneous outbreak of a multitude exasperated by the privations of war and by manifest inequality in the distribution of burdens.' This spontaneous outburst was 'welcomed and utilized by a broad stratum of the bourgeoisie and of the official class, which had lost confidence in the autocratic system of government and especially in the persons of the Tsar and his advisers.'[12]

Other historians have focused on one or more particular aspects of the situation as the key element. George Katkov thought the conspiracy among the elite was the decisive factor, that the nobles, the Duma and especially the generals pressurized Nicholas to abdicate in order to prevent a real mass revolution developing; the 'spontaneous' strikes and demonstrations in Petrograd were not so much a cause of the revolution as a symptom of it. Katkov was alone among historians in attaching vital importance to German attempts at stirring up revolution in Russia and to the machinations of a masonic group within the elite.[13] W.H. Chamberlin, writing nearer to the events (1935), came to the opposite conclusion: he argued that it was 'one of the most leaderless, spontaneous, anonymous revolutions of all time' – a revolution from below by the masses was decisive because it threw the privileged classes into a panic. Without the crowds on the streets and the mutiny of the troops, there would have been no need for the elite to act.[14] Most traditional liberal historians took the view that the mass uprisings were a direct result of the war and its deprivations, and had very little to do with the efforts of the revolutionary parties. Their organizations had been suppressed by the police, they were demoralized and nearly all their most influential leaders were living in exile. Even Lenin had admitted in a speech delivered in Switzerland in January 1917 that his generation would probably not live to see the revolution.

Soviet historians went along with the 'revolution from below' theory but felt that too much emphasis had been placed on spontaneity. In their view it *was* organized; they make the point that events don't just happen without origin or cause. Who fixed the timing of the strikes? Who decided on the formation and starting points of demonstrations? Who spread the news? For Soviet historians there was only one answer – the revolutionary groups, especially the Bolshevik Party. They argued that the local revolutionary committees had recovered from the secret police clampdown of December 1916 and were consciously using the situation to turn the strikes into demonstrations and the demonstrations into revolution. They claim to have found evidence of Bolshevik organizations in two hundred towns, and in the navy and in the army at the front. There were no fewer than 18 different illegal Bolshevik periodicals in circulation. Although Lenin was in exile, he was in constant touch with Bolshevik activists inside Russia, and it was his brilliant leadership which guided the party throughout the war. In contrast the SRs and Mensheviks were largely ineffective, their organizations in disarray and their membership tiny. They could not begin to match the discipline, the commitment and the unity of the Bolshevik Party.

Leon Trotsky also argued that the idea of a spontaneous revolution, that is, a revolution with no planned leadership from above, was insufficient to explain the events of February. While admitting that most of the main SR and SD leaders were not present, he claims that Social Democrats led the revolution in the sense that people who had been influenced by their propaganda during recent years, spread their radical ideas among their fellow workers and soldiers, thus acting as catalysts for revolution. 'In every factory, in each guild, in each company, in each tavern, in the military hospitals, among the troops of the garrison, the work of revolutionary thought was in progress ... in the working classes there was a deep process of growth, not only of hatred for the rulers, but of critical understanding of their impotence. To the question, Who led the February revolution? we can then answer definitely enough: conscious and tempered workers educated for the most part by the party of Lenin.'[15]

Most recent Western historians have played down the role of the Bolsheviks in the February revolution, pointing out that it is impossible to differentiate the extent of Bolshevik influence from the influence of the SRs and Mensheviks, and from the part played by underground workers' and trade union groups. Some surprising statistics have emerged from late Soviet sources which cast serious doubts on how influential the Bolsheviks really were in February 1917. For example in the Petrograd Soviet, the great forum of the most militant workers, only 40 out of 600 deputies were Bolsheviks at the beginning of March 1917. Out of 242 workers' Soviets formed by the end of March, only 27 had a Bolshevik majority.[16] More emphasis is therefore laid on the contribution of worker activists with no party affiliations, such as for example, the Labour group who became increasingly militant and influential during the latter part of 1916, and who joined in the call for a general strike on 9 January 1917. Christopher Read reaches the conclusion that 'workers were only weakly identified with political parties ... after all, there had only been some 150 Bolsheviks among the 26,000 workers at the Putilov factory in February.' It was the issues at stake that really mattered – the desire for better living and working conditions and for more control over their own lives.[17] Diane Koenker was one of the first historians to investigate the activities of factory workers, in her study of what was happening in Moscow; she discovered that over 90 per cent of the strikes in Moscow factories in 1917 included demands for higher wages and were clearly motivated by economic issues.[18] Steve Smith also emphasizes the economic context of the revolution: 'Western historians have been so mesmerized by the astonishing political developments that they have failed to see the extent to which the crisis in the economy underpinned the crisis in politics.' It was an outburst of desperation to secure the basic material needs and a decent standard of living.[19]

In his meticulously detailed study of the events, Orlando Figes comes to the conclusion that 'the crowd violence of the February Days was not orchestrated by any revolutionary party or movement. It was by and large a spontaneous reaction to the bloody repressions of the 26th, and an expression of the people's long-felt hatred for the old regime.' None of the main party leaders were present either in Petrograd or Moscow – they were all in exile, in prison or abroad. Only the second-rank leaders were there and they 'chased after events, telephoning from one apartment to another trying to find out what was happening on the streets. It was only on the 27th when the revolution had become an established fact, that the party leaders sprang into action.' Before then the real strike leaders were the skilled and literate workers on the shop-floor, 'daring young men in their twenties and thirties, most of whom did not belong to any political party ... they resented the huge profits of their employers, and this increasingly defined their sense of class solidarity with the unskilled workers, many of them fresh from the countryside, who followed them into industrial battle. Here were those unnamed leaders of the crowd during the February Days in Petrograd.'[20]

Richard Pipes highlights the role of the soldiers. He points out that, given the fact that the February revolution is often portrayed as a workers' uprising, it is important to stress that first and foremost it was a mutiny of peasant soldiers, whom the authorities had unwisely billeted in overcrowded conditions in Petrograd. This, according to one eye-witness, was 'like kindling wood near a powder keg' (see Document K). Since in the last resort the survival of the regime depended on the loyalty of the army, the fact that these raw recruits and the embittered veterans shared the same grievances as the workers was a fatal blow. Consequently, by the end of the day on 27 February, 'Petrograd was in the hands of peasants in uniform.'[21]

And finally Christopher Read gives yet another slant to the discussion. He believes that the abdication of Nicholas was the culmination of the unrest in Petrograd together with the nervous and incompetent blundering by the Duma politicians and the generals. He stresses that the revolution was not simply spontaneous. The elite played a vital role: whereas in 1905 they had remained united in support of Nicholas, in February 1917 they were divided – in fact a majority of them were prepared to drop him. Read also makes the point that the 'spontaneity' was itself 'created by tsarism's incorrigibly self-destructive tendencies. To the very end, through its inflexibility and ineptness, the autocracy had been the principal architect of its own downfall.'[22] That was the tragedy of Nicholas II; a more imaginative and flexible tsar might have reacted completely differently and saved the monarchy; but Nicholas was trapped in a demanding role which was completely beyond his limited capabilities.

Documents

Russian foreign policy

(A) Sergei Sazonov, the Russian Foreign Minister in 1914, later wrote about the aims of Russian foreign policy.

Russia's historical mission – the emancipation of the Christian peoples of the Balkan peninsula from the Turkish yoke – was almost fulfilled by the beginning of the twentieth century. Although these younger countries no longer needed the guardianship of Russia, they were not strong enough to dispense with her help in the event of any attempt upon their national existence by warlike Teutonism. Serbia in particular was exposed to this danger, having become the object of the decorously concealed covetousness of Austrian diplomacy. Russia's sole and unchanging object was to see that those Balkan peoples should not fall under the influence of powers hostile to her. The ultimate aim of Russian foreign policy was to obtain free access to the Mediterranean, and to be in a position to defend her Black Sea coasts against the threat of the irruption of hostile naval forces through the Bosphorus.

Source: quoted in Michael Lynch, *Reaction and Revolutions: Russia 1881–1924*, p. 60.

Russia during the First World War

(B) A Russian soldier describes an attack on an Austrian trench in December 1915.

After artillery preparation, we went about a mile forward under heavy enemy gunfire. Once we were within five hundred yards, we were hit, suddenly, by devastating machine-gun and rifle-fire that had hitherto been silent. There was the enemy, in solid trenches with great parapets and dug-outs; sitting behind ten or fifteen rows of uncut wire, waiting for us. We lay on the frozen ground, for hours, as the snow drifted down; if we were wounded there was no help because we were so close to the wire. But behind us there were artillery colonels and captains of the General Staff, drinking rum tea, and writing their reports – 'After brilliant artillery preparation our glorious forces rushed forward to occupy the enemy trenches, but were held up by counter-attack of strong reserves.'

Source: quoted in Stone, p. 224.

(C) Extracts from two soldiers' letters.

They still haven't given out overcoats. We run around in thin topcoats. There is not much to eat and what we get is foul. Perhaps we'd be better off dead!

> For the Tsar's inspection they prepared one company and collected all the best uniforms from the other regiments for it to wear, leaving the rest of the men in the trenches without boots, knapsacks, bandoliers, trousers, uniforms, hats, or anything else.

Source: quoted in Figes, p. 263.

(D) Letter from the Empress Alexandra to Nicholas, 25 June 1915.

> Deary,
> I heard that that horrid Rodzianko & others went to Goremykin to beg the Duma to be at once called together – oh please don't, it's not their business, they want to discuss things not concerning them & bring more discontent – they must be kept away – I assure you only harm will arise – they speak too much. Russia, thank God, is not a constitutional country, tho' those creatures try to play a part and meddle in affairs they dare not. Do not allow them to press upon you. It's fright if one gives in & their heads will go up.

Source: quoted in Bernard Pares, *Letters of the Tsaritsa to the Tsar, 1914–1916* (London, 1923), p. 110.

(E) Letter to Nicholas from the War Committee of the Duma, 4 September 1915, to which they received no reply.

> Sire
> We have learned that our valiant army, after losing more than four million men killed, wounded or taken prisoner, is not only retreating but will perhaps have to withdraw even further. We have also learned the reasons for this retreat ... that our army does not possess armaments of equal effectiveness as the enemy ... We have barely enough machine-guns to replace the ones we have lost or have had to scrap ... Furthermore though the enemy has plenty of rifles, hundreds of thousands of our men are without weapons, and have to wait until they can pick up the rifles dropped by their fallen comrades.
>
> We have learned that appointments to important military posts have been made in accordance with seniority or rank; it is thus neither bravery, nor talent, nor competence, that is decisive in the promotion of candidates ... really able persons, true leaders of men who could lead our troops to victory, attain only rarely the highest positions in the army. All these woes and muddles have begun to affect the morale of the army and of the people.
>
> Your Imperial Majesty! We make bold to say ... that it is impossible to conduct national defence successfully without a supreme authority that unites everything. The Tsar can order the civil and military leaders to work out in advance a plan of action and so put an end to these disordered moves that look only a few days ahead and lack any underlying general idea.

Source: quoted in Ferro, pp. 164–7.

(F) Article by the Kadet politician, V.A. Maklakov, in the newspaper *Russkie Vedomosti* (Russian Record), September 1915.

A TRAGIC SITUATION: THE MAD CHAUFFEUR

Imagine that you are in a car that is racing headlong down a steep, narrow road: one wrong turn and you will be gone for ever...Suddenly you realize that the chauffeur cannot drive...he is carrying you and himself to destruction. Fortunately, there are people in the car who know how to drive. Consequently it is necessary that they take over from the chauffeur as soon as possible. But doing this is highly dangerous when the car is travelling at such a speed. Moreover the chauffeur stubbornly refuses to give up the wheel. What is to be done? One move of his hand could hurl the vehicle into the abyss. You know that and so does he. And he laughs at your anguish and your helplessness. 'You won't dare touch me.' And he is right – you won't dare. Not only will you not interfere with him, you will help him with your advice. But how will you feel if you realize that even with your help, the chauffeur cannot drive, and if your mother, seeing the danger, begs you to help him and accuses you of cowardly indifference?

Source: quoted in Ferro, p. 171.

(G) Speech by Paul Milyukov, the Kadet leader, to the Duma, November 1916.

We now see and know that we can no more legislate with this government than we can lead Russia to victory with it. When the Duma declares again and again that the home front must be organized for a successful war and the government continues to insist that to organize the country means to organize a revolution, and consciously chooses chaos and disintegration – is this stupidity or treason? (*Voices from the left: 'treason'.*) Moreover, when on the basis of this general discontent the government deliberately busies itself with provoking popular outbursts – for the involvement of the police in the spring disturbances in the factories is proven – when provocation is used to incite disturbances, knowing that they could be a reason for shortening the war – is this done consciously or not? We say to this government, as the declaration of the Progressive Bloc stated: we will fight you, we will fight by all legal means until you go.

We have many different reasons for being discontented with this government. But all these reasons boil down to one general one: the incompetence and evil intentions of the present government. This is Russia's chief evil, and victory over it will be equal to winning an entire campaign. And therefore in the name of the millions of victims and of their spilled blood...we shall fight until we get a responsible government which is in agreement with the general principles of our programme. Cabinet members must agree unanimously as to the most urgent tasks, they must agree and be prepared to implement the programme of the Duma. A Cabinet which does not satisfy these conditions

---

does not deserve the confidence of the Duma and should go. (*Voices: 'bravo';* | *loud and prolonged applause.*)

Source: quoted in John Laver, *Russia 1914–41*, pp. 6–7.

The February revolution

(H) Petrograd Police report dated January 1917.

> The proletariat here are on the verge of despair. It is thought that the slightest explosion, due to the least of pretexts, will result in uncontrollable riots... The cost of living, which has trebled, the impossibility of finding food, the loss of time through queuing for hours outside shops, the rising death rate, the restrictions imposed on the workers, have become unbearable. The ban on moving from one factory to another or changing one's job has reduced the workers to the level of cattle fit only to serve as cannon-fodder. The ban on all meetings, even meetings held to form co-operatives or to organize canteens, and the ban on trade unions are causing the workers to adopt an openly hostile attitude towards the government.

Source: quoted in Ferro, p. 186.

(I) Proclamation by the Petrograd Central Workers' Group, 26 January 1917. The following day all the group's leaders were arrested.

> Ending the war will not improve the situation of the working class if it is carried out not by the people themselves but by the autocratic authority. Peace achieved by the monarchy will bring yet more terrible chains. The working class and democracy can wait no longer. Every day that is allowed to pass brings danger: the decisive removal of the autocratic regime and the complete democratization of the country are tasks that must be solved without delay.

Source: quoted in Pipes, p. 270.

(J) Impressions of the February Days by Pitirim Sorokin, a sociology lecturer at the university in Petrograd, and a Socialist Revolutionary.

> It has come at last. About three o'clock one of my students rushed in with the news that two regiments, armed and carrying red flags, had left their barracks and were marching on the Duma, there to unite with the workmen. Hastily leaving the house we hurried... to the central part of the city. As we turned into the Liteinyi the crowd grew larger and much louder grew the sound of
>
> (*continued*)

the guns. The frantic efforts of the police to disperse the crowds were utterly without effect . . .

We finally reached the Tauride Palace. The hall of the Duma presented a striking contrast to the tumult without. Here was comfort, dignity, order – the hall and corridors were packed with people. Soldiers behind rifles and machine-guns were there, but order still prevailed. The street had not yet broken in . . .

'What's the latest?' I asked of a deputy shouldering his way through the mass. 'Rodzianko is trying to get into communication with the Tsar. The Committee is discussing the organization of a new ministry responsible jointly to the Tsar and to the Duma.'

'Is anybody in control and regulation of this revolution?'

'Nobody. It is developing spontaneously.'

'How about the monarchy and the Tsar?'

'I know absolutely nothing.'

'Too bad if even you don't know about these things,' I remarked sarcastically . . . Outside people were growing hysterical with excitement and the police had retreated. Wild speeches and shrieks of applause filled the air. Excited in spite of myself, I too listened and applauded, and it was midnight before I could tear myself away.

Source: quoted in R. Pethybridge, *Witnesses to the Russian Revolution*, pp. 113–18.

(K) Mikhail Rodzianko, the President of the Duma, gives his account of events.

Unexpectedly for all, there erupted a soldier mutiny such as I have never seen. These, of course, were not soldiers but *muzhiki* [peasants] taken directly from the plough who have found it useful now to make known their *muzhik* demands. In the crowd all one could hear was 'Land and Freedom', 'Down with the dynasty', 'Down with the Romanovs', 'Down with the officers'. In many units officers were beaten. This was joined by the workers and anarchy reached its apogee.

Source: quoted in Pipes, p. 278.

Notes

1. David M. McDonald, *United Government and Foreign Policy in Russia, 1900–1914*, gives a good general survey of foreign policy.
2. J.N. Westwood, *Russia against Japan*, is probably the best recent account of the Russo–Japanese War.
3. Quoted in Peter Waldron, *The End of Imperial Russia, 1855–1917*, p. 122.
4. Dominic Lieven, *Russia and the Origins of the First World War* is still an excellent account of how Russia became involved in the war.
5. Fritz Fischer, *Germany's Aims in the First World War*.
6. Norman Stone, *The Eastern Front, 1914–1917* (1998 edition), pp. 236–54.
7. Leon Trotsky, *The History of the Russian Revolution*, p. 41.

8. Stone, pp. 208–11.
9. Robert Service, *The Russian Revolution, 1900–1927* (1999 edition), pp. 29–30.
10. T. Hasegawa, 'The February Revolution', in Acton, Cherniaev and Rosenberg (editors), *Critical Companion to the Russian Revolution 1914–1921*, p. 49.
11. T. Hasegawa, *The February Revolution: Petrograd 1917*; details in this section from pp. 232–8, 247–55, 267–9.
12. E.H. Carr, *The Bolshevik Revolution* (1966 edition), vol. 1, p. 81.
13. George Katkov, *Russia 1917 – the February Revolution*.
14. W.H. Chamberlin, *The Russian Revolution* (1965 edition), vol. 1, p. 73.
15. Trotsky, pp. 169–71.
16. For a detailed analysis of the different interpretations see Edward Acton, *Rethinking the Russian Revolution*, pp. 107–28.
17. Christopher Read, *From Tsar to Soviets*, p. 90.
18. Diane Koenker, *Moscow Workers and the Revolution of 1917*, p. 304.
19. Steve Smith, *Red Petrograd: Revolution in the Factories, 1917–18*, p. 145.
20. Orlando Figes, *A People's Tragedy*, pp. 301, 322–4.
21. Richard Pipes, *The Russian Revolution, 1899–1919*, pp. 278, 281.
22. Read, pp. 44–5.

■ M̌ 4 The failure of the Provisional Government and the Bolshevik seizure of power, February–October 1917

Summary of events

March 1917 Provisional Government and Petrograd Soviet formed
When the abdication of Nicholas II was announced and the Romanov monarchy came to such an unexpected end, the leaders of the Progressive Bloc formed what they called a Provisional Government with Prince Lvov at its head. Their intention was to introduce necessary reforms and prepare for democratic elections to choose a Constituent Assembly or parliament. The workers and soldiers of Petrograd elected their own representatives to the Petrograd Soviet. This meant that **there was a dual power in the capital**: the Provisional Government of the Duma members which was supported by the middle and upper classes, and the Petrograd Soviet which had the support of the working classes, soldiers and the revolutionary parties – Socialist Revolutionaries (SRs) and Social Democrats, who were divided into Mensheviks and Bolsheviks. **The two bodies agreed to work together to continue fighting the war,** but it was an uneasy relationship.

April
- **At the beginning of the month Lenin arrived in Petrograd from Switzerland,** after travelling through Germany in what was described as a 'sealed' train. He immediately published his *April Theses* setting out what he thought the Bolsheviks' aims should be, and insisting that the Bolsheviks must cease all co-operation with the Provisional Government.

- **Towards the end of April there were demonstrations in Petrograd** against the government and against the continuation of the war. In an attempt at compromise **Prince Lvov formed a coalition, bringing six of the socialist leaders from the Petrograd Soviet into the government.** Alexander Kerensky, a socialist lawyer, became Minister for War. No Bolsheviks joined the government.

*Figure 4.1   The 'July Days' in Petrograd, 1917. Provisional Government troops fire on
a demonstration in the Nevsky Prospekt.*

During the summer of 1917 nothing went right for the Provisional Government

- The war dragged on; **Kerensky began a new offensive** against the Austrians in
  Galicia (16 June), and although there were some initial successes, the Russians
  were forced to retreat, with heavy losses, when German troops arrived to help
  the Austrians.
- The economic situation continued to deteriorate and the government's popularity waned rapidly.
- **The July Days** – on 3 July there was a huge demonstration of workers, soldiers
  and sailors, many of whom were from Kronstadt, the naval base on an island
  in the estuary of the river Neva, just off Petrograd. They marched on the Tauride
  Palace where both the government and the Petrograd Soviet were meeting,
  and demanded that the Soviet take over. The Soviet refused to take the responsibility and the government brought loyal troops from the front to restore
  order. The Bolsheviks were accused of stirring up the trouble and trying to
  seize power. The government reported, falsely, that Lenin was a German
  agent. At this, public support for the Bolsheviks quickly declined; some of the
  leaders were arrested, and Lenin fled to Finland. About 400 people had been
  killed during the violence of these 'July Days'.
- **Prince Lvov**, deeply shocked by the 'July Days', **resigned as head of the
  government and was replaced by Kerensky.** However, the situation in Russia
  became steadily worse: unrest and frustration mounted, the economy was in
  deep crisis, unemployment was rising and real wages were falling.

August: The Kornilov affair

There was a further disaster on 21 August when the Germans captured Riga, only
300 miles from Petrograd. The popularity of the Bolsheviks soon revived, since they

were the only party not tainted by the failures of the Provisional Government. There was confusion in Petrograd: troops sent by the army supreme commander, General Kornilov, advanced towards the city, apparently intending to take over from Kerensky and set up a military dictatorship. However, Kornilov's real intentions are still a subject of debate among historians. Kerensky announced that a right-wing coup was in progress; he dismissed Kornilov, allowed arms to be distributed to the workers of Petrograd, and released most of the imprisoned Bolsheviks. Kornilov's troops began to desert and he was eventually arrested.

September–October: Bolshevik influence grows

- The so-called Kornilov rising had important results: it convinced workers and soldiers that there was a real danger of a counter-revolution and that the Bolsheviks were the only party that could be relied on to act independently in their interests.
- On 31 August the Bolsheviks won a majority in the Petrograd Soviet for the first time, and by late September they were in a majority in the Moscow Soviet as well.
- Lenin returned in secret to Petrograd early in October and convinced the Central Committee of the Bolshevik party that now was the time to attempt to seize power. Using forces **acting in the name of the Soviet,** the Bolsheviks took over the important points in the city (24–25 October). The ministers of the Provisional Government were arrested, except Kerensky who escaped, and it was announced that all power was in the hands of the Soviets.

Main areas of debate:

- Were the Bolsheviks planning to seize power by armed force during the July Days, or were they taken by surprise by a spontaneous uprising?
- Was there a Kornilov coup attempt or did Kerensky invent it?
- Did the Bolsheviks achieve power in October by a coup, without much popular support, or were they swept into power by the social and economic concerns of the masses which gave them a huge basis of popular support?

4.1   The failure of the Provisional Government

(a) The Provisional Government and the Petrograd Soviet

After the revolution of February/March the vast majority of people in Russia who had any views about the situation probably expected a democratic parliamentary republic to emerge. Even strict Marxists like the Mensheviks believed that the country would be ruled by a bourgeois liberal government until the industrial working class had become large and powerful enough to take control itself. This, it was assumed, would take years rather than months. However, the Provisional Government failed to consolidate its position, and only eight months later the Bolsheviks, still only a small party in February, were able to take power. One of the main reasons for the failure of the Provisional Government was that from the very beginning of its existence it had to function alongside the Petrograd Soviet – they even met in the same building, the Tauride Palace. The Soviet, the elected representatives of the workers and soldiers, had a great deal of power; via the trade unions they controlled all the railways in the Petrograd area, together with all postal and telegraph services. They had set up committees to deal with food supplies and military matters, and they published their own newspaper *Izvestiya* (News). There was a network of Soviets throughout the country and in June a national conference was held – the First All-Russia Congress of Soviets; this body had a Central Executive Committee (known as Ispolkom) which did its best to undermine the Provisional Government. The Petrograd Soviet and Ispolkom acted as self-appointed 'watchdogs' of the revolution.

Although Prince Lvov was the Prime Minister, probably the most influential member of the government was Paul Milyukov, the Kadet leader. The Soviet supported what was basically the Kadet programme of full civil rights, including freedom of the press, speech, assembly and religion, the right to strike, the abolition of the death penalty and an amnesty for all political and religious prisoners. Also promised were elections for a Constituent Assembly based on the principle of votes for everybody and a secret ballot. It was decided to set up a militia to take the place of the police, and the government ruled that none of the 250,000 soldiers of the Petrograd garrison were to be disarmed or moved from the city. This last point was included on the insistence of the Soviet and Ispolkom because the troops in Petrograd had helped to carry out the revolution and would continue to defend it, whereas troops brought in from elsewhere might be unreliable. On the same day that this programme was announced (1 March), the Soviet issued what it called Army Order Number One (see Document A): troops were to obey orders given to them by the government only after they had been approved by the Soviet. Soldiers and sailors were urged to set up their own committees which would take over control of all arms from the officers. A few days later Army Order Number Two gave soldiers the right to sack and replace their own commanders. These orders were a serious blow for the government because it meant that if any major policy disagreement arose, in the last resort it could not rely on the loyalty of the army. It wasn't long before there was a major disagreement over the conduct of the war and the question of war aims (see next section).

Given that it was apparently so powerful, why didn't the Petrograd Soviet take control during the summer of 1917? After all, as the elected representatives of the soldiers and sailors, they had a better claim to legitimacy than the Provisional Government – the remnants of the Fourth Duma which had been elected on a very limited franchise. The reason was that most of the members of the Soviet were extremely cautious. The Mensheviks were sticking to their strict Marxist views that the February Revolution was the expected bourgeois revolution, and that this must be consolidated before the workers' revolution could take place. They thought it was vital for them to co-operate with the liberal Provisional Government, at least for the time being. After all, times were difficult – it was better for the liberals to take the responsibility, and the blame, if necessary. The Mensheviks were happy to take the role of watchdog over the government, making sure that the workers' interests were looked after. The Socialist Revolutionaries, who drew most of their support from the peasants, were the largest party in the Soviet. But they were divided into a right wing which was prepared to support the government, a left wing, led by Maria Spiridonova, which gradually drifted towards the Bolsheviks, and a centre which couldn't make up its mind. Until Lenin arrived in Petrograd at the beginning of April even the Bolsheviks were content to let the Provisional Government have its way. Two major concerns among all these groups were firstly, that the middle of a war was the worst possible time for inexperienced politicians to take over the running of a country; and secondly, that if the Soviet took power in their own name, they would lose the support of the moderate bourgeoisie; these would then join the right wing reactionaries who might be provoked into launching a military coup to bring the revolution to an end.

Early in May the situation began to change: serious splits developed in the Soviet when some of its members joined the government. Prince Lvov took six socialists into his cabinet, including Viktor Chernov, the SR leader, and two leading Mensheviks, Irakli Tsereteli and Mikhail Skobelev. However, they were unable to change the government's policies to any great extent. In mid-June the government ordered some of the Petrograd regiments to the front, ostensibly to reinforce the faltering Kerensky offensive; the real reason was to get them away from Petrograd where they were seen as a major threat to the government. This breach of the promise not to move any of the garrison from the city outraged the troops, and many of their unit committees voted to overthrow the Provisional Government in an armed uprising. By the end of 3 July Petrograd was virtually in the hands of the soldiers, workers and Kronstadt sailors supported by many rank-and-file Bolsheviks. The following day an armed crowd of around 50,000 besieged the Tauride Palace brandishing placards bearing the slogan 'All Power to the Soviets'. When Chernov tried to calm the crowd he was roughly handled and almost lynched before he was rescued by Trotsky. A worker from the Putilov factory shouted in his face: 'Take power you son of a bitch when they give it to you.' Power was there for the taking but the Soviet, including the Bolshevik leaders, shrank from the fateful step; Lenin himself was not convinced that this was the right time – premature action could be disastrous. It was clear that the masses were far more militant than the Soviet and the leaders of the Bolsheviks, the only party which claimed to be in favour of insurrection; but without decisive leadership, the crowds didn't know how to make the unwilling Soviet take power. Confused and leaderless, they began to disperse, and in the evening loyal troops arrived from the front to restore order.

There has been a lively debate about what really happened during the July Days. Richard Pipes is convinced that Lenin and the Bolsheviks planned the whole affair from the beginning. He claims that it was the Bolsheviks who stirred up the garrison troops with a 'furious propaganda campaign urging them to refuse to go to the front. No country with a tradition of democracy would have tolerated such incitement to mutiny in time of war.' The Bolshevik Central Committee passed a resolution calling for the overthrow of the Provisional Government by armed force. The plan was that troops would arrest the Soviet Executive, whereupon Lenin would proclaim the new Soviet government, which would in reality be a Bolshevik government. Pipes claims that Lenin lost his nerve at the critical moment because he could not decide whether or not it was the right time. Pipes believes that the insurrection was Lenin's worst mistake, which could easily have caused the destruction of the Bolshevik party. He argues that to absolve themselves of responsibility, the Bolsheviks went to unusual lengths to 'misrepresent the July putsch as a spontaneous demonstration which they sought to direct into peaceful channels.'[1]

However, the evidence for this theory is far from conclusive; much more convincing is the argument that it *was* a spontaneous uprising. Although it was supported by the majority of rank-and-file Bolsheviks, the party leadership was much too cautious to be planning a coup. According to another American historian, Alexander Rabinowitch, the Bolshevik Central Committee seems to have spent most of its time trying to restrain the ordinary rank-and-file party members. It only issued its resolution calling for the armed overthrow of the government under pressure from the militants; even then it had no intention of the Bolsheviks taking power alone, but was hoping that a show of force would be enough to persuade the Soviet to take control.[2] As for Lenin, he was reluctant to speak in public, and on his only appearance he made a very short speech in which he failed to give the crowds any detailed instructions, except to remain calm and to keep the demonstrations peaceful. It seems unlikely that he would have been so hesitant if he had genuinely intended from the beginning to overthrow the government. Robert Service's view is that he was weighing up the pros and cons of a gamble: 'it was more likely by far that he was improvising and that he was testing the waters with the aim of discovering the strength of force and determination that the Provisional Government retained.' By the time he came to make his speech, he had reached the conclusion that it was too early to launch a violent uprising and that the leaders of the Bolshevik Military Organization and the Kronstadt Bolsheviks (who were in a majority in the Kronstadt Soviet) had been acting irresponsibly. Turning to the ones who were with him, he told them: 'You ought to be given a good hiding for this!'[3] Lenin was probably also influenced by the knowledge that the government was about to denounce the Bolsheviks as German agents, which would not exactly get a newly proclaimed Bolshevik government off to an auspicious start.

After the July crisis and the resignation of Lvov, Kerensky formed a government made up of eight mainly right-wing socialists (from the Soviet) and seven non-socialists. But although it might appear to the outsider that the socialists had succeeded in capturing control of the country, in reality the government's policies changed very little. The situation with the war and the collapsing economy was so disastrous that the socialists simply dare not try anything dramatic; they knew that if they did, they would arouse the bitter opposition of industrialists, landowners and the army command. Having committed themselves to this compromise with the liberals, the Soviet-based members of the government now had to bear the responsibility for their failures. The workers and soldiers of Petrograd and many of the peasant SR supporters were becoming increasingly exasperated with the caution of the moderate socialists and were pressing for more militant action. The only alternative was to turn to the Bolsheviks whose popularity gradually recovered after the crisis of the 'July Days'. By September Kerensky and his government were becoming increasingly isolated between, on the one hand, the counter-revolutionary forces of the right, particularly most of the army high command, and on the other, the Bolsheviks, together with their left SR supporters, who claimed to have answers to the problems of the war and the economy and who presented themselves as the chief defenders of the revolution. So long as the war and its associated failures continued, the Provisional Government would be in grave difficulties.

(b) The Provisional Government continues the war

Unfortunately for the Provisional Government, there could be no return to normality while the country was still at war. If peace could have been made within the first few weeks after the February revolution, the government would have been able to give all its attention to the pressing problems of the economy and the preparations for democratic elections. The left called for a negotiated peace based on the principle of no annexations of occupied territory. However, since it was hardly likely that the Germans would agree to hand back all their conquests, there seemed no alternative but to continue fighting. The new government was anxious to show solidarity with Russia's Western allies, who expected that the removal of the Tsar would bring about an immediate improvement in the war effort. After all, the Provisional Government, professing as it did to be a democratic government, would not want to be accused of abandoning its democratic allies who were fighting German and Austro–Hungarian autocracy. There were also suggestions that the government's ulterior motive in continuing the war was to keep as many peasants as possible away from home for as long as possible in order to reduce the danger of mass land seizures, and, in the case of Kerensky's summer offensive, to find something useful for the Petrograd garrison to do.[4]

It wasn't long before disagreements arose about the conduct of the war. The Soviet supported the decision to continue fighting, but only to the extent of recapturing lost territory and defending Russian lands from further invasion. They were not prepared to tolerate what they called an 'imperialist' war involving the capture and annexation of enemy territory. Chernov, the SR leader, insisted that the Foreign Minister, Milyukov, should send the allies a declaration of Russia's war aims which had been drafted by the Soviet, and which called for a lasting peace based on the 'self-determination of nations' and a renunciation of all annexationist claims by all the combatants. Milyukov was worried in case this gave the allies the impression that Russia was prepared to make a separate peace. He added a secret note to the declaration assuring the allies that Russia still stood by her obligations, which presumably included keeping to the secret treaty signed in 1915 promising Russia Constantinople and the Straits once the Central Powers were defeated.

When the 'secret' note was published there was uproar in the Soviet and among the left at this revelation of the government's 'imperialism'. There were massive protest demonstrations supported by troops from the garrison, and soon afterwards Milyukov resigned (2 May). Soldiers at the front were bitterly disappointed, since they had expected peace to follow very soon after the Tsar abdicated. Normal discipline and order began to break down, especially now that there was no death penalty to deter would-be mutineers. By April a system of soldier–officer committees from company level upwards had been set up and accepted by the High Command, since it seemed to be the only way of restoring some sort of order. Each committee at the front usually consisted of four soldiers and one officer from every division; many of the lower officers were socialists who became predominant in the leadership. Bolsheviks and other socialists played a significant role in committee activity and seemed to work well together during March and April. However, when Kerensky and the other socialists entered the cabinet, they committed themselves to the continuation of the war. This placed the soldier–officer committees in a difficult situation: the officers felt they must try to support their fellow socialists in government by trying to enforce discipline, whereas the rank-and-file peasant and working-class soldiers continued to press for peace, neglecting routine military duties and fraternizing with the Germans. When Kerensky's plans for an offensive became known, this gave the Bolsheviks their opportunity; 'Bolshevik agitation against the war at the front, which was a trickle in early May, became a flood by early June. Whole regiments mutinied, disobeyed orders on troop movements, and committed violence against their officers.'[5]

Public opinion too began to turn decisively against the war; each military setback caused a crisis on the home front and led to dwindling support for the Provisional Government. General Brusilov was convinced that the mood of the troops did not augur well for the June offensive (see Document B), but the government insisted that it should go ahead. Its failure was a bitter blow – thousands of troops were killed and thousands more ran away when the Germans counter-attacked. The official number of deserters during the offensive was 170,000, but the actual number was very much larger. At a meeting of one of the soldiers' committees somebody asked the question: 'What's the use of invading Galicia anyway? Why the hell do we need to take another hilltop when we can make peace at the bottom?' Some soldiers shot their officers rather than fight the Germans. When the government tried to reinforce the army by bringing some of the garrison troops from Petrograd, that precipitated the crisis of early July and the resignation of Prince Lvov (see section 4.1(a)). The capture of Riga by the Germans on 21 August threw Petrograd into a panic and was quickly followed by the Kornilov Affair (see section 4.1(d)).

The war hampered the government in other ways: it prevented any decisive action on land reform and it delayed elections for a Constituent Assembly. Or perhaps the politicians were using the war as an excuse for their inaction. Either way it did nothing to make the war or the government any more popular. A committee was set up to investigate the land situation, but the problem was how to organize the redistribution of land when so many peasants were away in the army. If they heard that estates were being carved up and handed out in their absence, there were likely to be mass desertions of peasant soldiers walking home to make sure that they didn't miss out. In some areas peasants soon grew tired of waiting for government action and began to seize land; on 8 April Prince Lvov gave local authorities permission to use troops to suppress disorders in rural areas. When Viktor Chernov, the SR leader, became Minister of Agriculture in May, he quietly allowed peasants to take over unused land, but the liberals in the government prevented him from introducing any general land reform policy.

It was almost the end of May before a council was formed to draw up legislation for the new electoral system, and even then progress was slow. They had problems deciding on which type of proportional representation to adopt and how to organize things so that around seven million troops and civilians still at the front could vote. The Kadets did their best to prolong the discussions since it was clear that they had no chance of winning a genuinely democratic election. This delay played into the hands of the Bolsheviks, enabling them to tell the public, with some apparent justification, that the government had no intention of holding elections and that the revolution was at an end. It was eventually announced that the elections would take place on 12 November, but by then the Bolsheviks had taken power.

(c) Economic chaos grows

Some historians see this as the major reason for the failure of the Provisional Government, though like so much else, it can be attributed to the continuation of the war. Inflation continued to soar, especially in the towns and cities where high grain prices were the main problem. In March the government tried to deal with the problem by introducing a state monopoly on the purchase of grain in order to keep supplies flowing and prices stable. This failed because peasants refused to sell their grain at the prices offered; they preferred to feed it to their livestock or consume it themselves, since the largest slice of profits was taken by the dealers who transported it to the urban areas. Prices of manufactured goods were so far above the prices that the peasants received for their produce that they preferred to revert to subsistence. In September the government was forced to double the price offered, but by this time the rouble was worth only 10 per cent of its 1914 value. Although wages increased, they lagged far behind price increases, and this led to demands for even higher wages. In some places traders refused to accept the almost worthless paper money and worked on a barter system.

By the autumn the economy was collapsing: towns and cities were starving; production of war materials had fallen by half and the army was approaching the point where it would be unable to fight even if it wanted to. There was a transport crisis with one train in four out of order. Hundreds of firms had been forced to close down, giving as their reasons shortages of raw materials and fuel, lack of orders and excessive wage demands. Meanwhile in the countryside peasants continued to seize land, livestock, farm equipment and stocks of timber and hay. In most areas this was carried out in an orderly way by the *mir* which formally took possession of the new land and divided it up among the villagers. This was embarrassing for the SRs who supported the principle of land seizure but wanted it carried out by local land committees. The government repeatedly warned peasants not to take matters into their own hands, but their warnings were ignored and they lacked the means to do anything about it. The government had lost all control of the economic system, and the situation was so dire that, in the words of Norman Stone, 'the way was open to Lenin, who promised a new system altogether. Economic chaos drove Russia towards Bolshevism, sometimes despite the Bolsheviks.'[6]

(d) The growing popularity of the Bolsheviks – the Kornilov Affair

From being a minority party in February 1917 the Bolsheviks gradually attracted more support; but it was not a smooth process – public opinion fluctuated, and after the 'July Days' many people thought the party was finished. Yet by October they had a majority in the Petrograd and Moscow Soviets and in the All-Russia Congress of Soviets. The first important milestone was the publication of Lenin's

April Theses, an aggressive and uncompromising document containing ten urgent proposals. He claimed that the leaders of the Soviet were completely misguided to co-operate with the Provisional Government; they had sold out to bourgeois capitalism; support for it should cease immediately and the misplaced confidence that the masses had in the government should be destroyed. Lenin claimed that the situation had already gone beyond the parliamentary democracy stage; the Soviets, under real revolutionary leadership, should now play the vital role in shifting power from the bourgeoisie to the workers. He urged that the power of the Soviets must be built up and that the Bolsheviks should do all they could to increase their membership of the Soviets. 'All Power to the Soviets' was one of his slogans – the Soviets must take control of the state, thus fulfilling the next stage in Marx's pattern. Another slogan was 'Peace, Bread and Land'. 'Peace' meant immediate withdrawal from the capitalist war, and therefore was only possible after the capitalist government had been overthrown. 'Land' meant the seizure of large estates and their transference into state ownership. Another task of the party was to create a revolutionary international movement; Lenin believed that the proletarian revolution in Russia would spark off similar movements in other countries – the socialist revolution in Russia could only be fully successful as part of a world-wide movement.

When Lenin first presented these ideas in a speech to a gathering of Social Democrats in the Tauride Palace there was uproar. The Mensheviks heckled and booed and even the Bolsheviks themselves were stunned. They had already committed themselves to support the Provisional Government, assuming that the bourgeois stage would last for some considerable time, and were hoping for a reconciliation with the Mensheviks, with whom they were already working quite amicably in the provincial Soviets. But here was Lenin talking about abandoning 'the old Bolshevism' and reducing the Marxist two-stage revolutionary process into one all-inclusive revolution at the end of which 'the proletariat and the poorest peasants' would have taken power. According to most reports Lenin was not dismayed by his reception – he had expected a struggle, and now he set about converting the party to support the *April Theses*. He threw himself into the campaign with incredible energy and will-power, speaking at mass meetings, writing articles for the Bolshevik newspaper *Pravda* (Truth), circulating pamphlets and cajoling the Bolshevik Central Committee. He was prepared to modify his slogans and ideas but even so, his programme was far more radical than that of any other party. He called for the nationalization of large-scale industry and banks, and insisted that only a genuinely socialist government run by the Soviets could achieve peace. At a conference of elected Bolshevik delegates held during the last week in April there was a remarkable turnaround – the delegates voted overwhelmingly to back the *April Theses*; less than a month after returning from abroad, Lenin was firmly in control of the party. His next struggle would be to win over the general public.

Events greatly helped the Bolsheviks: in May when the Mensheviks and SRs joined the government, many of their supporters were bitterly disappointed and began to turn towards the Bolsheviks, the only party which was anti-war and pro-working class. Lenin and the Bolsheviks took every opportunity to make use of the growing disillusionment among the masses and to spread the main points of the party programme. They used the factory committees, the trade unions, the

Soviets (of which there were around 900 by the autumn of 1917) and the Bolshevik newspapers; and of course there were more speeches in the Petrograd Soviet and the First All Russia Congress of Soviets held in June (see Document D). To gain the support of the peasants they dropped the idea of land nationalization and offered peasants more or less a free hand to divide the land up as they chose. There is evidence that this new attitude to the land question produced quite a marked swing to the Bolsheviks in the countryside, where previously they had had very little support. Peasants were losing patience with the over-cautious Social Revolutionaries; in fact many left-wing SRs were splitting away from the main body and moving towards the Bolsheviks. In the larger cities the Bolsheviks formed militia groups, a sort of Bolshevik private army consisting of workers armed with rifles; by July there were about 10,000 of them in Petrograd. The message was clear and simple – the Bolshevik party was the vanguard of the movement which would guide the mass of the workers, soldiers and peasants towards the socialist revolution. This revolution would take place when the Bolsheviks had gained a majority in the Soviets; this would show that public opinion was on their side and that the workers and soldiers were ready to take power.

The fiasco of the 'July Days' (see section 4.1(a)) was a temporary setback for the Bolsheviks. They had talked about insurrection, but when the Bolshevik sailors at the Kronstadt naval base had taken the initiative, the party leadership more or less disowned them. Worse still, the government was able to blame the Bolsheviks for the 'July Days', and accused them of being in the pay of the Germans and working for the defeat of Russia. It was true that the party had received cash from the Germans who were prepared to try anything which might destabilize the Provisional Government; this was the reason they had allowed Lenin and his party of supporters to travel back to Russia through Germany in the 'sealed' train. After the publication of the *April Theses* it was in Germany's interests to ease the way for a Bolshevik government, since they were the only party in Russia pledged to bring about a quick end to the war. In fact the amounts of cash involved were not large, but the right-wing press made the most of them. The government ordered the arrest of twelve Bolshevik leaders, including Lenin, and prepared to charge them with high treason. About 800 Bolsheviks were arrested altogether and the offices of *Pravda* were raided and closed down. The popularity of the Bolsheviks, especially among the troops, plummeted for the time being, and although Lenin himself escaped to Finland, Kerensky, who became leader of the Provisional Government soon afterwards, believed that the Bolshevik threat had been permanently removed.

Kerensky saw himself as a man of destiny and the saviour of Russia, and he soon began to act almost like a dictator.[7] He took up residence in the Winter Palace, slept in Alexander III's bed and worked at his 'swimming-pool sized' desk. He never took the Bolsheviks seriously enough, and believed that they were only a threat because their extremism encouraged a counter-revolutionary backlash, especially among those right-wingers who wanted to restore the monarchy. It was no doubt for this reason that he had the royal family secretly moved to Tobolsk in Siberia. Once Nicholas was safely out of the way, Kerensky felt he could afford to be lenient with the Bolsheviks. Eventually they were all released and the charges against them dropped.

It was the counter-revolutionary backlash in the shape of the Kornilov Affair[8] which helped the rapid revival of Bolshevik fortunes. The leaders of industry, business, commerce and finance were becoming increasingly worried at the apparent breakdown of law and order. In August they held a conference in Moscow at which they were joined by right-wing politicians and army officers, and they agreed that the most important step was to destroy the Soviets, especially the Petrograd Soviet, which they saw as the root of the revolution. There was another Moscow conference arranged by Kerensky later in the month and attended by representatives of all parties except the Bolsheviks. No agreement was reached but the most significant outcome was that General Kornilov, whom Kerensky had appointed as Commander-in-Chief of the Army, emerged as the leader of the right. Described by one of his colleagues as having 'the heart of a lion and the brain of a sheep,' Kornilov seems genuinely to have seen himself as the man to save Russia from the chaos. He believed that the key to success was to restore discipline in the army and he urged Kerensky to restore the death penalty for soldiers disobeying orders and deserting. Kerensky obliged but Kornilov demanded more – he wanted the death penalty restored at the rear as well, which would apply, for example, to reserves waiting to move up to the front. He wanted soldiers' committees banned and political agitators removed, and he remarked to one of his aides around this time: 'The time has come to hang the German agents and spies headed by Lenin, and to disperse the Soviet of Workers' and Soldiers' Deputies so that it can never reassemble.' However, these demands placed Kerensky in a difficult situation since he knew that the Petrograd Soviet would never agree to them. Some reports say that he wanted to introduce the measures and that the cabinet had discussed moving loyal troops into Petrograd to eliminate the Soviet when the new disciplinary measures were announced; but no decision on this had been taken.

What happened next is still not clear, and several different accounts have been produced. What seems to be beyond dispute is that a number of people on the right were urging Kornilov to carry out a military coup to remove both the Petrograd Soviet and Kerensky. The day after the Germans captured Riga, Kornilov ordered some of his troops to move to Petrograd. According to Christopher Read, 'Kornilov was deploying his most reliable troops with a view to suppressing the Petrograd Soviet, even paying *agents provocateurs* to start disorders in the capital as a pretext for his actions.'[9] However, what is not known for certain is whether Kornilov intended to overthrow Kerensky as well as suppress the Soviet. Also unclear is how far Kerensky supported Kornilov; certainly Kerensky would have been glad to get rid of the Soviet, and may well have given Kornilov the impression that he wanted him to go ahead.

Things were complicated by a go-between or mediator, Vladimir Lvov, who told Kerensky that he had heard rumours that Kornilov intended to set himself up as dictator. Horrified, Kerensky, who was in Petrograd, contacted Kornilov, who was still at army headquarters at Mogilev, by telegraph, to ask him if Lvov's story was true. Without bothering to check with Kerensky exactly what Lvov had told him, Kornilov said that it was true. After a short conversation full of misunderstandings, Kerensky decided that Lvov must have been telling the truth and ordered Kornilov to halt the advance on Petrograd. On 26 August he sent a telegram dismissing Kornilov from his post, but Kornilov refused to be dismissed, afterwards claiming that he thought Kerensky was acting under duress and that the Bolsheviks must already have taken over Petrograd (see Document C). Another reason which has been suggested for Kornilov's refusal to be dismissed is that he believed Kerensky had suffered some sort of breakdown, was no longer fit to rule and must be replaced.

As Kornilov's troops continued their advance, Kerensky appealed to the Soviet for help. Arms were distributed to workers and Red Guards, printers stopped the publication of newspapers supporting Kornilov, and railway workers diverted troop trains. Brigades of workers went out to talk to the troops and eventually they refused to march to Petrograd. The *coup* fizzled out without a shot being fired and on 2 September Kornilov, who was still at army headquarters, was arrested. After studying the tapes of the telegraph conversations between Kerensky and Kornilov, Richard Pipes concludes that to begin with, Kornilov had never intended a *coup* – misunderstandings arose because of the interfering Lvov, and then these were used by Kerensky to discredit Kornilov and enhance his own crumbling authority. It was only when Kornilov felt he had been betrayed by Kerensky that he decided to disobey orders.[10]

Whatever the truth about the intentions of Kornilov and Kerensky, the results were beyond doubt: the right was thrown into confusion and discredited. The army high command was demoralized; relations between officers and troops took a sharp turn for the worse, discipline seemed on the verge of complete breakdown and there were mass desertions. The army leaders turned against Kerensky, accusing him of betraying Kornilov, and General Alexeev, Kornilov's successor, resigned, saying that he could no longer take responsibility for an army in which discipline had collapsed and 'our officers are made martyrs.' It also emerged that the Kadets had been secretly encouraging Kornilov. The Soviets turned against Kerensky because they suspected that he had been plotting their downfall, and the left was strengthened because everything seemed to bear out what they had argued all along – that the right could never be trusted to put genuine democracy first. Many workers believed that only their prompt actions had saved the revolution.

The Bolsheviks benefited most, partly because they were seen as the chief target of the discredited right and because they were still the only party not to have compromised themselves by joining coalition governments with the middle class parties. In exchange for their co-operation in dealing with the Kornilov crisis, Kerensky ordered the release of all imprisoned Bolsheviks, including Trotsky, who had joined the party in July. Their reviving popularity was reflected in election results around the country for city councils and Soviets. In Petrograd itself another significant sign was the way in which the Bolsheviks came to dominate most of the factory committees. At the Lessner works in September the Bolsheviks won 471 votes, SRs 155, Mensheviks 23 and non-party candidates 186. At the Pipe works where they had won only 36 per cent of the votes in the committee elections in June, the Bolsheviks took 62 per cent in October. The First All-Russia conference of factory committees opened on 17 October and one of the main resolutions accepted called for a state-wide system of workers' control of production and distribution, to be achieved by giving workers two-thirds of the places on all institutions of economic regulation. This was a Bolshevik resolution, drafted by Lenin himself.[11] After the Bolsheviks came to power it became clear that Lenin and the factory committees meant different things by 'workers' control'; but at this stage, as far as ordinary workers were concerned, what mattered was that the Bolsheviks were the only party which claimed to support any kind of workers' control. This, together with their promises of land for the peasants, immediate peace and government by the Soviets, added up to an irresistible programme.

Clearly the Provisional Government was on the verge of collapse, having completely failed to solve the problems facing it. Hamstrung by the need to continue fighting the war, it had stumbled from crisis to crisis. Its handling of the economy and the land question satisfied nobody and its attempt to go on the offensive militarily backfired disastrously. During its last few weeks in office it consisted of an uneasy coalition between moderate politicians from right and left who were unable to give anybody what they really wanted. The government's continued failure to hold elections for the Constituent Assembly called into question its legitimacy, and by the end of September it was viewed at best with apathy and at worst with contempt. As it turned out, there were very few people willing to risk their lives to save it.

4.2   The Bolshevik seizure of power – October 1917

(a) Lenin urges immediate action

By the end of September 1917 there had been a polarization of political forces which left Kerensky and his dwindling band of supporters in a kind of void at the centre. Election results for Soviets and city councils demonstrated both the political polarization and the rapidly growing popularity of the Bolsheviks. In the elections for the Moscow city Duma on 24 September the Bolsheviks took 51 per cent of the vote as against only 11 per cent in June; the SR vote collapsed from 56 per cent to 14 per cent and the Menshevik vote from 12 per cent to only 4 per cent. On the other hand the Kadets, now seen as the main party to represent middle class interests, increased their vote from 17 per cent to 31 per cent. The Bolsheviks had already won majorities in the Petrograd and Moscow Soviets; on 25 September, Trotsky, now established as a Bolshevik leader, was elected chairman of the Petrograd Soviet and four out of seven seats on the executive were filled by Bolsheviks.

Lenin was still in Finland but he kept up a constant barrage of letters to the Central Committee of the Bolshevik party, first of all urging them to take power in the name of the Soviets and form a coalition socialist government along with the Mensheviks and SRs. Now that the Bolsheviks had majorities in so many elected bodies, that would make the transference of power to a socialist government with a Bolshevik majority perfectly legal. The Bolsheviks would not resort to violence provided the Mensheviks and SRs broke away from their association with the Kadets, so that the socialist government would be totally responsible to the Soviet. However, this golden opportunity was not taken – at a time when the vast majority of soldiers, workers and peasants would surely have supported the assumption of power by a socialist coalition government, incredibly the Menshevik and SR leaders still preferred to cling to Kerensky and the so-called bourgeois stage of government. So Lenin quickly changed his plan of campaign. By the middle of September he was urging the Central Committee to seize power immediately, either in Petrograd or Moscow. 'The Bolsheviks, having obtained a majority in the Soviets of Soldiers' and Workers' Deputies of both capitals, can and must take state power into their own hands,' he wrote; 'history will not forgive us if we do not assume power now.' But most of the members, especially Kamenev and Zinoviev, felt that it was too early to attempt this, since in the country as a whole the Bolsheviks were still in a minority in most of the Soviets.

Lenin was becoming increasingly frustrated by their lack of action: although warrants had been issued for his arrest, he slipped back into Petrograd and on 10 October attended a meeting of the Bolshevik Central Committee. He argued passionately in favour of armed insurrection and persuaded them to pass, by a vote of 10 to 2, a resolution committing the Central Committee to begin planning an insurrection. At a further meeting on 16 October the vote was again in favour of insurrection, this time by 19 to 2, but very little progress had been made with the planning. Although the party had adopted the principle of insurrection, there was still a strong feeling at this point that there would not be much support outside the big cities for a purely Bolshevik uprising. The majority view was to wait until the Second All Russia Congress of Soviets met on 20 October before a final decision was taken; if power was taken then, it would be in the name of the Soviets. But Lenin continued to argue that it was vital to seize power *before* the Congress met in case Kerensky took steps to prevent its meeting. Probably his real reason was so that Bolshevik control in the name of the Soviet could be presented as an accomplished fact. If power was transferred by a vote of the Congress, it would almost certainly be to a coalition of all the socialist parties. Two days later Kamenev and Zinoviev published an article in a left-wing newspaper, *Novaia zhizn* (New Life), explaining that they could not accept the idea of an uprising so soon. They advocated waiting until the Petrograd Soviet was ready to declare itself the new government, and expressed doubts as to whether the Bolsheviks could hold on to power alone, even if their armed *coup* succeeded. This infuriated Lenin: it not only showed that the Bolshevik leadership was divided, worse still it let out the secret that they were planning an armed insurrection.

This new crisis for the Bolsheviks served to precipitate events in their favour. The non-Bolshevik leaders postponed the opening of the All-Russia Congress of Soviets until 25 October to give their supporters time to get to Petrograd; but in fact it gave the Bolsheviks time to organize their *coup*. Kerensky took no action to restrain them and was reportedly hoping they would make a move so that he could crush them once and for all.

(b) The *coup* is launched

Lenin was determined to force the pace and found that Trotsky was willing to give him every support, even though the two men had not been on good terms for twelve years. Although it was Lenin who was the driving force behind the launching of the *coup*, it was Trotsky who planned and organized the details. They decided to act through the Military Revolutionary Committee of the Petrograd Soviet, a body formed on 12 October to organize the defence of Petrograd in case the Provisional Government decided to abandon the city to the Germans. Activists from the Bolshevik Military Organization went to talk to army units in and around Petrograd to explain the situation. On 21 October Trotsky himself addressed a large gathering of representatives of the Petrograd garrison at the Smolny Institute, and persuaded them to adopt a resolution supporting the Soviet against the forces of counter-revolution, by which he meant the Provisional Government (see Document E). On 23 October thousands of rifles were distributed to the Bolshevik Red Guards.

At this point Kerensky decided to take action to secure control of the capital. Troops were brought in to defend strategic points around the city; telephone lines to the Smolny Institute, the Bolshevik and Soviet headquarters, were cut and the Bolshevik press closed down. The Military Revolutionary Committee responded immediately, Kerensky's action enabling them to claim that they were defending democracy against the counter-revolution (see Document F). During the night of 24–25 October, Soviet forces consisting mainly of Red Guards and workers' militia, supported by some of the garrison troops, took control of the telephone exchange, post offices, railway stations, banks and the two bridges over the river Neva. There was hardly any resistance – the small numbers of government troops guarding these places were persuaded to disobey orders and hand over their arms (see Document G). Kerensky had underestimated the strength of support for the Bolsheviks and overestimated the reliability of the garrison, which, its commanders had assured him, were very much against a Bolshevik *coup*. In fact the vast majority of the garrison troops stayed neutral, unwilling to defend a government which had just reintroduced the death penalty for them. When Kerensky appealed for assistance to the military commanders at Mogilev, none was forthcoming. The members of the Provisional Government waited in vain in the Winter Palace for help to arrive.

While the action was taking place, Lenin came out of hiding and arrived at the Smolny Institute. At 10 am on 25 October he released a declaration to the press: 'The Provisional Government has been deposed. Government authority has passed into the hands of the organ of the Petrograd Soviet of Workers' and Soldiers' Deputies, the Military-Revolutionary Committee, which stands at the head of the Petrograd proletariat and garrison.' The Second All-Russia Congress of Soviets was due to begin in Petrograd later that same day, 25 October. Lenin planned to stage a sensational opening to the Congress, announcing the overthrow of the government and the arrest of the ministers. However, the Winter Palace was the only important building not yet under Soviet control. Here government troops put up more of a fight, and it wasn't until the late evening of 25 October that they eventually withdrew, after the cruiser *Aurora*, which was moored across the river Neva from the Palace, had fired a few shots, causing some slight damage. It was not exactly the dramatic and heroic event portrayed in Eisenstein's famous film *October*, made in 1927, but it was enough to achieve what the Bolsheviks wanted – the arrest of the Provisional Government. Only Kerensky escaped – he slipped out through a side entrance and drove off towards Pskov in a car belonging to the American embassy, flying the American flag.

The delay in capturing the Winter Palace spoiled Lenin's plan for a dramatic opening of the Congress of Soviets. The start was delayed for two hours and eventually they had to go ahead before the Palace had been taken. It was just after 3 am on the morning of 26 October that Kamenev was able to announce that the Palace had been occupied and that the ministers were under arrest. In the meantime some fierce arguments had taken place in the Congress. Of the 670 delegates, 300 were Bolsheviks, 193 SRs and 82 Mensheviks. A large majority of the delegates was in favour of forming a coalition government of all the socialist parties in the Soviet, and a leading Menshevik, Martov, made a proposal to this effect. However, just when it seemed that the proposal was about to be adopted, a large group of right-wing Mensheviks and SRs began to object. They protested that the *coup* had been a conspiracy organized and carried out by the Bolsheviks, in the name of the Soviets but behind the backs of all the other parties. If the Provisional Government was arrested, they argued, it would provoke civil war, and they demanded immediate talks with the government ministers. About 70 of them walked out of the hall in protest, which turned out to be a great mistake. Trotsky dismissed their arguments contemptuously: 'What has taken place is an insurrection, not a conspiracy,' he retorted; 'an insurrection of the popular masses was victorious and needs no justification. And now we are told: renounce your victory, make concessions, compromise. No, a compromise is no good here. To all those who have left and those who make proposals like these we must say "You are pitiful isolated individuals; you are bankrupts; your role is played out. Go where you belong from now on – into the dustbin of history".' At this, Martov and a group of his supporters also walked out of the conference.

When the Congress reconvened in the evening the Bolsheviks called for the transfer of power to the workers', soldiers' and peasants' Soviets throughout the country. Many of the non-Bolsheviks still expected that a standing committee elected by the Congress and including members from all the socialist parties would take over the central government. But all the walk-outs had played into the Bolsheviks' hands, and since they could count on the votes of the left SRs, they now had a comfortable majority in the Congress. It was announced that a new Council of People's Commissars had been formed consisting solely of Bolsheviks and with Lenin as its chairman. This was to be the new government of Russia – until the elections for the Constituent Assembly.

4.3   *Coup* or mass insurrection?

(a) The Soviet view

The official Soviet interpretation of events[12] was that the Bolshevik takeover was the result of pressure from a mass movement: workers, peasants and most of the soldiers and sailors – in fact a majority of the population – were attracted by the revolutionary policies of the Bolsheviks, hence the Bolshevik majorities in the Petrograd and Moscow Soviets and city councils, and in the factory committees. These policies included peace, land for the peasants, worker control, government by the Soviets and self-determination for the different nationalities. The party benefited from its complete unity, its strict discipline and its centralization. Lenin was a charismatic leader who inspired his party and the people; a brilliant propaganda campaign succeeded in converting the masses. Between February and October 1917 party membership rose from only 24,000 to around 350,000. When they were sure that the best moment had arrived, Lenin, together with Trotsky, planned and organized the seizure of power. The Bolsheviks were successful precisely because they had the support of a majority of the population. In only 16 out of 97 major centres did they have to use force in order to assert their authority. It was important for the Bolsheviks, or Communists, as they later called themselves, to emphasize the popular nature of the revolution because that gave the regime its legitimacy.

(b) The liberal view

Earlier Western historians never accepted the Soviet view, refusing to acknowledge that there was any significant popular support for the Bolsheviks. They were simply a minority group of professional revolutionaries whose efficient organization and ruthlessness enabled them make use of the chaos in Russia which they themselves had done so much to create. According to Adam Ulam, 'the Bolsheviks did not seize power in this year of revolutions. They picked it up. First autocracy, then democracy capitulated to the forces of anarchy. Any group of determined men could have done what the Bolsheviks did in Petrograd in October 1917: seize the few key points of the city and proclaim themselves the government.'[13] Other liberal historians claimed that whatever support the Bolsheviks did have came from the most ignorant levels of the population. These people were totally without political experience or understanding of what was happening; 'there was no such thing as mass political consciousness in Russia in 1917.'[14] They were easily taken in when the Bolsheviks offered them what they wanted, but in reality the party had never been genuinely democratic. This was proved beyond doubt by the way in which the Bolsheviks dealt with all opposition after they came to power, most notably when they disbanded the Constituent Assembly and introduced a dictatorship backed by terror.

Although revisionist research (see section 4.3(d)) has all but destroyed the traditional liberal interpretation, Richard Pipes has continued to pursue his own 'neo-liberal' or conservative interpretation. He almost ignores the role of the masses, and attributes the October revolution almost entirely to Lenin's overwhelming desire for power. In *The Russian Revolution 1899–1919* (1990), the first volume of his massive history of the revolutionary period, Pipes devotes 120 pages to the 'Bolshevik Bid for Power and the October *Coup*'. He makes scarcely any mention of the grievances and social concerns of the people or their contribution to the events leading up to the *coup*, except to deny their significance. He insists that the events of October were a classic *coup d'état* – the seizure of power by a small minority, carried out in such a way as to give the impression of a mass operation, but in reality without any participation by the masses. The demonstrations were not in the least spontaneous, and were actually organized by the Bolsheviks. Similarly, during the July Days the Bolsheviks brought to the Tauride Palace a large contingent of Putilov workers, and although the scene might have appeared to be spontaneous, it was closely organized by Bolshevik agents interspersed with the crowd. In the conclusion to his second volume, *Russia under the Bolshevik Regime 1919–1924* (1994), Pipes continues the same theme: 'Lenin rode to power on the anarchy which he did so much to promote. He promised every discontented group what it wanted...Lenin and Trotsky concealed their bid for one-party dictatorship with slogans calling for the transfer of power to the soviets and the Constituent Assembly, and they formalized it by a fraudulently convened Congress of Soviets.' He claims that most industrial workers and peasants had no interest in politics and that even if they had, 'industrial labor in Russia was numerically too insignificant to play a major role in revolution; they represented a mere 2 per cent of the population.' He points out that during the actual *coup*, the masses in Petrograd acted as spectators, ignoring Bolshevik appeals to storm the Winter Palace. Pipes is critical of revisionist professors and students, especially in the USA, who, he thinks, have spent too much time combing historical sources in the hope of finding evidence of worker radicalism. 'The results are weighty tomes, filled with mostly meaningless events and statistics, which prove that while history is always interesting, history books can be both vacuous and dull.'[15]

(c) The libertarian view

The libertarian view challenges both the Soviet and liberal interpretations of the Bolshevik success in October. Libertarians believe that the October revolution was the result of a popular uprising which had very little to do with the Bolsheviks. The masses were not responding to Bolshevik pressure but to their own aspirations and motivations – the peasants wanted land, industrial workers wanted better conditions, better treatment and the right to control their own lives; they had no need of the Bolsheviks to tell them these things. During the summer of 1917 their attitudes, particularly those of the industrial workers, became more sophisticated. The numbers of factory committees increased; according to Alexander Berkman 'the shop and factory committees were the pioneers in labour control of industry, with the prospect of themselves, in the near future, managing the industries entire.'[16] The peasants too had perfectly clear aims – a network of freely organized communes in which they owned all the land. The masses in fact were way ahead of the political parties most of the time and the only role of the Bolshevik leaders was to try and restrain them.

The tragedy was that the Bolsheviks muscled in on the popular revolution; they pretended that their aims were the same as those of the masses; they invented slogans which matched those of the masses; but in reality they distrusted the masses, especially the peasantry, and their aims were totally different. They had no intention of allowing factory committees to control actual production and they did not believe in genuine democracy and freedom. The masses had been strong enough to overthrow the autocracy in February, but in October, just as they were about to destroy the existing state and take power themselves, it was wrenched from their hands by the Bolsheviks.

(d) Revisionist views

Most revisionist historians tended to concentrate their researches on what was happening among ordinary people. In many ways their approach and some of their conclusions came close to those of the libertarians, though they drew on a much wider spectrum of evidence. Their conclusions were wide-ranging: peasants were not all primitive, illiterate animals – they *were* interested in events, in newspapers, in education and in a better future; and they were militant – throughout the summer of 1917 they were taking direct action on their own initiatives, not those of the Bolsheviks. Industrial workers too showed that their radical ideas were their own, not those of Bolshevik agitators; nor were they naive or utopian – in fact their behaviour 'suggests a working class which was both highly rational in its responses to the political and economic pressures of 1917 and extremely patient as well.'[17] Steve Smith showed that there was a growing political awareness among industrial workers in Petrograd, in the spring of 1917. They were involved in trade unions and Soviets; but increasingly they were active in factory committees. The aim of these committees, elected on the shop-floor, was to maintain production, in the face of attempts by employers to close the factories down; this, so the employers hoped, would deprive the workers of their income and cool their revolutionary ardour. The committees acted in a highly responsible way: they maintained discipline, organized guards to defend the factories at night, ordered raw materials, and made sure the management was not attempting to sabotage production. They were the very opposite of revolutionary anarchists, and were not trying to turn the factories into worker-communes. They were determined to keep the factories running throughout the economic crisis, and they often demanded that the government should help by nationalizing the plants.[18]

It was a similar story in Kronstadt, the island naval base about twenty miles off Petrograd. Kronstadt was in many ways a special case: it was a fortress and a town as well as a naval base; in 1917 it had a civilian population of 50,000, along with 20,000 soldiers and 12,000 sailors. The tensions there arose from brutal discipline, inadequate supplies of food and clothes and general exhaustion. Within a very short time of the February revolution, the Kronstadt Soviet of Workers' and Soldiers' Deputies had established itself as the central and sole authority. It encouraged a return to work and normality after the disturbances, abolished the death penalty and allowed soldiers and sailors to choose their own officers. Other decrees introduced minimum wages and an eight-hour working day, and provided for democratic elections. By May 1917 Kronstadt had virtually declared itself an independent republic. The Bolsheviks emerged as the largest group in the Kronstadt Soviet; it was their resolution, condemning 'this pernicious war', and in particular the Kerensky offensive, which in June was accepted by a huge majority, thus preparing the way for the July Days.[19] Clearly the role of the Bolsheviks was important, even though they were certainly not the unified and strictly disciplined party of the traditional Soviet view. Their great achievement in the summer of 1917 was to align themselves with the policies of the people throughout the country, to harness the support of the people, and then to judge the right time to use that support. Though relatively few in number, the Bolshevik members of the factory committees and Soviets were able to influence the rest, in the same way that the Menshevik members of trade unions were able to spread their ideas.

Richard Pipes's criticisms of the revisionists have not discouraged other historians from continuing to trawl the archives, especially the newly opened ones, for evidence about the experiences of ordinary people all over Russia, not just in Petrograd and Moscow. Christopher Read in his book *From Tsar to Soviets* (1996) examines what was happening in the villages, in the provinces, and in the army and navy during these revolutionary years. He deliberately subtitles the book *The Russian People and their Revolution, 1917–1921*, and he shows how peasants, workers, soldiers and sailors had serious economic and social grievances – they wanted to take control over their own lives, and by the autumn of 1917 they were convinced that the only way to achieve this was through a government of the Soviets. Read points out that the emergence of the network of Soviets all over Russia – 900 of them by October 1917 – was one of the great, original features of the revolution. For many workers, the trade unions and the factory committees 'became the engine-room of worker organization and of integration into political parties, which themselves showed enormous growth in 1917.' However, for most workers, the main motivation was what was happening to them in their immediate circumstances, where they lived and worked. Read looks at the massive Putilov factories in Petrograd, which by the summer of 1917 employed 31,000 workers producing mainly armaments. He shows that internal stresses in the factory coincided with outbursts of revolutionary activity in the city. In February there were serious strikes over wages, working conditions and heavy-handedness by foremen and overseers, and on 22 February the management closed the works. 'It is just possible,' Read argues, 'that the February revolution might not have taken place, at least in the way it did, were it not for the struggle going on inside the Putilov factory.' Similarly the violence of the July Days coincided with the government's rejection of a new wage and bonus scheme which had just been worked out, and 30,000 workers came out onto the streets. 'Leaders in the factory, including Bolsheviks, were still doing their utmost to stop the demonstrations, but to no effect. The workers' frustration was too intense and whatever influence the political parties had on them completely broke down.' Shortly before the October coup it had been announced that a third of the Putilov workforce were to be made redundant, a move which was justified by the Soviet newspaper *Izvestiya*. This betrayal by their own representatives – right-wing Mensheviks and SRs – was a stunning blow for the workers, reducing them to something close to resignation and apathy. But although they did not come out onto the streets to demonstrate in the vast numbers of February and July, they were sympathetic towards the Bolsheviks, as the election results show. Similar situations were occurring in other parts of Russia – among the miners of Ukraine and the textile workers of Ivanovo for example; workers, motivated by workplace tensions, were 'moving towards their own, local October revolution through the logic of events rather than as a result of organization and propaganda.'

On the question of the role of the peasants, Read believes that the experiences of 1917 'were a series of self-generating mini-revolutions.' Dramatic events like land seizures and cases of violence against landlords and officials were probably not as widespread as some writers have suggested, although they did take place. The first step was to organize peasant committees at district or *volost* level; these were an extension of the village commune, and although they rarely called themselves Soviets, they functioned in the same way as the urban Soviets. They were democratically elected and took the lead in trying to bring unsown land into cultivation, and in pressurizing landlords to reduce rents by withdrawing labour. Although there was no general violent uprising of peasants, there were some serious outbreaks. In September 1917, for example, after a landowner in Kozlov (Tambov province) had killed two peasants suspected of stealing his property, the local peasants launched a general attack on 57 landowners in the region. The authorities in Tambov sent troops to restore order, but it was only when reinforcements arrived from Moscow that the situation was brought under control, with the arrest of 1500 peasants. Yet although such dramatic incidents were fairly rare, over the country as a whole there was a massive change in the relations between landowners and peasants. 'Where peasants had been cowed into submission for decades ... they were quick to realize that the power of the major proprietors to defend their wealth and privilege was diminishing by the week.' The weakness of the government made it possible for the peasants to fulfil their most cherished ambition – the acquisition of the land by those who worked it. 'The rural revolution of 1917 was a formidable component of the many events that erupted in that tumultuous year.'

As for the military, many of their grievances were soon addressed, as we have seen; but when Kornilov became Commander-in-Chief, the death penalty was brought back. Read argues that the Kornilov Affair 'had an electric effect' on the army and navy. Reports soon began to come in from all fronts of worsening relations between officers and men, of 'waves of Bolshevism' and of calls for the handing over of power to the Soviets. The more the officers tried to tighten discipline, the more open the resistance became. There were widespread reports of refusal to obey orders, demands for peace and mass fraternization with enemy troops. This was the growing opposition to the Provisional Government that the Bolsheviks were able to harness. Read's conclusion is that 'the revolution was constantly driven forward by the often spontaneous impulse given to it from the grass roots.' Events at the centre in Petrograd obviously had a great impact in both February and October, but 'they should be seen against the background of grass roots and peripheral events ... it was only the profoundly revolutionary situation that made the October takeover possible. *Coup de grace* it certainly was but it was too deeply linked with the broader situation to be considered a *coup d'état* in the true sense of the word.'[20]

Robert Service goes along with the notion of a combination of events at the centre of politics and events taking place among the masses – he calls it 'a process of dynamic interaction.' He stresses the contribution of Lenin himself; there can be no doubt that Lenin wanted power and used the already potentially revolutionary situation brilliantly. He cleverly manipulated public opinion and adopted slogans which he knew would appeal to the masses – slogans like 'All Power to the Soviets' and 'Land, Peace and Bread'. These fitted in well with workers' and soldiers' ideas of democracy based on the network of Soviets, in which local Soviets would govern on a decentralized basis. At the same time Lenin kept quiet about parts of the Bolshevik programme which might lose him support among the masses; as Service puts it in his most recent book about Lenin, 'he was keeping his political cards close to his chest. He was a party boss, and wanted Bolshevism to be attractive to those workers, peasants, soldiers and intellectuals who had not yet supported it. And so terms such as dictatorship, terror, civil war and revolutionary war were quietly shelved...his every pronouncement was directed towards encouraging the "masses" to exercise initiative. His wish was for the Bolsheviks to appear as a party that would facilitate the making of Revolution by and for the people.'[21] And indeed this seems to be exactly what happened. The aims and concerns of the great mass of ordinary people coincided with the carefully chosen slogans of the Bolsheviks. The Bolsheviks did have popular backing, even though it was fairly passive, for their October *coup*, because the popular movement thought it was going to get government by the Soviets. In reality therefore, the coincidence of aims between the party and the people was very shortlived. Although some of the hopes of the masses were achieved, it wasn't long before disappointment with the way the new regime was developing was to lead to civil war.

In the end the seizure of power by the Bolsheviks turned out to be remarkably straightforward – the Provisional government could find no forces of any significance who were prepared to fight for it, and there was hardly any real resistance. It was 'like picking up a feather' as Lenin put it later. But no matter how favourable the circumstances were, it still needed that small group of people with the nerve and the resolve to use the situation. That was the contribution of Lenin and Trotsky – they judged to perfection the point of maximum unpopularity of the Provisional Government and then they actually 'made' the revolution happen. It would not have been possible without the popular movement – it was the popular movement which determined that there would be so little resistance to the Bolsheviks. But equally, it would not have been possible without Lenin and Trotsky. As Trotsky himself put it: 'If neither Lenin nor I had been present in Petersburg, there would have been no October Revolution; the leadership of the Bolshevik Party would have prevented it from occurring – of this I have not the slightest doubt! If Lenin had not been in Petersburg I doubt whether I could have managed to conquer the resistance of the Bolshevik leaders.'[22]

Documents

Problems of the Provisional Government

(A) The Order No. 1 of the Petrograd Soviet which appeared in *Izvestiya* on 2 March 1917.

To the garrison of the Petrograd Military District, to all soldiers of the guard, army, artillery and fleet for immediate and exact execution, and to all the workers of Petrograd for their information. The Soviet of Workers' and Soldiers' Deputies has decreed:

Committees are to be elected immediately in all companies, battalions, regiments, batteries, squadrons...and in all naval vessels, from the elected representatives of the lower ranks of the above-mentioned units...

The orders of the military commission of the State Duma shall be executed only in such cases as they do not conflict with the orders and resolutions of the Soviet of Workers' and Soldiers' Deputies.

All types of arms, such as rifles, machine-guns, armoured automobiles and others, must be kept at the disposal of company and battalion committees, and under their control, and must in no case be turned over to officers, even upon demand.

When off duty, in their political, civil and private lives, soldiers should enjoy fully and completely the same rights as all citizens. In particular, standing at attention and compulsory saluting when off duty are abolished.

The addressing of officers with the titles 'Your Excellency', 'Your Honour', and the like, is abolished, and these titles are replaced by the address of 'Mr General', Mr Colonel', and so forth. Rudeness towards soldiers of any rank is prohibited . . .

Source: G. Vernadsky and others, *A Source Book of Russian History*, vol. 3, p. 882.

(B) General Brusilov's visit to a division which had just thrown out its officers and was threatening to go home – June 1917.

When I arrived at their camp I demanded to speak to a delegation of the soldiers: it would have been dangerous to appear before the whole crowd. When these arrived I asked them which party they belonged to, and they replied that before they had been Socialist Revolutionaries, but that now they supported the Bolsheviks. 'What do you want?' I asked them. 'Land and Freedom,' they all cried. 'And what else?' The answer was simple: 'Nothing else!' When I asked them what they wanted now, they said that they did not want to fight any more and pleaded to be allowed to go home in order to share out the land their fellow villagers had taken from the squires and live in freedom. And when I asked them: 'What will happen to Mother Russia if no one wants to defend it, and everyone like you only thinks of themselves?' they replied that it was not their job to think about what should become of the state, and that they had firmly decided to go home.

Source: quoted in Figes, p. 416.

(C) After his dismissal by Kerensky, General Kornilov sent the following message to all commanders and to the Russian people, 27 August 1917.

The telegram of the Prime Minister [stating that Kornilov had demanded supreme power for himself] is an out-and-out lie.

Russian people: our great homeland is dying! The moment of death is near! Forced to speak out publicly, I, General Kornilov, declare that the Provisional

(continued)

Government, under pressure from the Bolshevik majority in the Soviet, acts in full accord with the plans of the German General Staff and, concurrently with the imminent landings of enemy forces on the coast of Riga, destroys the army and convulses the country from within . . .

I, General Kornilov, the son of a Cossack peasant, declare to each and all that I personally desire nothing except to save Great Russia. I swear to lead people to victory over the enemy to the Constituent Assembly, where it will decide its own destiny and choose its new political system.

Source: quoted in Pipes, pp. 459–60.

Lenin and the October Revolution

(D) Report on the First All-Russia Congress of Soviets, June 1917, by an English observer, M. Philips Price.

There now arose from an obscure corner of the room a thick-set little man with a round bald head and small Tartar eyes. He was leading a small group of delegates who had set themselves down on the extreme left and at the back of the hall. Nobody seemed to pay much attention to the corner where they sat . . . But as soon as this short thick-set little man rose and strode with firm step, and even firmer look upon his countenance, up the gangway, a hush came upon the whole assembly. For it was Lenin, the leader of that small Bolshevik minority at this Congress. No uncertain words came from his lips. Straight to the point he went from the first moment of his speech and pursued his opponents with merciless logic. 'Where are we?' he began, stretching out his short arms and looking questioningly at his audience. 'What is this Council of Workers' and Soldiers' Delegates? Is there anything like it anywhere else in the world? No, of course not, because nothing so absurd as this exists in any country today except in Russia. Then let us have either one of two things: either a bourgeois government with its plans of so-called social reforms on paper, or let us have that government which *you* [pointing to Tsereteli – a Menshevik leader] seem to long for, but which you apparently have not the courage to bring into existence, a government of the proletariat . . .'

Source: M. Philips Price, *My Reminiscences of the Russian Revolution*, p. 44.

(E) Resolution by representatives of the Petrograd garrison at the Smolny Institute on 21 October 1917.

Endorsing all political decisions of the Petrograd Soviet, the garrison declares: the time for words has passed. The country is on the verge of ruin. The army demands peace, the peasants demand land, and the workers demand bread and work. The Coalition Government is against the people. It became the tool of the enemies of the people. The All-Russia Congress of Soviets must take the power into its own hands in order to give to the people peace, land and bread. Only thus can the safety of the revolution and of the people be ensured. The Petrograd garrison solemnly pledges itself to put at the disposal of the All Russian Congress all its forces, to the last man, to fight for these demands. Rely on us . . . we are at our posts, ready to conquer or die.

Source: Quoted in Isaac Deutscher, *The Prophet Armed: Trotsky 1879–1921*, pp. 304–5.

(F) Trotsky describes the beginning of the October *coup.*

An attempt to suppress the papers, a resolution to prosecute the Military Revolutionary Committee, an order removing commissars, the cutting-off of Smolny's telephones – these pinpricks were just sufficient to convict the government of preparing a counter-revolutionary *coup d'état*. Although an insurrection can win only on the offensive, it develops better the more it looks like self-defence. A piece of official sealing wax on the door of the Bolshevik editorial rooms – as a military measure that is not much. But what a superb signal for battle! Telephonograms to all districts and units of the garrison announced the event: 'The enemy of the people took the offensive during the night. The Military Revolutionary Committee is leading the resistance to the assault of the conspirators.' The conspirators – these were the institutions of the official government.

The *Aurora* in the Neva meant not only an excellent fighting unit in the service of the insurrection, but a radio station ready for use. Invaluable advantage! The *Aurora*'s radio broadcast that the counter-revolution had taken the offensive, and the garrisons guarding the approaches to Petrograd were ordered by radio to hold up the counter-revolutionary echelons. It was a question of taking full possession of Petrograd in the next twenty-four hours.

Source: Leon Trotsky, *The History of the Russian Revolution*, pp. 1055–7.

(G) A report from General Polkovnikov, the Military Commander in Petrograd, to army headquarters, 25 October 1917.

The situation in Petrograd is menacing. There are no street disorders, but a systematic seizure of government buildings and railway stations is going on. None of my orders is obeyed. The cadets surrender their posts almost without resistance, and the Cossacks, who were repeatedly ordered to come out refused to do so. I must report, conscious of my responsibility to the country, that the Provisional Government is in danger. There is no guaranty that the insurrectionists will not next attempt to arrest the Provisional Government.

Source: quoted in R.W. Clark, *Lenin, The Man behind the Mask*, pp. 270–1.

Notes

1. Richard Pipes, *The Russian Revolution, 1899–1919*, pp. 419–31.
2. Alexander Rabinowitch, *Prelude to Bolshevism: the Petrograd Bolsheviks and the July 1917 Uprising*, pp. 174–6.
3. Robert Service, *Lenin: A Biography*, p. 284.
4. See L.C. Heenan, *Russian Democracy's Fateful Blunder: The Summer Offensive of 1917*, for a development of this theory.
5. Allan Wildman, 'The Breakdown of the Imperial Army in 1917', in Acton, Cherniaev and Rosenberg (editors), *Critical Companion to the Russian Revolution 1914–1921*, pp. 70–1. See also his great two-volume, massively detailed work *The End of the Russian Imperial Army*, vol. 2, pp. 73–111.
6. Norman Stone, *The Eastern Front, 1914–1917*, p. 284. See pp. 282–301 for a detailed analysis of the economic chaos.
7. R. Abraham, *Alexander Kerensky: The First Love of the Revolution* is a good biography.
8. See George Katkov, *The Kornilov Affair: Kerensky and the Break-up of the Russian Army* for a detailed account.
9. Christopher Read, *From Tsar to Soviets*, p. 56.
10. Pipes, pp. 451–64.
11. Steve Smith, 'Factory Committees', in Acton, Cherniaev and Rosenberg (editors), *Critical Companion to the Russian Revolution 1914–1921*, pp. 352–3. See also his *Red Petrograd: Revolution in the Factories, 1917–1918*, for a detailed analysis of Petrograd factory committees and trade unions. Also useful is D. Mandel, *The Petrograd Workers and the Soviet Seizure of Power*.
12. Edward Acton, *Rethinking the Russian Revolution*, and Acton, Cherniaev and Rosenberg (editors), *Critical Companion to the Russian Revolution* are extremely helpful for a survey of the different interpretations.
13. Adam Ulam, *Lenin and the Bolsheviks*, p. 409.
14. Roger Pethybridge, *The Spread of the Russian Revolution. Essays on 1917*, p. 196.
15. Pipes, *The Russian Revolution 1899–1919*, pp. 385, 428; *Russia under the Bolshevik Regime 1919–1924*, pp. 494, 498.
16. Alexander Berkman, *The Russian Tragedy*, p. 58.
17. Diane Koenker, *Moscow Workers and the 1917 Revolution*, p. 359.
18. Steve Smith, *Red Petrograd: Revolution in the Factories, 1917–1918*, pp. 65–8, 80–98, 139–67.
19. Israel Getzler, *Kronstadt 1917–1921*, pp. 29–40, 66, 81, 109–10.
20. Read, pp. 5, 65, 68–71, 102–3, 117–18, 140–2.
21. Robert Service, *Lenin: A Biography*, p. 315.
22. Leon Trotsky, *Diary in Exile*, p. 54.

◼ ⌄ 5 Lenin and the Bolsheviks in power, 1917–24

Summary of events

Although the Bolsheviks took control easily enough in Petrograd, in the name of the Soviets, it was more difficult in Moscow; there was fierce house-to-house fighting and they had to use artillery fire to capture the Kremlin. Other cities soon came under Bolshevik control, but in the rural areas they had only limited influence, and most of the non-Russian provinces looked on the Bolshevik takeover as a chance to assert their independence. In fact very few people, including some of the Bolshevik leaders themselves, expected the new government to last very long. It faced enormous problems, and the new ministers, or 'commissars' as they called themselves, had spent so much time thinking about revolution that they had no clearly thought out plans ready.

Early Bolshevik reforms

Whether or not they could stay in power depended very much on whether they could deliver what they had been promising – **peace, land and bread** – and whether they could put the economy right. There could hardly have been a more testing and desperate time for a new government to take over. They began right away – during an all-night session of the Congress of Soviets on 26–27 October **Lenin announced their first decrees:**

- Negotiations for peace were to begin immediately with Germany and her allies and there was to be no more secret diplomacy.
- Land owned by landlords and the church was to be confiscated without compensation and handed over to village Soviets for the time being – final arrangements would be made by the Constituent Assembly, but it was understood that the land would be redistributed among the peasants. Official Bolshevik policy was for the land to be nationalized (taken over by the state), so this was a concession to win the support of the peasants.
- A third decree set up the new government of 15 commissars (ministers), known as the Council of People's Commissars (Sovnarkom), with Lenin as chairman, Trotsky as Commissar for Foreign Affairs, and Stalin as Chairman for Nationality Affairs.

The Left Socialist Revolutionaries join the government

But there were tensions between the Bolsheviks and the other socialist groups: Lenin had invited the Left SRs to join the government but they refused; they wanted all shades of SR and Menshevik opinion to be represented in a coalition of all the left-wing parties; but Lenin was determined that the Bolsheviks should exercise power alone. This problem was eventually resolved for the time being when three Left SRs agreed to join Sovnarkom. There were also disagreements over policy within the Bolshevik Central Committee: for example, was industry the property of the people or the state? What was to be the role of trade unions and factory committees now that a 'dictatorship of the proletariat' was in operation? Was the land to be the property of the peasants who worked it or was it going to be nationalized?

November 1917: Constituent Assembly election
The first big milestone was the election for the Constituent Assembly on 12 November. The results were disappointing for the Bolsheviks who came second with 175 seats out of a total of 717; the Socialist Revolutionaries led by Viktor Chernov emerged as easily the largest single party with 370 seats.

January 1918: end of the Constituent Assembly
But Lenin had no intention of letting the SRs take power and the Constituent Assembly was dissolved at gunpoint after only one day and one all-night sitting (5–6 January 1918); it never met again. The justification for this was that the Assembly must take second place to the Congress of Soviets and Sovnarkom.

January–March 1918: the struggle for peace and the Treaty of Brest–Litovsk
The stream of decrees setting up the 'new socialist order' (including the nationalization of banks and industry) continued to flow and peace negotiations with the Central Powers got under way at Brest–Litovsk in Poland. For much of the time the Russian delegation was led by Trotsky; a cease-fire had been agreed on 23 November, but progress was slow and German demands were harsh. There was fierce argument in Russia about whether or not to accept the terms, but the Russians were desperate for peace, and it was decided that the sacrifice had to be made. **The Treaty of Brest–Litovsk, ratified on 16 March 1918, was humiliating for Russia, depriving her of a vast area of land and 55 million people.**

The drift toward Civil War
The government was becoming increasingly unpopular; peace had been secured but the cost was high, and every one of the new decrees caused resentment in some quarter or other. During May and June the Bolsheviks began to lose their majorities in the big urban Soviets, but used force to keep control. **The SRs and the Mensheviks came out in open resistance** and Lenin narrowly survived two assassination attempts. With the help of their new secret police, **the Cheka,** the Bolsheviks turned more and more to violence, terror and extreme measures to keep themselves in power; in the summer of 1918 uprisings staged by SRs were ruthlessly dealt with: there were hundreds of arrests and over a thousand people were executed.

1918–20: Civil War (Reds against Whites)
Meanwhile the anti-Bolshevik forces, who became known as the Whites, were beginning to gather themselves together in several areas – major armies were

Figure 5.1   Bolshevik Civil War poster: 'Kazak! Whose side are you on? Ours or theirs?'

formed in Siberia, the Caucasus and Estonia. By the summer of 1918 the country was in the grip of a full-scale Civil War; White armies advanced on Moscow (now the capital) from the south, the east and the north-west. Britain, France, the USA and Japan sent troops to help the Whites, and the Reds seemed in a hopeless position. In July the Tsar and his family were murdered to prevent them being rescued by the Whites and used as a focus of opposition to the Bolsheviks. In reality, though, the Bolsheviks had all the advantages; the Red Army was successfully reorganized by Trotsky, who was now the Commissar for War; and an effective new policy known as **War Communism** was introduced. This extended state control over the entire economy, and included requisitioning grain from the peasants. The Bolsheviks were able to defeat the White armies one by one; but it wasn't until November 1920 that the Civil War formally ended.

1920–21 – War between Russia and Poland ended in defeat for Russia.

1921 – Russia devastated after the Civil War
After six years of almost non-stop war, Russia, or what was left of it, was in a state of complete chaos:

- The economy was in a state of collapse, industrial and agricultural production had fallen alarmingly and the peasants were resentful of War Communism and the government's grain requisitioning policy.
- During 1921 and 1922 there were constant famines and epidemics.
- In some places, open revolt broke out; the most disturbing one for the Bolsheviks took place in March 1921 when there was **a mutiny of the 15,000 soldiers and sailors who made up the garrison of Kronstadt**; they were joined by several thousand workers from Petrograd who crossed over to the island to lend their support. These people had been the Bolsheviks' strongest supporters in 1917, but now they denounced the government as 'enemies of the people'. Once again force was used to restore order; many former Bolshevik supporters were outraged that the Red Army had fired on 'the heroes of the revolution', as Trotsky had earlier described them.

1921: The New Economic Policy (NEP) brings concessions and a mixed economy
Soon after the Kronstadt rising Lenin began to change his approach to the economy. The New Economic Policy (NEP) was brought in, dropping the requisitioning of grain, allowing private trading and handing back smaller firms to private ownership. There was **a general move away from complete state control of the economy towards a mixed economy in which there were elements of capitalism and socialism**. Many of the leading Bolsheviks were unhappy about this trend, seeing it as an unacceptable departure from Marxism. However, Nikolai Bukharin supported Lenin strongly and the new policy went ahead. Statistics suggest that by 1924 the NEP had helped to bring about an economic revival, though it was far from being a magic solution to all the problems of the economy.

1921–22: Political control tightens
Although Lenin was willing to make concessions on the economy, he kept firm political control:

- At the same time as NEP was introduced, another resolution entitled 'on party unity' tightened discipline by banning factions within the party.
- In 1922 all other political parties except the Communist Party (as the Bolsheviks were now called) were banned and hundreds of Kadets and Mensheviks were deported from Russia.

- The government redoubled its efforts to influence people's minds through popular culture and tried to create a new 'Soviet man and woman'.
- At the same time Lenin was sympathetic to the non-Russian nationalities and wanted them to have some elements of self-government. Over this question Lenin clashed with Stalin who was a Russian nationalist and wanted the Russians to be dominant.
- **USSR comes into existence** – on the last day of 1922 a new constitution was ratified; it began to go into operation immediately and the Soviet state became the Union of Soviet Socialist Republics (USSR). Seemingly against all the odds, Bolshevik power had been maintained and consolidated; all the vital elements of a one-party dictatorship were now in place.

January 1924: Death of Lenin

By the end of 1922 when the new constitution was ratified, Lenin was a sick man; he suffered a stroke in May 1922 and another more serious one in December. After this he had less and less influence on the course of events and a third stroke in March 1923 left him paralysed and unable to speak. He died on 21 January 1924. During his last months, one of his greatest disappointments was that the revolution in Russia had still not been followed by successful proletarian revolutions anywhere else.

Lenin's premature death leaves many unresolved questions:

- The vital dilemma for the communist government was: should they continue to try to bring about world revolution or concentrate on developing socialism in one country – Russia? This problem left Soviet foreign policy full of contradictions – on the one hand Russian communists working with other European communist parties in an organization known as the Communist International were trying to provoke revolutions, while on the other hand the Russian government was trying to get economic help from the very countries they were trying to destabilize.
- Would NEP continue for the foreseeable future?
- Who was to be Lenin's successor? Or would there be a collective leadership?
- Would there be a relaxation on the political front with the emergence of a genuinely democratic socialist system?

Main areas of debate:

- **Did the Bolsheviks have any real popularity or was it simply violence and terror that kept them in power?**
- **Did Lenin have violent intentions from the beginning or was he pushed into these policies by the difficult circumstances?**
- **Were the Bolsheviks militarized and brutalized by the civil war or were they like that all along?**
- **Were they any worse than previous regimes in their use of repression and terror?**

(continued)

- Was NEP just a temporary retreat from strict Marxism or, as Bukharin believed, a policy that 'must be followed seriously and for a long time'?
- How important was Lenin's contribution to the events of 1917–23?
- Did Lenin genuinely believe in the 'dictatorship of the proletariat' or was he an evil genius whose main concern was his lust for personal power?

5.1 The political situation – the Constituent Assembly

(a) Coalition or not?

The main political issue facing Lenin was that the Second All-Russia Congress of Soviets was under the impression that the new government was a Soviet regime, not a purely Bolshevik one. The Mensheviks and Socialist Revolutionaries were hoping to join a coalition government of all the socialist parties, though they had few illusions about Lenin's intentions. Some of the leading Bolsheviks, including Lev Kamenev, Grigori Zinoviev and Alexei Rykov, tried to reason with Lenin that this was the right democratic course and that the Bolsheviks could only survive as part of a coalition. Lenin was unmoved: he had very little time for the Mensheviks and SRs since they had compromised themselves by entering a coalition with the Kadets, and he believed that if he allowed them a share of the power, they would prevent him from carrying out the full Bolshevik programme.

The forces of the right too must be kept under control and at the end of October a strict press censorship was brought back; this was ostensibly intended to close down the right-wing and liberal press, but could also be used against any socialist newspaper if necessary. However, the SRs had wide support among the peasants, and the railway workers' union wanted a coalition and threatened to go on strike unless one was formed. This could be serious – food and fuel supplies to the capital and other cities would be held up and the already chaotic situation would become much worse. Kamenev had discussions with Menshevik, SR and union representatives and at one point actually agreed to a plan for a socialist coalition, but excluding Lenin and Trotsky.

Lenin and Trotsky, supported by Stalin, soon dealt with that problem – there was a decisive confrontation with Kamenev at a Bolshevik Central Committee meeting early in November in which Kamenev was left in no doubt about what was going to happen: there would be no socialist coalition and he and his supporters would be expelled from the party unless they agreed. After a browbeating from Lenin, Kamenev and his four strongest supporters – Zinoviev, Rykov, Miliutin and Nogin – resigned from the party Central Committee. It seemed as though the Bolsheviks were fatally divided and most people thought their days in power were numbered. But support came from the left wing of the SRs who were now functioning more or less as a separate party from the Right SRs. The Left SRs were happy with the Bolsheviks' land decree which was the basic item of their programme and they were prepared to go along with Bolshevik policies in the hope of moderating them and achieving more of their own programme. Three Left SRs were allowed to join Sovnarkom and five others were given lesser jobs, but the

Bolsheviks kept all the most important posts; according to Orlando Figes, 'the Left SRs were really no more than a fig-leaf used by Lenin to conceal the nakedness of his dictatorship.'[1] But it was enough to mollify the trade unions, and the threat of a railway strike was removed. As for the five moderates who had resigned from the Central Committee, they all lacked the leadership qualities and the ruthlessness to form a breakaway party, and by the end of November 1917 they had capitulated to Lenin's will. The Bolshevik party was united and surviving.

(b) Bolshevik power extended

The first few weeks brought other problems for the Bolsheviks: there was a strike of civil servants protesting against their seizure of power; the post and telegraph office workers did their best to be unco-operative, and the State Bank refused to release any funds. Even teachers and pharmacists went on strike. Finally on 17 November a detachment of troops accompanied by a military band was used to take control of the bank and forcibly remove the necessary funds. Eyewitnesses remarked that it was more like a bank hold-up than a government taking what it was legally entitled to. Little by little the government was able to extend its control: some strike leaders and hostile civil service chiefs were arrested and replaced by Bolshevik sympathisers. It was announced that in the countryside power now rested in the hands of the local Soviets, while in industrial areas factory committees were given the right to supervise the management, thereby making the concept of 'worker control' a reality. In this way the old pre-revolutionary administrative and control systems would be destroyed.

Sovnarkom acted as the government, taking precedence over the Executive of the Congress of Soviets, and a whole stream of new decrees and resolutions poured out. National self-determination was offered to the non-Russian peoples of the Empire, and in particular Finland and Poland were promised complete independence. Lenin hoped that this would encourage revolutions leading to Soviet governments in these regions. The new Soviet states would then voluntarily join Russia to form a huge multi-national Soviet state. Turning to the workers, as well as the decree on workers' control, there was to be a maximum eight-hour working day, free education for all children, and full civil and religious rights for all citizens. Sovarnakom was given the authority to regulate industry, agriculture, trade and banking, and all banks were nationalized. During December 1917 the government took control of some of the larger factories.

Much of this was popular – it was the sort of programme designed to help the working class that the Bolsheviks had been promising before October. One move which had not been talked about earlier was the creation in early December of an Extraordinary Commission to root out counter-revolution; soon to be known as the Cheka, this organization was not subject to ordinary legal procedures. Under its ruthless leader, Felix Dzerzhinsky, a Polish communist, it became a huge organization whose function was to look after state security. Its members were instructed to use their revolutionary consciences and take whatever action was deemed necessary to protect the revolution. This soon degenerated into a campaign of mass terror. In December 1917 all this was still in the future, and not many people at the time realized the significance of the Cheka's creation. The attention of the country at large was focused on something else – the elections for the Constituent Assembly which began on 12 November and were spread out over two weeks. It was confidently expected among the opposition parties that the election results and the meeting of the Assembly would see the end of the Bolshevik regime.

(c) The Constituent Assembly comes and goes

Kerensky had fixed 12 November as the starting date for the elections, so the Bolsheviks, having continually criticized the Provisional Government for post-poning them, could hardly put them off again.[2] Lenin was afraid that the Bolsheviks would lose the election; it was one thing for them to win majorities in the Soviets and in the Congress of Soviets, where only workers and soldiers had the vote; but when the peasants and all the rest of the population voted, the most likely winners were the SRs. The election was the most democratic and free that the country had ever seen – everybody aged 20 and over, both men and women, was allowed to vote. It proved to be the last free election until 1993. Lenin's fears were justified: the Bolsheviks came a poor second to the SRs. The full figures were:

Socialist Revolutionaries	370	(16 million votes)
Bolsheviks	175	(10 million votes)
Left Socialist Revolutionaries	40	
Mensheviks	16	
Kadets	17	
Various national groups	80	

Under a Western-style democratic system the SRs would have been expected to form a government, with their leader, Viktor Chernov, as Prime Minister. How-ever, Lenin, supported by all the leading Bolsheviks and the Left SRs, had decided to ignore the election results and get rid of the Constituent Assembly as soon as possible. Having made a good start, as they saw it, on setting up the workers' state, they were not prepared to see it threatened by a Constituent Assembly full of Right SRs with their bourgeois tendencies. Sovnarkom agreed that the Assembly should be allowed to meet in January 1918 but that it should be sent packing soon after its first meeting.

How could this apparently undemocratic decision be justified? To begin with, the Bolsheviks claimed that the arrangements for the elections, which had been made by the Provisional Government, were flawed, because in the majority of areas the ballot papers did not distinguish between Left and Right SRs. This pre-vented peasants who were pleased with Lenin's land decree from voting specific-ally for Left SRs, whose main support was among younger peasants who had served in the army and navy. The argument was that if the split in the SR party had been clearly shown on the ballot papers, the Left SRs, who were still allies of the Bolsheviks, would have won many more than 40 seats, and the Right SRs correspondingly fewer. Some of the SR representatives were non-Russians, and it was by no means certain that they would vote with the Russian SR group. In fact it is doubtful whether the SRs would have been able to muster an overall majority in the Assembly. Given that the Bolsheviks held a majority in the Soviets of all the big urban industrial areas, the SRs would have found it extremely difficult to govern the country.

In several of his writings around this time Lenin justified the rejection of parliamentary democracy. He argued that there were two forms of democracy: *bourgeois democracy* which was exercised through a parliament elected by the whole country, and *revolutionary democracy* which was exercised by the Soviets elected by working people – the majority of the population. Soviet democracy was a higher form of democracy than parliamentary democracy because it abolished exploitation of the workers by the ruling class. The exploiters had enjoyed their day – now it was time for the workers to enjoy their form of democracy. The Bolsheviks had never claimed to represent the whole population – they had seized power in the name of the working class. The dictatorship of the proletariat meant the workers overthrowing and smashing the remnants of the old capitalist system, which included parliaments dominated by the bourgeoisie and their 'hirelings' and 'accomplices' (SRs and Mensheviks). Lenin also quoted a speech made in 1903 by Plekhanov, the founder of Russian Social Democracy, who said:

'The success of the revolution is the supreme law. And if, for the sake of the revolution, it should become necessary to restrict the action of one or another democratic principle, then it would be criminal not to do so . . . one must view even the principle of the universal vote as one such fundamental principle of democracy . . . one can conceive of a situation where we Social Democrats would oppose the universal vote. If in an outburst of revolutionary enthusiasm the people elect a very good parliament, then we should try to prolong it; but if the elections turned out unfavourably, then we should try to disperse the parliament – not in two years, but, if possible, in two weeks.'[3]

Meanwhile supporters of the Assembly formed a Union for the Defence of the Constituent Assembly and on 28 November held an impressive demonstration outside the Tauride Palace. The Bolsheviks responded by banning the Kadet party and arresting a number of its leaders. On the opening day, 5 January 1918, the Tauride Palace was surrounded by thousands of reliable government troops armed with machine-guns and artillery (see Document A). An unarmed demonstration in support of the Assembly was fired on by Red Guards positioned on rooftops, and at least ten protesters were killed. When the opening session of the Assembly eventually got under way the SRs, as the largest party, attempted to begin the discussions but were shouted down by the Bolshevik deputies and by some of the soldiers who were there to 'keep order'. They succeeded in getting Chernov elected as chairman, but then the Bolsheviks introduced a Declaration of the Rights of Working People, one of the clauses of which required the Assembly to renounce its authority to pass laws. Naturally the SRs could not accept this and they were able to defeat it by a large majority. However, this was what the

Bolsheviks had been angling for: it enabled them to claim that the Assembly had been hi-jacked by 'counter-revolutionaries'. The Bolsheviks walked out of the session and at a separate meeting chaired by Lenin it was decided that this was the time to dissolve the Assembly. Lenin gave orders that the Red Guards should allow the session to continue for a time and that force must not be used. At just after 4 o'clock in the morning on 6 January the commander of the guard informed Chernov that the guards were tired and the session must end. At 4.40 am the deputies filed out at gun-point; when they returned next day the Tauride Palace was locked and they were told that the Assembly had been dissolved. And that was the end of it. Two days later the Third All-Russian Congress of Soviets opened; the Bolsheviks and Left SRs had a huge majority in this assembly which proceeded to approve all the recent new decrees. It recognized Sovnarkom as the legitimate government and announced that Russia was to be known as the Russian Soviet Socialist Republic.

Surprisingly perhaps, there was no violent reaction to this unceremonious closure of the Constituent Assembly; and yet it isn't difficult to explain (see Document B). Chernov and the SRs were not prepared to use force against the Bolsheviks at this stage, arguing that they 'must proceed by legal means alone.' Most of the action was taking place in Petrograd and Moscow where much of the Bolsheviks' support was concentrated. The main SR supporters, the peasants, were getting what they most wanted – the redistribution of the land through their local Soviets – and they seemed not to care whether the government in distant Petrograd was the Constituent Assembly or not. The Assembly's strongest sup-porters, the intelligentsia, had very little military strength to call on and so for the time being there was no serious challenge to the developing Bolshevik dictator-ship. Lenin could feel pleased with progress so far, although there was no room for complacency; two big problems remained: a peace settlement had not been reached, and the economy was still in crisis.

5.2   Land and economic problems

(a) The Bolsheviks and the land

The Bolsheviks' second decree ordered that land should be taken from land-owners, the church, monasteries, the state and the monarchy without com-pensation, together with livestock and farm equipment, and handed over to the local Soviets, for redistribution among the peasants. During the following three months, the vast majority of this land was taken and redistributed to members of the village commune according to their needs – the larger the family, the more land they received. Orlando Figes has carried out a detailed analysis of what happened in Saratov province around the river Volga, some 500 miles south-east of Moscow.[4] He discovered that the Saratov peasants also took over farms belonging to those who had separated from the communes as a result of Stolypin's policies (see section 2.4(a)). In fact some of these so-called 'separators' beat them to it by voluntarily coming back into the commune in the hope of getting a share of the spoils taken from the wealthy landowners. On the whole the peasants in Saratov province did well out of the land redistribution, on average doubling the size of their individual holdings.

Although the peasants had at last achieved their greatest wish – and with the encouragement of the government – the redistribution of land brought fresh problems. The big estates and the 'separator' farms which had been broken up were the most efficient units in the agricultural system. Russia was now dependent for its food supply and its main export commodity on some 25 million smallholders working tiny plots and using the traditional, less efficient methods of the peasant commune. It was inevitable that grain output would fall and that there were going to be serious food shortages. These developments caused great controversy within the Bolshevik party. The traditional Bolshevik land policy had been to end private ownership, to bring all the land under state control and to reorganize it into large collective farms. This would enable modern farming methods and mechanization to be used on a large scale; although individual peasants would not actually own a separate piece of land, overall productivity would be much higher and the whole community would be much better off. Many of the leading Bolsheviks thought that Lenin was completely misguided to allow the peasants a free hand with the land redistribution; but he rightly pointed out that there was very little the government could do in those early months to resist almost the entire peasant population. Lenin argued that it was a temporary tactical retreat. He believed that broadly speaking there were two classes of peasants: the majority, like the industrial working classes, were poor; the better-off peasants, known as *kulaks*, were seen by Lenin as enemies of socialism, who would resist the setting-up of collective farms. He seems to have believed that there was a class war in progress in the countryside which he could use to achieve his ultimate aims. The poor peasants could be used to dispossess the kulaks.

By February 1918 Lenin was beginning to move more towards the original Bolshevik position. He announced that in time they hoped to organize 'the collective system of agriculture as being more economic both in respect of labour and of products, at the expense of individual holdings, in order to bring about the transition towards a socialist economy.' In June 1918 the government set up committees of poor peasants, known as *kombedy*; they were intended to stir up the class war in the countryside in which, it was hoped, the great mass of poorer peasants would seize kulak land to be incorporated into collective farms. But the *kombedy* were a failure: they were unpopular with most types of peasants who saw them as just another example of government interference, especially when some of them advocated forced collectivization, and they often seemed to be in conflict with local Soviets over exactly what their role was. The government further discredited itself in the eyes of the peasants by banning private trade and introducing a policy of confiscating surplus grain from peasants in order to feed the cities and the army. This had disastrous effects: unable to market their surplus grain and unwilling to see it taken from them at giveaway prices, peasants produced only enough for their own needs. Before very long the cities were beginning to feel the pinch, and during the winter of 1918–19 droves of industrial workers left the cities for the countryside. Early in December 1918 the *kombedy* were abolished.

It wasn't long before the peasants' satisfaction with the land redistribution turned into resentment and resistance to government policies. The Cheka reported over a hundred peasant uprisings in the European part of Russia between July and November 1918. In Saratov province there were a number of violent incidents; in one village eleven members of the local *kombed* were murdered by irate villagers who went on to organize neighbouring villages in an armed campaign to resist the groups sent to confiscate their grain. The villagers fought them off, describing them as 'alien food brigades which have given power to hooligans calling themselves members of the "rural poor".' However, the government did not allow this challenge to go unanswered: a detachment of Red Guards was sent to restore order and escort the food brigade as it went about its duties.[5] Lenin blamed such problems on the kulaks who, he claimed, were trying to sabotage attempts to develop the new socialist state. His critics in the party claimed that this was the inevitable consequence of launching the proletarian revolution too soon after the bourgeois revolution, before the industrial working class was large or powerful enough to exercise its dictatorship. Kamenev and Zinoviev had always argued that this would leave the revolution at the mercy of the peasants. So the Bolsheviks turned to more forceful methods which only caused more resentment (see section 5.4).

(b) Industry and finance

At the end of 1917 these areas of the economy were in serious difficulties: factory production in 1917 was 30 per cent less than in 1913, through a combination of transport problems, shortage of raw materials, lack of investment and continued massive inflation. Lenin intended a gradual transition to a socialist system through an intermediate stage in which Soviets and workers' committees would 'supervise' the management; it would be a sort of joint management in which the workers' committees would learn how to do the job. Full control by the workers would come later, though just how much later was not made clear; once the working population was free from exploitation by capitalists, the economy would right itself. The government began in mid-November 1917 by bringing large factories under state control; owners had to make accounts and other documents available to workers' committees, and in the last resort, workers' decisions were to be binding on owners. But there was also pressure from below: according to Robert Service, many workers in medium and small factories ignored the authorities and carried out their own 'nationalization'; often this was in order to forestall the threatened shutdown of their factories by the owners.[6] But the expected intermediate stage of 'supervision' did not materialize: many managers and owners refused to co-operate; some simply abandoned their factories while others were thrown out by workers' committees. These developments were extremely popular with urban workers; in their view this was what the revolution had been for – freedom from exploitation and the right to organize their own lives. Hundreds of them, including many Bolshevik party members, volunteered for work in administration and public service.

Worker control did not bring the expected benefits. Without the skills and experience of managers and engineers, factories were thrown into chaos and in

1918 production fell catastrophically to only one-third of the 1917 figure. In this desperate situation Lenin realized that concessions would have to be made; he resorted to a policy of bringing managers back into the factories, and attracted them by paying them much higher wages than ordinary workers. He defended this apparently regressive step in a long article, *Immediate Tasks of the Soviet Government*, published in April 1918. 'The transition to socialism,' he wrote, 'will be impossible without the guidance of experts in the various fields of knowledge, technology and experience . . . , and the specialists are, in the main, inevitably bourgeois. Now we have to resort to the old bourgeois method and to agree to pay a very high price for the "services" of the top bourgeois experts . . . Clearly this measure is a compromise, a departure from the principles of the Paris Commune and every proletarian power, which call for the reduction of all salaries to the level of the wages of the average worker.'[7]

More ominous for the workers was Lenin's call for 'iron discipline'. He complained that at present the government was too weak – 'very often it resembles jelly more than iron.' He argued that Russians were 'bad workers' compared with people in advanced countries; although this was the fault of the tsarist regime, the main task for the people was: 'learn to work.' Astonishingly for the leader of the proletarian revolution, he advocated adopting the theories of Frederick W. Taylor (1856–1915), an American engineer and inventor who is regarded as the founder of scientific management. The most controversial aspect of Taylor's system was his time and motion study – efficiency in factories could be greatly improved by close observation of individual workers with a view to eliminating wasted time and unnecessary motion. While the value and influence of Taylor's ideas are beyond doubt, they provoked great resentment and opposition among workers, who felt that this was the height of exploitation. 'We must organize in Russia the study and teaching of the Taylor system,' wrote Lenin, 'and systematically try it out and adapt it to our own ends . . . we must make wages correspond to the total amount of goods turned out.'[8] It would not be possible to build socialism, he argued, without using the most up-to-date methods and achievements of capitalism. The difference was that under capitalism these methods aimed at increasing the exploitation of workers, while under socialism they aimed at increasing production, and thereby raising the workers' standard of living.

However, left-wing Bolsheviks objected strongly to this change of course which seemed to them the opposite of worker control. They also believed that since the proletarian revolution had now taken place, the state, in the words of Marx, should be withering away. These latest developments suggested that the state was becoming stronger. Instead of local Soviets and committees running their area and their factory, everything was being brought under central control by state commissars. Russia had exchanged private capitalism for state capitalism, and ordinary workers were no better off. It is clear that Lenin and Trotsky had intended some degree of central control right from the early days of the Bolshevik government. Early in December the Supreme Council of National Economy (*Vesenkha*) was set up. Always known by its initial letters – VSNKh – its function was to plan, guide and co-ordinate the national economy, though the details were vague. But in the spring of 1918 the economy was showing no signs of recovery: there was widespread and ever-increasing unemployment and severe food shortages in the cities. In February 1918 the daily bread ration in Petrograd fell to only two ounces (50 grams) per person, even for workers. Hundreds, probably thousands of people fled to the countryside in search of food, but this caused a labour shortage and even more factories had to close.

By this time the workers were losing their enthusiasm for the Bolsheviks, and party membership was falling. The Petrograd party had about 40,000 members in October 1917, but by August 1918 this had slumped to around 7000.[9] In the elections to some town Soviets in central Russia in the spring of 1918 the Bolsheviks lost their majorities and they resorted to the use of force in order to keep control. Paradoxically, however, at the time when support among industrial workers seemed to be dwindling, the Bolsheviks were able to tighten their grip on the state administration. This was possible because many workers *had* done well, thanks to the Bolsheviks; hundreds of party members, for example, who had started off as ordinary workers, had been promoted from the factory-floor to become civil servants, public officers, organizers, managers and so on; it was in their interests for the Bolshevik government to survive, and so this new bureaucracy did its best to strengthen the Soviet state.

The ending of the war in March 1918 brought no immediate improvement; it simply meant that the state stopped financing armaments production, leaving all the factories producing war materials without any orders. It took some time to switch back to ordinary peace-time production, and this caused further chaos and unemployment. Russia lost so much territory by the Treaty of Brest–Litovsk that it was bound to have an adverse effect on the economy.

5.3   Russia withdraws from the First World War

(a) The Bolsheviks' dilemmas

Lenin was anxious to deliver as soon as possible the peace which his slogans had been promising. Only two weeks after the Bolsheviks seized power all Russian troops were ordered to cease fire. The Germans welcomed this move and peace talks opened at the German military headquarters at Brest–Litovsk in Poland, just inside the German lines. During the negotiations the Bolsheviks faced two different dilemmas. The first problem was that although they wanted to keep their promise and bring Russia back to something like peace and normality, there had still been no successful revolutions in other parts of Europe. Lenin thought these were vital to the survival of his regime and that they were less likely to happen if peace was restored. So the Bolsheviks' tactics were to try and spin the talks out in the hope that revolutions would break out in the states of central Europe, particularly in Austria where the population was showing distinct signs of unrest.

The other great dilemma for the Russians was caused by the German attitude at the peace talks. The Russians were hoping, unrealistically, that goodwill would prevail on both sides, and that the Germans would be so grateful to secure an end to the fighting on their eastern front that they would not insist on annexing any Russian territory. But the Germans had their own designs on the Russian empire: for Germany to feel secure she needed a weak Russia on her eastern frontier; German businessmen and bankers were interested in getting their hands on Russia's economic resources. The best way to achieve both of these aims was to break up the Russian empire and either annex the western provinces directly or have them set up as small independent states which Germany could dominate. Consequently the Germans refused to withdraw from the provinces around the southern Baltic – Lithuania and Courland – and from Poland. In addition Austria–Hungary demanded part of the Ukraine, which was a valuable source of wheat. In fact the Bolsheviks had already made it known that they would allow independence to all these provinces as well as to Finland, although the intention was that they would eventually all become Soviet republics. This was another reason why the German government wanted to keep these territories under their control; if Soviet governments came to power, revolution might spread from these states into Germany itself. This situation was complicated further when an anti-Bolshevik Ukrainian nationalist delegation turned up at Brest–Litovsk; the nationalists had already declared an independent Ukrainian republic, and they now demanded that the conference should officially recognize their independence.

The German demands caused the most bitter disagreement so far in Sovnarkom. A majority of members wanted to reject the terms and begin hostilities again. In the Bolshevik Central Committee the voting was much closer, but Nikolai Bukharin and his supporters had a majority in favour of fighting a 'revolutionary war' against Germany and her allies, which, they argued, was the best way of sparking off more revolutions. Lenin opposed this; he reasoned that the terms must be accepted in spite of their harshness, and pointed out that the Russian army by this time was not even capable of organizing a retreat. A temporary compromise was reached early in January 1918: no final decision would be taken on whether to accept or reject the terms until a plan suggested by Trotsky had been tried. Trotsky had taken over the leadership of the Russian delegation at Brest–Litovsk in December 1917; on 28 January he revealed his proposal to the astonished Germans and Austrians. He told them that their terms were unacceptable, but that his government had decided on a policy of 'no peace, no war'. The Russians would stop fighting but they would not surrender and they would not sign a treaty. Nothing like this had ever been experienced in the entire history of peace negotiations. Leaving the Germans in a state of shock, Trotsky walked out of the conference and took the Russian delegation back to Petrograd.

The Russians' reasoning was that if the Germans continued to advance deeper into Russian territory, it would seem to the rest of the world like an act of pure aggression against a country which wanted only peace. The Russians were too weak to stop the Germans anyway, if they did choose to advance, so at least Trotsky's plan would leave them in possession of the moral high ground. But the Germans did not co-operate – they soon announced that hostilities would begin again in two days' time. Lenin wanted to accept the treaty immediately to forestall the threatened German advance, but was outvoted. Only a week after Trotsky had walked out the Germans began to advance through Estonia, and in five days covered 150 miles, as much as they had achieved during the previous three years. There was no Russian resistance. There was consternation in Petrograd; Lenin was afraid that the Germans were aiming to capture the capital and overthrow the Bolshevik government. Still the Bukharin–Trotsky faction wanted to delay signing a peace treaty; only after Lenin had threatened to resign did Trotsky change his mind and support Lenin's proposal to send an immediate telegram accepting the German terms. But the Germans were in no hurry to reply; they continued to advance until they were only 150 miles from Petrograd. Preparations were started to move the government to Moscow, and panic set in as thousands of people tried to flee from the city. There was no electricity, no fuel and no medical services, and the railway stations were crammed with people hoping to find a train to take them to safety.

At last on 23 February the Germans responded; they had decided not to capture Petrograd – they preferred to keep the Bolsheviks in power, believing that Russia would be weaker under their control. As one German writer put it: 'the Bolsheviks are ruining Great Russia, the source of any potential Russian future danger, root and branch. They have already lifted most of that anxiety which we might have felt about Great Russia, and we should do all we can to keep them as long as possible carrying on their work, so useful to us.'[10] However, their terms were now much more harsh – they demanded to keep all the extra territory which they had occupied during the previous ten days. Russia would therefore lose Estonia, Livonia, Ukraine (where the independent republic had been officially recognized and promised support by the Germans) and Finland. Other demands were that Georgia was to be given independence, land in south-eastern Russia, including Batum, was to be given to Turkey, and Russia was to pay reparations of 6000 million marks. The Russians were given two weeks to decide whether or not to accept these new terms.

(b) Final discussions and the Treaty of Brest–Litovsk, March 1918

Agonized discussions took place in the Central Committee. For Lenin it was a question of peace at any price; Russia had no effective army and he was convinced that if they refused to sign now, the Germans would take Petrograd, which would mean the end of the Soviet government. Peace was desperately needed so that the Bolsheviks could consolidate their power and set Russia on the road to recovery. Lenin seemed to have given up hope of immediate revolutions breaking out, and talked about sacrificing space in order to gain time. He still seemed to believe that Russia would regain all the lost territory when the revolutions did occur and socialist governments came to power in Germany and Austria–Hungary.

Against this, Bukharin and his supporters argued that Russia would be economically crippled by these territorial losses, especially Ukraine which was their main food supply area. They wanted to take up the fight again and claimed that it should be possible to raise a new and enthusiastic army to defend the revolution; the nearer the Germans got to Petrograd, the more inspired the Russian masses would become. Lenin won the argument, pointing out that Bukharin was to blame for the harshness of the latest terms – if it hadn't been for Bukharin's stubborn refusal, Lenin would have accepted the earlier offer. In the end, after further

Map 5.1   **Russian losses by the Treaty of Brest–Litovsk, 1918.**

threats of resignation, Lenin carried the day by seven votes to four with four abstentions. The Treaty of Brest–Litovsk was finally ratified on 16 March 1918.

The terms of the treaty were a national disaster (see Map 5.1): Russia lost most of its non-Russian territories in Europe – Poland, Estonia, Courland, Lithuania and Finland, together with Belorussia and Georgia were given independence, but under German 'protection'. Ukraine was occupied by German troops and the Germans replaced the Ukrainian nationalist government with a puppet regime of their own and suppressed the Ukrainian Soviet. In total these areas contained 34 per cent of the empire's population (some 55 million), 32 per cent of agricultural land, 54 per cent of all heavy industry and 89 per cent of her coalmines. In addition the Germans were allowed important economic privileges in Russia – for example German-owned property was exempt from nationalization. This 'shameful' and 'obscene' peace, as Lenin's critics described it, meant that economic recovery was going to be even more difficult and it left the country politically unstable: instead of a cordon of friendly Soviet-run states along her western frontier, Russia now had potentially hostile countries under German influence. The loss of Ukraine, the main grain-producing area, was especially serious and meant that famine was almost inevitable in some areas. Within Russia there was widespread opposition to the treaty. The Left SRs resigned from Sovnarkom and the Right SRs began to build up forces in preparation for armed resistance against the Bolsheviks in Siberia and in the Don area. On 6 July 1918 two Left SR members assassinated Count Mirbach, the new German ambassador in Moscow (which became the capital on 10 March) in a vain attempt to destroy the peace with Germany. It was too late for that now, but clearly the communist government (the name of the party was officially changed from Bolshevik to Communist on 8 March) was in serious crisis.

5.4   The drift towards violence

(a) Was violence an inevitable part of Bolshevik rule?

Almost immediately after the October coup the Bolsheviks began to resort to coercion in order to get things done and to stay in power. This raises the question: were coercion and violence inevitable in these circumstances, or could the Bolshevik programme have been achieved peacefully? Soviet historians played down the violence and claimed that the Bolsheviks had no choice, given the attitude of their enemies (see Document D(ii)). After the signing of the Treaty of Brest–Litovsk, it was the Socialist Revolutionaries who launched a campaign of assassination and terror, and before long Russia was engulfed in the Civil War. There is some evidence that in those crucial early months before the Civil War proper got under way, Lenin and other Bolshevik leaders would have preferred to avoid violence. The socialist writer and novelist Maxim Gorky probably knew Lenin as well as anybody and he was certainly not an uncritical admirer. His newspaper *Novaya Zhizn* (New Life) often carried articles denouncing Bolshevik excesses and in 1917 he had condemned Lenin as a fanatic and as the destroyer of the Social Democratic tradition. Later he wrote letters to all the Bolshevik leaders, protesting about unnecessary arrests (see Document F(i)). After the assassination attempt on Lenin on 30 August 1918 the two men renewed their friendship and Gorky eventually came to have a clearer understanding of Lenin's reasoning. He later wrote: 'I have never met anyone in Russia, nor do I know of anyone, who hated, loathed and despised all unhappiness, grief and suffering as Lenin did.' Gorky also reported that Lenin had once said to him: 'Our ideal is not to use force against anyone.'[11]

According to Christopher Hill, 'there was no wholesale suppression of the opposition press during the six months immediately after the Bolshevik revolution, and no violence against political opponents, because there was no need for it. The death sentence was even abolished at the end of October, though Lenin thought this very unrealistic. When the first attempt was made to assassinate Lenin in January 1918, he treated the matter as a joke and insisted that his assailant should be liberated. The terror came later and was a direct consequence of allied military intervention.'[12] Lenin himself remarked early in November: 'We do not use the sort of terror as was used by the French revolutionaries who guillotined unarmed people, and I hope we shall not have to use it. When we have made arrests we have said: "We will let you go if you sign a piece of paper promising not to commit acts of sabotage". And such signatures are given.' This was certainly the case with the members of the Provisional Government who were arrested, together with large numbers of officers who had supported them.

They were almost all eventually released after promising 'not to take up arms against the people any more;' but that did not prevent them from joining the Whites during the civil war. Even the Cheka, Lenin's new secret police, got off to a quiet start: in the first six months of its existence it only had 22 people executed, and they were described as bandits and speculators rather than political opponents; most of those arrested were released after a few weeks.[13]

It was the chronic food shortages which first caused the Bolsheviks to take desperate measures – and the situation really was desperate. Early in January 1918 Lenin sent telegraph messages to government agents in the provinces: 'For God's sake use the most energetic and revolutionary measures to send grain, grain and more grain. Otherwise Piter [Petrograd] may perish.' Lenin was convinced that the kulaks were hoarding huge quantities of grain in an attempt to force up the price. Although he was probably mistaken about the existence of a distinct kulak class, there is evidence of hoarding – according to one historian of the Civil War, W. Bruce Lincoln, 'at midsummer [1918] kulak storehouses probably still contained nearly three-quarters of a million tons of grain from the 1917 harvest plus a great deal more from earlier years.' In addition there were enormous amounts of grain which the peasants distilled into rough vodka known as *samogon*; it is estimated that in just one province in Siberia, a quarter of a million tons of precious grain were distilled during the winter of 1917–18. One village was discovered where peasants had distilled enough grain to feed a town of ten thousand people through the winter. Vodka could be sold much more profitably than grain and since the peasants were unable to buy consumer goods such as tools and boots because factories had concentrated on war supplies, they simply refused to sell their grain at the low prices on offer.[14]

The dire food situation gave the Cheka (set up in December 1917) its first important role – to deal with people hoarding grain or trying to speculate with important supplies. 'There will be no famine in Russia,' Lenin said in April 1918, 'if stocks are controlled, and any breach of the rules laid down is followed by the harshest punishment – the arrest and shooting of takers of bribes and swindlers.' In May he announced: 'Those who have grain and fail to deliver it to properly designated railway stations and shipping points are to be declared enemies of the people.' Shortly afterwards he launched 'a great crusade against grain speculators, kulaks, and bloodsuckers, who . . . after growing fat and rich during the war, now refuse to give bread to starving people . . . it must become a pitiless struggle . . . Until we apply terror – shooting on the spot – to speculators, we shall achieve nothing.'[15]

It was after the signing of the humiliating Treaty of Brest–Litovsk early in March 1918 that things took a turn for the worse. The loss of the Ukraine, a vitally important source of wheat, was a terrible blow to hopes of ending the food crisis. The Left SRs were determined to wreck the treaty and began a campaign of terror: in June they shot dead a leading Bolshevik member of the Petrograd Soviet, and on 6 July they assassinated Count Mirbach, the German ambassador in Moscow. This turned out to be the beginning of an attempted SR coup in Moscow, Petrograd and some other cities – the same day SRs arrested some leading Bolsheviks including Dzerzhinsky, the head of the Cheka, and occupied the main Moscow post office. Messages were sent out to all Soviets announcing that the Left SRs were now 'the party in power'. However, their plans to kill Lenin and

Trotsky somehow went adrift and the whole coup attempt deteriorated into a fiasco. Order was soon restored by Red Guards in both Moscow and Petrograd and in the other centres of uprising. It is now widely believed that the SRs were not aiming to seize power themselves but were hoping to spark off a popular uprising to force the Bolsheviks to change their policies. There is evidence too that the Bolsheviks knew of the SRs' intention to assassinate Mirbach but allowed them to go ahead so that the SRs could be blamed, giving the Bolsheviks an excuse for an attack on their former allies. Whatever the truth of the SR 'coup' attempt, the Bolsheviks certainly made the most of it; mass arrests began immediately, 13 of the ringleaders were shot the next day, and the Socialist Revolutionaries soon ceased to exist as a viable political force.

The pace of violence and terror intensified after the second assassination attempt on Lenin (30 August 1918). Earlier in the day Moise Uritsky, the head of the Petrograd Cheka, had been shot dead by a young army officer. Lenin had just made a speech in a Moscow factory and was walking to his car when a woman shot him twice with a revolver at point-blank range. Although he was wounded in the neck and in one of his lungs, Lenin seemed to make a quick recovery and was able to resume work after only three weeks. However, some accounts claim that it was shortly after this that his health began to deteriorate, and that he never again possessed the same degree of vitality. The woman, Fanny Kaplan, who said she had shot Lenin because he had betrayed the revolution, was executed a few days later. The attacks were the signal for a policy of all-out terror in which thousands of people perished.

All this evidence can be interpreted as supporting the view that it was the desperate circumstances of the time – the food shortages, the unemployment in the big cities, the threat from the Left Socialist Revolutionaries, and the attacks on Lenin and other Bolshevik leaders, which drove the Bolsheviks towards violence and terror, rather than any inherent ideological motive. The problem was that however well-intentioned the Bolsheviks were, Lenin's reasoning was fatally flawed in two vital respects. First of all his insistence that the two revolutions – bourgeois and proletarian – could be successfully telescoped together, led to the situation in which the Bolsheviks were in power before their most reliable supporters – the industrial workers – had become a large or powerful enough class to sustain them. This left the Bolsheviks as a minority government, uncomfortably dependent on the largest, but most self-absorbed class in Russian society – the peasants. Secondly, Lenin had always expected that a successful revolution in Russia would occur as part of a European or even a world-wide socialist revolution. He was convinced that socialist revolutions would quickly follow in central and western Europe, so that the new Russian Soviet government would be supported by sympathetic, comradely neighbouring governments. None of this had happened, so Russia was left isolated facing a capitalist Europe which was deeply suspicious of the new regime. This meant therefore that both internally and externally the regime was under pressure from the forces of counter-revolution. Law and order seemed to be breaking down and local Soviets simply ignored the government's decrees. If the Bolsheviks intended to stay in power and rebuild the country, regrettably they would more than likely have to resort to violence to achieve anything significant.

Traditional liberal and neo-liberal historians emphasize that Lenin and Trotsky, if not all the Bolshevik leaders, were committed to the use of violence and terror right from the beginning, whatever the circumstances. Richard Pipes believes that Lenin regarded terror as an absolutely vital element of revolutionary government and was prepared to use it as a preventive measure, even when no active opposition to his rule existed. In a 1908 essay about the failure of the French revolutionaries, Lenin wrote that the main weakness of the proletariat was 'excessive generosity – it should have exterminated its enemies instead of trying to exert moral influence over them.' Lenin was highly indignant when the death penalty was abolished, retorting: 'This is nonsense, how can you make a revolution without executions.' Yet this was at a time when no organized opposition had been formed. Again, the Cheka was set up early in December 1917 before there was any opposition threat or foreign intervention – the reason suggested by Christopher Hill for the resort to violence. Some of Trotsky's utterances were of a similar nature to those of Lenin; on 2 December 1917 he said: 'There is nothing immoral in the proletariat finishing off the dying class . . . You are indignant at the petty terror which we direct against our class opponents. Be put on notice that in one month at most this terror will assume more frightful forms, on the model of the great revolutionaries of France.' This is the sort of evidence which leads Richard Pipes to conclude that 'it is absurd to talk of Red Terror as an "unfortunate" policy "forced" upon the Bolsheviks by foreign and domestic opponents . . . terror served the Bolsheviks not as a weapon of last resort, but as a surrogate for the popular support which eluded them. The more their popularity eroded, the more they resorted to terror, until in the fall and winter of 1918–19 they raised it to a level of indiscriminate slaughter never before seen.'[16]

(b) The violence unfolds

As soon as the grain detachments began to operate, taking grain away from peasants who were thought to have surpluses, there were violent responses. The committees of poor peasants (see section 5.2(a)) aroused ferocious resistance in many villages and the Red Army was used increasingly to enforce the food procurement policy. The government eventually ordered that every food-requisitioning detachment must consist of at least 75 men with two or three machine guns. In June 1918 there were about 3000 of these detachments, and by the end of August the number had risen to over 17,000. Increasingly the Cheka became involved – in 1918 the Cheka suppressed no fewer than 245 peasant uprisings against the food detachments and 99 in the first seven months of 1919. In the course of these operations, 3057 peasants and 1150 on the Red side were killed; by the end of 1918, according to official Cheka figures, 6300 people had been executed for taking part in uprisings or 'embezzlement', and during 1919 there were a further 3456 executions. However, it is certain that the actual death toll during this period was much higher.[17]

One of the most disturbing aspects of the violence was that many of the victims were arrested or executed not for any particular offence, but simply because they were 'bourgeois' – a term of abuse levelled against people like businessmen, employers, army officers, landowners, priests, students, or indeed any sort of professional or well-dressed person. The government encouraged this class war by labelling them all as 'enemies of the people' and using slogans like 'loot the looters'. Not that the masses needed much encouragement: a policy of terror could hardly have been carried out without the willing co-operation of large sections of the population. Some of the most violent incidents occurred independently of any central direction, and often the strongest demands for executions came from local Soviets rather than the Cheka. This desire for revenge and retribution against the privileged – 'the scoundrel fleas, the bedbug rich,' as Lenin once described them – was strong and widespread. In fact Orlando Figes believes that 'the Terror erupted from below. It was an integral element of the social revolution from the start. The Bolsheviks encouraged but did not create this mass terror. The main institutions of the terror were all shaped, at least in part, in response to these pressures from below ... For however much one may condemn it, and however hard it may be to admit, there is no doubt that the Terror struck a deep chord in the Russian civil war mentality, and that it had a strange mass appeal.'[18]

It has to be remembered that there was a climate of violence and repression in Russia stretching back over many years. There was a long history of peasant revolts, like the ones led by the Cossacks Stenka Razin in 1670–71 and Emilian Pugachev in 1773. The collapse of such outbreaks was always followed by severe reprisals against their supporters; both Razin and Pugachev were brought to Moscow, tortured and then executed. During 1906 the tsarist regime carried out a harsh campaign against those who had taken part in the uprisings – estimates put the number executed at 15,000, with 20,000 shot or wounded and 45,000 exiled. The right-wing Black Hundreds waged campaigns of terror against Jews – over 3000 were murdered in the two weeks following the announcement of the October Manifesto in 1905. There were more anti-Jewish pogroms during the Civil War – some sources suggest that during 1919 in Ukraine alone, as many as 200,000 Jews were murdered by White forces.[19] Not that any of this excuses the Bolshevik terror, particularly since they claimed to have humanitarian ideals, but it certainly goes a long way towards explaining it.

One of the worst incidents of the Terror was the murder of the ex-Tsar Nicholas and his family. When the Bolsheviks took power the royal family were moved from Tobolsk in Siberia to Yekaterinburg in the Urals, where they were kept under guard in a large house which had belonged to a merchant called Ipatiev. Trotsky wanted Nicholas to be brought to Moscow and put on trial, but Lenin would not agree. By the summer of 1918 when the Civil War was in full swing, the question of what to do with the royal family became more urgent. White forces were advancing from the east towards Yekaterinburg and there seemed a strong possibility that the family would be rescued; they might then become the focus of all the anti-Bolshevik forces. Whether he seriously believed this, or whether he simply used it as an excuse is not clear; but there is no doubt that it was Lenin who gave the order for them to be killed. In the early hours of 18 July 1918 Nicholas and Alexandra, their four daughters and their son Alexei, were taken from their beds and into the cellar of the Ipatiev house. There, together with their doctor, cook, valet and housemaid, they were lined up against the wall and shot by members of the local Cheka. After sulphuric acid was poured on their faces, the bodies were buried; the graves were only discovered after the collapse of the Soviet empire. In 1992 some of the bones were subjected to DNA analysis which showed conclusively that they were the remains of the Romanovs; it seems certain that the whole family perished together in the cellar of the Ipatiev house on 18 July.[20] The following day the official announcement of the death of Nicholas appeared in *Izvestia*, but no mention was made of the deaths of the rest of the family. This was kept secret because the Bolsheviks were afraid of public outrage if it became known that they had murdered innocent women and children; also there was the fear that the Germans would be incensed by the murder of Alexandra, who was a German princess. Coming so soon after the assassination of their ambassador (6 July), this could spark off a renewal of the war. According to Robert Service, Lenin 'exterminated the Romanovs because they had misruled Russia ... but also because he enjoyed – really enjoyed – letting himself loose against the people in general from the *ancien regime*. He hated not only the Imperial family but also the middling people who had controlled Russia before 1917.'[21]

5.5   The Civil War

(a) When did the war start and what caused it?

There is still disagreement among historians as to exactly when the Civil War started. The majority date the war proper from the summer of 1918, though there had been several military engagements before then. One British historian of the war, Evan Mawdsley, argues that it really began as soon as the Bolsheviks took power, since almost immediately afterwards there was bloodshed, with Russian fighting Russian. Throughout the winter of 1917–18 there was 'internal fighting of an intensity that can only be called "civil war".'[22] Lenin and his colleagues had expected some resistance but assumed that it would be easily dealt with. And so it was in the early days. In December 1917 Bolshevik forces invaded Ukraine and by the end of January had chased out the anti-Bolshevik council known as the Rada. However, this success was only short-lived – the Treaty of Brest–Litovsk signed in March made the Ukraine into an independent state, under German influence. Successful actions took place against the hostile Don Cossacks in January 1918 and the important Cossack centres of Rostov and Novocherkassk were captured towards the end of February. Another challenge to the Bolsheviks was being prepared by generals Alexeev, Kornilov and Denikin who formed the Volunteer Army; in April they attacked Ekaterinodar, capital of the Kuban Soviet Republic, north-east of the Black Sea. They met fierce resistance and disaster struck when Kornilov, the hero of the right during the Provisional Government, was killed. His successor, Denikin, abandoned the siege; Lenin celebrated this as a great victory and announced that the Civil War was over. In fact it was just about to erupt into a full-scale military conflict. Why did the war escalate in this way?

Opposition had been growing for some time among most social and political groups in Russian society – peasants, industrial workers, the middle classes, army officers, Socialist Revolutionaries, right-wingers and monarchists. Better-off peasants soon turned against the Bolsheviks when the government launched its drive to get sufficient food supplies to the cities. Private trade in grain was banned, so that peasants could only sell to government officials. They were paid for their produce, but they felt that the prices were too low and refused to sell. Lenin sent out armed requisitioning detachments who seized whatever grain they could find, whether it was surplus to the peasants' requirements or not. At the Fifth All-Russian Congress of Soviets which opened in the Bolshoi Theatre in Moscow on 5 July 1918, Maria Spiridonova, one of the SR leaders, launched a bitter attack on Lenin for his 'dictatorship of individuals in love with their theories...I accuse you of betraying the peasants, of making use of them for your own ends...When the peasants, the Bolshevik peasants, the Left Social Revolutionary peasants and the non-party peasants are alike humiliated, oppressed and crushed, in my hand you will still find the same pistol, the same hand grenade...'[23]

Another important cause of the growing opposition was the Bolsheviks' treatment of the local Soviets. The workers, soldiers and sailors who had supported the Bolshevik coup believed they were going to get Soviet rule, which they took to mean self-rule, not rule by the Bolshevik party. Their expectation was that every city, town and factory would elect its own Soviet to run its affairs; in this way workers and ordinary people would take control of their own lives. There would be only minimal interference from the government in Moscow; this was the sense in which the state would 'wither away', as the Marxists believed. But the reality was different: as the Bolsheviks began to lose their majorities on local Soviets, the government responded by sending commissars supported by Red Guards and often some Cheka officers as well. They threw out all non-Bolshevik members of the Soviets and sometimes dissolved the local Soviet altogether, leaving the commissar in control. There was resistance in several places and the popular slogan became 'Long live the Soviets and down with the commissars'. As for the question of workers running their own factories, this became almost irrelevant in some cities; in Petrograd, for example, by mid-March 1918, the daily bread ration had reached its lowest ever – 50 grams per person. By June about 60 per cent of the workforce had left the city in search of food, and the total population of Petrograd had fallen from three million to less than two million.

There was a nationalist element in the growing resistance to Bolshevik rule. Nationalities such as Ukrainians and Georgians hoped to gain independence from Russia, but the Bolsheviks were not interested in giving way to what they called 'bourgeois nationalism'. They claimed that the majority of the people – peasants and workers – were happy with the Bolshevik reforms and wanted to stay with their Great Russian comrades. The nationalist armies became known as the Greens, of which the most famous was that led by the anarchist Nestor Makhno in the south-eastern Ukraine. By the summer of 1918 no fewer than 30 regions had declared themselves independent republics, and all but one were hostile to the Bolsheviks.

Foreign intervention in Russia complicated the situation and at first there was confusion about what the real motives of the foreign powers were. Britain and France were desperate to keep Russia in the First World War so that the Germans would be unable to divert their eastern-front forces to the west. They offered the new Bolshevik government the same support in the way of military equipment and funding which they had given the Provisional Government. During the German advance into Russia in February 1918 Trotsky decided to accept any help on offer from Russia's allies. The first to arrive was a small party of 170 British marines who landed at Murmansk, a port north of the Arctic Circle, the day after the Treaty of Brest–Litovsk was signed. A further 600 arrived in June, followed in August by a small joint Anglo–French force which arrived at Archangelsk, also in the far north, on the White Sea. These were the only Russian ports in Europe that the allies could reach so long as the First World War continued. The first arrivals were quickly followed by other foreign contingents: in April a Japanese force arrived at Vladivostock, Russia's main port in the far east. Later they were joined by troops from France, Britain, the USA and Italy. The French set up a base at the port of Odessa on the Black Sea, and more British forces moved into Transcaucasia in the south and into Central Asia. Initially the British and French claimed that their motive was to prevent war supplies, which they had previously brought to Russia and which were still there, from falling into German hands. They all claimed that they were in Russia to protect their interests, but Lenin and Trotsky had no doubts that their real motive was to help overthrow the Bolshevik regime, which the rest of the world viewed with the greatest suspicion, since it was advocating 'world revolution' and refusing to honour debts incurred by previous Russian governments.

A number of former Tsarist generals had fled from the Bolsheviks and built up White armies: Generals Denikin and Alexeev were in southern Russia in the Caucasus region with the White Volunteer Army of tsarists and former Kadets. In Siberia Admiral Kolchak was at the head of an army and was being hailed as 'Supreme Ruler of Russia'. Another apparently more serious threat, since he was much nearer Petrograd and Moscow, came from General Iudenich who formed a White Army in Estonia; he was one of the few successful Russian generals in the First World War and had never lost a battle. In Finland General Gustav Mannerheim led the Finnish White army which overthrew the Finnish Reds and took control of the country in April 1918. They received help from German troops who landed on the south coast of Finland and captured Helsinki from the Red Finns. Petrograd seemed under threat from this direction as well as from Estonia. In May 1918 a group of leading SRs gathered in Samara on the Volga and set up what they called a Committee of Members of the Constituent Assembly (known as Komuch), claiming that it was the legal government of Russia. The Volga region was one of the strongholds of the SR party and there seemed every chance that the population would rally behind them.

What seemed to galvanize all these disparate groups into action was the presence in Siberia of an army of around 40,000 Czechoslovaks. They had a strange history: the army had started with several thousand Czechs who were working in Russia in 1914 when the war broke out. Their homeland was part of the Austro–Hungarian empire, the enemy of Russia, but they decided to stay on and fight on the Russian side in the hope that the defeat of Austria–Hungary would mean freedom for their nation and a Czechoslovak state. The force grew with the recruitment of thousands of Czech and Slovak prisoners taken by the Russians

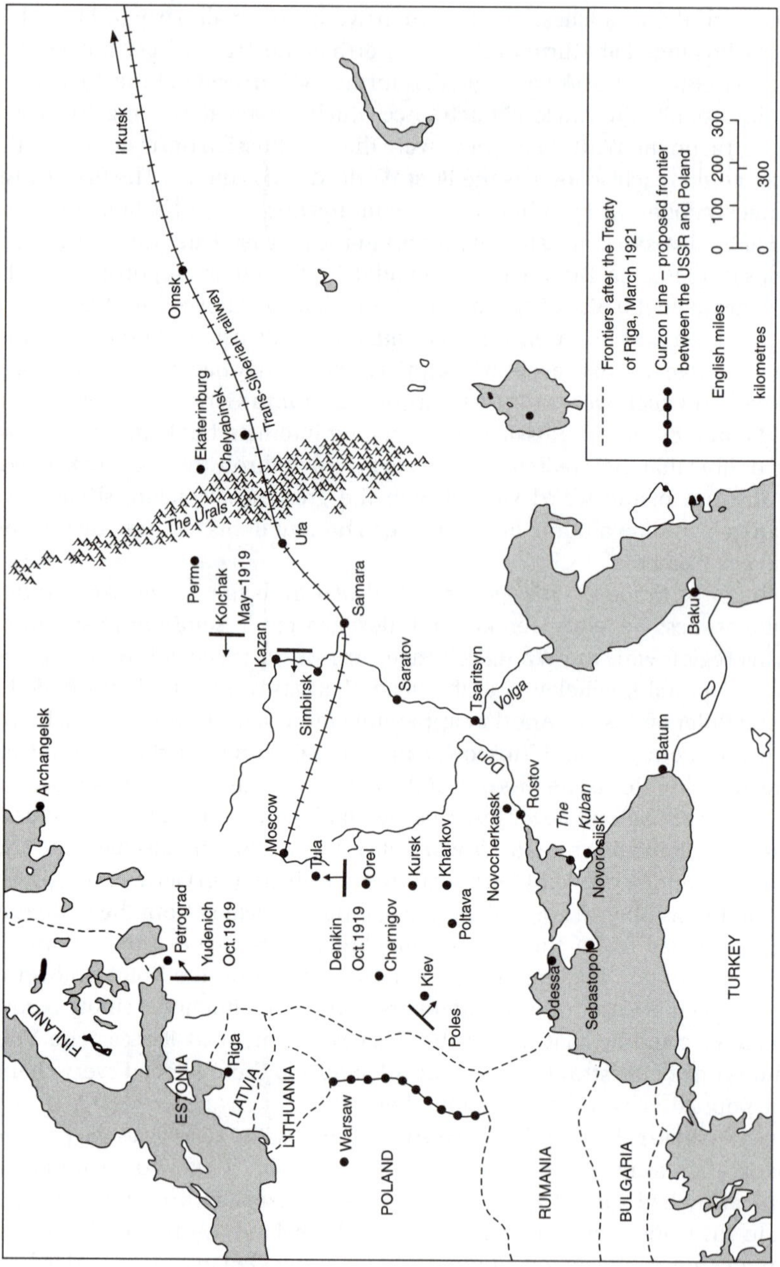

Map 5.2 The Civil War.

during their successful offensives against the Austro–Hungarian fronts. In March 1918 when Russia left the war, there seemed to be no longer any role for them. Their main interest was national independence, but with Austria–Hungary still involved in the war, they could not simply go straight home, since this would involve crossing the battle-lines from the Russian side. So the Bolshevik government agreed to let them leave the country from Vladivostock in the far east, to which they would travel along the Trans-Siberian Railway. Their intention was to make their way around towards the western front and rejoin the allies in the struggle against the Central Powers. However, tensions mounted along the way; the Czechs had been allowed to keep their weapons for self-defence, but this caused suspicion among local Soviets who kept holding up the trains. The Czechs also distrusted the Bolsheviks whom they suspected of planning to hand them over to the Germans.

The threatened violence eventually erupted on 14 May 1918 when one of the trains reached Chelyabinsk just east of the Ural Mountains. A brawl developed between a group of Czechs and some Hungarian prisoners of war; the local Soviet ordered the arrest of the Czechs, to which other Czechs responded by taking control of the town until their comrades were released. Trotsky, now Commissar for War, ordered that all further movement of the legion eastwards must cease immediately and all Soviets along the railway were to disarm the Czechs, who must be made to join either the Red Army or a labour battalion. Any Czech found on the railway in possession of weapons was to be executed on the spot. This was an unnecessary overreaction by Trotsky; all the Czechs wanted was to escape from Russia as quickly as possible, and in any case government forces in the area were too weak to carry out the order. The Czechs, who were spread out in six separate groups along the railway, replied that they would only surrender their arms when they reached Vladivostock. Fearful that the Bolsheviks would hand them over to the Germans, they decided to take control of the Trans-Siberian Railway. During the next two weeks they occupied Mariinsk, Novonikolaevsk, Chelyabinsk, Penza, Tomsk, Omsk and Samara (9 June 1918). Vladivostock was taken on 29 June, Ufa on 6 July and Irkutsk, where the Bolsheviks put up the strongest resistance so far encountered by the Czechs, was captured on 11 July. By this time the government had completely lost control of the Trans-Siberian Railway east of Samara. It was ironic that this foreign army, trying to fight its way out of Russia, provided the stimulus for the Whites to take decisive action to bring down the Bolshevik regime.

(b) Military events in the Civil War

The war was an extremely complex and confusing affair, but the basic story line was simple: the Reds (Bolsheviks or Communists), who by the summer of 1918 controlled a relatively small but compact area of European Russia around Moscow and Petrograd, were attacked by the Whites on four main fronts. There was Kolchak in the east in Siberia, Denikin and his Volunteer Force in the south in the Caucasus, in the west there was Iudenich advancing from Estonia, and the Czech legion was in control of the Trans-Siberian Railway. Fortunately for the Reds there was no co-ordination between the various White armies, and after

Trotsky had created a new Red Army, the Reds were able to defeat the challenges one by one. The Civil War proper was over by November 1920. It was a war of movement over large distances determined mainly by the layout of the railway network; and it was a war marked by extreme brutality on both sides.

The main action during the remainder of 1918 took place in the east and south. The Czechs continued their successes by capturing Simbirsk (Lenin's birthplace) and Kazan. Trotsky took personal command of the forces in this theatre of war and soon recaptured Simbirsk and Kazan together with Ufa and Samara. Meanwhile in the south Stalin successfully organized the defence of Tsaritsyn which was being besieged by Denikin's forces. However, the year ended in defeats for the Reds; supporters of Admiral Kolchak overthrew the newly formed SR dominated, anti-Bolshevik government at Omsk and took control; Kolchak was declared Supreme Ruler of Russia. In December Kolchak's forces advanced westwards and captured Perm.

The ending of the First World War in November 1918 had important implications for Russia. Now that Russia's former allies had defeated the Central Powers, there seemed a strong possibility that they would turn their forces against the Bolsheviks, whose activities were viewed as increasingly unacceptable. These actions included the terror, the murder of the royal family, the formation of the Communist International (known as the Comintern) in 1919, an organization dedicated to the incitement of revolutions in other countries (see section 5.7(a)), and the announcement that the Bolsheviks would not honour the debts incurred by previous Russian governments. However, the threatened anti-Bolshevik crusade failed to materialize. More important was that the German defeat got rid of German troops from Ukraine and other parts of western and central Russia.

The year 1919 saw fierce fighting on three fronts as the Whites launched three separate offensives. All three had some initial successes, but by the end of the year they had all been halted and forced to retreat. In the east Kolchak captured Ufa and advanced towards the Volga. At the end of April the Reds began a counter-offensive which drove Kolchak back eastwards; Yekaterinburg fell to the Reds in July and Omsk in November; Kolchak retreated to Irkutsk in central Siberia. Meanwhile in May Denikin's Volunteer Army moved northwards again, this time with more success than in 1918. Kharkov and Tsaritsyn were captured in June, followed by Kiev, the capital of Ukraine (August). On 12 September Denikin gave the order to advance on Moscow, and on 14 October his forces captured Orel, less than 250 miles from Moscow. Their next objective was the city of Tula, half-way between Orel and Moscow. The Reds decided that the fall of Tula must be prevented at all costs. What made the situation more difficult for them was that Iudenich was at the same time advancing on Petrograd. However, the Reds were able to rush troops from the eastern front where the threat from Kolchak seemed to be over. Red troops moved against the Volunteer Army and it was clear that this would be one of the decisive battles of the war. Denikin had almost 100,000 troops whereas the Reds commanded by general Yegorov had around 186,000. The battle took place on 18–20 October; as the White forces were advancing towards Tula, the Reds launched a surprise attack on their left flank, and after heavy fighting Denikin was forced to evacuate Orel and retreat southwards to Kursk. When Yegorov's troops were joined by reinforcements, including cavalry divisions, the retreat became a rout, discipline broke down and what was left of the Volunteer Force fled towards the Black Sea.

The attack from the west was the one which came closest to ultimate success. Iudenich began his advance against Petrograd on 11 October and within five days he had reached Tsarskoe Selo, only 15 miles from the city. The Red forces were apparently demoralized by the appearance of tanks manned by British soldiers, although there were only six of them. The British navy helped by bombarding the naval base at Kronstadt, severely damaging two Red battleships. Lenin seemed to have given up hope of holding Petrograd, feeling that it was more important to save Moscow from Denikin. But Trotsky had other ideas: he went to Petrograd, took charge of the army himself, and somehow succeeded in restoring morale. He had the Putilov factory produce some mock-ups which looked like tanks, and riding on horseback, he actually led a detachment of troops into battle. Within a couple of weeks Iudenich's army was forced to retreat into Estonia where it was disarmed (see Document D). In December an armistice was signed between Estonia and Russia.

In 1920 most of the loose ends were tied up. First of all, in February, a formal peace treaty was signed between Russia and Estonia. Later in the year Latvia, Lithuania and Finland signed agreements in which Russia recognized them all as independent states. In the east Kolchak came to a tragic end; deserted by most of his army and betrayed by the Czech legion, he was handed over to the Bolsheviks who executed him. In the south Denikin's retreat continued to the Black Sea port of Novorossiisk where about 50,000 of his troops embarked on British and French ships and sailed to Sebastopol in the Crimea. On 2 April 1920 Denikin resigned and was replaced by Wrangel; although he was able to restore discipline and morale in the Volunteer Army, he was unable to prevent the Reds from occupying the whole of the Crimea. However, he succeeded in organizing the evacuation of over 80,000 troops and refugees aboard British and French ships. This was completed on 14 November, the date taken by many historians as the official end of the Civil War.

One problem still remained for the Reds to deal with – in April 1920 the Poles had invaded Ukraine, though strictly speaking, this was not part of the *civil* war – it was an attack on Russia by a foreign country. The Poles aimed to liberate Ukraine from Russian control (Ukraine had passed back into Russian control following the defeat of Germany in the First World War) and secure Ukrainian recognition that eastern Galicia belonged to Poland. By 7 May the Poles had captured Kiev, but the invasion seemed to cause outrage among all shades of Russian opinion and rallied support for the government. With morale high, Red forces drove the Poles out of Kiev and chased them back into Poland all the way to Warsaw, which they prepared to attack in August. The Poles meanwhile had offered to begin peace talks and to drop all their claims against Russia. This offer was conveyed to the Russians by Lord Curzon, the British Foreign Secretary, who suggested that the River Bug might serve as an armistice line. Lenin rejected the offer, hoping that the Russian capture of Warsaw would spark off a proletarian revolution in Poland which would in turn spread to other countries. However, there was no uprising of the Polish masses, and when the Poles counter-attacked on 16 August, the Russians were caught off guard and thrown into retreat.

Thanks to tactical blunders by the Russian commanders and inspired general-ship from Marshal Pilsudski, the Polish leader, the Russians accepted that their attempt to control Poland had failed; an armistice was agreed in October 1920 followed by a formal peace treaty signed at Riga in March 1921. Russia made some territorial gains, but overall it was a much worse deal than if they had accepted the Curzon Line (see Map 5.2).

(c) Why did the Reds win the Civil War?

Although the Reds may have looked to be in a weak position, surrounded on all sides by White armies, in fact they had vital advantages. Militarily they had the advantage of a unified command and numerical superiority over the Whites. In October 1918 the Red Army had about 430,000 men; Trotsky as Commissar for War was responsible for building up the numbers – conscription was intro-duced and by the end of 1919 the total was approaching three million, including 61 rifle divisions and 12 cavalry divisions. The first commander, Ioachim Vatsetis, had told Lenin that he needed such numbers since he had to think about cam-paigns 'on all parts of the compass.' Lenin probably thought they would be needed later to carry the revolution forward into the rest of Europe. By contrast the White armies never totalled more than 250,000 at any one time. The Reds had a great advantage in the supply of armaments since they controlled about three-quarters of all the arms dumps and the factories capable of producing arms.[24] In the early days of the war the Reds lacked sufficient experienced officers, but Trotsky solved this problem by conscripting about 50,000 former Tsarist officers. Some of the other Communist leaders were dismayed at this, fearing that they could not be trusted; Trotsky made it work by pairing each officer with a com-missar or sometimes two; these were always reliable Bolsheviks, whose job was to shadow the officer and countersign all orders. Sometimes members of an officer's family were taken as hostages to ensure his good behaviour. Discipline was extremely strict; the army was supervised by the Cheka and Trotsky insisted that 'all cowards, self-seekers and traitors will not escape the bullet.' If a regiment abandoned its position, he had its commissar and commander executed and then had selected soldiers shot at random from the ranks (see Document C).

This was all part of the 'Red Terror' first proclaimed officially on 2 September 1918 immediately after the assassination attempt on Lenin; it was intended to gal-vanize the masses into active support for the regime and to crush anti-Bolsheviks. Although some leading Bolsheviks protested at this 'bloody discipline', it probably played an important part in ensuring the final Red victory. It certainly brought remarkable results in the army and Trotsky continued to use it. He described the policy as 'a red-hot iron applied to a festering wound.'[25] Trotsky's overall contri-bution to the Red victory has been a matter of some debate. Soviet historians would not allow him any credit whatsoever, but this is not surprising given that Trotsky and Stalin had never got on and that Trotsky was disgraced and exiled after Stalin came to power. But there can be no doubt that Trotsky does deserve the credit for the creation of a regular army and for providing a focus for it to rally around. His famous double-headed train, in which he was said to have covered 65,000 miles during the war, contained a printing press, a telegraph system, a radio station, an electricity generating station, a library and a garage which held several cars.

Although the area controlled by the Reds looked small on the map in comparison with White areas, it had the advantage of being central and compact. It contained the majority of the country's population, heavy industry and administrative apparatus. The railway network radiated outwards from Moscow, which was the centre of the country's communications and the Reds had much shorter lines of communication than the Whites. The closer the White armies drew towards their objectives – Moscow and Petrograd – the longer their lines of communication became and they overreached themselves. On the whole it is probably true to say that the urban working classes supported the Reds and so did the army of new administrators and bureaucrats who owed their positions to the regime.

The communist government took decisive measures to make sure that all the economic resources of the state were channelled into the war effort. This policy became known as War Communism; it involved the extension of state control over as much of the economy as possible. Nearly all industry was nationalized and stocks of raw materials were allocated wherever necessary to meet the demands of the military situation. Private trade was banned, though this was very difficult to enforce, and a special Commissariat of Supplies (*Narkomprod*) was given the job of getting sufficient food to the cities. This led to an intensification of grain requisitioning which was extremely unpopular with the producers. In the words of Alec Nove, the essence of War Communism was 'all these factors combined with terror and arbitrariness, expropriations, requisitions. Efforts to establish discipline, with party control over trade unions. A siege economy with a communist ideology. A partly organized chaos. Sleepless, leather-jacketed commissars working round the clock in a vain attempt to replace the free market.'[26] Lenin also experimented cautiously with collective farms which he thought would provide the magic solution to the food problem – though he knew that this was a long way in the future. By the end of 1918 some 3000 had been formed, but their first harvests were not especially impressive and after that the pace slowed down – by 1920 there were still only 4400 of them altogether. War Communism was not a complete success – it failed to end the food shortages in the cities but it did enable the government to feed and equip the Red Army.

Compared with these Red strengths the Whites had all the disadvantages. The various White armies were widely separated geographically, they had very little contact with each other and tended to operate as individual units, each with its own distinct aims. There was no central control, no overall plan and no joint strategy; the Reds were able to eliminate them one by one. The Whites lacked first-rate politicians – neither Kolchak nor Denikin had any political experience or instinct and both thought only in military terms, whereas the Reds had both efficient generals and astute political leaders. Heavily outnumbered, the Whites began to suffer from exhaustion and disease, especially typhus. There were problems with the Whites' non-Russian supporters; at first many Finns, Estonians, Latvians, Ukrainians, Armenians, Georgians and Cossacks supported the Whites; in fact the vast majority of Denikin's army consisted of non-Russians. But as it became clear that Denikin was a passionate Russian nationalist, whose slogan was 'Russia great and undivided', and was against giving independence to non-Russians, his support gradually melted away. The Whites refused to recognize the independence of Finland, Estonia and Latvia, which lost them vital support.

Another problem for the Whites was harassment from the armies of anarchist irregulars known as Greens, who opposed all authority. They were specialists in guerrilla warfare and attacked both Reds and Whites. The most influential Green army was probably that led by the Ukrainian anarchist, Nestor Makhno, which at one point was thought to have numbered around 30,000 men. According to W.B. Lincoln, Makhno had a deep belief in an egalitarian revolutionary order. He was fighting for 'a stateless communist society in which slavery will vanish and state authority will have no place, where the land belongs to nobody and it can be used only by those who care about it and cultivate it.' Makhno viewed Denikin as the greatest enemy; operating in the south – in the Ukraine, the Crimea and the Kuban – he and his partisan army did everything in their power to harass Denikin. They raided his ammunition dumps and destroyed vital reserves of shells just as he was about to launch his attack on Orel. They continued to attack his supply lines so successfully that Denikin was forced to detach troops to deal with them. An American pilot helping the Whites reported that 'Makhno was looting trains and depots with impunity, and White officialdom was losing what little control over the civilian population it had.' In the end Makhno probably contributed as much to the defeat of Denikin as the Reds did.[27]

Both Reds and Whites used methods of terror in the areas they controlled, to conscript peasants and to seize their grain – usually without payment. As far as ordinary people were concerned there was probably not much to choose between them, but the Whites had one big disadvantage – they were seen by the peasants as the representatives of the former landlords. The Reds were able to claim that if the Whites won the war, the peasants would lose the land they had gained from the revolution. The Whites did nothing to reassure the peasants on this score, and so, as Kolchak moved into central Russia, it became more and more difficult for them to get peasant support. White leaders seemed to assume that it was the duty of the peasants to fight for the White armies in the same way that they had served in the tsarist army. If they refused they were whipped, flogged and tortured, and villages were burned. General Graves, the American commander in Siberia, described how Kolchak's cavalry would ride into towns on market days and round up the young men at gunpoint and take them off to join the army. But this tactic was disastrous – it destroyed the discipline and the morale of Kolchak's army because four out of every five peasants conscripted in this way deserted, and many of them went to join the Reds, taking with them their weapons, uniforms and supplies. The American troops were there in a neutral capacity to help maintain the Trans-Siberian Railway, and Graves had plenty of opportunity to observe what went on. He became increasingly disenchanted with Kolchak's regime which he regarded as corrupt, brutal and reactionary. 'At no time while I was in Siberia,' he wrote, 'was there enough popular support behind Kolchak for him to have lasted one month if all allied support had been removed from him ... I am well on the side of safety when I say that the anti-Bolsheviks killed a hundred people to every one killed by the Bolsheviks.'[28]

Finally Lenin was able to make great propaganda by claiming that the Whites were responsible for the intervention of all the foreign troops in Russia.

He presented the Bolsheviks as the real patriots who were trying to clear the foreigners out and preserve Russia's independence. In fact the foreign intervention never became a serious threat to the Bolsheviks, mainly because the victorious powers were sick of war and were not impressed by the Whites who wasted much of the war supplies sent to them and were generally seen as corrupt and incompetent. As the White armies began to suffer defeats, the interventionist states lost interest; by the end of 1920 all the foreign troops except the Japanese had been withdrawn. Lenin was able to present this as a great victory and it did much to restore Russia's prestige after the humiliation of Brest–Litovsk.

(d) Effects of the Civil War

The war was a terrible tragedy for the Russian people – the most obvious effect was the enormous cost in human lives and suffering. It is impossible to give any accurate statistics since no records were kept and the administration was chaotic. Evan Mawdsley quotes estimated statistics from several different sources which suggest that the Red Army may have lost as many as 632,000 men killed in battle and 581,000 who died from disease. The Whites may have lost a total of 1.29 million from deaths in battle and disease; typhus and typhoid were the main killer diseases. In addition there were the victims among the civilian population and the people killed in both the Red and White Terrors. No figures are given for victims of the White Terror, but taking into account the White operations against the Greens and against peasant partisans, and the White anti-Jewish pogroms, the total number must have been in the tens of thousands. Estimates for those killed in the Red Terror vary widely: the lowest figure given is 50,000 and the highest a figure of 200,000 executed, plus 400,000 who died in prison or were killed in the suppression of anti-Red revolts. It is when the deaths from disease and famine are taken into account that the full horror of the Civil War becomes apparent. Typhus and typhoid epidemics killed 890,000 people in 1919 and just over one million in 1920; there were also innumerable deaths from dysentery and cholera as well as hunger and starvation. The total number of deaths which can be attributed to the Civil War was between seven and ten million – more than four times the number of Russian deaths in the First World War (1.7 million); seven million children were left homeless, and a further one million people are thought to have emigrated during the war. These included tens of thousands of right-wing political opponents of the communists and huge numbers of intellectuals, professionals, scientists and engineers. This was one of the reasons why there was a chronic shortage of such qualified people in the USSR during the inter-war years. 'The Civil War unleashed by Lenin's revolution,' concludes Mawdsley, 'was the greatest national catastrophe Europe had yet seen.'[29]

The war left the economy in a state of collapse; half the labour force of Moscow and Petrograd (see Document E) had fled into the countryside in search of food, and the industrial centres of the Donbas, the Ukraine and the Urals had suffered heavy damage. Thus the class which had been the Bolsheviks' strongest supporters in 1917 was rapidly disappearing. To cope with its cash shortage the government had simply printed more banknotes to meet its immediate expenses; by October 1920 the rouble was worth only one per cent of its value in October 1917.

The Baltic states of Estonia, Latvia and Lithuania had been given their independence, so it was only to be expected that production in all areas of the economy would be well down on the pre-World War levels. However, output was not just lower – it was catastrophically lower, as these statistics provided by Alec Nove show:[30]

	1913	1921
Factory production (million roubles)	10,251	2004
Coal (million tons)	29.0	8.9
Electricity (million kWhs)	1945	520
Pig iron (thousand tons)	4216	116
Steel (thousand tons)	4231	183
Cotton fabrics (million metres)	2582	105
Grain harvest (million tons)	80.1	37.6
Rail freight carried (million tons)	132.4	39.4
Exports (million roubles)	1520	20

The area which has interested historians most is the extent to which the Bolshevik regime was affected by the Civil War. Many changes took place in the nature and policies of the regime in both the political and economic spheres. Politically the regime became militarized and brutalized; economically it became centralized, and state control was extended over all areas of the economy. The question is: was the regime forced into these changes by the crisis of the Civil War, or would they have taken place anyway because of the nature of communism, as a deliberate drive towards socialism? If the second alternative is the correct one, did the government try to blame the changes on the crisis situation once they were seen to be ultimately failing?

American historian Robert C. Tucker argues that the Civil War was responsible for the political developments. 'War Communism militarized the revolutionary political culture of the Bolshevik movement. The heritage of that formative time in the Soviet culture's history was martial zeal, readiness to resort to coercion, centralized administration and summary justice.' It brutalized the party and gave them a siege mentality which they found it difficult to break away from; and it made centralization, strict discipline and mobilization of the population in order to achieve the regime's targets an integral part of the system. Tucker believes that already at the height of the Civil War there were signs of Lenin's later, more 'civilized' NEP thinking. For example in May 1919 Lenin wrote: 'the dictatorship of the proletariat is not only the use of force against the exploiters, and not even mainly the use of force.' Lenin was convinced that the main obstacle to socialism was the culture of backwardness left over from centuries of the tsarist regime, which was so deeply ingrained in the mentality of the population; the best way to change this was not by forcible means but by education, and that would take a long time.[31] Already in March 1919 the party had adopted a new programme which aimed to raise 'the low cultural level of the masses' as a vital preliminary to 'the abolition of state authority.' One of the key clauses in Lenin's *April Theses* was that the army should be abolished and replaced by a democratic militia in which everybody would have a chance to serve. This would guarantee that it could not be used against the people, since the people would hardly choose to attack themselves. However, the growing military threat to the new government arguably forced it to abandon such utopian hopes and return to more traditional military thinking.

Other historians believe that although the Civil War was one of the influences which militarized the Soviet system, it was by no means the only one. Christopher Read makes the point that the Bolshevik leaders were products of the tsarist environment, which was itself extremely authoritarian and did all it could to stifle criticism and opposition. The revolutionaries had been brought up under this system and had suffered at its hands. 'In the prevailing circumstances,' claims Read, 'it is hard to see why opposition should be tolerated when the Russian tradition was to eradicate it as heresy.' Even without the Civil War then, the Bolsheviks would have resorted to strong-arm methods because they were a minority party, which, in the eyes of the strict Marxists, had seized power too soon. They saw themselves as teachers and guides of the masses, knowing what the people wanted better than the people did themselves. Inevitably many of the masses were reluctant to accept this leadership and withdrew their support and co-operation. Whenever a minority party tries to force its will on the majority, coercion is more or less inevitable. In the case of the Bolsheviks, 'where consent was lacking, force, in varying degrees, filled the gap.'[32]

Among the older generation of liberal historians, Adam Ulam claims that Lenin fully expected civil war to break out and even welcomed it because it gave him the justification to continue with the violence, the terror, the suppression of an independent press, the persecution of opposition within the party and all the other elements that went to make up War Communism. When the Civil War was over he used other crises – the famine in the Volga area in 1920–21 and the Kronstadt uprising in 1921 – as excuses to prolong the 'state of siege'. 'How can one allow the luxury of free political discussion, he would ask, when there are two million Russian refugees abroad? Or when the capitalists have not desisted from their plans to overthrow the Soviets?'[33]

There is the same debate about the main economic features of War Communism – nationalization and state control of the whole economy: would they have been introduced with or without the Civil War because they were central to Bolshevik aims and ideals, or were they forced on the government by the need to gear the economy totally to the war effort? Even Soviet historians differ in their interpretations; A. Venediktov, writing in 1957, believed that the party did have a basic plan for nationalizing all the major branches of industry as soon as possible. The Sixth Party Congress (July–August 1917) passed a resolution to this effect, and Lenin had already said in his *April Theses* that they must 'bring production and distribution under the control of the Soviets.' In December 1917 Lenin said that he intended to declare all limited companies to be state property and on 15 December he set up the Supreme Council of National Economy (known as Vesenkha or VSNKh). Its function was 'the organization of the national economy and state finance ... and to plan for regulating the economic life of the country – food supply, trade and industry, agriculture, finance, army and navy; also activities of factory and trade union working class organizations.' It had the power to issue orders on all economic matters, which were binding on everybody, including the commissars. On 17 January 1918 the government announced that its policies were designed 'to guarantee the power of the working people over the exploiters, and as a first step towards the complete conversion of the factories, mines, railways and other means of production and transport into the property of the workers' and peasants' state.'

All this seems a very clear statement of intent, and some steps had been taken to carry it into practice before the Civil War proper began. Banks were nationalized, the state monopoly on grain introduced and the railways and merchant fleet placed under government control. By June 1918, 487 large factories had been nationalized. However, some other Soviet historians feel that Venediktov's evidence is not convincing. F. Samokhvalov, writing in 1964, feels that Lenin intended to develop a mixed economy in which some capitalist activity would be allowed. He pointed out that the wording of the official documents setting up VSNKh was vague: at no point was the word 'nationalization' used, nor was any timetable mentioned. The 487 nationalized factories were only a minute proportion of the total – when War Communism eventually took off fully, 37,000 enterprises employing 1.5 million workers had been nationalized by 1920. The interesting point is that over two-thirds of those first 487 nationalizations were carried out not on the orders of the government, but by local Soviets. In fact the government was alarmed by the large numbers of unauthorised nationalizations taking place and actually ordered that no more should be undertaken without permission from VSNKh. This hardly suggests that all-round nationalization was an immediate aim when VSNKh was set up. The Bolsheviks themselves were divided on the issue: some, including Nikolai Bukharin, were horrified by War Communism because they believed that small-scale trade and agriculture should remain in private hands. Others fully approved of it and saw nationalization as their main socialist goal. For them the difficulties of the Civil War were an excuse to introduce full state control. Alec Nove concludes that 'Lenin and his colleagues were playing it by ear...we must allow for the interaction of Bolshevik ideas with the desperate situation in which they found themselves.' In a sense therefore War Communism was both a response to the war emergency and an attempt to leap into full socialism.[34]

5.6 The New Economic Policy (NEP)

(a) The shift to the New Economic Policy

In 1921 Lenin suddenly introduced a dramatic change in the government's economic policies, ending grain requisitioning from the peasants and allowing small-scale manufacturing and trade to be returned to private ownership. Again there is much debate about Lenin's motives: was the NEP forced on him by difficult circumstances – the Kronstadt mutiny and various other crises – or had he intended to introduce it anyway once the Civil War was over? Some Bolsheviks claimed that they had been on the point of starting it when the Civil War prevented them. If this is true then NEP was intended to be a permanent policy; but at the time of its introduction most Bolsheviks saw it as a temporary retreat from real socialism. But how long was temporary? Even Lenin himself made contradictory statements about this at different times.

There is no doubt that early in 1921 Russia was still in crisis, despite the ending of the war. War Communism was extremely unpopular with the peasants who felt that they had no incentive to produce as much grain as possible; they were quite content to grow just enough for their own needs, and so production fell sharply. In 1921 the peasants sowed only about half the area sowed in 1913 and the harvest was less than half the 1913 total. In 1921–22 Russia experienced the worst famine ever in its history – probably about five million people died from starvation and disease, and there were reports of cannibalism and body-snatching. The government was forced to appeal to the outside world for help, and many organizations responded, including the international Quakers and Herbert Hoover's American aid project (see Document F(iii)). There was a wave of peasant revolts across most of European Russia; now that the Whites had been defeated there was no need for the peasants to continue supporting the communists as the lesser of two evils. By March 1921 the government had virtually lost control of rural Russia; large armies of rebel peasants led mainly by Left SRs roamed the countryside raiding grain-collecting stations and carrying the requisitioned grain back to the villages. Almost all the new collective farms were destroyed and their livestock shared out among local peasants. Some of the rebel leaders had been Bolshevik supporters during the Civil War but had now had enough of the Bolshevik dictatorship. Terrible revenge was taken against government officials, commissars and members of the grain brigades – thousands of Bolsheviks were tortured and murdered; the classic symbolic torture was to slice open stomachs and stuff them with wheat (see Document F(ii)). The growing disaffection with the regime was reflected in the increasing numbers of Mensheviks and SRs elected to rural Soviets.

The government was unpopular in the cities too. Food was in short supply and extremely expensive. Unusually heavy snow disrupted transport throughout January 1921 and hundreds of factories were forced to close through lack of fuel. In February 1921 the appalling conditions brought the workers of Moscow to breaking point, and thousands came out on strike. There were massive demonstrations calling for free trade and the recall of the Constituent Assembly. The strikes soon spread to Petrograd where similar demands were made – freedom of speech and the press, an end to the police terror, and free elections for factory committees, trade unions and Soviets. Martial law was declared in both cities and the Cheka arrested hundreds of strikers as well as many Mensheviks and SRs who were said to be playing a leading role in the demonstrations. This only inflamed the situation further and the government was not confident that it could rely on the army to restore order if called upon.

There were disagreements within the communist party leadership as to how best to proceed. Trotsky felt that the fate of the Revolution was delicately balanced and he suggested that the workers needed stricter discipline to get the economy moving again. He demanded that trade unions should be put in their places – that is, strictly subordinated to the state. This outraged some of the other leading Bolsheviks who felt strongly that trade unions should remain independent and were horrified at the prospect of 'military discipline' for workers. This group, the so-called 'Workers' Opposition', was led by Alexander Shlyapnikov and Alexandra Kollontai, who wanted power to be shared between the party, the trade unions and the Soviets. In the end Lenin acted as a peacemaker – both Trotsky and the trade union supporters had to acknowledge defeat and accept Lenin's middle way policy. Unfortunately this preoccupation with the 'trade union problem' delayed proper discussion of the food crisis, and by the end of February 1921 there was a serious threat that the unrest would bring down the regime. The situation was strikingly similar to the one which had led to the overthrow of the monarchy exactly four years earlier. It was the mutiny of the Kronstadt naval garrison which brought matters to a head.

(b) The Kronstadt Mutiny, February–March 1921

As the news of the strikes in Petrograd reached the island naval base, the garrison of around 15,000 soldiers and sailors became increasingly restless. They were mainly peasants from rural village backgrounds and they were well-informed about the hardships suffered by their families – the continuation of grain requisitioning even though the Civil War was over, the brutality of the grain detachments and the complete insensitivity of many of the commissars. Already they had complained about the corruption and special privileges of the Bolshevik elite and they bitterly resented the dictatorial attitude of the party. In 1917 the Kronstadt garrison had been the most dedicated Bolshevik supporters, but by the end of January party membership on the island had fallen by half and the party itself was being denounced as 'an enemy of the people'.

On 28 February a meeting on board the battleship *Petropavlovsk* passed a resolution calling for free elections for the Soviets by secret ballot, freedom of speech and the press for peasants, workers, soldiers and the left wing parties (but not for 'the bourgeois and the landlords'), freedom of meetings for peasant associations and trade unions, abolition of grain requisitioning and the right of peasants to cultivate their land as they saw fit, provided they did not employ hired labour. The resolution was almost unanimously approved at a huge open-air meeting the following day attended by around 16,000 people, which included soldiers, sailors and a fair proportion of the 30,000 civilian inhabitants of Kronstadt. There was no hint of counter-revolution in their demands – they had simply had enough of the communist one-party dictatorship. They did not want the Constituent Assembly; what they wanted was genuine Soviet democracy of all the working class parties, a return to democratically elected soldiers', sailors' and factory committees and the release of all workers from the Cheka prisons. They took no aggressive action and waited, apparently hoping that the rest of the country and the army would rally to their support; perhaps too they were hoping that the government would negotiate.

However, to make any major political concessions would be the beginning of the end of the one-party dictatorship. The leadership saw the Kronstadt programme simply as an attack on Bolshevik power, and had no hesitation in deciding that the mutineers must be crushed, before they were joined by the Petrograd strikers and the rest of the country. Lenin and Trotsky announced that the rising was being organized by 'White Guards' and claimed that the sailors were not the same as the staunch Bolshevik supporters of 1917 – they were young recruits who were bringing 'anarchist' and 'petty-bourgeois' attitudes with them from their villages. Both claims were untrue. Efforts were now made to appease the workers of Petrograd. Zinoviev, the communist leader in the city, increased the daily food ration (though this depleted the rapidly dwindling reserves) and dropped hints that the government was preparing to abandon the hated grain requisitioning. On 1 March he ordered the removal of the road blocks set up around Petrograd to prevent private trade, and these gestures did something to defuse the situation in Petrograd itself.

Pressure could now be brought to bear on Kronstadt. Trotsky was sent to Petrograd to take charge of operations and on 5 March he ordered the mutineers to surrender immediately or they would be 'shot like partridges'. The mutineers rejected this ultimatum and Trotsky ordered the Red Army to attack Kronstadt. On 8 March, after a long artillery bombardment, the troops set out on the five-mile march across the ice. They soon came under heavy machine-gun fire; many ran away, about a thousand joined the mutineers, two thousand were killed and the attack ended in fiasco. A week later General Tukhachevsky had assembled a larger and more reliable force of 50,000 men consisting of Cheka troops and elite communist regiments known as Units of Special Designation. A second assault was launched on Kronstadt using different tactics – the troops crossed the ice at night and succeeded in getting close to the island before they were spotted. By the morning of 18 March, after vicious house-to-house fighting which brought heavy losses on both sides (about 10,000 of the communist troops were killed), the communists had regained control of Kronstadt. About 8000 of the rebel garrison troops escaped across the ice to Finland, but those who were taken prisoner could expect no mercy. Zinoviev ordered the immediate execution of 500 leading mutineers, and almost 2000 more were executed later, most of them without trial. Lenin ordered hundreds of other prisoners to be sent to a concentration camp in the far north, on an island in the White Sea; here conditions were so bad that very few of them returned. The American anarchist Alexander Berkman, who was in Petrograd at the time, wrote in his diary: 'My heart is numb with despair; something has died within me ... the last thread of faith in the Bolsheviks is broken.'[35] The ruthless suppression of the Kronstadt mutiny stunned socialists the world over (see Document D(iii)). It was now clear beyond all shadow of doubt that the Bolsheviks were not interested in listening to the political arguments of the ordinary people of Russia. In the words of Israel Getzler, 'the sailors, soldiers and workers of Red Kronstadt had enthusiastically enlisted in the front ranks of the October revolution and in the civil war, trusting that Soviet power would make the whole of Russia into one large Soviet democracy like their Kronstadt. Now it was they who found themselves in brutal confrontation with a Bolshevik power which had snuffed out their dream of egalitarian democracy.'[36] Before long the same brute force had successfully crushed the peasant revolts in Tambov, where 15,000 rebels were shot, and in Siberia, the Don and the Kuban. The Mensheviks and SRs were suppressed and as many as 5000 Mensheviks arrested during the course of 1921.

(c) The Tenth Party Congress and the beginning of NEP

The Congress opened in Moscow on 8 March 1921 at the height of the Kronstadt mutiny. The first few days were taken up by debates about the role of the trade unions and party unity. It wasn't until 14 March that Lenin eventually announced the proposal to replace grain requisitioning with a tax in kind; in other words peasants would hand over a fixed amount of grain and would then, presumably, be free to sell the rest privately. Although none of the Bolshevik leaders was enthusiastic about the new policy, which was seen as a betrayal of socialism, Lenin was able to persuade them that it was the only way to win the co-operation of the peasants. The Congress approved this change as well as the proposal to grant concessions to foreign capitalists to set up factories in Russia.

On the surface it might look as though the strikes and the Kronstadt mutiny forced Lenin into economic retreat. But recent biographers have shown that he may well have changed his mind as early as November 1920 after visiting the village of Yaropolets near Moscow and talking to peasants about their difficulties. He paid other visits to villages in December and talked to peasants at the Congress of Soviets held in December 1920. If he still needed convincing, his meeting on 2 February 1921 with V.N. Sokolov, a Bolshevik representative from Siberia, perhaps did the trick: he reported on the peasant unrest and disturbances in his area and told Lenin that some urgent action was needed to pacify the peasants; otherwise there could be a catastrophe. The same day Bukharin brought news of another peasant uprising – in Tambov province. When the Politburo met on 8 February Lenin sketched out his first proposals for the reversal of policy. The aim of the new tax in kind was 'to expand the freedom of the cultivator to use his surpluses over and above the tax in local economic exchange ... and to reward those who increase their output.'[37] As yet, however, the proposed change was not made public – it would take time to persuade the rest of the party that, given the huge scale of opposition to them, some drastic action was urgently needed. The importance of Kronstadt was not that it changed Lenin's mind, but that it gave him the weapon with which to overcome the opposition and win over the Party Congress.

Although Lenin was prepared to allow some relaxation of economic control, the opposite was true in the political sphere. In the weeks leading up to the Congress he had become increasingly impatient with the disputes and arguments going on within the communist party. In his 1902 pamphlet *What Is To Be Done?* Lenin laid great emphasis on party discipline, and most Bolsheviks had accepted the idea of democratic centralism – that is, members were free to debate issues, but once an issue had been voted on at a Congress or a Central Committee meeting, they were bound to accept that decision as final. Since the party took power in 1917 a tendency had developed for factions to continue pressing their point of view even after a decision had been taken against them. Alexander Shlyapnikov and the Workers' Opposition for example, who believed that the workers were not receiving the benefits they deserved from the revolution, were continually trying to whip up support for their programme of more power to the trade unions. The factions acted almost like separate political parties within the communist party; this was a healthy sign in the sense that it enabled genuine discussion of many important issues to take place. But Lenin thought otherwise – at a time when the Bolsheviks' popularity was at its lowest ebb since 1917, divisions in the party were a luxury they simply could not afford; at this time of economic and political crisis they were an open encouragement to the enemies of the regime. The Tenth Party Congress therefore passed Lenin's resolution 'On party unity' which banned factions within the party and allowed the leadership to expel any member who persisted in opposing a policy once it had been adopted as official. It seemed that the one-party dictatorship with Lenin as the dictator was now complete.

(d) The NEP in operation

The introduction of NEP was a great victory for the peasants; the government expressed its regret that grain requisitioning had been forced upon them by the Civil War. The first payments of grain and other agricultural products were set at a considerably lower level than under War Communism. Peasants were allowed to sell their surplus produce privately; it was hoped that this would encourage them to produce as much as possible and thus alleviate the food shortages. After 1923 they were allowed to pay the tax in cash. At first private trade was restricted to local markets and fairs, but before long middlemen were allowed to trade so that the surplus grain could be brought to the towns where it was most needed. Many of these private traders, who were soon known as 'Nepmen', flourished and became quite wealthy. Small private shops were allowed to open again. The government promised to buy manufactured goods from abroad so that there would be something worthwhile for the peasants to spend their profits on. As soon as the beneficial effects of the new policy were felt, the relaxation of control began to spread to industry. The goal of complete nationalization was abandoned and about 80 per cent of small-scale industry had been restored to private ownership by 1923. However, Lenin insisted that most heavy industry – what he called 'the commanding heights of the economy' – including the railways and banking should remain under state control, which meant that around 84 per cent of all industrial workers were employed in state-owned enterprises. The economy was an odd mixture in which one section – heavy industry – was totally dominated by the state, while the other section – agriculture – was controlled by some 25 million independent small producers. Many of the Bolshevik leaders felt highly aggrieved at this return of capitalist activities and Lenin had a very rough ride at the Party Conference in May 1921. Other aspects of NEP included foreign investment to help develop Russian factories and mines, and attempts to stabilize the currency by cutting government spending. This resulted in the introduction of charges for schooling and health care, which had been free, and contributory old-age pensions.

Lenin defended the NEP vigorously. It would be a great crime, he argued, not to admit that they had made mistakes in dealing with the peasants; 'only agreement with the peasantry can save the socialist revolution in Russia . . . the needs of the middle peasants must be satisfied . . . we must adapt our state economy to the economy of the middle peasant.' He told the Eleventh Party Congress in 1922 that the communists had failed to run the economy successfully; therefore they must make use of the experience of the capitalists. 'The capitalist is the possessor of the secret to make the economy bloom; they are operating like robbers; they make profit; but they know how to do things ... The mixed companies that we have begun to form, in which private capitalists, Russian and foreign, and Communists participate, provide one of the means by which we can learn to organize properly, so that we can help the peasant make progress. Communists must learn from ordinary capitalists.'[38]

On the question of how long it was intended to continue NEP, it is difficult to be certain. At first the impression given was that it was only temporary; according to Bukharin: 'we are making economic concessions in order to avoid political ones. The NEP is only a temporary deviation, a tactical retreat, a clearing of the land for a new and decisive attack of labour against the front of international capitalism.' Lenin himself compared it with the Japanese attack on Port Arthur during the Russo–Japanese War: the first attack had failed, so then the Japanese halted, retreated for some distance and rethought their strategy; later on a second attack was launched but with more careful preparation, and this time it succeeded. The lesson to be drawn was that some failures were necessary in order to find the best method. About the length of time involved, Lenin was vague – in May 1921 he told the party that NEP must be pursued 'seriously and for a long time – not less than a decade and probably more ... we must definitely get this into our heads and remember it well, because rumours are spreading that this is ... a form of political trickery that is only being carried out for the moment. This is not true.' In October 1921, when asked when NEP would be halted he replied: 'This question is incorrectly posed because only the further implementation of our turnabout can give an answer to it. We shall retreat until we have learned for ourselves, until we have prepared ourselves to go over into a solid attack.'

At other times Lenin seemed to be suggesting that the NEP was not a retreat – it was a return to something like the correct road to socialism along which they had scarcely begun to advance before the Civil War distracted them. He admitted that by taking power in 1917 the Bolsheviks had prevented the bourgeois revolution from running its course; so instead of introducing socialism immediately in a country dominated by a large industrial proletariat, it had to be developed more gradually in a backward peasant-dominated society. NEP was not a retreat – it was an attempt to find an alternative road to socialism in less than ideal circumstances.[39]

The dissenting Soviet historian Roy A. Medvedev, writing in 1971, argued that judging by Lenin's last thoughts on the economy which were expressed in articles which he dictated, and in conversations with Bukharin in 1923 after he had suffered two strokes, he envisaged NEP as consisting of two stages. In the first stage the plan was to increase agricultural production as much as possible using the existing system of small peasant farms by giving all possible help to poor and middle peasants. He did not see the kulaks as a threat to socialism during this first stage and even proposed giving prizes to kulaks for increased production. But he did believe that in the long run the kulaks were the enemies of socialism and of the Soviet regime, and so it would be wrong to make the future of Russian agriculture dependent on them. The second stage of NEP therefore was the development of agrarian co-operatives which would lead to the triumph of socialism. He acknowledged that this would not be easy and would involve a long campaign stretching over many years to develop literacy and general culture among the peasants. They would have to be taught how to work together and how to use agricultural machinery and tractors, and they would have to be convinced of the benefits of a co-operative system of farming in terms of efficiency, productivity and profit. In an article written in January 1923 Lenin explained that 'to achieve through NEP the participation of the entire population in the co-operative movement requires an entire historical epoch. We may get through this epoch successfully in one or two decades' (see Document H).

There were no precise details given; clearly at this stage it was all experimental, and the details would be worked out from actual experience. As Lenin remarked to H.G. Wells: 'Those who are engaged in the formidable task of overcoming capitalism must be prepared to try method after method until they find the one which answers their purpose best.'[40] One thing was very clear, however, at least according to Bukharin – Lenin had turned his back on the use of force and was anxious to rely on peaceful methods; it was to be communism with a human face. Some later historians have questioned the reliability of Bukharin's claims which he made in the late 1920s when he had fallen out with Stalin over whether or not to continue the NEP. Stalin wanted to abandon it and introduce a tougher policy towards the kulaks, whereas Bukharin was keen to continue without the use of force. Obviously it was to Bukharin's advantage if he could show that Lenin too was in favour of an evolutionary and peaceful approach.

(e) How successful was the New Economic Policy?

The NEP continued until the spring of 1928 when it was abruptly abandoned on the orders of Stalin. Judging from the statistics, the policy seems to have been reasonably successful and by 1926 the government could claim with some justification that it had achieved its immediate aim. Production in all sections of the economy had improved significantly and in most commodities it was not far off the 1913 levels. Given the territorial losses at the end of World War One and the war with Poland, this was a considerable achievement.[41]

	1913	1921	1922	1923	1924	1925	1926
Industrial output (million roubles)	10,251	2004	2619	4005	4660	7739	11,083
Coal (million tons)	29.0	8.9	9.5	13.7	16.1	18.1	27.6
Electricity (million kWhs)	1945	520	775	1146	1562	2925	3508
Pig iron (thousand tons)	4216	116	188	309	755	1535	2441
Steel (thousand tons)	4231	183	392	709	1140	2135	3141
Cotton fabrics (million metres)	2582	105	349	691	963	1688	2286
Sown area (million hectares)	105.0	90.3	77.7	91.7	98.1	104.3	110.3
Grain harvest (million tons)	80.1	37.6	50.3	56.6	51.4	72.5	76.8

Especially impressive were the sown area which was slightly greater than in 1913, and the electricity output which almost doubled. This was one of Lenin's favourite schemes; in December 1921 he wrote in his report to the Congress of Soviets: 'Communism is Soviet power plus the electrification of the whole country. Otherwise the country will remain a small peasant country...Only when the country has been electrified, and industry, agriculture and transport have been placed on the technical basis of modern large-scale industry, only then shall we be fully victorious.'[42]

One can never be quite sure how reliable statistics are; the problem with these particular statistics is that they are mainly from Soviet sources and so could have been exaggerated to make the communists' achievement appear better than it really was. On the other hand the 1913 statistics are from official tsarist sources, so they too could have been inflated. Although they give the impression of a fairly steady improvement, the sources conceal many problems. The dreadful famine continued into 1922, partly because of transport problems. The railways were in a bad way – at least half the locomotives had broken down and it was difficult to get hold of spare parts. The government solved this problem by importing locomotives and parts, though they had to spend precious foreign currency to pay for them. In the long run this paid off, and in 1926–27 the amount of rail traffic surpassed the 1913 figure.

There were also serious industrial problems because the government insisted that under the NEP heavy industry must produce commercially. This meant that it must do without the state subsidies which it had been receiving since 1917, and it must make a profit – or at least avoid making a loss. Factories tried to cut expenses by reducing their workforces, and so unemployment rose rapidly. The country experienced a problem with inflation which caused its currency to dwindle dramatically in value; by 1922 the rouble was worth 60,000 times less than it had been in 1913. In rural areas money went out of use and its place was taken by a barter economy. Sometimes poods (a pood was approximately 36 pounds) of grain were used as a unit of exchange. Lenin was determined that the country must have a stable currency, but this could only be achieved by balancing the budget. Somehow the government had to increase its income, and that meant imposing more taxes and higher taxes: the grain tax was changed to a cash payment, and taxes were introduced on income and property, and on private businesses and workshops. People were encouraged to buy government bonds, and sometimes the 'encouragement' was little short of coercion. The situation was helped by the communists' repudiation of millions of roubles worth of foreign debts and interest payments incurred by the Tsarist government before 1917. A new Soviet bank was set up in October 1921 which worked so well that the government succeeded in balancing the budget in the financial year 1923–24. In February 1924 the newly stabilized rouble became the sole official currency and then in the following financial year the government had a surplus for the first time since 1917.

But before that was achieved there was another problem to be faced – this was the strange situation in which industrial and agricultural prices moved rapidly in opposite directions. It was Trotsky who nicknamed it the 'scissors crisis': the scissors of the economy were opened as the blades of industrial and agricultural prices moved apart – industrial prices rose substantially while agricultural prices fell. In October 1923 industrial prices stood at 276 per cent of their 1913 level, whereas agricultural prices had fallen to only 89 per cent of their 1913 level. There were a number or reasons for this: agriculture recovered rapidly, no doubt because of the greater incentives to produce more; by 1923 the sown area was back to 90 per cent of the 1913 total, there was a good harvest, food shortages were no longer a major problem, and so prices fell. However, industry, short of equipment and supplies of raw materials, recovered far more slowly; for example in 1923 output of textiles was still only about a quarter of the pre-war figure, and iron and steel output was even lower than that, which tended to push industrial prices up. The peasants suffered most from this: although their incomes had increased, the government was still the main buyer of grain, in spite of the activities of the private traders, and the government always paid the lowest prices it could get away with. The peasants reacted as they always did in these circumstances – they stopped releasing their grain; they were the main buyers of manufactured goods, but now they could not afford to buy as much as they would have liked. Eventually the scissors crisis partially solved itself: the lack of peasant spending power meant that state-owned industry had difficulty selling its consumer goods and machinery, and so prices began to fall, encouraged by the government which did its best to bring prices down. By mid-1924 the blades of the scissors had closed appreciably.

To sum up, economic progress under the NEP was modest but it was such a marked improvement on what had happened in the years before it was introduced that it was widely accepted up until 1927. By then industrial workers who had a job were being paid real wages on a level with pre-war values and they had the benefits of new social legislation brought in under the NEP. They were entitled to an eight-hour working day, two weeks' holiday with pay, sick pay, unemployment pay and health care. As for the peasants, it seems likely that they too were better off; statistics suggest that the percentage of the harvest leaving the countryside fell between 1913 and 1927, which is taken by some historians to mean that peasants and their livestock were eating more; the peasant standard of living was probably far higher than in 1913. The fact that hardly any peasant protests took place in the mid-1920s seems to bear out this view.[43] Electricity came to many villages along with hospitals, schools, libraries and cinemas. On some of the larger peasant farms advanced methods were being used – multi-field crop rotation was introduced on around 20 per cent of all farmed land, along with chemical fertilizers and modern machinery. Unfortunately, however, the NEP had some major weaknesses: it led to high unemployment – by 1923 about 16 per cent of the industrial workforce had been made redundant as factories tried to cut costs; and in 1927 unemployment was still at the same level. Industry needed new plant and new machinery and therefore massive new investment which the NEP was not providing (see Document I). And NEP meant that the urban areas were still dependent on privately-owned agriculture for their basic food supplies. Given the fact that grain marketings remained well below pre-war levels, this was bound to cause the government serious concern.

5.7 Foreign affairs and the Communist International

(a) The Bolsheviks and world revolution

Lenin and Trotsky attached vital importance to the theory of 'permanent revolution'. Since in the eyes of the strict Marxists, the proletarian revolution had taken place in Russia too early, before the country was sufficiently industrialized, it was crucial that the Bolshevik revolution should spark off revolutions in more advanced countries like Germany. They genuinely believed that Germany was the most likely candidate for the next revolution because her people were weary of the war and her armies were in retreat in the west in October 1918. Their theory was that when dictatorships of the proletariat were established in advanced states like Germany, they would give their Russian comrades all the economic and political support they needed. There was a rising of left-wing socialists known as Spartakists in Berlin in January 1919, but it was soon suppressed. More promising for the Bolsheviks was an uprising in Munich, the capital of Bavaria, in March 1919 – a Soviet republic was declared but it collapsed after only two months. The nearest thing to a successful revolution outside Russia occurred in Hungary, where in March 1919, Bela Kun set up a Soviet republic in Budapest. Again, however, it was short-lived – it lasted only until August when Kun was overthrown and forced to flee, eventually settling in Russia.

In order to encourage world revolution Lenin called together representatives from communist parties all over the world in a Congress in Moscow in March 1919. It was known as the Third International or the Comintern; Lenin was hoping to use it to organize the world's communists under Russian leadership, showing them how to provoke strikes and insurrections. The chairman was Zinoviev who confidently predicted that 'in a year the whole of Europe will be Communist.' Comintern agents were active in most European countries during the next few years, doing their best to 'export the revolution'. They had very little success: by the time the next Comintern Congress met in the summer of 1920, the revolutionary tide in Europe had clearly ebbed. The Russian invasion of Poland in July 1920 was the last desperate attempt to provoke revolution and it ended in failure (see section 5.5(b)). The Bolsheviks had to accept at last that their dreams of world revolution were not going to be realized. At its 1921 Congress the Comintern adopted new tactics – the goal now was to form a United Workers' Front in which the world's communist parties pledged themselves to work with other socialist parties and trade unions for common aims. This was a major climb-down from its original strategy, although it did not entirely abandon its subversive activity. Comintern agents were involved in an attempted rising in Germany in 1923 which was a failure. Foreign governments assumed that its activities were sponsored by the Soviet government and this made it more difficult for Russia to regain the trust of the great powers.

(b) Communist Russia and the West

The realization that Russia was in danger of being isolated for the foreseeable future brought about a radical change in communist foreign policy. Lenin took the humiliating lesson of defeat by the Poles to heart, and at the Third Comintern Congress in June 1921 he denounced any further attempts at armed uprising. He acknowledged that Russia needed peaceful co-existence and co-operation in the form of trade with, and investment from the capitalist world. Britain was one of the first countries to resume diplomatic relations with Russia, and in March 1921 the two countries signed an agreement in which Britain promised to begin trading again. Later in 1921 the Russians agreed to pay back some of the loans which the Tsarist government had accepted before 1917. In April 1922 the Russians attended an international conference in Genoa, along with the British, French, Italians and Germans. This in itself was a significant step, showing that communist Russia was being accepted as an equal among the other European states. But they all had their own ulterior motives: Britain hoped to persuade the Russians to repay all their debts in full, and to manoeuvre the French into reducing their reparations demands from Germany. Germany was hoping that some of the harshest terms of the 1919 Versailles Peace Settlement would be toned down; and the Russians hoped to attract investment and aid from the West in order to revive their economy.

The Russian delegation was led by Georgi Chicherin, the Commissar for Foreign Affairs, but he had strict instructions from Lenin not to reach any general agreement with all the powers – Lenin felt that Russia's interests would best be served if the other European states remained divided; once they were united and in full agreement, they might well turn against Russia. Lenin had also decided that Russia would refuse to pay *all* her outstanding debts, and he was suspicious that any deal with Britain or France over trade or investment would have strings attached which would enable them to interfere in Russian economic affairs. Not surprisingly the conference failed: the French were unco-operative on the question of reducing German reparations, and the British and French would not do a deal on Russia's terms. However, the Russian and German delegations withdrew from the conference and met at Rapallo about 20 miles further along the coast. A treaty was signed in which the two defeated black-sheep states of Europe promised to cancel their mutual debts; Russia would supply Germany with grain in return for machinery, and Russia was to allow German pilots to train in her territory (the Versailles Treaty forbade them to train in Germany). This agreement was something of a triumph for the communist government – Russia was no longer completely isolated and the economic co-operation with Germany was valuable. In 1924 the First Labour government in Britain gave official recognition to what was now the USSR.

Meanwhile, at the same time as the Moscow government was trying to improve relations with individual Western states, the Comintern, despite its 1921 declaration, could not resist interfering. When there was an economic crisis in Germany in 1923, the Soviet government backed a Comintern plan to help German communists to seize power. The attempt went badly wrong and the communists were crushingly defeated. Although the German government continued to co-operate with Russia under the terms of the Rapallo Treaty, they were now beginning to feel that there was more to be gained from closer ties with the West, rather than from the USSR. Similarly Britain became more suspicious of Russian interference; just before the election of October 1924 *The Daily Mail* published a letter signed by Zinoviev which, it was claimed, he had written to the British Communist Party giving instructions about forming cells in the British army as a step towards revolution. Although it was a fake, the letter helped to turn British public opinion against the USSR, and may well have contributed to the Labour government's defeat in the next election. During the British General Strike of 1926 the Russians encouraged the strikers and at the same time Comintern agents were trying to stir up trouble for the British in India. In 1927 the British Conservative government broke off diplomatic relations with the USSR. These apparently contradictory foreign policies on the part of the Moscow government left the USSR almost isolated again. Stalin in particular among the Russian leaders was worried at the increasing co-operation between the Western powers (the 1924 Dawes Plan and the 1925 Locarno Treaties – see section 7.1(a)), which he felt boded ill for Russia.

5.8 Russia, government, nationalities and the 1922 constitution

(a) The nationalities and the Bolsheviks

In 1917 only just over half the population – the people in the central core of the empire – was Russian; around the peripheries there was a bewildering variety of different national minorities. To the north there were the Finns, around the Baltic there were Germans, Estonians, Latvians and Lithuanians, in the west there were Poles, Belorussians and Ukrainians, and in Transcaucasia (the area between the Black Sea and the Caspian Sea) there were Armenians, Azerbaijanis, Georgians, Chechens and Dagestanis. In the east, where most of the people were Muslims, there were the Iranian-speaking Tadjiks, and there were Kazakhs, Kirgiz, Uzbeks, Turkmen and many others. The Tsarist regime had made no distinction between those who were likely to be loyal to Russia, like the Finns and the Baltic Germans, and those who were likely to want independence, like the Ukrainians and Poles. The policy was simply to Russianize everybody, so by 1917 all the nationalities were bitterly opposed to tsarist rule.

Before they came to power the Bolsheviks claimed to be sympathetic to demands for independence, if any national group felt strongly enough about it. In 1913 Lenin spoke of the need for a gentle approach to the Poles: 'The Poles hate Russia, and not without reason. We cannot ignore the strength of their nationalist feeling. Our revolution will have to treat them very gently and even allow them to break away from Russia if need be.' Stalin agreed with Lenin at this point and in 1913 published an essay entitled *Marxism and the Nationalities*, in which he argued that all oppressed peoples should be allowed the right of self-determination. However, he went on to express the hope that after gaining independence the nationalities would stage their own socialist revolutions and then voluntarily rejoin Russia in one large multi-national socialist state. Stalin's essay, plus the fact that he was himself a non-Russian (he was a Georgian and spoke Russian with a strong Georgian accent), earned him the reputation of being something of an expert on the nationalities problem. When the Bolsheviks took power, Lenin appointed him Commissar for Nationalities. Together they drew up *The Declaration of the Rights of the Peoples of Russia*; these rights included the equality and sovereignty of all the peoples of Russia, free self-determination 'even to the point of separating and forming separate states' and the abolition of all national and national–religious principles.[44] Only a few weeks later the government began to carry out the policy by granting Finland full independence. Between January and March 1918, Ukraine, Georgia, Armenia and Azerbaijan took Lenin and Stalin at their word and declared themselves independent. In February–March 1918 Belorussia and the Baltic states of Estonia, Latvia and Lithuania were occupied by the Germans who encouraged them to declare independence from Russia. In Belorussia the communist party eventually gained control and formed the Belorussian Soviet Socialist Republic; however, the three Baltic states were allowed to remain outside the USSR until 1939 when they were again occupied by the Russians on the outbreak of the Second World War.

Before very long though, the attitude of the Bolshevik leaders changed and Stalin in particular became hostile to the independence movement. In fact although he was a Georgian he ended up being far more of a Russian nationalist than many of the Russians themselves. There were several reasons for this reversal of policy. The recognition of Finnish independence was followed by a disastrous civil war. The struggle for independence had been led by the Social Democrats who had won a majority in the Finnish parliament in the elections of 1916; the Russian Bolsheviks were happy to recognize the independence of Finland under a socialist government. However, right-wing groups or Whites under the command of General Mannerheim, and helped by the Germans, attacked the socialists, and by May 1918 were in control of the whole country. In the following White terror, thousands of people were murdered and an estimated 12,000 Red prisoners died in prison camps. The new governments in the Ukraine, Georgia, Armenia and Azerbaijan were also anti-communist. The Ukrainians were the most troublesome: their leader, Petliura, ordered all Ukrainian troops fighting in the Russian armies to walk away and return home. During the Civil War, when Moscow wanted to send troops against the White armies in the south, Petliura refused to allow them to pass through the wedge of Ukrainian territory separating northern and southern Russia. Worse still, he began to attack the Ukrainian Bolsheviks who were rapidly getting stronger.

Many of the Russian Bolshevik leaders, most notably Bukharin, had argued all along that it was foolish to grant independence to nationalities *before* they had become communist, in case Russia found herself surrounded by a ring of hostile states. Exactly that situation had now arisen and was threatening the survival of Russia's revolution. Stalin came round to agreeing with Bukharin and in January 1918 the government announced a change of policy: a nation could have self-determination only if the working-class demanded it, and not just to satisfy the middle-classes. The ultimate aim was for a federal constitution in which the smaller nations must accept overall control from Moscow but would have their own parliaments for internal affairs. In other words a nation could only have its independence if it was being ruled by communists, and even then it would immediately have to surrender a large measure of that independence by joining a Russian federal state. During the Civil War the government took decisive action: in the Ukraine a communist regime was imposed by force; after initial brutality Lenin insisted that Ukrainian national culture must be respected, and gradually the communists won the support of a substantial proportion of the peasants.

In Transcaucasia a similar process took place. Azerbaijan was the first to return to the Russian fold. In Baku, the main city, there was a large Bolshevik party membership who championed the cause of the (mainly Muslim) working classes and who were demanding that the Red Army should come and rescue them from the bourgeois nationalists who had declared Azerbaijan independent in May 1918. At the end of April 1920 there was very little resistance when the Red Army entered Baku. The Christian Armenians, who lived on both sides of the frontier between Russia and Turkey, had gone through a troubled period. With Russia and Turkey on opposite sides during the First World War, the Turks systematically murdered thousands of the Armenians living in their territory and deported thousands of others. Estimates of those killed between 1915 and 1922 vary from 600,000 to 2.5 million; tens of thousands of refugees managed to escape to Russian Armenia. The Armenian government, led by the party known as the Dashnaks (Armenian Revolutionary Federation), made the mistake of launching an invasion of the eastern part of the Turkish province of Anatolia, claiming it for Armenia. This only provoked a Turkish counter-attack which by November 1920 had brought the Armenians to the verge of defeat. Moscow took advantage of this situation, demanding that the Dashnaks agree to accept a Soviet government in Armenia. In the circumstances they had very little choice, and in December 1920 the independent republic of Armenia came to an end.

Georgia, the third of the Transcaucasian states, was a different case: it already had a socialist government of Mensheviks, who were supported by a large majority of the Georgian people – they won 75 per cent of the votes in the elections for their parliament. They were providing stable government and had introduced a programme of social and economic reform, including land reform – breaking up large estates and redistributing land among the peasants. Georgia was already being hailed by world socialist leaders as a shining example of how to organize the classic Marxist state. In May 1920 the Moscow government signed a treaty with Georgia, recognizing its independence and promising not to interfere in its internal affairs. But in reality the Soviet leadership was determined that Georgia must be 'sovietized', as they put it. Lenin hoped that it could be achieved gradually and peacefully, but Stalin was impatient. In February 1921, he and his close associate, Sergo Ordzhonikidze, another Georgian, stirred up the Georgian Bolsheviks to stage a rising against the Menshevik government; the Red Army moved in to help, the Mensheviks were forced to flee, and Georgia once again became part of Russia.

In the vast area to the east of the Caspian Sea, bordering on Iran, Afghanistan, India and China, the inhabitants were mainly Muslim. Relations between Russians and Muslims varied, but in some areas, progressive Muslim intellectuals joined the communist party in the hope of modernizing Muslim society. During and shortly after the Civil War, sometimes by force, sometimes with local co-operation, the Soviet government set up a series of Soviet Socialist Republics – Bashkir, Tatar, Turkmen, Kirghiz, Kazakh, Uzbek and Tadjik. By March 1921 therefore, apart from the loss of Finland, the three Baltic states and some territory to Poland and Turkey, the communists had more or less restored the frontiers of the old Russian empire.

(b) The formation of the Transcaucasian republic

Lenin and Stalin both thought Georgia, Armenia and Azerbaijan should be amalgamated into one republic of Transcaucasia. This would make it easier for Moscow to control the area, and it would help to improve relations between the three states, which were constantly squabbling over frontiers and territory. There was also the hope that Turkey would be less likely to interfere in Armenian affairs if Armenia became part of a larger state, and, so it was argued, amalgamation would help the economies of the three states to develop more successfully. The leading Georgian communists objected, claiming that their sovereignty would be curtailed and their separate identity lost in a large Transcaucasian state; they demanded that they should be admitted to the USSR on the same terms as Ukraine. Nevertheless enough of them were persuaded to enable the scheme to go ahead, and in March 1922 the Federal Union of the Soviet Socialist Republics of Transcaucasia formally came into being.

(c) The development of the party state and the background to the new constitution

In his book *State and Revolution* written in August–September 1917, Lenin put forward the traditional Marxist view that the state was repressive and should 'wither away'; when freedom existed there would be no need for a state. The early decrees of the Sovnarkom (the Soviet of People's Commissars) laid stress on 'popular initiative and social reconstruction from below' by workers and peasants. In 1918 the first constitution was introduced for the new state, which was called the Russian Soviet Federated Socialist Republic (RSFSR). The constitution was based on the Soviets, and it attempted to be democratic and decentralized so that workers and peasants could exercise some power and initiative through the network of elected Soviets. Ordinary workers and peasants elected their local Soviets, whose members chose delegates to their provincial Congress of Soviets. They in turn chose delegates to the All-Russian Congress of Soviets, which had 3000 members. They elected the 300-member Central Executive Committee of the Congress of Soviets. At the top was Sovnarkom which usually had ten members and was chaired by Lenin. In theory Sovnarkom was supposed to submit decrees to the Central Executive Committee for approval. In the early days it was still a multi-party state and the Soviets were open to all parties such as Mensheviks and SRs which accepted Soviet power. While Lenin was in reasonable health most of the important government decisions were taken by Sovnarkom.

Alongside the official soviet government structure there was an equivalent communist party organ at each level. At the top was the Political Bureau (Politburo), the party equivalent of the Sovnarkom; at local level there were the local communist party groups, who sent delegates to the Party Congress, and above that there was the Central Committee of the communist party, known as the

Praesidium. During the Civil War the Bolshevik or communist party gradually began to take on more power. After the Mensheviks and the SRs were outlawed for 'counter-revolutionary activities', the communist members of Sovnarkom were left as the acting government, and since they were all members of the Politburo, in effect the governing body of the party, the Politburo began to act as the government. The circumstances of the war required quick decisions and so the Politburo members got into the habit of regarding themselves as the government and continued to do so when the war was over.

By 1921 therefore the government situation had been completely transformed. Decision-making was concentrated firmly in the hands of the party leadership, and the dictatorship of the proletariat was nowhere in evidence. Lenin defended this development on the grounds that the working class was 'exhausted and is naturally weak in a country that is in ruins.' If the workers were exhausted and their level of 'political culture' was low, then the most advanced workers and their leaders must rule the country – and that meant the communist party. This also meant increased centralization of the state at the expense of local power; many communists had now come round to the view that the party should have primacy over the government structure. Lenin and Trotsky were not happy about this latest development and wanted to keep the party and the government structures separate. Stalin on the other hand approved of the party becoming dominant because by the time of Lenin's death he had built up enormous personal power within the party. Lenin aimed to strengthen the governmental structures, but after May 1922 when he became increasingly incapacitated, Sorvnarkom declined in importance and it was the Politburo that became the most powerful political body in the country. It was against this background that the new constitution, which went into operation in January 1923, was drawn up.

(d) Lenin and Stalin fall out over the new constitution

The general feeling among the party leadership was that there was a need to formalize the developments that had been taking place and to bring the separate republics into a closer and more centralized union with the Russian republic. It was felt that this would help economic reconstruction and it would enable them to present a united front of Soviet republics against the threat of encirclement by hostile capitalist states. Some communists saw the new constitution as a counterbalance to NEP – to tighten up control from Moscow in the face of an emerging new capitalist class. Stalin saw it as a chance to increase his own power via the party machine; as Lenin's health deteriorated there was clearly going to be a struggle for power before very long, and Stalin was determined to be as well-placed as possible when that time came.

It was over the exact nature of the USSR that Lenin and Stalin disagreed. Lenin wanted all the republics to join together in the Russian Federation in which they would all have equal status and which would be ruled by a Federal Union government, 'presided over in turn by a Russian, a Ukrainian, a Georgian, etc.', and not by the government of the Russian republic in Moscow. However, Stalin, by now an intense Russian nationalist, disagreed with this – although he was a non-Russian, he wanted the other nationalities to be subordinate to the

Figure 5.2   Lenin and Stalin looking pleased with themselves at Gorky in 1992.

Russians; the Russian government in Moscow must be the dominant one; there was no question of an equal partnership. He called this idea 'autonomization'; it meant that although in theory the non-Russian republics would have some rights of self-government, in practice overall control would be in the hands of the RFSR in Moscow. He even accused Lenin of being 'soft on the nationalities.' Although Lenin was ill by this time, he was determined to have his way and he persuaded the Politburo to support him. Stalin wisely decided to avoid a confrontation and

Lenin's plan was adopted. On 31 December 1922 the new constitution was approved in principle by an All-Union Congress of Soviets, and the Union of Soviet Socialist Republics (USSR) officially came into existence. The Georgians welcomed this but were still not happy about amalgamation and they resented the overbearing attitude of Stalin and Ordzhonikidze, the Politburo representative in Georgia. It was reported that Ordzhonikidze had beaten up one of the Georgian leaders who had called him 'a Stalinist arsehole'. Lenin was dismayed by such violent behaviour, and began to take steps to have Stalin removed from his position as Party Secretary. Sadly Lenin's health and influence declined during 1923, and no steps were taken against Stalin (see sections 6.1(a) and (b) for details).

At first the USSR consisted of four republics – Russia, Ukraine, Belorussia and Transcaucasia; Uzbekistan and Turkmenistan joined in 1925. The governmental structure of the new constitution was in many ways similar to that of the 1918 constitution. Each republic had a Congress of Soviets which sent a number of delegates to the Union Congress of Soviets, proportionate to the size of its population. The Union Congress elected a Central Executive Committee composed of two chambers: the larger one was the Council of the Union, again consisting of delegates chosen according to the size of population of the individual republics. The delegates from the Russian republic were in a large majority because of Russia's much larger population. The smaller chamber was the Council of Nationalities in which each national group had equal representation – five delegates from each republic. The Central Executive Committee appointed the Sovnarkom for the USSR. Correspondingly each republic had its own Central Executive Committee and Sovnarkom.

The USSR government in Moscow was to have full control over foreign and military affairs, defence, overseas trade and 'the struggle against counter-revolution'; the republics were to have some control over their own internal economic affairs, agriculture, health and education; and they had the right, in theory, to withdraw from the Union. Although the new constitution stressed the equality of the republics and seemed to give them considerable control over their internal affairs, in practice this turned out not to be the case. Because it was now a one-party state, the local communist party leaders controlled the governments of the republics; most of the time they simply carried out Moscow's orders. If there was a conflict of interest, the All-Union government could overrule any laws passed by the republics; and the All-Union government had control of the budgets of the republics. In effect, therefore, the constitution was a significant step towards centralized control of the USSR from Moscow. So although Lenin thought he had got his own way and solved the nationalities problem, the long-term outcome was not at all what he had intended. Stalin had got what he wanted over Georgia and had managed to steer the new constitution a substantial part of the way along the road to domination by Moscow.

In the central government the Congress of Soviets and the Central Executive Committee turned out to be merely discussion bodies; no voting on important issues took place and no vital decisions were taken. In theory the Sovnarkom was the body which decided on policy and issued decrees, but as we saw earlier, it was the Communist party Politburo acting as Sovnarkom which was the real power in the country. The Politburo, working through the bureaucratic party

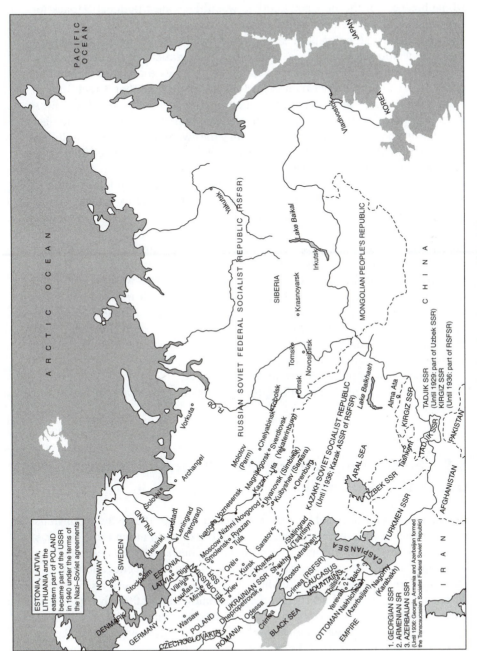

Map 5.3 The USSR before the Second World War.

ESTONIA, LATVIA, LITHUANIA and the eastern part of POLAND became part of the USSR in 1940 under the terms of the Nazi–Soviet agreements

1. GEORGIAN SSR
2. ARMENIAN SSR
3. AZERBAIJAN SSR
(Until 1936: Georgia, Armenia and Azerbaijan formed the Transcaucasian Socialist Federal Soviet Republic)

TADJIK SSR (Until 1929: part of Uzbek SSR)
KIRGIZ SSR (Until 1936: part of RSFSR)

machine, was the body which ran the USSR; and it was not even mentioned in the constitution. Lenin's attempt to strengthen the governmental structure at the expense of the party machine had failed. In fact Robert Service believes that this whole business of the new constitution 'was the greatest political setback for Lenin in his party since before the February Revolution of 1917.'[45]

In spite of the tightening political control, most of the party leaders recognized that they would have to tread carefully in their treatment of the nationalities. It would be unwise to attempt to 'Russianize' them as the tsarist regime had done. At the Twelfth Party Congress in 1923 it was decided that 'Great Russian chauvinism' was as great a danger as nationalism within the republics. Even Stalin accepted for the time being a new official policy of denouncing Russian chauvinism and encouraging and heightening the awareness of national cultures. Self-government was given to the Bashkirs, the Tatars, Kirghizia and Dagestan. The Tatar and other languages were accepted as equal in status to Russian; thousands of new schools were built and Russians were forbidden to settle in Kirghizia so that the local nomadic tribes would be free to move around unhindered. The party claimed that national minorities received more sympathetic treatment in the USSR than anywhere else in eastern or central Europe; it was hoped that this would help to recruit more party members among the non-Russian population in order to strengthen the local organizations. In the mid-1920s there was a period of stability when it seemed that the nationalities were accepting the centralized Soviet regime. The policy had one drawback: it resulted in a great flowering of national cultures; this inevitably stimulated nationalist pride and patriotism and so the desire for more independence grew. In the early 1930s Stalin took steps to dampen nationalist enthusiasm. Even in the 1920s there were limits to the Politburo's patience; persistent trouble-makers were dealt with by the Cheka (known from 1923 onwards as the United Main Political Administration, or OGPU); and in 1924 an attempted uprising in Georgia was crushed by the Red Army.

5.9 Education, culture, the arts and religion under the Bolsheviks

One of the better features of life under the Bolsheviks was that, with the obvious exception of religion, there was more freedom of expression than there ever was under the Tsars.[46] This was partly because the Bolsheviks felt they needed to win the support of as many intellectuals as possible to help spread education and the cultural changes necessary for building a socialist society. There was a feeling among many writers and artists that they must move out of their 'ivory towers', make contact with the workers, become involved in everyday life, and help to create the new 'Soviet man and woman'. As the poet Mayakovsky put it: 'Let us make the streets our brushes, the squares our palette.' The first reaction of most intellectuals to the Bolshevik takeover was not encouraging: many left Russia and never returned, while others refused to co-operate with the new regime. However, as the Bolsheviks became established, some of the *émigrés*, like the composer

Sergei Prokofiev and the writer Maxim Gorky, returned and became at least partially reconciled with the regime. Lenin actively encouraged experimentation in all forms of the arts, although he did not always like the results. At the end of the 1920s, as Stalin moved into the ascendant, a new phase of intolerance began.

(a) Education

The Bolsheviks saw universal education as absolutely vital for achieving the great cultural transformation, and Lenin's wife, Nadezhda Krupskaia, was a great advocate of high-quality mass education. Anatoli Lunacharsky was made Commissar for Education in 1917; he was responsible for all schools, although in theory the church schools came under the supervision of local Soviets. Hundreds of new schools were built, especially in rural areas. By 1927 education was free and compulsory for all up to the age of 12; the government had intended to provide free education up to the age of 17, but resources and numbers of teachers were insufficient. Institutes or workers' faculties were set up so that ambitious workers could prepare themselves to enter higher education; any Red Army recruits who were unable to read had to attend classes as part of their training. It was estimated that in 1927 about 51 per cent of the population were literate, as opposed to only 35 per cent in 1907. In the universities, workers and peasants were given preference over young people from 'bourgeois' backgrounds. Another innovation was the Proletkult organization which was meant to encourage and develop working-class culture. It worked through factory clubs which organized theatre groups, choirs, music groups, art and creative writing classes and sporting events.

Lunacharsky had a grand vision which went far beyond simply teaching the children of the workers to read and write; he wanted them to have a wide general education so that they could rise to the level of the intelligentsia, and he intended to take class differences out of education. All this would be offered in a new type of school – the United Labour School – where mixed courses of vocational and academic education could be followed by all children, whatever their class background. He encouraged progressive teaching methods – more relaxed discipline and project work instead of examinations. There was opposition to these schools from other Bolsheviks who thought they were encouraging bourgeois values, or more seriously, that they were not developing the skills needed to modernize the economic life of the country. Although Lunacharsky never came anywhere near achieving his full programme, he was allowed to persevere until 1930 and great progress was made. Under Stalin's leadership, however, education for workers' children concentrated more on narrow vocational training in order to produce the required number of apprentices for the factories. Progressive teaching methods were abandoned and class divisions were brought back into education; Lunacharsky was removed from his post.[47]

(b) Literature and the theatre

When the First World War broke out in 1914 Russia was enjoying a great cultural revival known as the Silver Age (see section 2.1(k)) in which avant-garde writers, artists and musicians led the way. Many of the avant-gardistes welcomed the

revolutions; the Symbolist poet Alexandr Blok stayed in Russia and soon produced two of his greatest poems, *The Twelve* and *The Scythians* which glorified
the revolution as an irresistible force destroying the old capitalist system of Europe.
The Futurist poet Vladimir Mayakovsky was another committed Bolshevik supporter, although Lenin was not an admirer of his work. Writers who were in
sympathy with the regime formed the All-Russian Association of Proletarian
Writers (RAPP); they wanted working-class values to be dominant and did all
they could to encourage cultural activities in factories; they claimed to be the
official voice of the communist party. Writers who were not communists were
allowed to publish, provided they were not critical of the regime; they were known
as 'fellow-travellers'.

But there was a limit to the tolerance of the Politburo; the secret police kept
a close watch on all the leading intellectuals, including writers and artists.
In August 1921 the poet Nikolai Gumelev was arrested by the Petrograd Cheka,
accused of being involved in a right-wing plot and executed without trial; although
Gumelev was known to have monarchist sympathies, there was not a shred of
evidence to support the accusation. Blok became disillusioned with the Bolsheviks,
his health deteriorated and he died shortly before the execution of Gumelev.
These two events were the last straw for Maxim Gorky who left Russia in October
1921. In the spring of 1922 a large group of around 160 writers and academics,
who were considered to have overstepped the mark and were held responsible
for 'the growing influence of a revitalized bourgeois ideology in the young Soviet
Republic,' were expelled from the country. All writings were now to be strictly
censored. Under the NEP remaining writers were encouraged and well paid.
A great clutch of Civil War novels appeared, of which the best known was *And
Quiet Flows the Don* (1929) by Mikhail Sholokhov, which dealt with the experiences of the Don Cossacks during the war years. Also popular with the general
public was a new genre of satirical stories poking gentle fun at the Soviet system.

Lunacharsky gave the job of relating the theatre to everyday life to the well-
known director Vsevolod Meyerhold. He experimented with new techniques,
dispensing with the curtain and the proscenium arch; he made use of platforms
of varying levels and ramps sloping down to the first row of seats, multi-purpose
movable sets, and eventually complete theatre in the round. The idea was to
break down the division between the actors and the audience and encourage the
audience to participate and express its reactions to the drama. Not many new
Russian plays were written in the early years of the regime, but the ones which
were produced were based on the theme of the struggle between the evil capitalist
and the noble worker; it was all part of the attempt to win over the support of the
general public. Although Meyerhold was forced to resign after only a few months
because his ideas were too avant-garde for the authorities, he continued to work
and experiment in the theatre.

Another famous actor, director and producer who stayed in Russia after the
revolution was Konstantin Stanislavsky, founder of the Moscow Arts Theatre in
1898. His new style of acting technique was extremely influential both in the
USSR and abroad – actors were encouraged to use memories of their own experiences and emotions and to empathize with the characters they were playing. He
wanted them to actually feel the emotions which the characters were supposed

to be feeling, in order to achieve convincing performances which were more appropriate to the greater realism of the twentieth century. His production of a new play by V.V. Ivanov about the revolution, *Armoured Train 14–69*, in 1927, was regarded as a milestone in the progressive Russian theatre.

Public interest in the theatre spread rapidly as workers' drama groups flourished. It was reckoned that by 1920 there were three thousand theatres in the Russian Republic alone, and the Red Army and Navy ran over a thousand theatres. The regime used the theatre for propaganda, telling the approved version of the Revolution and the Civil War. Among the most spectacular productions were the massive street theatre events, like *The Storming of the Winter Palace* which was performed in 1920 on the third anniversary of the Bolshevik coup. It was enacted in Petrograd on three huge stages in Palace Square, with the Winter Palace itself as part of the set. There was a cast of 10,000 and an audience estimated at 100,000.

(c) Art, architecture and music

In the world of art things seemed to be getting off to a good start under the Bolsheviks. Wassily Kandinsky, the great pioneer of abstract art, who had considerable sympathy with the revolution and its aims, was appointed Professor at the newly founded Free State Art Studios. In 1920 he was made an honorary Professor at the University of Moscow and was responsible for creating the Russian Academy of Artistic Sciences in Moscow in 1921. He also worked in Lunacharsky's Commissariat for Enlightenment where he was responsible for deciding which works of art should be bought; one of his greatest achievements was in organizing 22 museums throughout the Union.

Marc Chagall was another famous artist who supported the revolution and he was appointed Commissar for Art in his native Vitebsk in Belorussia. He launched himself enthusiastically into projects for a local academy and museum and on the first anniversary of the revolution he decorated the streets of Vitebsk with murals which portrayed, among other things, green cows and horses, and a smiling Lenin hovering over a newly married couple. Sadly there were soon bitter disagreements between Chagall and local party leaders who found his work too avant-garde and claimed that the workers could not understand it. He moved to Moscow and worked for a time designing sets and costumes for theatre productions. Both Kandinsky and Chagall became disenchanted with the regime when some of the officials began to put pressure on artists to produce art to which the workers could relate. This was dismissed by the avant-gardists as 'five-kopek art'. Kandinsky left Russia in December 1921 and Chagall in 1922; neither of them returned.

A group known as the Constructivists, which included the artists Malevich and Rodchenko, and the architect Tatlin, tried to bring contemporary art into everyday life by designing clothes and furniture for use in the factory. In the realms of architecture, the 1920s saw some remarkable new designs. There was Tatlin's model for a monument to the Third International, which took the form of a spiral tower (1919–20); Leonidov's design for the new Lenin Institute (1927); experimental houses in Moscow, Saratov and Sverdlovsk designed by Moses Ginsburg (1928–30), and the designs for the new town of Magnitogorsk drawn up by a group of architects led by Leonidov, which were much more humane than the high-rise blocks which became familiar as typical Stalinist architecture.

In one sense music came off well since the new regime gave musical opportunities to all sections of the public. A great deal of talent was discovered that might otherwise have been missed. In another sense, however, music was not as successful as the other arts. Russia's two greatest composers of the pre-war era, Stravinsky and Rachmaninov, both left the country; Dmitri Shostakovich (born 1906) tried to produce music to appeal to the working class; but much of his output during the early years was not among his best work. Most of the musical experimentation had a mildly eccentric air and was soon abandoned: some orchestras played without conductors, since a conductor was not considered to be socialistically correct; some music was composed to be played in factories using factory sirens and hooters as instruments (even Shostakovich used factory whistles in his Second Symphony). Probably most bizarre was the changing of well-known opera titles and librettos to make them politically acceptable – thus Glinka's popular opera *A Life for the Tsar* had its libretto rewritten and it was renamed *The Hammer and the Sickle*. In fact, with the possible exception of Shostakovich's First Symphony (1926), no really outstanding music was composed in Russia during the 1920s. Classical orchestral music, opera and ballet were certainly popular with ordinary people who had been unable to afford to see and hear them before the revolution – but what they wanted most was Tchaikovsky, Borodin, Rachmaninov and Rimsky-Korsakov.

(d) The cinema

Lenin was extremely enthusiastic about the cinema; he saw it as possibly the most important of the arts, and the film industry was nationalized in August 1919. He thought it could turn out to be a more powerful propaganda medium than the written word, since at least half the population was illiterate. He wanted films to be informative 'like the best of our soviet newspapers,' full of the new socialist ideas, but entertaining and amusing as well. Lunacharsky promised that in the new Soviet films there would be 'no glorification of bloodshed and violence, no appeal to race or religious bigotry and hatred: the cinema will be used to teach citizenship and love of humanity.' A group of talented young directors emerged which included Sergei Eisenstein, Vsevolod Pudovkin and Alexander Dovzhenko. Eisenstein was greatly influenced by Meyerhold and was the director mainly responsible for staging *The Storming of the Winter Palace* in 1920. He performed plays in factories and a gasworks before turning to the cinema. His first major film, *Strike*, about the brutal repression of a strike which took place just before the First World War, came out in 1924, and this was followed in 1925 by *Battleship Potemkin*, to mark the twentieth anniversary of the 1905 revolution. This film turned out to be the finest example of Eisenstein's montage technique, in which some scenes were shot using several cameras, making possible a dramatic mixture of close-up and long-shot. For the tenth anniversary of the Bolshevik coup he produced *October* which recreated the revolution (not altogether accurately) so graphically and dramatically that some of the shots were often taken for authentic newsreel clips.

Pudovkin's films concentrated more on individual heroes and heroines rather than on the grand sweep of events. He focused on the actors who were encouraged to use Stanislavsky's realistic methods, so that he was probably the director who came closest to social realism. His most important films were *Mother* (1926), based on Maxim Gorky's novel, which tells the story of a mother who is gradually converted to the idea of revolution through the influence of her son; *The End of St Petersburg* follows the experiences of a young peasant during the war and the revolution which changed St Petersburg into Leningrad (1927); and *Storm over Asia* (1928) which deals with incidents in the Civil War. The Ukrainian Dovzhenko began his film career in 1926 as a scriptwriter with the Ukrainian Film Company. As a director he was responsible for *Svenigora* (1928), *Arsenal* (1929), which is a portrayal of the revolution in Ukraine, and *Earth*, which came out in 1930. Each one of these films is a masterpiece in its different way, and they all won great critical acclaim abroad. They were popular with Russian audiences too, but ironically the Russian public tended to prefer American thrillers and Tarzan adventures.

Film also played an important role in the more direct mass propaganda campaigns of the Agit-ships and Agit-trains which travelled all over the country. They contained cinemas which showed newsreel, documentary and lecture films, and they carried collections of propaganda art and posters. Usually there would be poets and writers on board who would read out their work, and there would be artists who decorated the ships and trains with images presenting topical messages. Whether the regime succeeded in creating the new 'Soviet man and woman' with this barrage of propaganda during the 1920s is open to question. The problem was that the 'ordinary person in the street' was more interested in being entertained than politically educated. The best of the writers and film-makers had some success in combining the two, but the traditional popular culture continued to exist in the cafes, bars, music halls and homes, where people shared jokes and irreverent stories about the communists. R.G. Suny tells a popular joke which circulated in the mid-1920s – an old man on a trolley-bus, feeling sad at the miserable conditions of his life, sighs long and deeply, 'Oi'. His wife quickly hushes him with a warning: 'Fool, don't talk counter-revolution in public.'[48]

(e) Religion

Lenin and the Bolshevik leaders were atheists who accepted Marx's claim that religion was merely an invention of the ruling classes to keep the people docile and under control – the 'opium of the masses'. The Orthodox Church was seen as a rival in the struggle for control of the country's soul. For the Bolsheviks, communism was the only religion, and they were determined that people should worship the Soviet state instead of God. All the Church lands had been taken away in 1917; Church schools were taken over and even the Church buildings were now owned by the local Soviets which hired them out for services. Hundreds of priests were arrested by the Cheka, but the peasants were not happy about this and began to elect their own priests instead. The government ridiculed religious believers as backward; they tried to replace the religious holidays with secular holidays like May Day and Revolution Day; Red baptisms and weddings were encouraged – children were said to be 'Octobered' instead of baptized and couples took their marriage vows in front of a portrait of Lenin instead of at the altar. These ceremonies were popular with young party members, but most peasants resisted and stayed with the traditional sacraments.

In 1921, probably because of their lack of success, the Bolsheviks stepped up their anti-religion campaign. The shooting of priests began and Lenin accused the Church of refusing to sell their consecrated valuables to help the famine relief fund. In fact the Church had been giving generous help to the campaign and there was no need for the sale of treasures; but Lenin needed an excuse for the vicious attack he was about to launch. In February 1922 local Soviets were ordered to remove all valuable objects from churches; violent clashes were reported from all over the country as people resisted. Some members of the Politburo felt that the campaign was proving to be counter-productive and voted to end the confiscations. However, Lenin was furious at this and overruled the Politburo; the memorandum containing his instructions (which was not published until 1990) does not reveal him in a good light at this time when, some historians have claimed, he was trying to achieve his aims without violence: the time had come, he argued, to destroy the Church 'for many decades . . . to assure ourselves of capital worth several hundred million gold roubles . . . to carry out governmental work in general . . . I have come to the unequivocal conclusion that we must now wage the most decisive and merciless war against the Black Hundred clergy[49] (see also Document G). Some estimates put the 1922–23 death toll in the campaign as high as 7000 clergy killed in clashes, and 8000 people executed, including a group of bishops.

Since many of the leading Bolsheviks were Jewish, the Jews had a better time at the hands of the new regime than under the Tsars, and restrictions on their activities were removed after 1917. But during the Civil War they suffered vicious attacks from the Whites, and also from Ukrainian nationalists who resented the fact that Ukrainian Jews opposed separation from Russia. Consequently many Jews joined the communist party and Jews became influential in the party hierarchy and the bureaucracy. The Bolsheviks also tried to win over the Muslims, of whom there were over 15 million living in Central Asia, the Volga region (the Tatars) and Transcaucasia (the Azerbaijanis). Traditional Muslims remained hostile to the regime, and although progressive Muslims tended to side with the Russians, very few actually went so far as to join the communist party. The Koran remained their Bible, not the works of Karl Marx.

5.10 Assessments of Lenin

(a) Lenin and Marxism

One of the debates which used to occupy historians a great deal is the extent to which Lenin's ideas and actions deviated from Marxism. It is difficult to be precise about this, firstly because Marx himself modified his principles during the forty years that he was writing, and secondly because Lenin had no absolutely fixed ideas: he had basic aims which were reasonably consistent, but when it came to the question of how best to achieve his aims, he was a practical realist who adapted and changed his methods and policies in response to circumstances. What Lenin did was to build on Marx's ideas and refine them to suit the circumstances in Russia at the time. Not all of Lenin's modifications and additions were original – many of them had their roots in earlier Russian history. It is possible to identify several areas in which Marx's ideas were developed further. In his 1902 pamphlet *What Is To Be Done?* Lenin first put forward the idea of the small elite group of full-time dedicated professional revolutionaries who might come from any class provided they were totally committed. They were the advanced guard who would show the workers how to develop a 'modern socialist consciousness'. This was probably the most original aspect of Leninism; most of the strict Marxists strongly disapproved because they believed it would lead to dictatorship; however, others thought it was a realistic approach, given the political and social conditions of Tsarist Russia.

Lenin disagreed with the Mensheviks and most other Bolsheviks in the timing of the revolution. They followed Marx in the belief that there must be a long gap, probably years rather than months, between the bourgeois revolution and the workers' revolution, and that industry, technology and education must be highly developed before there was any attempt to establish a socialist state. Lenin had rejected this idea of fixed historical stages as early as 1905, and in fact in 1881, shortly before his death, Marx himself had suggested that in certain circumstances it might be possible to carry out both revolutions together and introduce a socialist state, even in a peasant society. The circumstances needed for this to be possible were some sort of massive international catastrophe (like the First World War) brought about by the failings of capitalism, and at the same time revolutions in other countries. Lenin came to the conclusion that capitalism had reached its final form with imperialism, which had led to colonial rivalry and thus helped to cause the First World War. Capitalists would therefore be opposed not only by the workers but also by their oppressed colonial peoples, who were the natural allies of the workers.

In his 1917 *April Theses* Lenin argued that the opportunity provided by the situation in Russia at the time was too good to miss and urged an immediate seizure of power by the Bolsheviks. The strict Marxists objected on the grounds that Russian society was not yet sufficiently industrialized for socialism to be established; the peasants would never co-operate. But Lenin believed that an alliance with the poorer peasants could play a vital part in the revolution.

Another divergence of ideas was over the question of how the new state would be organized after the revolution. Marx had given only minimum guidelines – the old bourgeois system would be destroyed by force, the state would wither away, and there would be a classless society and a dictatorship of the proletariat in which the workers would run the country in their own interests. In *State and Revolution*, which he wrote during the summer of 1917, Lenin added more details. He argued that the apparatus of state authority would have to be maintained for some considerable time in order to achieve the destruction of the capitalist system and the substitution of the dictatorship of the proletariat. This would be the period of class war, when the collective dictatorship would establish socialism; this would involve, among other things, worker control of the factories and the highest level of social welfare systems ever seen anywhere in the world. When this was achieved and all resistance from the former ruling class had been finally crushed, dictatorship would no longer be needed and the state would start to wither away; however, no timetable or time-scale was given for this. Arguably these ideas were not a significant departure from Marxism since Marx himself was quite clear that it would take some time to kill off bourgeois institutions. Unfortunately it didn't work out quite as Lenin had hoped; remarkably generous welfare schemes were introduced, but the state did not wither away. As we have seen, the party bureaucracy grew larger and the state became even stronger.

After coming to power Lenin also had to revise his ideas about the role of the workers in running industry. Although the idea of workers' control was supported by the 'workers' opposition', it soon became clear that workers lacked the necessary expertise; a return to some of the previous capitalist practices was thought to be unavoidable, and so the workers soon lost one of their main gains from October – worker management of the factories. This was quickly followed during the Civil War period by the terror, the forced requisition of grain from the peasants, the militarization and the centralization of the regime; all of which gave rise to the claim that the ordinary workers were no better off. Was all this an integral part of Leninism or was it forced on him by the circumstances? (see section 5.4). The last and most startling of Lenin's deviations from Marxism were NEP, the apparent trends away from violence and the adoption of a more gradual, more 'civilized' approach to socialism. Clearly Lenin's ideas were constantly changing according to circumstances. Three distinct phases can be identified: first of all his pre-1918 ideas; these had to be drastically revised when the Bolsheviks came to power and were faced with the reality (Civil War, absence of other revolutions, international isolation of Russia) of having to govern the country; and thirdly the return to state capitalism and a more relaxed approach economically in the NEP phase.

(b) Lenin – the evil genius?

After Lenin's death the Politburo, against the wishes of his widow, decided that his body should be embalmed and put on display in a glass case in a special mausoleum to be built in Red Square. The apparent success of the NEP had increased respect for Lenin, and the Politburo members, especially Stalin, hoped to share in the popularity by presenting themselves as Lenin's heirs who would continue his policies. They encouraged the Lenin cult for all they were worth: all his main works were published (with careful editing), and no shred of criticism was allowed, Petrograd was renamed Leningrad, and Stalin launched a new drive called 'the Lenin Enrolment' to recruit more workers. As a result the party gained around 240,000 new members. Stalin gave a series of lectures which were published under the title *Foundations of Leninism*. Lenin was revered almost as a saint and the faithful flocked to Moscow to view his remains as though they were a religious relic.

A quite different view of Lenin was current among *émigré* Russians, Social Democrats, Mensheviks and Social Revolutionaries, who had known him and worked with him for many years. Many of them commented on the strange mixture of attractive and repellent qualities in Lenin. The Menshevik Alexander Potresov described him as an 'evil genius'. He claimed that nobody else among the revolutionary leaders possessed the mysterious hypnotic effect on people that emanated from Lenin, not even Plekhanov and Martov, and this was what enabled him to dominate people. They respected Plekhanov and they loved Martov, but only Lenin did they follow unquestioningly as their sole and indisputable leader. Lenin was the rare phenomenon of a man with an iron will and indomitable energy, who combined a fanatical faith in the movement and the cause with a no lesser faith in himself. 'Behind these virtues, however,' Potresov wrote, 'lurk equally great defects, negative features which might be more appropriate in some medieval or Asiatic conqueror.'[50]

Inside the USSR the saintly view of Lenin survived intact until the late 1980s. When in 1956 Khrushchev began to denounce the excesses of Stalin's regime, no criticisms were voiced of Lenin; the official view was that Stalin had betrayed Leninism, and Lenin was elevated to an even higher pedestal. During the *glasnost* (openness) era after 1985, Gorbachev intended to preserve the Lenin cult, but he gradually lost control and the critical spotlight spread from Stalin to Lenin as well. As the archives became accessible, details were published in the USSR for the first time about Lenin's role in the Red Terror, the murder of the Tsar and his family, and the building of the one-party state. After the collapse of the USSR most Russian historians presented a hostile picture of Lenin. Dmitri Volkogonov in his massive 1994 biography blamed all the unpleasant features of Soviet history on Lenin – Stalin merely followed Leninist traditions.[51] Lenin's reputation in Russia probably reached its nadir in 1997–98; in 1997 Alexander Yakovlev, who had once been a member of Gorbachev's Politburo, claimed in an interview that Lenin was the one who had set up a 'criminal state'; 'villain number one was Lenin. Stalin and Hitler were secondary.'[52] The following year Volkogonov, in his final book before his death, further sharpened his attack on Lenin. 'Politics, to be sure, tends to be immoral,' he wrote, 'but in Lenin immorality was exacerbated by cynicism. Almost every one of his decisions suggests that for him morality was totally subordinated to political realities . . . and his main goal – the seizure of power.'[53] On the other hand some Russian historians are trying to present a more balanced interpretation of Soviet history. Robert C. Tucker mentions Irina Pavlova whose researches suggest that Lenin was not a dictator and that while he was alive, there was still a certain amount of 'democratic' discussion within the party.[54]

Among Western historians there have been several revisionists who took a sympathetic view of Lenin. Moshe Lewin in his 1968 book *Lenin's Last Struggle* portrayed Lenin as having been forced unwillingly into policies of violence and terror, and in his last years, in the face of ill-health and the evil ambitions of Stalin, struggling unsuccessfully to steer communism into a more peaceful and civilized phase. In a later book published in 1985, Lewin continued the same theme. By 1922 'an older and wiser Lenin was proposing a new and final series of innovations known as his "testament" . . . it does not mention revolutionary terror of any sort. Its message is very different: no violent measures as a way of transforming the social structures of the country! The cultural revolution first, an understanding with the peasants, and slowness as the supreme virtue; in addition, a new vision on Lenin's part of socialism as a regime of "civilized co-operators". It is well known that that set of ideas was disdainfully labelled "liberalism" by Stalin himself.'[55]

This sort of interpretation is at opposite poles from the traditional liberal interpretation, and was roundly condemned by Richard Pipes in his two-volume work on Russia from 1899 until 1924. He emphasized that Lenin had a strong streak of cruelty, that he advocated terror on principle, and that he condemned thousands of completely innocent people to death. Nor did he show the slightest remorse at the great loss of life which he had caused. The success of the Bolshevik seizure of power in 1917 was nothing to do with social forces – it was simply because Lenin wanted power.[56] Orlando Figes seems to reach a similar conclusion: 'In everything he did, Lenin's ultimate purpose was the pursuit of power. Power was for him not a means – it was the end in itself.'[57]

A more balanced picture of Lenin is presented by Robert Service, who must have written more words about Lenin than any other historian over the last twenty years. His conclusion is that Lenin was certainly ruthless, intolerant and repressive, and even seemed to enjoy unleashing terror; but although he sought power, and believed that dictatorship was desirable, power was not an end in itself. In spite of all his faults, he was a visionary; 'Lenin truly thought that a better world should and would be built, a world without oppression and exploitation, a world without even a state; and it was his judgement, woeful as it was, that the Dictatorship of the Proletariat would act as midwife to the birth of such a world . . . He had in many ways an appealing temperament; friends and relatives found him boundlessly attractive.' It seems that Lenin did not become a dictator; the Bolshevik party never was a unified monolithic organization totally under his control. Although he usually got his way in the Politburo, it was not always easy; he did it by skilful persuasion and 'perpetually impressed his colleagues with his intellectual breadth and depth.' Time and again Lenin's wishes prevailed at the vital turning-points of the revolution – the decision to seize power in October 1917, the signing of the Brest–Litovsk Treaty in 1918, and the introduction of NEP in 1921. None of these would have happened without Lenin. But he did not get everything right: it was his idea to invade Poland in 1920 and that ended in humiliating defeat; and there was his mistaken conviction that other revolutions would follow the Bolshevik seizure of power in Russia. But his achievements make him one of the great political figures of the twentieth century. 'He led the October Revolution, founded the USSR and laid down the rudiments of Marxist–Leninism. He helped to turn a world upside down.'[58]

(c) Leninism and Stalinism

So what was Lenin's real legacy? Does he bear the responsibility for the even greater excesses and atrocities of the Stalinist era, as his detractors claim, or did Stalin betray his vision of a society free from injustice and exploitation? Was Stalinism merely a continuation of Leninism or something quite different? This question has been very much in the forefront of historical debate since the Second World War and the beginning of the Cold War. At first the 'straight line' theory – that Stalin was just a continuation of Lenin – was widely accepted among Western historians. In other words, the forced collectivization of agriculture, the purges, the Great Terror of the 1930s, the tens of thousands of executions and the network of labour camps, were the logical conclusion, the inevitable completion of Leninism. Historians like Adam B. Ulam and Robert H. McNeal point out that Lenin founded the Cheka which became the KGB under Stalin; Lenin could be ruthless when he thought it was necessary, for example when he initiated the Red Terror. Like Stalin during collectivization, Lenin treated the peasants badly during War Communism. Lenin destroyed the multi-party system in Russia and created the highly authoritarian structures of the Bolshevik party which Stalin was able to use.

The revisionists of course take a different view: Moshe Lewin, Robert C. Tucker and Stephen F. Cohen, on the other hand, argue that there was a fundamental discontinuity between Lenin and Stalin; things changed radically under Stalin. As Cohen put it, in a 1977 article, 'Stalinism was excess, extraordinary extremism. It was not merely coercive peasant policies, but a virtual civil war against the peasantry; not merely police repression, or even civil-war style terror, but a holocaust by terror that victimized tens of millions of people for twenty-five years ... not merely a leader cult, but deification of a despot.'[59] In fact Lenin strongly opposed the cult of the individual leader, whereas Stalin began his own personality cult with his lavish 50th birthday celebrations in 1929. Lenin's nationalities policy was the opposite of Stalin's. Lenin wanted to keep the party bureaucracy as small and manageable as possible, but Stalin enlarged it. Lenin encouraged discussion and criticism and got his way by persuading the Politburo; Stalin allowed not the slightest criticism. By the time Lenin died in January 1924 the Russian people had accepted his communist party. After all, it *was* the people's party: in the period between 1917 and Lenin's death well over a million ordinary people – some of them educated people from a peasant background – had joined the party and many of them had good jobs in the party bureaucracy. Even Prince Lvov, the former Provisional Government Prime Minister, acknowledged this: 'The people supports Soviet power,' he wrote at the end of 1923; 'they see that their own type of people are entering into the apparatus, and this makes them feel that the regime is "their own" '[60] (see Document J).

However, in the 'Great Terror' of 1935–39 Stalin in reality destroyed Lenin's communist party. At least a million members were 'purged', its leaders were murdered and its whole ethos was changed. This was quite different from anything that had happened under Lenin. As Robert Conquest points out, 'Lenin's Terror was the product of the years of war and violence, of the collapse of society and administration, of the desperate acts of rulers precariously riding the flood, and fighting for control and survival ... Stalin, on the contrary, attained complete control at a time when general conditions were calm ... and the country had accepted, however reluctantly, the existence and stability of the Soviet Government ... It was in cold blood, quite deliberately and unprovokedly, that Stalin started a new cycle of suffering.' This destruction of Lenin's party and the Old Bolshevik elite leaders was 'a revolution as complete as, though more disguised than, any previous changes in Russia.'[61] In the words of Ronald G. Suny, 'devoted to Karl Marx's vision of socialism, in which the working class would control the machines, factories and other sorts of wealth production, the communists led by Lenin believed that the future social order would be based on the abolition of unearned social privilege, the end of racism and colonial oppression, the secularization of society, and the empowerment of working people. Yet within a generation Stalin and his closest comrades had created one of the most vicious and oppressive states in modern history.'[62]

Documents

The Constituent Assembly

(A) Mark Vishniak, a Right SR deputy and Secretary of the Assembly, describes the scene at the Tauride Palace on 5 January 1918, the opening day of the Constituent Assembly.

> The closer one approached the palace, the fewer pedestrians were to be seen and the more soldiers, Red Army men and sailors. They were armed to the teeth: guns slung over the shoulders, bombs, grenades and bullets, in front and on the side, everywhere, wherever they could be attached or inserted...
>
> The entire square in front of Taurida Palace was filled with artillery, machine guns, field kitchens. All the gates to the palace were shut, except for a wicket gate on the extreme left, through which people with passes were let in. The armed guards attentively studied one's face before permitting entry: they inspected one's rear, felt the backside... After more controls the guards directed delegates into the Assembly Hall. Everywhere there were armed men.

Source: quoted in Richard Pipes, *The Russian Revolution 1899–1919*, p. 550.

(B) Boris Sokolov, a Right SR who had worked as an SR propagandist in the army, gives the soldiers' view of the Constituent Assembly.

> The Constituent Assembly was something totally unknown and unclear to the mass of the front-line soldiers... their sympathies were clearly with the Soviets. These were the institutions that were near and dear to them, reminding them of their own village assemblies... I more than once had occasion to hear the soldiers, sometimes even the most intelligent of them, object to the Constituent Assembly. To most of them it was associated with the State Duma, an institution that was remote to them. 'What do we need some Constituent Assembly for when we already have our Soviets, where our own deputies can meet and decide everything?'

Source: quoted in Orlando Figes, *Peasant Russia, Civil War: The Volga Countryside in Revolution (1917–1921)*, p. 68.

The Civil War and the Terror

(C) Extracts from Trotsky's order to the Red Army troops on the southern front, 24 November 1918.

Krasnov and the foreign capitalists who stand behind his back have thrown on to the Voronezh front hundreds of hired agents who have penetrated, under various guises, Red Army units and are carrying on their base work, corrupting and inciting men to desert...I declare that from now on an end must be put to this by using merciless means:

(i) Every scoundrel who incites anyone to retreat, to desert, or not to fulfil a military order, will be shot.

(ii) Every soldier of the Red Army who voluntarily deserts his military post, will be shot.

> Death to self-seekers and to traitors!
> Death to deserters and to the agents of Krasnov!
> Long live the honest soldiers of the Workers' Red Army!

Source: quoted in John Laver, *Russia 1914–1941*, pp. 23–4.

(D) Viktor Serge writes about the saving of Petrograd, and the Terror. Serge was an Anarchist, a Bolshevik and a close associate of Trotsky. This led to his arrest and imprisonment in 1933, though he was later released and allowed to leave Russia.

(i) On 7 October Iudenich captured Gatchina, about twenty-five miles from Petrograd. Two days later his advanced forces entered Ligovo, on the city's outskirts, about nine miles away...It seemed quite plainly to be our death agony. There were no trains and no fuel for evacuation, and scarcely a few dozen cars...I spent my nights with the Communist troops in the outer defences. The news from the other fronts was so bad that Lenin was reluctant to sacrifice the last available forces in the defence of a doomed city. Trotsky thought otherwise. He arrived almost at the last moment and his presence instantly changed the atmosphere at Smolny. He arrived with a train, that famous train which had been speeding to and fro along the different fronts since the previous year...It was magical. Trotsky kept saying, 'It is impossible for a little army of 15,000 ex-officers to master a working-class capital of 700,000 inhabitants'...This session of the Soviet took place beneath the lofty white columns of the Tauride Palace. Trotsky was all tension and energy: he was, besides, an orator of unique quality, whose metallic voice projected a great distance. The decision to fight to the death was taken enthusiastically, and the whole amphitheatre raised a song of immense power...

(continued)

Capable regiments of infantry, recalled from the Polish front, now marched through the city to take up their positions in the suburbs...Petrograd was saved on 21 October at the battle of the Pulkovo Heights...Iudenich's troops rolled back in disorder towards the Estonian frontier...

(ii) The atmosphere was often sharpened because of the perpetuation of the Terror, by an element of intolerable inhumanity. A notable saying of Lenin kept rising in my mind: 'It is a terrible misfortune that the honour of beginning the first Socialist revolution should have befallen the most backward people in Europe.' Nevertheless, within the current situation of Europe, bloodstained, devastated, and in profound stupor, Bolshevism was, in my eyes, tremendously and visibly right. It marked a new point of departure in history...

(iii) I am well aware that terror has been necessary up till now in all great revolutions...but at the same time I saw that the perpetuation of terror, after the end of the Civil War and the transition to a period of economic freedom, was an immense and demoralizing blunder. I was and still am convinced that the new regime would have felt a hundred times more secure if it had henceforth proclaimed its reverence, as a Socialist government, for human life and the rights of all individuals without exception... I did not feel disheartened or disorientated, but I was disgusted at certain things, psychologically exhausted by the Terror and tormented by the mass of wrongs I could see growing, which I was powerless to counteract.

Source: Viktor Serge, *Memoirs of a Revolutionary*, pp. 90–4, 113–14, 153–5.

(E) Emma Goldman, a Russian Anarchist who had lived in the USA for 30 years, returned to Petrograd in January 1920; but she found it very different from the brilliant city she remembered from the 1880s.

It was almost in ruins, as if a hurricane had swept over it. The houses looked like broken old tombs upon neglected and forgotten cemeteries. The streets were dirty and deserted; all life had gone from them. The population of Petrograd before the war was almost two million; in 1920 it had dwindled to five hundred thousand. The people walked about like living corpses; the shortage of food and fuel was slowly sapping the city; grim death was clutching at its heart. Emaciated and frost-bitten men, women and children were being whipped by the common lash, the search for a piece of bread or a stick of wood. It was a heart-rending sight by day, and an oppressive weight by night. The utter stillness of the large city was paralysing. It fairly haunted me, this awful oppressive silence broken only by occasional shots...the Nevsky Prospect was lined with young girls selling themselves for a loaf of bread or a piece of soap or chocolate.

Source: Emma Goldman, *My Disillusionment in Russia*, pp. 8–11.

(F) Maxim Gorky, the famous writer and novelist, was a Bolshevik sympathizer and a friend of Lenin, but he was an outspoken critic of the Terror and the general culture of violence.

(i) [Letter to Zinoviev protesting about the arrest of academics (March 1919)] In my view such arrests cannot be justified by any political means. The disgusting crimes you have perpetrated in Petersburg during the past few weeks have brought shame to the regime and aroused universal hatred and contempt for its cowardice . . .

(ii) In Tambov province Communists were nailed with railway spikes by their left hand and left foot to trees a metre above the soil, and they watched the torments of these deliberately oddly-crucified people. They would open a prisoner's belly, take out the small intestine and nailing it to a tree or telegraph pole they drove the man around the tree with blows, watching the intestine unwind through the wound . . .

(iii) [An Appeal to All Honest People, 13 July 1921, printed in the Western press] Tragedy has come to the country of Tolstoy, Doestoevsky, Mendeleev, Pavlov, Mussorgsky, Glinka and other world-prized men. If humanitarian ideals and feelings – faith in whose social import was so shaken by the damnable war and its victors' unmercifulness towards the vanquished – if faith in the creative force of these ideas and feelings, I say, must and can be restored, Russia's misfortune offers a splendid opportunity to demonstrate the vitality of humanitarianism. I ask all honest European and American people for prompt aid to the Russian people. Give bread and medicine. Maxim Gorky.

Source: quoted in Orlando Figes, *A People's Tragedy*, pp. 648, 775, 778.

(G) Lenin's secret orders to the members of the Politburo, 19 March 1922, urging them to launch an attack on the Orthodox Church.

Precisely now and only now, when they are eating human flesh in the famine regions and hundreds if not thousands of corpses are lying on the road, we can (and therefore must) carry out the seizure of church valuables with the most desperate and the most ruthless energy . . . In Shuia as many as possible [clergymen and bourgeois who had demonstrated against the seizure of church property] must be arrested and put on trial. The trial must end with the shooting of a very large number of the most influential and dangerous Black Hundreds of the city of Shuia, and also of Moscow and . . . other spiritual centres. The more representatives of the reactionary clergy and reactionary bourgeoisie we manage to shoot on this occasion, the better. Now is the time to teach those types such a lesson that for a few dozen years they won't even be able to think of resistance.

Source: quoted in Sheila Fitzpatrick, *The Russian Revolution* (1994 edition), pp. 97–8.

Lenin's ideas for the future

(H) Extracts from Lenin's article *On Co-operation*, written in January 1923, in which he argued that the way forward was to organize the peasants into co-operative communities.

All we actually need under NEP is to organize the population of Russia into co-operative societies on a sufficiently large scale . . . But it will take a whole historical epoch to get the entire population into the work of the co-operatives through NEP. At best we can achieve this in one or two decades. Nevertheless it will be a distinct historical epoch, and without this historical epoch, without universal literacy, without a proper degree of efficiency, without training the population sufficiently to acquire the habit of book-reading, and without the material basis for this, without a certain sufficiency to safeguard against, say, bad harvests, famine, etc. – without this we shall not achieve our object . . . Two main tasks confront us, which constitute the epoch – to reorganize our machinery of state, which is utterly useless . . . and our second task is educational work among the peasants . . . But the organization of the entire peasantry in co-operative societies presupposes a standard of culture among the peasants that cannot, in fact, be achieved without a cultural revolution.

Source: Robert C. Tucker, *The Lenin Anthology*, pp. 708–12.

(I) Extracts from Lenin's last article, *Fewer, But Better*, dictated in February 1923. It appeared in *Pravda* on 4 March 1923. It was a criticism of the grow-ing party bureaucracy and therefore of Stalin, but Lenin also speculates about the final outcome of the world revolutionary process.

Thus, at the present time we are confronted with the question – shall we be able to hold on with our very small peasant production, and in our present state of ruin, until the West-European capitalist countries consummate their development towards socialism? . . . It is only by thor-oughly purging our government machine, by reducing to the utmost everything that is not absolutely essential in it, that we shall be certain of being able to keep going . . . Morever we shall be able to keep going not on the level of a small-peasant country, but on a level steadily advan-cing to large-scale machine industry. These are the lofty tasks that I dream of . . .

Source: Robert C. Tucker, *The Lenin Anthology*, pp. 744–6.

An aristocrat's view of Soviet Russia

(J) Prince Lvov, the former Prime Minister during the 1917 Provisional Government, gave his impressions in this letter written in November 1923.

> Russia has changed completely in the past few years. It has become a completely new Russia. The people and the power are, as usual, two different things. But Russia more than ever before belongs to the people. To be certain, the government is hostile to the people and their national feelings, standing as it does for international goals, it deceives the people and turns them into slaves, but nonetheless it still receives the support of this oppressed and enslaved people. They would still defend the regime if it was attacked by an intervention or by an organization within Russia fighting under the old slogans or in the name of a restoration... The people supports Soviet power. That does not mean they are happy with it. But at the same time as they feel their oppression, they also see that their own type of people are entering into the apparatus, and this makes them feel that the regime is 'their own'.

Source: quoted in Orlando Figes, *A People's Tragedy*, pp. 815–16.

Notes

1. Orlando Figes, *A People's Tragedy: the Russian Revolution 1891–1924*, p. 512.
2. O.H. Radkey, *Russia Goes to the Polls: the Election to the Russian Constituent Assembly, 1917* (second edition, 1989) for full details.
3. Quoted in Leonard Schapiro, *The Origin of the Communist Autocracy* (second edition, 1977), p. 87.
4. Orlando Figes, *Peasant Russia, Civil War: The Volga Countryside in Revolution, 1917–21*, pp. 56, 127.
5. Figes, *Peasant Russia*, p. 198.
6. Robert Service, *The Russian Revolution, 1900–1927*, p. 59.
7. Robert C. Tucker (editor), *The Lenin Anthology*, pp. 443–4.
8. *Ibid.*, pp. 448–9.
9. Mary McCauley, *Bread and Justice: State and Society in Petrograd, 1917–22*, pp. 27–8, 162.
10. Quoted in Richard Pipes, *The Russian Revolution, 1899–1919*, p. 574.
11. Quoted in Christopher Hill, *Lenin and the Russian Revolution* (1971 edition), p. 158.
12. *Ibid.*, p. 96.
13. L.D. Gerson, *The Secret Police in Lenin's Russia*, pp. 31–2.
14. W.B. Lincoln, *Red Victory: A History of the Russian Civil War*, pp. 59–64.
15. *Ibid.*, p. 65.
16. Pipes, pp. 789–93.
17. Gerson, pp. 83, 295, 145, 159.
18. Figes, *A People's Tragedy*, p. 525.
19. Richard Pipes, *Russia under the Bolshevik Regime, 1919–1924*, p. 112.
20. For a full analysis of the last days of the Romanovs and the testing of the bones see R.K. Massie, *The Romanovs: the Final Chapter*. Recently Shay McNeal, in *The Plots to Rescue the Tsar*, questions the authenticity of the bones and argues that the Tsar and his family may have survived after all.
21. Robert Service, *Lenin: A Biography*, p. 364.
22. Evan Mawdsley, *The Russian Civil War*, p. 4.

23. Quoted in Lincoln, pp. 126–7.
24. Mawdsley, pp. 181–4.
25. Lincoln, p. 189.
26. Alec Nove, *An Economic History of the USSR, 1917–1991*, p. 68.
27. Lincoln, pp. 325–7.
28. Figes, *A People's Tragedy*, pp. 656–7; Pipes, *Russia under the Bolshevik Regime*, p. 47.
29. Mawdsley, pp. 285–7.
30. Nove, pp. 62, 89.
31. Robert C. Tucker, 'Stalinism as Revolution from Above', in Tucker (editor), *Stalinism: Essays in Historical Interpretation*, pp. 90–2.
32. Christopher Read, *From Tsar to Soviets: The Russian People and their Revolution, 1917–21*, pp. 220–2, 289.
33. Adam B. Ulam, *Lenin and the Bolsheviks*, p. 610.
34. Nove, p. 40; for a detailed analysis of the debate, see pp. 39–77.
35. Quoted in Figes, *A People's Tragedy*, pp. 767–8.
36. Israel Getzler, *Kronstadt 1917–1921*, p. 258. See pp. 205–258 for a full account of the 1921 rising.
37. Robert Service, *Lenin: A Political Life, volume 3, The Iron Ring*, p. 169.
38. Robert C. Tucker (editor), *The Lenin Anthology*, pp. 520–2.
39. Quoted in Figes, *A People's Tragedy*, pp. 769–70; Service, *Lenin: The Iron Ring*, p. 216.
40. Roy A. Medvedev, *Let History Judge: The Origins and Consequences of Stalinism* (1989 edition), pp. 213–14.
41. Nove, statistics from the table on p. 89.
42. Tucker, *The Lenin Anthology*, p. 494.
43. R.W. Davies, *The Socialist Offensive: The Collectivisation of Soviet Agriculture*, pp. 17, 25–7.
44. Isaac Deutscher, *Stalin*, p. 188. For a full analysis of the nationalities problem see Helene Carrere d'Encausse, *The Great Challenge: Nationalities and the Bolshevik State, 1917–1930*.
45. Service, *The Iron Ring*, p. 282.
46. An excellent book which deals with the first phase of Soviet culture is a collection edited by Abbott Gleason, Peter Kenez and Richard Stites, *Bolshevik Culture: Experiment and Order in the Russian Revolution*.
47. See T.E. O'Connor, *The Politics of Soviet Culture*, and Sheila Fitzpatrick, *The Commissariat of Enlightenment: Soviet Organization of Education and the Arts under Lunacharsky*.
48. Ronald G. Suny, *The Soviet Experiment*, p. 206.
49. Figes, *A People's Tragedy*, p. 749.
50. Quoted in Dmitri Volkogonov, *The Rise and Fall of the Soviet Empire*, pp. 5–6.
51. Dmitri Volkogonov, *Lenin: Life and Legend*.
52. Robert C. Tucker (editor), *Stalinism: Essays in Historical Interpretation*, Introduction to the Transaction edition (1999), pp. xi–xii.
53. Dmitri Volkogonov, *The Rise and Fall of the Soviet Empire*, pp. 8–9, 82.
54. Tucker, *Stalinism*, p. xii.
55. Moshe Lewin, *The Making of the Soviet System*, pp. 205–6.
56. Pipes, *The Russian Revolution 1891–1919*, p. 350.
57. Figes, *A People's Tragedy*, p. 504.
58. Service, *The Iron Ring*, pp. xiii–xix; *Lenin: A Biography*, p. 494.
59. Stephen F. Cohen, 'Bolshevism and Stalinism', in Tucker (editor), *Stalinism: Essays in Historical Interpretation*, p. 12.
60. Figes, *A People's Tragedy*, p. 816.
61. Robert Conquest, *The Great Terror: A Reassessment*, p. 251.
62. Suny, *The Soviet Experiment*, p. xiv.

6 Stalin in control – Russia transformed

Summary of events

After Lenin had suffered a second stroke in December 1922, it became clear that he was unlikely to be able to remain in control. He gave no positive suggestions as to who might succeed him, except that it should not be Stalin. Trotsky seemed the most obvious candidate, but he was unpopular with the other leading members of the communist party. During the final year of Lenin's life, Kamenev, Zinoviev and Stalin concentrated on trying to block Trotsky; Lenin's criticisms of Stalin were ignored and his attempts to have Stalin demoted failed. After Lenin's death in January 1924, **Stalin skilfully outmanoeuvred his rivals, expelling them from the party one by one, until by 1929 he was the unchallenged leader. He remained in control right through the Second World War and until his death in 1953 at the age of 73.**

Under Stalin's leadership Russia was transformed almost out of recognition:

- By 1929 the idea of world revolution had been abandoned and the communist aim was to consolidate socialism in the USSR – **the concept of 'socialism in one country'**.
- Stalin's great goal now was **to transform the USSR into a leading industrial and military power** so that it would be possible to withstand any attack which might be launched against it by the capitalist West. This programme would need massive investment, which Stalin hoped to finance with profits from agriculture.
- **Collectivization of agriculture completed by 1936.** Stalin thought that the key to success was to increase agricultural efficiency and output by **putting an end to Lenin's NEP and introducing collective farms**. There was resistance from the better-off peasants, but Stalin had no hesitation in pushing the collectivization programme through by brute force. In many ways it was a disaster – millions of peasants died, and grain and meat production did not recover until the end of the 1930s. From Stalin's point of view though, it meant that the countryside was now under government control for the first time; agricultural output, though much reduced in the early years of collectivization, was at the disposal of the government, not the peasants.

- **The Five-Year Plans for industry, 1928–41**. Meanwhile the industrial modernization programme went ahead with the implementation of three Five-Year Plans between 1928 and 1941; all three were said to have been successful and their targets achieved early. But again, as in the case of collectivization, industrial progress was achieved only at great human cost – regimentation of the workers became the order of the day, and living standards deteriorated.
- **1934 – The Purges begin**. Many of the Old Bolsheviks disagreed with Stalin's policies – particularly the speed of industrialization and the harsh treatment of peasants and industrial workers. However, Stalin was determined to eliminate all critics and opponents. Beginning in 1934, he embarked on what became known as 'the Purges': hundreds were arrested and forced to appear in 'show-trials' in which they were invariably found guilty of 'plotting against the Soviet state', and sentenced to death or imprisonment in labour camps. The army leadership was purged. Some estimates put the number of those who disappeared during the 1930s as high as ten million. All possible alternative leaders were eliminated and the ordinary population was terrorized into obedience.
- **1936 – A new constitution introduced**. This had some appearance of democracy, but in reality it merely underlined the fact that Stalin and the communist party ran everything. The freedom of artists, writers, musicians and film producers was severely restricted; everybody was expected to produce works of 'socialist realism' glorifying Soviet achievements, and anyone who did not conform was soon 'purged'.

By June 1941 when the USSR was forced into the Second World War by the German invasion, a huge gulf had opened up between the visionary ideals and expectations of the original 1917 Bolshevik revolutionaries and the dismal realities of Stalinism.

Main areas of debate:

- If Stalin was a 'grey blur', how did he succeed in getting to supreme power?
- Were there genuine policy disagreements among the communist leaders between 1924 and 1929, or were the disputes caused by struggles for power?
- Was Stalinism a distortion of Marxism–Leninism or its natural offspring?
- Was there an alternative to Stalin's policy of forced collectivization?
- Was Stalin's subjection of the countryside to the state a substitute for the process of capital formation which might have been expected to precede the expansion of heavy industry?
- Was Stalinism simply a 'revolution from above' or did it have popular support?
- Was the Stalinist system totalitarian?

6.1 Trotsky or Stalin? The struggle for power after Lenin's death

(a) Stalin – the least likely leadership candidate

There were five main contenders to take over the leadership of the party and the country, although at first they all denied that they were interested. They claimed that nobody could adequately replace Lenin, and talked about a collective leadership. However, for most of 1923 they all seemed to be manoeuvring for position. The obvious candidate was Trotsky – viewed by many people as Lenin's second-in-command and right-hand man. Other possibilities were the 'old' Bolsheviks Kamenev (head of the Moscow party organization) and Zinoviev (head of the Leningrad party organization and the Comintern), and Bukharin, the rising intellectual star of the party. The vast majority of people at the time felt that the least likely candidate for the leadership was Stalin. Of the Politburo members, he was the least known to the general public, and in some ways was an outsider. Born in 1879 in Georgia, of poor parents – his father was a shoemaker who had been a serf – Joseph Djugashvili was educated for four years at Tiflis Theological Seminary, since his mother wanted him to be a priest. He hated its repressive atmosphere and was expelled in 1899 for spreading socialist ideas. He had joined the Bolsheviks in 1904 and eventually took the surname Stalin – man of steel. He gained a reputation as an outstanding administrator, but although his job as Party General Secretary meant that he was head of the party bureaucracy, it also meant that he was not greatly in the public eye. In 1925 when a series of ten postcards entitled 'Leaders of October' was published to mark the eighth anniversary of the revolution, Stalin was not included.[1]

Stalin seemed to have none of the characteristics normally expected of a great leader: he had nothing like the charisma of Lenin and Trotsky, all his rivals were better public speakers than he was, he was not a war hero, and he was certainly nowhere near the intellectual equal of Trotsky or Bukharin. The Menshevik Nikolai Sukhanov wrote in his memoirs that 'in the political arena Stalin was nothing more than a vague, grey blur;' Trotsky was devastating about him, describing him as 'the Party's most eminent mediocrity . . . his mind is devoid of creative imagination . . . a man destined to play second or third fiddle.'

By the end of 1922 Lenin had turned against Stalin after a number of disagreements, even though he recognized his great abilities. Lenin was critical of Stalin's handling of the Georgian problem, and Stalin accused Lenin of being 'soft on the nationalities' (see section 5.8(d)). Lenin felt that the party bureaucracy was becoming too big and unwieldy and wanted the state and party organizations to be kept separate; Stalin of course approved of the party dominating the government structures because of the enormous personal power that he had built up within the party machine. In December 1922 Lenin dictated a document which became known as his political testament. In it he reviewed the qualities of his possible successors, and was unable to summon up much enthusiasm for any of them. Stalin as General Secretary, he said, 'has concentrated unlimited power in his hands, and I am not convinced that he will always manage to use this power with sufficient caution.' Trotsky, he admitted, was extremely able; 'he is distinguished not only by his outstanding talents. To be sure, he is personally the most capable person in the present Central Committee – but he also over-brims with self-confidence and with an excessive preoccupation with the purely administrative side of things.' Lenin was afraid, with good reason in view of their long history of mutual hostility, that Stalin and Trotsky would fall out and cause a split in the party. The party must therefore take measures to prevent such a split taking place. As for Kamenev and Zinoviev, Lenin had very little to say except to give a reminder of 'the October episode' in 1917, when they had both disagreed with him about whether or not the time was right to seize power.

A few days later, on 4 January 1923, Lenin dictated a postscript to the political testament, after discovering that Stalin had spoken abruptly and rudely on the telephone to Nadezhda Krupskaya, Lenin's wife. This was evidently the last straw for Lenin and he made up his mind that Stalin must be removed from his power-ful position: 'Stalin is too crude, and this defect which is entirely acceptable in our milieu and in relationships among us as communists, becomes unacceptable in the position of General Secretary. I therefore propose to comrades that they should devise a means of removing him from this job and should appoint to this job someone else who is distinguished from comrade Stalin in all other respects only by the single superior aspect that he should be more tolerant, more polite and more attentive towards comrades, less capricious etc.'[2] At this point, however, the political testament was not made public. It was headed 'Letter to the Congress', and Lenin presumably intended it to be read out at the Twelfth Party Congress later in 1923, with the aim of having Stalin voted out of office. However, with Lenin's worsening health and his death, it did not become public until the Thirteenth Congress in 1924, when the party leaders, meeting in private, decided to ignore it.

More public was Lenin's article published in *Pravda* (Truth) on 25 January 1923, in which he criticized the People's Commissariat of Workers' and Peasants' Inspection (known as Rabkrin), a body of which Stalin had been the head since it was set up in 1919 until April 1922. It was an organization which had the power to go into all government institutions and look at their records to make sure that the 'experts' and the bureaucracy were doing their jobs properly. It had never func-tioned very efficiently and Lenin had often criticized its work, though without actually blaming Stalin. The January *Pravda* article, entitled *How We Should Reorganize the Workers' and Peasants' Inspection*, was widely interpreted as an attack on Stalin. Lenin sent a letter to Trotsky asking him to lead the attack on Stalin at the party Congress over his handling of the Georgian affair. Sadly, Trotsky proved unequal to the task and the opposition to Stalin remained fragmented.

(b) Trotsky's failure

Charged with leading the attack on Stalin, Trotsky was strangely half-hearted and ineffectual. In spite of having Lenin's full authority behind him, Trotsky did nothing at all about attacking Stalin over his handling of the Georgian question; in fact he even failed to attend the meetings of the Party Congress in 1923 when the Georgian issue was being discussed. Adam Ulam suggested that the reason for this was that Trotsky still saw Zinoviev as his chief rival, and to discredit Stalin would only increase Zinoviev's chances of taking over Lenin's position.[3] A similar thing happened in May 1924 with regard to Lenin's political testament; this was considered by the Central Committee, and when Lenin's criticism of Stalin was read out, Stalin seemed devastated and offered to resign. However, Kamenev and Zinoviev spoke up in defence of Stalin, arguing that he had made amends for any earlier misdemeanours; there was no need to have him replaced as Party General Secretary, and they 'persuaded' him to withdraw his resignation. It was also agreed that the testament should be kept secret; and although a version of it appeared in *The New York Times* in 1926, it was not published in Russia until after Stalin's death. Kamenev and Zinoviev acted in this way because they were afraid of Trotsky and were determined to prevent him from becoming leader. They were extremely ambitious themselves, and ironically they did not perceive Stalin as a danger; they seem to have expected him to continue quietly with his work as General Secretary, leaving the two of them in the top positions. Trotsky went along with all these decisions, and in fact uttered not a word at the Central Committee meeting; these two incidents were his last chances to attack Stalin with the backing of Lenin.

What were the reasons for this apparently limp reaction? The most obvious one is that by May 1924 Trotsky was extremely unpopular with the rest of the party leadership and knew that he had no chance of winning the argument. Isaac Deutscher described Trotsky's attitude as one of 'moody aloofness', caused partly by a recent illness and partly because he knew full well that 'the tide was running against him'. He did not covet personal power and 'in his whole being he shrank from the scramble.'[4] There is evidence that he told Lenin the day after the Bolshevik seizure of power that he would never accept the leadership of the country because he knew that the fact that he was Jewish would arouse a lot of opposition in some quarters. Martin McCauley comments on how often, during this period after the death of Lenin, Trotsky was ill at critical moments when he needed to be on top form, and suggests that the illnesses may have been psychosomatic.[5]

Trotsky's unpopularity with the most influential of the leading Bolsheviks greatly reduced his chances of success. Many could not forget that he had only joined the party at the last minute shortly before the October revolution; others were jealous that he rose to the top so quickly after joining so late. Although he had support among students and former students, and in the Red Army, he was not popular with industrial workers who remembered his advocacy of strict military discipline for workers. He could be extremely arrogant: he often treated Kamenev, Zinoviev and Stalin with condescension and even contempt. He made himself more unpopular by some of his actions during Lenin's illness, which showed an odd lack of political skill and sensitivity. In October 1923 for example, during the 'scissors crisis' (see section 5.6(e)), he launched a bitter attack on the party leadership, which in effect meant Stalin, Kamenev and Zinoviev, who were acting as a triumvirate during Lenin's illness. Trotsky was supported by a group of Bolsheviks who had signed what they called the 'Platform of 46'. Their criticisms of the leadership were that there was no plan for the future of the revolution, no vision; Trotsky claimed that military methods were the way forward in both industry and agriculture, criticized the lack of democracy in the party and accused the Secretariat of amassing too much power. An augmented meeting of the Central Committee condemned Trotsky, who was supported by only two out of the 114 members who took part.

In October 1924 Trotsky published a book called *The Lessons of October* in which he criticized Zinoviev and Kamenev over their disagreements with Lenin about the timing of the October revolution; this outraged the other Politburo members who responded angrily. Bukharin wrote an article attacking Trotsky's version of events, entitled *How Not to Write the History of October 1917*. Kamenev produced the most devastating reply in an article in *Pravda* in November 1924. He said that Trotsky had always in reality been a Menshevik, and he quoted from letters written by Trotsky in 1913, in which he condemned the whole foundation of Leninism as being 'built on lying and falsification', and went on to call Lenin 'a professional exploiter of all that is backward in the Russian workers' movement.' Stalin also defended Kamenev and Zinoviev – their disagreement with Lenin in October 1917 was only a passing aberration that was over in a few days. 'Why does Trotsky have to keep dragging the party backwards to new debates?' Stalin asked in one of his speeches. 'What is the meaning, the point of this, when the party does not want to debate, when the party is overloaded with pressing tasks, when the party needs united work to restore the economy? The motivation is that Trotsky is making another (yet another!) attempt to substitute Trotskyism for Leninism.'[6] Stalin went on to orchestrate a press campaign against Trotsky who reacted by having a sort of breakdown and failing to defend himself. Several historians have commented on Trotsky's poor timing; Dmitri Volkogonov points out that Trotsky had a strange habit of starting up every discussion at a time least favourable to himself, so that he must have known in advance that he would be defeated.[7] The conclusions to be drawn are either that deep down, he did not want the leadership, or that, if he did want the leadership, he was so overbearingly arrogant that he totally underestimated Stalin's political abilities. Whatever Trotsky's true motives, the reality was that by the end of 1924 almost all his support had disappeared. In January 1925 he was more or less forced to resign as Commissar for Military and Naval Affairs, and Zinoviev even tried to persuade the others to expel Trotsky from the party. Ironically it was Stalin, taking a stand as a moderate, who was responsible for the defeat of this proposal, and it was the votes of Stalin and his friends which kept Trotsky as a member of the Politburo. In spite of that, however, it was clear that Trotsky was finished as a contender for supreme power.

(c) Stalin triumphant

Stalin was appointed to the new post of Party General Secretary in April 1922, apparently at the instigation of Lenin and Kamenev; two of Stalin's allies – Molotov and Kuibyshev – were appointed as secretaries. Stalin was able to use his position to build up enormous personal influence. One of his major jobs was to appoint the secretaries of local Communist Party organizations, and he also had the power to dismiss them. He quietly filled these positions with his supporters and gained control over the local parties. These local organizations chose the delegates to national Party Conferences, and so the Party Conferences gradually filled with

Stalin supporters. The Party Congresses elected the Party Central Committee and the Politburo; as the 1920s progressed, all the top bodies and congresses became more and more packed with people who supported Stalin, so that by 1928 he was unassailable. In many ways Stalin was lucky: if Lenin's health had held out for another year, it is almost certain that Stalin would have been removed from the post. The death of Dzerzhinsky (head of the Cheka and VSNKh) in 1926 opened the way for Kuibyshev, one of Stalin's closest allies, to be appointed in his place. And Stalin was fortunate too that his other two rivals, Kamenev and Zinoviev, both had serious weaknesses: they were good team members but lacked leadership qualities, and their political judgement was suspect – for a long time they were so busy attacking Trotsky that they failed to recognize the real danger from Stalin and missed several opportunities to get rid of him.

Although he could never be described as an intellectual, Stalin nevertheless had great political skill and intuition. He had the ability to cut through the complexities of a problem and focus on the essentials. He was always careful to present himself as the pupil and dedicated follower of Lenin, whereas Trotsky, Kamenev and Zinoviev considered themselves more as Lenin's equals. Stalin was an excellent judge of character and had the gift of being able to work out people's weaknesses and then exploit them to maximum effect. He was adept at using disagreements over policy in the Politburo in order to side with one faction against another, eliminating his rivals one by one until he was left supreme.[8] His manoeuvrings fell into four phases:

1922–25 Stalin sided with Kamenev and Zinoviev against Trotsky, mainly over Trotsky's theory of 'permanent revolution'. Both Lenin and Trotsky believed passionately that the lasting success of the revolution in Russia depended on the spread of revolution world-wide. Trotsky wanted Russia to continue to do everything in its power to spread the revolution. In opposition to this Stalin put forward the theory of 'socialism in one country'. Stalin had picked up the idea from an article by Bukharin, and he proceeded to develop it. Socialism, he argued, must be firmly established in Russia first, and Russia's economic and military strength must be built up so that she could defend herself against the inevitable capitalist attacks which would come sooner or later. Only when Russia was strong enough would it be realistic to think of carrying the campaign of revolution to the rest of the world. This was a genuine policy disagreement, but there was also the personal rivalry element. Hostility between Stalin and Trotsky went back as far as the Civil War when Trotsky was Commissar for War and Stalin was in charge of the defences of Tsaritsyn (later called Stalingrad). Trotsky thought that Stalin was too independent and asked Lenin to dismiss him. Lenin recalled Stalin to Moscow to explain himself, and Stalin never forgave Trotsky for this humiliation. Trotsky's rivalry with Kamenev and Zinoviev was less bitter, but they both resented his arrogance and his criticism of them. This phase ended, as we saw, in January 1925 with Trotsky's isolation and his resignation from his post of Commissar for Military Affairs.

1925–26 With Trotsky safely out of the running, Stalin now began to turn against Kamenev and Zinoviev. There were a number of policy debates going on in the Politburo. Should NEP be continued? Should they press ahead with rapid industrialization? Should they stick with Stalin's 'socialism in one country'? Although NEP was a success in many ways, there was still a problem with insufficient grain supplies reaching the cities. Nikolai Bukharin, who was now on the right of the party (he had been a Left Communist and had supported War Communism during the Civil War) emerged as the champion of NEP. He was in favour of encouraging the peasants to produce more by giving them more concessions; in fact he wanted an intensification of NEP. In a speech in April 1925 Bukharin exhorted the peasants: 'We must say to the whole peasantry, to all its strata: enrich yourselves, accumulate, develop your economy.' In theory the whole economy of the state would benefit: there would be a great improvement in agricultural productivity and peasants' incomes would increase correspondingly, enabling them to buy more consumer goods; this, together with the increased demand for agricultural machinery, would stimulate industry. At this stage Stalin supported Bukharin's policy which was in operation from 1923 right through to 1926. The 1925 harvest was an excellent one, probably the best since 1917, and this seemed to vindicate the Bukharin–Stalin policy.

However, Kamenev and Zinoviev, known as the Left Opposition, vigorously opposed Bukharin and Stalin, feeling that their policy was favouring peasants at the expense of industrial workers. Both men had their power bases and main support in industrial areas and feared that they would lose popularity if Bukharin's policy continued. More concessions to peasants would mean moving too far away from socialism in the direction of capitalism; if this trend continued, it would never be possible to return to strict Marxism. Zinoviev began a series of speeches criticizing Bukharin; he demanded that there should be no more concessions to the peasants and that rapid industrialization should be made the top priority. He even attacked the theory of 'socialism in one country'. Many saw this as Zinoviev's bid for the leadership – belatedly he and Kamenev had wakened up to the danger from Stalin. At the Fourteenth Party Congress in December 1925 Kamenev delivered a blistering speech criticizing Stalin personally for the first time: 'We are against creating the theory of a leader . . . we think it is harmful to the Party to prolong a situation in which the Secretariat combines politics and organization, and, in fact, decides policy in advance . . . I have reached the conclusion that Comrade Stalin cannot perform the function of uniting the Bolshevik general staff.' But it was all too late to damage Stalin; the Left Opposition could muster only 64 votes against 559 who voted for Stalin and Bukharin. In the elections for the Politburo (whose membership was increased from seven to nine), Kamenev was voted off and the three new members were Molotov, Kalinin and Voroshilov – all close allies of Stalin. Although Zinoviev remained a member of the Politburo, within a few weeks he had been voted out of his position as head of the Leningrad party organization. He was replaced by another Stalin supporter, Sergei Kirov.

1926–27 This third phase of events saw the unlikely alliance of Kamenev and Zinoviev with Trotsky, the man they had tried to get expelled from the party only two years earlier; it was a last desperate attempt to defeat Stalin. Calling themselves 'The United Opposition', in July 1926 they issued the 'Declaration of the

Thirteen' in which they continued to criticize the government's 'soft' policy towards the kulaks and insisted that NEP could not be relied on to produce sufficient grain. They also criticized 'socialism in one country' as being far too narrow – communism should be international. Again they called for a speeding-up of industrialization so that workers' conditions and wages could be improved. Stalin cunningly turned the opposition's arguments against them. He pointed out that Trotsky's support for 'permanent revolution' rather than 'socialism in one country' proved that he cared more for foreign countries than he did for Russia; Trotsky therefore was a traitor! Stalin also emphasized that he wanted rapid industrialization just as much as Trotsky did; he accused Trotsky of being insincere in his concern for industrial workers, raking up Trotsky's earlier policy of strict military discipline for workers. When the United Opposition persisted in their campaign Stalin accused them of factionalism – a breach of party discipline. Trotsky called Stalin 'the gravedigger of the revolution.' Trotsky and Zinoviev, as members of the Politburo, were severely reprimanded, expelled from the Central Committee of the Party (October 1927), and expelled from the party itself the following month, along with 25 other members of the Left Opposition, including Kamenev. Trotsky was exiled to Alma-Ata in Kazakhstan, Central Asia, where he stayed for a year before being expelled to Istanbul in Turkey. Kamenev and Zinoviev later confessed that their views were anti-Leninist and recanted; they were allowed back into the party. The Left Opposition was finished; Stalin and Bukharin were now supreme.

1928–29   In this final phase of Stalin's triumphant rise to supreme power he made a dramatic policy change: in some areas in the spring of 1928 he suddenly launched campaigns to seize grain by force. Bukharin, the great advocate of NEP, and his supporters, could not go along with this, and so found themselves in opposition to Stalin – the Right Opposition. To be fair to Stalin, it does seem to have been a genuine policy decision, not just a ploy to eliminate the Right. The problem was that NEP had run into serious crisis; the 1927 harvest had been disappointing. Peasants felt that the grain prices being offered by the government were too low, so they withheld their grain and sold meat, vegetables and dairy produce instead. By the time the Party Congress met in December 1927 there were already food shortages in the cities. The Congress accepted that more pressure would have to be exerted on the peasants, that Lenin's idea of co-operatives was the way forward, but that these must be introduced without coercion. Even Bukharin was prepared to go along with this; Stalin himself spoke in favour of a cautious approach, and Molotov followed the same line, rejecting the idea of grain confiscations: coercion, he said, was inadmissible; 'whoever tells us to apply a policy of compulsory extraction of two to four million tons of grain . . . then that person is an enemy of the workers and peasants, however well intentioned his proposal.'[9]

In January 1928 Stalin paid a visit to the Urals and Siberia to investigate for himself why grain supplies from these areas were dwindling.[10] While he was there, on his own initiative and without consulting any of his colleagues, he began to order grain requisitioning. Gradually over the next few months this policy was extended to most parts of Russia, not by order of the Politburo, but on

Stalin's orders given to local party secretaries. Already he was acting as a dictator; over the next two years all aspects of NEP were phased out, with the use of force whenever necessary (for a full explanation of the abandonment of NEP and Stalin's agricultural policies see section 6.2). This provoked intense opposition from Bukharin and his allies, Rykov and Tomsky, now known as the Right Opposition. They claimed that Stalin was exaggerating the danger from the kulaks and they deplored the use of violence. For a time it seemed as though Bukharin might be gaining the advantage – Bukharin, Rykov and Tomsky were all members of the Politburo, Bukharin was greatly respected in the Party, he was popular, he was the editor of *Pravda* and he genuinely believed that his policy – to continue NEP 'for the foreseeable future' (Lenin's phrase) – was what Lenin himself would have wanted. But there was also considerable support for Stalin from communists who had no patience with wealthy peasants. By April 1929 the Right Opposition were also criticizing the breakneck pace of Stalin's First Five-Year Plan for industry (1929–32) which was well under way (see section 6.4). Stalin responded by quietly removing Bukharin supporters from their posts all over Russia and replacing them with his own allies. In November 1929 Stalin delivered a scathing three-hour speech, full of sarcasm and insults directed against Bukharin, and shortly afterwards Bukharin was voted off the Politburo. The Right Opposition was crushed and Stalin was the undisputed ruler of the USSR.

It was an astonishing achievement that the most obscure and apparently least gifted of the Bolshevik leaders should reach this position. Stalin's rise to power was made possible through a combination of his control of the Party Secretariat, his own political skill and ruthlessness, the weaknesses of his opponents and a certain amount of good fortune. One of his most successful devices was constantly identifying his own views with those of Lenin, which made it difficult for anybody to win an argument against Stalin without appearing to criticize Lenin. Robert Service believes that most of Stalin's biographers, including Dmitri Volkogonov, have failed to emphasize another important factor: that Stalin's policies were actually popular with a majority of party members. The Lenin Enrolment of 1924 brought a quarter of a million new members, almost all of them workers, into the party. Many of these new members soon began to be promoted into the management and the ever-growing party bureaucracy and so became part of the Bolshevik political culture. These people were doing well and rising in the social scale; they enjoyed their new-found power in society and saw Stalin as the leader most likely to enable them to continue. Service argues that most officials were impatient with the problems caused by NEP – the constantly recurring crises over food supplies to the towns, the mass unemployment in industrial areas, and the wealthy peasants blocking the progress to socialism. Unless a modern economy could be developed quickly, the USSR might collapse and their influential positions would be lost. The inclinations of Bolsheviks at all levels of the party therefore coincided with Stalin's inclinations in the late 1920s: 'a wish to complete the revolution at home, to suppress opposition both outside and inside the party, to build a strong centralist state, to promote working-class Bolsheviks into positions of power, and to settle accounts with the "bourgeois specialists".'[11]

Historians have speculated about the point at which Stalin began to think in terms of becoming supreme leader. Had he planned his every move from the time Lenin first became ill in 1922 or even earlier? Or did it only dawn on him later that events might move in his favour if he played his cards correctly? It is impossible to be sure even now, since Stalin kept his innermost thoughts to himself. What does seem clear is that when he did change his policies, it was not simply for his own personal advantage – there were always good political or economic reasons as well. As Ronald Suny puts it: 'for Stalin, as for many politicians, personal power and political goals were complexly intertwined, and he probably saw little contradiction between what was good for him personally and what was good for the country.'[12]

6.2 The end of the New Economic Policy: why was it abandoned?

(a) Failures in agricultural policy

Although the NEP had been moderately successful for the first few years, by 1927 it seemed to be faltering and the results were disappointing. Whether this was because of inherent weaknesses within the NEP or whether it was because the government did not pursue it efficiently enough is still debatable. Certainly food production seemed to have reached an upper limit which was still well below the amounts produced and marketed in 1913 – and this to feed a population which was growing by at least two per cent per annum. Critics blamed this failure on the division of the land into large numbers of tiny uneconomic farms, and the continuing use of old-fashioned farming methods. But the situation was made worse by the government's policy of paying low prices for grain procurements; this was a deliberate ploy because the government wanted a price policy which ran counter to market forces. But it was fatal for hopes of increasing grain marketings – in the year 1926–27 the general level of agricultural procurement prices fell by about six per cent from the previous year, but grain prices on offer fell by as much as 25 per cent in some areas. Sometimes these prices were so low that they failed to cover the cost of production, and there was no incentive for peasants to try and produce more grain. Many concentrated on livestock and other crops, for which the prices were better, and they held on to their grain and sold it later for a better price to private traders (known as Nepmen) who were still legal.

By December 1927 when the Fifteenth Party Congress met, the food situation had reached crisis-point, although the Stalinists denied that there was a crisis. At the end of the year the state had bought up only 300 million poods (a pood = approximately 36 pounds) of grain compared with 428 million a year earlier. The situation was worst in Siberia, the Urals and the Volga: even though the harvest had been good in the Urals, grain sales to the state in that area were only 63 per cent of the previous year's figure; significantly, meat sales had increased by 50 per cent and bacon had quadrupled.[13] Peasants were waiting and hoping for an increase in grain prices offered by the state, which had happened in 1925. But not this time: Stalin was losing patience. Not only were there bread shortages in the big cities, even peasants in non-food producing areas were feeling the pinch; for example, the cotton-growers of Uzbekistan in Central Asia were short of food. It was against this background that in January 1928, Stalin himself, accompanied by a large posse of officials, travelled to the Urals and Siberia and personally ordered military-style operations against peasants. Free markets were closed and private traders – Nepmen – were banned; peasants were ordered to deliver their grain and were arrested if they failed to do so. Offenders could be sentenced to three years in jail if convicted of hoarding grain. Stalin was harsh with local party officials, blaming them for allowing the 'kulak gentry' to get away with 'specula-tion', and telling them that private farming in the villages could not go on like this indefinitely. Other senior officials organized similar campaigns in other areas, and this sort of operation became known as the 'Urals–Siberian method'. The government claimed that these measures had originated from local initi-atives and would not admit publicly that NEP had been abandoned. But Stalin and his supporters had clearly decided by the spring of 1928 that NEP was no longer a viable policy.

Some historians believe that NEP could have been much more successful in the agricultural sphere if only the government had made more of an effort to make it work. Lenin and Bukharin believed that the second stage of NEP should involve the state encouraging and educating the peasants (see section 5.6(d)) to prepare them for working together in agrarian co-operatives. However, there was little sign of encouragement or education of the peasants in the mid-1920s. The government's low-price policy was a disaster and almost destroyed the incentive to produce and market more grain. There were already several thousand state-owned (*sovkhozy*) and privately-owned collective farms (*kolkhozy*) in existence, but the government neglected them completely and they were not successful. If the state had encouraged and supported them, their output was bound to have increased and the crisis of 1927–28 may have been avoided. Instead, as Moshe Lewin points out, 'the leadership seemed to be relying on NEP to function "automatically" ... and gave very little thought to any preparation of alternative policies. The responsibility for this blindness must lie with Stalin, as well as with those of the future right. Their absorption with the struggle against the left cannot obscure the fact that the administration was guilty of a lack of foresight and perspicacity.'[14]

(b) Industrial failures

However, it wasn't only in the agricultural sphere that NEP turned out to be disappointing. Although by 1926 industrial output had recovered generally to around or just below its 1913 levels (see section 5.6(e)), it had somehow failed to make a great leap forward. The labour force seemed to be available – in fact there was a high level of unemployment; but what seemed to be lacking was planning and above all finance. There could be no life-saving French loans and investment now – no capitalist country would invest in a communist state which until recently had been trying to spread world revolution. Yet all the party leaders agreed that rapid industrialization was vital; the only disagreement was about the pace of the expansion – how 'rapid' should it be? In October 1925 Stalin announced that the government had decided to push ahead with a programme of industrialization based on a Five-Year Plan (although this did not actually begin until October 1928). His new slogan was 'socialism in one country'. This was an acknowledgment that revolutions elsewhere in the world were unlikely and that consequently the USSR would have to rely on its own strength for survival. The USSR must catch up with the Western countries as quickly as possible, so there must be a great drive to expand and modernize heavy industry – metallurgy, coal and machinery. A fully industrialized USSR would dissuade the capitalist powers from attacking, and if they did presume to intervene, a Soviet victory would be much more likely.

Stalin appeared to take the threat of war seriously, especially at the time of the famous 'war-scare' crisis in 1927. First of all, in April, Soviet relations with China took a disastrous turn. China was in the grip of a civil war in which the nationalist Kuomintang (KMT) party led by General Chiang Kai-shek, were trying to establish control. The Chinese Communist Party, founded in 1921, co-operated with the KMT, and both received support and encouragement from Moscow. However, as Chiang Kai-shek gradually gained control over more and more of China, he decided he could do without the help of the communists. He began to see them as potentially dangerous rivals and decided to destroy them. In April 1927 the attack began – thousands of communists were arrested, a workers' rebellion in Shanghai was brutally suppressed and a terrible 'purification movement' was launched in which thousands of communists, trade union leaders and peasants were massacred; some estimates put the total number of deaths as high as a quarter of a million. The Chinese nationalists seized the Chinese Eastern Railroad which, it had been agreed, would be managed jointly by the Chinese and Russians. The Russian government hurriedly brought all the Soviet advisers in China back home, and the Chinese broke off diplomatic relations with the USSR. This was a bitter blow for Stalin who had pressed the policy of co-operation with Chiang Kai-shek, against the advice of Trotsky. In May 1927 Britain broke off diplomatic relations with the USSR after police raided the premises of Arcos, a Russian trading organization in London. The police claimed to have found evidence that Russian agents were trying to stir up revolution in Britain. In June the Soviet ambassador in Poland was assassinated; and in addition to all this bad news there was evidence of deepening Japanese involvement in Manchuria, a further threat to Russian interests in the Far East.

Although the situation might have seemed serious, there was no real danger of war at that point, as Stalin's Foreign Minister, Chicherin, assured him. But Stalin chose to exaggerate the fears in order to strengthen his case for rapid industrialization – there was no time to lose! He also used the 'scare' to justify a tougher policy against opponents and 'enemies' at home. One of the first manifestations of the new approach, apart from the grain procurement campaigns against the peasants, were the Shakhty trials. In March 1928 it was announced that a group of about 50 engineers, including some Germans, in the Shakhty region of the Donbass in the Ukraine, were to be put on trial for deliberate sabotage of the mining industry and for conspiring with foreign capitalist powers. It was said to be a counter-revolutionary plot. The trials, reported every day in the press throughout May and June, were a complete travesty. The accused, some of whom had been beaten or tortured, were forced to make false confessions. They were all found guilty, five were shot and most of the others were given long prison sentences. This was the first of the so-called 'show-trials' in which the case against the defendants was based on confessions extracted by torture or threats. Stalin's aim in this instance was to frighten the leaders of industry – economists, managers, engineers and 'experts' in general – at this time when the government was preparing to launch its Five-Year Plan for industry. The Shakhty trials were a warning against experts of all types: to members of the bourgeoisie who might be tempted to put less than one-hundred per cent effort into making the forthcoming plan a success; to communist experts who worked with 'old' experts that they had better be on guard against the wiles of the class enemies; and to anybody who felt inclined to criticize the Five-Year Plan on any grounds whatsoever. All such people now ran the risk of being labelled 'wreckers' and 'saboteurs', of being sacked from their jobs and, at worst, of facing trial and execution.

Having softened up the potential opposition, Stalin was ready to launch the great industrial leap forward in 1929. However, there was still one huge question-mark: where was the finance coming from to sustain such an intense programme of expansion over a period of five years? For example, until the Russian machine-tool industry could be expanded, it would be necessary to import machinery from abroad; but how could this be paid for? This is where the close links between industry and agriculture became apparent: the only possible source of cash was from massive exports of grain. This was the crux of the entire NEP problem: the Russian peasants were required to produce not simply enough food to feed the rapidly growing population, but enough to finance the industrial expansion as well. To achieve this they needed to adopt more modern farming methods; but only the wealthiest peasants could afford, for example, to buy tractors, which were badly needed and expensive. NEP would clearly have to go, but as yet Stalin was undecided about what should take its place. Bukharin and the Right were against any form of coercion being used against peasants and blamed much of the trouble on Stalin for trying to rush industrialization too quickly.

(c) Political motives

All these were understandable economic motives for abandoning NEP. But there were clear political motives too. The Left Communists had believed passionately from the inception of NEP that it was impossible to justify the permanent survival of a largely privately-owned system of agriculture in what was intended to be a socialist state. Even more galling for them was the existence of the wealthy peasants or kulaks, as Stalin labelled them, who, so it seemed to them, took every opportunity of holding the country to ransom by hoarding their grain. Many workers resented the unemployment in industry while, they were told, kulaks and Nepmen were making big profits. 'What did we fight for?' was a question often put during the mid-1920s when it was becoming clear that society as a whole had not yet been transformed. Stalin encouraged these feelings for all he was worth; it was vital, he argued, to keep the revolutionary impetus going, to guard against a revival of the old middle classes; this is what the 1928 Shakhty trial was really all about. Bukharin, Rykov, Tomsky and the Right seemed over-cautious in comparison, offering only a very gradual change and rejecting all suggestion of toughness towards the wealthy peasants. The majority feeling in the party was apparently not one of satisfaction at a job well done. In the words of Sheila Fitzpatrick, 'it was a mood of restlessness, dissatisfaction and barely subdued belligerence and, especially among party youth, nostalgia for the old heroic days of the Civil War; for a young party still perceiving itself as (in Lenin's phrase of 1917) "the working class in arms", peace had perhaps come too soon.'[15] For Stalin, the Left and probably a majority of the party therefore, an attack on those wealthy peasants they described as kulaks was the best way forward and would give the party new direction. This policy had the additional advantage, from Stalin's point of view, of enabling him to defeat Bukharin and his supporters, leaving him in supreme control.

6.3   The collectivization of agriculture

(a) The decision taken

Although by the spring of 1928 Stalin had decided that NEP must go, it seems unlikely that he had any clear idea of what should take its place. The change to a policy of full collectivization took place only gradually. At first Stalin seemed to be toying with the idea of developing the kolkhozy and sovkhozy, which, he was told, could produce four times more from the same area of land than small peasant farms. At this stage nobody seemed to be thinking of total collectivization, and it was expected that a large private sector of farming would remain. During the three to four years which it could be expected to take before the collectives reached full capacity, Stalin intended to continue with the grain-requisitioning campaigns already started, calling it a war against the kulaks. The forces sent out had orders to seize grain from kulaks and 'middle peasants', but it soon became obvious that many of the 'middle peasants' were far from rich. All peasants resented requisitioning and resisted as best they could, eventually falling back on their old weapon – they sowed less. The relationship between the Soviet state and the peasants, which had gradually developed since 1917 into one of at least mutual tolerance, now broke down. The grain crisis continued, there were bread shortages in the cities and in February 1929 food rationing was introduced in some areas. Living standards were falling in industrial areas, and output was adversely affected. The weak agricultural system was jeopardizing the whole economy. Bukharin and his supporters reiterated their policies: a return to the free market for grain and a slow-down in the pace of industrialization. Once again the majority rejected their suggestions and criticisms and the Right was soon defeated. It was probably some time in September 1929 that Stalin was converted to total collectivization. It must have seemed to some of the leaders that the country was in a real crisis. They wanted an even faster rate of industrialization, and they accused the kulaks of trying to sabotage the country's future. Perhaps what finally convinced Stalin were the encouraging statistics of collective farm output released in the autumn of 1929: peasants working in collectives, who were only about five per cent of total peasants, produced fourteen per cent of the marketable grain. The decision was taken: rapid and total forced collectivization of all Soviet agriculture.

(b) Was collectivization the only alternative?

For many years most historians did not question the assumption that Stalin had no choice but to introduce forced collectivization because of the seriousness of the crisis. Isaac Deutscher claimed that 'Stalin acted under the overwhelming pressure of events...he was precipitated into collectivization by the chronic danger of famine in 1928 and 1929.'[16] Alexander Gershenkron argued that by the mid-1920s NEP had become restrictive and that conditions for further economic growth were therefore unfavourable.[17] More recent historians, including Robert C. Tucker, Moshe Lewin, James R. Millar and Dmitri Volkogonov, believe that there were alternatives. Lewin argues that agriculture was not exclusively to blame for the crisis, and that the rate of industrial growth at the time was excessive. The First Five-Year Plan (see section 6.4) for industry had ridiculously high targets which involved a great wastage of scarce resources and a forcing of the pace, which put an enormous strain on agriculture. The obvious alternative was to have started the industrialization programme much earlier so that it could have been pursued at a more modest pace, with, in the end, results which were just as impressive. The concept of the mixed private sector and state-collective sector was another perfectly viable alternative which was neglected by the regime. There were already several thousand kolkhozy and sovkhozy in existence in 1929. Kolkhozy were collective farms in which members farmed the land as a co-operative and were allowed a small private plot. Wages were paid at the end of the harvest, though if the farm failed to make a profit, no wages would be paid. In 1928 the government defined a 'large' kolkhoz as one with a sown area of 2000 hectares (one hectare = two and a half acres). Sovkhozy were state-owned collective farms, directed by the state and usually formed to bring previously virgin land under cultivation. They were looked on as grain factories and members were treated as industrial workers with a guaranteed minimum wage and social benefits. The first sovkhoz, started in 1928, was a huge one of 41,000 hectares in the Northern Caucasus.

There were also examples of spontaneous co-operative movements already taking place in the villages; these included 'simple producers' associations' and a kind of voluntary collectivized form of organization known as the TOZ; these were popular both with peasants and with local party activists who were involved with the problem, and thousands of poorer peasants rushed to join them during the first half of 1928. However, the government ignored them and they were banned early in 1930 once the decision for forced collectivization had been taken.[18] James R. Millar argues that the problem could have been solved by a sensible, more flexible pricing policy which gave peasants reasonable incentives. He came to the conclusion that 'mass collectivization of Soviet agriculture must be reckoned as an unmitigated economic policy disaster.'[19] There is also the strongly held view that even if total collectivization was the only answer, it could have been achieved gradually and without the use of force.

(c) The drive for collectivization

'The events of 1929–34 constitute one of the great dramas of history ... affecting virtually every aspect of Soviet life;' so wrote Alec Nove about this period of Stalin's 'revolution from above.'[20] Basically what happened in agriculture was that about 25 million small peasant farms were consolidated into some 200,000 large collective farms (kolkhozy), and hundreds of thousands of other peasants were taken on as paid labourers on state farms (sovkhozy). The theory was that these larger farms would be much more efficient, enabling the use of modern farming methods and machinery, especially tractors. Kulaks were not allowed to join the collectives; their land and stock were taken away from them and they were expelled from the area. There was untold suffering and later on a famine; the death toll ran into many millions. By 1936 about 90 per cent of all peasant households in the USSR had been collectivized.

Stalin himself explained the policy in an article in *Pravda* in November 1929: 'if the development of kolkhozy and sovkhozy proceeds at an accelerated pace, there are no grounds for doubting that in three years or so, our country will become a great grain country, if not the greatest in the world.' As for the kulaks, their fate had been decided: 'We have gone over from a policy of limiting the exploiting tendencies of the kulak as a class ... Now we are able to carry on a determined offensive against the kulaks, eliminate them as a class. Dekulakization is being carried out by the masses of poor and middle peasants themselves ... it is now an integral part of the formation and development of collective farms. Consequently it is ridiculous and foolish to discourse at length on dekulakization. When the head is cut off, you do not mourn for the hair. There is another question no less ridiculous: whether kulaks should be permitted to join collective farms. Of course not, for they are sworn enemies of the collective farm movement.'[21] It is difficult to be certain whether or not the Communist leaders actually believed their own propaganda against the 'malicious kulaks', but it certainly fits in with Marxist ideas of an 'exploiting class' manipulating the state for their own benefit. Beginning early in 1930, a huge batch of villages was declared ready to be collectivized each month, and it was hoped that the main grain-producing areas like the Volga and the Northern Caucasus would all be completed by the spring of 1931. The actual process of collectivization was carried out by the Red Army and secret police troops together with cadres of industrial workers and party members from the cities who descended upon the villages to help 'socialize' the countryside. The first 25,000 of these workers were only given two weeks' training before being sent out as shock brigades. Local officials were very anxious to push through collectivization in their area as quickly as possible; if it took too long, they risked being branded as 'Right-deviationists' – Bukharin sympathizers.

In theory force was only allowed against the kulaks; but the question was: who exactly were the kulaks? In fact, historians now believe that there was no such thing as a separate kulak class; they were simply the more successful and richer peasants who were an integral part of every village. They were the leading farmers in their village, often pioneers of new techniques and machinery, and respected by most of their neighbours. Nevertheless the government insisted on dividing them into three categories: 'dangerous' peasants known to be counter-revolutionaries –

Figure 6.1   A poster of the early 1930s advocating collectivization. The banner reads: 'We are completing unbroken collectivization'. The caption below reads: 'We are completing victory in making socialist changes in agriculture'.

they were to be sent to labour camps or shot; the most wealthy peasants, described as 'arch-exploiters' – they were to be exiled to distant provinces; and the least dangerous or loyal kulaks – they could stay in their native area but were only allowed a small piece of the worst land. The 'twenty-five thousanders', as the workers' cadres became known, had been told that the kulaks were responsible for the bread shortages in the cities, and they were determined on revenge at the slightest provocation. When they arrived in the villages they had problems deciding which were the kulaks and which category they fitted into. It was obvious that many of the peasants who were being less than co-operative were hardly rich, and so a new category of 'sub-kulaks' was introduced; these were middle or poor peasants who opposed collectivization, and therefore were to be treated as though they were kulaks. So in fact lots of middle and poor peasants became involved in the violence as well as the rich peasants. As well as being driven from their homes, they had their livestock and other property confiscated. It was like War Communism all over again, except much worse. Meanwhile the local officials spoke at village meetings, trying to persuade the other peasants to sign up for the kolkhoz. If they did so, their animals were declared the property of the kolkhoz; on the other hand if they refused they were likely to be labelled as kulaks. On 20 February it was announced that 50 per cent of all peasant households had been collectivized, though it seems highly unlikely that this could have been achieved properly in under two months in the middle of the Russian winter. Some writers have suggested that this figure was based on exaggerated reports from nervous officials who were anxious to impress their superiors.

The situation during the first few months of 1930 was chaotic and frenzied. There was tremendous anger among the vast majority of peasants at the crude and brutal behaviour of the collectivizers, and especially at the loss of their livestock. There were violent scenes: officials were beaten and stoned, and many peasants slaughtered their animals rather than hand them over to the collective. Thousands of dispossessed kulaks and peasants left the countryside and went to the towns in search of jobs. Outraged groups shouted slogans like 'down with the kolkhoz' and 'Long live Lenin and the Soviets'. The secret police responded by arresting thousands of 'trouble-makers' who were mainly exiled to Siberia and the far north. Even Stalin seemed shaken by the resistance and decided to call a temporary halt to the crash collectivization programme. On 2 March 1930 an article by Stalin headed 'Dizzy with Success' appeared in *Pravda*. In it he blamed local officials and the party cadres for the chaos, accusing them of becoming over-enthusiastic and 'drunk with success'. He pointed out that collectivization was a matter of voluntary choice by peasants, and that force was inappropriate; and he condemned the confiscation of cows and poultry. This left local officials confused and embarrassed and some felt angry and betrayed by central government whose orders they were carrying out. The famous edition of *Pravda* in which Stalin's article appeared became a best-seller in the countryside as beleaguered officials tried desperately to limit its circulation. Delighted peasants rushed to leave the kolkhozy: by the end of May around half of all collectivized households had walked out. Collectivized peasant households had reached a peak at 55 per cent of total households at the end of February 1930, or so it was claimed; but by the end of May this figure had fallen to only 23.6 per cent. These were averages over the whole country; some of the statistics for individual areas were startling enough to suggest that collectivization must have been all but abandoned: in the central Black-Earth Region the percentage of collectivized households fell from almost 82 to 15.7, while in Moscow province the fall was from 73 per cent to only 7.2 per cent.[22] But this was only a breathing-space so that the spring sowing could be completed. Once this had been achieved, Stalin had every intention of resuming the assault on the countryside later in the year.

(d) The assault renewed

Amazingly in view of all the disruption and violence, the 1930 harvest was a good one – the best since 1926. There was sufficient grain to feed the cities and even some left over to export, earning vital income with which to help finance industrialization. Unfortunately, grain exports earned less than had been hoped because of a fall in world grain prices. Most recent historians believe that the good weather was responsible for the successful harvest rather than any special contribution from the kolkhozy. Often these were being farmed by the poorest and least expert peasants, since the most efficient farmers – the kulaks – had not been allowed to join. The government had promised large numbers of tractors but only a small proportion had actually been delivered, and even they were often not properly used because there was a shortage of experienced drivers and mechanics. Nevertheless, one set of statistics sug-gested that although only 25 per cent of all peasants had joined collectives, those kolkhozy actually produced 40 per cent of all grain delivered to the state. This was only to be expected, given that the state controlled the marketing of the kolkhozy produce, but it was enough to convince many leading commun-ists and officials that collectivization was the answer to the country's problems and must be persevered with. However, the authorities played down the fact that animal products were in shorter supply than usual because so many peas-ants had slaughtered their livestock.

In 1931 the campaign began again; this time it was more carefully planned, it was carried out more slowly and there was perhaps less brutality. As an incentive peasants were allowed to keep some cows and chickens; they were each given a small plot of land and could spend part of the week working on it. Again the technique was the same: communist party members and cadres of industrial workers arrived in the villages to organize the kolkhozy, and some stayed on to act as chairmen. The upheaval was enormous, and accurate statistics are impos-sible to obtain; but it is clear that during the first three years of the collectivization drive, starting from the autumn of 1928, several million people – so-called kulaks and their families – were uprooted from their homes and deprived of everything they possessed. Some were resettled locally on the poorest land and some fled to the towns. But the vast majority were less fortunate: by the end of 1930, accord-ing to official police statistics, 63,000 heads of households had been executed or imprisoned; between 1929 and 1932 some 450,000 kulaks were deported to the Urals, 375,000 to Siberia, almost 200,000 to Kazakhstan and over 130,000 to the far north. Dmitri Volkogonov calculated that between eight and nine million men, women, old people and children were affected by dekulakization, most of them simply uprooted from the villages where their families had lived for genera-tions. Many were shot for resisting, and many died en route. In some places the process also swept up many middle peasants. Volkogonov came to the conclusion that, one way or another, perhaps as many as eight per cent of peasant households were 'sucked into the vortex'.[23] By 1936 it was reported that 90 per cent of peasant households had been collectivized.

There has been some controversy over whose was the responsibility for this appalling policy with all its attendant chaos and misery. The traditional 'totalitarian' view is that it was a 'revolution from above' and that Stalin must bear the responsibility; the famous *Short Course* of the history of the Communist Party, which Stalin himself edited in 1938, stated quite clearly that 'the distinguishing feature of this revolution is that it was accomplished from above, on the initiative of the state,' and it went on to explain that it was 'directly supported from below by the millions of peasants, who were fighting to throw off kulak bondage and to live in freedom in the collective farms.'[24] While the first part of the statement may well be true, there is very little evidence that the revolution had support from the great mass of the peasants, who only joined the collectives because the alternatives were so unattractive. Revisionist and social historians have argued that a revolution of this magnitude could not have been achieved simply by the use of force from above. They showed that there were large groups of people in Soviet society, especially young people from worker or peasant backgrounds who had moved up in society, who actively supported the Stalinist system, because they were doing well out of it. Members of the party bureaucracy, managers, experts, trade union leaders, kolkhoz chairmen – these were the people who benefited most from the regime and who did their best to stabilize it and prolong it. But there were other groups of people who supported the regime, not simply because they benefited from it, but because they genuinely believed in the ideals of the communists and the new Soviet society which they were trying to build. For them collectivization was not just about squeezing more grain out of the peasants; it was about control of the countryside – the extension of Soviet 'culture' and Soviet 'structures' over the whole of the USSR. The old-Leftist Trotskyite, Yurii Pyatakov, who became a strong supporter of the First Five-Year Plan and collectivization, may well have been wrong, but he was not alone when he declared that it was impossible to solve the problems of agriculture within the existing framework of individual farming. 'Therefore,' he explained, 'we are obliged to adopt extreme rates of collectivization of agriculture. In our work we must adopt the rates of the Civil War. Of course I am not saying we must adopt the methods of the Civil War, but that each of us is obliged to work with the same tension with which we worked in the time of the armed struggle with our class enemy. The heroic period of our socialist construction has arrived.'[25]

During the late 1980s and 1990s a so-called 'new cohort' of young American, European and Russian historians emerged, including J. Arch Getty, Lynne Viola, Stephen Kotkin and Jochen Hellbeck. They do not all agree on everything, but there is some consensus over this concept of a revolution from below, motivated by genuine ideological conviction and not just self-interest. There is evidence of initiatives being taken from below: Lynne Viola argues that the party's 'revolutionary-heroic' tradition was epitomized in the activities of people like the 'twenty-five thousanders', and that in its early stages collectivization was developing a momentum of its own and slipping out of central control.[26] Many young people were genuinely inspired by Bolshevik ideas of what people should be like and how a society should be organized; they wanted to identify with the new socialist society and 'culture' and become New Soviet people. Jochen Hellbeck, in his analysis of the diary of Stepan Podlubnyi, a young man living in Moscow in the early 1930s, charts one person's struggle to become a New Man. Podlubnyi was the son of a well-to-do peasant in the Ukraine who was designated a kulak. Stepan was only 15 when his father was dekulakized and deported to the far north in 1929; somehow the boy and his mother obtained false papers showing that they were from a working-class background and they escaped to Moscow. There Stepan worked as an apprentice in the *Pravda* printing plant and joined the Komsomol, the communist youth organization. He seemed to bear no ill-will towards the regime for the way his family had been treated; he concentrated on throwing off the stigma attached to him as the son of a kulak, trying to 'reconstruct' himself and devote himself to the state. As Hellbeck puts it: 'Only the state could imbue him with the notion of being a free agent. It was through the Soviet state that Podlubnyi acquired a sense of purpose, indeed the norms to define and guide his personal life. As his case makes clear, Soviet man could realize himself only by working for the state.'[27] It was only later, around 1935, that Podlubnyi became critical of Stalin's brutal methods and the regime's failure to live up to its promises; even then, however, he did not criticize the overall Bolshevik vision of the ideal society.

(e) The results of collectivization

Naturally Stalin claimed that collectivization was a great success; the press simply repeated the official line, and no criticism was allowed. Incidents which did not reflect well on the regime were not reported. The main achievement was that state grain procurements increased impressively, more than doubling between 1928 and 1933. Grain exports increased dramatically, especially in 1930 and 1931, and although they fell away after that, the 1933 export figure was still ten times greater than the 1929 total:[28]

State grain procurements (in millions of tons)

1928	1929	1930	1931	1932	1933
10.8	16.1	22.1	22.8	18.5	22.6

Grain exports (in millions of tons)

1927–8	1929	1930	1931	1932	1933
0.029	0.18	4.76	5.06	1.73	1.69

However, what Stalin did not reveal was that, apart from the exceptionally good year of 1930, *total grain production did not increase at all – in fact it was less in 1934 than it had been in 1928*:

Grain harvest (in millions of tons)

1928	1929	1930	1931	1932	1933	1934	1935
73.3	71.7	83.5	69.5	69.6	68.4	67.6	75.0

There were a number of reasons for this failure: the most obvious was that the best producers – the kulaks – were excluded from the collective farms, and most of the party activists who came from the cities to organize collectivization did not know a great deal about agriculture. Many peasants seemed demoralized after the initial seizure of their land and property, and according to Moshe Lewin, for every three peasants who joined a kolkhoz, at least one soon left to try and find a job in the city. Many peasants had slaughtered their horses rather than hand them over to the kolkhoz; since the government had not yet provided sufficient tractors, there were serious problems involved in trying to get the ploughing completed in time.

And then there was the problem of wages. Collective farmers or kolkhozniki, as they were called, were not paid wages; at the end of the agricultural year the profits of the farm were divided out in proportion to the number of workdays put in by each farmer. But for many years the cash payments on most kolkhozy were tiny; as Robert Service puts it, 'in reality most kolkhozniki could no more make a profit in the early 1930s than fly to Mars.'[29] The state fixed the quotas that each kolkhoz (typically consisting of between 50 and 100 households managed by the farm chairman) had to supply, at very low prices. Once the quota was met, any surplus could be sold at the local market. Peasants were also allowed to sell produce from their own private plots; this was one of the concessions made by the government to try and improve relations with the surviving peasants. They soon found that they could sell their vegetables, meat, eggs, butter and fruit at good prices and they could make much more profit from their home produce than from the collective farm. This meant that they worked much harder on their own plots and did the bare minimum that they could get away with for the collective. Since there were fewer peasants working than before, thanks to all the deportations and migrations, productivity fell; in fact in some areas it took three times as long to get the harvest in as it did before collectivization. From Stalin's point of view, the success of the new system was that it made it easier for the state to get its hands on the available grain without having to be constantly haggling with the peasants. For the first time the state had taken significant steps towards controlling the countryside. No longer would the kulaks hold the socialist state to ransom by causing food shortages in the cities; it was the countryside that would suffer now if there was a bad harvest.

It wasn't long before the countryside *was* ravaged by famine – in the winter of 1932–33. As the statistics show, the grain harvests of 1931, 1932 and 1933 were all disappointing in comparison with 1930. Yet in 1931 the state took more grain and exported more grain than in 1930. During those years of 1930 and 1931 the state exported almost ten million tons of grain, which ran down the reserves. So already in 1931 there were food shortages in some rural areas. In 1932 the government increased the quotas, especially in the Ukraine, which was the greatest grain-producing area. Stalin seems to have been convinced that the Ukrainians, motivated by nationalism, were holding back too much of their grain, although in 1931 they had handed over 42 per cent of their harvest. Stalin demanded over 50 per cent in 1932, but the Ukrainian Communist Party officials protested that this was impossible. Some reductions were agreed, but even so, the grain-collecting brigades had great difficulty in squeezing out the required quotas, and were forced to take everything they could find. As many as half the local party officials were arrested for being too lenient with the peasants, and anybody found with more grain than they should have had was arrested under a law passed in April 1932, which made 'pilfering foodstuffs' a crime punishable by death. Some 55,000 people were convicted and most received sentences of forced labour. The result of all this was that by the autumn of 1932 there was a disastrous food short-age throughout the Southern Ukraine. Other grain-producing areas had similar experiences, especially the Northern Caucasus, the Volga region and Kazakhstan. The situation was worsened by the slaughter of so many animals – throughout the USSR as a whole, almost half the cattle, two-thirds of the sheep and goats, and well over half the pigs and horses had been killed between 1928 and 1933. In Kazakhstan almost the entire sheep and goat population was wiped out. After collectivization animals were on average much smaller and weaker than they had been in the 1920s. Admittedly peasants were able to save on fodder, but it severely limited their options on alternative foods. The decline in numbers of animals showed itself in other ways – shortage of horses for ploughing and other farm work, reduction in the supply of hides for leather and footwear, and of wool for textiles.[30]

Nobody knows how many people died of starvation during the famine; estimates range from about five million to around eight million. Hundreds of thousands of people tried to move from the countryside into the nearest city or into a more prosperous area, hoping to find food. But this proved difficult: in December 1932 the government introduced an internal passport system to prevent starving people from seeking refuge in the towns. Country people were not given passports, and very few succeeded in getting through. Stalin was apparently anxious to keep the unfortunate peasants bottled up in the country-side, so that as few people as possible knew about the enormity of the famine. Roy Medvedev, the dissident Soviet historian, describes how 'military barricades and checkpoints were set up on highways and at railway stations to halt and turn back peasants from the famine-stricken regions. Even those who reached the cit-ies did not receive help. The peasants did not have ration cards, and stores would not sell them bread. In Kiev and in many other cities in the south the gathering of the corpses of dead peasants began early in the morning; they were loaded onto wagons and brought outside the city to be buried in large anonymous graves.'[31]

How did the young party activists, the members of the grain brigades, recon-cile their own roles with the terrible things they saw happening? Lev Kopelev, a bright young enthusiast who later became disillusioned with Stalinism, wrote: 'I was convinced that I was accomplishing the great and necessary transformation of the countryside; that the sufferings of the people who lived there were a result of their own ignorance or the machinations of the class enemy; that those who sent me knew better than the peasants how they should live, what they should sow and when they should plough.'[32] Stepan Podlubnyi confided similar thoughts to his diary, after his mother had written to tell him about the situation in their home village in the Ukraine: 'an incredible famine is going on over there. Half of the people have died of hunger. Now they are eating cooked beet tops. There are plenty of cases of cannibalism... All in all it's a terrifying thing. I don't know why, but I don't have any pity for this. It has to be this way, because then it will be easier to remake the peasants' smallholder psychology into the proletarian psychology that we need. And those who die of hunger, let them die. If they can't defend themselves against death from starvation, it means they are weak-willed, and what can they give to society?'[33]

The famine was not reported in the Russian press and Stalin consistently denied that there was a famine. When one of the Ukrainian party leaders tried to tell him about the dire situation in the Kharkhov area and appealed for grain to be sent, Stalin told him: 'You have made up quite a fable about famine, thinking to frighten us, but it won't work! You should join the Writers' Union; then you can write your fables and fools will read them.' Many people were arrested for uttering the words 'famine in the south' and it was not until 1956 that it was possible to write about it. In fact, of course, the famine was man-made – it need never have happened. Most historians agree that it was a deliberate policy carried out by Stalin with a political aim: the total subjugation of the countryside. Otherwise why were no relief measures taken? During the 1921 famine the government, as well as organizing its own relief campaign, had also appealed for help from abroad, and assistance came flooding in from all over the world. This time there was no appeal for help and the outside world hardly knew that there was a problem; and yet there was a great glut of agricultural produce which could have been rushed in to ease the crisis. There is still no consensus as to exactly what Stalin's motives were; many Ukrainian historians, together with Robert Conquest,[34] believe that his aim was to destroy Ukrainian nationalism. Certainly at the same time Moscow started a campaign against what it called Ukrainian 'national Communists', and over two thousand of them were arrested. On the other hand it seems more likely that Stalin was aiming at all peasants in grain-surplus areas generally, not just in the Ukraine. So many other areas were affected by the famine and even in the Ukraine itself other nationalities – Germans and Russians – suffered in the same way as the Ukrainians.

In many ways collectivization changed rural life less than might have been expected. The press circulated reports giving the impression that Soviet agriculture now consisted entirely of huge mechanized collective farms, but this was greatly exaggerated, certainly during the 1930s. The mir – the village commune – was abolished in 1930, but the kolkhoz which took its place consisted, in most cases, of the same village lands farmed by the same people, living in the same huts, except that they worked together as a team. The main difference was that a chairman appointed from outside acted as the manager and organized the marketing of the crop. Most of the traditional village leaders, the elders, had been classified as kulaks and removed. There were some giant kolkhozy and sovkhozy, but they were not especially successful, and some of the kolkhozy were broken up again into smaller units. From the peasants' point of view the main change was that they were worse off under collectivization: they had lost their land, their animals and much of their freedom; for a time their movements were restricted by the passport system, and they were expected to do forced labour repairing roads and cutting timber, as they did in the old days of serfdom. There is evidence of a gradual decline in the peasants' standard of living. The most productive farmers had been excluded, there was barely any improvement in productivity, *per capita* food consumption decreased and the birthrate fell. The peasants felt embittered and demoralized and they looked back on the period of NEP as a golden age. And ironically there is no evidence that grain exports made a worthwhile financial contribution to the development of industry. The millions of tons of grain that were exported in 1931 and 1932, and which could have more or less alleviated the famine in Russia, only contributed to the glut of grain on the world market; the prices were at rock bottom and the profits made available for investment in industry were negligible. In fact some economists calculate that the state was forced to use valuable resources to help agriculture recover, and that this cancelled out whatever profits had been made from grain exports. It was only in 1953 that the livestock figures recovered to their 1928 levels again.

Probably the biggest change was the departure of millions of people heading for the towns and cities. Sheila Fitzpatrick has shown that between 1928 and 1932 the urban population increased by some twelve million people, and at least ten million peasants left the countryside and became wage-earners in industry. A large proportion of them were young, able-bodied peasants; this, together with 'dekulakization' and the disappearance of the most efficient peasants, goes a long way towards explaining the future weakness of collectivized agriculture and the demoralization of the remaining peasants.[35] On the other hand this migration provided the necessary labour force for the rapid development of Soviet industry.

6.4 Industry and the Five-Year Plans

(a) The First Five-Year Plan takes shape

Discussions about the further development of industry began about August 1925, during meetings of the State Economic Planning Commission (Gosplan), and other discussions took place among economists. By this time it was becoming clear that NEP, although modestly successful, had serious limitations (see section 6.2(b)). Further significant increases in production could only be achieved through massive capital investment in new plant, and this needed careful centralized planning. All the leaders agreed that industrialization was a priority, but they could not agree on the rate of industrialization. As we saw earlier (see section 6.1(c)), in late 1925 and early 1926 the argument raged between those on the left of the party (Kamenev and Zinoviev) who wanted to industrialize as rapidly as possible and to raise the necessary funds by squeezing the peasants, and those on the right (Bukharin, Rykov and Tomsky) who favoured a more measured approach based on co-operation with the peasants. At first Stalin supported the moderates, but once the left was defeated, he came out in favour of rapid industrialization. In 1928 Gosplan brought out a plan which contained both 'basic' and 'optimum' estimates of industrial production and investment over the next five years; whichever variant was adopted, it was due to go into operation in October 1928. Having already defeated the left, Stalin now turned against the right and placed the party firmly behind the optimum plan, the very policy which he had opposed earlier. The main emphasis was to be on heavy industry, iron and steel, and on producer goods – machines which would be used to produce other tools; the coal and oil industries were also to be involved. Over the next five years it was intended that coal and oil production should roughly double, while iron ore and pig iron should treble. Many economists thought these targets were far too ambitious, but after the Shakhty trials earlier in 1928 (see section 6.2(b)), they were afraid to speak out. According to Isaac Deutscher, Stalin 'seemed to live in a half-real and half-dreamy world of statistical figures and indices, of industrial orders and instructions, a world in which no target and no objective seemed to be beyond his and the party's grasp. He coined the phrase that there were no fortresses which could not be conquered by the Bolsheviks.'[36] During the course of the plan the estimates were revised upwards: coal output was to treble, oil output to increase four times, and iron ore and pig iron to increase five times. In fact the plan was changed so often that some historians claimed it never actually existed in the first place.

Stalin told the Russian people that this breakneck pace of industrialization was vital for the survival of their socialist fatherland which, he felt sure, would inevitably come under attack from the capitalist nations. He wanted the country to be self-sufficient and prepared. Russia must be converted from a country 'that imports machines and equipment into a country that produces machines and equipment.' The Party Conference of April 1929 adopted as its main aim 'the maximum development of the production of the means of production as the foundation of the industrialization of the country.' Early in 1931, in one of his most famous speeches, Stalin told a group of business executives: 'It is sometimes asked whether it is possible to slow down the tempo somewhat, to put a check on the movement. No, comrades, it is not possible; the pace must not be slackened! On the contrary, we must quicken it as much as is within our powers and possibilities ... To slacken the pace would mean to lag behind; and those who lag behind are beaten. We do not want to be beaten. The history of old Russia was [to be] ceaselessly beaten for her backwardness ... for military backwardness, for cultural backwardness, for political backwardness, for industrial backwardness, for agricultural backwardness ... We are fifty or a hundred years behind the advanced countries. We must make good this lag in ten years. Either we do it or they crush us.'[37] There were political motives too – Stalin continued to see industrial workers as the main allies of the communists; greater industrialization would increase the proportion of workers to peasants, the 'class enemies'. Incidentally, the policy of rapid industrialization also fell in conveniently with Stalin's campaign to defeat Bukharin, who wanted to follow the basic variant of the plan.

(b) The First Five-Year Plan goes into operation

The plan began officially in October 1928, and was declared to have been completed in December 1932 – nine months early. New work had already started before the plan was officially inaugurated. In the year 1926–27 investment in new projects more than doubled, and the great Dnieper Dam was begun. A new tractor factory was completed at Stalingrad in June 1930, and all over the country work went ahead on massive projects, some 1500 of them: a new railway line (the Turksib Railway) linking Turkestan and Siberia; a tractor factory at Kharkhov; many new iron and steel works; a huge plant at Nizhny Novgorod (Gorky) for the manufacture of turbines, cars and lorries; mining projects in Kazakhstan; and engineering works in Georgia. There were several major canals and a series of thirteen dams along the Volga providing water for electricity and irrigation. One of the great showpieces was Magnitogorsk, a brand new industrial (mainly steel) city built in what was previously virgin wilderness in the south-eastern Urals, safe from invading forces. All these were new projects which did not reach full production until well on in the Second Five-Year Plan (1933–37).

It was a remarkable campaign by any standards; there were incredibly difficult problems to overcome; conditions in some areas were primitive and there were many disasters on the way. In spite of the announcement that the plan had been completed nine months early, the targets had not been reached. However, experts agree that a huge leap forward had been made with an annual industrial growth rate of between 15 per cent and 22 per cent during the four years of the plan. In the early days there was tremendous enthusiasm among many of the young party members and Komsomol members who were prepared to throw all their energies into 'the great construction projects of socialism'. According to Alec Nove, 'many seemed to have been fired by a real faith in the future and in their own and their children's part in it . . . with a will to self-sacrifice, accepting hardship with a real sense of comradeship.'[38] Some volunteered for the 'shock brigades', gangs of committed workers who descended on the factories to show ordinary workers how it should all be done, by setting new production records and sharing out their earnings equally. Hiroaki Kuromiya argues that in spite of all the hardships endured by the workers, the enthusiasm for the First Five-Year Plan was shared by the vast majority of the working class, who were in fact the main supporters of Stalin's regime in the early 1930s.[39] However, Donald Filtzer believes that Kuromiya exaggerates the proportion of workers who were genuinely enthusiastic and politically motivated; he argues that the shock-workers were never more than a small minority and were not typical of the overwhelming mass of ordinary workers on the shop-floor.[40]

There was intense government propaganda linking the industrialization drive to national defence and the danger of foreign invasion. The constant upward revision of targets was designed to keep workers on their toes and galvanize them into superhuman efforts. Other attempts to encourage greater efforts included a return to some capitalist practices – wage differentials, piece-work, bonuses, and offers of better food and lodging for those who improved their productivity. Great attention was paid to the ideas and methods of F.W. Taylor, the American time and motion expert (see section 5.2(b)) much admired by Lenin. Where expertise was lacking, the government brought in foreign experts, including British, Germans and Americans; American planners and engineers were heavily involved in the construction of Magnitogorsk.

At the halfway stage of the plan Stalin claimed to be dissatisfied with progress and launched an attack on 'experts', accusing them of 'wrecking' and 'sabotage'.

The new slogan was 'Destroy the Wreckers'; Stalin told the 1930 Party Congress: 'people who chatter about the necessity of *reducing* the rate of development of industry are enemies of socialism, agents of our class enemies.' Hundreds of economists, planners and engineers were arrested; in the Donbass half the engineers and technicians had been arrested by the end of 1931, and these included many foreign experts accused of sabotage. One group of economists and engineers was put on trial on the unlikely charge of aiding the French to attack the USSR. At the end of 1930 a group of 48 officials from the People's Commissariat of Trade was shot for sabotage in the food trade. Hundreds of older experts trained before the revolution were removed and replaced by younger graduates trained under the Soviet system. Stalin put two of his most reliable friends in top positions: Kuibyshev became head of Gosplan and Ordzhonikidze took over VSNKh (Supreme Council of National Economy); when that was abolished in 1932 Ordzhonikidze became People's Commissar of Heavy Industry. By this time the terror campaign against the 'bourgeois experts' had had the desired effect – all open criticism and opposition was stifled. Ordzhonikidze now felt able to relax the hard-line towards experts and skilled workers, and tried instead to promote co-operation and good industrial relations.

How did the government raise the cash to finance these enormous projects? Given the disappointing profits from grain exports, they had to look elsewhere for revenue. Much came from the sale of government bonds which people were more or less forced to buy. Duties on vodka, salt and matches were increased and a tax was place on the sale of goods. Agriculture did contribute something, but not in the expected way; the grain procurement agencies paid very low prices to the peasants and then sold the grain to the state flour mills at sometimes four times the price paid; the government taxed the difference, which boosted government revenue by some 30 per cent. One of the simplest devices was to print more banknotes, so that the amount of money in circulation increased five-fold between 1928 and 1933. The government increased its control over the economy in general so that it was transformed into what was known as a 'command economy'. This enabled ruthless decisions to be taken about which were the priority projects so that scarce cash and other resources could be channelled to where they were most urgently needed. For example it was decided that the targets for consumer goods such as textiles, which were considered to be less important, should be revised downwards, while those for metals were revised upwards.

(c) Successes and failings of the First Five-Year Plan

Whatever the criticisms and failings of the plan and Stalin's methods – and there are many – the evidence suggests that there was a remarkable increase in industrial output. Official Soviet statistics show that targets for gross industrial production, producers' goods and machinery were not only fulfilled but 'over-filled'. However, the official statistics are extremely suspect, and even they show that there were shortfalls in several important areas. Even so, most economists and historians agree that a great leap forward did take place. American economist Holland Hunter estimated that Soviet industry expanded by at least 50 per cent in the five years from 1928, and that between 1928 and 1940, industrial output grew on average by 17 per cent per year.[41] Alec Nove came to the conclusion that 'there is no doubt at all that a mighty engineering industry was in the making, and output of machine-tools, turbines, tractors, metallurgical equipment, etc. rose by genuinely impressive percentages.'[42] It was a time of laying the foundations on which the further expansion of industry could take place during the second and third Five-Year Plans. All privately owned enterprises and workshops ceased to exist and even small craftsmen and shopkeepers were either forced out of business or made to join state-supervised co-operatives. The state took over almost total control of the economy.

There was an improvement in transport: the Turksib Railway was opened in January 1931, making raw cotton from Central Asia more readily available for the textile industry, while food and fuel could be brought more easily to Central Asia and Kazakhstan from western Russia. There was still a long way to go, however, to bring the transport system up to the high standards of western Europe. On the railways there was a constant shortage of spare parts and skilled engineers and not enough time for proper maintenance. In 1932 the average speed of a Russian goods train was just under nine miles per hour. As for the canals, many of them froze during the winter and were therefore of only limited value.

Progress was made with armaments; during the course of the plan Stalin diverted more and more investment into the defence sector of industry, in order to build up Russia's military strength. No statistics are available, for obvious reasons, but the aircraft industry was a top priority, closely followed by the production of tanks. The government claimed that the plan had enabled the USSR to avoid the worst effects of the world economic crisis which developed after the Wall Street Crash of October 1929. While the USA and western Europe suffered all kinds of economic disaster – share prices and banks collapsed, firms went out of business, and millions of people were thrown out of work – the people of the USSR continued to enjoy stability and full employment. Soviet propaganda made the most of the industrial successes and there was no mention of accidents, delays, shortages, faulty planning, falling standards of living and strikes. Marx had been right after all, they argued; the capitalist system was collapsing and the Soviet system was the model for the rest of the world to follow. Western economists began to sit up and take notice of Russian achievements, and in some quarters, a grudging respect began to develop.

If they had known the true situation their assessments would no doubt have been very different. There were two main weaknesses in the plan: a large proportion of the products were of poor quality, and the workers were shamefully exploited, many of them having to endure totally unacceptable living and working conditions. Poor-quality products were common because high targets and quotas forced workers to speed up and caused shoddy workmanship, even among older experienced workers. Much of the new labour force consisted of peasants who had come into industry to escape from collectivization; they were completely unskilled and had no experience of industrial discipline or time-keeping. Although some learned very quickly, it took time to train them, and in the meantime a lot of damage was done to machinery through sheer ignorance. Another contributing problem was the high turnover of labour: newly arrived peasants, bewildered and dismayed by the appalling conditions, moved from job to job trying to find something better. In the coal industry, for example, the average worker changed jobs three times during 1930. Many of the new factories had been built in a slipshod way using poor materials. New equipment was often made out of defective metal, so that it did not function efficiently. As Donald Filtzer points out, although this was all shown in the statistics as growth, defective products could not be used; they had to be scrapped or remade. This meant that 'fuel and raw materials were squandered, overconsumed, or simply lost; over the economy as a whole the endemic inefficiencies of industry, transport and construction caused them to soak up inordinately large amounts of inputs relative to the output they produced.'[43] The Stalingrad tractor factory provides a good example: completed in June 1930, its target was 500 tractors a month; however, in July none at all were completed, in August there were 10, and in September 25. Unfortunately, after a few weeks' normal usage, the tractors began to fall apart. John Scott, an American engineer who was full of socialist ideals, went to work on the building of Magnitogorsk. He described how 'during the winters of 1933 and 1934 the whole blast furnace department was periodically shut down. The cold winds played havoc with the big furnaces ... tons of ice hung down all around, sometimes collapsing steel structures with their weight ... One job we all remembered was the demolition work after the disastrous explosion on No. 2; the blast blew the roof off the cast house, badly damaged the side of the furnace and seriously injured everybody who was near at the time. Several people were tried in an attempt to fix responsibility.'[44]

Industrial workers came under intense pressure to achieve their targets; the nervous-breakdown rate increased alarmingly and many older workers who failed to cope were simply forced out of their jobs. By 1929 there was considerable labour unrest; workers began to speak out about the physical and mental stress they were suffering as they tried to reach impossible targets; articles appeared in the trade union newspaper complaining that their treatment was worse than 'capitalist exploitation'. Some workers refused to carry out orders and others resorted to 'go-slows', alcohol or persistent absenteeism. There were strikes and demonstrations all over the country in protest against the raising of targets, delays in paying wages and the deduction of compulsory loans to the state. In 1932 there was a major strike in the textile city of Ivanovo–Voznesensk when almost the entire workforce refused to go back to work after the May Day holiday in protest against food shortages. The government felt that this could not be allowed to continue; in March 1929 factory directors were given the power to ignore the usual arbitration procedures and the trade unions and to sack people on the spot; trade union powers to protect workers were reduced and they were now required to devote themselves to increasing production and furthering the plan; in effect they were little more than tools of the management. Things got even more nasty in 1932 as the number of strikes increased: a single day's unjustified absence (which could be interpreted as being twenty minutes late for work) could be punishable by instant dismissal, denial of food ration cards and access to food shops, and by eviction from lodgings. Managers could be arrested if their performance was thought to be below standard; if a machine broke down or was used incorrectly, the manager was likely to be charged with 'wrecking' or 'sabotage'. Scapegoats had to be found for any failures or disasters, like the explosion at Magnitogorsk; the regime would never admit that the cause might be any fault of the plan. Strikes were broken up by force and the ring-leaders arrested; every worker had an individual production record and could expect trouble if he came at the bottom of the league table.

Donald Filtzer believes that a major aim of this harsh campaign, as well as mass mobilization of the workforce in order to achieve the targets, was to break down working-class solidarity and destroy its ability to act collectively. All the evidence suggests that the regime was successful in its aim: 'the old working class ceased to exist *as a class*. A new workforce took its place, but the atomization it encountered at work and in daily life made it impossible for it to function as a militant class able collectively to articulate and pursue its own radical needs.' A combination of circumstances contributed towards the regime's success in causing this fragmentation of the labour force: the dwindling number of older workers with traditions of trade union organization and militancy; the influx of so many peasants with no experience of collective action; the presence of the young enthusiasts – the Komsomol members – who were keen to join the shock brigades; the rapid turnover of labour as 'workers roamed the country looking for any job that offered better wages, rations or housing.' Even many older skilled workers left their traditional industries in the search for something better. In 1930–32 the average industrial worker changed jobs once every eight or nine months. All this against a background of difficult working conditions deprived workers of any coherence; they were reduced to waging a struggle for personal survival and had little time or energy left for political organization and militancy. There was a way out for a minority of workers: to work their way up to positions in management or in the party bureaucracy, which was achieved by perhaps 15 per cent of the labour force during the First Five-Year Plan. On the other hand the workers were not entirely helpless; there were constant labour shortages and many managers, anxious to achieve their targets, were reluctant to dismiss people who broke the rules. As the 1930s progressed, a kind of unwritten mutual collusion agreement emerged between workers and management, since it was in both their interests to ignore the law.[45]

It wasn't only at work that the labour force seemed to be under attack – living conditions were often atrocious as well. The plan estimated an urban population by 1932 of 32.5 million, but the actual figure turned out to be 38.7 million. The targets for new housing were reduced to less than half so that more factories could be built, and consequently there was serious overcrowding in industrial areas. Again much of the new housing was of poor quality, maintenance was poor, and there was a shortage of water, shops and other amenities. Apartments and kitchens had to be shared and this put appalling strains on family life, creating, in the words of Moshe Lewin, 'the specifically Soviet (or Stalinist) reality of chronically overcrowded lodgings, with consequent attrition of human relations, strained family life, destruction of privacy and personal life, and various forms of psychological strain. All this provided a propitious hunting ground for the ruthless, the primitive, the blackmailer, the hooligan, and the informer. The courts dealt with an incredible mass of cases testifying to the human destruction caused by this congestion of dwellings.'[46] The birth rate fell dramatically, the child mortality rate was increasing, and by 1936 the big industrial cities were experiencing a net loss of population. City dwellers also suffered from recurrent food shortages; by the end of 1929 all basic foodstuffs were rationed and gradually most consumer goods were rationed too. The worst time was the winter of 1932–33 when the countryside was experiencing the disastrous famine (see section 6.3(e)). There was rapid inflation, partly caused by the government's policy of printing more paper money; although actual money wages rose, real wages fell dramatically, and there was a marked fall in the workers' standard of living. Stalin would not admit publicly that there was any problem; in January 1933 he claimed that wages had risen by 67 per cent and completely ignored the rising prices. 'We have unquestionably reached a position,' he told his audience, 'where the material conditions of the workers and peasants are improving from year to year. The only ones who can have doubts on this score are the sworn enemies of the Soviet regime.'

(d) The Second and Third Five-Year Plans

The Second Five-Year Plan began immediately the first one was declared completed at the end of December 1932. It ran from January 1933 until it too was declared to have been completed early in 1937. It did not begin well: at the start of the year the country was still in the grip of the famine, there was a transport crisis and shortages of all kinds. Even Stalin realized that the targets set were totally impossible, and the industrialization drive was allowed to slow down for a time while the economists carried out a recalculation. The revised plan aimed to consolidate the achievements of 1928–32 and to increase the output of consumer goods to enable living standards to improve. However, during 1934 the plan was changed again, with more investment being diverted towards heavy industrial production. The probable reason for this was the need to increase armaments in view of the rise to power of Hitler in Germany in January 1933. Consequently the targets for consumer goods and housing were once again not achieved. On the other hand there were some good features in 1934: food rationing was brought to an end, statistics suggest that real wages doubled, and many of the new factories and plants which had suffered teething-troubles earlier now came on full stream. The years 1935 and 1936 were also successful. Highly impressive were the growth rates in the machinery and metal-producing sectors, and in coal and electricity production. Although targets were not attained, output of consumer goods nevertheless increased and more was available for sale. Great progress was made in developing a more educated working class; there were numerous training schemes and opportunities for workers to receive higher level technological education at universities.

One of the most interesting features of the second plan was the Stakhanovite movement. Alexei Stakhanov was a miner in the Donbass in the Ukraine. In September 1935, with a team of assistant workers to help him, Stakhanov set a new record by cutting 102 tons of coal in a single shift, which was about fourteen times greater than the norm. His achievement was widely publicized and Stakhanov was elevated to the status of a national hero – a champion shock worker whom everybody should emulate. The government urged workers in all branches of the economy to follow his example by introducing new techniques and work patterns. Soon every industry had produced its Stakhanovite – the champion workers who had established new production records and whose pictures now appeared all over the country. The campaign gathered momentum, pressurizing both workers and managers to work harder and faster. It was all very misleading – these champions were not achieving new records on their own but as leaders of teams; nevertheless the government used it as an excuse to increase output norms in a number of industries. 'All saboteurs, routinizers, and bureaucrats will be swept away by the glorious march of the Stakhanovites,' warned Andrei Zhdanov, the new Leningrad party boss. Needless to say, the Stakhanovites became unpopular with ordinary rank-and-file workers who were likely to respond to their new targets by going-slow. In some places Stakhanovites were attacked and beaten up; in the long term the Stakhanovite movement may well have done more harm than good. Donald Filtzer believes that 'at its high point Stakhanovism led to greater disruption than it alleviated, as the efforts of the record-breaking minority created bottlenecks by disrupting the smooth flow of production.' As soon as the novelty had worn off by mid-1937, the old pattern of work practices quickly came back in. Admittedly by 1940 techniques had become more modern, but this was due more to new technology than to the Stakhanovites.[47]

In 1937 there was a sudden slowdown caused by a sharp fall in investments as more and more resources were diverted into armaments. Another contributing factor was undoubtedly the purges (see next section) which removed from the scene thousands of engineers, managers, technicians, planners and economists who were said to be saboteurs or spies in the pay of enemies of the people. Many were executed and the rest sent to labour camps in remote areas. Not only did this cause a serious shortage of experts, it also stifled initiative among the remainder, since any mistake or accident would be construed as 'wrecking'. Apart from Stalin's political motives – his desire to hold on to supreme power – there was an economic motive behind some aspects of the purges. It enabled him to claim that all the economic shortfalls, shortages, poor-quality goods and trans-port difficulties were the work of class enemies who were trying to discredit the government. For example, *Pravda* reported that the shortage of eggs had been caused by wreckers who deliberately smashed eggs in transit just to deprive the Soviet people of the fruits of their labour and to turn them against the govern-ment.[48] Five men were shot in Minsk for 'wilful contamination of flour; another five were shot in the village of Tabory in the Urals for 'disrupting the kolkhoz'.

The Third Five-Year Plan (1938–42) was cut short by the USSR's involvement in the Second World War in June 1941. The plan aimed to double production in all sectors of heavy industry and to increase consumer goods substantially. Another important aim was secondary education for all children living in cities and a minimum of seven years' education for children living in the countryside. Once again, in spite of official claims, targets were not achieved, although industrial output did continue to rise. There was a shortage of labour, the effects of the purges continued to be felt, and there was a shortage of iron ore and sometimes coal. As the pace began to flag, the regime decided that discipline, which had been relaxed somewhat in the three good years of 1934–36, must be tightened up again. In 1939 an old tsarist practice was brought back – the labour book, with which every worker was issued. It was like a student's report card, listing the worker's qualifications, jobs, special achievements and offences. Stalin genuinely hoped that the gradual improvement in living standards during the second plan would win over both workers and peasants to the regime; but by 1940, after a decade of mobilization and assaults on their freedom, the vast majority of workers and peasants must have been reduced to, at best, complete apathy, and at worst, outright hostility.

Most historians and economists agree that during the 1930s the USSR, under the leadership of Stalin, experienced a remarkable expansion and modernization of industry. Even those most critical of Stalin himself allow this; Roy Medvedev wrote: 'I am not about to deny the major successes achieved by the Soviet Union during the first five year plan. In the period from 1928 to 1933 alone, 1500 big enterprises were built and the foundations laid for branches of industry that had not existed in tsarist Russia: machine-tool production, automobile and tractor manufacturing, chemical works, aircraft factories, the production of powerful turbines and generators, of high-grade steel and so on ... The eastern part of the country became a second major centre for metallurgy and the oil industry. A modern defence industry was established. And hundreds of new cities and workers' settlements were founded. Stalin put considerable effort into the huge task of building a modern industry in the Soviet Union.'[49] The question which has exercised historians greatly is this: did it need Stalin and his brutal methods to force the USSR into this great leap forward, or could it have been achieved by more conventional methods? It was Alec Nove who once put the question in an article in *Encounter*: was Stalin really necessary? One line of argument is that after the great spurt around the turn of the century, Russian industry had stagnated and had fallen even further behind the West. Work practices and techniques remained so inefficient and chaotic that something really drastic was needed to wake people up to the necessity of rapid expansion and modernization to make the USSR into a great industrial power. Thus Martin McCauley suggests that 'the First Five-Year Plan was a period of genuine enthusiasm, and prodigious achievements were recorded in production. The impossible targets galvanized people into action and more was achieved than would have been the case had orthodox advice been followed.'[50]

Alec Nove leans towards a similar view; he believes that as far as industrial planning is concerned, given the inheritance from the tsarist period, it is difficult to conceive that there was any genuinely viable alternative to the course Stalin took. 'Under Stalin's leadership an assault was launched against the fortress, defended by class enemies, and on obstacles to rapid industrial growth. The assault succeeded in part, failed in some sectors, but failures could be said to be inherent in the process of learning. The later improvements in planning technique were based on lessons learnt in the course of storming the heavens ... A great industry was built ... and where would the Russian army have been in 1942 without a Urals–Siberian metallurgical base?' On the other hand Nove also points out that Stalin made vast errors: he tried to go too far much too fast, ignored sound advice, resorted to unnecessarily brutal methods in both town and country, and treated all criticism, even when it was justified, as evidence of subversion and treason.[51]

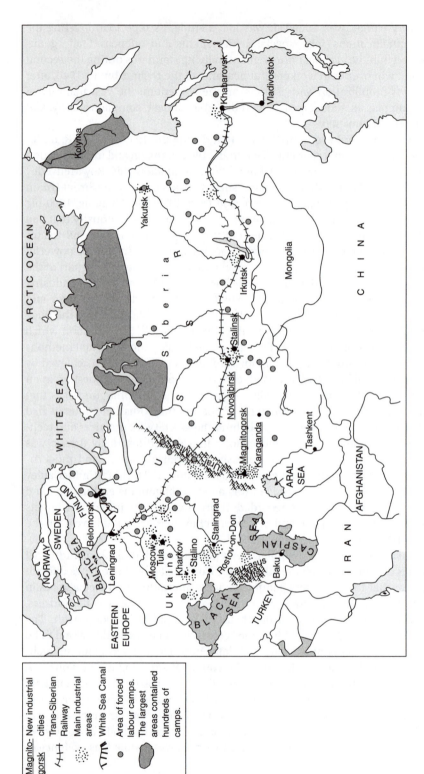

Map 6.1 The expansion of Soviet industry and labour camps under Stalin.

Legend:
- Magnito- gorsk — New industrial cities
- Trans-Siberian Railway
- Main industrial areas
- White Sea Canal
- Area of forced labour camps.
- The largest areas contained hundreds of camps.

It is these excesses which lead others to the conclusion that similar or even better results could have been achieved without Stalin. As Medvedev puts it: 'There are many examples of Stalin's incompetence and adventurism, which greatly complicated the already complex job of industrialization . . . It is possible to say with certainty that industrialization during the first five year plan proceeded at a slower pace and higher price not least of all because Stalin was the head of the party and the government. If the extreme exertions and sacrifices which the people made for the sake of industrialization are compared with the results, the conclusion cannot be avoided: the results would have been far greater *without* Stalin.'[52] James R. Harris has recently shown how constant pressure from Moscow hindered production in the Urals region by causing all kinds of unnecessary tensions. The government's refusal to accept any excuses or delays made it impossible to raise and discuss genuine problems with central officials. Local managers were blamed for any serious accidents and other problems and were put on trial. And so the local ruling clique in the Urals region muddled on until well over half way through the Second Five-Year Plan, using a range of cover-up strategies – sending in exaggerated production figures and underestimates of production capacity; worst of all, they often deliberately turned out poor quality goods just to increase the production figures. Unfortunately for them, it was impossible to conceal underfulfilment indefinitely, and in 1936 the Central Committee demanded explanations; in the ensuing purge of 'enemies of the people', hundreds of conspirators were arrested and shot. Since these practices were repeated all over the country, from the economic point of view the Stalinist approach was disastrous – it forced people to make personal survival rather than the modernization of industry their first priority.[53]

Donald Filtzer is even more damning: he argues that Stalin's methods caused the emergence in the USSR of an industrial system which was neither capitalist nor socialist, but which was, in fact, a 'deformed productive apparatus.' Because so many industrial units had been built in a hurry, using poor materials, they continued to produce poor-quality goods. Although this might have been expected in the early stages of industrialization because of normal teething troubles, the problem in Russia was that the new system of production and of industrial relations proved impossible to reform, and the Soviet state was left with a set of economic problems which could not be overcome within the existing framework of society. It was for this reason that 'Stalinism proved historically unstable and transient . . . from the late 1980s onwards its breakup was simply a matter of time . . . The system could digest neither internal reform nor the attempt at a full-scale restoration of capitalism, launched by Gorbachev from mid-1990 onwards.'[54] Another important legacy of the Stalinist industrialization was the ecological disaster; not only were safety and decent working conditions neglected, but no consideration was given to the effect of these vast 'smoke stack' plants on the environment, which suffered massive pollution.

Some historians still hold to the view that similar results could have been achieved by sticking to the sensible and realistic NEP framework. American economist Holland Hunter has calculated that if the growth rates under NEP had continued throughout the 1930s, the USSR would have reached the same industrial and military capacity; there would have been a more even spread of expansion, less waste, less expense both in financial and human terms, and less defective output.[55] One thing seems certain: the Soviet people under Bukharin's leadership would have been less shell-shocked and happier with the government. Arguably Bukharin, with his shrewd eye for foreign affairs, would not have made Stalin's mistake of underestimating the threat from Hitler and Nazism, and certainly would not have executed almost the entire army high command in the years 1937–38 (see section 6.5(c)). Nor, presumably, would Bukharin have indulged in the great Purges of the later 1930s. As R.W. Davies puts it: 'the arrest of officials, managers and engineers in industry and other sectors of the economy … was a major factor in the economic disruption. Economic crisis in the Soviet Union of the 1930s cannot be understood outside its political context.'[56]

6.5 Politics and the Purges

(a) The Stalinist political system and the background to the Purges

During the years 1928–40 Stalin and his closest allies gradually tightened their grip on the party, the government and the local party organizations, until by 1938 all criticism and disagreement had been driven underground and Stalin's personal dictatorship was complete. By the summer of 1930 the government's popularity had fallen sharply with the general public because of collectivization and the rigours of the First Five-Year Plan. Some prominent communist leaders, including Beso Lominadze, the party chief in Transcaucasia, appalled by the brutalities of collectivization and the excessive cost of industrialization, called for more moderate policies and suggested 'a clean sweep of the party leadership.' 'If there is to be a spring cleaning,' he remarked unwisely to a friend, 'every piece of furniture has to be removed, including the biggest one.' Lominadze and several others were sacked, though as yet, they suffered no further punishment. Even Stalin at this stage was sticking to Lenin's warning that although the death penalty was acceptable for non-party opponents, Bolsheviks should never exterminate each other. But it was clear that there was a substantial body of communists, some in the Central Committee and some in the Politburo, who were unhappy with Stalin and were prepared to resist his drive for dictatorship. Martemian Ryutin, head of the party committee in Krasnaya Presnya (a district of Moscow), and a member of the Central Committee, organized a small opposition group in Moscow which circulated a document known as the 'Ryutin Platform'. This called for an easing of the pressure on the countryside, more democracy in the party and the removal of Stalin from the leadership by force. Stalin, who had informers everywhere, soon found out, and Ryutin and seventeen members of his group were arrested. The charge was that they had attempted to set up a 'a bourgeois kulak organization to re-establish capitalism'. Stalin wanted them executed, but Sergei Kirov (the Leningrad party boss) and other moderates in the Politburo defeated Stalin; the culprits survived for the time being – they were simply expelled from the party, Ryutin was given a ten-year gaol sentence and the rest were sent to remote areas (September 1932). Early in January 1933 a third group of plotters was uncovered; these were Old Bolsheviks who included the highly respected A.P. Smirnov who had been Commissar for Agriculture and a party member since 1896. He had not been associated with either the Left or Right opposition, but now he and his supporters wanted the removal of Stalin, the break-up of most of the collective farms and the return of full powers to the trade unions. They were all expelled from the party, but once again Kirov, Ordzhonikidze and Kuibyshev voted against the death penalty and Stalin was thwarted in his bid to have them executed.

At the same time Stalin resorted to the technique of blaming the famine, the chaos in the countryside, industrial problems and transport difficulties on saboteurs. 'The nearer we get to achieving socialism,' he warned, 'the more evident will be the counter-revolutionary character of every oppositional tendency.' The Politburo called for a purge of party members, many of whom, Stalin claimed, had been involved in organizing 'kulak sabotage'. An atmosphere of suspicion and fear was created in which everybody was encouraged to inform on 'enemies of the people'. It is impossible to say whether Stalin himself genuinely believed that he was in danger of being overthrown; but he must have known that his government was deeply unpopular, especially in the countryside; he didn't trust the Old Bolsheviks and the former Left and Right oppositionists, who were still at liberty; and his close allies, who owed their positions to Stalin, no doubt felt insecure, and distrusted many of the party and government officials below them. And so the purge of party members went ahead: over 800,000 were expelled during 1933 and a further 340,000 in 1934. By the end of 1933 there were already about two million people in prison, in forced labour camps and deportation camps.

As the economic situation began to improve during 1934 there was something of a relaxation of tensions. The more moderate members of the leadership, especially Kirov and Ordzhonikidze, were probably responsible for the range of concessions made in agriculture and industry sometimes described as the 'Great Retreat'. This was partly an attempt to improve relations between the government and ordinary people, and it seems to have had some success. Even Dmitri Volkogonov admits that in the mid-1930s 'Stalin's popularity was genuine among the masses.' They believed what they were told about Stalin, that he was 'the great helmsman', steering the nation through all the perils and threats of counter-revolution from the 'class enemies', and many of them accepted the fabrication that the failures and hardships were caused by saboteurs. Unfortunately 'they had neither the opportunity nor the inclination to delve deeper into what was going on.'[57] The Seventeenth Party Congress which met in February 1934 was presented as the Congress of the Victors: it was a celebration of the successes of collectivization and industrialization, and the defeat of the enemies within the party.

Behind the scenes, however, there were disagreements: Stalin and his allies Molotov and Kaganovitch wanted to continue the hard line, while Kirov and Ordzhonikidze spoke in favour of moderation. Kirov wanted better relations with writers and other members of the intelligentsia. In a rare example of public disagreement, Ordzhonikidze objected to Molotov's proposal to increase the industrial growth rate by five per cent and suggested three per cent instead;

when a vote was taken, Ordzhonikidze's proposal was carried. According to Roy Medvedev, there is evidence that during the congress some of the moderates held discussions about transferring Stalin from his post of General Secretary to some other job and replacing him with Kirov. They went as far as to ask Kirov whether or not he would be willing to stand, but he was strongly against the idea. So unpopular had Stalin become among the rank-and-file party members that when the voting was held for the new Party Central Committee, he only just scraped enough votes to become a member. On the orders of Kaganovitch, who was the organizer of the election, the normal practice of publishing the number of votes cast for each candidate was not followed. But Stalin knew the statistics and he knew about the talks aimed at demoting him. It seems likely that by the end of the congress Stalin cannot have been feeling too secure. 'Events had shown a growing lack of confidence in Stalin among wide circles of party activists. Stalin was always extremely sensitive to such signals. He felt that his position and power were in danger, and this danger was personified for him by Sergei Mironovich Kirov.'[58]

(b) The murder of Kirov and the beginning of the Purges

On the afternoon of 1 December 1934, a young Communist party member, Leonid Nikolaev, walked into the Smolny, the party headquarters in Leningrad, and hung around unchallenged in a corridor near Kirov's office. Shortly afterwards, as Kirov came along to his office, Nikolaev stepped out and shot him dead from behind. The murder caused a sensation and Stalin and his entourage rushed to Leningrad from Moscow to investigate. What happened over the next four years must have seemed like an endless nightmare to the Russian people. Stalin used the murder as a pretext to claim that a huge and wide-ranging plot had been uncovered to assassinate not only Kirov, but Molotov and himself as well. A campaign was launched against party members whom he distrusted or disliked for some reason, and from 1936 until 1938 this was intensified into what became known as the Great Terror. The number of victims is still in dispute, but even the more modest estimates put the total executed and sent to labour camps at well over three million in the two years 1937 and 1938. The vast majority of those sentenced to concentration and labour camps never returned.

What could possibly be the motives for such an extraordinary policy – a campaign of violence so unrestrained and so monstrous as to be almost beyond belief? The traditional view, put forward by Robert Conquest, is that Stalin was driven by his lust for power. 'The one fundamental drive that can be found throughout is the strengthening of his own position. To this, for practical purposes, all else was subordinate. It led him to absolute power.' Anybody against whom Stalin had a personal grudge was automatically included on the death list. But even Stalin could hardly have had personal grudges against four million people. Conquest believes that Stalin's terror has to be looked at as a mass phenomenon rather than in terms of individuals. The effect of terror is produced in any group or society when a given proportion of that group has been seized and shot. 'The remainder will be cowed into uncomplaining obedience. And it does not much matter, from this point of view, which of them have been selected as victims, particularly if all or almost all are innocent.'[59] Political scientist Zbigniew Brzezinski took a less personalized view, arguing that in any totalitarian system where there are no genuinely democratic elections, continued random purging is needed to keep people in a constant state of fear and uncertainty.[60] Revisionist historian J. Arch Getty argues that the purges were really an extreme form of political infighting at the top; he plays down the role of Stalin himself and claims that it was the obsessive fears of all the leaders which generated the terror.[61] Sheila Fitzpatrick suggests that the purges must be seen in the context of a continuing revolution. 'Suspicion of enemies – in the pay of foreign powers, often masked, involved in constant conspiracies to destroy the revolution and inflict misery on the people – is a standard feature of revolutionary mentality ... In normal circumstances, people reject the idea that it is better that ten innocent men perish than that one guilty man go free; in the abnormal circumstances of revolution, they often accept it.'[62] And there was the added advantage that sensational purges would divert attention away from the country's economic and social problems. On a more mundane level, the purges made room for the promotion of ambitious party apparatchiks.

Ironically some of the most recent evidence to emerge from the Soviet archives seems to bear out the simple traditional view that Stalin's ambition and paranoia were responsible. Dmitri Volkogonov reached the conclusion that Stalin had an exceptionally evil mind, that there was a gap in his personality where the moral sense should have been. This moral gap in the personality 'can reduce even a powerful mind to the functions of a calculating machine, a logical mechanism to the level of a rational but pitiless apparatus.' He went on to argue that the chief responsibility for all the horrors of the terror rested with Stalin. It was Stalin who personally gave Yezhov instructions on the direction and scale of the repressions, and he approved long lists of people to be executed. This went on until 1938, when Stalin seemed to have become bored with this procedure, and thereafter gave courts and tribunals the right to decide for themselves.[63] There is no real evidence that Stalin felt himself in danger; early in 1939, when he felt that the terror had served its purpose, it was Stalin who quite calmly called a halt. Of course, he needed help in his extraordinary campaign; his two most faithful assistants, Molotov and Kaganovitch, seem to have been very similar in mentality. Molotov, who survived everything and lived to the ripe old age of 96, was unrepentant to the end. 'In the main it was the guilty, those who needed to be repressed to one degree or another, who were punished,' he said forty years later. 'Obviously one or two out of ten were wrongly sentenced, but the rest got their just desserts.'[64]

And it was the murder of Sergei Mironovich Kirov on 1 December 1934 which became the starting point of the Great Purges. This murder, according to Robert Conquest, 'has every right to be called the crime of the century. Over the next four years, hundreds of Soviet citizens, including the most prominent political leaders of the Revolution, were shot for direct responsibility for the assassination, and literally millions of others went to their deaths for complicity in one or another part of the vast conspiracy which allegedly lay behind it. Kirov's death, in fact, was the keystone of the entire edifice of terror and suffering by which Stalin secured his grip on the Soviet peoples.'[65] Although it is probably not possible at this distance in time to prove it conclusively, there seems little doubt that Stalin himself was responsible for Kirov's death. The official Soviet version, held from 1938 until 1956, was that Zinoviev, Kamenev and Trotsky had ordered the murder, and that Yagoda, who was head of the NKVD (The People's Commissariat of Internal Affairs), had arranged for the murderer to be given uninterrupted access to his victim. Conquest argues that Yagoda had indeed been involved but that it was Stalin who had given the orders, not directly but through certain intermediaries.

The circumstances surrounding the murder were certainly suspicious. In the preceding six weeks Nikolaev had twice been arrested by Kirov's bodyguards for threatening behaviour, and twice the NKVD had released him, even though he was carrying a loaded pistol. Just before the killing, Kirov's bodyguards mysteriously disappeared, although they had been seen with him at the Smolny entrance. Borisov, the leader of the bodyguard, who was known to be devoted to Kirov and who had thwarted the two earlier attempts on Kirov's life, was reported as having been killed in a motor accident as he was being taken for questioning; but in 1956 two of the doctors who had signed his death certificate admitted that he had died from being beaten on the head with iron bars. Nikolaev himself was executed without being questioned too deeply, and several others, including the men who had killed Borisov, were also shot soon afterwards. It is difficult to resist the conclusion that Stalin was deeply involved; it was all so convenient: Kirov's murder destroyed his most influential rival, and the blame could be laid on his other rivals and critics. On the day of the murder, even before any investigation had begun, a new decree was issued on Stalin's orders giving the NKVD full authority to arrest and try all those accused of acts of terror; death sentences must be carried out immediately; there was no right of appeal and no possibility of a pardon. This decree was published before the Politburo had even seen it.

The first important victims of the new purge were Kamenev and Zinoviev; on 16 January 1935 they were both found guilty of complicity in Kirov's murder; Zinoviev was sentenced to ten years' imprisonment and Kamenev to five years. This was followed by literally thousands of arrests in Leningrad, in which hundreds of supporters of Zinoviev (who had earlier been the Leningrad party boss) and anybody considered to be enemies of the Communists were rounded up; many were former nobles who were guilty of nothing except belonging to the wrong social class. Over 30,000 people were deported to Siberia from Leningrad alone, and there were similar purges in other cities. There is evidence that after this first wave of terror the remaining Politburo moderates, particularly Valerian Kuibyshev, argued against any further purges. However, on 26 January Kuibyshev died suddenly from a heart-attack; later it was suggested that he had been murdered by his doctors who deliberately gave him the wrong medical treatment, on the orders of Yagoda. Either way, it was another convenient death for Stalin, and the hard line continued. In May 1935 a letter was sent from the Central Committee to all regional party organizations calling for the rooting out of 'enemies of the Party and the working class' who still held party membership cards. Within a few weeks over 280,000 people had their membership cards taken away and were in effect expelled from the party. New and stricter penalties were introduced for certain offences: anyone leaving the country without permission automatically incurred the death penalty and relatives of the culprit were to be arrested; all penalties, including death, were to apply to children aged twelve and over. This was to give Stalin an extra weapon in his struggle against the opposition: he could now threaten their children if they refused to co-operate. According to Conquest, by mid-1935 'Stalin had men of his personal selection, who were to prove themselves complete devotees of the Purge, in control of Leningrad [Andrei Zhdanov] and Moscow [Nikita Khrushchev], and in the Transcaucasus, where Beria ruled; in the Control Commission and the key departments of the Party Secretariat, and in the Prosecutor-Generalship.'[66] Discussion still took place in the Politburo, but it had almost reached the point where nobody dared to make a strong stand against Stalin. Apparently even Kaganovitch and Molotov were not strongly in favour of a continuation of the purges, but Stalin was determined to press on.

(c) The Great Terror, 1936–38

In the summer of 1936 the NKVD claimed to have discovered evidence that Trotsky had been in touch with a wide range of people – students, Komsomol members and Old Bolsheviks – all plotting to murder Stalin. Most of the evidence seems to have been fabricated, as Stalin must have been aware, but it was enough to justify the launching of a bloody campaign. Kamenev and Zinoviev were the first to come under attack; they were brought from prison and dealt with in the first of the great show-trials, along with a group of so-called Trotsky-ites. They were pressurized to confess that they had organized an Anti-Soviet Trotskyist–Zinovievite Centre. At first they refused, but after threats that Kamenev's son would be shot, and promises from Stalin that their lives would be spared if they complied, they both confessed. In August 1936 they were found guilty, sentenced to death and shot the following day. These were the first executions of Old Bolsheviks who had been right at the top of the party and the government; and it was the first breach of the unwritten rule that Bolsheviks should not kill their own colleagues. But Stalin had got away with it and there was no stopping him now. Kamenev's wife and elder son, and Zinoviev's son were arrested and eventually shot. Some of the evidence given during the trial implicated Bukharin, Rykov and Tomsky. Vyshinsky, the chief prosecutor, ordered an investigation into their activities. After a stormy meeting between Tomsky and Stalin, Tomsky shot himself. Apparently most of the general public accepted these events at face value. Throughout the trial the press carried lurid reports giving the impression that the entire country was in the grip of Trotskyite plotters. The newspapers now began to demand the death penalty for Bukharin and Rykov. Volkogonov claims that Stalin gradually created this atmosphere of suspicion; 'the constant massage of the public mind produced results, and the people became indignant when they heard about the baseness of those who had managed to stay out of sight for so long.'[67] Even if they found the confessions astonishing, there were very few people now who dared voice what they were thinking.

Only a few days after the executions Stalin ordered Yagoda, the head of the NKVD, to pick out five thousand political oppositionists – Trotskyites, Old Bolsheviks and Zinovievites – who were already in labour camps and have them shot. In September Yagoda himself was removed on the grounds that he had been too lax in rooting out enemies of the people; he was replaced by Nikolai Yezhov, one of Stalin's favourites. It was Sergo Ordzhonikidze, Stalin's old friend from Georgia, who made the final attempt to moderate the terror. As Commissar for heavy industry, Ordzhonikidze had consistently objected to the extension of the purges into the economic sphere. Accusations of sabotage, mass arrests of managers and workers, and the constant raising of targets were, in his view, not the way to improve results; however, Molotov and Kaganovitch could usually be relied on to support Stalin against him in the Politburo. Ordzhonikidze had opposed Stalin on other occasions as well. Robert Conquest's theory is that Stalin now decided to undermine Ordzhonikidze's position. Yuri Piatakov, Ordzhonikidze's deputy and close friend, was arrested and put on trial along with Karl Radek and a group of fifteen other prominent communists, charged with leading a totally imaginary Parallel Anti-Soviet Trotskyist Centre and planning terrorist acts, including the murder of Kirov. This was the second of the great show-trials and it ended in the usual way – no convincing evidence was produced, and yet the defendants all made full confessions; most of them were sentenced to death and shot (January 1937). On 19 February, after several uncontrollably angry conversations with Stalin, Ordzhonikidze shot himself. He had been heard to say to Stalin that he could not share the responsibility for what he had no power to prevent, and that he would not become a corrupt timeserver. The press reported that he had died of a heart-attack; it has also been suggested that he was shot on Stalin's orders, although there seems to be no conclusive evidence of this.[68]

Stalin's next target for radical purging was the army. In June 1937 Marshal M.N. Tukhachevsky, one of the top generals in the Red Army and Deputy Commissar for Defence, and several other generals were arrested and charged with treason. They were tortured to make them sign confessions, tried in secret, found guilty and shot immediately. This came as a surprise to the public since, unlike the two big public show-trials, the affair had received no previous publicity in the press. Marshal K.Y. Voroshilov, one of Stalin's closest associates, and Commissar for Defence, explained in a *Pravda* article that they had all confessed 'their treacherousness, wrecking and espionage.' Evidence had been produced that Tukhachevsky and his supporters had been planning a military *coup*. According to Isaac Deutscher, 'the main part of the *coup* was to be a palace revolt in the Kremlin, culminating in the assassination of Stalin. A decisive military operation outside the Kremlin was also prepared. Tukhachevsky was the moving spirit of the conspiracy.'[69] Many historians do not believe in the existence of any conspiracy; it was claimed that the incriminating documents had originated in Germany during the course of Tukhachevsky's plotting with the German secret service, but the evidence was never made public. One theory is that the documents were fabricated by the Gestapo in order to try and weaken the Soviet army. Another idea is that they were forged by anti-Soviet *émigré* Russians living in Paris.

If there was no plot, why did Stalin launch his attack on the army, which until then had seemed to be largely immune from the purges? Perhaps Stalin was genuinely afraid of a military *coup*, which he well knew was the only way he could be removed by 1937. By striking first at the generals most likely to oppose him, Stalin would encourage the rest to behave themselves. There was probably also a personal motive: Tukhachevsky was by far the most intelligent and forward-looking of the Red Army generals and had a distinguished military career in the Civil War. Unfortunately he did not get on with Voroshilov: Tukhachevsky was well-informed about the latest military thinking and about ways of avoiding the horrific stalemate caused by trench warfare in the First World War. He wanted the Soviet army to follow the German practice of building up mechanized units with motorized transports and tanks which would be capable of either launching a swift invasion of enemy territory or delivering a decisive counter-attack against an enemy invasion of the USSR. However, Voroshilov, who was Tukhachevsky's political superior, dismissed the new ideas; he did not believe that a rapid victory would be possible and insisted that the USSR should prepare for a long defensive war in which infantry and artillery, not motorized divisions, were the crucial element. Stalin knew about the disagreements; some sources claim that he had grown to dislike Tukhachevsky for his independence, arrogance and progressive ideas.[70]

The execution of Tukhachevsky and the seven other generals was only the beginning of a wholesale attack on the army. It is said that Stalin killed more generals and commanders than perished in the Second World War: 15 out of 16 top generals, 60 out of 67 corps commanders, and 136 out of 199 divisional commanders were executed. In addition, about 37,000 officers were arrested and mostly sent to labour camps. In many cases their wives and families suffered too; Tukhachevsky's wife and two brothers were arrested and shot, his three sisters were sent to labour camps, and his daughter was arrested later when she came of age and given a five-year sentence in a labour camp. At the same time there was a similar purge of the top ranks of the navy. In 1938 there was a second wave of arrests and executions in which many officers who had replaced those slaughtered in 1937 now perished themselves. Whatever else all this achieved, it did very little to help the country's security, especially as Voroshilov cancelled Tukhachevsky's plans for building up motorized and tank units (see section 7.2(a)).

The climax of the Great Terror was the third big political show-trial, known as 'the trial of the twenty-one'. It involved Nikolai Bukharin himself, together with Rykov, a group of eighteen other Rightists, and ironically, Yagoda. Yezhov had been preparing the case for most of 1937, and the trial eventually opened in March 1938. The main charges were that they belonged to an anti-Soviet bloc of Trotskyites, they had repeatedly organized acts of sabotage, and they were spying for foreign powers. Bukharin and several of the others were determined not to confess to crimes they had not committed; Bukharin stoutly denied that he had been involved in the murder of Kirov or that he had been working as a spy for foreign intelligence services. However, after Stalin ordered Yezhov to use 'all means', threats were made against Bukharin's wife and nine-month old son. Bukharin crumbled immediately and agreed to sign anything. Eighteen of the defendants, including Bukharin, Rykov and Yagoda, were sentenced to death and executed the next day; the other three were given prison sentences ranging from fifteen to twenty-five years.

These spectacular show-trials of leading political figures were only the tip of the iceberg; in the background, week by week throughout 1937 and 1938, in the hands of NKVD chief Yezhov, the Great Terror continued against literally hundreds of thousands of ordinary people. Although the campaign was directed from the centre, there was a great deal of scope for local initiative; it was the job of the local NKVD officials to decide who were the class enemies. Managers, engineers and administrators were prime targets, and ordinary workers were not safe: engine drivers were sometimes shot if their trains were late, or if they drove too fast or too slowly. Lorry drivers were arrested for driving too fast and therefore using too much petrol. Other groups at risk were priests, kulaks who had gone to work in industry, anybody who had a 'doubtful' background (for example, sons and daughters of priests and kulaks) and the 'former people' from the old privileged classes. Ordinary people were encouraged to denounce or 'unmask' class enemies; soon workers began to get revenge on unpopular managers and foremen by denouncing them for incompetence or harassment and then testifying against them in local trials. Another favourite group for denunciation were arrogant or unhelpful local officials. The government also began to introduce a sort of social cleansing by arresting what were described as 'degenerates' whose presence was said to be corrupting and disruptive; these included prostitutes, beggars, travelling tinkers and tailors, and gypsies. In one sweep in the summer of 1933 about 5000 gypsies were arrested in the Moscow region and sent to a labour colony at Tomsk in Siberia. Recently released documents from the Soviet archives suggest that the social cleansing of 'marginals' went further than Western historians had previously thought. Sheila Fitzpatrick has shown that in 1937–38 the regime began a policy of rounding up criminals, troublemakers, and people who had returned from exile illegally. Each region was given a quota; the total target figure for the USSR was 200,000 to be sent to labour camps and 70,000 to be executed.[71] Paul Hagenloh argues that in one sense this was separate from the party, industrial and military purges which were taking place at the time; it was the culmination of a decade-long police campaign against all kinds of people – the misfits of society 'who did not or could not fit into the emerging Stalinist system.' These were not tightly controlled political purges, but are best understood as 'chaotic, poorly planned, brutal police campaigns intended to eliminate the social by-products of the upheavals associated with collectivization and forced industrialization.'[72]

By the summer of 1938 Stalin had decided that the terror must end soon; perhaps he thought it was threatening to get out of control. He began to prepare the ground so that an official announcement could be made at the Eighteenth Party Congress in March 1939. Stalin planned to make Yezhov the scapegoat and in October 1938 he was replaced by Lavrenti Beria; about a year later Yezhov was arrested and shot. Beria soon purged most of Yezhov's staff at the NKVD and replaced them with his own appointments who were equally vicious. All the blame for the Great Terror was laid on the excesses of Yezhov and his subordinates. Stalin himself remarked later: 'that scoundrel Yezhov! He finished off some of our finest people. He was utterly rotten ... that's why we shot him.' In this way Stalin succeeded in diverting responsibility for the terror away from himself and kept at least a certain level of popularity. Addressing the Party Congress in March 1939 he admitted that mistakes had been made but claimed that they were not too serious. He told the delegates that the party membership had shrunk by over a quarter of a million since the previous Congress in 1934, but he made no mention of what had become of those who were no longer members. 'But there is nothing bad in that,' he said. 'Our Party is now somewhat smaller in membership, but on the other hand it is better in quality. This is a great achievement.'[73] There was still one major piece of unfinished business: Trotsky was still at large, though he was living in exile in a suburb of Mexico City. He had continued to infuriate Stalin by publishing a constant stream of articles and letters in the Western press criticizing Stalin's policies with his usual biting wit and sarcasm. In a 1938 article Trotsky wrote: 'Trotsky has only to blink an eye and it is enough for the veterans of the revolution to become agents for Hitler . . . railwaymen destroy military transports in the Far East, while highly respected doctors poison their patients in the Kremlin. This is the amazing picture drawn by Vyshinsky, but here a difficulty arises. In a totalitarian regime it is the apparatus which implements the dictatorship. But if my hirelings are operating all the key posts in the apparatus, how is it that Stalin is in the Kremlin and I'm in exile?' Stalin had had enough of this sort of thing, and in April 1940 he told Beria to get on with the job of disposing of Trotsky. In August 1940 a young man who was a friend of one of Trotsky's secretaries and who was trusted by the family, entered Trotsky's study. He was, in fact, employed by the NKVD and had been chosen as the assassin. He took out an ice-axe and struck Trotsky on the head with all his strength; Trotsky died 24 hours later. The delighted Stalin promoted Beria to the position of General Commissar of State Security.

What was the reaction of ordinary people to the purges? It is important to realize that on the whole people were not aware at the time of the vast scale of the purges. Many of those who did not themselves suffer believed that the victims were guilty and deserved to be punished. Often the reaction of workers was concern lest their corrupt managers got off too lightly. Most people had experienced incompetent and deliberately unco-operative local officials and had no sympathy for them when they were arrested. Peasants, especially those who had suffered personal hardship during collectivization, were pleased for a different reason: they were delighted that there were so many enemies of Soviet power around. But many ordinary members of the general public simply did not believe that so many people could be guilty of deliberate 'wrecking' and espionage. The inimitable Russian sense of humour survived unscathed and a wide variety of grim jokes circulated. In one of the stories Stalin lost his pipe. He telephoned the NKVD and ordered them to find it immediately. Two hours later he found the pipe himself – it had fallen into one of his boots next to the sofa in his apartment. He telephoned the NKVD again and asked what progress had been made. 'We have arrested ten men already,' he was told, 'and the investigation is continuing.' 'As it happens,' said Stalin, 'I have found my pipe, so free them instantly.' 'But Comrade Stalin,' came the reply, 'seven of them have already confessed!' Another story which came in several variants concerned a group of rabbits who turned up at the frontier with Poland in the hope of being admitted. When asked why they wanted to leave the USSR they replied: 'The NKVD has given orders to arrest every camel in the Soviet Union.' 'But you are not camels.' 'Yes, *we* know that,' said the rabbits, 'but we can't prove it.'

(d) The aftermath of the Purges and the Great Terror

The main victim was Lenin's old Bolshevik/Communist party, which more or less ceased to exist. Although the political forms remained much the same, the party was now completely different even from that of 1934; the power of the old Bolshevik elite had been eliminated. By the time the Party Congress met in March 1939, nearly 80 per cent of the Central Committee (98 out of 139) elected at the 1934 Congress had been arrested and shot. Sixty per cent of those who had been party members in 1934 had been expelled from the party. Over 80 per cent of the party elite in 1934 had joined the party before 1921; in 1939 that percentage had fallen to only 19. At the end of 1940 the only survivor among the 14 members of Lenin's first government was Stalin; only four of them died a natural death, five were executed during the purges, three died in labour camps and Trotsky was murdered. The army and the intelligentsia had also suffered and so had tens of thousands of ordinary, innocent people. Non-Russian groups, especially those like Poles, Koreans and Kurds, who had compatriots living outside the USSR, were removed from their homelands and deported to Kazakhstan where they would be less likely to cause trouble in the event of war. Historians are still arguing about how many people fell victim to the purges. Robert Conquest gave relatively high figures: just for the years 1937–38 he estimated about seven million arrests, about one million executed, two million who died in the camps, about eight million in camps at the end of 1938 (this was assuming five million in camps at the end of 1936), and about one million in prison. He also estimated that of those in the camps, not more than ten per cent survived. Other writers argued that these estimates were too high; Jerry Hough, for example, claimed that executions and prison deaths were, at most, a few hundred thousand or even a few tens of thousands in 1937–38, and that ordinary everyday life was not affected. In the early 1990s official KGB figures were released which show that in the two years 1937–38 just under 700,000 people were executed and that at the end of the 1930s there were about 3.6 million in labour camps and prison. Ronald Suny points out that if you add the four to five million people who perished in the famine of 1932–33 to the total figures of those executed and exiled during the 1930s, 'the total number of lives destroyed in the 1930s runs from ten to eleven million.' A similar conclusion was reached by S.G. Wheatcroft and R.W. Davies who calculated that 'the total number of excess deaths in 1927–38 may have amounted to some 10 million persons, 8.5 million in 1927–36, and about 1–1.5 million in 1937–38.'[74]

There can be no doubt that the purges left the USSR in a seriously weakened condition. Economically, militarily and intellectually, the country was worse off than it had been in 1928. In the words of Robert Service: 'The blood-purge of the armed forces disrupted the USSR's defences in a period of intense international tension. The arrest of the economic administrators in the people's commissariats impeded industrial output. The destruction of cadres in party, trade unions and local government undermined administrative co-ordination ... Stalin had started the carnage of 1937–38 because of real hostility to his policies, real threats to his authority, a real underlying menace to the compound of Soviet order. Yet his reaction was hysterically out of proportion to the menace he faced.'[75]

Nevertheless, from Stalin's point of view, the internal menace was now at an end: the central government, local government, government in the republics, the army and navy, and the nation's economic structures had all been violently subdued; power was concentrated in the hands of Stalin who ruled unchallenged, with the help of his supporting clique (Molotov, Kaganovich, Mikoyan, Zhdanov, Voroshilov, Bulganin, Beria, Malenkov and Khrushchev) until his death in 1953.

(e) The Constitution of 1936

Ironically, in November 1936, in the midst of the campaign urging Communists to unmask hidden enemies, the mass arrests, the trials and the purges, a new constitution was introduced. It was known as the Stalin Constitution, although it had mostly been drafted by Bukharin and Radek, and the regime claimed that it was the most democratic constitution in the world. It certainly looked democratic on paper; it stated that the USSR was a federation of eleven Soviet Socialist Republics: Russia, Ukraine, Belorussia, Georgia, Armenia, Azerbaijan, Kazakhstan, Kirgizia, Uzbekistan, Turkmenistan and Tadzikhistan, plus a number of autonomous areas and regions. The union (or federal) government in Moscow controlled defence, foreign policy and budgetary matters, but the republics controlled some of their own internal affairs (see section 6.6(i)). Any republic could leave the union if it so desired. The main law-making body was the Supreme Soviet of the USSR, which had two houses: the Soviet of the Union consisted of members elected by electoral constituencies in which one member represented 300,000 people; the Soviet of Nationalities consisted of 25 members from each union republic plus some extras from the autonomous republics and regions. The franchise (the right to vote) was to be universal, which meant that 'former people' such as ex-nobles, kulaks, priests and White Army officers who had been deprived of the vote were now enfranchised again. There were to be universal civil rights such as freedom of thought, the press, religion, organization and public assembly, and the right to work. In fact 'work in the USSR' said the Constitution, 'is a duty and a matter of honour for every able-bodied citizen, in accordance with the principle: "He who does not work shall not eat".' A new social and economic order had been built, according to Stalin, in which there were only three classes – the working class, the peasantry and the working intelligentsia, by which he meant anybody in a managerial, educational or administrative job. Since the capitalist system had been eliminated and the means of production were no longer privately owned, any exploitation of workers by capitalists had ceased to exist.

In practice, however, very little of the so-called democracy seemed to come through. The elections, which were to be held every four years, were not competitive – there was only one candidate to vote for in each constituency, and that was the Communist Party candidate. Stalin justified this on the grounds that there was no need for a multi-party system in a state where there were no conflicting classes. The Communist Party represented everybody's best interests. The aim of the candidates at elections was to get as near as possible to 100 per cent of the votes, thereby showing that the government's policies were widely popular. The Supreme Soviet only met twice a year for a few days each time, when the government presented its policies for approval; the Supreme Soviet did not actually make the laws – it simply rubber-stamped whatever the government told it. Its members then reported back to their districts about what was happening at the centre. The other function of the Supreme Soviet was to elect two smaller bodies: the Presidium, whose chairman acted as President of the USSR, a figurehead position which carried no real power; and the Council of People's Commissars, which had more power. The Commissars were heads of departments and formed a sort of cabinet; in a sense, however, they were more bureaucrats than politicians. Although it was not specifically stated in the Constitution, the real power remained with the Politburo, the leading body of the Communist Party. According to Article 126, 'the most active and most politically conscious citizens…unite in the Communist Party of the Soviet Union, which is the vanguard of the working people in their struggle to strengthen and develop the socialist system and is the leading core of all the public and state organizations of the working people.' In fact no party congress was called between 1939 and 1952; all important decisions were taken in the Politburo, and Stalin, as its general secretary, seemed to act very much as a dictator. T.H. Rigby compares him to Al Capone – he was good at 'keeping the boys in line', and this meant keeping them intimidated.[76] Amazingly, even Molotov's wife was arrested on Stalin's orders in 1939 and kept in prison for a time. Not surprisingly, very few people in the USSR took the 1936 Constitution seriously.

(f) Was the Stalinist regime totalitarian?

There has been great and sometimes acrimonious controversy among historians about the exact nature of Stalin's regime and its relationship with society. The traditional critical Western liberal–democratic view held by historians such as Adam Ulam, Robert Conquest and Leonard Schapiro, was that Stalin's regime was totalitarian, in many ways like Hitler's Nazi regime in Germany. A 'perfect' totalitarian regime is one in which there is dictatorial rule in a one-party state which totally controls all activities – economic, intellectual, political and cultural; all activities are directed towards achieving the state's goals, which are decided by the dictator. Every individual is considered to be the property of the state, and the interests of the individual are subordinate to the interests and requirements of the state. Obviously the state will not be able to control absolutely all human activities – it will have difficulty, for example, with family matters, emotional and sexual relationships, and private thoughts and opinions on things like politics, culture and religion. But a genuine totalitarian regime will strive to extend its control to the limits by attempting to indoctrinate everybody with the party ideology and to mobilize society in its support. Inherent in this kind of system is the use of both mental and physical terror and violence to crush opposition and keep the regime in power. There is ample evidence of all these characteristics at work in Stalin's system: the dominating role of Stalin himself in policy and decision making – especially collectivization, dekulakization, the suppression of information about the famine in 1932–33, the Purges and the Great Terror; the personality cult which portrayed Stalin as 'The Father of the Peoples', 'The Great Helmsman', 'The Greatest Genius in History', 'Shining Sun of Humanity' and other equally absurd titles; the awesome power of the state in the economic sphere;

the gradual coalescing between the party and the state, and the ever-growing party bureaucracy; the control of the press, the arts and religion; the constant propaganda and attempts at indoctrination at all levels of society; and above all the executions, the overflowing prisons and the labour camps with their atrocious conditions and high death rates.

On the other hand, during the 1970s, 'revisionist' Western historians, among whom Sheila Fitzpatrick was one of the leaders, began to look at the Stalin period from a social viewpoint. They criticized the 'totalitarian' historians on the grounds that they ignored social history and presented society as the passive victim of state policies, whereas in fact, during the late 1920s and 1930s the regime was supported by many people who benefited from the system. These included officials in the party–state bureaucracy, the army and the trade unions, members of the Komsomol, administrators, experts and key industrial workers – in other words, the new elite. The social historians suggested that to some extent certain groups in society were able to show 'initiatives from below' and even negotiate and bargain with the regime, so that they were able to influence policy. Yet another twist occurred during the 1980s when a group of historians, notably the American J. Arch Getty, criticized the totalitarian historians for exaggerating the personal dictatorship and role of Stalin and the extent to which the one-party state operated as an efficient centralized system of control. Getty claims that Stalin was not much more than a power-broker trying to manoeuvre his colleagues, who stumbled into policies almost by accident; the party, far from being a highly organized and finely honed instrument, was inefficient, chaotic and unco-operative. By the mid-1930s Stalin had actually lost control of the party.[77] Most controversially, this group of historians, which also includes Roberta Manning and G.T. Ritterspoorn, plays down the role of Stalin in the Great Terror, seeing it as the outcome of a series of circumstances which 'boiled over' almost unintentionally.

The basic difference between the various groups is that the totalitarianists emphasize the total ruthlessness of the Stalinist regime in its determination to impose its policies on society regardless of all opposition, while the rest, including the so-called social historians or 'structuralists', believe that the regime was moulded by institutional, economic and social pressures from below, which caused its policies to be modified if they became too unpopular. The totalitarian writers criticized the others, especially Arch Getty and those who took a similar line, because they felt that they were attempting to whitewash Stalin; they accused them of trying to gloss over the downright criminal and evil aspects of his policies. On the other hand the structuralists accused the totalitarians of refusing to give fair and objective consideration to the Communist System and the processes which formed it, simply because their own political Cold War prejudices would not allow them to concede that anything good could come out of a socialist system.

Now that the dust has settled somewhat and historians have had time to digest the new information emerging from the archives, it is possible to arrive at a more balanced conclusion. It seems clear that there are elements of truth in both these interpretations. It is impossible to ignore the central role of Stalin himself: overwhelmingly the evidence suggests that increasingly after 1928, it was Stalin's policy preferences that were carried out, until by 1936 he had acquired the powers of a dictator. As E.A. Rees puts it: 'the depiction of Stalin as a pragmatist, an organizational man, who responded to evolving political circumstances and pressures with no conceived plan, initiating policies which had unforeseen consequences, reflects an under-estimation of his central role.'[78] On the other hand the regime could not completely ignore public opinion – even Stalin needed and wanted to feel popular; he needed and secured the support of the new elite groups, the younger people who had been promoted. And it was these groups, mainly from worker and peasant backgrounds, who were participants in, rather than victims of, Stalinism. There is evidence too that although the regime had totalitarian aims, in practice it was far from successful. Streams of orders issued forth from the top, which would have been obeyed without question in a genuinely totalitarian state. But this was not the case in the USSR: whether through fear, or apathy, or hostility, as both Donald Filtzer and Sheila Fitzpatrick have shown, peasants and workers found ways of resisting and evading government orders.[79] The more the government tried to tighten controls, the more counterproductive its efforts became; there was conflict between the centre and the regional leaderships; attempts to control the media and suppress information about, for example, the excesses of dekulakization and the horrors of the famine, must have struck a jarring note with millions of people who knew the truth from their own experiences. The Stalinist system was over-centralized, disorganized, inefficient, corrupt, sluggish and unresponsive.

Finally it has to be said that there is a danger in this academic debate, in the preoccupation with the extent to which pressures from society shaped the regime, of forgetting that looming over the entire system were the Purges and the Terror. Concentrating on social history can give the impression that everyday life under Stalin was a normal sort of existence. But this was not the case. Martin Malia argues in a recent review article that the revisionists make too much of the so-called 'negotiation' between state power and the people. For the vast majority of people, the concept of negotiating with, or attempting to influence the regime simply did not arise. Nobody was safe, not even members of the elite; in fact in the earlier rounds of the purges the party elite suffered proportionately more than anybody else. The term 'negotiation,' Malia points out, 'carries connotations of equality and normality incongruous in a situation of institutionalized terror.'[80] Even Sheila Fitzpatrick herself acknowledges the all-pervasive nature of Stalinist violence: 'Terror – meaning state violence against groups and randomly chosen citizens – was so frequently used that it must be regarded as a systemic characteristic of Stalinism in the 1930s ... Anybody could be exposed as "an enemy of the people"; the enemies, like witches in earlier ages, bore no reliable external marks.'[81] Extremely inefficient the regime may well have been, but it still succeeded in being extremely murderous.

6.6   Everyday life and culture under Stalin

As we saw at the end of the previous section, everyday life in the USSR during the 1930s was dominated by the state, which controlled, or attempted to control, as much of human activity as possible. Ordinary people could not avoid contact with the state – being educated, finding a job, getting promotion, getting married and bringing up children, finding somewhere to live, shopping, travelling, reading literature, going to the theatre and concerts, enjoying the visual arts, practising your religion, reading the news, listening to the radio – in all these activities people ran up against the state. The communists had a mission – to eradicate 'backwardness'; most things belonging to pre-revolution Russia were viewed as backward – like small-scale peasant farming, the illiteracy of the peasants and many of the poorer working class, private trade, petty bourgeois culture, and religion, which was dismissed as superstition. The Soviet state must become modernized and socialist, and the new Soviet citizen must be educated and 'cultured'. The state considered that it was the duty of artists, musicians and writers to play their part in the attack on bourgeois values by producing works of 'socialist realism' which glorified the Soviet system. They were to be 'engineers of the soul,' as Stalin put it, helping to indoctrinate the population with socialist values. This placed all artists under tremendous pressure, since it was not always clear exactly what was 'socialist' and acceptable to Stalin.

(a) A hard life

These were impressive ideals, but by all accounts the most striking thing about everyday life in the 1930s was that everything, including food, seemed to be in short supply. This was partly because of the concentration on heavy industry at the expense of consumer goods, and because of the famine of 1932–33, followed by bad harvests later in the decade. People no longer talked about 'buying' something, but about 'getting hold of' it. If they saw a queue, they would join it first and then ask what was on offer. In 1933, the worst year, the average married worker in Moscow consumed less than half the amount of bread and flour that his counterpart had consumed around 1900. From all over the country there were reports of people having to queue from the early hours of the morning to get hold of a loaf. Meat, vegetables and fruit were also hard to come by, and so were clothing and shoes, and household goods such as pans, kettles and cutlery. Even when they were available, the quality of manufactured goods was usually poor. In 1937 average real wages were about three-fifths of what they had been in 1928.

Other hardships were caused by the rapid growth of the urban population which brought serious housing shortages and placed untold strain on town amenities. Between 1926 and 1939 the population of Moscow grew from 2 million to 3.6 million, while Sverdlovsk (formerly Yekaterinburg), an industrial city in the Urals, mushroomed from under 150,000 to over half a million. Magnitogorsk, the new metallurgical centre in the Urals, which did not exist in 1926, had grown to over 100,000 in 1939. In total, the urban population increased by 31 million between 1926 and 1939. The local Soviet controlled all the housing in a town and decided how much space a person was entitled to; in Moscow in 1930 this was fixed at 5.5 square metres per head, although in 1940 it dropped to about 4 square metres. The Soviet had the power to evict residents and move new residents into houses already occupied; it was common for middle-class families living in large houses to be told that they were taking up too much space and to find their home suddenly transformed into a 'communal apartment' as two or three other families were moved in. Kitchens, bathrooms and toilets were shared between families, and most large houses had people living in corridors and under staircases. Even less fortunate were the workers who lived in barracks. At Magnitogorsk in 1938 half the housing consisted of barracks, which was the usual accommodation for unmarried workers and students. One barracks in Moscow in 1932 housed 550 men and women, and the space worked out at 2 square metres per tenant. City conditions were generally poor; most of them lacked effective sewage systems, running water, electric lights and street lights. Zara Witkin, an American engineer working in the USSR in the early 1930s, wrote: 'the physical aspect of the cities is dreadful. Stench, filth, dilapidation batter the senses at every turn.'

Getting to work in most cities could be a nightmare. In Leningrad the trams were dilapidated and always hopelessly overcrowded, and in most other cities and large towns public transport was limited. For example, Pskov, a city of 60,000 people half-way between Riga and Leningrad, had no paved roads in 1939, no trams and only two buses. The exception to this grim situation was Moscow itself where the government made a real effort to make the capital city something to be proud of. There was an efficient system of trams and buses, and by 1940 three-quarters of the inhabitants had sewage systems and running water. The showpiece was the Moscow underground, opened in the mid-1930s, which boasted deep escalators and spacious stations complete with chandeliers and murals.

One of the most irritating aspects of everyday life for the majority of people was that there were certain privileged groups who seemed to escape the worst of the hardships. These included members of the party, important government and trade union officials, members of the intelligentsia – writers, composers, artists and so on who fulfilled their duty and produced acceptable works of social realism, engineers and other technical experts, and shockworkers and Stakhanovites. Privileges took the form of extra food parcels, deliveries of bread to their homes, separate works canteens, special stores where prices were usually lower, preferential treatment in the provision of accommodation and dachas (country houses), passes for long stays in rest homes and summer camps for their children. The existence of such a privileged class resulted in a 'them and us' attitude – ordinary people felt aggrieved that they were still the underdogs. The propaganda constantly told them that power in the USSR belonged to the people – workers and peasants. But in reality they felt excluded from power and resentful that they were still being exploited; in a so-called socialist state, exploitation of one class by another was no longer meant to exist. This is no doubt one reason why the purges against members of the elite were popular in many quarters.[82]

How did people cope with these difficulties? Since the state shops were inadequately stocked with goods, there was a flourishing illegal 'second economy' which in a way was a continuation of NEP private trading. This ranged from large-scale operators who did deals with corrupt store and factory managers, to individuals who bought a few metres of cloth, a few items of clothing or some sausage, and sold them later for a small profit. But whatever the scale of the operation, this was a criminal offence, and the authorities labelled the culprits as 'speculators' – people who bought goods and sold them at a higher price. The kolkhoz markets were a good place to take advantage of the second economy – here it was legal for people to sell their own produce, but in fact all sorts of things were bought and sold, and it was difficult for the authorities to enforce the rules. Another coping strategy was the widespread use of the system known in Russian as *blat* – which means something like 'pull' or 'influence' – a system of informal networks of people who could do each other favours in the way of providing goods and services. Somebody who worked in a factory or a warehouse might be able to get hold of clothes, shoes, household goods or even flour and sugar; somebody else might be able to arrange medical certificates, university entrance, places in convalescent homes, somewhere to live; there were people who could get hold of railway tickets, radio sets, firewood and fuel; and there were those who could do engineering or building work. Although people were not usually willing to talk openly about *blat* since it was frowned on by the authorities, it was not an offence, and there is no doubt that it was widely practised.[83]

(b) Signs of improvement?

There is some evidence that life began to improve during the second half of the 1930s. In a speech in November 1935 Stalin told his audience of Stakhanovites: 'Life has become better, life has become more joyous;' this claim was taken up as a motto and was even set to music. His statement was not entirely wishful thinking: food supplies improved and all rationing was abolished in 1936. The provision of cheap meals in factory canteens and free work clothes was a great boon. Education and health care were free and the network of schools and medical centres was spreading all the time during the 1930s. Soviet citizens who left Russia during the Second World War usually mentioned this welfare-state provision as one of the best aspects of life in the USSR. The government worked hard at the concept of state paternalism – the idea that the population were like children who must be looked after, protected and guided by the state which acted as a sort of guardian. For example, the state provided facilities for leisure: by the end of the 1930s there were close on 30,000 cinemas, there were sports facilities for players and spectators – football, athletics, gymnastics and ice-hockey, and there were public gardens and parks of culture – the largest and most famous was Gorky Park in Moscow, named after Maxim. Also provided were 'houses of culture' and libraries, and most towns of any size had a theatre.

Another important aspect of the state's role was to encourage what the Russians called *kul'turnost'* – culturedness. This involved taking care with one's appearance, dress and personal hygiene – washing with soap, cleaning one's teeth and not spitting on the floor. Ordzhonikidze himself, the Commissar for Industry, stressed the need for men to look tidy and shave regularly. Some industrial enterprises issued orders that all engineers and managers must make sure that they were clean-shaven and had their hair properly cut. The workers' barracks were a special target for improvement; these were viewed, in the words of Vadim Volkov, as 'repositories of deviance, violence, filth, offensive smells, and coarse speech . . . "unculturedness" emanated from there.' Gradually conditions were improved by the use of partitions to divide the space up so that each person had his own space. In March 1936 the Komsomol press launched a campaign condemning 'dirty talk' which, it was argued, was unacceptable from a 'cultured' person, and encouraging good table manners and correct behaviour in public.[84] Other signs of culture were sleeping on sheets, eating with a knife and fork, and not beating your wife and children. Household items encouraged as signs of culture were curtains, lampshades and tablecloths. According to Stephen Kotkin, as a person ascended to a higher level of culture, he learned to 'speak Bolshevik'. In other words, he learned all the rituals of being a genuine Soviet person and how to conduct himself in the workplace. Not only did he not spit on the floor, he also knew how to make a speech and propose a motion at a meeting, he understood the basic tenets of Marxism and he was well-informed about the international situation.[85]

The government extended culturedness to shopping: in the last few months of 1934 no fewer than 13,500 new bread shops opened across the country; the assistants wore white smocks and caps and had lessons in how to be polite to the customers. Strict new sanitary regulations were brought in and loaves had to be wrapped. The campaign for cultured trade was aimed at every shop in the country, from the largest Moscow department store to the smallest bread shop. Delegations visited the USA, Britain and Germany to find out how the large stores operated. They were most impressed with those in the USA, especially Macy's in New York; trying to copy what they had seen in America, the Russians set up 'model' stores in most big cities, which were meant to serve as a pattern for others to follow. Unfortunately, goods in these stores tended to be extremely expensive, so that only the privileged class could afford them. Life may well have been better for the few, but for most ordinary Soviet citizens, the lavish commodity exhibitions in the model department stores remained something to be gaped at in wonder.

(c) The state, women and the family

The 1930s were a difficult time for many families because of the 'disappearance' of so many men during collectivization, the famine and the purges. There was a high desertion and divorce rate, and millions of women were left as the sole breadwinner in the family. During the rapid industrialization of the 1930s more than 10 million women became wage-earners for the first time, and the percentage of women at work rose from 24 per cent to 39 per cent of the total paid workforce. By 1940 about two-thirds of the workforce in light industry were women, and many were even engaged in heavier jobs such as construction, lumbering and machine-building which were traditionally thought of as men's work. The government faced the dilemma that it needed women to provide much of the workforce for the industrialization drive, while at the same time it wanted to encourage and strengthen the family unit. One way of coping was to build more daycare centres and nurseries for children – the number of places doubled in the two years 1929–30. In the mid-1930s new laws were passed encouraging women to have as many children as possible; abortion was made illegal except in cases where the mother's life was in danger; maternity leave of up to 16 weeks was allowed and there were to be various subsidies and other benefits for pregnant women. Even so this placed a heavy burden on working-class and peasant women, who were expected to produce children, take jobs, increase output and look after the household and family.

Things were different for the more privileged women – wives of the elite and educated women, either married or single, who had professional jobs. They were seen by the state as part of its campaign to 'civilize' the masses. The movement began in May 1936 with an All-Union Meeting of Wives of Industrialists and Engineering Personnel held in the Kremlin and attended by Stalin. It was followed by similar meetings of wives of members of other branches of industry, of the Red Army and of the bureaucracy. The Wives' Movement, as it became known, was expected to do everything in its power to raise the culturedness of the people its members came into contact with, particularly those in their husbands' workplaces. Wives of managers were expected to brighten up workers' barracks and dormitories with curtains, lampshades and carpets, organize study groups and plant trees and flowers. Some went further and started child-minding groups, literacy groups and libraries for their workers. But above all, their main duty was to make a comfortable and well-organized home life for their husbands and families. Towards the end of the 1930s, as war began to seem more likely, the Wive's Movement began to emphasize the need for women to learn to drive lorries, shoot and even to fly planes, so that they would be ready to take men's places if they had to go off to war.[86]

(d) Education

One of the greatest achievements of the Stalinist regime was the expansion of free, mass education. In 1917 under half the population could be described as literate. In January 1930 the government announced that by the end of the summer, all children aged eight to eleven must be enrolled in schools. Between 1929 and 1931 the number of pupils increased from 14 million to around 20 million, and it was in rural areas, where education had been, to say the least, patchy, that most of the increase took place. By 1940 there were 199,000 schools, and even the most remote areas of the USSR were well provided. Lots of new training colleges were set up specifically to train the new generation of teachers and lecturers. According to the census of 1939, of people aged between 9 and 49, 94 per cent in the towns and 86 per cent in rural areas were literate; by 1959 these percentages had increased to 99 and 98 respectively. Of course the regime had an ulterior motive – education was the way in which it could turn the younger generation into good, orthodox Soviet citizens, with modern, cultured attitudes and values; religion and other bourgeois practices were presented as superstitious and back-ward. Ironically, the educational experts decided that a return to traditional teaching methods would be better than the experimental, more relaxed techniques tried in the 1920s. These had included the abolition of examinations and punish-ments, and emphasis on project-work. All this began to be reversed from about 1931. Teachers were given more authority and were to impose strict discipline, examinations and the old marking-systems were brought back and more teaching time was to be spent on mathematics and science.

At the same time some elitist steps were taken: in 1932 the rule that universities should take two-thirds of their entry from the working class and peasants was dropped. This meant that it was easier for children of the elite class to gain admission. In 1940 Stalin approved the introduction of fees for higher education and for the final three years of secondary education. These final years were voluntary anyway (the first seven years of education were still compulsory and free), but the fees meant that it was mainly the children of better-off elite families who could take advantage of the final three years.

(e) Religion

After Lenin's attack on the Russian Orthodox Church in 1922–23 (see section 5.9(e)), the regime became more tolerant towards religious groups. Many priests were sympathetic towards communist ideals which, after all, do have some similarities to Christian attitudes to the poor and oppressed. Some writers have even referred to Jesus Christ as the first communist on account of his, for the time, revolutionary teachings. Some priests formed a breakaway group called the Living Church, deposed the Patriarch Tikhon (the head of the Orthodox Church) and took over the leadership themselves. Any bishops and priests who continued to oppose the communists were sacked. Eventually Tikhon himself publicly renounced his opposition to the regime and became leader again. When he died in 1925 it was revealed in his will that he advised all Christians to support the government. There seemed a good chance of complete reconciliation between church and state, and with careful handling, the church could have been a useful tool in the state's campaign to bring the peasants under control. However, many militant young communists continued to believe that the church was a 'harmful superstition' which must be eliminated. In 1925 they formed the League of the Militant Godless and launched an anti-religious propaganda campaign with lectures, pamphlets and journals, mainly directed at the peasants.

With Stalin in the ascendant, tolerance was not destined to last long. Many priests opposed collectivization and so relations between church and state deteriorated again. Stalin never publicly announced the start of an anti-religion campaign, but secret instructions were sent to local party organizations encouraging physical attacks on churches and priests. Membership of the Godless League rose to a peak of five million, and they responded with enthusiasm. Hundreds of churches and cemeteries were vandalized and literally thousands of priests were killed. The number of working priests fell from about 60,000 in 1925 to under 6000 by 1941. Not all of them were murdered – many country priests fled to the towns and tried to avoid the secret police and make a living incognito. The slaughter was not confined to Christians: hundreds of Muslim and Jewish leaders – mullahs and rabbis – also fell victim. The campaign was relentless: by 1941 only one in 40 church buildings was still functioning as a church. In the new cities like Magnitogorsk no churches were allowed to be built, and in Moscow the Cathedral of Christ the Saviour was blown up to make way for the Palace of Soviets (which was never built). The campaign against religion caused outrage, especially in rural areas where priests, mullahs and rabbis were popular and respected members of the local communities. Most peasants looked on them almost as part of the family; a village community which had lost its church, mosque or synagogue and its spiritual leader felt bereft and lacking a sense of direction. And what was the point of it all? Apparently the League of the Militant Godless believed that communities in such a state of shock would submit to collectivization more readily; the disappearance of so many priests removed the most likely focuses of opposition to collectivization and other unpopular government policies.

During the Second World War the regime and the church were to some extent reconciled. In 1942, with the war going badly for the Russians, and both Leningrad and Moscow under threat from the Germans, Stalin decided that the church had a role to play after all, as a force for patriotism. An understanding was reached with Christians, Muslims and Jews that past differences would be forgotten in their joint struggle against the invader. Churches, mosques and synagogues were allowed to open again, and priests, mullahs and rabbis were released from jail. By most accounts it seems that the various religious groups played a vital role in maintaining morale among the general public.

(f) Literature and the theatre

It was during the years 1928 to 1931, the period known as the Cultural Revolution, that the regime began to systematically mobilize writers, artists and musicians to wage a cultural war against 'bourgeois intellectuals'.[87] There were two rival groups of writers; the convinced communists were members of the All-Russian Association of Proletarian Writers (RAPP) and they were committed to 'socialist realism' and what they called 'working-class values'. Some of the young hotheads among them got carried away and began to suggest that the time was approaching for the state to wither away. Bukharin described them as suffering from 'revolutionary avant-gardism'. Stalin was happy to give RAPP free rein for the time being because it enabled him to claim that his 'revolution from above' was a response to the surge of militancy from below. The other group of writers were the non-communists who wanted to keep politics out of literature and were labelled dismissively by the communists as 'fellow-travellers'. They were members of the All-Russian Union of Writers (AUW), and they included most of the leading writers who had made their names before the revolution. RAPP did not approve of the attitude of the AUW and in 1929 began a campaign against it, accusing some of its members of publishing anti-Soviet works abroad. They were found guilty and the government dissolved the AUW, replacing it with a new organization called the All-Russian Union of Soviet Writers (AUSW). About half the former AUW members were refused admission to the new union; this was a serious blow for them, since only union members were allowed to publish. Their choice was simple – they either had to recant and beg to be readmitted, or cease having their works published in the USSR.

RAPP was now very much the dominant literary organization, but from Stalin's point of view it had one unfortunate fault: it believed in portraying society as it really was, whereas Stalin wanted it portraying as he would like it be. But RAPP members felt that if there were failings in the system, these must be exposed; if this meant criticizing the party, then so be it. However, in 1930 Stalin announced that nothing should be published which showed the party in a poor light or which went against the party line. Many RAPP members were slow to respond to this clear warning; therefore in April 1932 the regime disbanded both RAPP and the new AUSW and replaced it by one organization – the Union of Soviet Writers; each branch of the arts was given the same treatment – one union for all members. Maxim Gorky (whose works Stalin admired) became chairman of the Writers' Union, and Andrei Zhdanov emerged as the politician most involved in the arts. In August 1934 he opened the First Congress of Soviet Writers. He repeated Stalin's earlier pronouncement that the guiding principle of Soviet literature must be 'socialist realism', whose main goal was 'the ideological remoulding and re-education of the toiling people in the spirit of socialism ...Our literature must not shun romanticism, but it must be a romanticism of a new type, revolutionary romanticism.'

Among the most popular new works were Nikolai Ostrovsky's novel *How the Steel was Tempered* which came out in 1934, and Mikhail Sholokhov's *Virgin Soil Upturned* which dealt with collectivization; the first part of this appeared in 1931, though the general opinion seemed to be that it was not up to the standard of his real masterpiece, *Quiet Flows the Don*, the first part of which had appeared in 1929. There were other works of lesser quality sometimes known as five-year plan novels, in which the heroes were ordinary people who bravely achieved their targets in spite of all kinds of obstacles. There was the bus driver who reduced petrol consumption by careful driving; the engine driver who repeatedly overcame all the efforts of wreckers and brought his train in on time; and the engineer who successfully completed a new dam despite bad weather, landslides and the evil machinations of foreign spies and saboteurs. These were not great literature, but arguably they served a purpose – they were easily understood by ordinary workers and peasants, they raised morale and they inspired people to greater efforts.

Writers who did not succeed in producing the right kind of 'socialist realism' ran the risk of arrest. Stalin himself sometimes read the novels in typescript and would add comments and suggested changes which the authors were expected to take note of. He insisted on extensive changes being made in later editions of Sholokhov's novel *Quiet Flows the Don* because he thought some passages implied criticism of the Red Army. In the later 1930s many writers, whose work was considered to be beyond redemption, were denounced as Trotskyites or wreckers and were arrested; some were kept in jail or labour camp for long periods and others were executed. Among the best-known victims were the poet Osip Mandelstam who had written a poem critical of Stalin in 1933 (Document J); he tried to make amends later by writing an ode in praise of Stalin, but he was eventually arrested and died in a labour camp. Evgenia Ginsburg spent 18 years in prison and labour camps for having allegedly organized a writers' terrorist group (Document E). Isaac Babel, a well-known writer of short stories and author of *Red Cavalry*, died in a labour camp, and the writer Boris Pilniak was arrested in 1937 and shot. Some of the best writers, like the poetess Anna Akhmatova and the novelist Boris Pasternak, felt unable to adjust to the demands of 'socialist realism', and either stopped work altogether or kept their new work locked away. Pasternak's great novel *Dr Zhivago* was published abroad after Stalin's death. Mikhail Bulgakov's wonderful novel *The Master and Margarita* lay unpublished for years until after Stalin's death. Soon after Khrushchev came to power in 1956 the authorities admitted that at least 600 writers had perished in prison and labour camps during Stalin's rule. Theatre people also came under attack: a number of actors, actresses and ballet dancers were sent to labour camps. Natalia Sats, founder of the Moscow Children's Theatre, was arrested and sent to a labour camp in 1937 and survived for seven years until she was eventually released. The most celebrated victim in the theatre was the great experimental director Vsevelod Meyerhold. He had gradually fallen out of favour because his productions were thought to be too avant-garde. In 1938 his theatre in Moscow was closed down on the grounds that it was 'alien to Soviet art.' In June 1939 he was summoned to appear before a meeting of producers chaired by the notorious prosecutor Vyshinsky in order to defend himself. Apparently he made a good show of self-criticism but could not resist a final swipe at the regime: 'the theatre of socialist realism has nothing in common with art ... Where once there were the best theatres in the world, now everything is gloomily well-regulated, stupefying and murderous in its lack of talent. Is that your aim? If it is, you have done something monstrous! In hunting down formalism, you have eliminated art.'[88] A few days later Meyerhold was arrested and tortured in prison. His wife, a famous actress, was found brutally stabbed to death in their flat, but the police carried out no investigation of the crime. This was taken by all writers and artists as a warning to wives of potential 'enemies of the people'. Meyerhold himself was shot in February 1940.

Ironically in view of all this obsession with 'socialist realism', after the first flush of the Cultural Revolution in the early 1930s, the regime decided to reinstate nineteenth century classical Russian literature into the body of acceptable reading. The works of the poet Pushkin, the novels of Leo Tolstoy, Nikolai Gogol and Ivan Turgenev and the plays of Anton Chekhov were back in fashion again, since the government had now decided that, after all, these writers were 'revolutionary democrats'. However, Fyodor Dostoevsky, author of the great novels *Crime and Punishment* and *The Brothers Karamazov*, was still frowned on as being too conservative.

(g) Art, architecture and music

After the experimentation in art in the 1920s, once 'socialist realism' took hold, painters and sculptors had to fall into line. Abstract art was rejected and paintings were expected either to portray workers straining every muscle to fulfil their targets and other 'events' in the economy, or to show scenes from the revolution or Civil War, and revolutionary leaders in portraits or other settings. They were to be photographic in style and finely detailed. There was a steady flow of paintings of Lenin and Stalin in various revolutionary and heroic poses – a striking one entitled *Stalin and Voroshilov in the Kremlin*, and innumerable others with titles like *The Steelworker* and *The Milkmaids*. The French novelist Andre Gide visited the USSR in 1937 and afterwards wrote: 'At Tiflis I saw an exhibition of modern art of which it would be charitable not to speak ... episodes of Stalin's life being used as the themes of these illustrations ... In the USSR, however fine a work may be, if it is not in line, it scandalizes. Beauty is considered a bourgeois value.

What is demanded of the artist is that he shall conform.'[89] Busts of Lenin and Stalin were about the only items that sculptors were permitted to produce. As for architecture, it too deteriorated into the uninspiring and dull, with grandiose neo-classical facades and featureless tower blocks being popular.

Music followed a similar pattern to literature; in the Cultural Revolution years (1928–31) the more aggressive, committed communist members of the Russian Association of Proletarian Musicians (RAPM) condemned what they described as the 'modernism' of contemporary Western music. This included not only the atonal 12-note music of the Austrians Schoenberg, Webern and Berg, but also jazz, music hall style 'light' music and even the fox-trot. However, in the mid-1930s the regime relaxed its attitude towards non-classical music, and jazz, dance and 'light' music were permitted; after all, Stalin had just told people 'life has become more joyful, comrades.' There were two outstanding classical composers who had gained international reputations by the 1930s – Sergei Prokofiev and Dmitri Shostakovich. Prokofiev had left Russia soon after the revolution but decided to return in 1933. He was particularly successful at producing music of a high quality which could be readily appreciated by ordinary people – his film score for *Lieutenant Kije* (1934), his ballet *Romeo and Juliet* (1936) and his musical story for children, *Peter and the Wolf*, were highly popular with audiences and the authorities. Shostakovich[90] was not quite so successful; his first opera, *The Nose*, based on a short story by Gogol and first performed in 1930, was condemned by RAPM and banned. His second opera, *Lady Macbeth of Mtsensk*, was well received by audiences and critics in 1934 and it ran for over 80 performances in Leningrad and over 90 at the Bolshoi Theatre in Moscow. Unfortunately in January 1936 Stalin himself decided to go to a performance at the Bolshoi and took Molotov along with him. They did not like what they heard and walked out before the end. Two days later a devastating article, thought to have been written by Stalin himself, appeared in *Pravda*; the opera was dismissed as 'a cacophony, primitive, crude and vulgar – the music shouts, quacks, explodes, pants and sighs, so as to convey the love scenes in the most naturalistic manner.' It was too much influenced by Western formalism and experimentation and negative to the nth degree, according to the writer of the article. Within a few days all Shostakovich's work had been banned, and he himself decided to withdraw his Fourth Symphony which was just about to go into rehearsal. *Lady Macbeth* was not performed again until 1962, long after Stalin's death, and Shostakovich had been so shaken by the whole episode that he never composed another opera. After the appearance of the *Pravda* article he expected to be arrested and kept a bag packed so that he would be ready when the dreaded knock at the door came in the early hours of the morning. However, for some reason, possibly because Alexei Tolstoy, one of Stalin's favourite authors, defended him to Stalin, Shostakovich was spared, although he remained in official disgrace for over a year.

The *Lady Macbeth* incident was enough to frighten Soviet composers into writing music which was melodic, approachable, stirring and inspiring, like the music of the great Russian composers of the nineteenth century – Tchaikovsky, Rimsky-Korsakov and Borodin. With his Fifth Symphony (1937) Shostakovich succeeded in producing a great piece of music which also fulfilled the requirements of the regime. He was gradually rehabilitated: he was allowed to teach at the Leningrad conservatoire, in 1940 he was awarded the Stalin prize for his Piano Quintet, and during the Second World War he became something of a hero, staying on in Leningrad during the German siege and working on his Seventh Symphony which was eventually performed in 1943 and became known as the Leningrad Symphony.

(h) The cinema

Like Lenin, Stalin considered that film was probably the most important form of communication; he loved films and had a private cinema in the Kremlin and in his dacha. As the Cultural Revolution got under way in 1928, the party conference demanded that film-makers should play their part and make films which were 'intelligible to the millions;' the avant-garde and experimental films of the 1920s were to be abandoned in favour of films which told a simple but powerful story. In 1930 Boris Shumyatsky was given the job of modernizing the film industry. He aimed to develop the mass production of films that were genuinely entertaining as well as being full of 'socialist realism', and he wanted to extend the network of cinemas to the most remote parts of the USSR. He was hampered by an unexpected development – the arrival of sound films, which were more expensive to make and which created language problems in a country where so many different languages were spoken. Another difficulty was the almost impossible demands of the regime which wanted film-makers to incorporate sometimes contradictory themes into their work – proletarian values, classless Soviet nationalism, the problems experienced by ordinary people in the drive towards a socialist state, the heroic exploits of the revolutionaries, and the glorious communist future as it would be. Film-makers were aware of what happened to writers and theatre directors whose work did not win the approval of the authorities, and many of them were reluctant to risk a similar fate. The output of new films declined rapidly in the early 1930s. Shumyatsky decided to go and see how the real experts did things, and in 1935 he took a small group of Russian film-makers to Hollywood to look for new ideas. He soon became convinced that the Russian film industry needed a Soviet equivalent of Hollywood, and he chose the Crimea as the site for his project because the agreeable climate would allow filming all year round. Unfortunately, the government refused to provide the necessary finance and the project never got off the ground. Stalin was not satisfied with Shumyatsky's progress, and in 1938 he was arrested and shot.

Nevertheless, in spite of all the obstacles, over 300 Soviet films came out between 1933 and 1940, some of which were of high quality. There was a huge increase in the number of cinemas in the same period – from about 7000 to nearly 30,000. Good examples of socialist realism in film were *Road to Life* (1931) about a group of homeless boys who are redeemed by a wise educator who wins their respect and turns them into excellent Soviet citizens; *Counterplan* (1932), probably the best of the films about industrialization, and boasting a score by Shostakovich; and, most famous of all, *Chapayev* (1934), a film by the brothers Sergei and Giorgii Vasiliev, a powerful and romantic story about a Civil War hero, which was extremely popular with audiences. Most popular of all were the Hollywood-style musical comedies by Grigori Alexandrov, who had started his film career as Eisenstein's assistant. The three best ones were *The Happy Guys* (1934), which broke all box-office records, *The Circus* (1936) and *Volga-Volga* (1938). These films tried to put over the message that life in the USSR was happier and better in every way than anywhere else in the world. Stalin became so obsessed with making sure that the film-makers were presenting an acceptable picture of life in Soviet Russia that he vetted a large number of scripts himself. 'It is a telling comment on his state of mind', points out Richard Taylor, 'that the editors of the unpublished fourteenth volume of his *Works* could find nothing to include for the year 1940, when the rest of Europe was engulfed in war, but Stalin's comments on some film scripts.'[91] Some that did not find favour were by Sergei Eisenstein who failed to repeat his great masterpieces of the 1920s – *Strike, The Battleship Potemkin* and *October*. He was forced to abandon his work on the film *Bezhin Meadow* (1935) which dealt with collectivization and told the true story of a boy who denounced his father to the authorities as a kulak, and was then murdered by his relatives. The party wanted the boy to be portrayed as a hero on whom young people should model themselves. The censors decided that Eisenstein had somehow not struck the right note and insisted that the film should be withdrawn. He salvaged his reputation in 1938 with his great patriotic film *Alexander Nevsky*. It had a magnificent score by Prokofiev and told the story of the invasion of Russia by Teutonic knights in medieval times. In a spectacular final scene the great Russian hero, Prince Alexander, defeats the Germans as they flee across the ice on a frozen river. It was a clear warning about what the Germans could expect if they dared to invade Russia again, but perhaps Hitler did not see the film.

(i) The nationalities

As we saw earlier (section 5.8(d)) the government encouraged the awareness of national cultures, allowed local languages and promoted non-Russians into important positions. The Communists hoped that liberal treatment of the non-Russians would attract Ukrainians, Armenians, Belorussians and Moldovans who lived outside the USSR to join; there were, for example, Ukrainians and Belorussians living in what was now Poland, and there were Moldovans in Rumania. Ukraine was the republic most conscious of its national culture, and by 1936 over 80 per cent of school-age children were being taught in Ukrainian. The government even went so far as to employ scholars to invent written languages for smaller ethnic groups who had never had one. Although the governments of the republics did not have a great deal of control over their internal affairs, ordinary citizens had some reason to feel grateful to Moscow, at least until Stalin began his agrarian reforms.

The tolerant attitude towards the nationalities ended suddenly in December 1932 because of widespread resistance to Stalin's collectivization policy. In Ukraine, Kazakhstan, Uzbekistan and the Northern Caucasus there was much fiercer resistance than in Russia itself, and it was reported to Stalin that resistance was being fuelled by local nationalism. In Ukraine the situation was exacerbated by the famine and the Ukrainian Communist Party infuriated Moscow by admitting that collectivization had been a failure in their republic. Stalin decided that the Ukrainian party leadership needed 'strengthening'; a team of top officials and thousands of trusted party workers descended on Ukraine to carry out a purge of 'bourgeois nationalist deviationists'. This was done with utter ruthlessness – many thousands of people were deported from their villages, and many were sent to prisons or labour camps. This was followed by similar purges in Belorussia, Transcaucasia and Central Asia, after which the regime abolished most of the nationality districts and Soviets that it had recently created to represent non-Russian minorities within the different republics. Non-Russian nationalities were not suppressed, but within each republic only the nationality of the republic was recognized as official. So, for example, Ukrainians living in the Northern Caucasus had their schools closed down; and Belorussians living on (for them) the wrong side of the border with the Russian republic were no longer officially recognized as a Belorussian minority. This meant a sharp reduction in the number of ethnic groups from 188 in the 1926 census to 107 in the 1937 census.

The government began to promote pro-Russian patriotism; in 1938 Russian was made compulsory in all schools in the USSR, and although non-Russian languages continued to be taught, non-Russians could choose to be taught in Russian. Everyone had the right to choose their own nationality and an increasing number of non-Russians chose to become assimilated with the Russians. Yet at the same time the new 1936 constitution increased the number of republics: Transcaucasia was split up so that Armenia, Azerbaijan and Georgia became full union republics within the USSR; Kazakhstan and Kirgizstan (which were previously autonomous republics) were elevated to full union republics; and the five autonomous regions became autonomous republics (see section 6.5(e)). In 1939–40 five more full republics were added to the USSR – Latvia, Lithuania, Estonia, Moldavia and Karelo–Finland (see section 7.1(d)). The constitution mentioned the nurturing of national cultures provided they were 'socialist in content'. The republics were encouraged to hold official celebrations of their important historical events and their writers, artists and musicians, though at the same time they were left in no doubt that Russian culture was in prime position. It was a strangely ambivalent policy in more than one sense: in spite of Stalin's 'socialism in one country', the communists were still arguably an internationalist party, and yet they were genuinely anxious to preserve the non-Russian nationalities, and encourage national identity and have them all living happily together in one big family. Russian historian Yuri Slezkine describes the USSR as a 'communal apartment' in which each national family had its own room.[92] But the encouragement was only up to a point: so long as it did not conflict with the continuation of a unitary, socialist state. Stalin himself said, in a famous phrase, that he wanted cultures to be 'national in form, socialist in content'. At the first sign of any opposition to Moscow or any national *political* aspirations, there was an immediate clamp-down. In Georgia the secret police leader, Lavrenti Beria, dealt ruthlessly with any potential nationalist threat and also with any peasant resistance.

The relationship between Moscow and the non-Russian republics was almost imperial/colonial; the Moscow government took over more and more of the republics' powers – in areas such as agriculture, taxation, higher education, media, justice and public health. After the nationalist/communist leaders had been purged, all the really important decisions were taken in Moscow. Kazakhstan was forced to undertake collectivization and meet agricultural quotas, a policy totally inappropriate in that region where the population were mainly nomads who knew nothing about growing wheat. It is calculated that between 1.3 and 1.8 million Kazakhs died during this ill-fated campaign. Similarly in Ukraine so many people perished that nationalist leaders began to feel that Stalin was hell-bent on exterminating the entire Ukrainian nation. And yet on the other hand in 1939 the Ukrainians were allowed to hold lavish celebrations of the 125th anniversary of the birth of the Ukrainian writer and poet Taras Shevchenko. By 1940 therefore the regime's policy towards the nationalities had produced a paradoxical situation: at the same time as its main drive was towards modernization, it found itself encouraging a revival of traditional cultures which in some areas had been dying out. As Terry Martin puts it: 'Communism's folkloric national identities were the invention of the state, usually with the enthusiastic participation of national elites ... Modernization is the theory of Soviet intentions; neo-traditionalism, the theory of their unintended consequences.'[93]

Documents

(A) Trotsky explains why he thought Stalin would become the dictator of the USSR.

In the spring of 1924, after one of the Plenums of the Central Committee at which I was not present because of illness, I said to Smirnov: 'Stalin will become the dictator of the USSR.' Smirnov knew Stalin well. They had shared revolutionary work and exile together for years, and under such conditions people get to know each other best of all.

'Stalin?' he asked me with amazement. 'But he is a mediocrity, a colourless nonentity.'

'Mediocrity, yes; nonentity, no,' I answered him. 'The dialectics of history have already hooked him and will raise him up. He is needed by all of them – by the tired radicals, by the bureaucrats, by the nepmen, the kulaks, the upstarts, the sneaks, by all the worms that are crawling out of the upturned soil of the manured revolution. He knows how to meet them on their own ground, he speaks their language and he knows how to lead them. He has the deserved reputation of an old revolutionist, which makes him invaluable to them as a blinder on the eyes of the country. He has will and daring. He will not hesitate to use them and to move them against the Party. He has already started doing this. Right now he is organizing around himself the sneaks of the Party, the artful dodgers ... '

Source: quoted in F.W. Stacey, *Stalin and the Making of Modern Russia*, p. 9.

(B) Alexander Barmine, a party member and worker, remembers Trotsky's short-comings (memoirs published in 1945).

As soon as he [Trotsky] had finished he left the hall. There was no personal contact in the corridors. This aloofness, I believe, may partly explain Trotsky's inability as well as his unwillingness to build a large personal following among the rank and file of the Party. Against the intrigues of Party leaders, which were soon to multiply, Trotsky fought only with the weapons he knew how to use: his pen and his oratory. And even these weapons he took up only when it was too late.

Source: Alexander Barmine, *One Who Survived*, pp. 93–4.

(C) Stalin's speech to local party and soviet workers in Siberia in January 1928, usually taken to mark the beginning of collectivization.

'You're working badly! You're idle and you indulge the kulaks. Take care that there aren't some kulak agents among you. We won't tolerate this sort of outrage for long...Take a look at the kulak farms; you'll see their granaries and barns are full of grain; they have to cover the grain with awnings because there's no more room for it inside. The kulak farms have got something like a thousand tons of surplus grain per farm. I propose that:
(a) you demand that the kulaks hand over their surpluses at once at state prices;
(b) if they refuse to submit to the law, you should charge them under Article 107 of the RSFRS Criminal Code and confiscate their grain for the state, 25 per cent of it to be redistributed among the poor and less well-off middle peasants.

Source: quoted in Dmitri Volkogonov, *Stalin*, pp. 164–5.

(D) John Scott, an American engineer who went to work in the USSR, describes his experiences during the 1930s.

One of the most important projects was the creation of a heavy industry base in the Urals and Siberia out of reach of any invader, and capable of supplying the country with arms and machines in immense quantities... It was necessary to start from scratch. There were no supply bases, no railroads, no other mills in or near Magnitogorsk and Kuznetsk. But Stalin and his Political Bureau decided that the job must be done. Stalin was probably one of the few men in the Soviet Union who realized how catastrophically expensive it was going to be. But he was convinced that it was just a matter of time until the Soviet Union would again be invaded by hostile capitalist powers seeking to destroy the first Socialist State. Stalin considered it his sacred obligation to see to it that when the time came the attackers would not be able to accomplish it...As the Arctic winter suddenly broke into

(continued)

spring, Magnitogorsk changed beyond recognition. In early April everything was still frozen solid. By May the ground had thawed and the city was swimming in mud ... Welding became next to impossible as our ragged cables short-circuited at every step. Bubonic plague had broken out in three places not far from Magnitogorsk ... The resistance of the population was very low because of undernourishment during the winter and consistent overwork. Sanitary conditions, particularly during the thaw, were appalling. Within two weeks the sun had dried the earth and the summer was upon us. By the middle of May the heat was intolerable. In the barracks we were consumed by bed-bugs and other vermin, and at work we had trouble keeping to the job.

The history of actual construction of Magnitogorsk was fascinating ... Brigades of young enthusiasts from every corner of the Soviet Union arrived in the summer of 1930 and did the groundwork of railroad and dam construction necessary before work could begin on the plant itself. Later groups of local peasants and herdsmen came because of bad conditions in the villages, due to collectivization. A colony of several hundred foreign engineers and specialists arrived to advise and direct the work. Money was spent by the millions ... From 1928 until 1932 nearly a quarter of a million people came to Magnitogorsk. About three quarters of these new arrivals came of their own free will seeking work, bread-cards, better conditions. The rest came under compulsion.

Source: John Scott, *Behind the Urals*, pp. 52–4, 61, 110.

(E) Evgenia Ginzburg, a writer who survived 18 years in prisons and labour camps, describes her interrogation.

I was put on the 'conveyer belt'. The interrogators worked in shifts; I didn't. Seven days without sleep or food. Without even returning to my cell. The object of the 'conveyer' is to wear out the nerves, weaken the body, break resistance, and force the prisoner to sign whatever is required. The first day or two I still noticed the individual characteristics of the interrogators – Livanov, calm and bureaucratic, urging me to sign some monstrous piece of rubbish as though it were no more than perfectly normal, routine detail; Tsarevsky and Vevers always shouting and threatening – Vevers in addition sniffing cocaine and giggling as well as shouting. 'Ha, ha, ha! What's become of our high-brow beauty now! You look at least forty ... and if you go on digging your heels in, we'll turn you into a real granny. You haven't been in the rubber cell yet, have you? You haven't? Well, there's a pleasure in store.'

Major Elshin was invariably courteous and humane. He asked me why 'I was so becomingly pale' and was 'amazed' to hear that I had been questioned without food or sleep for four or five days on end. 'Is it really worth torturing yourself like that rather than sign a purely formal, unimportant record? Come on now, get it over with and go to sleep.' The 'unimportant record' stated that, on Elvov's instruction I had organized a Tartar writers' branch of a terrorist group of which I was a member: there followed a list of Tartar writers I had 'recruited' ... I have no idea what answers I gave the colonel. I think I was silent most of the time, only repeating occasionally: 'I won't sign.' He used threats and persuasion in turn, promising that I would see my husband, my children. Finally I blacked out.

Source: Evgenia Ginzburg, *Into the Whirlwind*, pp. 71–2.

(F) A British diplomat, Fitzroy Maclean, describes the opening of the show-trial of Bukharin and Rykov in March 1938.

For sheer blood and thunder the indictment left nothing to be desired. The prisoners were charged, collectively and individually, with every conceivable crime: high treason, murder, attempted murder, espionage and all kinds of sabotage. With diabolical ingenuity they had plotted to wreck industry and agriculture; to assassinate Stalin and the other Soviet leaders; to overthrow the Soviet regime with the help of foreign powers; to seize power themselves and restore capitalism...One after another, using the same words, they admitted their guilt: Bukharin, Rykov, Yagoda...Bit by bit, as one confession succeeded another, the fantastic structure took shape. Each prisoner incriminated his fellows and was in turn incriminated by them. Readily, glibly, they dwelt on their crimes and on those of their companions, enlarged on them, embroidered them...And yet what they said, the actual contents of their statements, seemed to bear no relation to reality. The fabric that was being built up was fantastic beyond belief...As the trial progressed, it became ever clearer that the underlying purpose of every testimony was to blacken the leaders of the 'bloc', to represent them, not as political offenders, but as common criminals, murderers, poisoners and spies.

Source: quoted in F.W. Stacey, *Stalin and the Making of Modern Russia*, pp. 31–3.

(G) The closing speech by the Public Prosecutor, Andrei Vyshinsky, at the trial of Bukharin and Rykov, March 1938.

The whole country, from the youngest to the oldest, are waiting for and demanding one thing: that the traitors and spies who sold out our motherland to the enemy be shot like vile dogs! The people demand one thing: that the accursed vermin be squashed! Time will pass. The hated traitors' graves will become overgrown with weeds and thistles, covered with the eternal contempt of honest Soviet people, of the entire Soviet people.

While over our happy land, bright and clear as ever, our sun will shine its rays. We, our people, will as before stride along our path now cleansed of the last trace of the scum and vileness of the past, led by our beloved leader and teacher, the great Stalin.

Source: quoted in Dmitri Volkogonov, *Stalin*, p. 293.

(H) Letter from A.M. Volkova, a worker on a sovkhoz (state collective farm) in the Ivanovo district, in reply to a questionnaire sent out by the Department of Cattle and Dairy Sovkhozes in September 1935.

You wrote about an apartment. Our apartment is 3 metres wide and 5 metres long. We have lived for two years without windows, in winter wearing coats. I have two children, both in school, one in the fourth grade, the other in the second. They have no shoes or coat and go barefoot and only in a shirt. You wrote about the cafeteria. We don't go to the cafeteria. I earn 108 to 116 and no more. You wrote about health. My health is very bad and all this depends on food, and you wrote about vouchers to the health resort, but with whom can I leave the children? I am completely illiterate. I am 48 years old and it is late to learn. You wrote about animals. We don't have any. We were given a pig but it was undernourished and diseased. I have been forgotten in this respect. Nowhere is there a work corner where my children can write or read. There are no tools or materials for a labour corner. They don't give milk to schoolchildren who must go with crusts of bread. We live badly. Give help.

[The letter is signed Volkov, V.K. – probably the older of the two children]

Source: quoted in Lewis H. Siegelbaum, 'Dear Comrade, You Ask What We Need', in Sheila Fitzpatrick (editor), *Stalinism: New Directions*, p. 239.

(I) Victor Serge writes about the hardships of the winter of 1934–35. He had already spent some time in prison for being an associate of Trotsky, and although he had been released, he was expecting to be arrested again. However, he was eventually allowed to leave the USSR.

The winter of 1934–5 was frightful, despite the lessening of the famine towards the New Year and the abolition of bread-rationing. For a long while my wife, a victim to crises of insanity, had been away from me for treatment in Leningrad, and I was alone with my son ... We rationed ourselves to the limit, so that all we fed on now was a little black bread and 'egg-soup' which I made to last two days with some sorrel and just one egg. Fortunately we did have wood. Soon I began to suffer from boils...An enormous anthrax tumour under my left breast laid me flat on my back... This was a little after Kirov's assassination. I left for the hospital lying in straw on a low sledge. My son walked along beside the sledge.

The hospital was run as efficiently as the general destitution permitted; what it treated primarily was poverty...chronic undernourishment aggravated by alcoholism. The worker who lived on sour-cabbage soup, without fat content, would acquire an abscess as a result of a simple bruise. Children were covered in cold sores; whole wards were full of peasants with frozen limbs; bellies empty, clothes worn and threadbare, they offered small resistance to the cold. I saw gangrenous flesh being torn from the frozen limbs with pincers; indescribable scars resulted.

Nor shall I forget how on the most wretched of our days of misery we all heard a radio broadcast from a regional meeting of kolkhoz workers. Passionate voices went on endlessly thanking the Leader for 'the good life we lead'. And twenty or so patients tormented by hunger, half of them kolkhoz workers themselves, listened to all in silence.

Source: Victor Serge, *Memoirs of a Revolutionary*, pp. 310–13.

(J) Poem by Osip Mandelstam attacking Stalin in 1933. It led to his eventual arrest and death in a labour camp.

We live, deaf to the land beneath us,
Ten steps away no one hears our speeches,
But where there's so much as half a conversation
The Kremlin's mountaineer will get his mention.
His fingers are fat as grubs
And the words, final as lead weights, fall from his lips,
His cockroach whiskers leer
And his boot tops gleam.
Around him a rabble of thin-necked leaders –
Fawning half-men for him to play with.
They whinny, purr or whine
As he prates and points a finger,
One by one forging his laws, to be flung
Like horseshoes at the head, the eye or the groin.
And every killing is a treat
For the broad-chested Ossete.

Source: Nadezhda Mandelstam, *Hope Against Hope: A Memoir*, p. 13.

Notes

1. Roy A. Medvedev, 'New Pages from the Political Biography of Stalin', in Robert C. Tucker (editor), *Stalinism: Essays in Historical Interpretation*, p. 204.
2. Robert Service, *Lenin: A Biography*, pp. 465, 469.
3. Adam B. Ulam, *Lenin and the Bolsheviks*, p. 757.
4. Isaac Deutscher, *The Prophet Unarmed – Trotsky: 1921–1929*, pp. 136–7.
5. Martin McCauley, *Stalin and Stalinism*, p. 15.
6. Dmitri Volkogonov, *Stalin: Triumph and Tragedy*, p. 109.
7. *Ibid.*, p. 87.
8. For a full account of this process see Catherine Merridale, *Moscow Politics and the Rise of Stalin*.
9. Volkogonov, p. 163.
10. See J. Hughes, *Stalin, Siberia and the Crisis of the New Economic Policy*.
11. Robert Service, 'Joseph Stalin: The Making of a Stalinist', in John Channon (editor), *Politics, Society and Stalinism in the USSR*, p. 25.
12. Ronald G. Suny, *The Soviet Experiment*, p. 167.

13. Alec Nove, *An Economic History of the USSR 1917–1991*, p. 149.
14. Moshe Lewin, *The Making of the Soviet System*, p. 94.
15. Sheila Fitzpatrick, *The Russian Revolution*, pp. 218–19.
16. Isaac Deutscher, *Stalin*, pp. 319, 322.
17. Alexander Gershenkron, *Economic Backwardness in Historical Perspective: A Book of Essays*, pp. 144–60.
18. Lewin, pp. 114–20.
19. James R. Millar, 'Mass Collectivization and the Contribution of Soviet agriculture to the First Five-Year Plan: A Review Article', *Slavic Review*, December 1974, pp. 764–6.
20. Nove, p. 159.
21. *Ibid.*, p.165.
22. *Ibid.*, p. 171.
23. Volkogonov, p. 166.
24. Quoted in Robert C. Tucker, 'Stalinism as Revolution from Above', in Tucker (editor), *Stalinism:Essays in Historical Interpretation*, p. 83.
25. Quoted in R.W. Davies, *The Socialist Offensive 1929–30*, p. 148.
26. Lynne Viola, *The Best Sons of the Fatherland. Workers in the Vanguard of Soviet Collectivization.*
27. Jochen Hellbeck, 'Fashioning the Stalinist Soul. The diary of Stepan Podlubnyi, 1931–9', in Sheila Fitzpatrick (editor), *Stalinism: New Directions*, pp. 89–90.
28. All the statistics in this section are from Nove, pp. 180, 186.
29. Robert Service, *A History of Twentieth-Century Russia*, p. 183.
30. R.W. Davies, Mark Harrison and S.G. Wheatcroft (editors), *The Economic Transformation of the Soviet Union, 1913–1945*, pp. 113–14.
31. Roy A. Medvedev, *Let History Judge: The Origins and Consequences of Stalinism*, p. 241.
32. Quoted in Suny, p. 227.
33. Hellbeck, p. 102.
34. Robert Conquest, *Harvest of Sorrow*.
35. Sheila Fitzpatrick, 'The Great Departure. Rural–Urban Migration in the Soviet Union, 1929–33', in W.R. Rosenberg and L.S. Siegelbaum (editors), *Social Dimensions of Soviet Industrialization*, pp. 21–2. See also Sheila Fitzpatrick, *Stalin's Peasants. Resistance and Survival in the Russian Village after Collectivization*.
36. Deutscher, *Stalin*, p. 322.
37. *Ibid.*, p. 328.
38. Nove, p. 193.
39. Hiroaki Kuromiya, *Stalin's Industrial Revolution: Politics and Workers, 1928–1932*, chapter 5.
40. Donald Filtzer, 'Stalinism and the Working Class in the 1930s', in John Channon (editor), *Politics, Society and Stalinism in the USSR*, pp. 166–7.
41. Suny, p. 240.
42. Nove, p. 195. For more about the First Five-Year Plan see Nove, pp. 189–225.
43. Filtzer, p. 180.
44. John Scott, *Behind the Urals: An American Worker in Russia's City of Steel*, p. 110.
45. Filtzer, pp. 166–78; see also his *Soviet Workers and Stalinist Industrialization. The formation of modern Soviet production relations, 1928–41* (New York, 1986).
46. Lewin, p. 220.
47. Filtzer, p. 178.
48. Nove, p. 240.
49. Medvedev, p. 248.
50. Martin McCauley, *Stalin and Stalinism*, p. 27.
51. Nove, pp. 224–5.
52. Medvedev, p. 254.
53. James R. Harris, 'Purging Local Cliques in the Urals Region', in Sheila Fitzpatrick (editor), *Stalinism: New Directions*, pp. 262–80. See also his *The Great Urals: Regionalism and the Evolution of the Soviet System* (Ithaca, NY, 1999), chapter 6.

54. Filtzer, p. 180.
55. Holland Hunter, 'The Overambitious First Soviet Five-Year Plan', *Slavic Review*, 32: 2 (1973), pp. 237–57. See also H. Hunter and J.M. Szyrmer, *Faulty Foundations. Soviet Economic Policies, 1928–1940*.
56. Davies, Harrison and Wheatcroft, p. 157.
57. Volkogonov, p. 263.
58. Medvedev, pp. 330–4.
59. Robert Conquest, *The Great Terror: A Reassessment*, pp. 67–9.
60. Zbigniew Brzezinski, *The Permanent Purge*.
61. J. Arch Getty, *The Road To Terror: Stalinism and the Self-Destruction of the Bolsheviks, 1932–9*.
62. Sheila Fitzpatrick, *The Russian Revolution*, pp. 166–70.
63. Volkogonov, pp. 225, 308.
64. Quoted in Ronald G. Suny, *The Soviet Experiment*, p. 267.
65. Conquest, p. 37. For a full account of Kirov's murder see Robert Conquest, *Stalin and the Kirov Murder* (New York, 1989).
66. *Ibid.*, p. 74.
67. Volkogonov, pp. 280–1.
68. Medvedev, pp. 399–403.
69. Deutscher, *Stalin*, p. 376.
70. For a full account of the Tukhachevsky affair, see Conquest, *The Great Terror*, pp. 182–225; Volkogonov, pp. 316–29.
71. Sheila Fitzpatrick, *Everyday Stalinism*, pp. 126–7.
72. Paul M. Hagenloh, ' "Socially Harmful Elements" and the Great Terror', in Sheila Fitzpatrick (editor), *Stalinism: New Directions*, pp. 286–7.
73. Quoted in H. Montgomery Hyde, *Stalin: The History of a Dictator*, p. 377.
74. Conquest, pp. 485–9; Jerry Hough, *How the Soviet Union is Governed*, p. 176; Suny, p. 266; Davies, Harrison and Wheatcroft (editors), pp. 67–77 for a detailed examination of the statistics.
75. Service, pp. 225–6.
76. T.H. Rigby, *Political Elites in the USSR*, p. 132.
77. J.A. Getty, *Origins of the Great Purges. The Soviet Communist Party Reconsidered, 1933–1938*, pp. 16–17, 27, 56, 91, 153, 196–206. Gabor T. Ritterspoorn, *Stalinist Simplifications and Soviet Complications: Social Tensions and Political Conflicts in the USSR 1933–1953*.
78. E.A. Rees, 'Stalinism: The Primacy of Politics', in John Channon (editor), *Politics, Society and Stalinism in the USSR*, p. 63.
79. Filtzer, pp. 167–80; Sheila Fitzpatrick, *Stalin's Peasants*.
80. Martin Malia, 'Revolution fulfilled. How the revisionists are still trying to take the ideology out of Stalinism', in the *Times Literary Supplement*, 15 June 2001.
81. Sheila Fitzpatrick, *Everyday Stalinism*, p. 7.
82. Sarah Davies, ' "Us Against Them": Social identity in Soviet Russia, 1934–41', in Sheila Fitzpatrick (editor), *Stalinism: New Directions*, pp. 47–67.
83. Much of the information in this section is from Sheila Fitzpatrick, *Everyday Stalinism*, pp. 1–114.
84. Vadim Volkov, 'The Concept of Kul'turnost', Notes on the Stalinist civilizing process', in Sheila Fitzpatrick (editor), *Stalinism: New Directions*, pp. 210–28.
85. Stephen Kotkin, *Magnetic Mountain. Stalinism as a Civilization*, chapter 5.
86. Fitzpatrick, *Everyday Stalinism*, p. 161.
87. There is a huge literature on Soviet culture; perhaps the two best to serve as an introduction are James von Geldern and Richard Stites (editors), *Mass Culture in Soviet Russia: Tales, Poems, Songs, Movies, Plays and Folklore, 1917–1953*, and Hans Gunther (editor), *The Culture of the Stalin Period*.
88. Quoted in Conquest, p. 306.
89. Andre Gide, *Back From the USSR*, p. 78.
90. An excellent recent biography is by Elizabeth Wilson, *Shostakovich, A Life Remembered*.

91. Richard Taylor, 'Soviet Cinema – The Path to Stalin', in *History Today*, vol. 40, July 1990, p. 48. For a full treatment of Soviet cinema see Peter Kenez, *Cinema and Soviet Society, 1917–1953*.
92. Yuri Slezkine, 'The USSR as a Communal Apartment', in Sheila Fitzpatrick (editor), *Stalinism: New Directions*, pp. 313–39.
93. Terry Martin, 'Modernization or Neo-traditionalism?', in Sheila Fitzpatrick (editor), *Stalinism: New Directions*, pp. 360–1.

■ ⏷ **7** The Great Patriotic War and Stalin's last years, 1941–53

Summary of events

For the whole of the period from the mid-1920s until his death in 1953, Stalin remained in supreme power. During the later 1920s the USSR continued to be treated very much as a state to be shunned by the world's other major powers, especially as the Comintern still seemed intent on stirring up trouble wherever possible. Only Germany was consistently friendly towards the USSR, as both countries saw the advantages of having at least one ally. Stalin's great fear was that the capitalist states would form an alliance with the express purpose of destroying the Soviet Union and communism, thus removing the danger of world revolution; his foreign policy was directed towards preventing such developments. At the beginning of the 1930s the USSR's international position seemed to be improving; all the other leading states except the USA had granted official diplomatic recognition to the Soviet government, and a number of countries had signed trade agreements and non-aggression pacts with Moscow.

But the situation soon changed dramatically for the worse:

September 1931 – the Japanese invaded the Chinese province of Manchuria, bordering on the USSR in the Far East. Stalin was suspicious of Japanese motives and feared they might try to expand into Soviet territory.

January 1933 – Hitler, the sworn enemy of Communism, came to power in Germany; although Stalin tried to continue good relations, the Soviet Union's only close ally now became her most dangerous potential enemy. The USSR felt threatened from both east and west, and a radical change was clearly needed in Soviet foreign policy.

Maxim Litvinov, collective security and the popular front. Litvinov, the Soviet Commissar for Foreign Affairs from 1930 until 1938, sought protection with his policy of collective security – trying to persuade the peaceful nations of the world, particularly Britain, France and the USA, to act together to curb the aggressive powers – Germany, Japan and Italy. Even the Comintern agreed to co-operate with non-communist parties, encouraging the formation of a 'popular front' in the attempt to defeat Fascism. But Britain, France and the USA were desperate to avoid war; Litvinov failed to galvanize them into action, and Hitler and Mussolini were allowed to get away with a long series of breaches of the Versailles peace settlement. Stalin, also anxious to avoid war, was convinced that Britain and France were planning to embroil the USSR in a war with Nazi Germany.

August 1939 – the Nazi–Soviet Non-Aggression Pact. Apparently aiming to delay the outbreak of war between the USSR and Germany as long as possible, Stalin amazed the rest of the world by signing this agreement, which included secret clauses providing for the division of Poland between Stalin and Hitler. With his eastern front secure, Hitler was able to invade Poland and overrun most of western Europe, except Britain, without any interference from the Russians.

June 1941 to May 1945 – war between the USSR and Germany – The Great Patriotic War. Although Stalin did his best to keep his side of the Pact and refused to accept that Hitler was planning to attack, the USSR was forced into the Second World War on 22 June 1941 when the Germans launched a massive invasion – Operation Barbarossa. The Russians, unprepared for such an onslaught, at first suffered widespread defeats on all fronts: an enormous area in the west of the country was overrun, Leningrad was besieged for 900 days but was eventually relieved, and Moscow was almost captured but managed to survive. In the south the Germans captured Rostov-on-Don and were pushing towards Stalingrad and the oilfields of the Caucasus.

The Battle of Stalingrad – August 1942 to January 1943 – was the great turning point in the war. The German Sixth Army captured probably three-quarters of the city, but was then surrounded by vast Soviet reinforcements and compelled to surrender. The Russians gradually pushed the Germans back, although they resisted fiercely, and it was August 1944 before Soviet forces reached Poland. In January 1945 the Red Army entered East Prussia and on 2 May completed the capture of Berlin. Although the USSR had received considerable help from Britain and the USA, there can be no doubt that it was Soviet forces which played the major role in the defeat of Hitler's Germany and her allies.

The beginning of the Cold War. Towards the end of the Second World War relations between the USSR and her two main allies, Britain and the USA, began to deteriorate. In spite of the extensive help which they had sent to Russia in the shape of supplies and war materials, Stalin suspected that they still wanted to destroy communism. He believed that their delay in launching a 'second front' – an invasion of France (which did not take place until June 1944) – was a deliberate ploy to keep most of the pressure on the Russians and bring them to the point of exhaustion. Two conferences were held between the allies – at **Yalta and Potsdam (February and July 1945)** – and although the first one seemed to be a success, at Potsdam there were disagreements over the future of Poland and Germany. Eventually relations between the USSR and the West became so strained that although no actual conflict took place, the decade after 1945 saw the first phase of what became known as the Cold War. It was a period in which the rival powers attacked each other with propaganda and economic measures, and generally refused to co-operate.

Stalin takes over eastern Europe. Between 1945 and 1949 Stalin, wanting to put as much space as possible between the USSR and the West, took control of most of the states of eastern Europe, doing whatever was necessary to enable communist governments to come to power in Poland, Hungary, Romania, Bulgaria, Yugoslavia, Albania, Czechoslovakia and East Germany. At the same time the USA, as the main enemy of communism, did its best to build up an anti-communist bloc of states.

The Soviet Union devastated at the end of the war. The entire western part of the country which had been occupied by the Germans was a complete ruin, and many people would have been happy to see the end of Stalin. However, Stalin and his system had survived the test of war, and **he was determined that his dictatorship and the one-party state should continue.** The terror methods of control, and other harsh policies which had been relaxed somewhat during the war, were resumed. More politicians were executed and when he died in 1953 he was on the point of launching another purge. He left behind enormous problems – in agriculture, industry, administration and above all in the ludicrous over-centralization of the State.

Main areas of debate:

- Why did Stalin leave the USSR so unprepared for the German invasion in June 1941?
- Was Stalin preparing for a 'preventive' war with Germany?
- Could the USSR have won the war without Stalin and his methods?
- Who was to blame for the Cold War, Stalin or the West?
- Is there anything positive to be said for Stalin and his 'achievements'?

7.1 Foreign relations and the background to war

(a) The USSR and its place in the world

The capitalist states continued to view the USSR with the utmost suspicion, although as we saw earlier (section 5.7(b)) the Soviet state was not completely isolated in world affairs since the signing of the Rapallo Treaty with Germany in 1922. It seemed a rather unlikely alliance between the two outcast nations of Europe, but the link was that both of them were opposed to the Versailles peace settlement; the agreement benefited both sides. The USSR was hoping to get access to the latest military technology and strategic thinking, while Germany needed iron ore and oil, and somewhere to develop armaments and carry out military training which was forbidden in Germany itself by the peace settlement. However, relations were not entirely smooth: the Comintern (see section 5.7(a)) continued to try and stir up revolution in Germany, so it should have come as no surprise to Moscow that in the mid-1920s the Germans, with Gustav Stresemann in charge of foreign policy, began to aim for better relations with Britain and

France. At a conference in London in 1924 an agreement known as the Dawes Plan was reached allowing Germany longer to pay war reparations to the victorious powers and providing the Germans with a large American loan. In 1925 a series of agreements known as the Locarno Treaties was signed by Germany, France, Britain, Italy, Belgium and Czechoslovakia. Germany, France and Belgium promised to respect their joint frontiers, and Germany, Poland and Czechoslovakia agreed to submit any disputes between the three of them to arbitration. Although there were some glaring omissions from the treaties – for example, Germany did not promise to guarantee her frontiers with Poland and Czechoslovakia – it seemed that reconciliation between the Germans and their former enemies in the West was well under way. In 1926 Germany was allowed to join the League of Nations.

These developments caused consternation in the People's Commissariat of Foreign Affairs (Narkomindel) in Moscow. The readmittance of the Germans into European affairs was seen by Georgi Chicherin, the Commissar for Foreign Affairs, as a deliberate attempt to lure them away from their alliance with the USSR, leaving the Russians totally isolated. However, it was not a complete disaster for the USSR: the Germans wanted to keep all options open, and there were good reasons for wanting to continue the relationship with Moscow. Both Germany and the USSR were united in their distrust of Poland; their secret military arrangements and their trade links were working well. Consequently, in April 1926 a new agreement was signed by the Germans and Russians in Berlin, providing for a continuation of the Rapallo Treaty; each of the two powers also promised not to take part in any hostile military or economic action against the other, and to remain neutral if the other state was attacked. Britain and France were not too happy about this new agreement, but did not protest, since they were anxious to maintain their own good relations with Germany.

The year 1927 proved to be full of problems for the USSR. Relations with Britain deteriorated sharply when the British Conservative government ordered a police raid on the London premises of Arcos, a Soviet trade delegation which was suspected of being the centre of a spying organization. The British claimed to have found incriminating documents; the trading mission was expelled and diplomatic relations with the USSR were suspended. Stalin retaliated by ordering the arrest of some British residents in Moscow. At the same time there were problems with China. During 1915 and 1916 China disintegrated into hundreds of small states, each controlled by a warlord and his private army. General Chiang Kai-shek, leader of the Chinese Nationalist Party since 1925, was struggling to destroy the warlords and unite the country again. The Nationalists were working together with the Chinese Communist Party (founded in 1921), and the Soviet government was providing aid to both parties in the hope that a reunited China would be friendly towards the USSR. However, in spite of his Soviet connections, Chiang was not a communist; by 1927 he had decided that the nationalists were strong enough to do without communist help and that the Communist Party must be destroyed before it became powerful enough to challenge the nationalists. He launched a brutal 'purification' campaign in which thousands of communists and trade unionists were killed, and yet Stalin insisted that the communists should try and continue the alliance. Stalin's reasoning was that the Chinese

Communist Party was as yet too small to be able to bring about a full-scale pro-letarian revolution; they should therefore work with the middle-class nationalists to unify China, and the workers' revolution could come later. Stalin's attitude aroused bitter criticism from Trotsky, Kamenev and Zinoviev who accused him of betraying the Chinese communists. Eventually Mao Zedong, one of the communist leaders, rejected Stalin's orders and concentrated on survival. The failure of its Chinese policy was a serious embarrassment for the Soviet government. Even more uncomfortable were developments on the USSR's western frontier: the Polish leader, General Pilsudski, was clearly aligning his country with the West and taking a strong anti-Soviet stance. This did nothing to quell Stalin's fears of a capitalist plot for a joint attack on the USSR. On the other hand, the activities of the Comintern did nothing to lessen Western suspicions of the Soviet government.

By the early 1930s there were signs that the USSR's international position might be improving. In 1927 a Russian delegation had attended a meeting in Geneva called to plan and prepare a major Disarmament Conference. Maxim Litvinov, who was to become Soviet Commissar for Foreign Affairs in July 1930, impressed delegates with his demand for immediate disarmament. In 1929 the new British Labour government resumed diplomatic relations and opened negotiations with Moscow for a fresh trade treaty. Another trade agreement was signed with Germany in 1931, and the same year, non-aggression and trade agreements were signed with Turkey and Afghanistan. Most of the world's important states, with the exception of the USA, had by this time given formal recognition to the Soviet government; and in 1932 the USSR signed more non-aggression pacts – with Poland, France, Finland, Latvia and Estonia. With the capitalist nations still suffering the effects of the world economic crisis which began with the 1929 Wall Street Crash, Stalin was able to present the USSR as an economically successful state, which wished only for peace and international recognition.

In spite of this network of non-aggression and trade agreements, there were some worrying signs for the USSR – from Japan and from Germany. Japan, like the other capitalist states, was suffering severe economic difficulties because of the world depression. Desperate to find new outlets for their exports, the Japanese cast envious eyes towards China, which was still torn by civil war between Chiang Kai-shek's nationalists and the communists. In 1931 the Japanese invaded and occupied the Chinese province of Manchuria which, with its population of around 30 million, would provide a valuable new market for Japanese exports. China appealed to the League of Nations, which condemned the Japanese action and ordered them to withdraw their troops from Manchuria. However, when the Japanese refused and withdrew from the League (March 1933), no action was taken against them. League action depended on the attitude of its two most powerful members – Britain and France; since both of them were suffering the effects of the depression, they decided against economic sanctions in case they led to war, which they felt ill-equipped to win. The USA was in its isolationist phase – not wanting to get involved in European affairs; it had declined to join the League of Nations at its inception, and now it refused to intervene against Japan. The League had suffered a humiliating blow and the Japanese were firmly established in Manchuria, which they set up as the puppet state of Manchukuo.

This was an alarming development for the Russians, since Manchuria bordered on the Soviet Far East. They were afraid that the Japanese might attempt to expand into Siberia, and some leading Russians suspected that Britain, France and the USA were deliberately working to bring about war between Japan and the USSR. How else could their lamentable response to Japanese aggression against China be explained except as an encouragement to Japan to engage in further aggression, this time against the USSR?

Even more worrying for the Soviet government were the developments in Germany which led to the appointment of Hitler as German Chancellor in January 1933. In fact, Russian policy was to some extent to blame for what happened in Germany. Stalin had consistently underestimated the threat from Hitler and the Nazis, and had allowed the Comintern to dictate a disastrous policy to the German Communist Party (KPD). The series of abortive uprisings prompted by Comintern agents in Germany did much to nurture the growing fear of communism which Hitler was able to exploit. Worse still, at its Sixth Congress, in 1928, the Comintern resolved that non-communist left-wing parties, such as the German Social Democrats (SPD), were just as dangerous as fascism; communists therefore must not co-operate with social democrats or trade unions, and must expel any members who were thought to be 'Rightists'. This policy had the most catastrophic effects in Germany where the KPD, instead of allying with the SPD to defeat the Nazis, actually campaigned against the SPD, dismissing them as 'social fascists' whose aim was to delay genuine revolution. This fatally split the left during the crucial period in the early 1930s when Nazi strength was growing and Hitler was manoeuvring for power, and perhaps destroyed the best chance of creating a barrier to keep the Nazis out. Once Hitler was in power, Soviet–German relations took a sharp turn for the worse: within a few months the German Communist Party and the SPD had been outlawed, the socialist trade unions had been dissolved, and Hitler was almost undisputed dictator. Germany's military co-operation with the USSR was brought to an abrupt end by Hitler, and although economic co-operation continued, Hitler's anti-communist and anti-Soviet views were well known. In the long term there could be no realistic future for the alliance with Germany, and it was clear that some dramatic changes would have to take place in Soviet foreign policy.

(b) Litvinov and the shift to collective security

Maxim Litvinov, the People's Commissar for Foreign Affairs from 1930, was given a fairly free hand in foreign policy. He had the full confidence and backing of Stalin, and survived the Purges and the Terror; even after 1939, when he was replaced by Molotov, he was allowed to live quietly in retirement with his wife. Many observers were surprised at the close relationship between Litvinov and Stalin, since they seemed to be poles apart. Litvinov was Jewish and an 'old' Bolshevik – he had first joined the party in 1903, whereas Stalin was personally anti-Semitic and was busy eliminating most of the old Bolsheviks during the 1930s. Litvinov was an internationalist who had travelled widely, spoke several languages and was married to an Englishwoman who was also Jewish. Stalin had travelled very little outside the USSR, and knew nothing of foreign languages.

This is probably the reason why Stalin allowed Litvinov such freedom; lacking confidence in his own knowledge of international affairs, he felt that foreign policy was not really his metier, and he depended heavily on the experienced and sophisticated Litvinov.[1]

Even before Hitler came to power Litvinov was convinced that it was time to move away from the Rapallo strategy of entente with Germany and to aim for improved relations with Britain and France and also with the USA, which had still not formally recognized the Soviet government. With Hitler firmly in power, new approaches became more urgent, especially after the Germans walked out of the World Disarmament Conference and the League of Nations in 1933 and signed a non-aggression pact with Poland in 1934. As a Jew, Litvinov was bound to feel a personal antipathy towards the violently anti-Semitic Nazi regime, and he was keen to take advantage of the anxieties of the Western powers at the growing threats from Germany and Japan. Litvinov aimed to strengthen the security of the USSR by forming a network of alliances with these powers, which would act together to curb the potential aggressors. This was known as a policy of 'collective security'. However, Soviet foreign policy continued to be confused: Stalin himself was so anxious to avoid war between the USSR and Germany that he seemed prepared to go to almost any lengths to try and maintain reasonable relations. Another trade agreement was signed in March 1934 and regular economic meetings took place between German and Soviet representatives throughout the 1930s. The Russians were continually angling for improved political relations but their proposals were invariably rejected by the Nazis.

Meanwhile Litvinov pressed ahead, with some success, with his policy of collective security, making a good impression on the Western powers. 'The portly, jolly, bustling Litvinov,' in the words of Nikolai Tolstoy, 'appeared a genuinely humane and civilized statesman ... in contrast to the bloody past of the Soviet regime.'[2] In November 1933 he went to Washington and agreement was reached with the new Roosevelt government on formal recognition of the USSR. The American change of heart came when they realized that the USSR might be useful in restraining Japanese expansion. Before the end of the year the Politburo voted in favour of collective security, and the following year the USSR became a member of the League of Nations. In May 1935 a Franco–Soviet pact of peace and friendship was signed and two weeks later a similar agreement was reached with Czechoslovakia.

At the same time the Comintern also began to change its policy, under the influence of the Bulgarian Communist leader, Georgi Dimitrov. He had gained an international reputation when he was arrested and tried in Germany on charges of involvement in the burning of the German Reichstag building in 1933. At his trial in Leipzig he defended himself so brilliantly that he was acquitted; when he arrived in Moscow early in 1934 he was greeted as a conquering hero, and was summoned to appear before the Politburo. He argued passionately that communists should work with social democrats against fascism; after some initial hesitation, Stalin seems to have decided that Dimitrov's ideas were at least worth a try. In April 1934 it was agreed that Dimitrov should become Secretary-General of the Comintern, with the promise of full support from the Politburo. The French communists did not wait for official instructions from the Comintern:

in July 1934 they signed an agreement with the French Socialist Party on a joint strategy against fascism and promised to stop criticizing each other. The rift in the French left had been healed and the new alliance of communists and social democrats soon became known as the Popular Front. The Comintern approved this new Popular Front strategy for all communist parties and it was adopted as official policy at the Seventh Congress of the Communist International in August 1935.

This new twin policy of collective security and the Popular Front did not please everybody in Soviet government and Comintern circles. Some members of the Comintern continued to believe that revolution was still a practicable possibility in central and western Europe and deplored the fact that the new strategy seemed to postpone it indefinitely. There was criticism of Litvinov's pacts with France and Czechoslovakia, two countries which, until recently, had been consistently denounced by the Soviets – France because it was capitalist and imperialist, and Czechoslovakia because it was a creation of the Versailles settlement which the USSR had always opposed. On close examination, the agreements seemed to be very weak affairs: although the USSR had promised to help its allies in case of 'an unprovoked attack on the part of a European state', this was only on condition that France acted first. Since the 'European state' in question was obviously Germany, this raised another problem: the USSR had no common frontier with either Germany or Czechoslovakia, so Soviet troops would have to pass through Poland or Romania in order to take any effective action. Neither state was likely to give permission for such action, especially since Poland had just signed the ten-year non-aggression pact with Germany. The capitalists were afraid of the threat from Germany, but they distrusted the communist USSR even more. Moreover, in some ways the twin policies even seemed to work against each other. As Jonathan Haslam explains: 'The very governments which Litvinov was so persistently attempting to win over in an alliance against Germany were the governments which looked with alarm at the Popular Front as a threat to their survival. As well as facilitating and complementing the policy of collective security, the Popular Front unfortunately also complicated and undermined the fulfilment of an already impossible task.'[3] Nevertheless, once Stalin had given his blessing to the new strategy, all open criticism was stifled.

(c) The failure of collective security

Sadly Litvinov's attempts to galvanize the Western powers into collective action against aggression ended in failure. Time and time again between 1935 and 1939, Britain and France failed to take decisive measures against acts of aggression by Italy, Germany and Japan. This was partly because their economic weakness made them desperate to avoid war, but it was also to some extent because they did not trust Stalin. Although Litvinov seemed convincing, British and French ruling circles found it difficult to believe that Stalin himself would be prepared to commit Soviet troops to fight alongside them to curb German aggression. For his part Stalin certainly distrusted the West: he suspected that they were planning either to involve the USSR in war with Germany, so that both communism and fascism would be weakened, or that they might form an alliance with Hitler aimed at destroying the USSR. Stalin's primary aim was to keep out of war and prevent the formation of a European alliance against the Soviet state, and it was for this reason that he continued Soviet trade contacts and discussions with Germany.

The catalogue of breaches of the Versailles settlement and acts of aggression began in March 1935 when Hitler announced the reintroduction of conscription in Germany. Britain, France and Italy protested at this violation of the peace agreement, but their solidarity was short-lived: in June 1935 the British, without consulting anybody else, signed a naval agreement with Hitler allowing the Germans to build submarines (another breach of Versailles) and a battle-fleet, provided this was limited to 35 per cent of the size of the British fleet. In October 1935 Mussolini launched an Italian invasion of Abyssinia (Ethiopia), against which the League of Nations offered only ineffective economic sanctions. In March 1936 Hitler sent German troops into the Rhineland, an area which had been demilitarized by Versailles; again Britain and France protested but took no action to expel the Germans. Encouraged by this series of limp responses, Hitler and Mussolini signed a pact of friendship known as the Berlin–Rome Axis (October 1936); the following month Hitler signed the Anti-Comintern Pact with Japan; Italy joined in 1937 and the three states pledged themselves to destroy communism. This opened up the possibility of a nightmare scenario for the USSR – a war on two fronts – which the Soviet army was in no state to cope with. When the Spanish Civil War broke out in 1936, Hitler and Mussolini sent help to the rebel right-wing forces of General Franco; the USSR sent help to the opposing republican government forces, but Britain and France refused to intervene and in 1939 the war ended in victory for Franco. Meanwhile in the Far East the Japanese advanced from Manchuria and by the autumn of 1938 had occupied a huge area of China as far south as Nanking and Shanghai. In Europe Hitler sent his forces to occupy Austria (March 1938) which was incorporated in Germany – a move specifically forbidden by Versailles. When no counter-measures were taken, Hitler began to look towards neighbouring Czechoslovakia for his next project.

The USSR's part in many of these events was minimal. In the case of Mussolini's invasion of Abyssinia, the USSR protested strongly and imposed economic sanctions banning the export of war materials to Italy. However, Britain and France, although they imposed some trade sanctions, carefully avoided a ban on vital goods such as oil and coal. This rendered all the sanctions ineffective, Mussolini consolidated his hold on Abyssinia, and the Russians were left complaining bitterly against 'British perfidy'. When German troops marched into the Rhineland in 1936, the French were best placed to send troops to clear the Germans out. Litvinov urged France to act, arguing that it was a question of preventing German hegemony over the whole continent of Europe. However, the British, anxious to keep on good terms with Hitler, pressurized the French to take no action, and the French government succumbed to Britain's wishes, in spite of their pact with the USSR. On every occasion it was the USSR which urged decisive action only to be let down primarily by the British with their policy of appeasing the aggressors, and by a weak France, which usually followed the British lead. When the Germans annexed Austria (an operation known as the *Anschluss*), Litvinov told the Politburo 'the seizure of Austria represents the most important event since the world war, fraught with the greatest dangers and not least for our Union;' Ivan Maisky, the Soviet ambassador in London, warned the British that Hitler's next target was clearly going to be Czechoslovakia; but no response was forthcoming, either from Stalin or the Western powers. During the Spanish Civil War even the Popular Front government in France failed to send help to the Spanish left. By March 1938 the USSR still had no reliable allies, and Litvinov's collective security policy seemed close to collapse.

The USSR's contradictory policies in Spain served to heighten the general distrust of Stalin and his motives. This was an example of the Soviet government and the Comintern carrying out their new policy of encouraging 'popular fronts' against fascist aggressors. Soviet agents went to Spain to help organize the pro-republican forces, and large amounts of military equipment were sent, although the republic was required to pay the USSR for its assistance. Stalin's motives were devious to say the least; the Spanish left was split between the communists and more extreme Trotskyites and anarchists, who were aiming for a complete socialist revolution at the expense of the 'bourgeois' republic. Stalin did not want this sort of revolutionary republican victory because he was afraid that it would frighten France and Britain into forming an anti-Soviet front with Germany. Consequently, he ordered the communists to fight for the 'bourgeois' republic and tried to curb the extremists. This was bitterly resented by the Trotskyites and anarchists, and in Barcelona in 1937 the communists ended up fighting and defeating the anarchists who were trying to take control of the republican government. This internal strife on the left contributed to the ultimate defeat of the republican forces in 1939. It is difficult to see what advantages the USSR gained from its intervention in Spain apart from getting its hands on the republic's gold reserves in payment for assistance. True, it demonstrated that the Soviet government was prepared to take military action, but in the main the policy succeeded only in confusing and alienating those on the political left in other countries who should have been sympathetic.

It was Hitler's designs on Czechoslovakia which brought the final collapse of collective security. Soon after the takeover of Austria in March 1938, Hitler began to demand an area known as the Sudetenland from Czechoslovakia. This was an area bordering on Germany and containing a large German minority, and it had been included in Czechoslovakia against the wishes of Germany by the Versailles settlement in 1919. Hitler threatened to use force against Czechoslovakia if necessary. The USSR, invoking the 1935 treaties with the Czechs and the French, made it clear that it would defend Czechoslovakia if the French also came to its aid; hints were also dropped that some sort of aid would be forthcoming even if the French did nothing. The Red Army began to prepare for action and some 90 divisions were mobilized; the Czechs also prepared to resist the threatened German invasion. However, both Britain and France were unwilling to go to war over Czechoslovakia and began to put pressure on the Czechs to give way to Hitler. As Maisky put it, British policy was directed 'not at curbing the aggressor, but at curbing the victim of aggression.'

In the midst of the Czech crisis there was more trouble for the USSR in the Far East, along the frontier with Japanese-occupied Manchuria. At the end of July 1938 Japanese forces launched an attack on the hills above Lake Khasan, which were an important surveillance point occupied by Soviet troops. After some sharp exchanges lasting just over a week, in which the Japanese failed to make any headway, a cease-fire was agreed on 11 August. The Russians apparently had intelligence information that the Japanese government was merely testing Soviet resolve and had no intention of escalating the conflict into an open war. The Soviet government made great propaganda use of their success, emphasizing the strength of their forces and pointing out the value of showing firmness and the will to resist aggressors. In September Soviet troops began to move up to the frontier with Poland which was also now demanding territory from Czechoslovakia. But it made no difference to the attitudes of Britain and France: British Prime Minister Neville Chamberlain was determined to pursue his policy of appeasing Hitler, and suggested a conference, an offer which Hitler accepted. On 30 September 1938 the conference was held in Munich, attended by Chamberlain, Daladier (the French Prime Minister), Mussolini and Hitler. The Russians were not invited and not even consulted; even the Czech representatives took no part in the discussions. It was agreed that the Sudetenland was to be handed over to Germany and that if the Czechs refused, they would receive no help from Britain and France when the Germans invaded. In the end the USSR was spared having to decide whether or not to act alone – the Czechs felt they had little choice but to accept the conference decision, and there was no further question of resistance to Hitler.

There has been much speculation as to whether Stalin would have supported the Czechs if they had decided to reject the conference ultimatum. There is some evidence, though it is not entirely conclusive, that Stalin did intend to take some action. As well as the troops already on the Polish frontier, a further 330,000 Soviet reservists were called up, and leave cancelled in all military districts west of the Urals; 700 aircraft were offered to the Czech government; even Romania agreed, after some pressure, to allow the passage of 100,000 Soviet troops to go to the aid of Czechoslovakia.[4] It may all have been a huge bluff, but from the latest military memoirs to appear, it seems certain that Soviet troops would have moved against Poland if the Poles had attacked Czechoslovakia. As to Germany, Stalin himself was probably undecided on exactly what action to take. The Munich settlement came as a great shock to the Russians who felt betrayed by the West. Stalin was convinced that it was part of a conspiracy by all the anti-Soviet nations of Europe to encourage Hitler to turn eastwards and to give him a free hand to destroy the now isolated Soviet Union. Collective security had failed and neither Litvinov nor Stalin knew which way to turn next. For a time the Soviet government seemed to be retreating into isolation, but it wasn't long before dramatic events precipitated by Hitler changed the international situation again.

(d) The Nazi–Soviet Pact and the outbreak of war in Europe

In March 1939 German troops occupied the Czech capital, Prague, and the provinces of Bohemia and Moravia, and the eastern province of Slovakia was declared an independent state, but in effect became a German puppet state. These actions provoked a sudden change in the attitude of the British who were outraged that Hitler, without any negotiations, had seized territory not inhabited by Germans, the neutrality of which he had promised to respect at Munich. Chamberlain now abandoned his appeasement policy and began to sound out the USSR, Poland, Yugoslavia, Turkey, Greece and Romania as to whether they would support Britain and France in action against any further German aggression. Suddenly collective security seemed to be on the cards again; however, when Litvinov responded by proposing an immediate conference in Bucharest to discuss common action, Chamberlain rejected the idea as 'premature'. On 17 April the USSR offered to sign an alliance with Britain and France, to guarantee the integrity of every state from the Baltic to the Mediterranean. Again the two Western powers hardly responded, evidently assuming that Stalin was not sincere, but also probably because they were unwilling to guarantee the Baltic states. In fact there was a problem: the Poles refused to sign any agreement which also included the USSR; they hated the Soviet government and would rather fight Germany alone than accept 'help' from the USSR which might turn into a permanent occupation; they were afraid that co-operation with the USSR might provoke Hitler, who was now making territorial demands on Poland. At the end of March Chamberlain announced that Britain and France would help the Poles if any action threatened their independence and the Poles felt it vital to resist. However, the British and French realized that it would be impossible for them to offer any effective help to Poland without Soviet co-operation, and so they continued to work for an agreement with the USSR, even though they had doubts about Soviet military capability and trustworthiness. Another advantage of such an agreement was that it would presumably prevent a pact between Stalin and Hitler. Ironically, Hitler had also decided to seek an agreement with the USSR, even if only a temporary one, in order to isolate Poland and thwart Britain and France. In April 1939, in a major speech on foreign affairs, Hitler omitted his usual tirade against the Soviet Union. The USSR, instead of being an outcast nation, suddenly found itself eagerly wooed by both opposing blocs in Europe. It was no doubt in order to cope better with this new situation that Stalin decided to have a change of Foreign Minister. According to Donald Watt, 'a new man was needed, more senior, closer to Stalin, hard, obstinate, unclubbable, uncharmable, a man to keep everything in his own hands, a man capable of calculated obtuseness or deliberate rudeness if necessary.'[5] On 3 May 1939 the pro-Western and Jewish Litvinov was dismissed and replaced by Vyacheslav Molotov, Stalin's right-hand man since 1917.

Throughout the summer of 1939 the Western powers and Germany continued negotiations with the USSR. Stalin may well have preferred an alliance with Britain and France, but pinning them down proved difficult. The British Foreign Minister was invited to Moscow but when a negotiating team eventually went to the USSR, it contained nobody of cabinet rank and no leading military figure; the most senior member was a military attaché, Admiral Drax, who had not been given any bargaining powers and had to keep contacting the Foreign Office. The lack of urgency was shown by the fact that instead of flying directly to Moscow, they travelled by slow passenger boat which took five days to get to Leningrad. Although progress had already been made on political matters, the talks soon stalled when it came to military details. In spite of strong pressure from the French and British, the Poles expressed the most extreme distrust of the Russians and refused point blank to allow Soviet troops to cross Polish territory to take up positions on the Polish frontier with Germany, although it was obvious to the whole of Europe that Hitler was preparing to invade Poland in the near future. Since the British and French had no specific military plans of their own to bring aid to Poland, the talks broke up on 21 August without any agreement. Britain and France seemed so irresolute that Stalin and Molotov could not imagine either of them standing by their guarantee to help Poland.

Developments were pointing more and more to an agreement with Germany, especially since during the summer there was further trouble with the Japanese in the Far East. In May 1939 Japanese forces occupied Mongolian territory right on the frontier with the USSR, and early in August they were planning a new offensive. An understanding with Germany would relieve the USSR of the fear of an attack in the west and leave Soviet forces free to take a more active role against the Japanese. Stalin began to respond to Germany's overtures and it was arranged that the German Foreign Minister, Ribbentrop, should come to Moscow. When Stalin, Molotov and Ribbentrop met on 23 August, it soon became apparent that the Germans were prepared to make major concessions; by the end of the day they had drawn up a Nazi–Soviet Non-Aggression Treaty in which the two states pledged themselves for the next ten years to avoid war with each other and to increase trade – the USSR buying more German machinery and supplying Germany with more coal and oil. But it was the secret clauses in the agreement which were the most explosive: in effect they agreed to partition Poland, the eastern section coming under Soviet control and the western part under Germany. As for the Baltic states, Lithuania was to be taken by Germany, and Estonia, Latvia and Finland by the USSR, which was also to be allowed to take Bessarabia, given to Romania in 1918. This was a triumph for Stalin: the USSR was about to recover all the territory lost in 1917–18 and that taken by Poland in 1920, plus more of Poland. Hitler was pleased with the Pact because it meant that he could go ahead with his invasion of Poland knowing that no help would be forthcoming for the Poles from the USSR; Ribbentrop assured him that the British and French guarantees to Poland would no longer count.

The announcement of the Nazi–Soviet Pact caused consternation in the capitals of Europe. The unthinkable had happened – the two bitter ideological arch-enemies had shelved their differences and come together. In London, however, the resolve of the British government to honour its guarantee to Poland remained strong. It was the Japanese who reacted with the greatest dismay, feeling humiliated and betrayed by their ally in the Anti-Comintern Pact. At the same time Soviet forces, commanded by General Georgi Zhukhov and using tanks for the first time in Russian military history, inflicted a heavy defeat on the Japanese in Mongolia. On 15 September a ceasefire was agreed. For the time being the USSR could feel safe from invasion on both eastern and western fronts.

Having secured the neutrality of the USSR, Hitler wasted no time: on 1 September German forces invaded Poland; Britain and France sent an ultimatum ordering them to withdraw, and when this was rejected, Britain and France declared war on Germany. Hitler was surprised by this unexpected decisiveness, though after some initial hysterics, he calmed down since he could not imagine what action they could possibly take to save Poland. On 17 September, with the frontier in the Far East now secured, Soviet troops invaded and occupied their allotted parts of Poland. The Poles were defeated and on 27 September the USSR and Germany signed a formal agreement dividing Poland between them. Stalin assured Ribbentrop personally that he would never break the pact between their two countries. A second agreement was reached over the future of Lithuania which Hitler conceded could now come into the Soviet sphere instead of Germany's. Control of Lithuania was seen as vitally important by Stalin because it would enable the Russians to block the entrance to the route around the Baltic towards Leningrad. All three Baltic states – Lithuania, Latvia and Estonia – were soon pressured into signing mutual defence treaties which allowed the USSR to base troops on their territory.

Frontier talks were also taking place between the USSR and Finland. Stalin was concerned about the vulnerability of Leningrad, since the border with Finland was only some 18 miles to the north-west of the city. In October 1939 Stalin put some proposals to the Finns: the existing frontier should be moved 25 miles further away from Leningrad; the USSR should take over the islands in the Gulf of Finland and lease the port of Hanko (to the west of Helsinki) which could be used as a Russian naval base to control the entrance to the Gulf of Finland; in return the USSR would give Finland a large bloc of territory further north. Although these demands were not entirely unreasonable, the Finns were nervous that once the Russian forces gained access there would be no way of controlling them. Stalin's proposals were rejected and consequently Soviet troops invaded Finland on 30 November, expecting an easy victory. But the Finnish army was far better equipped for a winter war than the Russians, whose first invasion attempt was driven back with heavy losses. Time and again massed attacks by Soviet infantry on defensive strongpoints were driven back with heavy losses because the preceding artillery bombardment had been ineffective. Stalin was forced to rethink the campaign: he appointed Timoshenko as commander and gave him the full resources of the Red Army; in January 1940 the Soviet army launched a massive artillery bombardment of the Finnish defences known as the Mannerheim Line and then threw nearly a thousand tanks and 140,000 men into the attack. Even then it took almost three weeks before the Finns were forced to withdraw. It had not been a total rout, but the Finns were exhausted and running out of men. A settlement was reached in March 1940 in which the Finns agreed to hand over much more than Stalin had originally demanded: a larger slice of territory to the north of Leningrad including the north-eastern shore of Lake Ladoga, the city of Viborg and the port of Hanko; however, the Finns were allowed to keep their independence. The Winter War with Finland was in reality a mixed success for Stalin. The Red Army's performance had been far from impressive and over 200,000 men had been lost against 25,000 Finns killed. The Commissar for Defence, Kliment Voroshilov, was replaced by Semyon Timoshenko, who was at least an efficient organizer and was determined to make the Red Army into a professional, rather than just a revolutionary force. The German General Staff took careful note of events, and came to the conclusion that the Red Army, in spite of its huge size, would be no match for their well-trained and well-equipped army with its superior leadership. It probably helped to convince Hitler that no Slav army could stand up to the racially superior Germans. In the words of Alan Bullock, 'Nothing did more to convince him in 1941 that he was justified in gambling on defeating the Russians in a single campaign than their performance against the Finns.'[6]

Stalin was in no mood to put up with any more resistance; in July 1940 the governments of Lithuania, Latvia and Estonia were ordered to request their incorporation into the USSR as new Soviet republics. Since the alternative was to be invaded by the Red Army anyway, the governments complied. In the same month Stalin annexed Bessarabia from Romania, which had been promised him in the Nazi–Soviet Pact; he also annexed northern Bukovina from Romania, which had not been included in the agreement. Having been incorporated into the USSR the inhabitants of these territories found themselves reorganized along Soviet lines: industry, land, trade, banks and mines were nationalized and a start was made on collectivization. But the process was carried out with great brutality, especially in eastern Poland where Russians, Ukrainians and Belorussians took revenge for grievances suffered during the 20 years of Polish rule. In all the territories leading people were arrested – intelligentsia, politicians, landowners, businessmen, clergy, teachers and army officers – and either executed or sent to labour camps. The aim was to eliminate everybody who might possibly have organized resistance to the Soviet takeover. The Poles were especially hated because they had tried to exploit the exhaustion of the Red Army towards the end of the Civil War in 1920 by invading the Ukraine; this 'treachery' still rankled with the Soviet leaders 20 years later. The most notorious case was that of 15,000 Polish reservist officers, all professionals of various types, who were arrested by the NKVD in September 1939 and sent to labour camps in western Russia. Nothing further was heard about them after May 1940, but in April 1943 the German invaders uncovered over 4000 bodies in a camp at Katyn near Smolensk. The Russians claimed that it was the Germans themselves who had killed them, but the Germans consistently denied this. In 1989 the Soviet government finally admitted that the Russians had indeed executed all 15,000.

Meanwhile Hitler's war was going brilliantly for the Germans; in the spring of 1940 their forces overwhelmed Denmark, Norway, Belgium, Luxembourg and the Netherlands. By 15 June they had defeated France; only the British were left still undefeated in the west and even they had been forced to evacuate their troops from the European mainland at Dunkirk. It seemed only a matter of time before they too were eliminated. However, Hitler soon suffered his first major setback: in the Battle of Britain throughout the late summer of 1940, the RAF gradually got the better of the German *Luftwaffe*. Hitler dared not begin his planned invasion of Britain without superiority in the air; in mid-September he decided to postpone it for the time being and turned his attention eastwards again. Hitler's quick victories were a stunning blow for Stalin, who was hoping that the war in the west would drag on like the First World War; he expected the Germans to win eventually, but thought they would be too exhausted to think about attacking Russia for several years. Tensions were already beginning to show in the Nazi–Soviet alliance: Hitler, annoyed at Stalin's annexation of Bukovina, decided to intervene in the Balkans himself and sent troops into Romania. At a meeting in Berlin in November 1940 the Germans tried, without success, to persuade Molotov to switch Soviet expansion in the direction of India and Central Asia, leaving the Balkans as a largely German sphere of influence.

In fact Hitler had already made the decision at the end of July 1940 for an attack on the USSR in the spring of 1941. For years he had been thinking vaguely about a war to win *Lebensraum* (living space) for the Germans in the east. Euphoric at his successes in western Europe, he now made grandiose plans to seize the entire area right up to the Urals. Some of the population would be kept as slaves for the master race, while the rest of the Soviet people would be allowed a 'homeland' east of the Urals. Once the Soviet Union was defeated, Britain would quickly be subdued. By 18 December Hitler had approved plans for the invasion of the USSR, code-named Operation Barbarossa, to be launched in May 1941 (Document A). In the event the invasion was delayed for a month because Hitler was sidetracked into helping out his ally Mussolini, who was trying to build up an Italian empire in the Balkans and expand Italian territory in North Africa. Italian troops invaded Greece and Egypt, but quickly ran into difficulties, and German troops had to be sent to help in both areas. On 5 April Yugoslavia signed a non-aggression pact with the USSR, much to the annoyance of Hitler who immediately declared war on Yugoslavia. By the end of April German forces had defeated both Greece and Yugoslavia and occupied Bulgaria. Final preparations could now be made for the invasion of the USSR, and the date was fixed: the early hours of 22 June. After the abysmal showing of the Soviet forces in the war with Finland, Hitler was convinced that the USSR would be crushed in a short campaign: 'we have only to kick in the door and the whole rotten structure will come crashing down,' he told General Jodl. The target was Moscow; but in the words of Martin Gilbert: 'although the day was to come when the tall spires of the Kremlin were to be visible through the binoculars of his front line commanders, Moscow was never to be his, and his march to Moscow, Napoleon's downfall in 1812, was to lead, through suffering and destruction, to the end of all Hitler's plans, and, within four years, to the downfall of his Reich.'[7]

7.2   The USSR at war, 1941–45

(a) Stalin and the USSR unprepared

Hitler had gathered an awesome invasion force along the frontiers with the Soviet Union: 5.5 million troops, 2800 tanks, 5000 aircraft and 47,000 pieces of artillery. At 3.15 on the morning of 22 June 1941, Operation Barbarossa began. German bombers attacked 66 Soviet airfields, destroying hundreds of aircraft on the ground; several important cities including Minsk, Odessa and Sevastopol were bombed, and the German army entered the USSR along a front stretching almost a thousand miles. The Soviet forces facing them had not been placed on alert and had been given orders not to respond to provocation; although Stalin was informed within 15 minutes about the start of the invasion, he rejected requests for permission to respond, apparently believing that Hitler was simply trying to provoke the USSR; it was only at 6.30 am that he gave orders to retaliate. Gradually over the next few days the scale of the catastrophe became apparent: on the first day almost a thousand Soviet aircraft were destroyed; by the end of the fifth day the Germans had captured Dvinsk, 185 miles inside the border, and had seized the road and rail bridges over the River Dvina. All along the front no steps had been taken to destroy important bridges, and although the frontier had been moved westwards after the incorporation of parts of Poland into the USSR, no effective fortifications had been put in place along the new frontier, while some of the fortress defences along the old frontier had been dismantled.

Yet Stalin had been given plenty of warning during the preceding weeks of an impending German invasion. As early as January 1941 the American Under Secretary of State, Sumner Welles, gave a warning to the Soviet ambassador in Washington, based on information picked up in Berlin, that the Germans intended to attack in May or June. Churchill had sent Stalin a message on 3 April that an attack was imminent, and Anthony Eden, the British Foreign Secretary, told Soviet ambassador Maisky the same thing in London at least five times between April and June. The British intelligence service had even passed on to Moscow, via a Soviet spy-ring in Switzerland, the correct date of the invasion and exact details of where attacks would take place. If Stalin did not trust British and American sources, similar information was arriving in Moscow from other informants. The most remarkable was Richard Sorge, a German communist and intelligence agent based in Tokyo, who was acting as a Soviet spy. He was on close terms with the German ambassador in Tokyo, Hermann Ott, who kept him supplied with all the latest military and diplomatic information. On 5 March Sorge informed Moscow that the Germans planned to attack in mid-June; he continued to send a stream of reports adding more details until a week before the actual invasion, when he gave the date and the dispositions of the nine German armies which would be involved. At about the same time the German ambassador in Moscow, Count von Schulenburg, who was no supporter of Hitler, and was against the idea of war between the two states, warned his Soviet counterpart of the impending attack on 22 June. Stalin's own intelligence forces reported on 5 May about the ominous build-up of German troops close to the border with the USSR: 'Military preparations are going forward openly in Poland. German officers and soldiers speak openly of the coming war between Germany and the Soviet Union as a matter already decided. The war is expected to start after the completion of spring planting.' At the end of May came reports that the Germans were moving all civilians out of border areas, and on 6 June the German border guards were replaced by field troops. The signs and the warnings multiplied daily until by 21 June, in the words of Harrison Salisbury, 'the preparations for attack could hardly have been overlooked by a ten-year old child.'[8]

All the evidence seems to suggest, however, that in spite of so much advance warning, Stalin was stunned and devastated by the German attack. He could not believe that Hitler would risk invading the USSR before Britain had been decisively defeated, because it would mean a repeat of the fatal scenario – a war on two fronts – which had led to Germany's defeat in the First World War. He was under no illusions that the Nazi–Soviet Pact would last for anything like its full ten years; he told an audience of young officers on 5 May that war was certain to come, but that he hoped to stave it off until 1942. On 6 June he approved a detailed plan for switching Soviet industry over to war production by the end of 1942.

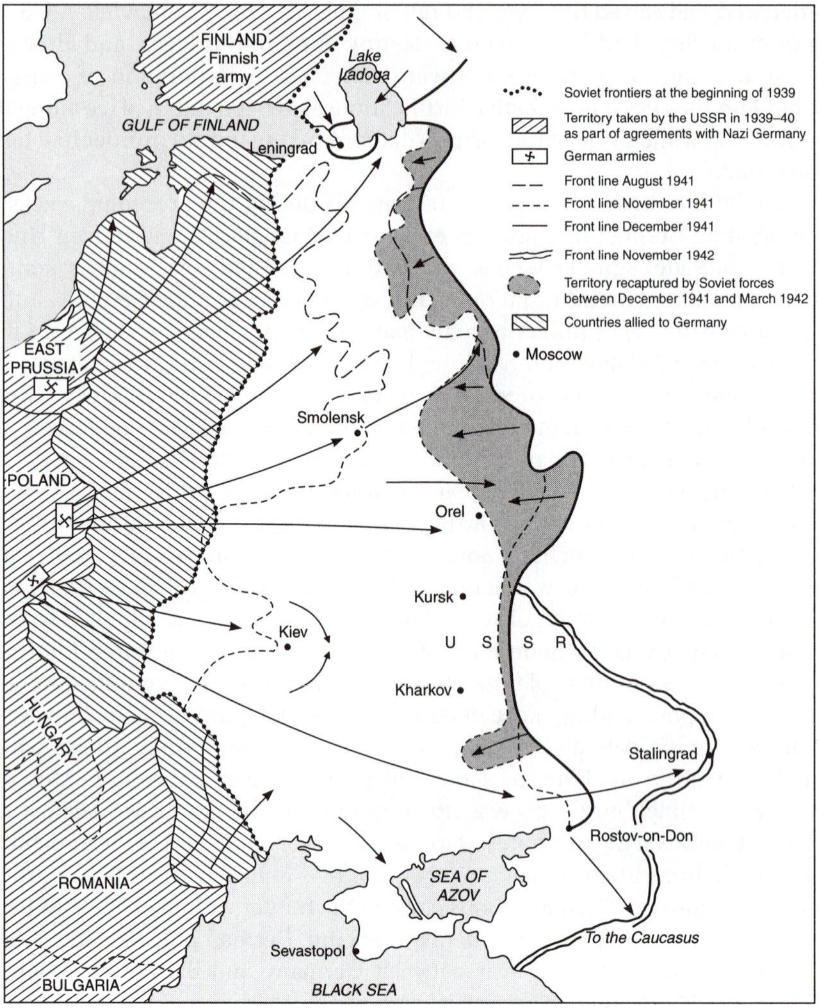
FINLAND
Finnish army
Lake Ladoga
GULF OF FINLAND
Leningrad
Soviet frontiers at the beginning of 1939
Territory taken by the USSR in 1939–40 as part of agreements with Nazi Germany
German armies
Front line August 1941
Front line November 1941
Front line December 1941
Front line November 1942
Territory recaptured by Soviet forces between December 1941 and March 1942
Countries allied to Germany
Moscow
EAST PRUSSIA
Smolensk
POLAND
Orel
Kursk
Kiev
U S S R
Kharkov
HUNGARY
Stalingrad
Rostov-on-Don
SEA OF AZOV
ROMANIA
To the Caucasus
Sevastopol
BULGARIA
BLACK SEA

Map 7.1 **The German invasion of the USSR.**

This terrible catastrophe which befell the people of the USSR in June 1941 has naturally been one of the most controversial and sensitive topics in Soviet historiography. How could Stalin possibly have been so mistaken about the timing of the German invasion? Did he actually see and read the intelligence reports? And if he did, why did he not take more decisive action? The evidence suggests that Stalin did indeed receive and read the reports, although they were edited to some extent by the General Staff Intelligence Administration, but that he ignored information which did not fit in with his own theories and beliefs. However, it seems likely that he did not show all of them to his military chiefs who were kept very much in the dark. One strand of his thinking was that Britain was the real enemy of the USSR; ever since the British had intervened in the Civil War, Stalin suspected that they were just waiting for a suitable opportunity to destroy the Soviet Union. Their betrayal of Czechoslovakia at Munich and their reluctance to sign an alliance with the USSR in the summer of 1939 convinced him that they had not changed. During the Soviet–Finnish War there were plans to send 50,000 British and French troops via northern Norway to help the Finns, and Stalin was genuinely worried about the possibility of British bombing raids on Leningrad. Even after the defeat of Finland the British Chiefs of Staff prepared a report exploring the possible options of an attack on the USSR, for example, raids on her oil installations in the Caucasus. In March and April 1940 British reconnaissance flights were made over the oil towns of Baku and Batum revealing that Baku had virtually no anti-aircraft defences. In conversation between the British and French Prime Ministers, there was mention of 15 May as a possible date for an aerial attack on Baku. The Germans were depending heavily on the USSR continuing to supply them with oil; a few well-directed air attacks from bases in Iraq could put the Soviet oil industry out of action and deal a severe blow at both countries.[9] There was no attack on 15 May, and after the fall of France in June 1940 the British abandoned the idea; but there is no doubt that information about British plans was passed on to Stalin's intelligence services by Gestapo agents. By this time Winston Churchill, a sworn enemy of communism, was British Prime Minister, and Stalin completely distrusted any information which emanated from British or American sources. He believed that Churchill would stoop to anything to bring the USSR into the war against Germany. When Rudolph Hess suddenly flew to Scotland on 10 May 1941 to try and negotiate peace, Stalin was convinced that Hess had been invited over by the British secret service to work out plans for a joint British and German attack on the Soviet Union.

The other main strand in Stalin's thinking was rather confused: he believed that although war with Germany was inevitable in the end, it would not come until 1942, and perhaps not even then if Britain was still undefeated. British and American warnings he saw as attempts to get the Russians to take some sort of defensive measures which would upset Hitler and provoke him to attack. This is why Stalin continued to give the strictest possible orders that his forces must avoid any action that could be interpreted as provocation. For the same reason he scrupulously kept the Soviet side of the agreement with the Nazis, actually stepping up supplies of wheat and oil which continued right up until the invasion; the last Russian goods train carrying supplies crossed the border into Germany at midnight on 21 June. By the end of the first week in June 1941 Stalin felt certain that there would be no attack that year simply because the huge distances that the German armies would have to cover would make it impossible for them to complete the conquest of the USSR before the winter set in. Stalin seemed confident that the Red Army was strong enough to repel the invaders; even if they penetrated deeply, their lines of communication would become impossibly long and they would eventually suffer the same fate as Napoleon's Grand Army in 1812. Yet Stalin *was* perturbed at the German troop build-up in the western part of Poland; how could that be explained away? Evidence suggests that Stalin genuinely believed that Hitler was building up threatening military pressure on the Soviet Union as a bluff or blackmail, as a preliminary for some new demands for economic or territorial concessions; when these were eventually presented Stalin would be able to negotiate with Hitler and reach a satisfactory agreement, as they had done earlier, and war would be avoided. Another possibility considered by Stalin was that it was the German generals who wanted to provoke war with the USSR; in that case there was no need to worry because Hitler himself would make sure that it did not happen in 1941. Stalin even wrote a personal letter to Hitler saying how surprised he was by the German military preparations which gave the impression that Hitler was preparing to attack the USSR. Hitler sent a personal letter back explaining, in confidence, that troops were being concentrated in Poland so that they would be safe from the heavy British bombing of western and central Germany. He gave his word of honour as head of state that he would keep the Pact. According to General Zhukov, Stalin believed this explanation.[10] Why Stalin felt he could trust Hitler remains a mystery – he certainly trusted nobody else. Once Stalin had made his mind up it was usually impossible for the people around him to make him change it. And Stalin had made up his mind that Hitler could be trusted; Hitler had told him, in confidence, that he would honour the Nazi–Soviet Pact; therefore there would be no war in 1941. This made it extremely difficult for his subordinates to make preparations to meet an attack without risking the wrath of Stalin – and they all knew what that could mean.

During Khrushchev's period of de-Stalinization in the late 1950s and early 1960s (see section 8.1(b)), a great deal of evidence came out about Stalin's mistakes in the period leading up to the German invasion. According to Admiral Kuznetsov in his memoirs, Stalin fully expected war with Germany and regarded the Nazi–Soviet Pact as a ploy to gain time for further preparation. His mistake was in overestimating the length of time he had available to make these preparations. Another of Kuznetsov's criticisms of Stalin was his secretiveness – most of the top officers in the Red Army had no idea what the strategic plans were in case of a sudden attack, or even whether any such plans existed. The people immediately surrounding Stalin were so dominated by him that they were not used to taking any initiatives and dared not challenge his authority. Soviet historian A.M. Nekrich in his book *22 June 1941*, published in 1965 under the auspices of the Marxism–Leninism Institute, laid the blame for Russia's lack of preparedness entirely on Stalin; it wasn't that Stalin ignored the warnings being presented to him, he simply put the wrong interpretation on them and refused to believe that there would be any invasion before the spring of 1942; this, argued Nekrich, showed how completely out of touch Stalin was with the real world. Very soon though, the climate of Soviet thinking changed again. Khrushchev had already fallen from power in 1964, and Stalin gradually began to be rehabilitated. To begin with, military leaders and historians were encouraged to write memoirs and articles about Stalin's role as war leader; they were not forbidden to make fair criticisms, but the main point of the exercise was to encourage a positive evaluation of Stalin's contribution. Nekrich's work, which had been well reviewed both in the USSR and in the eastern European countries and recommended to the general public, now came under attack. His book was discussed at a conference of historians who came to the conclusion that it was 'politically harmful'. Nekrich himself was severely censured and expelled from the Communist Party in June 1967 and his book was banned. The new official line was put by another historian, G.A. Deborin, who claimed that although Stalin had certainly made mistakes and reached false conclusions, this was because he had received false information. 'Stalin's estimate of German intentions was endorsed by those around him. So Stalin cannot be considered solely responsible for his mistakes.'[11]

With the coming of Gorbachev's *glasnost* and the subsequent collapse of communism in the USSR, Stalin's reputation came under attack once more. Dmitri Volkogonov was scathing about Stalin's miscalculations which 'stemmed from his personal rule. It is hard to blame the Commissars of the Chief War Council when their boss's image was that of the wise and infallible leader ... To please Stalin, everyone talked about the "invincibility of the Red Army" ... Zhukov probably put it best when he said that all Stalin's actions and thoughts on the eve of the war were subordinated to the single effort to avoid war, and this generated in him the certain belief that it would not occur.' Zhukov also made the point that Stalin resisted all attempts by the military leadership to put the troops on alert on the western front for fear of provoking Hitler. As Volkogonov comments, 'one can understand the desire not to give Hitler an excuse to attack, but he can hardly have imagined that Hitler would attack if provoked, if invasion of the USSR did not already figure in his plans.[12]

On the other hand, there were still some Russian historians who felt this interpretation was too simplistic. In 1990 a book called *Icebreaker: Who Started the Second World War?* was published in English; written by Viktor Suvorov, who had defected to Britain from Soviet Military Intelligence, the book claimed that Stalin had intended to attack Germany first, on 6 July 1941. Hitler's invasion of the USSR in June was a 'preventive war' to forestall Stalin. Some German historians eagerly seized on this theory since it enabled them to portray Hitler's invasion as a justifiable action designed to save western Europe from communism. The book caused a sensation in the USSR; in 1995 a collection of essays was published based on the latest evidence and generally supporting Suvorov's interpretation. For instance in his speech to the officer graduates on 5 May 1941, Stalin had this to say: 'Now that we have reconstructed our army, built up sufficient technology for contemporary warfare, become strong – now is the time to move from the defensive to the offensive. We have to move from defence to a policy of attack. The Red Army is a modern army, and a modern army is an offensive army.' Zhukov was also thinking along the same lines, or so he claimed in his memoirs; on 15 May he sent a note to Stalin proposing that 'we deprive the German command of their initiative by forestalling their forces during deployment, by attacking them at the moment they are at the deployment stage.' More recently, two Russian historians, Gabriel Gorodetzky and Dmitri Volkogonov, have both dismissed the theory. In his last book, *The Rise and Fall of the Soviet Empire*, published in 1998, Volkogonov argued that although the possibility that Stalin *was* planning to attack Hitler first cannot be ruled out, there is absolutely no evidence or documentation that he intended to do it in July 1941. Nor was there any evidence to show how Stalin had reacted to Zhukov's note. 'It was impossible to contemplate a large-scale offensive against Germany without a detailed and documented operational analysis, without creating the necessary army groupings and many other undertakings. It would be possible to send a unit into battle on verbal orders only, but never a multi-million-man army. If Stalin was planning to attack Hitler first, he must have been planning to do it later.'[13] The latest British thoughts on the question have come from John Erickson, in an article in *History Today*, marking the 60th anniversary of the invasion. 'The Suvorov fantasies, fictions and inventions,' he concludes, 'do not bear comparison with a horrendous reality.'[14]

Wherever the blame lies, it seems indisputable that the USSR was not in a state of preparedness for the German invasion which began on 22 June 1941. True, the Russians had been rearming since the beginning of the First Five-Year Plan and had spent huge amounts of money on it, but as Mark Harrison points out, 'because the Soviet rearmament pattern aimed at some future war, it was never ready for war in the present. Changing forecasts and expectations meant that military plans were always under revision. The armed forces were always in the midst of re-equipment and reorganization. Military products already in mass production were always on the verge of obsolescence; defence industries were always half-way through re-training and re-tooling.'[15] During the Spanish Civil War, for example, Soviet weapons and aircraft were obviously inferior to those produced in Germany. However, the 20 months of extra preparation time gained by the Nazi–Soviet Pact had not been wasted; in fact some estimates reckon that defence output doubled and the size of the Red Army trebled during that period. By June 1941 there were some 5.5 million men in uniform, and every month

Figure 7.1   German soldiers execute five young men from Velizh, Smolensk district, suspected of being partisans, summer 1942.

industry was managing to produce 230 tanks, 700 military aircraft, 4000 guns and mortars, over 100,000 rifles and more than a million shells.

These statistics look encouraging but the overall picture was not nearly so impressive. A large proportion of the troops were untrained and were using obsolete weapons, and most of the tanks were obsolete. The most up-to-date tanks were only just coming into mass production in June 1941, and it was a similar story with aircraft – the new YAK-1 and MiG-3 fighters. The army command had not recovered from the purges of 1937–38 when all the most experienced generals and officers had been executed. Their immature and inexperienced replacements obediently accepted Stalin's view of military strategy, which was quite simply that if the Germans attacked, the Red Army would immediately plug any breaches of the defences that the Germans might make, and then it would drive them out and 'crush the enemy on his territory;' it would be a short war and an easy victory. Those who had suggested that German forces might be strong enough to penetrate deeply and that therefore plans should be made for defence in depth in the interior, had been accused of being in league with the enemy; many had been shot and others were still in prison. Stalin seemed so confident that obvious precautions were ignored; discussion had taken place about relocating armaments factories much further eastwards, but very little had actually been done; work had started on fortifying the newly annexed territories in the west, but there was no sense of urgency. Advisers suggested that supply dumps should be moved further eastwards, beyond the Volga; Stalin ordered that they should be concentrated in the frontier areas, where the Germans captured them in the first few weeks. Stalin was responsible for another strategic mistake: his military advisers told him that Hitler was likely to head straight for Moscow, since his earlier campaigns had been won by making straight for the capital of the country under attack. This would mean that the main German thrust would be in the direction of Minsk and Smolensk. However, Stalin believed that the south-west was the most likely area to attract Hitler so that he could get his hands on Ukraine's wheat and the coal of the Donbass. The defence plans were designed according to Stalin's wishes; although all available military intelligence suggested that the Germans were preparing to direct three-quarters of their attacking forces towards Smolensk and Moscow, none of the generals dared argue with Stalin, with the result that 25 Soviet divisions were switched to the south-western front. This made the German advance easier: on 9 July they captured Minsk and on 16 July they began to surround the city of Smolensk, half-way between Minsk and Moscow. In fairness, it has be said that some preparations to meet an attack had been made, but they were the wrong preparations.

(b) The USSR in retreat – June to December 1941

Some reports say that Stalin was so devastated by the invasion that he suffered a nervous collapse and left it to Molotov to broadcast to the Soviet people, telling them that the war had begun. The vast majority of ordinary people were stunned by the news, since for nearly two years government propaganda had been telling them about the great achievement of the Nazi–Soviet Pact and the power of the

Red Army. Stalin shut himself away in his dacha, and when Molotov and a group of Politburo members went to see him to find out what to do next, he was afraid they had come to arrest him. This was the perfect opportunity for them to get rid of him, but nobody seems to have thought of that as a serious option; they evidently thought he was indispensable. Molotov proposed the formation of a small group able to take quick decisions, and this idea was accepted. On 23 June a Main Headquarters known as the Stavka (as in Tsarist days) was set up and Stalin became chairman of the State Defence Committee. By early August he had taken the title of Supreme Commander of the Armed Forces, and had replaced Timoshenko as Commissar for Defence. He quickly pulled himself together sufficiently to broadcast to the nation on 3 July. 'Comrades! Citizens! Brothers and sisters! My friends,' he began. 'A grave threat hangs over our country; this war with fascist Germany is not simply a war between two armies, but a total war of the whole Soviet people against German–fascist forces. The goal of this great patriotic war against the fascist oppressors is not only to liquidate the danger hanging over our country, but to help all the peoples of Europe groaning under the yoke of German fascism.' He went on to appeal to the people to form partisan units behind the lines, to blow up bridges and roads, damage telephone and telegraph lines, and set fire to forests, stores and transports. 'The enemy and all his accomplices must be hounded and annihilated at every step' (Document D). According to Volkogonov, the speech had a powerful effect, boosting people's confidence in Stalin and in the possibility of ultimate victory.[16]

The first five months of the war were one long disaster for the USSR. Time after time Soviet troops were encircled by the Germans and forced to surrender. The main invasion consisted of a three-pronged attack: Army Group North was heading for Leningrad, Army Group Centre had Moscow as its target, and Army Group South was aiming for Ukraine and ultimately the oilfields of the Caucasus. The Germans were using a new type of warfare known as *Blitzkrieg*, which had been spectacularly successful in the west. It involved air strikes to soften up the enemy, followed by rapid tank and artillery attacks. The invasion on the central front made the most rapid progress: on 27 June the Germans captured Minsk, the capital of Belorussia, and eventually over 550,000 Soviet troops were encircled in that area and forced to surrender. A month later the encirclement of Smolensk was completed and a further 100,000 troops were taken prisoner. By 1 September Leningrad was completely cut off from the rest of Russia, except for the route across Lake Ladoga and the link by air, and the city began an appalling 900-day siege in which over 800,000 of its citizens died from starvation, disease and German shelling. Meanwhile on the southern front Kiev, capital of Ukraine, was captured on 16 September, and another 600,000 prisoners were taken.

The Germans might have advanced even further if Hitler had not kept on switching strategies. He and many of his generals suffered from over-confidence; General Halder wrote in his diary as early as 3 July: 'It is no exaggeration to say that the campaign against Russia has been won in 14 days.' So confident was Hitler that on 14 July he ordered a reduction in the number of troops on the eastern front, and switched some divisions from the Moscow front to reinforce the attacks on Leningrad and Kiev. Then Hitler changed his mind again and decided to concentrate on Moscow as the main target – it was vital that the capital should be taken before winter set in, and a crucial couple of weeks had been lost. The German advance on Moscow was resumed at the beginning of October, and the Germans won another huge encircling victory, capturing the towns of Vyazma and Bryansk and taking another 650,000 prisoners on 12 October. Hitler told the German people that the Soviet enemy was now beaten and would never rise again. In Moscow preparations began to evacuate the government to Kuibyshev, 600 miles south-eastwards on the Volga. By this time well over half of the total number of Soviet troops at the beginning of the invasion had been killed or captured, and most of the original aircraft and tanks had been destroyed. One reason for the huge number of prisoners was Stalin's refusal to allow his troops to retreat to safety before the German encirclements were completed. Massive areas of territory had fallen into German hands, containing about two fifths of the population of the USSR and probably about half its industrial and agricultural assets. The capital itself seemed doomed as German forces penetrated to within a hundred miles. General Zhukov, the most competent of Stalin's military leaders, was placed in charge of the defence of Moscow. He organized the building of new fortifications; the work was done by hundreds of thousands of women and children who dug anti-tank ditches and built tank traps and gun emplacements. Soviet troops resisted fanatically and the German advance began to slow down. Fortunately the weather also came to the rescue – first there were heavy snowfalls followed by bitter cold – it turned out to be the coldest winter in living memory. By the end of November the advance had ground to a halt. Although the Germans continued to make progress in the south, occupying the Crimea and penetrating as far as the outskirts of Rostov-on-Don, both Leningrad and Moscow held out until the end of the war.

Quite early in the campaign some Germans began to express surprise at how fiercely the Russian soldiers were resisting. At the end of the first week General Halder was writing in his diary: 'Information from the front confirms that the Russians are generally fighting to the last man,' and the Nazi Party newspaper was reporting that 'the Russian soldier surpasses our adversary in the West in his contempt for death. Endurance and fatalism make him hold out until he is blown up with his trench, or falls in hand-to-hand fighting.' By the middle of July disquiet and alarm began to creep into German accounts of unexpected Russian counter-attacks. German soldiers had been repeatedly told that the average Soviet soldier hated the harsh Stalinist system and would desert at the first opportunity. It is true that the system *was* vastly unpopular both because of its policies before the war and because of some of Stalin's actions during the war. For example, he ordered the NKVD to round up and deport groups of non-Russians – including Kalmyks, Chechens and Crimean Tatars – whom he wrongly suspected were traitors. Stalin caused more resentment among Soviet troops by forbidding them to retreat, resulting in huge numbers being taken prisoner unnecessarily. Lieutenant-General A.N. Vlasov, who had been captured in this way by the Germans in 1942, was so incensed that he turned against Stalin and agreed to form a Russian Liberation Army of Soviet prisoners-of-war. He hoped to use it to overthrow Stalin first and then turn against the Nazis; but Hitler had only permitted the army to be formed for propaganda purposes, and it was never allowed to get anywhere near Moscow. However, the fact that so many Soviet prisoners were willing to join Vlasov's army showed how widespread the hatred of Stalin was.[17] Yet although there were a number of mass panics, desertions and retreats in the early months of the invasion, these quickly dwindled.

One reason for the new tenacity of the Soviet troops was the increasingly strict army discipline; NKVD agents were active within every army unit, reporting on potential subversives and deserters, who were quickly dealt with; sometimes they were shot in front of their assembled units; more often they were sent to join penal regiments who were given the terrifying and deadly job of marching out in front of their own tanks and armoured vehicles to clear away mines. Much more important in stiffening the Soviet troops' determination to fight was the barbaric way in which the Germans treated the population in the occupied territories. Many Soviet citizens were at first inclined to look on the approaching Germans as liberators, but that was before they actually arrived. The Nazis looked on the Slavs and the Jews as inferior and sub-human peoples, and set out quite deliberately to exterminate as many of them as possible, along with communists, gypsies and other unacceptable groups of people. In the words of Hitler, 'a Communist is not and can never be considered a fellow soldier. This war will be a battle of annihilation; it will be very different from the war in the West. In the East harshness will guarantee us a mild future.' Goering told his commanders in the east: 'I do not care if you say the people are dying of hunger. So they may so long as not a single German dies of hunger.' On 8 July Halder noted in his diary: 'Fuhrer is firmly determined to level Moscow and Leningrad to the ground, and to dispose of their populations, which otherwise we shall have to feed during the winter.'

The Germans set up Special Task Forces whose job was to move from town to town and 'liquidate' Jews and other people suspected of resistance; systematic reports and statistics were sent back to Berlin every week: 1150 Jews shot in Dvinsk, 7000 Jews rounded up and shot in Lvov, 1460 in Lutsk, between 300 and 500 at Zolochew, and 3302 at Tilsit. When some German officers protested about the killings, Hitler responded on 16 July: 'The necessary rapid pacification of the countryside can be attained only if every threat on the part of the hostile civil population is ruthlessly taken care of. All pity and softness are evidence of weakness and constitute a danger.' In every town and village the communist officials were shot; at a village in Belorussia a group of 45 Jews was forced to dig a pit; they were roped together and thrown into the pit alive. The SS (*Schutzstaffel* – protection units) ordered a group of about 40 local Russians to shovel earth on top of the Jews; the Russians refused, so the Germans opened fire with machine guns and killed both the Jews and the Russians. By the end of July the numbers of Nazi victims was rising steadily: at Kishinev in Bessarabia the SS indulged in a two-week campaign of slaughter in which over 10,000 Jews were murdered. In August and September German barbarism reached unspeakable depths; in just two days at the end of September almost 34,000 Jews were murdered in a ravine at Babi Yar, on the outskirts of Kiev in Ukraine (Document B); and almost 36,000 people described as Jews and Communists were killed in the cities of Nikolayev and Kherson on the Black Sea. At Odessa at least 75,000 Jews were killed. Any non-Jew who tried to hide or protect Jews in any way was unceremoniously shot along with the Jews and Commissars. No wonder the approach of the German armies filled the Russian civilians with terror and inspired the Russian soldiers to fight like tigers (Document C). It also inspired thousands of Russians to join the partisans, who harassed the invaders in all sorts of ways with guerilla attacks, scorched earth policies and raids on enemy lines of communication. Predictably the Germans took ruthless reprisals – at least 50 Russians were to be shot for every German killed by partisans. Any village suspected of housing or supplying partisans would be burned down and its people shot. 'This partisan war has its advantages,' remarked Hitler; 'it gives us a chance to exterminate anyone who turns against us.' But there were always those who were prepared to collaborate with the invader; in the Crimea some of the locals helped the Germans to murder Jews, and at Babi Yar, Ukrainians helped to round up Jews to be marched to execution. The Germans came to rely on informers who betrayed Jews and partisans in return for bread or protection for their village.

Russian prisoners-of-war, estimated to number over three million by the end of 1941, were also shamefully treated. The Nazis issued a directive that as communists, Soviet soldiers had forfeited every claim to be treated as an honourable foe, and that therefore the most ruthless methods were justified in dealing with them. Many of them were shot without any pretext, simply to reduce the numbers needing to be fed. Others were starved, beaten, refused medical treatment and denied adequate shelter and sanitation. Hundreds of thousands were forced to march long distances to places where new camps were being set up. Anybody who could not keep up, or who dropped from exhaustion, was shot. The Germans opened a new prisoner-of-war camp near Minsk in which conditions were so appalling that hundreds of Soviet soldiers were dying every day from starvation, disease and brutal treatment at the hands of their guards. In August 600 Russian prisoners were used at Auschwitz in experiments to test a new method of mass killing – the gas chamber. The experiments proved satisfactory and the Nazis soon adopted the gas chamber, using prussic acid (known as Zyclon-B), as the normal method of mass murder in their extermination camps. A German report dated 19 February 1942 reveals that almost three million of the four million Russian prisoners taken up to that time had died. Unfortunately for the Russian soldiers, their government had never signed the Geneva Convention which laid down rules for the correct treatment of prisoners-of-war; this gave the Germans the excuse to ignore it. Ironically, the more the German army and the SS became committed to a war of annihilation, the more determined the Russians became to resist them, and the more people joined the partisans.[18]

(c) The USSR fights back

'If they want a war of extermination, they shall have one,' declared Stalin in a speech on 6 November 1941; the following day, the anniversary of the October Revolution, the traditional military parade went ahead as usual in Red Square. Stalin himself reviewed his troops and delivered a stirring speech invoking Russian nationalism and the heroic military leaders of the past. With the Germans less than fifty miles away, it was a defiant gesture; as John Erickson puts it: 'His words were meant first to steady and then to stimulate Russian nerves, his phrases were at once defiant and gloomy, but he hammered on the conscious-ness of Russian achievement and historical self-respect. He gave notice that the *Untermensch* intended to fight back.'[19] Work had started many weeks before on moving armaments factories and other industrial plants from the threatened areas to cities such as Magnitogorsk in the Urals, and Sverdlovsk, Chelyabinsk and Kurgan in Siberia, east of the Ural Mountains. Since early July the Red Army had been carrying out a scorched earth policy; as they withdrew from an area they took with them everything movable that could be of use to the enemy – trucks, locomotives, rolling stock, fuel, food and cattle; anything that could not be moved had to be destroyed. The numbers of partisan units grew rapidly in all areas captured by the Germans until by the middle of 1942 they included some-where in the region of 700,000 men. Both the Red Army and the partisans were helped by information about German positions and plans passed on to them by the British, who in July 1941 had broken the Enigma code which the German army used to direct its campaigns on the eastern front. In September large quantities of war materials supplied by Britain and the USA began to arrive in Archangelsk; they included tanks, anti-tank guns, fighter aircraft, lorries, barbed wire, copper, aluminium, rubber, soldiers' overcoats and boots, and medical supplies.

The first achievement of the Soviet fight-back was the recapture of Rostov-on-Don on 28 November, which the Germans had only succeeded in holding for one week. This was the first German reverse and it gave a great boost to Russian morale. Next came the successful defence of Moscow in November and December 1941. The German commander, von Bock, was trying to carry out the classic encircling movement with his Panzer divisions, but Zhukov had prepared the defences well and German progress was slow. The fighting was heavy and by the end of November, although the advance had been halted, the German pincers had edged around to the north and south of Moscow; the most forward German troops were only 20 miles from the Kremlin. By this time the weather was bitterly cold with temperatures of –20 °C and deep snow. The wheels of the Panzers froze solid and it was too cold for the lubricating oil to work. The Germans, who lacked proper winter clothing, began to suffer from frostbite. Meanwhile Russian re-inforcements were arriving, some of them from the Far East on the Mongolian front. Stalin had decided that it was safe to withdraw them, after he had received information from Richard Sorge, the Soviet spy based in Tokyo, that the Japanese intended to attack south-east Asia rather than the USSR. The Soviet leaders had learned lessons from the failures of the winter war against Finland. These Siber-ian troops were vastly experienced in winter conditions and the Red Army as a whole was now better equipped, padded and furred, to cope with intense cold. On 5 December Zhukov launched a series of Soviet counter-attacks with 700,000 troops along a 500-mile front. Fierce blizzards were raging and in some places the snow was waist high; the Germans were gradually pushed back, and as they retreated they were attacked by Soviet ski-troops. By the end of February the Germans had fallen back by as much as 100 miles along the front; pressure on Moscow was relieved and the city was not threatened again. It was a tremendous psychological victory for the Soviet forces; this was the first large-scale German military reverse of the war. They lost around half a million men and thousands of guns and tanks; their troops had suffered terribly, since in the intense cold even a relatively minor wound could lead to severe shock and death. In one day alone at the end of December, more than 14,000 German soldiers were forced to undergo amputations because of frostbite; a further 62,000 were suffering from frostbite which did not require amputation, but was serious enough to prevent them taking any further part in the fighting. Hitler removed the three main generals – von Leeb, von Bock and von Runstedt – and made himself Commander-in-Chief on the Eastern Front.

Early in 1942 the activities of Soviet partisans began to cause the Germans serious difficulties in most of the occupied areas. On 20 February a German officer reported that 'the area east of the Dnieper is infested with well-armed partisans under unified command. The roads are heavily mined. The whole male population is being recruited and is trained in special training areas. It would appear that the partisans are constantly reinforced by airborne troops.' They were well armed with machine guns and anti-tank guns. All these partisan groups had become expert at disrupting the movement of German troops and supplies, and it was beginning to tell on German morale. In March 1942 the Germans launched Operation Munich, striking at partisan bases in the Minsk and Smolensk areas. Their treatment of the local civilian population was brutal in the extreme: villages were set on fire and their inhabitants shot; but the only achievement of these tactics was to strengthen the resolve of the partisans and their local supporters. The success of the partisans and the victory outside Moscow encouraged Stalin, against the advice of his generals, to attempt three more offensives: one in the north to try and lift the siege of Leningrad, one in Ukraine to recapture Kharkov, and one aimed at Kerch in the Crimea. But all three were premature and not one of them was successful; the Red Army lost a further half a million men – a personal failure for Stalin, who had insisted on the offensives (Document F). The best that could be said for them was that they at least delayed the next German offensive. The German forces were also very much reduced by this time, but Hitler hoped to make up for this by holding their positions in the north and centre while launching the main offensive on the southern front. For the time being, Moscow was to be spared any further assault.

Hitler intended his next strike to begin in May, and it was to be directed towards capturing Stalingrad and recapturing Rostov-on-Don, which they had held for a week in November 1941. The Germans would then advance into the rich oil-producing region of the Caucasus as far as the Caspian Sea. But Hitler made two crucial changes of plan: he had come to the conclusion that Russian resistance was crumbling, so he decided to strike at Rostov without waiting until the capture of Stalingrad was completed. The attack on Rostov began on 23 June, but the city was not taken until 23 July. Most military historians agree that this four-week delay was vital: if Hitler had concentrated on Stalingrad in early July, the city could probably have been captured quite easily. Stalin also made a mistake which could have proved fatal; he believed that the Germans would concentrate their spring offensive against Moscow, and reinforcements were sent to that front. When it became clear that the main German offensive was being launched in the south, Stalin and his generals had to do some rapid reorganization of their fronts and rush more troops to the Stalingrad area. Stalin was learning from his mistakes in other ways too: at Rostov-on-Don the Germans were expecting to encircle the Soviet troops and take the usual huge numbers of prisoners, but Stalin allowed his forces to withdraw; the majority escaped and survived to fight another day.

After the capture of Rostov Hitler issued his orders for the next move: the capture of the eastern Black Sea coast all the way down to Batum on the frontier with Turkey, and the seizure of the oil-wells at Maikop, Grozny and Baku. Further to the north, Stalingrad on the River Volga still had to be taken. But this was the second of Hitler's miscalculations; Stalingrad was still vulnerable, and a concerted attack would have had an excellent chance of success. However, when Rostov fell, Hitler became even more confident that the Russians were finished, and he decided to spread his forces out. Without waiting for Stalingrad to be captured, he split the German forces into three: Army Group A was to advance round the Black Sea coast and aim for Batum; part of Army Group B was to head straight for the oilfields at Maikop, Grozny and Baku; and the remainder of Army Group B was ordered to capture Stalingrad. At first the Germans advanced rapidly through the Caucasus, capturing Maikop and Stavropol in August; but in September, as Soviet resistance stiffened and more reinforcements arrived, the invaders ground to a halt about 35 miles from Grozny. Some of the German troops were diverted to reinforce the attack on Stalingrad, and Grozny was never captured. Field Marshal List, the German commander in the Caucasus, was sacked by Hitler for failing to reach the Caspian Sea coast. All attention was now focused on Stalingrad where a titanic struggle was developing. Hitler was determined to capture the city and had ordered that when it was eventually taken, the entire male population was to be eliminated. Stalin was totally obsessed with his commitment to save the city which bore his name.

(d) Stalingrad – August 1942 to January 1943

Stalingrad was in a pivotal position on the frontier between European and Asian Russia; it was also a vital communications centre both by rail and by river. It stretched for some twenty miles along the west bank of the River Volga which flowed southwards into the Caspian Sea at Astrakhan. It was a university city and also an important industrial and commercial centre, a symbol of Soviet achievement; there were tall white apartment buildings and beautiful gardens all along the high west bank of the river. There were still around 600,000 people in the city, since Stalin had forbidden any evacuation across the Volga, in case it led to panic. Already at the end of July Stalin had issued his famous Order No. 227, which became known as 'Not One More Step Backwards' (Document G). 'Panic-mongers and cowards must be destroyed on the spot. The retreat mentality must be decisively eliminated.' Commanders who allowed their troops to abandon positions were to be removed and sent for immediate trial. Each army had to organize 'three to five well-armed detachments (up to 200 men each)' who would form a second line; their orders were to shoot any soldier who attempted to run away. Zhukov carried out this order using tanks manned by specially selected officers; they followed up each attack and opened fire on any soldiers who hung back or tried to retreat.

The German Sixth Army, commanded by General von Paulus, began their great push towards Stalingrad on 21 August, crossing the River Don some 80 miles west of the city. Two days later the Luftwaffe carried out a massive air-raid on Stalingrad with up to a thousand bombers. Incendiary bombs completely destroyed most of the wooden houses in the south-west of the city, and the huge petroleum-storage tanks on the river bank were hit, sending a ball of flame 15,000 feet into the sky. People crowded into the cellars as the city became an inferno, but 40,000 were killed. In the late afternoon the first of the Germans reached the Volga just north of the city, while another army was closing in from the south-west. Stalin appointed General Vassily Chuikov to take charge of the city's defence and its 40,000 defending troops. Tough and blunt, he told Khrush-chev, who was the leading political commissar in the city: 'We will defend the city or die in the attempt...Time is blood.' His first achievement was to stiffen the nerve of his army commanders who were beginning to waver; NKVD troops were placed in charge of every landing stage and jetty on the west bank with orders to shoot anybody, whatever their rank, who attempted to escape across the river to the east bank. There was nowhere for the soldiers to go and nothing they could do except fight the Germans; and this they did with increasing ferocity. The Russian forces included women, many of whom operated anti-aircraft batteries. Try as they might, the Germans failed to make a breakthrough into the city.

On 12 and 13 September the Germans launched a terrific onslaught by air and on the ground. One Russian corporal wrote: 'A mass of Stukas came over us, and after their attack, one could not believe that even a mouse was left alive.' The main part of the city was now completely destroyed, and the streets were blocked with burnt-out vehicles and fallen masonry. Gradually the Germans forced their way in and began to take over the city block by block. In some places they man-aged to push through to the Volga, splitting Chuikov's forces. Still the defenders held on, all the time being squeezed into a narrowing strip along the river bank. The Germans now began to suffer the results of their own devastating bombing; it was extremely difficult to make progress through the ruined city – the streets were almost impassable and the empty shells of buildings provided the perfect cover for the defending Russians. There was fierce hand-to-hand fighting as each block and each building was fought over. The main railway station changed hands fifteen times in five days, but it was eventually held by the Germans. This was not what the German soldiers had been led to expect; as Antony Beevor explains, 'they found artillery fire far more frightening in the city. Whenever a tall building was hit, shrapnel and masonry showered from above...there was the danger of snipers in tall buildings...noise assailed their nerves constantly... They loathed house-to-house fighting. They found such close-quarter combat, which broke conventional military boundaries and dimensions, psychologically disorientating.'[20] One of the most famous incidents in the battle was the defence of 'Pavlov's house'. At the end of September Sergeant Jakob Pavlov of the Soviet 42nd Guards Regiment and about 60 men seized a large four-storey building on the corner of a square, only about 300 yards from the river. They had plenty of mortars, heavy machine guns and anti-tank guns, and they succeeded in holding off tanks and Panzers for 58 days, in spite of artillery, mortar fire and bombing. By mid-November Chuikov held only a narrow strip of land less than a thousand yards deep along the river bank; but both sides had fought each other to a standstill; the Germans were completely exhausted and von Paulus decided to break off the attack for the time being.

In the meantime Generals Zhukov and Vasilevsky were planning an ambitious counter-attack, known as Operation Uranus, on the same lines as the earlier German encircling tactics. Stalin was at first critical of the plan, but eventually approved it; he was beginning to learn to trust the experts. Huge reinforcements were assembled consisting of 12 armies, and the plan was to surround the entire German forces besieging Stalingrad. After some delays because of bad weather, the Soviet forces were ready; on 19 November just over one million men in three army groups swept round from the north-east, behind the German Sixth Army, and within five days it was completely encircled. Between 250,000 and 300,000 German troops were trapped in and around Stalingrad. Von Paulus asked Hitler for permission to break out while there was still time, but Hitler refused. 'We are not budging from the Volga,' he told von Paulus. The Luftwaffe would keep the troops supplied until a relieving army commanded by von Manstein arrived. He had been hurriedly recalled from the Leningrad front; he was ordered to form a new army group, take it to Stalingrad and break through the Soviet ring from the outside. Hitler had clearly learned nothing from the earlier events on the eastern front, and this plan was completely unrealistic. The Luftwaffe did not have sufficient transport planes at its disposal to deliver even the minimum supplies that von Paulus needed, even in perfect weather conditions. But the winter weather was predictably bad – ice and fog were the main problems for aircraft – and the Soviet anti-aircraft defences became more effective. As for von Manstein's relief army, it too was in danger of being encircled, the closer it advanced towards Stalingrad. At the end of December it was itself attacked by yet another Soviet army and brought to a halt well short of the city. Von Manstein urged Hitler to allow von Paulus to try and break out of Stalingrad while he still had enough fuel, but Hitler again refused. 'The Sixth Army must stand fast, even if I cannot lift the siege until the spring; retreat would sacrifice the whole meaning of the campaign.'

However, the end was fast approaching for von Paulus. His troops were running short of food, ammunition, fuel and medical supplies, and were forced to eat their horses – 39,000 were consumed before the Germans surrendered. On 9 January General Rokossovsky, who had been given the job of finishing off the operation, sent two envoys to call on von Paulus to surrender. When he refused, Rokossovsky launched a devastating artillery barrage, killing thousands of Germans. The surviving troops were in a terrible state, starving, exhausted, and suffering from frostbite and various ailments, mainly dysentery and jaundice. Von Paulus informed Hitler that further resistance was impossible but again Hitler refused to hear of surrender. German soldiers, he told von Paulus, were required to fight to the death; he wanted a heroic example for the German people. He promoted von Paulus to Field Marshal, since no German Field Marshal had ever surrendered. By 26 January large numbers of senior officers were giving themselves up, and some were committing suicide. However, von Paulus, who was suffering from dysentery, is said to have remarked: 'I have no intention of shooting myself for this Bohemian corporal.' On 31 January 1943 he surrendered what was left of the once formidable German Sixth Army; 91,000 German soldiers were taken prisoner and 50,000 of them died during the next few weeks in the prison camps. During the battle over 150,000 Germans had been killed.

The Battle of Stalingrad was the great turning-point of the war on the eastern front. For the first time the Germans had not only been checked, they had been decisively defeated. This came as a stunning shock to the German people, and many began to have doubts about Hitler and the chances of ultimate victory. Russian losses had been even heavier: in the entire Stalingrad campaign the Red Army had lost almost half a million men killed and about 600,000 seriously wounded. But in spite of the losses, it was the first great Soviet victory of the war. The Kremlin bells were rung to announce the surrender of von Paulus, and Stalin was hailed as 'the wise leader and the great architect of victory.' For the Russians it was a wonderful confidence-booster; their generals had shown themselves capable of learning successfully from the Germans. Stalingrad was not decisive: the Russians had shown their superiority to the Germans in winter conditions, but it still remained to be seen whether the Germans could be defeated in summer conditions when they were at their most effective. However, Stalingrad did mean that for the first time the Soviet leaders could begin to think realistically about the possibility of ultimate victory. The German defeat was a great encouragement too for Russia's allies, Britain and the USA, and for the peoples of occupied Europe and their anti-German resistance movements.

(e) The siege of Leningrad

When Hitler launched Operation Barbarossa on 22 June 1941 Leningrad was in immediate danger of attack from the south-west by the Germans, and from the north by the Finns, who declared war on the USSR on 26 June. Thousands of civilians were set to work digging anti-tank ditches and building concrete gun-emplacements; factories, especially those producing armaments, were evacuated further eastwards and so were many of the most precious art treasures from the Hermitage. On 20 August the Germans reached Gatchina, only 25 miles from Leningrad, and the following day they were able to block the railway line from Leningrad to Moscow. Soon afterwards Finnish forces, advancing from the north, recaptured Terioki which they had been forced to hand over to the USSR in 1940; east of Lake Ladoga, more Finnish troops pushed towards the other great northern lake, Lake Onega. By early September all road and rail links with the rest of the country had been severed, although the airfield was still in Russian hands, and there was the route across Lake Ladoga. The siege had begun, and almost three million civilians were trapped inside the city.

The Russians threw everything into the defence of Leningrad. There were 30 Soviet divisions in the city attempting to beat off the invaders. Guns were brought from the Kronstadt battleships and mounted on land, and even the guns from the old cruiser *Aurora* were brought and positioned on the Pulkovo heights to the south-west of the city, facing the advancing Germans. But the noose was closing more tightly; on 8 September the Germans carried out their first air-raid, dropping some six thousand incendiary bombs. Among the buildings destroyed was a large warehouse complex containing hundreds of tons of food supplies

Figure 7.2   The siege of Leningrad – women mourn the shrouded corpse of a child who has died from starvation.

intended to see the Leningraders through the winter. In spite of the continued bombing the outer defence line held, and on 12 September Hitler made one of his notorious changes of plan. He decided that it was more important to capture Moscow first, so he switched several tank and motorized divisions from the Leningrad front to Moscow, and announced that Leningrad would be starved into surrender. But this did not mean any slackening of the air attacks; on 19 September almost 300 German bombers launched a terrifying raid, killing over a thousand people and destroying one of the city's hospitals. One of the few bright spots at this time was that during September, October and November, Soviet transport planes succeeded in flying in thousands of tons of armaments, ammunition and food. Stalin was furious with his old friend Voroshilov, the military commander, and Zhdanov, the party boss in Leningrad, who began to talk about giving up the city. Stalin angrily dismissed any such suggestions, calling Voroshilov and Zhdanov 'specialists in retreat.' He appointed Marshal Zhukov to take over the defence of Leningrad, and he too flew in during September.

Like Stalingrad, Leningrad took on symbolic importance: it was the cradle of the Revolution and Communism, and Stalin was determined that German soldiers should never set foot on its streets. And they never did, except as prisoners-of-war: in July 1942 several thousand of them were paraded along the Nevsky Prospekt in order to boost civilian morale.

For the civilians trapped in Leningrad it was a nightmarish experience; the first winter of the siege was one of the coldest in living memory, and there was no electricity and very little fuel to keep people warm. As the food supplies slowly dwindled, people began to die of starvation; by the end of 1941 between three and four thousand people were dying every day (Document E). On Christmas day 1941 some 3700 people died of starvation and related diseases; in January and February 1942 a total of at least 200,000 succumbed. Pavel Luknitsky, a writer and war correspondent, wrote in his diary on 29 December: 'To take someone who has died to the cemetery is an affair so laborious that it exhausts the last vestiges of strength in the survivors, and the living, fulfilling their duty to the dead, are brought to the brink of death themselves.' He went on to describe the deathly quiet of the city; there were no cars moving about the streets, only frail people pulling sledges which often carried a corpse wrapped in a sheet. When they arrived at the cemeteries the ground was frozen like iron, too solid for them to dig a grave. The body was just dumped, and sometimes those who pulled the sledge fell beside the corpse, themselves dead, without a sound, without a groan, without a cry. The corpses lay on the surface and were gradually covered by snow and ice.[21] Most people were forced to eat their dogs and cats and there were many cases of cannibalism.

During February 1942 the situation began to look slightly better with the improvement of the ice road across the frozen Lake Ladoga. When it first became passable in December 1941 it did not work well – the link from Leningrad to the lake side was slow and the organization of the road was chaotic. By the end of January the teams of trucks which travelled almost non-stop along the road were actually bringing food into Leningrad faster than it was being eaten. This was partly because of the large number of people who were dying but also because Zhdanov decided to evacuate 500,000 people, about a quarter of the surviving population. This target was achieved: between 22 January and 15 April 1942 over 550,000 people were moved from Leningrad and across the lake in buses, while in the opposite direction came food, fuel and arms and ammunition. It seemed that the worst horrors might be over and as the spring came the survivors came out and set to work to clean up the city and bury the dead. On 15 April 1942, the 248th day of the siege, the trams ran again for the first time in months. On the other hand the ice road was rapidly becoming impassable and the Road of Life, as it had become known, was severed until the following winter. People continued to die of starvation during the summer, although in much smaller numbers. Zhdanov tried to boost morale in all sorts of ways: in July German prisoners were paraded; and on 9 August there was a performance of Dmitri Shostakovich's 7th Symphony, his latest work, which he had dedicated to Leningrad. Shostakovich had been in the city when the siege began, and had completed the first three movements there when in October 1941 the government ordered him to leave. He was evacuated to Moscow and later to Kuibyshev, where the first performance of the completed symphony took place. In June 1942 the score was flown into

Leningrad; the performance of the Leningrad Symphony in the Philharmonic Hall was an incredibly emotional occasion; it was broadcast all over the USSR and on shortwave to Europe and the USA, and in the background could be heard the sound of heavy guns.

Between August and October 1942 Soviet forces tried four times without success to break out and lift the blockade. But at least they inflicted heavy casualties on von Manstein's army; when von Manstein himself was later sent to Stalingrad it was clear that there would be no further German attempt to take Leningrad in 1942. In January 1943 the Russians at last succeeded in capturing Schusselburg, making the first breach in the blockade. Many people in the city thought the siege would soon be over, especially after the news reached them of the surrender of von Paulus at Stalingrad. But they were soon bitterly disappointed: the capture of Schusselburg had opened up only a narrow corridor through which the railway ran; at one point the German guns were only 500 yards away; journeys were hazardous and casualties high. Nevertheless 'the corridor of death' as it soon became known, proved to be a life-saver – during the rest of 1943 some 4.5 million tons of supplies were brought through into the city, and the daily food ration was gradually increased. But the problems were not over; all through the summer of 1943 the Germans continued to shell the city, and it was not until 15 January 1944 that the iron ring was broken and the siege finally raised. In the words of Harrison Salisbury: 'Nothing can diminish the achievement of the men and women who fought on despite hunger, cold, disease, bombs, shells, lack of heat or transportation in a city which seemed given over to death. The story of those days is an epic which will stir human hearts as long as mankind exists on earth.'[22]

(f) The Germans in retreat – the end of the war

After Stalingrad the Red Army was elated and full of confidence; they pushed rapidly westwards and by mid-February 1943 had captured Kursk and Kharkov. But the German forces were not about to fall apart without a desperate fight. They succeeded in stabilizing their line and threw the Soviets back, recapturing Kharkov on 14 March. On 5 July Hitler began his attempt to recapture Kursk by attacking the great westward salient around the city. He sent a personal message to his troops: 'This day,' he told them, 'you are to take part in an offensive of such importance that the whole future of the war may depend on its outcome. More than anything else, your victory will show the whole world that resistance to the power of the German Army is hopeless.'[23] The Russians had been warned what to expect by a captured German sapper, and about two hours before the offensive was due to begin they directed a great artillery bombardment on the German forming-up positions. This inflicted considerable damage and put paid to German hopes of taking the Russians by surprise. The battle at Kursk lasted almost two weeks and developed into the biggest tank battle so far in military history. John Erickson describes it vividly: 'these were tank armadas on the move, coming on in great squadrons of 100 or 200 machines or more ... Now that Soviet tank armies were moving up into the main defensive fields, almost 4000 Soviet tanks and nearly 3000 German tanks and assault guns were steadily drawn into this gigantic battle, which roared on hour after hour leaving ever greater heaps of the dead and dying, clumps of blazing or disabled armour, shattered personnel carriers and lorries, and thickening columns of smoke coiling over the steppe. With each hour also, the traffic in mangled, twisted men brought to steaming, blood-soaked forward dressing stations continued to swell.' [24]The climactic engagement of the battle took place near the village of Prokhorovka on 12 July, when two rival armies of about 900 tanks each engaged each other. At the end of the day the Germans had lost over 300 tanks including 70 out of 100 of their superior 'Tigers'. The Soviets had lost even more, but the important thing was that the German attack had been held. The same day the Soviets also launched an attack on Orel, north of Kursk, just in case the Germans were thinking of sending reinforcements from Orel to Kursk. This amazed and dismayed the Germans, showing as it did the increasing confidence of the Soviet forces and their willingness to take tactical initiatives.

When Marshal Zhukov began a counter-attack, the Germans soon began to withdraw from the Kursk salient (16 July). Their retreat was certainly not a rout, but it was steady and consistent – Kharkov was liberated again on 23 August, Smolensk on 25 September and Kiev on 6 November. In the meantime Hitler had lost his ally Mussolini, who was overthrown towards the end of July; to make matters worse for the Germans, Italy eventually changed sides. After the siege of Leningrad was broken in January 1944, ultimate Soviet victory was assured. Some German troops had been withdrawn from the Russian front to try and stabilize the situation in Italy. In May 1944 the Russians at last succeeded in driving the Germans out of the Crimea. On 22 June – the third anniversary of Hitler's invasion – Stalin opened his summer offensive, Operation Bagration, along a 200-mile front around the Baltic and into Belorussia; this was the ideal follow-up to the successful British and American invasion of Normandy on 6 June. The Germans were under increasing pressure from both directions, making it very difficult for Hitler to switch troops from one front to the other. The Soviet forces massed in the east for Operation Bagration were awesome – 1.7 million troops, 2700 tanks, 24,000 pieces of artillery, 2300 rocket launchers, 6000 aircraft and 70,000 lorries. The Germans were overwhelmed; in the first week their entire front was broken; 38,000 soldiers were killed and over 100,000 taken prisoner. The Russians advanced rapidly – by the middle of July they had inflicted a stunning defeat on the German Army Group Centre which lost 350,000 men killed or taken prisoner. German defeats were now assuming similar proportions to those suffered by the Russians during the first few months of the war; by 1 August Soviet forces had liberated Lublin and Lvov and had reached the suburbs of Warsaw, where they halted. A few days earlier they had come upon the German concentration camp at Majdanek, near Lublin, where they found hundreds of unburied corpses and seven gas chambers. This was the first of the Nazi death camps to be discovered by allied forces; photographs of the corpses were the first to reveal to the rest of the world the unspeakable horrors of the concentration and extermination camps. It later emerged that over 1.5 million people had been murdered at Majdanek, including Jews, many Soviet prisoners of war and Poles who had opposed the German occupation.

As the Red Army began to move further into Poland, the question of the country's political future arose. Naturally Stalin wanted a Polish government which would be, ideally, communist and friendly to the USSR; Britain and the USA wanted a Polish government which was democratic and non-communist. They had no intention of allowing communism to spread across Europe, filling the vacuum left by the destruction of fascism. Inevitably tensions increased among the allies. There was already in existence a Polish government-in-exile based in London which was anti-Stalin and anti-communist. It controlled Polish partisans and resistance fighters who were organized into the Polish Home Army. However, Stalin announced that a Polish Committee of National Liberation had been formed which would become a pro-Soviet Polish government when the country was liberated. He would have nothing to do with the government-in-exile and refused to recognize the Home Army; as Soviet troops occupied Poland, they began to organize regular forces who were equipped and controlled by the Red Army. On 22 July Stalin set up the Polish Committee of National Liberation in Lublin to form what he called 'the core of a provisional Polish government made up of democratic forces.' But it was obvious that a 'liberated' Poland was going to be under close Russian supervision.

This left the Polish government-in-exile in a very difficult situation; their only alternative, apart from doing nothing at all and allowing Stalin to have his way, was to bring about an uprising in Warsaw, drive the Germans out and take control of the capital themselves before the Russians arrived. Hoping that the approach of the Soviet forces would throw the Germans into a panic and cause them to abandon the city, the local Home Army leaders decided to attack the German forces in Warsaw on 1 August 1944. They had about 150,000 men but they were poorly trained and short of weapons. Nevertheless the Germans were caught off guard and within the first week the Poles succeeded in taking over most of the city on the left bank of the River Vistula. Unfortunately they failed to capture three vital targets: the airport, the bridges over the Vistula and the suburb of Praga on the right bank. The Germans, who were in retreat almost everywhere else, decided to make a stand in Warsaw and crush the rising. 'Destroy tens of thousands,' Himmler ordered the general in charge. Reinforcements were brought in, and although the Poles fought bravely and held out for over two months, in the end they were savagely crushed; they surrendered officially on 2 October. Himmler's orders were brutally carried out by SS troops; even the patients in the city's main hospital were lined up and shot dead; other hospitals were set on fire; wounded Poles were drenched with petrol and burnt alive, and poisoned gas was used to kill hundreds of people who were trying to escape through the sewers. It was calculated that about 300,000 Polish civilians were killed, over half a million were sent to concentration camps, and another 150,000 were deported to forced labour camps in Germany. When everybody had been removed, the Germans blew up what remained of the city.

One of the most controversial aspects of the Warsaw uprising was that the Poles received no effective help from the allies. The British and Americans did what they could to fly in urgently needed arms and ammunition from their nearest bases in southern Italy, but Stalin refused to allow them to land on Soviet airfields, and supplies therefore had to be dropped by parachute. The allied losses in aircraft and pilots were high, and a large proportion of the supplies fell into German hands. Stalin himself sent no material help, and although Rokossovsky's army was only a few miles away across the Vistula, he made no move against the Germans until 5 September. But by then it was almost too late – the insurgents were being squeezed into an ever-dwindling area in the city centre. Western historians were critical of Stalin, suggesting that the Red Army deliberately sat on the other side of the river and allowed Warsaw to be destroyed. Stalin himself gave several explanations for this inaction: he claimed that the uprising was a 'reckless adventure' launched by a group of criminals who wanted to seize power for themselves. He said that the Soviet troops were exhausted and that the unexpected German counter-attack on the Vistula and the concentration of German forces made it necessary for Rokossovsky to pause and regroup his army. Stalin claimed that they had hoped to take Warsaw on 6 August but the Germans had forced them back on the defensive. The Germans had certainly inflicted severe damage on the leading Soviet tank corps, which had been forced to withdraw for refitting. When the Soviets, helped by two Polish divisions, did eventually start to move again on 5 September it took them over a week of fierce fighting to capture the suburb of Praga. Although some of the Polish troops managed to cross the river into the main part of Warsaw, it was too late – the insurgents were on the point of annihilation and the Polish troops were soon driven back onto the east bank. It also needs to be remembered, as Richard Overy points out, that 'the Warsaw rising was instigated not to help out the Soviet advance but to forestall it. Polish Nationalists did not want Warsaw liberated by the Red Army but wanted to do so themselves, as a symbol of the liberation struggle and the future independence of Poland.'[25] Stalin had used the rising cleverly to his own advantage; it seems fairly certain that his real motive was to allow the Germans to destroy the non-communist Poles, who would have resisted any Soviet attempts at domination. This the Germans did with savage efficiency, making it relatively easy for Stalin to establish his Soviet-sponsored Polish Committee of National Liberation once Warsaw was taken by the Russians (17 January 1945). At the same time Stalin had done just enough to enable him to claim that he had not simply abandoned the Poles to their fate; a breach with the West was avoided and the alliance of the Big Three – the USSR, the USA and Britain continued, for the time being.[26]

Although the Germans had succeeded in crushing the Warsaw rising by the beginning of October, Hitler had reached the point where he was drawing on his last reserves of men and war materials. It was vital therefore that he should make the best possible use of his resources, and that meant on the eastern front to stop the massive Soviet attack which was being prepared against Germany itself. However, against the advice of all his generals Hitler insisted on launching an attack in the west on 16 December 1944 through the Ardennes towards Antwerp. This was a pointless exercise at that stage of the war and made the job of the Red Army considerably easier. Although the Germans made some initial advances, by 16 January 1945 the Americans had been able to push them back to the original line; the Germans had lost 100,000 men killed or wounded, 600 tanks and 1600 aircraft with nothing to show for it. In the east the Soviet forces were massed along a front stretching some 350 miles. The Soviet generals Zhukov and Koniev opened their attack in January a few days before the final failure of Hitler's Ardennes offensive. They were brilliantly successful and by 3 February had reached the River Oder; some of the Soviet troops were only about 50 miles from Berlin. However, while the Yalta Conference was in session (4–11 February) Stalin slowed down the advance, and there was fierce German resistance. It was not until 16 April that the Red Army began its final great offensive – the push to take Berlin; 2.5 million troops moved towards the capital where Hitler was now spending most of his time in his underground bunker. The battle for Berlin was ferocious – the Red Army lost about 300,000 men killed and the Germans some 200,000 before the Soviets at last forced their way into the city on 21 April; Hitler shot himself on 30 April and that same evening a Russian soldier raised the Red Victory Banner on top of the Reichstag. General Chuikov, the heroic defender of Stalingrad, accepted the surrender of Berlin on 2 May; all remaining German forces surrendered unconditionally on 5 May. Stalin was pleased that the Americans and British had made no attempt to capture Berlin first. The war in Europe was over, but Japan still had to be defeated. Stalin's main concern was that Japan should not be exclusively under American control. Although the Japanese were on the point of surrender after the Americans had dropped atomic bombs on Hiroshima and Nagasaki (6 and 9 August 1945), Stalin insisted on declaring war on Japan, and the Red Army invaded Manchuria. When the Japanese signed an unconditional surrender on 2 September, he could claim to have played a part in their defeat. Stalin was at the pinnacle of his power and achievement. Fascism had been defeated, largely thanks to the efforts of the USSR, which had worn the Germans down; peace had been restored and the USSR was one of the three most powerful nations in the world.

(g) How was the Soviet victory made possible?

In the late summer of 1941, with triumphant German forces at the gates of Moscow and Leningrad, there cannot have been many people who expected Stalin and the USSR to survive much longer. After only three months of war the Red Army had lost two million men killed, well over two million taken prisoner, and almost all their tanks and aircraft had been destroyed. Yet only just over three years later the situation had been reversed, the Red Army had crossed the River Oder into Germany, and it was Hitler and his Fascist system which were on the verge of annihilation. It was an almost unbelievable transformation, perhaps the greatest reversal in military history. The Russians were fortunate that Hitler squandered much of his advantage by refusing to listen to the advice of his generals. The Germans had several fronts to think about – after November 1942 things became more difficult for them: they had to send troops to North Africa to help the Italians out and more troops had to be kept in France in case the Allies launched their 'second front'. The Russians were fortunate that they had vast human resources to call upon, and millions of new recruits were called up and hurriedly given some training. Thousands of officers who had been convicted as 'spies' in the purges before the war were brought out of their labour camps and recommissioned. But sheer numbers would not have been enough if tactics had not changed. One of the key reasons for the eventual Soviet success was that their military leaders – particularly Generals Shaposhnikov, Zhukov, Vasilevsky and Rokossovsky – were willing to learn from the Germans. They examined closely the Germans' techniques – massed air power, tank and motorized divisions used in rapid encircling movements – and they began to reorganize the Red Army so that it could attempt similar tactics. New tank armies were formed supported by mobile infantry, which were the equivalent of the German Panzer divisions. Each tank army was a self-sufficient striking force, with its own artillery, anti-aircraft guns, engineers and anti-tank battalions. At the end of 1942 new divisions were brought into action which contained fewer tanks and more motorized infantry; at the same time ordinary infantry divisions were given much more weaponry. As Richard Overy explains: 'The firepower of a typical infantry division quadrupled during the war, from 250 pounds for each artillery salvo in 1941 to over 900 pounds in 1944. The Soviet army was transformed from a labour-intensive military machine to one that was capital-intensive, from reliance on men to reliance on machines. As junior commanders became more familiar with the tactics of modern armoured warfare . . . the Red Army began to approach the German battlefield performance. In 1941, six or seven Soviet tanks were lost for every German one; by the autumn of 1944 the ratio was down to one to one.[27] Similarly the air force, instead of being split up a few planes to each army unit along the front, was reorganized into air fleets, on German lines, consisting of fighters, bombers and ground-attack aircraft in each strike fleet. One glaring Soviet weakness in the early months of the war had been communications, or lack of them; commanders sometimes knew neither the positions of their own troops nor those of the enemy. This was put right by the introduction of radios and radar for the air force, radios in tanks, and field telephone systems which enabled the Russians to plan and carry out complex strategies and operations – like the encirclement of Stalingrad – without the whole plan falling apart.

Another vital improvement was a change in the relationship between the Red Army and the Communist Party. Once Stalin had recovered from the initial shock of the German invasion, he took over supreme command of all Soviet forces; but as disaster followed disaster, he began to take more notice of his generals and listen to their advice. Vasilevsky became Chief of the General Staff in July 1942, and Zhukov was appointed deputy supreme commander. Zhukov, who was as tough and ruthless as Stalin himself, was allowed to argue with Stalin in a way that no German general dared speak to Hitler. And Stalin respected his expertise and took his advice; three times he sent Zhukov speeding off to organize the emergency defence of beleaguered cities – Leningrad, Moscow and then Stalingrad. According to Dmitri Volkogonov, Stalin 'learned a number of important truths from his military advisers, for instance that one could and should go over to defence not only when the enemy dictates it, but also, as in a number of operations in 1942, in one's own good time, for the purpose of preparing offensive operations.' After the victory at Stalingrad, although he continued to make suggestions, Stalin was usually content simply to approve the plans drawn up by Zhukov, Vasilievsky, Antonov and the front commanders.[28] The military leaders were delighted when Stalin abolished the practice of army officers at every level having to share their command with political commissars, who usually knew very little about military matters but insisted on interfering in military decision-making. Officers always felt, with good reason, that they were being spied on by the commissars, who were looking out for evidence of 'bourgeois' or anti-communist thinking, and who, given half a chance, would report them to the NKVD. From December 1942 the powers of the commissars were much reduced, so that in effect they were no more than assistants to the commander. At the same time special officers' uniforms, gold braid and shoulder epaulettes were brought back, together with the old ranks which had existed in the Tsarist army, and soldiers were required to treat officers with more respect. Some people saw this as a ludicrous betrayal of the 'proletarian' army, but in fact it helped to restore the confidence of the officer corps and to remove the influence of the party. However, discipline remained extremely strict for all ranks. Any soldier guilty of desertion or other dereliction of duty would be sentenced to be shot, although not all of them were actually executed. Another punishment was to be sent into a penal battalion. These measure certainly put an end to the mass panics and retreats of the early part of the war; as we saw earlier, the brutality of the German soldiers was probably just as effective in encouraging the Soviet troops to stand firm.

Soviet leaders acknowledged that the government was unpopular because of collectivization and the purges, so they were shrewd enough to present the war as a desperate struggle to save, not the communist system, but Mother Russia, from destruction at the hands of fascism. They began to use the term 'The Great Patriotic War', and the propaganda made great use of heroic stories from Russian history. In his speech on the anniversary of the revolution in 1941, with the Germans only a few miles from Moscow, Stalin urged the people to take encouragement from the great military heroes of the past – Alexander Nevsky, and generals Suvorov and Kutuzov who had helped to defeat the French in 1812, when Napoleon had been forced to retreat from Moscow. Stalin also decided that religion had a role to play as a force for patriotism; in 1942 the Orthodox Church and the state were reconciled, and an understanding was reached that they would forget their differences in their joint struggle to defeat the evils of Nazism. Churches were allowed to be restored, monasteries and seminaries were reopened and persecution stopped. Hundreds of gaoled priests were freed and Stalin allowed the Church to elect a new spiritual leader – the Patriarch – a position which the government had kept vacant since 1925. The new Patriarch, Sergei, sent a message to Stalin which began: 'I cordially and devoutly greet in your person the God-chosen leader of our military and cultural forces.' Muslims and Jews were given the same freedoms and encouragement. The Orthodox Church responded with enthusiasm: priests blessed soldiers before they went into battle, and the Church financed a whole new tank division. Churches all over the country were soon full again, and it seems that the religious groups generally played a vital role in maintaining the morale of the people.

Equally important was the industrial and economic recovery of the USSR. When the German occupation reached its greatest extent, the USSR had lost somewhere approaching half its food-producing area, three-quarters of its supplies of iron-ore and coal, and three-quarters of its steel production. The situation was saved by the rapid removal of industry and industrial equipment eastwards. It was an incredible operation involving the transportation of over 2500 major enterprises by train, before the Germans could lay hands on them. Some were reassembled in towns along the Volga and some further afield in the Urals region, in Siberia and in Kazakhstan. Some 25 million skilled workers and their families went with them and so did millions of refugees from the occupied areas. An oft-quoted example was the removal of the entire steelworks at Zaporozhe in the Ukraine, including all the machinery, rolling-mill equipment and generators, on 16,000 railway wagons, to a town on the Volga where it was reassembled. An aircraft factory reassembled on the Volga produced its first plane only two weeks after the last train carrying its equipment had arrived on 26 November 1941; by the end of December the factory had produced 30 MiG planes.[29] Incredibly the armaments industry managed to produce over 25,000 aircraft, 60 per cent more than in 1941, and 24,688 tanks, nearly four times more than in 1941. In 1943 Russian production of both tanks and planes passed the German production figures. In fact, arms production had already exceeded its pre-war figure by the middle of 1942. Some of the Soviet war material was superior to that of the Germans, especially their latest tanks and their Katyusha rocket launcher. The Urals area saw the greatest industrial expansion – 3500 new industrial enterprises were built there during the war, and by 1945 well over half the total metallurgical output of the USSR was being produced there (as against only one-fifth in 1940); coal production in the region increased spectacularly – from 12 million tons in 1940 to 257 million tons in 1945. Even the Gulag prisons were made to contribute to the war effort: it has recently been calculated that the labour camps produced approximately 15 per cent of all Soviet ammunition, including 9.2 million anti-personnel mines and 25.5 million shells. They also produced uniforms, leather goods and gas masks.[30]

The USSR received material help from its allies, though until recently Soviet historians were reluctant to admit just how important this assistance was. It was in food, raw materials and equipment rather than in weapons that the allied contribution was most helpful. Recent figures show that the allies provided 53 per cent of explosives, 58 per cent of aircraft fuel, and almost half the quantity of copper, aluminium and rubber tyres. Under the 'Lend–Lease' scheme, the USA supplied some half a million vehicles – Dodge trucks were especially popular – and 1900 locomotives, while the USA and Britain supplied 35,000 radio stations and 380,000 field telephones. Zhukov admitted in 1963 that the USSR could not have continued the war without foreign aid.[31]

This economic recovery was only achieved with iron discipline. Control over all resources was highly centralized, and Gosplan (the State Planning Commission) produced annual military–economic plans. Very strict priorities were applied and a new slogan was adopted – 'Everything for the Front'. Consumer goods were almost impossible to obtain and expensive, and wages were strictly controlled. Workers in industries producing war materials, together with transport workers, were placed under military discipline; holidays were suspended, overtime was compulsory and breaches of discipline were severely punished; anyone suspected of being a slacker, a saboteur or a collaborator with the enemy was in danger of being shot; no-one was allowed to leave his or her job without permission. With so many men involved in military service and such high casualties, the economy was heavily dependent on women – by 1943 half the workers in the war industry were women, and they made up two-thirds of the workforce in agriculture. Conditions were not pleasant, food was in short supply and ration cards were introduced in all cities and large towns. A common punishment for minor acts of indiscipline was the withdrawal of one's ration card. Peasants were not allowed ration cards; they were expected to survive on what was left over after the government had taken its quotas. In 1942 and 1943 the grain harvest and the potato crop were less than one-third of the 1940 total; farmers who had previously grown industrial crops such as cotton were forced to switch to growing food in order to survive. Imports of American tinned meat – the famous spam – helped to supplement the meagre diet.

In spite of all its faults and shortcomings the Soviet system proved to be sufficiently adaptable to meet the demands of the war situation. Many historians believe that Stalin deserves some of the credit for this. He flung himself single-mindedly into the direction of the war effort and worked long hours, usually into the early hours, as if to make amends for his mistakes at the beginning of the war. Other historians have pointed out that because of the prolonged crisis situation, it was not just the army which enjoyed more freedom from political control: administrators, officials, managers and planners also found that they had more freedom to use their initiative. In the end, the war was won through the incredible efforts of millions of ordinary Soviet citizens who, in the words of Richard Overy, 'were organized, bullied or coaxed by their political masters and responded to their task with a mixture of crusading zeal and fatalistic duty.' He quotes Alexander Nevsky's words at the end of Eisenstein's famous film (made in 1937, banned in 1939 after the signing of the Nazi–Soviet Pact, and then revived in 1941):

> He who comes to us with the sword, shall perish by the sword. On that the Russian land has stood, and will stand.[32]

7.3   The aftermath of the war and Stalin's final years, 1945–53

(a) The cost of victory

The Soviet victory was only achieved by enormous sacrifices of human life, far in excess of the losses of all the other participants put together. Soviet armed forces had casualties of over 29 million: 6.2 million killed, over 15 million wounded, 4.4 million captured or missing, and between 3 and 4 million incapacitated by illness and frostbite. This means that out of the 34.5 million men and women mobilized, 84 per cent died, were wounded or were captured. Recently published official figures give total military deaths from all causes as 8.6 million, although recent estimates by Russian historians put the figure much higher; one even suggests 26.4 million. As well as these, there were millions of civilian deaths – those who were murdered and those who starved to death or died from diseases. The most reliable recent estimate puts the total civilian deaths at around 17 million, giving a total Soviet war dead of over 25 million.[33] The surviving population were victims too: families were destroyed or disrupted, there were millions of widows and orphans, and for the government there was the problem of how to cope with the tens of thousands of disabled soldiers. The parts of the USSR which had been occupied by the Germans were left in ruins; factories and collective farms were all badly damaged, and in some rural areas farmers had almost stopped cultivating the land, except to keep themselves alive. It is estimated that over 1700 towns and some 70,000 villages were almost completely destroyed. Major cities like Minsk, Kiev, Vilnius, Smolensk and Stalingrad were heaps of rubble; 25 million people were homeless, and over one-third of total Soviet wealth had been destroyed. In effect, the entire modernization programme of the Five-Year Plans during the 1930s had to be started all over again almost from scratch in the western parts of the country. Yet the victory was seen by Stalin as the ultimate vindication of his entire system of government, which had passed the sternest test imaginable – total war. In Stalin's view, the situation at the end of the war needed something like another military campaign: the entire population had to be mobilized in the great battle to rebuild the Soviet Union.

(b) Stalin's final battles

Any Soviet citizens who were expecting more freedom and a more relaxed way of life as a reward for their superhuman efforts in winning the war were soon disillusioned. Stalin was well aware that his people were sick of the rigours of wartime life and that various groups were talking of radical change. Peasants, disgusted with the minimal wages paid on the collectives, began to take land back and farm it for themselves. Industrial workers were protesting about low wages and rising food prices. The peoples of the recently acquired territories – especially the Baltic states and the western Ukraine – bitterly resented Soviet rule. There was armed resistance from Ukrainian nationalists who were not finally crushed until 1949. The same happened in the Baltic states, Moldavia and Poland where nationalist guerrillas kept thousands of Soviet troops busy until the early 1950s. Stalin's first priority was to clamp down before the potential opposition began to threaten his own position. About 300,000 people were deported or imprisoned from western Ukraine alone, and the population of the labour camps, which had fallen during the war, more than doubled to about 2.5 million. Even ordinary industrial workers were subject to military-style discipline and peasants were compelled to return land to the collective farms. Anybody heard voicing subversive thoughts was likely to be arrested; telephone-tapping was commonplace.

Stalin saw enemies everywhere: Soviet soldiers who had been taken prisoner by the Germans were considered to be tainted, potential traitors. It seems almost beyond belief that some 2.8 million Red Army soldiers, who had survived the appalling treatment in Hitler's concentration camps, returned to their homeland only to be arrested and interrogated by the NKVD. Some were shot, some were sent into the Gulag system, and only about one-fifth were allowed home. One of Stalin's motives in sending so many people to labour camps was to ensure a constant supply of cheap labour for the coal mines and other projects, particularly the search for uranium needed for the Soviet nuclear programme. Also repatriated between 1945 and 1953 under the terms of the Yalta agreement (see next section) were almost 5.5 million other Soviet citizens who had come into the hands of the allies during the last months of the war. They were even more suspect in

Stalin's eyes because they had seen that life in the West was materially better than in the USSR. Some of them were found guilty of collaboration with the enemy and were executed; about 3 million were sent to labour camps. Stalin also demanded the return of people who had fled from the USSR before the war, some as long ago as the Civil War, and who were not even Soviet citizens. The British complied with this request, although the Yalta agreement did not require them to do so. The most notorious case was the forcible repatriation by the British of 50,000 Cossacks, including women, children and old men, in May and June 1945. Many committed suicide rather than cross the frontier into the USSR; the fate of the rest is still uncertain.[34]

Even more grotesque was the attack on some of the leading figures who had served Stalin best during the war, and whom he now saw as potential threats to his dictatorship. Marshal Zhukov, the hero of so many Soviet victories, was accused of planning a *coup* against Stalin and was condemned by the Politburo. In disgrace, he was sent off to be military commander in Odessa and later in the Urals; his name almost disappeared from the press and was hardly mentioned in the new school textbooks on the Second World War. A film was made about the capture of Berlin in which Stalin was portrayed as the man responsible for victory; no other generals and no staff officers were shown – just Stalin directing the battle single-handed. A similar fate befell Rokossovksy and Antonov; the latter was sent even further afield, down to Transcaucasia. They were the fortunate ones – several other senior generals were executed on false charges of treason and some were given long prison sentences.

Having secured his dictatorship, Stalin concentrated on the task of rebuilding the country, the first priority being to repair the material damage in the ruined western areas. Once again, as during the war, the people were mobilized to their task: in Leningrad every able-bodied person had to help with the rebuilding work – 30 hours a month for workers, 60 hours for those not working, and ten hours a month for students and children of school age. Most cities and large towns introduced similar programmes. In his election speech in February 1946 Stalin said that he was looking forward to a future in which industrial output would be treble that before the war, and that this would be achieved in three five-year periods. The general target of the Fourth Five-Year Plan, running from 1946 until 1950, was to exceed pre-war output. According to Alec Nove, if the statistics can be believed, the 1940 levels of industrial production were indeed achieved. In fact between 1945 and 1950 the output of capital goods, including armaments, rose by 83 per cent.[35] As the Cold War became more bitter, armaments remained the top priority – the 1952 budget provided for a 45 per cent increase in output of material for the armed forces. The outstanding achievement of the immediate post-war period was considered to be the successful explosion in Kazakhstan, in August 1949, of the first Soviet atomic bomb, which meant that the yawning technical gap in armaments between the USSR and the USA had been bridged.[36] The concentration on heavy industry and armaments meant the usual shortage of consumer goods. But agriculture was the greatest weakness in the economy; the 1946 grain harvest was even less than that of 1945, partly because of a severe drought. Ukraine was badly hit, but Stalin insisted that its full quota must be provided; the result was famine, starvation and reports of cannibalism. State control over the collective farms was tightened again; grain quotas were increased and new taxes placed on the peasants, even though their incomes were miserably low. At the time of Stalin's death in 1953, the average monthly pay of a collective farm labourer was about 16 roubles – less than one-sixth of the wages of a typical factory worker. It was as if Stalin was determined to make the peasants pay for the reconstruction. Most peasants managed to survive by working their individual plots, but conditions were so harsh that people left the countryside in droves. Between 1950 and 1954 around nine million people left the collective farms; for the first time, agricultural workers made up less than half the total labour force. It is not surprising that the recovery of agriculture was sluggish in all departments; in 1952 the grain harvest was still only about three-quarters of the 1940 harvest; as Alec Nove comments: 'How could it be tolerated that a country capable of making an A-bomb could not supply its citizens with eggs?'

Another aspect of Stalin's policies was the drive for Russification, which was pursued more rigorously than ever before. It took many forms: the introduction of Russian, or rather Soviet, institutions and practices in the newly acquired areas – collective farms and nationalized industries, communist party committees and state-controlled trade unions. Top officials in the non-Russian Soviet republics were usually Russian. In 1951, when the Georgian communist party leaders tried to take the Georgian Soviet Republic out of the USSR (which in theory was allowed under the 1936 constitution), Stalin had them removed and shot. Russia and Russian culture were seen as paramount, and other national cultures were played down and discouraged. The Baltic states – Estonia, Latvia and Lithuania – suffered especially from this; the Moldavians, who spoke Romanian, even had their language changed – they were made to use the Cyrillic alphabet, like the Russians, and lots of Russian words were added. Great Russian chauvinism was in the ascendant, and anything which smacked of foreign influence was immediately under suspicion. This is probably why, incredibly in view of all that had happened in the Holocaust, a new campaign of anti-Semitism was started. Stalin apparently resented the 'cosmopolitanism' of Soviet Jews – their contacts with fellow-Jews in the USA and in the new Jewish state of Israel, formed in 1948, and Jewish aid which kept flowing in from abroad. Solomon Mikhoels, a well-known playwright and leading Jewish spokesman, was murdered on the orders of Stalin in January 1948. The Jewish Anti-Fascist Committee set up during the war was disbanded and its leaders arrested; Jewish schools and libraries were closed down, and Jewish literature and newspapers banned. Jewish writers and artists were arrested, Jews in important positions were sacked and they were forbidden to travel abroad. Trials began in 1951 and were still going on when Stalin died in 1953. Most of the victims were tortured to make them confess to unlikely crimes such as taking part in a Zionist conspiracy and spying for the West; very few were acquitted – the usual sentence was execution or labour camp.[37]

It wasn't enough that Russian culture was dominant – it had to be Russian culture as approved by the party. The battle to re-establish control over the intelligentsia was launched in August 1946 when the Party Central Committee attacked the famous poet Anna Akhmatova and the popular satirical writer Mikhail Zoschenko for their writings in the Leningrad literary journals *Zvezda* and *Leningrad*. Both were expelled from the Writers' Union because Stalin felt that in the fields of literature and art, attempts were being made to go beyond the bounds set by the party, that is, by himself. Dmitri Volkogonov believed that Stalin saw this as a threat to uniform thinking and hence to one-man rule. This was the signal for the beginning of another purge, and it was aimed principally at the city of Leningrad.[38] Zhdanov, the Leningrad party boss and reliable Stalinist, led the attack, pointing out that the function of writers in Soviet society was to educate people in Bolshevik realism; at all costs modernism, liberalism and Westernism must be avoided. Hundreds of writers were expelled from the union, and other branches of the arts suffered similar repression. In January 1948 Zhdanov turned on Soviet composers, criticizing them for 'not reflecting our glorious victories, and for eating out of the hands of our enemies.' He informed musicians that they 'must protect Soviet music from infiltration by elements of bourgeois corruption; we should not forget that, as in all other fields, the USSR is the true protector of mankind's musical culture, a wall guarding human civilization and human culture from bourgeois decay.' All the leading Soviet composers – Prokofiev, Shostakovich, Miaskovsky and Khachaturian – were in disgrace and their music could not be played. They all came back into favour eventually, Shostakovich after only one year, but Zhdanov's campaign cast a blight over Soviet composers for the time being. Although Zhdanov died of a heart-attack in August 1948,[39] the campaign to discipline the intelligentsia, known as *Zhdanovshchina*, continued into the early 1950s. Scientists were not immune either; although he had little scientific training, Zhdanov did not hesitate to pronounce on Einstein's relativity theory, cybernetics and quantum mechanics, which he denounced as bourgeois and reactionary. Many biologists and chemists were arrested, though physicists enjoyed more freedom; this was because scientists working on the nuclear project convinced Beria, who was in charge of the Special Committee for the Atom Bomb, that if relativity theory and quantum mechanics were rejected as idealist, then they might as well reject the bomb itself. Stalin is reported to have remarked to Beria: 'Leave them in peace. We can always shoot them later.'[40]

Following the death of Zhdanov, it was not long before the Leningrad party leaders came under suspicion, particularly Nikolai Voznesensky, who had played a vital role in planning the Soviet war economy, and Alexei Kuznetsov, the outstanding leader of the struggle for survival during the siege. Both were talented and popular and both were being mentioned as possible successors to Stalin; that in itself was enough to place them in mortal danger. In 1949, in what became known as the 'Leningrad Affair', Georgi Malenkov, one of Stalin's yes-men who himself had leadership ambitions, was sent to Leningrad to look into alleged irregularities. After lengthy 'investigations', Voznesensky, Kuznetsov and the entire Leningrad party organization were arrested, charged with the usual variety of invented offences, beaten to make them confess, and put on trial in September 1950. All the main defendants were found guilty and executed. It seemed as if the nightmare scenario of the pre-war purges was being re-enacted. None of Stalin's close associates could feel safe: in 1949 Molotov was removed from his post as Commissar for Foreign Affairs which he had held for ten years, and his Jewish wife, Polina, was arrested, apparently because Stalin did not approve of the warm welcome she gave to Golda Meir, the first Israeli ambassador in Moscow.

Figure 7.3   A rare photograph of the leader and his henchmen, on their way to a sports meeting in Moscow in 1945. From left to right: Khrushchev, Stalin, Malenkov, Beria and Molotov.

Yet Molotov remained a member of the Politburo and Deputy Prime Minister, giving rise to the bizarre situation that the nominal second-in-command of the government was powerless to prevent his completely innocent wife being incarcerated in a labour camp for over three years. Some reports suggested that she was not in a camp – she was simply being kept in exile as a hostage to guarantee Molotov's good behaviour. Stalin even had his own personal physician arrested when he advised him to take things easy on grounds of failing health; the ageing dictator did not want the news to get round that his powers were declining, since that might encourage the others to remove him. In October 1952 Stalin caused consternation when during a speech to the Party Central Committee, he accused Molotov and Mikoyan of political cowardice and said he doubted whether they had the courage and firmness to stick to the agreed policies. Many of the members were convinced that Stalin was preparing the ground to remove some of his longest-serving comrades, although the subject was dropped for the time being.

The final act in the drama was the so-called Doctors' Plot. In November 1952 thirteen Moscow doctors, who at different times had treated Stalin and other leaders, were arrested and accused of conspiring to kill their eminent patients, and it was suggested that they had been responsible for Zhdanov's death four years earlier. Six of the doctors were Jewish and this was the signal for another outburst of anti-Semitism. Stalin talked of rounding up all Jews and sending them to Siberia; on 12 February 1953 the USSR broke off diplomatic relations with Israel. Preparations were being made for a show-trial of the doctors, and there is evidence that Stalin was working up to yet another bloody purge of leading figures in the party, the government, the army and the police, with Molotov, Mikoyan and Beria at the top of the list. Fortunately for them, on 1 March Stalin collapsed at his dacha; he often slept late, but when he had still not emerged from his room at 10.30 in the evening, his staff went in to investigate. They found him lying on the floor, conscious but unable to speak. They called Malenkov and Beria, but it was 3.00 am before they arrived. Beria took charge and there was a long delay before any doctors were called. Eventually doctors arrived and a cerebral haemorrhage was diagnosed; there was little that could be done, and Stalin died on 5 March. He had left no instructions about what should be done in the event of his death, but Beria clearly saw himself as the successor. 'Beria was behaving like the crown prince of a vast empire,' wrote Dmitri Volkogonov, 'with the power of life and death over all its citizens. For him, Stalin was already the past.'[41]

7.4 The beginnings of the Cold War

(a) The origins of tension

In one sense the origins of the Cold War can be traced back to the 1917 Bolshevik revolution which set up the Soviet system – an alternative model of political, economic and social organization which proclaimed itself as the enemy of, and the successor to the Western capitalist system. The communist system was therefore viewed with the greatest suspicion by Western capitalist governments, and when civil war broke out in Russia in 1918 several capitalist states – the USA, Britain,

France and Japan – sent troops to help the anti-communist forces. Although the intervention was ineffective, Stalin believed that the capitalist states still hoped to destroy the USSR and that there would be another attack from the West. Hitler's invasion in June 1941 showed that he had been right. The need for self-preservation against Germany and Japan caused the USA, the USSR and Britain to forget their differences and work together in a 'marriage of convenience'. But the tensions were there almost from the beginning: Stalin constantly complained that the material help he received from the allies was too little, and that they were deliberately delaying a second front in Europe in order to force the USSR to do the bulk of the fighting against the Germans. As soon as it became clear that the defeat of Germany was only a matter of time, both sides, but especially Stalin, began to plan for the post-war period.

Stalin's great fear was that the USA and Britain, having got rid of Hitler, might reach an agreement with Germany to turn their forces against the USSR. His aim therefore was to capture as much territory as possible as a buffer zone against invasion. This was why he pushed to occupy eastern Germany and to seize Berlin before the Americans and British arrived. In the months immediately following the defeat of Germany, Stalin's actions irritated and alarmed the West; the Russians expelled five million Germans from the area east of the Oder–Neisse Line, an area which had belonged to Germany but was now declared by the Soviet Union to be part of Poland. Stalin also began to interfere in the states of eastern Europe, setting up pro-communist governments. US President Franklin D. Roosevelt understood some of Stalin's concerns and wanted to maintain friendly relations, but at the Yalta Conference in February 1945 he did not tell Stalin that the USA had developed the atomic bomb. After Roosevelt's death in April 1945, his successor, Harry S. Truman, who admitted that he was a novice at foreign affairs, was more suspicious of Stalin's motives and decided to take a tough line. Stalin was only told about the atomic bomb shortly before it was used on Japan, and his request that the USSR should take part in the occupation of Japan was rejected.

(b) Which side was to blame?

The traditional interpretation among Western, particularly American historians, is that the responsibility for the Cold War must be laid firmly at the door of Marxism–Leninism, with its fundamental hostility towards capitalist states. The wartime alliance was only a brief interlude of co-operation against the common enemy; once Hitler was defeated the old ideological conflict was bound to re-emerge as Stalin tried to extend communist control over the whole of Europe. This view was first stated by George F. Kennan, an American diplomat with a long history of service in Russia before the war; he was asked by the State Department to write an analysis of Soviet foreign policy. In his reply, known as the 'Long Telegram' of February 1946, he claimed that Soviet policy was essentially expansionist. 'World communism,' he wrote, 'is like a malignant parasite that feeds on diseased tissue.' According to Kennan, Stalin, like previous Russian rulers before him, always needed an outside enemy in order to unite the Soviet people behind him. Now that Hitler had been defeated, the USA was the next obvious enemy. The Soviet leaders believed fanatically that there could be no peaceful co-existence with the USA, and that they would therefore do their utmost to disrupt and even destroy the traditional Western way of life. No amount of concessions from the Americans would change the aggressive nature of the USSR. No capitalist country would be safe – the Soviets would try to undermine and bring down any government, from Turkey right through to Britain, which resisted their demands. The capitalist nations must therefore draw together in a tightly-knit anti-communist bloc under the leadership of the USA.

Historians like William H. McNeill and Herbert Feis were critical of Roosevelt and Truman for being too accommodating to Stalin: the Russians were allowed to take Berlin, in spite of contrary advice from Churchill, and they allowed the formation of pro-Soviet states in eastern and south-eastern Europe. Even after Kennan's 'Long Telegram' Truman continued to work for co-operation with Stalin: the Americans offered joint US and USSR control over the production of nuclear weapons (June 1946), the withdrawal of all foreign troops from Germany (July 1946), and the participation of the USSR and its satellite states in the Marshall Plan. The USSR accepted none of these offers, and consequently, so the traditional explanation goes, the USA was forced to change its attitude to the USSR; there was no alternative but to embark on a policy of containing the expansion of communism. The Americans assumed the leadership of the remaining non-communist European states, and in order to avert their economic collapse, they launched a huge programme of aid. At this point the division of both Europe and the world into two rival blocs became unavoidable. The setting up of the North Atlantic Treaty Organization (NATO) and the Federal Republic of Germany were the West's self-defence against aggressive communism.

Revisionist historians, mostly American, soon began to challenge the traditional view, arguing that Stalin and the USSR should not be blamed for the Cold War. They suggested that, given the enormous losses which the Soviet Union had suffered during the war, it was only to be expected that Stalin would want to make sure that neighbouring states were friendly. In the view of the revisionists, Stalin's motives and actions were purely defensive; there is simply no evidence that Stalin was ready to do aggressive battle against the USA, and there was no real military threat to the West from the USSR. Even Kennan thought that the Soviets would use psychological rather than actual military warfare. The Americans should have been more understanding and should not have challenged the idea of a Soviet sphere of influence in eastern Europe. One of the earliest revisionists, William A. Williams, whose first work was published in 1959, laid much of the blame for the Cold War on the USA and its 'Open Door' economic policy. This was the demand that the USA should be given equal opportunity to trade wherever it wanted without restrictions such as tariffs, quotas and preferential systems. Since the USA was the most powerful economic state in the world, an 'Open Door' system would soon lead to American economic domination of the world, and consequently political domination too.[42] After its victory against Nazism the USA seemed to think it had the right to intervene wherever it wanted. It had already taken upon itself to hasten the break-up of the British empire and was forcing Britain to open its traditional markets to US competition.

The Americans also had their eye on south-eastern Europe as a valuable market, and there was every sign that they were out to weaken the USSR still further: Lend–Lease deliveries from the USA stopped immediately the war in Europe ended, the Americans refused to allow the USSR the high level of reparations from Germany that they asked for and needed to help their own economic recovery, and in May 1946 they stopped any further reparations from the American zone of Germany. In the revisionists' view, the dropping of atomic bombs on the Japanese cities of Hiroshima and Nagasaki in August 1945 was a deliberate demonstration to the USSR of American nuclear power and a warning of what to expect if they dared to challenge American domination. Stalin's response was to go all out to produce a Soviet atomic bomb, a feat which was achieved just four years later, marking the beginning of a terrifying nuclear arms race. The arms race assured American big business of enormous profits, and in order to ensure that this continued, the US government created the myth about Soviet aggression and expansion on a vast scale. True the USSR used force to set up the so-called 'people's democracies' in eastern Europe, but this was a reflex defensive action against American hostility. The revisionist camp was given a boost in the late 1960s when many people in the USA became critical of American foreign policy, especially American involvement in the Vietnam War. This caused some historians to reconsider the US attitude towards communism in general; they felt that successive US administrations had allowed themselves to become obsessed with their hostility towards the USSR, and they were prepared to take a sympathetic view of Stalin's difficulties. Prominent among the revisionists were Gabriel Kolko, a student of William A. Williams, whose first book, *The Politics of War*, came out in 1968, and Thomas G. Paterson.

Post-revisionist historians argue that both the traditional and the revisionist interpretations are too simplistic, given the complexity of the situation at the end of the war. The traditional interpretation ignores the weakness and exhaustion of the USSR, and overestimates its military strength, the extent to which it could control foreign communist parties, and the aggressive intent of its leaders. The revisionist interpretation turns a blind eye to some of Stalin's actions which seemed to go well beyond the needs of simple defence, and which contributed to a hardening of American policy towards the USSR. Neither group of historians used any Soviet sources. As access to official documents has increased, there has been a steady stream of post-revisionist investigations, mainly by American historians, who have tried to present a genuinely objective interpretation of the causes of the Cold War. Each study has its own emphases, but generally they all agree that both sides must share the responsibility. Influential post-revisionists include John Lewis Gaddis, Melvyn P. Leffler, Ralph Levering, Vojtech Mastny and the British historian Martin McCauley.

Gaddis[43] believes that Roosevelt was fully aware of Stalin's problems and thought his hostility to the West sprang from insecurity. Nor did Roosevelt regard communism as a threat to the West. As soon as the Americans showed Stalin that they had no intention of trying to destroy the USSR, his suspicions of the West would melt away. Roosevelt hoped that after the war, the USA, the USSR, Britain and China would act together to keep the rest of the world in order. Unfortunately for Roosevelt, Stalin would never trust another leader after his unfortunate experience with Hitler, and he was convinced that the pro-longed delay in launching the second front in Europe was designed to weaken the USSR. Even after the D-Day landings Stalin continued to complain and demanded more and more supplies from the USA, until American officials lost patience. Averell Harriman, the American ambassador in Moscow, who had fully supported Roosevelt's policy of winning over Stalin, now suggested that a more firm approach was needed. Truman told Molotov at their first meeting that relations must stop being all take and no give by the USSR, and that they must start keeping their agreements. However, the Russians responded by showing that they could be just as tough as the Americans; following Kennan's 'Long Telegram' of February 1946, the US government decided on a policy of no more concessions to the USSR. The main aim of US policy would be 'contain-ment' – the limiting of Soviet expansionism – hence the Truman Doctrine and the Marshall Plan (see next section). However, the post-revisionists also point out that Kennan himself did not believe that Stalin would resort to war, and was not entirely happy with some of steps taken in 1949 and 1950 – the formation of NATO and the German Federal Republic, and the American decision to build the hydrogen bomb; he wanted a policy of firmness, but these actions went much further than that, and seemed calculated to increase Stalin's feelings of insecurity.

Vojtech Mastny argued that Stalin's drive for control of eastern, central and south-eastern Europe was far more extensive than could reasonably be claimed on grounds of security requirements. The crude Soviet methods of forcing communist governments on the states of eastern Europe were bound to lend credence to the claims that Stalin's aims were expansionist. For Mastny, Stalin's policies were the main cause of the Cold War; but he also believes that if the Americans, particularly Roosevelt, had made it clear to Stalin very early on that, while they appreciated his desire for security, there were limits beyond which they would not allow him to go, he might well have trod more carefully. The fail-ure to stand up to Stalin early enough can be seen as comparable to Britain's appeasement of Hitler, and therefore must rank as an important contributory cause of the Cold War.[44]

Martin McCauley, looking at the origins of the Cold War from a western Euro-pean standpoint, sees the economic weakness of most of the non-communist states as an important factor in the development of the Cold War. The west Euro-peans, especially Britain, were in a desperate state economically, and so 'increas-ingly after 1945 they turned to the United States as their political, economic and military saviour. From a security point of view western Europe was incapable of defending itself. Hence the strategy of the containment of the Soviet threat owes its conception to the European, not the American, mind . . . The Truman Doc-trine, the Marshall Plan and, especially, the formation of NATO were articulated in the United States but were conceived in Europe.' In fact, the Americans were alarmed at the weakness of their allies and at the same time they overestimated the power of the USSR. McCauley believes that the Cold War was not inevitable, that up to the end of 1945 agreement could have been reached. Stalin got things wrong too: he could have done more in 1945 to form a good working relationship with the USA, so he must bear some of the blame for the Cold War.[45]

(c) The lost opportunities of 1945

As the eventual defeat of Germany became certain, the leaders of the Grand Alliance began to plan what should happen when the war ended. At a meeting in Moscow in December 1944 Churchill and Stalin came to a rough agreement about spheres of influence: the USSR was to have a 90 per cent influence in Romania, and Britain 10 per cent; in Greece the percentages were reversed; Bulgaria was to be divided 75/25 per cent in favour of the USSR, while in Hungary and Yugoslavia it was to be 50/50. Nothing final was signed and Churchill claimed that he had only meant the agreement to last until the end of the fighting. But this was not the sort of concession that Stalin was likely to let slip easily.

Next Stalin, Roosevelt and Churchill met at Yalta in the Crimea in February 1945. Agreement was reached on several points: the setting up of the United Nations Organization to replace the failed League of Nations; the division of Germany and Austria into three zones (Soviet, American and British; a fourth one, for the French, was included later); and free democratic elections in the states of eastern Europe. In addition Stalin agreed to declare war on Japan and in return would receive Sakhalin Island, the Kuriles, a group of 31 islands to the north of Japan, and part of Manchuria. The main source of disagreement was over the future of Poland: Churchill was prepared to make concessions to Stalin – some Polish territory was given to the USSR, and the West accepted the Polish pro-communist government installed by Stalin, on condition that some nationalists were allowed to serve in it. However, Roosevelt and Churchill were not happy about Stalin's demand that Poland should be given all German territory east of the Rivers Oder and Neisse. No agreement was reached on this point, but generally the atmosphere at Yalta was cordial. The Russians seemed genuinely to want to develop a good working relationship with the USA, and they wanted credit to enable them to buy American technology. In fact, Molotov had already formally requested a large American loan, somewhere in the region of one billion dollars; Roosevelt delayed making a decision on this, probably fearing that Congress would not approve it, and it was not discussed at Yalta.

However, a row soon broke out in March 1945 when the Russians discovered that a meeting had taken place between German, American and British representatives at Zurich in neutral Switzerland, to discuss the surrender of German troops in northern Italy. Stalin accused them of planning to sign a separate peace with Germany in the West behind the backs of the Russians. This of course was Stalin's recurrent fear, and according to one of Roosevelt's biographers, Stalin sent Roosevelt 'one of the most insulting communications ever addressed by one chief of state to another, in which he accused the president of being a liar or a dupe of his aides.' Roosevelt protested that Stalin was mistaken, and even after that, continued to try to be a peacemaker; on 12 April 1945, the day of his death, in his last message to Stalin, Roosevelt thanked him for his frank discussion of the 'Swiss incident,' which, he said, they now must now put behind them. 'There must not, in any event, be mutual mistrust,' he went on, 'and misunderstandings of this character should not arise in the future.'[46] Privately, however, Roosevelt was having serious doubts about Stalin; he now believed that either Stalin was not a man of his word, or that he did not have as much control over the Soviet government as Roosevelt thought he had.

The way in which the Soviets behaved in the areas occupied by the Red Army caused a revulsion of opinion against them in the West, even among those who were working for a good relationship. In Romania, for example, armed with the Stalin–Churchill percentages agreement, Andrei Vyshinsky, acting as spokesman for Stalin, gave King Michael a two-hour ultimatum to choose a Prime Minister acceptable to Moscow (February 1945). But it hardly mattered whom he chose, since the Red Army controlled the country anyway. Pro-communist governments were also installed in Bulgaria and Hungary, and Soviet forces occupied northern Iran. It was announced that the western border of Poland was the line of the Rivers Oder and Neisse (March 1945) which was not part of the Yalta agreement; the Russians proceeded to forcibly expel five million Germans who were living there. The Americans, still slow to appreciate the USSR's obsession with security, began to overreact and exaggerated the danger of Soviet expansion. The 'domino theory' emerged – the idea that if a country fell into the Soviet sphere of influence, its neighbour would soon follow, and the whole area would fall to communism like a row of dominoes. The Soviets didn't help their case at this point by demanding military bases in the Straits and a mandate over the former Italian colonies. Some influential Americans, including Joseph C. Grew, the Under Secretary of State, believed that war with the USSR was inevitable. As preparations were made for the next major conference – at Potsdam in July 1945 – pressure built up on President Truman to take a tougher line and make no more concessions.

By the time the Potsdam Conference met, relations had worsened; Stalin would make no concessions on major issues, except to reduce his reparations demands on Germany. Truman told Stalin that the USA possessed an atomic bomb, but this did not make Stalin any more amenable; if anything it made him even more determined to build up Soviet security. The conference ended reasonably cordially, however, since it was intended to continue discussion of the major issues at regular meetings of the three Foreign Ministers. At the first meeting, held in London in September 1945, the main sticking point was Molotov's demand that the West should formally recognize the governments of Romania and Bulgaria. The Americans would not agree and the meeting broke up in some disarray. In January 1946 Truman declared that both Romania and Bulgaria were police states and would not be recognized by the USA until changes were made. In February Stalin made a fairly conventional speech which was, however, interpreted by some Americans as an aggressive statement. George Kennan, who was the American *chargé-d'affaires* in Moscow, sent a report of the speech, along with his famous 'Long Telegram', to Washington, which gave, according to Dmitri Volkogonov, a misleading and biased account; Kennan reported that Stalin regarded a Third World War as inevitable, which was certainly not Stalin's view.[47] Then in March 1946 Churchill delivered a speech at Fulton, Missouri, in the presence of Truman, in which he said that 'from Stettin in the Baltic to Trieste in the Adriatic, an iron curtain has descended across the continent,' and he called for an American–British alliance to prevent further Soviet expansion. This drew a sharp response from Stalin which revealed his fears about Germany and the need to strengthen Soviet security. 'How can anyone, who has not taken leave of his senses,' he said, 'describe these peaceful aspirations of the Soviet Union as expansionist tendencies on the part of our state?' (Document K).

Thus by March 1946 both sides had lost a great opportunity to forge a successful working relationship. As Martin McCauley points out, 'the Soviets were their own worst enemies;' their crude behaviour in eastern and south-eastern Europe seriously offended the West and caused the change in US policy. On the other hand, there were so many different views on the Soviet Union circulating in the USA that it was difficult for the Truman administration to formulate a consistent policy. The problem for US Secretary of State James F. Byrnes had been to keep public opinion happy by not appearing to be too soft on the Soviets, while trying in private to co-operate with them. 'Given the confusion of views in the US administration, the Soviet government had a difficult task in judging whether American proposals were genuine or merely trial balloons.' After 1945 it was almost impossible to break the vicious circle of misinterpretation and suspicion.[48]

(d) Europe divided

The American policy of toughness and containment did not bear much fruit, except that Soviet troops did withdraw from Iran at the end of March 1946. Throughout 1946 and early 1947 one of the main contentious issues, which the Russians seemed to be taking as the test of American goodwill, was their demand for massive reparations from the Germans and their allies. The Americans consistently refused to agree to this, bearing in mind that the Soviets had already taken almost everything that was movable from their eastern zone of occupation. The Russians in turn refused to accept Byrnes's 'Open Door' policy, whereupon Byrnes ended discussions about a loan to the USSR. When Poland, Czechoslovakia and Hungary applied to the World Bank for loans, they were refused. Meanwhile the main problem in western Europe was economic: most of the countries were finding recovery extremely difficult – they all had trade deficits, the 1946 harvests were generally poor, the winter of 1946–47 was unusually severe, and there was a shortage of coal. The future of Germany was still undecided: the French were against all suggestions of treating the country as a single unit, either politically or economically, since they wanted the Rhineland and the Ruhr to be detached from the rest. All these countries needed economic help, and there was only one state in the world which could afford to provide it – the USA. But Truman, a Democrat president, was faced with a Republican Congress bent on reducing expenditure, and which was unlikely to agree to loans and credits to Europe on the vast scale that was needed.

Early in 1947 the Truman administration came up with what seemed a brilliant solution to this problem: the loans must be made to appear necessary to enable western Europe to pursue the fight against communist expansion. In February 1947 Britain announced that it could no longer afford to continue its military and economic aid to Greece and Turkey. The Greek government was fighting the communists, and Turkey was resisting Soviet demands for a base on the Straits.

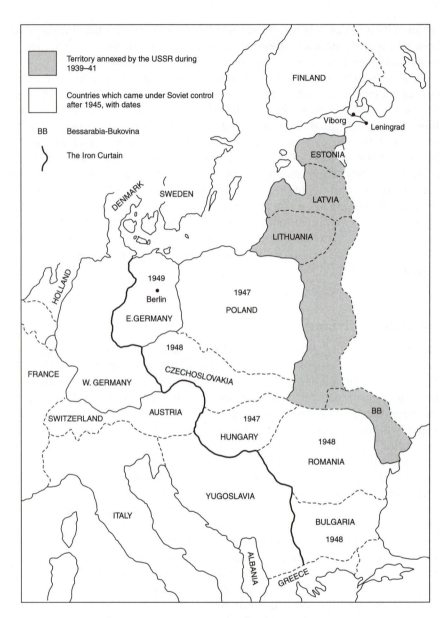

Map 7.2 **Soviet expansion 1939–49 and the Iron Curtain.**

Neither situation was critical, but Truman was able to use them to present the first part of his plan to Congress. In March 1947 he told both houses of Congress that every nation was faced with a choice between two alternative ways of life. 'One way of life is based on the will of the majority, and is distinguished by free institutions, representative government, free elections, guarantees of individual liberty . . . The second way of life is based on the will of a minority forcibly imposed upon the majority. It relies upon terror and oppression, a controlled press and radio, fixed elections, and the suppression of personal freedoms. I believe that it must be the policy of the United States to support free peoples who are resisting attempted subjugation by armed minorities or by outside pressures.' The Truman Doctrine, as it became known, impressed Congress sufficiently for it to vote the necessary funds for Greece and Turkey. An opinion poll showed that 75 per cent of Americans were in favour of Truman's policy; it was popular because it seemed to champion the American way of life and its success in winning the war against fascism.

The Soviet response was guarded; although his speech was clearly directed at the USSR, Truman had avoided mentioning either the Soviets or communism, and described the oppressive governments he had in mind as 'totalitarian'. Stalin could hardly protest publicly, since this would be to admit that his regime *was* totalitarian; privately, however, Molotov told the Soviet ambassador in Washington: 'the President is trying to intimidate us, to turn us at a stroke into obedient little boys. But we don't give a damn.' The second part of the American plan was unveiled in June 1947 by Secretary of State George Marshall (who had taken over after Byrnes resigned in December 1946) in a speech delivered at Harvard University. He explained that the USA was willing to make grants to European states provided they produced plans for European economic integration, which was seen by many Americans as the best way to bring about a prosperous Europe. 'Our policy,' he said, 'is directed not against any country or doctrine but against hunger, poverty, desperation and chaos.' The proposals were to apply to the USSR and the states of eastern Europe as well as to western Europe and Germany; if necessary the western zones of Germany would be developed as a separate unit. The Marshall Plan, as it was known, had a great deal to commend it: the French would have no need to fear the growth of a powerful German economy, because their economies would be integrated; a prosperous Europe would be less likely to fall to the communists and more likely to buy larger quantities of American goods. By offering aid to the states of eastern Europe, Marshall hoped that he could reduce their dependence on the USSR and enable them to escape from Soviet control.

The Marshall Plan put the USSR in a difficult situation: Stalin, Molotov and Mikoyan, the Foreign Trade Commissar, knew that they and the states of eastern and south-eastern Europe badly needed American aid, but they did not want the USA to get any sort of economic or political hold over the region, which they passionately saw as their sphere of influence. Yet if they rejected US aid, western Europe would become wealthy and prosperous while the east would languish in poverty and take much longer to recover. At the meeting of the leading Foreign Ministers in Paris a few weeks later, Molotov said that the USSR wanted the aid, but with no strings attached; the French and British and their American advisers insisted that a co-ordinated plan for the entire European economy must be drawn up. The USSR rejected the idea of their economy being integrated into a capitalist system; Molotov accused the West of simply using the Marshall Plan as a ploy to enable them to interfere in eastern Europe, and called it 'dollar imperialism.' Mikoyan tried to persuade Stalin that American aid would enable the USSR to recover much more quickly and on a higher technological level, which would actually make them more independent. But Stalin would not be convinced; he sent a telegram to Molotov in Paris, and the next day he rejected the proposals. The Americans at least were relieved – Washington would have been somewhat embarrassed if Molotov had accepted! The British and French still hoped that the east Europeans would join the plan, and invited all interested governments to send representatives to a meeting in Paris. Initially the Czechs, Poles and Hungarians seemed enthusiastic; but there was no way that Stalin would allow them to take part, once he had decided against it for the USSR. It was made clear that any state which accepted the invitation to Paris would incur the massive displeasure of the Soviet Union, and in the end all the governments of eastern Europe opted out.

Stalin wanted to offer something positive in place of the Marshall Plan; if western Europe was to have an integrated economy, why not something similar in eastern Europe? In August the USSR and the east European states began forming their own trade agreements and moving towards a separate trading bloc; before long Europe had divided into two hostile economic blocs. From then on it was inevitable that closer political links would develop between the USSR and the states of eastern Europe. The communist leaders in Poland, Czechoslovakia, Hungary, Romania, Bulgaria and Yugoslavia were invited to a conference in Poland in September 1947. Also present were the leaders of the French and Italian communist parties, the two most influential communist parties in western Europe. The main Soviet representative was Andrei Zhdanov, who told the conference that the world had now divided into two hostile camps. One was the capitalist–imperialist camp led by the USA which was bent on the 'enslavement of Europe'; the other was the anti-imperialist and democratic camp led by the USSR. While he did not consider that war between the two was inevitable, he said, nevertheless the communist parties of eastern Europe, France and Italy must prepare themselves for an economic and psychological struggle; he was critical of the French and Italian communists for being too conciliatory and urged them to become more militant. The conference ended with the formation of the Communist Information Bureau (Cominform) whose function was to encourage the setting up of fully communist governments with centrally controlled and planned economies like that in the USSR.

Gradually the Soviet grip on eastern Europe tightened. By the summer of 1948 all the countries of eastern Europe, apart from Greece and Finland, had communist governments. To be communist was not enough, however; it had to be communism according to Stalin. By this time he was so used to being the dictator at home that he expected to play the dictator over his allies (Document J). When Yugoslavia signed friendship treaties with Bulgaria, Romania and Hungary, and Bulgaria announced the formation of a Balkans customs union without consulting him first, Stalin was furious. Their representatives were summoned to a meeting in Moscow in February 1948. The Yugoslavs refused to be dictated to by Stalin; their leader, Josef Broz, known as Tito, had won power for his communist party without any help from Moscow by fighting the German occupying forces. He was tough and self-confident; he believed that there could be many different 'national roads to socialism' and that the leaders of each state, though communist, should be 'master in their own house'. It was the first serious resistance that Stalin had encountered for years; according to Milovan Djilas, one of the Yugoslavs present at the meeting, he treated them as though they were party leaders from one of his own republics who were expected to accept all his utterances as orders to be obeyed without question. Stalin reacted with a rush of blind fury; Djilas and Bokaric, the other Yugoslav representative, were taken at dawn to the airport and shoved into a plane without ceremony. Stalin decided that Tito must be removed; he seemed to think, as Khrushchev put it at the Twentieth Party Congress, that he had only to wag his little finger and Tito would be no more. Tito and his colleagues were accused of being Trotskyists, and Stalin expected that the Yugoslav communist party would remove them. But Tito was popular and his supporters remained loyal; it was the pro-Soviet Yugoslav communists who were expelled from their Central Committee and arrested. Stalin retaliated by having Yugoslavia expelled from the Cominform (June 1948), and all the other members broke off diplomatic relations with Yugoslavia, which was left isolated, outside both camps. Fortunately for Yugoslavia, the USA and Britain provided some help and Tito was able to survive to pursue his own brand of non-Soviet communism. Not one to give up easily, Stalin ordered Beria to 'get rid' of Tito; several assassination attempts were arranged but they all failed. Stalin had suffered his first major post-war defeat.

As the rift with Yugoslavia widened, Stalin became more determined than ever that the other states should be kept on a tight rein. Leaders who attempted to follow independent policies were arrested; Stalin had the power to make this happen because they lacked Tito's popularity and owed their positions to Soviet support. In Hungary the Foreign Minister Laszlo Rajk and Interior Minister Janos Kadar, both anti-Stalin communists, were arrested; Rajk was hanged, Kadar was tortured and gaoled, and about 200,000 people were expelled from the party (1949). In Bulgaria the Prime Minister, Traichko Koslov, was arrested and executed (1949), while in Czechoslovakia the party general secretary, Rudolph Slansky, and ten other cabinet ministers were executed (1952). In Albania the Communist premier, Koze Xoxe, was executed, and in Poland the party leader and Vice-President, Wladislaw Gomulka, was imprisoned; both had spoken out in support of Tito.

The remaining outstanding problem at the beginning of 1948 was the future of Germany. Stalin had originally been in favour of a reunited Germany, but the West, nervous about the potential threat, would not agree, and it seemed clear that Germany would remain divided. On 6 March 1948 the Western powers, anxious to speed up the economic recovery of their zones so that they could begin to pay their way, announced that a separate state of West Germany was to be created, with its own government. The USSR protested that this was a breach of the Potsdam agreement, but could do very little about it except instruct the Soviet representative on the allied council which controlled Germany to walk out. In June 1948, in preparation for the launching of the new state, the West introduced a new currency into their zones; on 23 June this was introduced into West Berlin as well. Stalin responded swiftly in the only area where it was possible for him to make an impact – against West Berlin. A blockade was placed on all road, rail and canal links between the western zones of Germany and West Berlin. His aim was primarily to pressurize the West into abandoning their plans for a West German state, though it would be a bonus if the blockade forced them out of West Berlin. However, the Western nations, always expecting the worst from Stalin, assumed that his main aim was to drive them out of West Berlin and then invade the rest of Germany. They resolved to hold on at all costs and began a massive airlift of supplies to keep the two and a half million West Berliners from starving, rightly judging that the Soviets would not risk shooting down the transport planes. Just in case, Truman sent a fleet of American B-29 bombers to take up positions on British airfields, showing that if necessary he was prepared to use nuclear weapons. Stalin had no intention of provoking a war and made no attempt to interfere with the airlift, which succeeded in keeping the West Berliners alive through the winter of 1948–49. In May 1949, when the blockade had obviously failed, Stalin called it off; with the help of the United Nations the four powers signed an agreement bringing the crisis to an end and restoring the status quo in Berlin. It was another failure for Stalin: he had gambled but the West had called his bluff. Instead of preventing the setting up of a separate West Germany, he had precipitated its formation – the newly elected federal government of West Germany first took office in August 1949. In the USA and Britain public opinion was outraged at the Soviet blockade and there was a great outburst of anti-communist feeling. Stalin's response, in October 1949, was to set up the Soviet zone as the German Democratic Republic.

Although it was a failure, Stalin's action had nevertheless shocked the states of western Europe; although he had never had any intention of launching an invasion of western Germany, many Europeans and Americans were left with the terrifying vision of vast Soviet tank armies rolling forward through Germany and into the West. Joint preparations seemed to be the best way forward; in April 1949 the North Atlantic Treaty Organization (NATO) was formed by the USA, Canada, Britain, France, the Netherlands, Belgium, Luxembourg, Portugal, Denmark, Eire, Italy and Norway. They agreed to regard an attack on any one of them as an attack on them all, and they placed their defence forces under a joint NATO command which would co-ordinate the defence of the West. To the USSR the formation of NATO was yet another challenge from American imperialism and militarism, to which Stalin responded by creating the Council for Mutual Economic Assistance (Comecon), designed to co-ordinate the economic policies of the eastern bloc states. Later, after Stalin's death, the USSR and its satellites signed the Warsaw Pact (1955), a military alliance which was the Soviet equivalent of NATO.

By 1950 the Cold War was spreading even more widely, involving China and Korea. In 1949, after many years of civil war, the Chinese communists under the leadership of Mao Zedong were at last victorious; Chiang Kai-shek and the remnants of his nationalist forces were driven off the mainland to the island of Taiwan. The USSR and the USA clashed repeatedly in the United Nations over the question of China. The Soviet Union proposed that Communist China should be admitted to the UN, taking the permanent Security Council place held by Nationalist China. This proposal was rejected, whereupon the Soviet representatives walked out of the Security Council session, and continued to boycott the meetings for several months. This turned out to be a serious mistake, when in June 1950, war broke out in Korea, as non-communist South Korea was invaded by troops from communist North Korea. The UN Security Council passed resolutions condemning North Korea and calling on member states to send help to the south. It was only possible to pass these resolutions because of the absence of the Soviet representatives who would have vetoed them if they had not still been boycotting the sessions. UN troops, mainly American, soon drove the North Koreans out of the south, invaded North Korea, occupying much of the country, and reaching the frontier with China. Afraid that the Americans would press on and invade China itself, Mao Zedong launched a massive counter-attack, driving the UN out of the north and occupying a large part of South Korea (January 1951). Stalin was anxious to avoid direct Soviet involvement, and he was shrewd enough to realize that this was an extremely dangerous moment. US General MacArthur, who was in command of UN troops, was shocked at the strength of the Chinese forces and wanted to attack Manchuria, using atomic bombs if necessary.

At about the same time other American military leaders were talking about using nuclear weapons against the USSR before the Soviets were able to make many atomic bombs themselves. Early in 1952 British naval intelligence warned the British government that the successful explosion of the Soviet atomic bomb in 1949 had produced a kind of paranoia in the USA. 'Many people in America have made up their minds that war with Russia is inevitable,' it was reported, 'and there is a strong tendency in military circles to fix the zero date for war.' One US general was reported to have remarked: 'We can afford to create a wilderness in Russia without serious repercussions on western civilization. We have a moral obligation to stop Russia's aggression by force ... Whether we call it a cold war or apply any other term, we are not winning; the only way we can be certain of winning is to take the offensive as soon as possible and hit Russia hard enough to at least prevent her from taking over Europe.' The report went on to describe the 'war-mongering fever in American cities whose inhabitants visualize in their own home town the ruins of Hamburg and Berlin.' Fortunately, moderation prevailed; the writer of the British report added that in his view, the USSR was far too cautious to start a war.[49] This was an accurate assessment: Stalin, Mao and Truman were anxious to avoid an escalation of the Korean War into a major conflict, and opted for negotiation; MacArthur was removed from his command and in June 1951 peace talks began. When Stalin died in 1953 the Cold War was still at its height; but at least his caution and moderation in the last two years had perhaps helped to head off a Third World War.

7.5   Assessments of Stalin

When Stalin died there was widespread and genuine grief; thousands of people flocked to view his body as he lay in state, and so great was the chaos that many were crushed to death. For 25 years the population had been brain-washed into regarding him as a kind of god, whose opinion on every subject was correct. Portraits of Stalin were everywhere – on street corners, on walls, on trains and trams, and in parks; towns and collective farms, schools, factories, power stations and even the highest peak in the Caucasus Mountains had been named after him. A large picture of Stalin was suspended from a balloon over Red Square in Moscow. His body was embalmed and placed in a glass case next to Lenin in what was now renamed the Lenin–Stalin Mausoleum. However, his reputation in the USSR soon went into decline when Khrushchev delivered his sensational speech at the Twentieth Party Congress in February 1956, denouncing Stalin's excesses. After another critical speech by Khrushchev in 1961, his body was removed from the mausoleum and buried beneath the Kremlin wall. In 1987 Mikhail Gorbachev also condemned Stalin, and two years later Dmitri Volkogonov's biography appeared in which he described Stalin and Stalinism as 'monstrously inhuman.' It is difficult not to be influenced by the general anger of Russian historians during the glasnost period directed against both Stalin and Lenin. This is why it is good to welcome the attempts by some of the younger generation of Western historians during the 1990s – the new cohort – to take a more detached view and emphasize the positive aspects of the Stalin period, treating it as though it were a normal regime. Stephen Kotkin even went so far as to subtitle his book *Magnetic Mountain*, which was published in 1995, *Stalinism as a civilization*.

So how does one begin to assess a phenomenon like Stalin, whose regime can by no stretch of the imagination be described as 'normal'? The important question surely is: what sort of impact did he have on the USSR? Was it for good or ill? Did he leave the USSR a better place than when he came to power? Did he achieve his aims? Of one thing there can be no doubt – he changed things dramatically, as we have seen. This was the time when the Soviet Union, in the words of Sheila Fitzpatrick, 'was at its most dynamic, engaging in social and economic experiments that some hailed as the future becoming manifest and others saw as a threat to civilization.'[50] Collectivization, the Five-Year Plans and the rapid industrialization, the new constitution, the rise of the new bureaucracy, the spread of mass education and social services, and the creation of the new 'cultured' Soviet citizen – all these can be traced either directly or indirectly to Stalin. But this was not simply a 'revolution from above'; there was a great deal of public support and initiatives springing from the grass-roots – a revolution from below. In fact the regime was extremely popular with the top and middle ranks of the bureaucracy in the party, in the various ministries, in the army and navy, in the security forces and among Komsomol members. These were the people who had risen from the working classes and owed their privileged positions to Stalin, and who would do their utmost to defend the Soviet state.

Stalin was also popular with the majority of ordinary people, which might seem surprising since most families must have lost at least one member during the course of the purges. Volkogonov asks the question: 'how was it that a man so unattractive and politically repellent as Stalin was able to make an entire nation love him?'[51] The answer is that he was extremely adept at manipulating public opinion, and had the knack of being able to rally support at vital moments by presenting himself as the great pupil of Lenin, the wise father-figure and the great Russian patriot who was devoting himself to the nation. Even some of his strongest critics admit that during the war he did much to keep morale high during the black days towards the end of 1941 and deserves some credit for the

Soviet victory. He never admitted he had made a mistake, always managing to shift the blame on to somebody else. If there were excesses, these were the fault of his underlings; he succeeded in giving the impression, rather like the Tsars before him, that injustices would be put right if only he knew about them. The public, unaware of the realities, believed what it was told, and was deeply shocked by Khrushchev's 'de-Stalinization' speech in 1956.

The policies themselves had, at best, mixed success; whichever way you look at it, collectivization was a disaster; industrial modernization was a great success in the areas of heavy industry and armaments and enabled the USSR to win the war. The development of the atomic bomb was a considerable achievement which came about through the insistence and determination of Stalin. On the other hand Soviet industry never solved the problem of how to produce enough household goods, shoes, clothes and furniture. Many of the faults caused by the rapid pace of industrialization still persisted – wasteful methods and poor-quality products. Living standards for the vast majority of people were lower than when Stalin became dominant; the real wages of workers were lower, living and working conditions were no better, and diet was if anything more limited; workers were restless and resentful but dare not go on strike. For a regime which had come into existence in 1917 with the express goal of creating a state run by and for the workers, this must be seen as something of a failure. Nor had the state got any nearer to 'withering away'; according to Robert Service: 'Stalin and his subordinates still talked about the eventual realization of communism, reaffirming that "the state will not last for ever". But how to create a communist society was not a question under consideration. Far from it. The specific aspirations of the Soviet working class no longer figured prominently in Soviet propaganda.'[52] Many historians believe that just as much, and perhaps even more industrial progress could have been made using more conventional methods, perhaps even by simply continuing NEP. Holland Hunter and Donald Filtzer both suggest that the Five-Year Plans, as well as reducing the Soviet workers to resentful unco-operativeness, also left the Soviet state on very shaky economic foundations. Some historians take a more sympathetic view; as we saw earlier (section 6.4(d)), Martin McCauley believes that more was achieved during the First Five-Year Plan 'than would have been the case had orthodox advice been followed.' Stalin aimed to create a totalitarian state (see section 6.5(f)) but he did not fully succeed; there were huge gaps between the orders from Moscow and what actually happened in the factories and on the collective farms. Those groups who actively supported the system made up only a tiny proportion of the total population – a very narrow base indeed.

Stalin's mistakes during the war almost caused the destruction of the USSR; his refusal to listen to warnings of the impending invasion led to the rapid loss of Ukraine, Belorussia and the western parts of Russia, together with much of the country's industrial strength. His refusal to listen to the advice of his military commanders in the early months of the war resulted in the death or capture of millions of soldiers when they were caught in the German encircling movements. The enormous Soviet casualties in the war seemed to leave Stalin unmoved, and never once is he recorded as having expressed regret or distress at the human suffering that must have been involved. Volkogonov claims that he was never tormented by conscience or grief at the enormous losses; 'there is not a single document in Staff HQ archives showing his concern about the number of human lives lost. He was oblivious of the fundamental principle of the military art, namely, that the objective should be gained at minimal cost in human life.'[53] Arguably, the USSR won the war *in spite of* Stalin rather than because of him. The evidence suggests that Stalin placed little value on human life; otherwise how could he have allowed so many of his people to die before their time? Collectivization caused the uprooting and deportation of hundreds of thousands of so-called kulaks, some 381,000 families, and there were many premature deaths. The famine of 1932–33, deliberately caused by Stalin in order to bring the countryside under control, resulted in between five and eight million deaths. The purges of the 1930s and the Great Terror of 1936–38 caused hundreds of thousands more people to be executed or sent to the Gulag. The brutalities continued during the war, alongside the normal war casualties: in the autumn of 1941 the government uprooted 400,000 Volga Germans and deported them to Central Asia and Siberia in case they tried to co-operate with the invading Germans. In 1943–44 Stalin ordered the deportation of about a million people – Crimean Tatars, Chechens, Balkars, Kalmiks and Turks – from their native homelands to Kazakhstan and Central Asia. Accused of helping the enemy, they were rounded up by the NKVD and crammed into freezing cattle-trucks. It was quite unnecessary, since only a handful of Chechens showed any inclination to collaborate with the Germans. Thousands died on the way and more died when they were simply abandoned at their destinations without any accommodation or food; about 40 per cent of those deported perished through hunger, cold and disease.

Was Stalin paranoid, psychologically unbalanced, as some historians have argued? Khrushchev claimed that he was 'a very distrustful man, sickly suspicious; we knew this from our work with him' (Document H). Roy Medvedev believes that he was perfectly sane and coolly ruthless: 'I still think that the main motives were Stalin's inordinate vanity and lust for power. He aspired to autocratic one-man rule, with no restraints whatsoever; he wished to take undeserved credit for building up the Soviet state and Communist party, and to those ends he promoted a personal cult of himself.' Stalin did not hesitate to destroy any section of people in the party or the state which seemed likely to be an obstacle to the achievement of his goals.[54] Even after the war there was no thought of rewarding the people for their efforts, only a continuation of the same harsh policies; at his death in 1953 there were still 2.5 million people in labour camps. This was the fundamental flaw in his whole philosophy and approach – that his regime had to be sustained by force and terror; the secret police and the forced labour camps were an integral part of his system, and this seemed to be perfectly acceptable in his eyes. He ruled his close associates by fear: Bulganin once remarked to Khruchchev that 'it has happened sometimes that a man goes to Stalin on his invitation as a friend. And when he sits with Stalin, he does not know where he will be sent next, home or to jail.' Alan Bullock compares him to a mafia boss who keeps his henchmen where they are, not out of sentiment, but because they are still useful to him. 'Having instilled fear like any other gangster boss by displaying his power to kill, he had the sense to see that the men he depended on for carrying out his orders needed a reasonable expectation of continued favour or they might decide that the dangers of betraying him were less than the dangers of continued loyal service.'[55] Even so there seems little doubt that just before his death he was planning to get rid of Mikoyan and Molotov, whose wife had been in prison, labour camp or exile for three years.

The lower ranks too were kept under control by fear. Stalin was responsible for the deaths of millions of people, although he always made sure that other members of the Politburo signed the death warrants as well as himself. Like Hitler, Stalin created the climate, the atmosphere in which this sort of terror could be possible, and there were huge numbers of people from those at the top like Yagoda, Yezhov and Beria, down to interrogators, torturers, guards, executioners and NKVD troops who were willing to carry out his orders. The evidence shows too that local party bosses – little Stalins – often initiated their own terrors, from below. It simply was not possible to express any sort of criticism of the regime in public and expect to survive; many people who lived through this period have said that it was like living a double life: one was the life in public where you said the acceptable things and used the correct language expected of the new Soviet person; the other was lived in private where you said what you really believed. The staggering fact is that Stalin and his system, whatever their genuine achievements might be, were responsible for the deaths of around 20 million of their own people, over and above those who died as a result of the war. This was more than twice the number of people put to death by Hitler and the Nazis.

The question of whether Stalinism was a continuation of Leninism, which was discussed earlier (see section 5.10(c)) is still being debated among Russian historians. The general trend is to demonize both of them, though there are some, like Irina Pavlova, who maintain that it was only under Stalin that the party apparatus became all-powerful and synonymous with the state. While Lenin was alive there was still a degree of discussion and democracy within the party, and the annual party congresses were not the sham events that they became under Stalin. Stalinism took time to evolve and can in no way be seen as inevitable; a different leader could have caused the system left by Lenin to have evolved in a different direction. In fact as Otto Latsis pointed out in 1989, 'Stalinism's first victim was Leninism.'[56] Lenin's communist party was eliminated and mainstream Bolshevik thinking was abandoned. So it seems that there was a clear break between Stalin and Lenin, and it is difficult not to agree with Stephen Cohen that 'Stalinism was excess, extraordinary extremism...a holocaust by terror that victimized tens of millions of people for twenty-five years.'[57] Stalin hi-jacked the revolution and turned it into his own personal dictatorship. The workers and peasants had exchanged one set of exploiters for another. Robert C. Tucker writes in his introduction to the 1999 edition of a collection of essays on Stalinism: 'one contention to which all the contributors to this volume would likely find themselves in agreement is the conclusion by Roy A. Medvedev that Stalin was "one of the greatest criminals in human history".' Perhaps the most sensible conclusion on Stalin and Stalinism is the one by Martin McCauley: 'Whether one approves or disapproves of it, it was a truly remarkable phenomenon, one that profoundly marked the twentieth century. One can only approve of it if one suspends moral judgement.'[58]

Documents

(A) Extracts from Hitler's directives for Operation Barbarossa and the treatment of the Ukraine, and his thoughts on how he intended to organize the USSR after the war.

Operation Barbarossa – directive signed on 18 December 1940

The German armed forces must be prepared to crush Soviet Russia in a quick campaign even before the conclusion of the war against England . . . the mass of the Russian army in western Russia is to be destroyed by driving forward deep armoured wedges; and the retreat of units capable of combat into the vastness of Russian territory is to be prevented . . . The ultimate objective is to establish a defence line running from the Volga river to Archangel. Then, the last industrial area left to Russia in the Urals can be destroyed by the Luftwaffe.

Directive dated 23 May 1941, concerning the Ukraine

The population of the northerly regions, especially the urban, will have to look forward to the severest famine. It will be essential to drive the population into Siberia. Efforts to save the population from starving to death by bringing surplus food from the black soil region can be made only at the expense of feeding Europe. This would undermine Germany's ability to hold out in the war. From this there follows the extinction of industry as well as of a large percentage of the human beings in the hitherto deficit areas of Russia.

Hitler in conversation – 27 July and 17 October 1941

It should be possible for us to control this region in the east with 250,000 men plus a cadre of good administrators. Let's learn from the English, who, with 250,000 men in all, including 50,000 soldiers, govern 400 million Indians. This space in Russia must always be dominated by Germans . . . We have undertaken the construction of roads that will lead to the Crimea and to the Caucasus. These roads will be studded along their whole length with German towns, and around these towns our colonists will settle . . . We shan't settle in the Russian towns and we'll let them go to pieces without intervening. And above all, no remorse on this subject! We're absolutely without obligations as far as these people are concerned. To struggle amongst the hovels, chase away the fleas, provide German teachers – very little of that for us! . . . Let them know just enough to understand our highway signs, so that they won't get themselves run over by our vehicles. For them the word 'liberty' means the right to wash on feast days. There's only one duty: to Germanize this country by the immigration of Germans, and to look upon the natives as Redskins . . . In this business I shall go straight ahead, cold-bloodedly.

Source: quoted in Alan Bullock, *Hitler and Stalin: Parallel Lives*, pp. 765, 773, 799–800.

(B) Extract from a report by German *Einsatzgruppe C* operating in the Ukraine.

> In Kiev the Jewish population was invited by poster to present themselves for resettlement. Although initially we had only counted on 5000–6000 Jews reporting, more than 30,000 appeared; by a remarkably efficient piece of organization, they were led to believe in the resettlement story until shortly before their execution.

Source: quoted in Bullock, p. 830.

(C) Extract from an article in the army journal *Red Star* by Ilya Ehrenburg, a well-known Russian writer.

> Now we know. The Germans are not human. Now the word 'German' has become the most terrible swear word. Let us not speak. Let us not be indignant. Let us kill. If you do not kill the German, he will kill you … If you have killed one German, kill another. There is nothing jollier than German corpses.

Source: quoted in Richard Overy, *Russia's War*, pp. 163–4.

(D) Stalin calls for a 'scorched earth' policy in his radio broadcast on 3 July 1941.

> In consequence of this war which has been forced upon us, our country has come to death grips with its bitterest and most cunning enemy – German fascism. Our troops are fighting heroically against an enemy armed to the teeth with tanks and aircraft. Side by side with the Red Army, the entire Soviet people is rising in defence of our native land …
>
> The enemy is cruel and implacable. He is out to seize our lands watered by the sweat of our brows, to seize our grain and oil secured by the labour of our hands. He is out to restore the rule of the landlords, to restore tsarism, to destroy our national cultures and our national existence, and to turn us into slaves of German princes and barons. Thus the issue is one of life and death for the Soviet State, of life and death for the peoples of the USSR.
>
> In case of a forced retreat of Red Army units, all rolling stock must be evacuated, the enemy must not be left a single engine, a single railway carriage, not a single pound of grain or gallon of fuel. The collective farmers must drive off all their cattle and turn over their grain to the safe keeping of the state authorities for transportation to the rear. All valuable property, including non-ferrous metals, grain and fuel that cannot be withdrawn must be destroyed without fail. In areas occupied by the enemy, guerrilla units, mounted and on foot, must be formed. Sabotage groups must be organized
>
> *(continued)*

to combat enemy units, to blow up bridges and roads, damage telephone and telegraph lines, set fire to forests, stores and transports. In occupied regions conditions must be made unbearable for the enemy and all his accomplices. They must be hounded and annihilated at every step, and all their measures frustrated.

Source: quoted in F.W. Stacey, *Stalin and the Making of Modern Russia*, pp. 50–1.

(E) Alexander Werth, a British war-correspondent, who spent some time in Leningrad during the later part of the siege, describes conditions.

To fill their empty stomachs, to reduce the intense sufferings caused by hunger, people would look for incredible substitutes; they would try to catch crows or rooks, or any cat or dog that had still somehow survived; they would go through medicine chests in search of castor oil, hair oil, vaseline or glycerine; they would make soup or jelly out of carpenter's glue (scraped off wallpaper or broken-up furniture). But not all people in the enormous city had such supplementary sources of 'food'.

Death would overtake people in all kinds of circumstances; while they were in the streets they would fall down and never rise again; or in their houses where they would fall asleep and never awake; in factories, where they would collapse while they were doing a job of work. There was no transport, and the dead body would usually be put on a handsleigh drawn by two or three members of the dead man's family. Often wholly exhausted during the long trek to the cemetery, they would abandon the body half-way, leaving it to the authorities to deal with it.

Source: quoted in Stacey, p. 53.

(F) Marshall Vasilevsky, the Deputy Chief of the General Staff, complains in his memoirs about Stalin's military performance (February 1942).

Stalin expressed great dissatisfaction with the work of the General Staff... At that time Stalin's performance suffered from miscalculations, sometimes quite serious ones. He was unjustifiably self-confident, headstrong, unwilling to listen to others. He overestimated his own knowledge and ability to guide the conduct of a war directly. He relied very little on the General Staff and made no adequate use of the experience and skills of its personnel. Often for no reason at all he could make hasty changes in the top military leadership... Stalin quite rightly insisted that the military abandon outdated strategic concepts, but he did not do so himself as quickly as we would have liked.

Source: quoted in Roy Medvedev, *Let History Judge*, pp. 768–9.

(G) Stalin's Order No. 227 – Not One More Step Backwards – 28 July 1942.

The enemy is creeping forward and breaking into the depths of the Soviet Union, seizing new districts, laying waste to our towns and villages, raping, looting and murdering the population. To retreat further would mean to destroy ourselves and with us our Motherland.

Not one more step backwards! That has to be our main slogan from now on.

We will no longer tolerate officers and commissars, political personnel, units and detachments abandoning their battle positions of their own free will. We will no longer tolerate them allowing a few panic-mongers to determine the position on the field of battle and to induce other fighters to retreat and open the front to the enemy. Panic-mongers and cowards must be destroyed on the spot. The retreat mentality must be decisively eliminated. Army commanders who have allowed voluntary abandonment of positions must be removed and sent to staff HQ for immediate trial by military tribunal. Three to five well-armed detachments (up to 200 men each) should be formed within an army and placed directly behind unreliable divisions and they must be made to shoot the panic-mongers and cowards on the spot in the event of panic and disorderly retreat.

Source: quoted in Dmitri Volkogonov, *Stalin*, pp. 459–60.

(H) Nikita Khrushchev criticizes Stalin during his speech to the Twentieth Party Congress, 25 February 1956. (For further extracts from the speech, see Chapter 8, Document A.)

Stalin very energetically popularized himself as a great leader; he tried to inculcate in the people the version that all victories gained by the Soviet nation during the Great Patriotic War were due to the courage, daring and genius of Stalin and to no-one else ... Not Stalin, but the Party as a whole, the Soviet government, our heroic army, its talented leaders and brave soldiers, the whole Soviet nation – these are the ones who assured the victory in the Great Patriotic War. [*tempestuous and prolonged applause*]

... Stalin was a very distrustful man, sickly suspicious; we knew this from our work with him. He could look at a man and say: 'Why are your eyes so shifty today?' or 'Why are you turning so much today and avoiding to look me directly in the eyes?' The sickly suspicion created in him a general distrust even toward eminent party workers whom he had known for years. Everywhere and in everything he saw 'enemies', 'two-facers' and 'spies' ...

It was determined that of the 139 members and candidates of the Party's Central Committee who were elected at the 17th Congress, 98 persons – 70 per cent – were arrested and shot [*indignation in the hall*]. The same fate met the majority of the 17th Party Congress. Of the 1966 delegates, 1108 were

(*continued*)

arrested on charges of anti-revolutionary crimes. Now when the cases of some of these so-called spies and saboteurs were examined it was found that all their cases were fabricated. Confessions of guilt of many arrested and charged with enemy activity were gained with the help of cruel and inhuman tortures. The vicious practice was condoned of having the NKVD prepare lists of persons whose sentences were prepared in advance. Yezhov would send these lists to Stalin for his approval of the proposed punishment... Stalin was convinced that this was necessary for the defence of the interests of the working class, in the name of the defence of the Revolution's gains. In this lies the whole tragedy!

Source: quoted in Stacey, pp. 58–9.

(I) Svetlana, Stalin's daughter, puts the blame on Beria.

Beria was a magnificent modern specimen of the artful courtier, the embodiment of Oriental perfidy, flattery and hypocrisy who had succeeded in confounding even my father, a man whom it was ordinarily difficult to deceive. A good deal that this monster did is now a blot on my father's name, and in a good many things they were guilty together. But I haven't the slightest doubt that Beria used his cunning to trick my father into other things and laughed up his sleeve about if afterwards. All the other leaders knew it...

But if a skilful flatterer like Beria whispered slyly in his ear that 'these people are against you,' that there was 'compromising material' and 'dangerous connections,' such as trips abroad, my father was capable of believing it... His opinion of people could be manipulated. It became possible to insinuate that so-and-so had turned out to be 'no good.' 'Even though he'd been well thought of for years, he only seemed to be all right. Actually, he's an enemy. He's been saying bad things about you; he opposes you. X, Y and Z have given evidence against him.' What my father didn't want to realize was that in the cellars of the secret police X, Y and Z could be made to testify to anything. That was the domain of Beria, Yezhov and the other executioners, whom nature had endowed with a special talent for that sort of thing.

Source: Svetlana Alliluyeva, *Twenty Letters to a Friend*, pp. 15, 74.

(J) Milovan Djilas, a leading member of the Yugoslav Communist Party, met Stalin several times, and later recalled their conversations.

He pointed out the meaning of his pan-Slavic policy. 'If the Slavs keep united and maintain solidarity, no-one in the future will be able to move a finger. Not even a finger!' he repeated, emphasizing the thought by cleaving the air with his forefinger. Someone expressed doubt that the Germans would be able to recuperate within 50 years. But Stalin was of a different opinion. 'No, they will recover, and very quickly. Give them twelve to fifteen years and they'll be on their feet again. And this is why the unity of the Slavs is important.'

It is time something was said about Stalin's attitude to revolutions, and thus to the Yugoslav revolution. Because Moscow had always refrained at the crucial moment from supporting the Chinese, Spanish and in many ways even the Yugoslav revolutions, the view prevailed, not without reason, that Stalin was generally against revolutions. This is, however, not entirely correct. His opposition was only conditional, and arose only when the revolution went beyond the interests of the Soviet state. He felt instinctively that the creation of revolutionary centres outside Moscow could endanger its supremacy in world Communism, and of course that is what actually happened. That is why he helped revolutions only up to a certain point – as long as he could control them – but he was always ready to leave them in the lurch whenever they slipped out of his grasp . . .

In his own country Stalin had subjected all activities to his views and to his personality, so he could not behave differently outside . . . He could not act in foreign affairs other than as a dictator. He became himself the slave of despotism, the bureaucracy, the narrowness, and the servility that he imposed on his country.

Source: Milovan Djilas, *Conversations with Stalin*, pp. 90, 103.

(K) Stalin's reply to Churchill's Iron Curtain Speech, in an interview for *Pravda*, 13 March 1946.

I regard it [Churchill's speech] as a dangerous move, calculated to sow the seeds of dissension among the Allied states and impede their collaboration . . . Mr Churchill now takes the stand of the warmongers, and he is not alone. He has friends not only in Britain but in the United States as well. Mr Churchill and his friends bear a striking resemblance to Hitler and his friends. Hitler began his work of unleashing war by proclaiming a race theory, declaring that only German-speaking people constituted a superior nation. Mr Churchill sets out to unleash war with a race theory, asserting that only English-speaking nations are superior nations . . . The English race theory leads Mr Churchill and his friends to the conclusion that the English-speaking nations, as the only superior nations, should rule over the rest of the nations of the world . . .

The following circumstances should not be forgotten. The Germans made their invasion of the USSR through Finland, Poland, Romania, Bulgaria and Hungary. The Germans were able to make their invasion through these countries because, at the time, governments hostile to the Soviet Union existed in these countries. As a result of the German invasion the Soviet Union has lost a total of about seven million people. In other words the Soviet Union's loss of life has been several times greater than that of Britain and the USA put together. The Soviet Union cannot forget about them. And so what can there be surprising about the fact that the Soviet Union, anxious for its future safety, is trying to see to it that governments loyal in their attitude to the Soviet Union

(*continued*)

should exist in these countries? How can anyone, who has not taken leave of his senses, describe these peaceful aspirations of the Soviet Union as expansionist tendencies on the part of our state?

Source: quoted in Martin McCauley, *The Origins of the Cold War 1941–1949*, pp. 133–4.

Notes

1. Jonathan Haslam, *The Soviet Union and the Struggle for Collective Security in Europe, 1933–39*, p. 52.
2. Nikolai Tolstoy, *Stalin's Secret War*, p. 74.
3. Haslam, p. 59.
4. G. Roberts, *The Soviet Union and the Origins of the Second World War*, p. 58.
5. Donald Cameron Watt, *How War Came*, p. 232.
6. Alan Bullock, *Hitler and Stalin – Parallel Lives*, p. 731.
7. Martin Gilbert, *Second World War*, p. 197.
8. Harrison E. Salisbury, *The 900 Days: The Siege of Leningrad*, p. 77. For more details about the reports and Stalin's interpretation of them, see pp. 55–81; also in John Erickson, *The Road to Stalingrad*, pp. 77–142.
9. Tolstoy, pp. 160–1.
10. Dmitri Volkogonov, *Stalin*, p. 399.
11. H. Montgomery Hyde, *Stalin: The History of a Dictator*, pp. 607–8; Salisbury, *The 900 Days*, p. 80.
12. Volkogonov, pp. 393–400.
13. Dmitri Volkogonov, *The Rise and Fall of the Soviet Empire*, pp. 112–13. Unfortunately the 1995 collection of essays by Soviet historians, *Gotovil li Stalin nastupatel'nuyu voinu protiv Gitlera?[Was Stalin preparing a military offensive against Hitler?]*, edited by G.A. Bordyugov, is not available in English. See also Gabriel Gorodetzky, *Grand Delusion: Stalin and the German Invasion of Russia*.
14. John Erickson, 'Barbarossa, June 1941: Who Attacked Whom?', in *History Today*, July, 2001.
15. John Barber and Mark Harrison, *The Soviet Home Front 1941–1945*, p. 16.
16. Volkogonov, *Stalin*, p. 414.
17. C. Andreyev, *Vlasov and the Russian Liberation Movement*, pp. 199–200.
18. The information in this section and the next is from Richard Overy, *Russia's War*, Martin Gilbert, *Second World War*, and John Erickson, *The Road to Stalingrad*.
19. Erickson, *The Road to Stalingrad*, p. 344.
20. Antony Beevor, *Stalingrad*, pp. 141–2, 148. Most of the information in this section is from Beevor.
21. Salisbury, *The 900 Days: The Siege of Leningrad*, pp. 436–7.
22. *Ibid.*, p. vii.
23. Gilbert, p. 441.
24. John Erickson, *The Road to Berlin*, p. 134. See pp. 115–180 for a detailed account of Kursk and its aftermath.
25. Richard Overy, *Russia's War*, p. 247.
26. For a detailed account of the Warsaw rising see Erickson, *The Road to Berlin*, pp. 329–88.
27. Overy, p. 191.
28. Dmitri Volkogonov, *Stalin*, pp. 474, 476.
29. Alec Nove, *An Economic History of the USSR, 1917–1991*, p. 276.
30. E.T. Bacon, *The Gulag at War: Stalin's Forced Labour System in the Light of the Archives*, p. 144.
31. Overy, pp. 194–6.
32. *Ibid.*, p. xxi.
33. *Ibid.*, pp. 287–9.

34. Nikolai Tolsoy, *Stalin's Secret War*, chapter 17, for more details about the repatriations; also Nicholas Bethell, *The Last Secret: Forcible Repatriation to Russia, 1944–47*.
35. Nove, pp. 294–330 for a detailed analysis of the economy during Stalin's last years.
36. Overy, pp. 313–16 for details of how the atomic bomb came to be developed. See also D. Holloway, *Stalin and the Bomb*.
37. N. Levin, *Paradox of Survival: The Jews of the Soviet Union since 1917*, pp. 393–4, 477–9, 512–24.
38. Volkogonov, *Stalin*, p. 519.
39. For a discussion of the theory that Zhdanov was murdered on Stalin's orders as a preliminary to the purge of Leningrad leaders, and in an attempt to 'wipe the Leningrad epic out of public memory', see Harrison Salisbury, *The 900 Days: The Siege of Leningrad*, pp. 579–83.
40. D. Holloway, *Stalin and the Bomb*, pp. 207–11.
41. Volkogonov, *Stalin*, pp. 571–4. See also E. Radzinsky, *Stalin*, pp. 549–58 for Stalin's death.
42. William A. Williams, *The Tragedy of American Diplomacy*.
43. John Lewis Gaddis, *The United States and the Origins of the Cold War, 1941–7*.
44. Vojtech Mastny, *Russia's Road to the Cold War: Diplomacy, Warfare and the Politics of Communism, 1941–1945*.
45. Martin McCauley, *The Origins of the Cold War 1941–1949*, pp. 106–8.
46. Ted Morgan, *FDR: A Biography*, p. 761.
47. Volkogonov, *Stalin*, p. 530.
48. McCauley, pp. 70, 108.
49. Richard Aldridge, *The Hidden Hand*.
50. Sheila Fitzpatrick, *Stalinism: New Directions*, p. 2.
51. Volkogonov, *Stalin*, p. 509.
52. Robert Service, *A History of Twentieth Century Russia*, p. 321.
53. Volkogonov, *Stalin*, p. 475.
54. Roy A. Medvedev, 'New Pages from the Political Biography of Stalin', in Robert C. Tucker (editor), *Stalinism: Essays in Historical Interpretation*, p. 220.
55. Alan Bullock, *Hitler and Stalin*, p. 704.
56. Robert C. Tucker (editor), *Stalin: Essays*, pp. x–xii; Tucker also provides the information about Irina Pavlova whose work has not been translated into English.
57. Stephen F. Cohen, 'Bolshevism and Stalinism', in Robert C. Tucker (editor), *Stalin: Essays in Historical Interpretation*, p. 12.
58. Martin McCauley, *Stalin and Stalinism*, p. 88.

8 The Khrushchev era and de-Stalinization, 1953–64

Summary of events

After Stalin's death in 1953 it seemed at first that there was going to be a collective leadership exercised by a group of his closest colleagues. However, Nikita Khrushchev gradually emerged as the dominant figure, cleverly outmanoeuvring his rivals, rather like Stalin did after the death of Lenin. Khrushchev believed that Stalin had derailed Lenin's revolution and he was determined to discredit Stalin and reform the distorted system which he had left behind. **In February 1956 he delivered his sensational de-Stalinization speech, accusing Stalin of developing 'the cult of personality' and diminishing the role of the party.**

Khrushchev was mainly responsible for the introduction of some new, more radical policies described by some historians as 'the Khrushchev revolution':

- The end of Stalin's system of terror.
- A more relaxed attitude towards the eastern bloc countries.
- An attempt to develop better relations with non-communist states – co-existence instead of conflict.
- Attempts to strengthen the Soviet economy by de-centralizing and streamlining agriculture, industry and the bureaucracy, in order to improve the standard of living of the Soviet people; his Seven-Year Plan, introduced in 1959, was one of his most ambitious innovations.
- A thaw in the cultural life of the USSR.

Khrushchev pursued all these policies with determination and enthusiasm and achieved some successes, most notably in the industrial parts of the Seven-Year Plan. Other aspects of his policies were much less successful; his agricultural reforms were disappointing, while his more relaxed attitude towards the Soviet satellite states caused problems in Poland and especially Hungary, where in 1956 there was a popular uprising against the communist government. Although there was something of a thaw in Soviet relations with the West, the USSR came to the brink of nuclear war with the USA in 1962 over the Cuban missiles crisis, and a bitter rift developed between the USSR and the world's other major communist state, China. These and other considerations caused Khrushchev's colleagues to drop him as leader in October 1964, and he was forced to retire into private life.

8.1   The rise of Khrushchev and the attack on Stalin, 1953–57

(a) The power struggle after Stalin's death

In many ways the situation immediately after Stalin's death was similar to that after Lenin's death in January 1924: neither Lenin nor Stalin had named a successor or left any instructions as to what should be done; at first there was a collective leadership exercised by Stalin's closest colleagues, but this quickly developed into a power struggle. Like Stalin, Nikita Khrushchev seemed the least likely candidate to become supreme leader, and his rivals underestimated him. He was born in 1894 in Kalnikovka, a village in Kursk province in southern Russia, close to the Ukrainian border. His parents were poor peasants and he had very little education beyond the normal four years in the village school. He worked first of all as a shepherd, then on the railways and in a brick factory before going into the mining industry. He served his apprenticeship as a metal fitter in the Donbass and was exempt from military service during the First World War because of the importance of the coal industry for the war effort. By October 1917 he was head of his local metalworkers' union; it was at a union conference that he first met Lazar Kaganovitch, who later brought him to Stalin's notice. Khrushchev joined the Bolsheviks in 1918 and was a Red Army commissar during the Civil War. During the 1920s he lived in Ukraine where he gradually rose through the party network. Returning to Moscow in the early 1930s, he attended courses at the Industrial Academy and by 1935 he was secretary of the Moscow party. He was completely loyal to Stalin and played his part in purging the Moscow party. In 1938 he moved to Ukraine again as first party secretary and carried out more purges; he was made a full member of the Politburo in 1939, no doubt as a reward for his labours. During the war he was a political commissar in the Red Army and fought at Stalingrad. In 1949 Stalin made him Central Committee Secretary with special responsibility for agriculture, but his work in that sphere was not especially successful. At the time of Stalin's death he was regarded by his colleagues as hardworking and enthusiastic, but not as one to be taken seriously as a contender for power. He was friendly, talkative and open, and seemed not in the least devious; he often drank too much vodka and acted the fool at the late-night gatherings in Stalin's dacha. It was easy to dismiss him as a cheerful nonentity; but in reality he was highly intelligent, ambitious, self-confident, courageous, and ruthless when necessary. By February 1956 when he delivered his famous 'Stalin Speech', he had succeeded in outmanoeuvring all his rivals.

The other main contenders were Georgi Malenkov, Stalin's favourite, so far as he ever had one, Lavrenti Beria, the former NKVD chief, who had slipped out of favour with Stalin, but clearly had ambitions for supreme power, and Vyasheslav Molotov, the former long-serving Foreign Minister. Within the first few days the leading jobs were distributed: Malenkov emerged with the posts of Chairman of the Council of Ministers and first secretary of the Communist Party Central Committee. This made him head of both the government and the party, the positions held by Stalin. Beria became head of the MVD (the new title of the NKVD) and Minister of the Interior, and Molotov was made Foreign Minister, while Khrushchev, although a member of the Presidium, was not given a top position. Other members of the Presidium (as the Politburo had been called since 1952) were Nikolai Bulganin, Lazar Kaganovitch, Anastas Mikoyan and Kliment Voroshilov. However, Malenkov's opponents on the Presidium, led by Khrushchev, soon began to protest; later in March they insisted that he should relinquish one of his posts and he decided to give up the secretariat, thinking that the Chair of the Council of Ministers would carry the greater authority; the secretariat was given to Khrushchev, which made him in effect the head of the party.

Malenkov and Beria had been allies for a long time, and made a formidable partnership; many of their ideas were adopted during the first few weeks. Beria in particular was anxious to introduce reforms: it was time to bring an end to the terror policy; an amnesty was declared for political prisoners and the first batches of the 2.5 million labour camp inmates were released, including Molotov's wife; the doctors who had been arrested and put on trial were rehabilitated; Beria announced that he wanted to follow a more relaxed policy towards the non-Russian nationalities and the Soviet bloc countries, and improve relations with Yugoslavia. However, Dmitri Volkogonov believes that any claims that Beria was a 'frustrated reformer' must be taken with a pinch of salt. Although he had ideas for changing the system, Volkogonov is convinced that none of them would have been fundamental, and that any idea that Beria was a genuine reformer is 'simply wrong-headed.'[1]

The first major disagreement came over East Germany: Beria wanted a united, neutral Germany, but Khrushchev was against reunification which he saw as dangerous to the USSR. Molotov agreed with Khrushchev – the German Democratic Republic (GDR) should be kept as a separate socialist state. However, they all agreed that moves towards socialism must take place gradually and cautiously, and that attempts must be made to reduce political tension. The GDR government was trying to introduce the full range of socialist policies as rapidly as possible – rather too rapidly for the liking of the industrial workers. In June 1953 there were strikes and demonstrations on the streets of Berlin and the situation seemed about to get out of hand; the Presidium decided that order must be restored, and Soviet tanks rolled in to crush the uprising. The events in Germany undermined Beria: it was a good excuse to blame his liberal ideas for encouraging the protests; also his was the overall responsibility for security throughout the Soviet bloc. By this time Khrushchev was becoming increasingly suspicious of Beria's intentions; he was obviously trying to build up a base of support in the non-Russian republics and was gradually increasing the power of the government apparatus over the party. His control of the MVD gave Beria enormous power – he had under his control several hundred thousand security troops as well as the ordinary police and border guards, plus some tanks and a small air force.

Khrushchev managed to persuade Malenkov, Molotov and Bulganin, one-by-one, that they were all in danger from Beria and that he must be arrested. They had the support of Marshall Zhukov, who was a particular admirer of Khrushchev because of his contribution during the war, and of many other generals who hated Beria and his secret police. Rumours began to circulate that Beria was pre-paring to surround Moscow with his troops as a preliminary to carrying out a *coup*.[2] This brought added urgency to the situation, and it was decided to arrest Beria at a Presidium meeting on 26 June. Malenkov acted as chairman and he soon handed over to Khrushchev who launched a fatal attack on Beria: 'I have formed the impression that he is no Communist,' he said. 'He is a careerist who has wormed his way into the party for self-seeking reasons. His arrogance is intolerable. No honest Communist would ever behave as he does in the party.' He went on to accuse him of preparing to seize power and of acting as an agent for the British. Beria was stunned and could only mutter incoherently; before he had the presence of mind to alert his bodyguards, Malenkov gave a pre-arranged signal, bringing Zhukov and a group of officers into the room. They arrested Beria and took him away to a secret location, successfully evading the MVD troops surrounding the Kremlin. Regular army troops were moved in to replace them and they took control of the MVD building. Khrushchev, with the support of a majority of the Presidium and the army, had outwitted Beria, who had thought himself unassailable. Together with six of his secret police associates, Beria was tried in secret, found guilty and executed in December 1953. Although it was not generally realized at the time, the fall of Beria marked an important turning point in Soviet politics: Khrushchev and the rest had mellowed since the bad old days before the war, and had had enough of terror and purges; there was a feeling of enormous relief that Beria was out of the way and that the secret police would never again be used against members of the ruling group. Power struggles were no longer going to be life-and-death affairs in which the losers were executed.

The new atmosphere meant that there could be open policy debates in the Presidium for the first time since the 1920s. The main bone of contention was over economic strategy; they all agreed that the most pressing need was to improve the standard of living – more food, more consumer goods, more incentives for farmers and industrial workers. One of their first reforms was to reduce the taxes on peasants by 50 per cent. Malenkov's idea – his 'New Course' – was to reduce expenditure on armaments and heavy industry and spend more on producing consumer goods. To increase food production he advocated the use of more mechanization and chemical fertilizers. Khrushchev argued that the quickest way to raise living standards was to provide more food, and that this could best be done by increasing the area under cultivation. He pointed out that there was plenty of uncultivated virgin land in the Volga area, southern Siberia, the Urals and Kazakhstan, and that the initial costs of bringing new land into cultivation would be recouped in three years, enabling the military budget to remain as before. Although Malenkov's ideas were more radical, the government decided to adopt Khrushchev's virgin land scheme. The 1953 harvest had been disap-pointing, and although the weather rather than Malenkov was to blame for this,

his reputation suffered. In the spring of 1954 millions of acres of new land were developed, and the weather was kind to Khrushchev – the 1954 grain harvest was a record one. *Pravda* switched its support to Khrushchev in January 1955, and by February he had rallied enough support to force Malenkov's resignation as Chairman of the Council of Ministers. Although Malenkov was defeated, he still remained a member of the Presidium and one of the four deputy prime ministers, and was made Minister of Power Stations. Marshall Bulganin, a close ally of Khrushchev, was promoted to be Chairman of the Council of Ministers, or prime minister, which made him head of the government. This meant that Khrushchev was not in complete control, but as the chief secretary of the party he was able to build up the party apparatus as his power base. He appointed officials who were loyal to him, many of whom had worked for him in Ukraine and Moscow.[3] By the time of the Twentieth Party Congress in February 1956 he had revived much of the power of the party which had dwindled during the years of Stalin's dictatorship. With the help of his close allies on the Presidium he was usually able to get his way.

(b) Khrushchev, the 'secret speech' and de-Stalinization

On 25 February 1956 Khrushchev electrified and stunned a closed session of the Congress with a four-hour speech criticizing Stalin (Document A). A few days earlier Mikoyan had already caused a commotion by talking about 'wrongly declared enemies of the people' and claiming that under Stalin 'a cult of personality flourished.' Perhaps he was testing audience reaction for Khrushchev; but nothing he said could have prepared the Congress for the sensational revelations Khrushchev was about to make. He told them about Lenin's advice in 1923 to remove Stalin from his post of Party General Secretary, and about the repressions, tortures, false confessions and wrongful executions of the 1930s. He gave them lists of names of perfectly innocent party members who had suffered at the hands of Stalin. Not only was Stalin a murderer, he was also an incompetent blunderer who had almost led his country to defeat by being unprepared for Hitler's invasion. He scoffed at the image Stalin had invented for himself as a great war hero and he revealed Stalin's errors of strategy. He gave full details of the deportations during the war, the Leningrad Affair and the imaginary Doctors' Plot, and criticized Stalin's handling of the eastern bloc states. The speech was frequently interrupted by gasps of dismay and disbelief, and several people fainted from shock. He condemned 'the cult of personality' introduced by Stalin and accused him of destroying party democracy; he pointed out that there had been a gap of 13 years between the Eighteenth and Nineteenth Party Congresses, and the Politburo had hardly met at all. Significantly, no criticisms were made of anything that had happened before 1934 – such as the horrors of collectivization and the less successful aspects of the First Five-Year Plan – otherwise the whole concept of the Soviet planned economy would have been called into question. Nor was there any reference to the millions of ordinary people who had suffered during the purges, and Khrushchev was careful to point out that he had not been a member of the Politburo until 1939 when the purges were over. Although the text of the speech was not published in full in the USSR until 1989, the general gist of what Khrushchev had said soon spread around the country, and translations found their way into the hands of foreign journalists. There can be no doubt that it was one of the most remarkable events in the whole of Soviet history. It produced mixed emotions in the USSR; there was dismay among many people that the image of their hero had been destroyed, and in Tbilisi, the capital of Stalin's native Georgia, there were protest riots. Among others, there was relief that at last the truth had been confronted and exorcised. There was a general feeling that the political atmosphere was more relaxed, and people felt able to talk about politics again in public. In the Lenin–Stalin mausoleum, the holy of holies of the Soviet regime, visitors were overheard muttering curses at Stalin.[4]

Why did Khrushchev make this attack on Stalin, which was a risky step to take bearing in mind that he and most of his colleagues owed their positions to Stalin and had gone along with his worst excesses without protest? He had difficulty persuading the Presidium that it was the right thing to do; the more conservative members – Molotov, Kaganovitch and Voroshilov – were strongly against it, but with the support of the younger members, Khrushchev secured the approval of the Presidium to appoint a commission to investigate and report on Stalin's activities. It was only towards the end of the Congress that the decision was taken to deliver the speech, and that was on condition that as much as possible of the blame was deflected from the Presidium on to Beria. The problem for the government was that sooner or later something would have to be said about the Stalin question, because of the increasing number of labour camp inmates who were being released. The innocent victims of Stalin's purges, many of whom had been in the camps for 20 years and who would have to be released eventually, would soon be talking about the repressions and the Gulag. Khrushchev genuinely believed that the truth about Stalin's crimes would have to come out, and that it was better if the party took the initiative itself and confronted the issue before it was forced to do so by public pressure. Having secured his colleagues' support with this argument, Khrushchev used his opportunity cleverly for his own political ends: without blaming them overtly for the bloodletting, nevertheless by emphasizing that he only joined the Politburo in 1939, and carefully omitting to mention his own role in the Moscow and Ukrainian purges, he gave the clear impression that his seniors – Malenkov, Molotov, Kaganovitch and Voroshilov – were infinitely more responsible than he was. Publicly condemning Stalin's behaviour in this way made it pretty certain that no future leader would attempt to imitate him.

Another probable motive for the speech is that Khrushchev genuinely felt that Stalin and his system had held up progress by stifling initiative; he wanted to get things back on the track that Lenin would have followed. In the words of Martin McCauley: 'Breaking the spell of psychological subservience to Stalin was the only way to release the pent-up creative energies of the people. The party would assume the task of guiding all these talents into productive channels, thus opening up exciting prospects for party functionaries and members. Khrushchev saw himself as the conductor of the whole enterprise: he sought Stalin's power but he wished to use it responsibly and humanely. He wanted to rule as Lenin would have done in a period of internal stability, as an enlightened dictator.'[5] Khrushchev's speech therefore began the process of de-Stalinization, although the phrase was not used at the time in the USSR; the leadership preferred to call it 'the attack on the cult of the individual.' This meant that Khrushchev had to tread a very fine line: he wanted Stalin's power, yet if he acted too much like a dictator he would lay himself open to similar charges. Nevertheless, over the next few months some remarkable changes took place. The labour camps began to empty and many people were rehabilitated; more freedom was allowed in the world of culture; in science, theories and disciplines which had been banned under Stalin were rehabilitated, the most recent developments in Western science were allowed into the USSR, and Khrushchev was keen to make use of the latest technology. Cybernetics and management science began to develop. There were new policies in industry and agriculture; managers were urged to be self-critical and to be willing to try new ideas; some of the more conservative Ministries were criticized for their 'inertia and stagnation which inflicts considerable damage on the state.' There were new initiatives in foreign policy, with Khrushchev calling for peaceful co-existence with the West, and a more relaxed attitude towards the eastern bloc countries; in April 1956 the Cominform, which had been an irritation to the USSR's partners since its creation, was dissolved. Khrushchev blamed Stalin for mishandling relations with Yugoslavia and did his best to heal the breach between the two countries. He twice visited Tito in Belgrade and Tito paid a return visit to Moscow in June 1956. Kaganovich was dropped from the Council of Ministers, and on 2 June, the same day that Tito arrived in Moscow, Molotov was replaced as Foreign Minister by Dmitri Shepilov.

(c) Trouble in the eastern bloc

The new policies carried dangers for Khrushchev and the party: people were not certain how far the changes were intended to go; was Khrushchev aiming for genuine liberalization? The first real crisis occurred in the eastern bloc states where people interpreted de-Stalinization as meaning more political freedom. If Stalin had been discredited, surely that meant that his puppets should go too. In June 1956 trouble flared up in Poland where, in Poznan, workers organized a general strike and held protest demonstrations against poor living standards, declining wages and high taxes. The Polish government used troops to suppress the violence, but tensions remained high throughout the summer and came to a head in October when Gomulka, the Polish communist leader who had been imprisoned on Stalin's orders, was elected to the Polish Politburo. Khrushchev flew to Warsaw, taking with him Mikoyan, Molotov and Kaganovitch, while Soviet troops in Poland were placed on alert; Warsaw was surrounded by Russian tanks. After difficult negotiations, a compromise was reached: the Poles were allowed more control over their domestic affairs, Gomulka was appointed First Secretary of the Communist Party, and in return the Poles promised to remain in the Warsaw Pact and to go along with the USSR in foreign affairs. Relations between the two states continued reasonably smoothly, though Stalin would not have approved of the Polish version of communism. For example, only about ten per cent of Polish farmland was ever collectivized. By presenting a united front and being prepared for reasonable compromise, the Polish communists won control of their own internal affairs, avoided bloodshed and preserved the unity of the eastern bloc.

The Hungarians were less fortunate. At the time of Stalin's death, the Hungarian leader was the pro-Stalin Matyas Rakosi, who had plunged the country into rapid Stalinization policies, including a collectivization drive which was almost as disastrous as the one in the USSR. Some 2000 people had been executed and about 200,000 put into prisons and concentration camps. The new Soviet leaders severely reprimanded Rakosi for his excesses and replaced him with Imry Nagy, a more moderate, reform-minded Communist. Rakosi and his supporters refused to be sidelined and in March 1955 Nagy was overthrown and Rakosi reinstated as leader. With the news of Gomulka's victory in Poland, Hungarian resentment exploded in a full-scale rising on 23 October 1956. Nagy was brought back as prime minister, and the popular Roman Catholic Cardinal Mindszenty, who had been under house arrest for six years for his outspoken anti-communist views, was released.[6] Nagy managed to negotiate a cease-fire which led to the withdrawal of a detachment of Soviet troops which had been vainly trying to restore order in Budapest. He made several other concessions to the insurgents, abolishing the one-party system and taking some non-communists into a new coalition government. Even this did not calm the tension and it seemed as though the government was on the point of collapse.

This placed the Soviet leadership in a dilemma: Nagy had already broken one main Leninist tenet by agreeing to a multi-party system, and even that was not enough for the insurgents. How much further was Nagy prepared to go? The Presidium agonized about whether or not to intervene; Khrushchev was strongly in favour of military action, arguing that if things were allowed to take their course, 'we would have capitalists on the frontiers of the Soviet Union... We cannot possibly permit it, either as Communists and internationalists or as the Soviet state.' Mikoyan was the main supporter of non-intervention and threatened to commit suicide if armed force was used. There is no doubt that the Soviet leaders would have preferred not to intervene, but the majority genuinely believed that the entire eastern bloc would be severely weakened if things were allowed to go any further in Hungary. In the meantime, Khrushchev explained their thinking to the other eastern bloc leaders, including Tito; all agreed that intervention should take place. On 31 October the Soviet troops which had just withdrawn from Budapest were therefore ordered to take up positions around the capital again, and more troops entered Hungary from Ukraine. Nagy protested strongly at these moves, arguing that they would only inflame the situation. When he got no satisfaction from the Soviet ambassador in Budapest, Nagy announced that Hungary was withdrawing from the Warsaw Pact and would become a neutral power. He appealed to the United Nations to help Hungary preserve its independence. This was the final straw for the Soviet leaders; even Janos Kadar, the leader of the Hungarian Communist Party and a member of Nagy's government, knew that he had overstepped the mark. Some sources claim that Tito played a vital part in what happened next; Nagy was invited to seek asylum in the Yugoslav embassy in Budapest, while Kadar became head of a new provisional government which requested Soviet intervention.[7]

On 4 November Soviet troops went into action; the Hungarians resisted bravely, but against Soviet tanks their defeat was only a matter of time. Casualties were high – some estimates put them at 20,000 Hungarians killed, with another

20,000 arrested; thousands fled the country and escaped to the West. Kadar was installed as the new Hungarian leader, and he stayed in power until 1988. About 300 people were executed, including Nagy, although he had been promised a safe conduct. The Soviet action in Hungary deeply shocked the West, where many observers had thought that de-Stalinization meant a general liberalizing of Soviet policies. It was clear now that there were strict limits to Soviet toleration; the USSR had every intention of using its military power whenever it felt its security was threatened. Khrushchev defended Soviet intervention in Hungary vigorously; he genuinely believed that Nagy had turned into a counter-revolutionary who simply had to be stopped before the infection spread to the rest of the eastern bloc. It was unfortunate for Khrushchev that the vision of Soviet tanks and troops crushing freedom fighters in Budapest rather dented his image of the new peaceful USSR. The West for its part had done nothing to help Nagy, beyond condemning Soviet action. The fact that Britain and France had just themselves intervened, unsuccessfully, in Egypt, spoiled any attempt they might have made to take the moral high ground.

(d) Khrushchev in crisis

By the spring of 1957 Khrushchev's opponents were gathering themselves together for an attack. He was blamed for the events in Poland and Hungary, but what really upset some of his colleagues was the announcement of his new economic policies in February 1957; these involved, among other things, a radical reorganization of the central industrial ministries, which seemed to be a deliberate challenge to the most conservative forces in the bureaucracy (see next section). The opposition to Khrushchev was organized by Malenkov, Molotov and Kaganovitch; they were not themselves in agreement about everything – in fact Molotov and Malenkov were not on good terms with each other; what united them was that they each opposed some area or other of Khrushchev's policies, but most importantly they were all afraid of Khrushchev's ambitions. He seemed intent on increasing his own power, and was taking more and more important decisions without any consultation; they suspected that he was planning to oust them from the Presidium and replace them with his own supporters, five of whom were candidate members of the Presidium. While Khrushchev was away on a visit to Finland, they decided to strike first, and persuaded Bulganin and Voroshilov to support them.

As soon as he returned from Finland Khrushchev was summoned to a meeting of the Presidium (18 June 1957). The conspirators had a majority, since three members who could be expected to support Khrushchev were away at other meetings or on holiday. They immediately launched a bitter attack on Khrushchev, criticizing his 'cult of personality,' his conduct of foreign affairs and the way in which he insisted on interfering with everybody and everything. If they expected Khrushchev to crumble under this sudden onslaught, they were very much mistaken; he defended himself with spirit and hit back at Malenkov, accusing him of being responsible for the deaths of innocent people in the Leningrad affair. The meeting proposed to abolish the position of First Secretary, the post held by Khrushchev, who was to be demoted to the position of Minister of

Agriculture. However, Khrushchev demanded that all the Presidium members and candidate members should be present, together with all the Central Committee Secretaries. He was supported by Mikoyan, Leonid Brezhnev and, most importantly, Zhukov, who controlled the armed forces; the conspirators dared not go ahead without his approval. A second meeting was held the following day, this time attended by the full Presidium and Secretariat, but there was still a majority of full Presidium members against Khrushchev. Still he would not give up; he reminded the meeting that every Central Committee member had the right to be present at Presidium meetings and argued that the fairest way to settle the issues was to call a full plenary session of the Central Committee. His opponents, confident of having a majority in the Central Committee as well, agreed to Khrushchev's proposal, and the session opened on 22 June. The Khrushchev camp had prepared their campaign meticulously; Zhukov and Brezhnev concentrated on discrediting the conspirators for their roles in the purges; statistics were produced to show the number of executions sanctioned by Molotov and Kaganovitch. Then Mikoyan revealed how the anti-Khrushchev group had been trying to limit the role of the Central Committee, and he accused them of being an 'anti-party group.' The opposition had begun to fall apart even before Khrushchev spoke; only Molotov put up a strong performance in his own defence. The final demolition was carried out by Khrushchev who made the big three look even more guilty than Stalin. He reserved his most scathing attack for Malenkov, placing him on a par with Beria and calling them 'the two evil geniuses;' he accused them of taking advantage of their ageing leader, who was out of touch with events and cut off from his people, and of manipulating him shamelessly for their own ends.

It was a wonderful team performance and it ended in a sweeping victory for Khrushchev. The Central Committee expressed full confidence in him as First Secretary, and condemned the anti-party group. Malenkov, Molotov and Kaganovitch were removed from the Presidium and the Central Committee, but to show how much things had changed since Stalin's time, they were not arrested. They were, however, spectacularly demoted, not without a touch of humour: Molotov was appointed as ambassador to Outer Mongolia, Kaganovitch was made manager of a cement works in Sverdlovsk and Malenkov was sent to look after power stations in Central Asia. Bulganin was left in his post as prime minister for the time being. A new Presidium was elected which was full of Khrushchev supporters and included Leonid Brezhnev who was later to play a leading role in Soviet politics. Zhukov became a full Presidium member and Minister of Defence, the first professional soldier to rise to a top position in the party. Khrushchev was soon in disagreement with Zhukov over a number of policy issues, particularly over the relationship between the party and the army. Zhukov wanted to reduce the party's control over the army, but this was unacceptable to Khrushchev, who suspected that Zhukov might try and seize power for himself in a military *coup*. In October 1957 Zhukov was sent on an official visit to Albania and Yugoslavia; while he was away it was announced that he had been replaced as Defence Minister by Marshal Malinovsky, and he was removed from the Presidium. Disgusted at this treatment after all he had done to keep Khrushchev in power, Zhukov retired into private life and concentrated on writing his memoirs.

To complete the consolidation of his power, in March 1958 Khrushchev removed Bulganin and became prime minister himself. He was now head of the party and the government, he had the support of a majority of the Presidium and the party Central Committee, and the army and the police were fully under his control. Although he was not exactly a dictator in the way Stalin had been – he still needed the approval of his colleagues – he was certainly the most powerful politician in the USSR, and remained so until October 1964.

8.2   Problems and new policies

(a) Agriculture

One of the most serious problems left behind by Stalin was the state of Soviet agriculture. The simple fact was that collectivization had come nowhere near achieving the ambitious targets which Stalin had set for it. Soon after Stalin's death Khrushchev told the Supreme Soviet the truth about Soviet farming, revealing details which had been kept secret for years. Ever since the introduction of collectivization, grain stocks had been lower than under Nicholas II; productivity was much too low; livestock herds were fewer than in 1928; peasants were paid too little and taxed too highly, so that they had no incentive to produce more, and the whole of agriculture was too bureaucratic. This would all be put right in the next two to three years.[8] Because of his peasant background Khrushchev considered himself an expert on agricultural matters. He toured round the countryside to meet peasants and talk to them in language which they understood, something which no previous Russian ruler had taken the trouble to do. One of his great contributions to agricultural policy was to persuade his colleagues that agriculture needed much more investment than ever before. He also realized that it was too centralized and that decisions needed to be made and carried out at local level; he urged that agricultural specialists and officials were needed on the spot in the countryside instead of sitting in offices hundreds of miles away. In 1957 even the USSR Ministry of Agriculture was moved from Moscow into premises on a sovkhoz (state collective farm) 70 miles from the capital.

Thanks to Khrushchev the state began to pay the peasants higher prices for their grain, their taxes were greatly reduced, and so were some of the procurement quotas, which left the collectives with more surpluses for private sale; for the first time they were brought into the social security system. The machine tractor stations (MTS) which had been built as part of the collectivization drive were disbanded, the tractors were sold to the collective farms, and the stations were used as repair depots. All this gave peasants greater incentive, and between 1953 and 1958 their average income more than doubled. One of Khrushchev's favourite ideas was the amalgamation of smaller kolkhozy to form larger units – the larger the unit, the greater the productivity, or so he thought. By 1967 the number of kolkhozy (collective farms) had fallen to just over 36,000, each including, on average, 418 households. The numbers of sovkhozy (state-owned collectives) had increased to almost 13,000, mainly because the virgin lands were organized as sovkhozy; the average sovkhoz was twice the size of the average kolkhoz.

These large collectives came in for criticism on the grounds that they were much too large, so that the individual was lost in a huge impersonal rural conurbation.

Krushchev's most famous project was the virgin lands scheme, carried into operation by tens of thousands of young volunteers, many of them from Komsomol. In the first three years some 36 million hectares of new land were brought under cultivation and the government provided over one hundred thousand tractors. Between 1953 and 1958 the new policies brought dramatic improvements in performance, largely because of the initial impact of the virgin lands scheme and some good weather. Total agricultural output more or less doubled during that period; grain output, which had averaged about 80 million tonnes in the years 1949–53, increased to an average of 110 million tonnes during 1954–58. Livestock numbers increased steadily: cattle numbers rose from 56 million to about 67 million and pigs from 28.5 million to 44 million. Output of meat and milk increased in roughly similar proportions.[9] These successes were extremely encouraging and contributed towards a steady increase in the standard of living.

It was after the bumper harvest of 1958 that things began to go wrong. Critics of Khrushchev within the party complained that there was too much investment in agriculture at the expense of other branches of the economy. Now that the virgin lands scheme was well under way, they argued, state investment should be reduced. Khrushchev found it difficult to resist their demands, and consequently the supply of vital agricultural machinery such as combine harvesters, seeders, mowers and trucks dwindled. Khrushchev tried to offset the effects of the investment slowdown by introducing new techniques and cropping patterns. On one of his visits to the USA he had seen huge plains of maize growing and he decided to experiment with it in the USSR, for use mainly as cattle fodder. Unfortunately the idea was carried to excess in some areas, where farms stopped growing crops such as rye and oats and changed to maize. By 1963, as the 'maize mania' took hold, the area growing rye had been reduced by a quarter and that growing oats by almost two-thirds. But in many of these areas – especially in Kazakhstan – the soil and climate were not suitable for maize, and the crop was so poor that it was hardly worth harvesting. Another idea was to farm land more intensively, ploughing up grass and fallow land to grow wheat every year, instead of alternating it. This was possible with the use of the right chemical fertilizers, but unfortunately these were not available in sufficient quantities. In the drive to maximize production Khrushchev adopted what seemed a rather petty policy of attacking the peasants' private plots and launched a campaign to 'persuade' peasants to sell their cows to the kolkhoz; peasants were required to work more hours at a time when their pay was getting less. All this only irritated peasants who responded in their usual way – by being unco-operative.

Some agrarian experts advocated early sowing of wheat, arguing that this would offset the risk of losing a late-sown crop if there was an early autumn frost. However, other experts warned that early sowing carried greater risk of soil erosion and weed infestation, and urged Khrushchev to stick to late sowing. Khrushchev went for early sowing which, by 1962, was being used extensively in the virgin lands areas. Sadly, he had backed the wrong horse – the warnings proved well-founded: there was massive weed infestation which choked the crops, and in 1963 there was a drought which dried out the soil in the virgin lands regions. The

Figure 8.1   *Khrushchev showing off the fruits of his maize campaign in Kazakhstan, 1961.*

harvest that year was a disaster and worse still, millions of hectares of land were lost through wind erosion. The early sowing technique could have worked, but it needed adequate supplies of weed-killer and careful irrigation and fertilization to safeguard against soil erosion; none of these measures had been taken, mainly because of the huge expense that would have been involved. The grain output was almost one-third less than that of the previous year and there was a looming food and fodder shortage. Many livestock were slaughtered because of the fodder shortage; for instance, numbers of pigs fell from over 70 million to only 41 million. The failure also showed up other weaknesses of the agricultural system: there were insufficient drying and storage facilities for crops, and the road system was poor; often the crops which had been harvested rotted before they could be distributed. This was the legacy of years of under-investment in agriculture, and it could only be put right by a massive state investment programme. Khrushchev was well aware of this, but it was only in late 1963, after the failure of the harvest, that he managed to persuade his colleagues to finance a programme to increase output of fertilizers and weed-killers. The problem was always the same – the demands of agriculture constantly had to be weighed against the requirements of defence and heavy industry. The ultimate humiliation for Khrushchev was that 20 million tonnes of grain had to be imported from the USA and Australia in order to prevent the food shortage turning into a famine. In October 1961 he had boasted at the Twenty-Second Party Congress that the USSR would soon overtake the USA in production per head of the population (Document B). The failure of the 1963 harvest was a severe blow to Khrushchev's prestige and one which contributed to his downfall in October 1964.

(b) Industry

Khrushchev's most radical step in general economic policy was to try to decentralize the administration. He believed that the ministries in Moscow had become overstaffed and stagnant; they showed no initiatives and seemed out of touch with local conditions and needs. In 1957 the central ministries were broken up and replaced by 105 regional economic councils (sovnarkhozy) which, it was hoped, because of their local knowledge, would be more efficient and dynamic. The Sixth Five-Year Plan, started in 1955, was abandoned within a year because of over-ambitious targets, and in 1959 a Seven-Year Plan was introduced, which aimed to increase the supply of consumer goods, chemicals and plastics. There can be no doubt that there were considerable economic achievements (apart from the grain harvest), as the statistics on the next page, provided by Alec Nove, show.[10]

Many changes beneficial to the workers were introduced: wage increases, a minimum wage, tax cuts on low incomes, price reductions on some manufactured goods, a shorter working week (reduced from 48 hours to 46 in 1956 and to 41 in 1960), a seven-hour day with six hours on a Saturday, a minimum of four weeks' holiday for workers under 18 and an increase of paid maternity leave to 112 days. A very popular move was the great increases in pensions and disability benefits, and the abolition of all tuition fees in secondary and higher education. In 1958 the trade union committees in the factories were given more powers and responsibilities.

	1958	Plan for 1965	Actual 1965 figure
National income	100	162–165	158
Producers' goods	100	185–188	196
Consumers' goods	100	162–165	160
Iron ore (million tons)	88.8	150–160	153.4
Steel (million tons)	54.9	86–91	91
Coal (million tons)	493	600–612	578
Oil (million tons)	113	230–240	242.9
Gas (thousand million cubic metres)	29.9	150	129.3
Electricity (thousand million kWhs)	235	500–520	507
Mineral fertilizer (million tons)	12	35	31.6
Synthetic fibres (thousand tons)	166	666	407
Machine tools (thousands)	138	190–200	185
Tractors (thousands)	220	–	355
Cement (million tons)	33.3	75–81	72.4
Wool fabrics (million square metres)	303	485	365
Leather footware (million pairs)	356.4	515	486
Grain harvest (million tons)	134.7	164–180	121.1
Meat (total) (million tons)	3.37	6.13	5.25
Housing (million square metres)	71.2	650–660	79.2
		(total for the 7 years)	

The achievements which gained most publicity both at home and abroad came in the Soviet space programme. Khrushchev was keenly interested in space research and made sure that no expense was spared to enable the USSR to take the lead in this area. In 1957 the USSR successfully launched the world's first artificial satellite (*Sputnik*). Most spectacular of all, in 1961 Yuri Gagarin became the first cosmonaut to orbit the Earth; at the reception held in Gagarin's honour in the Kremlin, Khrushchev said: 'this achievement is an accomplishment not only for our people, but for the whole of humanity.' Soviet prestige and Khrushchev's reputation were much enhanced. Unfortunately, the costs involved in these advanced technological projects, together with the military expenditure, especially on missiles, were so enormous that other areas of the economy suffered. Other weaknesses also became apparent in the system; one of the most disappointing was that the sovnarkhoz reform was not a success. The problem, as Alec Nove explained, was that 'any one of the 105 sovnarkhozy was unable to assess the needs of the other 104, unless they were conveyed to them by the centre. For how could an official in, say, Kharkov, or Omsk know the relative importance of requests received from all over the country?... The sovnarkhozy had only one independent criterion: the needs of their own regions. In the absence of clear orders to the contrary they therefore allocated scarce resources to their own regions.'[11] Apparently, Khrushchev had expected that the regional party secretaries would make sure that their sovnarkhozy kept an eye on national priorities and tried to reconcile them with their own local priorities; but this did not happen, and the disease known as 'localism' was diagnosed. Local officials were blamed, threatened and sacked, but it seemed to make little difference, since the defect was built into the system. So for a variety of reasons economic growth began to slow down, and 1963 saw the lowest peacetime industrial growth rate since 1933.

(c) Social policies

In some of his later writings, Karl Marx argued that the ultimate aim of a communist society was to make sure that everybody received what they needed to enable them to enjoy a standard of living which was, at the very least, above the poverty line, provided that they contributed to society by means of their labour. This stage of socialist development would only be reached, however, when society had achieved a high level of production and there was an abundance of most commodities. As we have already seen, at the time of Stalin's death, there had been no improvement in the standard of living, real wages were only about the same as they had been in 1928, and anyway, there was very little for people to spend their money on – food supplies were lower than they had been before the war, and there was a shortage of consumer goods. Also in short supply was adequate housing; this had been a serious problem in the 1930s, but the damage and destruction of the war years had made things worse. This would not do for Khrushchev; he did not seriously question the basic tenets of Marxism–Leninism, and genuinely believed that communism was unquestionably the best way to organize a state. He was convinced that communism *was* attainable, but his travels abroad showed him just how far the USSR was lagging behind the advanced countries of the West.

Khrushchev made a determined effort to identify exactly why progress towards the ultimate goal had ground to a halt, and then tried to come up with policies which would put things right. He was, for example, responsible for giving increased priority to consumer welfare; between 1955 and 1965, earnings increased at an average rate of almost three per cent a year, while prices on the whole remained fairly constant. New wage and salary scales were introduced which reduced the wide differentials that had existed, and there was a clear decline in poverty. Taking a poverty-line figure of 30 roubles a month per head, it can be estimated that in 1958 there were around 68 million state employees and their dependants living in families with a *per capita* income of less than 30 roubles, plus at least 33 million collective farm workers also receiving less than 30 roubles a month, so that at least one hundred million people were living below the poverty line in 1958. However, in 1967 this total had fallen to about 30 million people receiving less than 30 roubles a month; this was mainly due to the introduction of the minimum wage, which actually doubled in the 12 years following Stalin's death.[12] Great efforts were made to increase available living accommodation; the familiar five-storey blocks of pre-fabricated flats began to appear in the cities; they were much criticized for being dreary and badly built, but at least they were better than nothing at all.

Although Khrushchev himself only had the basic primary education, he was interested in education and wanted to introduce changes. There was a shortage of skilled labour; and he had a theory that the intelligentsia did not sufficiently value ordinary manual work. Secondary education was already free for all, and in the new educational programme started in 1958, all students were to receive eight years of compulsory schooling (from 7 to 15); after that, the student would take a job or go on to higher education. Those who chose higher education had first to do three more years' schooling during which ordinary lessons were combined with work on a farm or in a factory. In this way, it was hoped, people who were destined for professional or other 'educated' occupations would learn to appreciate and respect ordinary workers; the 'divorce from life and work' from which the intelligentsia suffered would be ended, and consequently they would be better citizens. Khrushchev was also responsible for the expansion of part-time and correspondence courses. A start was even made on trying to catch up with the West in the manufacture and use of computers. Some historians believe that Khrushchev has not been given enough credit for the progress that was made during this period. His immediate successors tried to write him out of Soviet history and claim the credit for themselves. But in the words of Alistair McCauley, 'he certainly consented to the changes and actively encouraged many of them ... it reflects his personal vision, and it is not wholly inappropriate to call it 'the Khrushchev revolution.'[13]

(d) 'Socialist legality' and culture

'Socialist legality' was Khrushchev's own phrase to denote the relaxation of the pressures and fears that Stalin had placed on pretty well everybody in society. The fear of arbitrary arrest and the death penalty was removed, the labour camps emptied and people were rehabilitated. For some it was too late; Nadezhda Mandelstam received a letter addressed to her husband Osip, informing him that he had been rehabilitated; tragically, he had died in a labour camp in 1938. But at least their families were no longer social outcasts and they could receive a pension. At the same time those who had hopes of a total thaw – a complete liberalization – were soon disillusioned; the legal system was still geared to the whims of the Communist Party, and anyone who persisted in openly criticizing the party or the government could not expect to remain free for long. The police probably showed rather more patience than in the past, but anybody who failed to heed warnings could still be arrested, tortured and sent to a labour camp.

The first reaction of many writers and artists once the dust had settled after Stalin's death was to test the new situation to see how far they could go. In

December 1953 the literary journal *Novy Mir* (New World) published a daring article by Vladimir Pomerantsev in which he attacked the need to stick to imposed rules, which stifled initiative and originality; the real test of a work was its sincerity and truth. The conservatives hit back, claiming that the true test was a work's value to the party; no matter how sincere it was, if it expressed ideologically incorrect attitudes, then a work could only be harmful to the party. This duel between conservatives and liberals went on right through the 1960s. Ilya Ehrenburg caused the next big stir with the publication of his novel, *The Thaw*, in May 1954, which was full of fascinating characters and implied criticisms of the late Stalinist era – the talented artists who can only make a living by painting pictures of 'socialist realism', the Jewish doctor almost driven to a nervous breakdown as the 'Doctors' Plot' unfolds, and the Stalinist factory manager who cares more about output targets than about the health of his workers, and is having his portrait painted to celebrate his successes. Although there was an outcry from the conservatives who called a congress of Soviet writers in December 1954, none of the new works were condemned or banned. The mid-1950s saw the rehabilitation of many writers who had been banned or were in disgrace. Dostoevsky was reinstated, and so were Babel, Bulgakov, Meyerhold and Anna Akhmatova. Mikhail Sholokhov delivered a bitter attack on the Writers' Union, blaming it for all the 'grey rubbish' which had appeared in the previous twenty years. After Sholokhov's wounding personal criticism, the secretary-general of the union, Alexander Fadeyev, committed suicide in May 1956. Clearly the liberals or reformers were in the ascendant.

Vladimir Dudintsev was the first writer to overstep the mark, as far as Khrushchev was concerned. His novel *Not by Bread Alone* appeared in serial form in *Novy Mir* during August, September and October 1956. It tells the story of Lopatkin, a talented young engineer and inventor, who comes up against a blank wall of opposition from the entrenched new ruling class – bureaucrats, party officials and managers. Their faces are set firmly against all innovation which they see as a threat to their vested interests, and they are powerful enough to get the hero sent to a labour camp. This was too near the truth for comfort, coming as it did at the time of the Hungarian uprising. Khrushchev denounced the novel as anti-Soviet; writers were summoned to his dacha and treated to a long harangue in which he warned them that the party would not tolerate literature which undermined the foundations of Soviet society. Yet he had a great respect for writers; he was prepared to forgive those who genuinely tried to 'improve', and no well-known writer was arrested, imprisoned or exiled. The greatest furore was over Boris Pasternak's new novel *Doctor Zhivago*, which he first submitted for publication in 1955. None of the publishers would handle it, and Khrushchev accepted the judgement of his conservative advisers and decided to ban it, though he had apparently only read short excerpts. The novel was eventually published in Italy in 1957 and was widely acclaimed. In October 1958 Pasternak was awarded the Nobel Prize for literature. By this time illegal copies were circulating in the USSR; Pasternak's critics in the Writers' Union whipped up a campaign of protest against the author, the novel and the Nobel Prize, and he was expelled from the Union. He declined the award, fearing that if he left the USSR to attend the ceremony, he would not be allowed to return. Later Khrushchev said that he regretted what had happened and proposed that Pasternak should be allowed to rejoin the Writers' Union.

Poetry had a special place in Soviet literature; public poetry readings were extremely popular during the Khrushchev era, and rising young poets like Yevgeni Yevtushenko and Andrei Voznesensky regularly drew huge audiences of mainly young people. Their work was critical of Stalinism, and therefore Khrushchev approved of them; the simple test of what his reaction was likely to be to any new work was: if it attacked Stalin and his system, it would be tolerated or even welcomed; if it attacked the party or present aspects of Soviet life, it would be denounced or refused publication. Yevtushenko's poem *Zima Junction*, published in 1956 when the poet was 23, vividly describes his childhood in the town of Zima on the Trans-Siberian Railway, his long absence in Moscow and his return at the age of 20, when his family questioned him closely about life in Moscow; his uncle Volodya complains:

> *Now the doctors have turned out innocent;*
> *well, why should people suffer in that way?*
> *It's an international scandal, of course it is,*
> *and all that bloody Beria, I suppose.*

Khrushchev strongly approved, but in 1961 when Yevtushenko brought out his poem *Babi Yar*, about the massacre of Jews near Kiev during the war, it was coolly received. It was clearly an attack on the anti-Semitism still prevalent in Soviet society, and therefore not welcome. Yevtushenko was in semi-disgrace for a time, and so was the composer Dmitri Shostakovich who set some verses from *Babi Yar* to music in his Thirteenth Symphony. On the other hand Alexander Solzhenitsyn's novel *One Day in the Life of Ivan Denisovich* was published thanks to the personal efforts of Khrushchev. The novel describes the experiences of an innocent man sentenced under Stalin to a labour camp, and was based on the author's own experiences of eight years in a camp. Solzhenitsyn's two long novels, *The First Circle* and *Cancer Ward*, were published in 1963, but after that there was a clampdown which lasted until after Khrushchev's downfall. The first signs of this had appeared in December 1962 when he paid a visit to an exhibition of contemporary paintings in Moscow. He made disparaging comments about the abstract exhibits, asking 'what's the good of pictures like this?' and dismissing one that he found particularly objectionable as 'dog shit'. The end of the thaw also showed itself with an attack on religion; Khrushchev believed that the Christian churches, particularly the Russian Orthodox Church, were gaining too much influence on Soviet life. By 1964 the number of monasteries and convents had been reduced from 69 to 10 and the number of theological seminaries from eight to three. Thousands of churches were compulsorily closed and the numbers dropped from 22,000 in 1958 to 7500 by 1964. It was illegal to hold gatherings in private houses without permission, and since this was never granted for religious meetings, it became extremely difficult for Christians to worship. Many Christian leaders who protested were either packed off to remote areas or arrested.

So although the thaw certainly existed under Khrushchev, it was a patchy affair, and nothing could be taken for granted. When some historians tried to reopen discussion on various aspects of the party's history, they were soon warned off. In 1961 a new party programme was produced promising that the USSR would overtake the USA in *per capita* output by 1971. The state would wither away, but the party would become stronger. According to the programme, the USSR was no longer a dictatorship of the proletariat, it was 'a state of the whole people'. But 'the people' had to be extremely careful what part they tried to play in their state; in June 1962 the factory workers of Novocherkassk went on strike and organized a big demonstration in protest against increases in meat and dairy prices. The demonstrators carried slogans demanding 'Meat, Milk and Wage Increases' and at the head of the procession was a large portrait of Lenin. But this did not save them: as the procession approached the offices of the local party, it encountered a line of tanks; troops fired into the crowd, killing 23 people and injuring dozens more – 49 people were arrested and the KGB held a public trial in the town. Five of the ringleaders were executed and the rest were given gaol sentences of between ten and fifteen years.

8.3   Foreign affairs: co-existence and the Cold War

(a) Khrushchev and peaceful co-existence

Krushchev and his colleagues believed that it was absolutely vital to improve relations with the USA. This was because, as Harry Hanak explains, 'it was clear to Khrushchev that the very survival of the Soviet Union and the camp of socialism did not depend on petty satraps in Eastern Europe or even on Mao Zedong, but on the USA. The Americans alone were in a position to inflict unacceptable damage on the USSR.'[14] The new Soviet leaders aimed to deal with this problem in two ways: first of all to build up Soviet military strength in terms of nuclear weapons to act as a deterrent to the USA; and secondly by preaching peaceful co-existence and nurturing personal relationships with leading politicians in the West. Khrushchev loved to travel abroad and believed that personal meetings and conversations were the best way of solving problems and avoiding serious conflict; the fact that his wife accompanied him on many of his trips helped to foster the impression that he was a humane and approachable statesman, not all that different from Western democratic politicians; Soviet communism, in fact, had a human face. Even before his de-Stalinization speech Khrushchev was talking publicly about peaceful co-existence; 'whether the capitalists like it or not,' he said in a speech in Bombay in November 1955, 'the socialists and the capitalists have to live side by side on one planet.' At the Twentieth Party Congress he emphasized that war was not inevitable and that it was possible for the USSR and the USA to share the domination of the world as partners. 'There are only two ways,' he warned, 'either peaceful co-existence or the most destructive war in history. There is no third way.' This did not mean that the Soviets had entirely given up the idea of a communist-dominated world, only that it would be achieved in a different way – when the capitalist world acknowledged the superiority of the Soviet economic system. The other main theme in his foreign policy was the idea of winning over to the socialist camp those newly emerging states which were just gaining their independence from the old colonial powers like Britain and France. The USSR aimed to attract them by supplying them with arms, economic aid and expert advice.

On the American side the rampant anti-communist feelings of the McCarthy era were beginning to moderate with the discrediting of Senator McCarthy in 1954. President Eisenhower announced that the American people wanted friendship with the people of the Soviet Union. An important step had already been taken in July 1953 with the signing of a peace agreement to end the Korean War. In 1954 the USSR, the USA and Britain took part in a conference held in Geneva to bring about peace in Indo-China and organize the withdrawal of French troops. Then in 1955 the Russians made some important concessions: they agreed to give up their military bases in Finland, lifted their long-standing veto on the admission of 16 new member states to the United Nations Organization, and hinted that there was to be more freedom for the states of eastern Europe. The rift with Yugoslavia was healed, and most important of all, in May 1955 the USSR signed a peace treaty with Austria and withdrew its army of occupation which had been there since 1945. In the summer of 1955 Khrushchev and Bulganin attended a summit conference in Geneva where they met Eisenhower and British Prime Minister Anthony Eden and established cordial relations. During his time in power Khrushchev visited numerous countries including Britain, India, France, Switzerland, Indonesia, Burma, Yugoslavia and China; but the one which attracted most attention was his first visit to the USA, in September 1959. He took with him an entourage of a hundred people, including his wife, Nina, and many of their family, and the whole party sailed to New York on board the cruise ship *Baltika*. Khrushchev and Eisenhower held a series of meetings at Camp David, and although no specific agreements were signed, the talks were constructive and mostly good-humoured, in spite of the tensions earlier in the year over Berlin (see below). Things went so well that both sides began to talk of 'the spirit of Camp David' to denote the 'thaw' in the Cold War.

Yet at the same time the arms race was building up; in 1952 the USA made a hydrogen bomb which was much more powerful than the atomic bombs which had caused such devastation in Japan. The Russians followed suit, producing their first hydrogen bomb in 1953, and soon afterwards they produced a bomber with a range long enough to reach the USA. The Americans remained well ahead in numbers of nuclear bombs and bombers; in 1955 they had about 1350 bombers capable of attacking the USSR with nuclear weapons, whereas the Soviets had perhaps 350 aircraft capable of reaching the USA. The Soviet leaders were no doubt pleasantly surprised when the West failed to take advantage of their problems in Hungary in 1956, and even more surprised when the USA failed to support the British and French action at Suez. This probably reassured Khrushchev and his colleagues that the West was not as aggressive as they had feared, and would only use their military strength if their vital interests were threatened. This was a great encouragement to the USSR; nevertheless the Soviets did not relax their efforts: in August 1957 they produced a new type of weapon – the inter-continental ballistic missile (ICBM). This was a nuclear warhead carried by a rocket so powerful that it could reach the USA even when fired from inside the

USSR. Not to be outdone, the Americans soon produced their own version of the ICBM, as well as some shorter-range nuclear missiles which could reach the USSR from launching sites in Europe and Turkey. When the Russians launched *Sputnik 1*, the world's first Earth satellite, the Americans also launched a satellite of their own within a few months.

The thaw in the Cold War was at best inconsistent; there were still some difficult questions to be settled, and it was the problem of East Germany and Berlin which caused strained relations again. The Western powers were still refusing to give official recognition to the German Democratic Republic, and Khrushchev was dismayed at the large numbers of East Germans who were fleeing to the West via West Berlin. He had been trying to find a way of blocking the exodus for some time, and in 1958 it seemed that he might have found the answer – an attack on the Western presence in West Berlin. In November he announced that the situation in West Berlin was 'a sort of malignant tumour. If that tumour is not removed, the situation is fraught with such danger that there might be some undesirable consequences. Therefore we have decided to do some surgery.' He demanded that the Western powers should join the USSR in signing a German peace treaty within six months; otherwise the USSR would sign a separate treaty with the East Germans, giving them full control of their own affairs; the East Germans would then be free to claim the whole of their capital, Berlin, enabling them to control access to the city, and excluding Westerners if they chose to do so. It seems likely that Khrushchev's main motive, apart from getting the West out of Berlin and stopping the drain of East Germans, was to limit West German rearmament, which was a worry even to some of West Germany's allies in NATO, as well as to Moscow. Khrushchev hoped to manoeuvre the West into attending a summit conference where a German peace treaty could be signed, setting limits to German rearmament and ratifying the post-war frontiers, including the division of Germany.

The Western powers did not reply immediately, and when they did, they made it clear that they objected strongly to being presented with an ultimatum, and they reasserted their right of free access to West Berlin. Khrushchev therefore tried a more gentle approach – in January 1959 he lifted the six-month deadline and agreed to attend a conference of foreign ministers, which met in Geneva for seven weeks in May and June. No progress was made with the German problem, but during Khrushchev's famous visit to the USA in September 1959, he agreed to drop his threat of unilateral action over Berlin, while Eisenhower agreed to the four-power summit for which Khrushchev had long been pressing. In January 1960, on the strength of the improving relations with the USA, Khrushchev announced a reduction of one-third in the size of Soviet armed forces, though he was quick to stress that this would in no way weaken the USSR militarily; the reduction in numbers of troops would be more than offset by an increase in numbers of missiles. Underlying this change of emphasis was the belief that it would be much cheaper to defend the country with rocket forces; this would make it possible to reduce the defence budget, spend more on consumer goods, and therefore raise the standard of living.

The long-awaited summit conference was to take place in Paris in May 1960, but unfortunately it had scarcely started when it broke up in disarray. On 1 May, two weeks before the summit was due to begin, the Russians shot down an American U-2 spy plane near Sverdlovsk, deep inside the USSR, and captured its pilot, Gary Powers. The Americans had been carrying out these flights regularly since 1956, in spite of several official protests from the USSR. Khrushchev hoped to make propaganda value out of the incident by embarrassing the Americans. 'Just imagine what would happen,' he asked the Supreme Soviet on 5 May, 'if a Soviet aircraft appeared over New York, Chicago or Detroit... How would the United States react?... What was this? A May Day greeting?' The wreck of the plane and its equipment were put on show in Gorky Park, where Khrushchev himself appeared and made another speech attacking the USA. However, his tactics were to blame the CIA rather than Eisenhower himself, so that relations between the two leaders would not be irrevocably damaged. Things began to go wrong for him when Eisenhower admitted responsibility for ordering the flights, and refused either to apologize or to end them. On the plane to Paris the Soviet delegation decided to ask Eisenhower for an official apology for the flights and a promise to end them. According to William Tompson, 'Khrushchev probably had little doubt that his demands would mean the break-up of the summit, but, faced with the prospect of only modest progress in Paris and under pressure from China, East Germany and Soviet hardliners, he concluded that he could not afford to go ahead with the meeting unless Eisenhower gave way on the U-2 issue. The political price would otherwise be too high for what Khrushchev might hope to achieve at the summit.'[15] When the four leaders met, Khrushchev put forward his demands; Eisenhower made one concession, announcing that the flights had been suspended, but he refused to apologize, claiming that there was nothing to apologize for. In spite of efforts by Macmillan, the British Prime Minister, and de Gaulle, the French President, to restrain him, Khrushchev stormed out of the meeting; the summit was over and so, apparently, was the thaw (Document C).

Khrushchev travelled to New York again in September 1960 in order to attend the opening of the UN General Assembly. He spent over three weeks in the USA, and seemed to be doing his best to annoy his hosts; he spent a lot of time attacking the Americans and the United Nations, while being as nice as possible to Third World leaders. He caused a sensation in one UN meeting when he interrupted a speech by Macmillan and started banging his shoe on the table; Macmillan upstaged him by calmly calling for a translation. Probably under pressure from hardliners at home, Khrushchev continued his tough stance when he met the new American President, John F. Kennedy, in Vienna in June 1961. He repeated his earlier demand that the Western powers must be prepared to leave Berlin within six months; the situation was becoming critical as the flow of refugees from East to West Germany via West Berlin became a flood – on average a thousand a day were leaving in the summer of 1961. Many of them were members of the intelligentsia and skilled people who were vital for the rebuilding of the East German economy. The climax was reached on 12 August when 4000 crossed into West Berlin on that one day. No progress had been made at the Vienna summit, and Kennedy had announced: 'We cannot and will not allow the Communists to drive us out of Berlin either gradually or by force.' In desperation the East German leader, Walter Ulbricht, ordered the building of the 28-mile long Berlin Wall all the way across the city, blocking the escape route. The West protested strongly and Kennedy sent 1500 troops to West Berlin to make sure that access was kept open. Tensions were high for a time, but neither side wanted war and the situation gradually calmed down. Both could claim some success in the episode: Khrushchev had managed to stem the flow of refugees, and arguably saved East Germany from economic collapse; and in fact Kennedy understood that the building of the wall was a defensive measure. Kennedy had shown firmness in the face of Khrushchev's attempts to browbeat him, and had secured the future of West Berlin, which was not challenged again for the rest of the Cold War. So in a strange sort of way the building of the wall seemed to stabilize the situation and Berlin ceased to be an issue.

(b) The Cuban missiles crisis

No sooner had tensions eased in one area than they began to build up in another. Cuba, a Caribbean island less than a hundred miles from the coast of Florida, became involved in the Cold War in 1959 when Fidel Castro seized power from the corrupt dictator, Batista, who had been backed by the Americans. Castro outraged the USA by nationalizing American-owned estates and factories, and the Americans responded by refusing to buy Cuban sugar and breaking off relations. This only drove Castro into the arms of the USSR: Khrushchev seized the chance to foster friendly relations with Cuba, agreeing to buy Cuba's sugar exports and providing other economic aid and military advisers. Kennedy believed that Cuba was now a communist state in all but name; he approved a CIA plan for a group of Batista supporters to invade Cuba from bases in Guatemala. There was a general view in the USA at the time that it was permissible for them to overthrow hostile regimes which they felt were too near for comfort; they had already got rid of the Arbenz regime in Guatemala, and they now planned to deal with Castro in the same way. The small invading force of 1400 men landed at the Bay of Pigs in April 1961, but the operation was so badly planned that it was easily defeated by Castro's army and his two jet planes. Kennedy continued his campaign to bring down Castro by economic and political means, trying to isolate Cuba, sinking Cuban merchant ships and sabotaging petroleum sites on the island, while some 40,000 American troops carried out invasion exercises around the neighbouring island of Puerto Rico. Seriously worried, Castro appealed to the USSR for military help, and Khrushchev sent over 40,000 troops.

It was Khrushchev's decision to install ballistic missiles on the island that caused the crisis. The Russians troops were already equipped with short-range nuclear weapons, and now Khrushchev ordered the building of launching sites for missiles with a range of up to 2000 miles, which meant that all the major cities of central and eastern USA would be under threat. There was absolute consternation in the USA when, on 14 October 1962, photographs taken from a U-2 spy plane clearly showed missile bases and launch pads under construction. Khrushchev could justifiably argue that it was the Americans who had caused the crisis by their aggressive attitude towards Cuba; he was simply responding to the Cuban request for protection. Clearly, he hoped that the missiles would make the Americans think twice before attempting another invasion. An additional motive was to even up the balance of power – to put the Americans under the same threat as the USSR faced from American missiles in Turkey. As he wrote in his memoirs: 'The Americans had surrounded our country with military bases and threatened us with nuclear weapons, and now they would learn just what it feels like to have nuclear missiles pointing at you.' And of course the Americans didn't like it; Kennedy was determined that the missiles must go, for the sake of his own prestige and that of the USA.

According to Andrei Gromyko, the Soviet Foreign Minister, the Cubans had already made it clear that if the USA would give effective guarantees that it would not carry out an armed invasion of Cuba, and not help other countries to invade either, Cuba would have no cause to reinforce her defences. However, in a meeting on 18 October Kennedy told Gromyko: 'the point is, the present regime in Cuba does not suit the USA. It would be better if there was a different one there.' In reply, Gromyko questioned his justification for supposing that the Cubans should decide their domestic affairs according to the wishes of Washington, and he warned Kennedy that if the USA took hostile action against Cuba, 'the Soviet Union cannot play the part of bystander.' But he stressed that the USSR did not want war and hoped to settle the matter through peaceful discussion.[16] Kennedy was under pressure from many of his advisers to launch air strikes against the missile bases in Cuba, but, perhaps influenced by his talks with Gromyko, he decided to take more cautious action. On 22 October he announced that the USA had introduced a naval blockade – he called it a 'quarantine' operation – to turn back 25 Soviet ships which were en route to Cuba carrying nuclear warheads. Without warheads, the missiles were useless; Kennedy also demanded that the missile sites in Cuba should be dismantled and the existing missiles removed.

The situation was extremely tense: Khrushchev placed Soviet troops in Cuba on full alert, and American troops moved into Florida; as the Soviet ships approached the American quarantine line, the world seemed to be on the brink of nuclear war. Neither side wanted to take the risk, and Khrushchev made the first move – he ordered the Soviet ships to turn back. There was enormous relief in the USA, but the crisis was not over yet; nothing had been decided about the missiles. On 26 October Khrushchev offered to remove them if the USA would promise not to invade Cuba. Kennedy did not reply immediately, knowing that such a promise would be unpopular with many people in the USA. Khrushchev raised his stakes, demanding a further concession – the removal of American Jupiter missiles from Turkey. When an American U-2 spy plane was brought down by a missile over Cuba, some people thought it was the first shot of the war. However, at this point both leaders kept their nerve and decided to compromise. Kennedy's brother Robert, who was the US Attorney-General, met the Soviet ambassador, Anatoly Dobrinin, informing him that the Americans accepted Khrushchev's proposals, on condition that the American promise to remove its missiles from Turkey was kept secret from the American public. The crisis was over: the Russians began to dismantle the missile sites almost immediately, and the Americans ended the blockade; in April 1963 they removed their Jupiter missiles from Turkey, although the public was not told for another six years.

It had been a close run thing, though. Some historians claimed that in reality the crisis was not as real as it seemed, since neither side intended to start a war. However, it later emerged that the Soviet forces had 36 nuclear warheads and

24 intermediate range missiles in Cuba, all of which were capable of hitting the US. The Soviet commanders in Cuba had been authorized to use the nuclear weapons without further authorization from Moscow, if the Americans invaded Cuba. American intelligence had got its information wrong – the President was informed that there were no actual warheads on the island, and that there were only 10,000 troops, whereas, in reality there were 42,000. If the USA had decided to risk an attack on Cuba, in view of the supposed weakness of the Soviet and Cuban defence forces, the Soviets would almost certainly have used their nuclear weapons.[17] Dmitri Volkogonov believed that Khrushchev was fully prepared to carry out nuclear strikes against the US. 'Twenty or twenty-five per cent of Soviet missiles could have found their targets, and in the first – and no doubt last – assault, ten or twelve nuclear devices would fall on American cities.'[18] Although Khrushchev had secured the removal of missiles from Turkey, the fact that it was not announced publicly deprived him of the credit, and his Cuban policy was seen as a failure. However, he had made sure that Cuba would not be invaded again by US forces (Document D). The crisis had one important beneficial outcome: both Khrushchev and Kennedy were shaken by the realization of how close they had come to a nuclear war, and of how easily it could have started. It seemed to bring both of them to their senses and led to an improvement in relations. A direct telephone link (known as the 'hot-line') was established between Moscow and Washington. This would allow swift consultations to take place and avoid the potentially dangerous delays that could occur if the two governments relied on communication by letter. Talks took place to explore the possibilities of limiting the spread of nuclear weapons. The first success was achieved in Moscow on 5 August 1963 when the USSR, the USA and Britain signed the Limited Test Ban Treaty, agreeing to ban the testing of nuclear weapons in the Earth's atmosphere, in space and under water. In January 1964 Khrushchev reached agreement with the new US President, Lyndon Johnson, to reduce the production of enriched uranium for making nuclear warheads.

(c) The USSR and the rift with China

When Mao Zedong finally won the civil war in China in 1949, it seemed that there could be a great future for world communism, with two giant states in alliance. In 1950 they signed a treaty of mutual assistance and friendship. After Stalin's death the new Soviet leaders were anxious to develop the relationship further; Khrushchev's first visit abroad was to China, in September 1954. When the Chinese requested that Soviet troops should give up their bases in the Chinese ports of Dairen and Port Arthur, which they had held since 1945, Khrushchev agreed. Chinese students were invited to come to the USSR to be educated and Soviet aid to China was increased. But relations soon began to turn sour; Mao was horrified by Khrushchev's attacks on Stalin, claiming that Stalin's mistakes should take second place to his great achievements. The Chinese recognized that the USSR was the leader of the communist world, but increasingly, they did not like the direction in which Khrushchev was trying to lead them. They disapproved of his policy of peaceful co-existence with the capitalist world, and believed that the USSR should be stirring up trouble for the capitalists and encouraging revolutions around the world. Khrushchev had promised to help the Chinese with their nuclear weapons programme, but then in June 1959 he changed his mind; if the USSR began supplying its allies with nuclear weapons, this would encourage the USA to do the same, which was exactly what Khrushchev was trying to prevent. Naturally Mao was furious at this and strongly disapproved of Khrushchev's visit to the USA in September 1959, when he agreed not to take unilateral action over Berlin. Mao felt that Khrushchev was kow-towing too much to the capitalists; Western imperialism, in the words of Mao, was no more than a 'paper tiger', which was really extremely weak underneath its surface glamour.

By the time Khrushchev went to Beijing for the tenth anniversary celebrations of the People's Republic in September 1959, immediately after his trip to the USA, the atmosphere was extremely chilly. Mao claimed that he was too busy to spend much time with Khrushchev, and when they did get together, their fundamental differences were all too obvious. Khrushchev's priorities were peaceful relations with the west, so that he could reduce the USSR's crippling defence budget, and friendship with Yugoslavia, which would help stabilize the other east European states. In Mao's book, Yugoslavia was even more lax than the USSR. When the Paris summit broke down in May 1960, Beijing was delighted; Mao obviously thought it served Khrushchev right for talking to the enemy. The quarrel between the two communist states was out in the open and there were bitter exchanges at a communist party conference in Bucharest later in May; Khrushchev denounced the hard-line Chinese leadership as 'left adventurists' who were recklessly willing to unleash a third world war. All the Soviet advisers were recalled from China and all aid was stopped. In November 1960 a conference attended by representatives of 81 communist parties met in Moscow to try and heal the rift, but it was a failure. There could be no agreement between the USSR and China on the question of peaceful co-existence. The Chinese labelled the USSR as 'revisionists' who were departing from strict Marxism–Leninism; this was a serious accusation in the eyes of communists, and Khrushchev responded vigorously, accusing Mao of 'dogmatism'. The vast majority of those present supported Moscow; among the states of eastern Europe, only Albania, which was ruled by the unreformed Stalinist, Enver Hoxha, supported Beijing. Relations continued to deteriorate over the next few years; the more the USSR tried to secure *détente* and restrict the spread of nuclear weapons, the more determined the Chinese became to develop their own independent nuclear power.

There were territorial disputes between the two states as well; during the nineteenth century the Russians had taken over large areas of Chinese territory which the Chinese now claimed back. The Soviet government refused their demands; by 1960 both sides had troops positioned along their joint frontier in Asia, and there were frequent incidents. China was also involved in a frontier dispute with India; when war broke out between the two in 1962, Mao Zedong expected that the USSR would support China; however, Khrushchev announced that the USSR would remain neutral in the dispute, while at the same time dropping hints that their sympathies lay with the Indians. Mao was full of contempt when, at the end of October 1962, Khrushchev agreed to remove Soviet missiles from Cuba. Relations probably reached rock bottom in August 1963 when China refused to join the USSR and the USA in signing the Limited Nuclear Test Ban Treaty. The two leaders continued to hurl insults at each other: Mao produced his famous criticism that 'Soviet revisionist collaborators are uniting with the running dogs of capitalism,' while Khrushchev began to talk of the Chinese as the 'yellow peril,' and about Mao as 'a living corpse.' From the West's point of view this was all very gratifying, since it meant that they no longer had any need to worry about the threat from an alliance of these two giant communist states.

8.4   Downfall and assessment of Khrushchev

(a) The fall

On 17 April 1964 Khrushchev celebrated his seventieth birthday and was awarded the title 'Hero of the Soviet Union' for his services to the state and the party. But behind the scenes, moves had already started to oust him. Leonid Brezhnev and Nikolai Podgorny were the prime movers, and they were determined to avoid the mistakes of 1957 when Khrushchev had rallied his support in the Central Committee to defeat the Presidium. Those in the plot were each given a group of Central Committee members to convert, and senior party officials in each region were recruited to convert their subordinates. Not all of them were amenable, and the plot would have come to nothing if Khrushchev had not given them plenty of cause for dissatisfaction. Khrushchev's policies had upset so many different people that by 1964 there were relatively few who would be sorry to see him go. His attempts to make the party and the government more efficient and decentralized were entirely laudable, but they brought him into conflict with the bureaucracy whose privileged positions were being threatened. In September 1962 he had pressurized the Presidium into accepting his plan to divide the party into two sections – agricultural and industrial – a move which aroused intense opposition. It meant that the authority of provincial officials would be cut in half, and those who were Central Committee members were afraid that they would lose their seats to their new colleagues at the next party congress. In many areas there was a deliberate go-slow on implementing the policy; some sources estimate that over a third of the provincial committees had still not carried out the division when Khrushchev left power. The policy was one of Khrushchev's greatest domestic failures: it angered provincial officials, caused bitter rivalries between the old and new secretaries, and had disastrous effects on both agriculture and industry.[19]

These latest reforms, together with his policy failures in other areas, were the decisive factors which sparked off the plot. The 1963 harvest was a disappointing failure, casting doubt on Khrushchev's entire agricultural policy, and particularly on the virgin lands scheme. The army and the hardliners disapproved of his cuts in defence spending and his proposal to reduce Soviet military manpower by one-third; they deplored the damage to Soviet prestige inflicted by his climbdown over Cuba, and the poor relations with China. Many of the elite wanted a rapid build-up of nuclear weapons, not Khrushchev's attempts at limiting nuclear proliferation. Above all, there was the fact that Khrushchev seemed to have developed the 'cult of personality' just as much as Stalin had. He never had the same authority as Stalin, and was always answerable to the Presidium and the Central Committee, but he became increasingly aggressive and arrogant, bullying his colleagues and delivering stinging attacks on party officials. During his early years in power Khrushchev always took care to cultivate the Central Committee and enhance its standing, but he became impatient with it and began to see it as a barrier to progress. After 1960 he tried to reduce the standing of the Central Committee by inviting supporters to take part who were not entitled to attend. As Martin McCauley puts it: 'he needed radicals who would tear the existing structure apart and build a new, dynamic vehicle of change. Career men and women would minimize risk-taking and seek compromise solutions...he wanted a revolutionary attitude to work, whereas officials wanted an administrative attitude to prevail. They wanted life and work to be predictable. Not surprisingly "Khrushchev's" Central Committee voted to remove him since he posed a powerful threat to their well-being.'[20]

In October 1964 Khrushchev went on holiday to Pitsunda on the Black Sea. He had received warnings that a plot was afoot but had not realized that Brezhnev and Podgorny were leading it. He made the mistake of telling Podgorny that he would clear it up after his holiday, when he would 'toss out those responsible like whelps.' The conspirators, knowing that they had to act quickly, took the decision to call him back from his holiday to attend a Presidium meeting. A long list of criticisms of his actions was put to him, and it was suggested that he should retire. He rejected some of the criticisms, but he apologized for his mistakes and his rudeness, and he agreed to resign, much to the surprise of most of his colleagues, who had expected him to put up a fight. The decision was confirmed by vote at a meeting of the Central Committee plenum, and it was announced that Khrushchev had retired because of his age and ill-health (14 October); he was the first Soviet leader to step down. It was also agreed that the posts of First Secretary of the Committee and Chairman of the Council of Ministers should never again be held by one person; Brezhnev was chosen as First Secretary and Kosygin as Chairman. Khrushchev was allowed to live quietly in retirement, where he spent much of his time recording his memoirs on tape. In spite of the efforts of the Soviet authorities to prevent it, these were first published in the USA in 1971, soon after Khrushchev's death.

(b) The importance of Khrushchev and his policies

For over 20 years Khrushchev seemed to have been forgotten; he was scarcely mentioned in the press – even his death and funeral in September 1971 merited only the briefest of announcements. With the arrival in power of Mikhail Gorbachev and the coming of *glasnost* (openness) and *perestroika* (restructuring), interest in Khrushchev revived; scholars were allowed to study his policies and people were keen to read what was written about him. So how important was Khrushchev? What sort of a leader was he? Did he achieve anything significant? In the immediate aftermath of his downfall the new leadership did all it could to discredit him; on 17 October *Pravda* carried a long article which, in the guise of explaining how the ideal communist leaderhip should work, delivered a devastating attack on Khrushchev without actually mentioning his name. In effect, it accused him of dreaming up hare-brained schemes, reaching half-baked conclusions, and taking hasty decisions and actions without regard to realities. 'Bragging and phrasemongering, bossiness, reluctance to take account of scientific achievement and practical experience' were also mentioned as characteristics which were alien to good leadership. The article gives the impression that Khrushchev's career had ended in complete failure. And of course many of his policies *did* seem to be ineffective or worse, even disastrous; the most obvious ones were his agricultural schemes, his decentralizing and streamlining policies, the division of the party into agricultural and industrial sections, the Cuban missiles fiasco, and the rift with China, which often seemed like a personal feud between Khrushchev and Mao Zedong. Some historians have criticized his lack of success in the area of science and technology, in spite of his determination to catch up with the West. Huge sums of money were spent and although this strengthened research and development, Soviet experts did not succeed in adequately bridging the gap between theoretical research and the application of the findings towards improved techniques in industry. On the contrary, some scientists claimed in 1965 that the gulf between the USSR and the USA in science had actually increased.[21] His other serious failure, in the eyes of some historians, was that he never developed a successful system to get the best out of industrial workers – either by providing workers with genuine political or economic incentives or managers with effective sanctions.[22]

On the other hand there are many historians who feel that Khrushchev deserves considerable credit. Alec Nove pointed out that because of his policies, supplies of food and consumer durables increased impressively, and life became more tolerable for ordinary citizens. 'An economic or political historian writing in the next century is, in my view,' he wrote in 1987, 'bound to evaluate Khrushchev's record positively, but would distinguish the period of his rise, 1953–58, as the most fruitful. After Stalin's grim remoteness, his much more approachable, human, folksy style was a welcome contrast.'[23] He had a good record on social welfare, there were higher growth rates and better harvests, and in his first years, much greater freedom of discussion, including discussion of economic shortcomings, and the publication of previously secret statistics was allowed. G.A.E. Smith thinks that Khrushchev's greatest contribution was that he persuaded his colleagues that coercive central control was not the way to secure the best results from agriculture; the way forward was more investment, a higher level of technical competence among farm-workers and managers, and more effective control over local decision-making. Unfortunately, he was badly let down by the powerful vested interests in the party and state administration, which opposed greater investment in agriculture in order to provide necessities like chemical fertilizers and weed-killers. The agricultural work force also let him down: 'the way in which apathetic farm workers misused and abused machinery and equipment resulted in enormous waste and low yields, a problem which could not be solved simply by pouring in even more resources.'[24] Khrushchev had the courage to break with the past in other ways too; if he had done nothing else, his bold denunciation of Stalin and his attempts to steer the system away from the cruelties and the rigidity of the previous 25 years should earn him a high place in Russian history. He wanted to reduce the tight grip of the bureaucracy and to 'return power to the people,' as he put it. Although his immediate successors, including Brezhnev, belittled most of his ideas, when they came to draw up the so-called 'Brezhnev' constitution in 1977, they incorporated in it Krushchev's concept of the all-people's state (see section 9.1(c)).

Khrushchev genuinely believed that Marxism–Leninism could work and that Stalin had hi-jacked the movement. Therefore it was vital to get back to the basic principles of Lenin. Khrushchev also recognized that to survive, communism must begin to 'deliver the goods;' the Soviet people must be able to start enjoying the time of plenty that the communists had been promising for so long. His attractive personality, his enthusiasm and his self-confidence drew great support among the younger generation; those who responded to his campaign to change things were known as 'Children of the Twentieth Congress'. In many ways, as we have seen, life did improve for most people; Robert Service sums it up succinctly: 'High-rise apartment blocks were put up in all cities. Diet went on improving. Meat consumption rose by fifty-five per cent between 1958 and 1965 alone. Fridges, televisions and even washing-machines entered popular ownership. The hospital and education services were free and universally available; rents, home heating and cooking fuel were very inexpensive. Labour discipline was relaxed. Unemployment was practically unknown. Wages rose after 1953 and kept on rising . . . The retention of cheap urban cafeterias meant that neither pensioners nor the working poor starved.'[25]

Martin McCauley sees Khrushchev as an original leader who, 'despite his modest success, was good for the Soviet Union and the world.' One of his achievements was to bring the Soviet Union on to the world stage, to reduce some of the fear it had aroused, and to increase respect for it. 'His policy of peaceful co-existence, the first *Sputnik* and the first man in space added immensely to the Soviet Union's prestige;' this gave the illusion that the USSR was ahead of the USA in science and technology. The reasons why Khrushchev's success was only modest was because he was trying fundamentally to change Soviet society; this involved 'systematically dismantling the system on which the privileges and power of the bureaucracy rested. He was forced to adopt reform after reform because his original solution had been blocked. His zigzagging is testimony to the strength of the bureaucratic opposition, but also to his refusal to concede defeat . . . Given time he could have fundamentally changed the Soviet system.' McCauley sees Khrushchev as a kind of heroic failure, a man with a noble vision which was eventually brought to naught, 'not because of its shortcomings, but because of the greed and concern for position of those in authority.'[26] Perhaps it is appropriate to allow a Russian historian the final word; Dmitri Volkogonov, who was not over-enthusiastic about any of the Soviet leaders, nevertheless conceded that Khrushchev had performed a great historical service: 'he had done the virtually impossible: as a fledgling from Stalin's nest, he had undergone a visible change in himself and in a fundamental way also changed society. However much his successor, Brezhnev, may have sympathized with aspects of Stalinism, he could not bring himself to restore it: the obstacles placed in the way by Khrushchev proved insurmountable.' The fact that when he was ousted, he was not exiled, shot or flung into jail, was a tribute to his own condemnation of such methods in 1956. Volkogonov approved of Khrushchev's memoirs too: '*Khrushchev Remembers* reveals Khrushchev's character as a bold and impulsive politician, and as both an orthodox Marxist and a heretic, and it is among the best works on the period.'[27]

Documents

(A) Extracts from Khrushchev's de-Stalinization speech delivered at the Twentieth
Party Congress, 25 February 1956. (For further extracts from the speech, see
Chapter 7, Document H).

Stalin acted not through persuasion, explanation and patient co-operation
with people, but by imposing his concepts and demanding absolute submission to his opinion. Whoever opposed this concept or tried to prove his
viewpoint and the correctness of his position, was doomed to removal from
the leading collective and to subsequent moral and physical annihilation...
Comrades, we must abolish the cult of the individual decisively and restore
completely the Leninist principles of Soviet socialist democracy, expressed in
the constitution of the Soviet Union, to fight the wilfulness of individuals
abusing their power. Comrades, the Twentieth Congress of the Communist
Party of the Soviet Union has manifested with a new strength the unshakeable
unity of our Party, its cohesiveness around the Central Committee, its resolute
will to accomplish the great task of building Communism. [*Tumultuous
applause.*]

We are absolutely certain that our Party, armed with the historical resolutions
of the Twentieth Congress, will lead the Soviet people along the Leninist path
to new successes, to new victories. Long live the victorious banner of our Party –
Leninism! [*Tumultuous prolonged applause ending in ovation. All rise.*]

Source: quoted in John Laver, *The USSR 1945–1990*, pp. 20–1.

(B) Khrushchev, at the Twenty-Second Party Congress, 31 October 1961, promises
a successful future for the people of the USSR.

In the current decade (1961–70) the Soviet Union will surpass the strongest
and richest capitalist country, the USA, in production per head of population;
the people's standard of living and their cultural and technical standards will
improve substantially; everyone will live in easy circumstances; all collectives
and state farms will become highly productive and profitable enterprises; the
demand of Soviet people for well-appointed housing will, in the main, be
satisfied; hard physical work will disappear; the USSR will have the shortest
working day.

The material and technical basis of Communism will be built up by the end of
the second decade (1971–80), ensuring an abundance of material and cultural
values for the whole population. Soviet society will come close to a stage where
it can introduce the principle of distribution according to needs, and there
will be a gradual transition to one form of ownership – national ownership.
Thus a Communist society will be built in the USSR...Active participation of

(*continued*)

---

all citizens in the administration of the state, in the management of economic and cultural development, improvement of the government apparatus, and increased control over its activity by the people – this is the main direction in which socialist statehood develops in the building of Communism . . .

Source: quoted in Laver, pp. 14–15.

(C) Khrushchev's impromptu speech at a press conference immediately after the breakup of the Paris summit, 16 May 1960, over the U-2 spy-plane affair – a typical example of his off-the-cuff style – aggressive, pugnacious and amusing.

Gentlemen, please forgive me, but I want to give a reply right away to the group who are doing all the booing here. I have been informed that Chancellor Adenauer [the leader of West Germany] has sent agents who were not beaten by us at Stalingrad, into the Soviet Union to boo at us. But we booed at them and chased them three metres into the ground. So, take a look around you when you boo us. We beat you at Stalingrad, in Ukraine and Belorussia, and we finished you off.

I am the representative of the great Soviet people; the people who made the great October socialist revolution under Lenin's leadership, a people who are successfully building a Communist society. If you boo at me you are only making me bolder in my class struggle . . . Gentlemen, I will not hide my satisfaction from you, I enjoy fighting the enemies of the working class. I like to hear the imperialist lackeys raging and unable to do anything.

Source: quoted in Dmitri Volkogonov, *The Rise and Fall of the Soviet Empire*, p. 223.

(D) Khrushchev, in his memoirs (published in 1971), gives his version of the Cuban missiles crisis.

We sent the Americans a note saying that we agreed to remove our missiles and bombers on condition that the President give us his assurance that there would be no invasion of Cuba by the forces of the United States or anybody else. Finally Kennedy gave in and agreed to make a statement giving us such an assurance . . . It has been, to say the least, an interesting and challenging situation. The two most powerful nations in the world had been squared off against each other, each with its finger on the button. It was a great victory for us though, a triumph of Soviet foreign policy . . . a spectacular success without having to fire a single shot! . . . We behaved with dignity and forced the United States to demobilize and to recognize Cuba. Cuba still exists today as a result of the correct policy conducted by the Soviet Union when it rebuffed the United States. I'm proud of what we did.

Source: Nikita Khrushchev, *Khrushchev Remembers*, p. 500.

(E) Sir Frank Roberts tells what he remembers about Khrushchev. Roberts attended the Yalta Conference, was British Minister in Moscow, 1945–47, and British Ambassador to Moscow, 1960–62. He worked closely with Stalin, Molotov and Khrushchev.

My first direct contact with Khrushchev came when I was Ambassador in Yugoslavia at the time he made his expedition in 1955 to persuade Tito to forgive and forget the breach made by Stalin in 1948. His behaviour then was typical of Khrushchev's approach to so many of the problems he thought he could solve. He started with a brainwave, calling for rapid action alien to the normal thought processes of his more plodding colleagues, and running serious risks of failure and even humiliation, but which, if successful, could bring big dividends and realize important policy objectives. His impulsive handling of the situation was clumsy and counter-productive, but he then retrieved from the apparent wreck enough of his original purpose to justify the enterprise ... At the reception he drank too much and had to be carried out through rows of diplomats and other guests on the arms of Tito and Rankovic, with his feet sketching out the motions of walking without ever touching the ground. But the end result ... did ensure that Yugoslavia resumed inter-state relations ...

I have never seen him more pleased with himself and his country than at his reception of Gagarin at Moscow Airport and at the subsequent Kremlin reception. It was at this time that he coined the slogan that the Soviet Union should not only catch up with, but overtake the USA, following on the misunderstood quip that the Soviet Union would see the US buried (not bury her itself). The Moscow wits were wiser when they commented that, while catching up was all right, there should be no overtaking, since this would only enable the Americans to see the patches on the seats of Russian trousers.

Khrushchev did not acquire the confident support of the Soviet population, despite all he had done to free them from Stalin's tyranny. They instinctively felt that his behaviour was not that expected of a Russian leader – as for example, in the shoe-slapping episode at the UN. However, for me he remains a man who, despite mixed motives and often confused thinking ... did make life less dangerous and more comfortable for most people in the Soviet Union ... He was a most accessible, communicative, human and stimulating leader, however adversarial, with whom to do business.

Source: Frank K. Roberts, 'Encounters with Khrushchev', in Martin McCauley (editor), *Khrushchev and Khrushchevism*, pp. 217, 219, 228.

Notes

1. Dmitri Volkogonov, *The Rise and Fall of the Soviet Empire*, p. 196.
2. William J. Tompson, *Khrushchev: A Political Life*, p. 121. For discussion of the power struggle, see pp. 114–42.
3. Martin McCauley, 'Khrushchev as Leader', in M. McCauley (editor), *Khrushchev and Khrushchevism*, pp. 12–13 for how Khrushchev built up his political 'tail'.

4. Tompson, p. 161.
5. Martin McCauley, *The Soviet Union 1917–1991*, p. 233.
6. Jonathan Luxmore and Jolanta Babiuch, *The Vatican and the Red Flag*, pp. 80–2.
7. Tompson, p. 169.
8. Alec Nove, *An Economic History of the USSR, 1917–1991*, p. 336. For a full account of Khrushchev's agricultural policies, see pp. 336–48, 372–7.
9. G.A.E. Smith, 'Agriculture', in Martin McCauley (editor), *Khrushchev and Khrushchevism*, p. 105.
10. Nove, p. 363.
11. *Ibid.*, p. 368.
12. Alistair McCauley, 'Social Policy', in Martin McCauley (editor), *Khrushchev and Khrushchevism*, pp. 146–7.
13. *Ibid.*, p. 144.
14. Harry Hanak, 'Foreign Policy', in Martin McCauley (editor), *Khrushchev and Khrushchevism*, p. 183.
15. Tompson, p. 225. For details of the U-2 crisis, the failure of the summit and Khrushchev's thinking, see pp. 219–28. For a detailed study of the U-2 crisis in the context of Soviet-US relations, see Michael R. Beschloss, *Mayday: Eisenhower, Khrushchev and the U-2 Affair*, London, 1986.
16. Andrei Gromyko, *Memories*, pp. 176–7.
17. Martin McCauley, *The Soviet Union 1917–1991*, pp. 244–5.
18. Volkogonov, pp. 235–47 for his account of the crisis.
19. Tompson, pp. 254–6.
20. Martin McCauley (editor), *Khrushchev and Khrushchevism*, pp. 23–4.
21. M.J. Berry, 'Science, Technology and Innovation', in Martin McCauley (editor), *Khrushchev and Khrushchevism*, pp. 90–4.
22. Donald Filtzer, 'Labour', in Martin McCauley (editor), *Khrushchev and Khrushchevism*, p. 137.
23. Alec Nove, 'Industry', in Martin McCauley (editor), *Khrushchev and Khrushchevism*, p. 70.
24. G.A.E. Smith, 'Agriculture', in Martin McCauley (editor), *Khrushchev and Khrushchevism*, pp. 113–14.
25. Robert Service, *A History of Twentieth Century Russia*, pp. 356–7.
26. Martin McCauley, 'Introduction' and 'Khrushchev as Leader', in *Khrushchev and Khrushchevism*, pp. 3, 26–9.
27. Volkogonov, pp. 248, 252. Khrushchev's memoirs are in two versions: *Khrushchev Remembers* (London and New York, 1971) and the much more detailed *Khrushchev Remembers. The Glasnost Tapes* (New York, 1990).

◼ ⊻ 9 The Brezhnev years – the USSR stagnates, 1964–85

Summary of events

Khrushchev's fall in October 1964 – he was the first Soviet leader not to die in office – was followed by the usual manoeuvring for power among his colleagues. Leonid Brezhnev soon became Secretary-General of the Party, with Alexei Kosygin as Chairman of the Council of Ministers. At first Brezhnev was in charge of the party, the administration and agricultural matters, while Kosygin was responsible for foreign affairs and industry. Of the two, Kosygin was the more go-ahead and reform-minded, but by the early 1970s, as the other members of the collective leadership either died or were dropped, **Brezhnev gained the ascendancy**. Reform disappeared from the agenda, and Brezhnev's years in control turned out to be a period of stagnation. Many of Khrushchev's reforms were abandoned and pressing economic problems were ignored:

*   Although agricultural yields increased, the government **failed to solve the built-in problems of the collective farm system**.
*   After a promising beginning during **the Eighth Five-Year Plan (1966–70), industrial performance was disappointing during the Ninth Five-Year Plan, (1971–75), and the decline continued during the Tenth Five-Year Plan (1976–80)**.

Brezhnev and his colleagues were less tolerant of criticism than Khrushchev, in all spheres of activity; anything that threatened the stability of the system or encouraged independent thinking was stifled, and this applied to the states of eastern Europe as well. When liberal trends developed in **Czechoslovakia in 1968**, a massive invasion took place by Soviet and other Warsaw Pact troops. The reforming government was removed and replaced by a strongly pro-Moscow regime. Soon afterwards Moscow announced **the Brezhnev Doctrine – Soviet intervention in the internal affairs of any communist state was justified if socialism in that state was considered to be threatened**. Brezhnev's record on human rights was not impressive, and so **by 1967 the human rights movement had developed;** leading figures in the movement were the scientist Andrei Sakharov, the writer Alexander Solzhenitsyn, and the historian Roy Medvedev and his twin brother Zhores, a biologist. The movement spread to Czechoslovakia where, in 1977, a human rights group calling itself 'Charter 77' was formed. There was trouble in Poland too – industrial unrest, food shortages and strikes forced the government to resign in 1980, and an independent trade union movement, known as Solidarity, was formed.

One area in which the Brezhnev regime did try to continue Khruchshev's work was foreign policy – pulling out all the stops to achieve parity with the USA in armaments, which they claimed to have reached by the early 1970s, and **trying to bring about a relaxation of international tension – a policy known as** *détente*. Brezhnev's efforts brought some success – he had three meetings with US President Nixon, and in 1972 **a Strategic Arms Limitation Treaty (SALT I) was signed.** However, there were setbacks, not least the Soviet invasion of Afghanistan on Christmas Day 1979. When the Russians removed the Afghan president and replaced him with a leader more favourable to the USSR, all the old Western suspicions of Soviet motives revived. All through the Brezhnev years the USSR was plagued by the same old problem – the enormous cost of the arms race and the attempt to play a global role imposed an ever-increasing strain on her economy.

When Brezhnev died in 1982 at the age of 76, he was succeeded first by **Yuri Andropov**, who hoped to introduce some reforms, but died after only 15 months in office. The Politburo chose **Konstantin Chernenko** as the next Secretary-General, but he was over 70 and already terminally ill; he died after only 13 months, leaving the country in dire need of a younger leader with energy and vision.

Main areas of debate:

- **Why did the USSR stagnate under Brezhnev?**
- **To what extent was life better during the Brezhnev era?**
- **How far can Brezhnev's foreign and eastern bloc policies be seen as a success?**

9.1 Personnel and policies

(a) The rise of Brezhnev

The leading group of Presidium members consisted of Leonid Brezhnev, Alexei Kosygin, Nikolai Podgorny, Anastas Mikoyan and Mikhail Suslov. For some months it seemed that there would be a genuinely collective leadership; Kosygin, the man in charge of foreign affairs and industry, gave the impression of being the senior figure in the government, and in 1965 was responsible for some important economic reforms, the last to be attempted until 1979. The 1968 Czech crisis was a turning point (see section 9.3(a)); Kosygin was not in favour of Soviet intervention, and since this left him very much in a minority in the Politburo (the Presidium changed its name back to the Politburo in March 1965), his influence began to decline. Meanwhile Brezhnev's position as Secretary General of the party enabled him gradually to build up his support, appointing his allies to important posts; for example, in 1967 Yuri Andropov was made head of the KGB, and Brezhnev's friend Marshal Andrei Grechko became USSR Minister of Defence. Relations with the Soviet satellite states in eastern Europe came under the heading of party matters, which is why Brezhnev found himself thrust into the limelight in 1968 when Warsaw Pact troops invaded Czechoslovakia. After that it was Brezhnev who took charge of foreign affairs and began to act increasingly as the head of state. By the end of the Twenty-Fourth Party Congress in March 1971, his supporters were in a majority on both the Politburo and the Central Committee, and he was, in effect, the leader.

Brezhnev was 58 years old when Khrushchev was removed. He was born in 1906 in Ekaterinoslav province, Ukraine, of working-class Russian parents. His father was a metalworker; the young Leonid also worked in the industry for a time, until the family moved back to Russia, where he took a course in agricultural methods. He joined the party in 1929 and later returned to Ukraine, qualifying as an engineer in 1935. He lived in the important industrial city of Dnepropetrovsk, where he began to rise through the party ranks, so that by the outbreak of war, he was a member of the Ukrainian party elite. During the war he was a political commissar, reaching the rank of Major-General. He attracted the attention of Khrushchev who, in 1950 recommended him to Stalin for the job of First Secretary of the Moldavian party. As a *protégé* of Khrushchev, Brezhnev's career continued to flourish and in 1956 he was promoted to candidate membership of the Presidium. According to Dmitri Volkogonov, 'he was a man of one dimension, with the psychology of a middle-ranking party functionary, vain, wary and conventional. He was afraid of sharp turns, terrified of reform, but was capable of twisting the party line in whatever direction the hierarchy desired.' He had a reputation of being good-humoured and sympathetic with his subordinates, and got his way not by harshness and threats, but by patience and persuasion. But with his long experience as a member of the party apparatus, he had learned that the most important requirement was to avoid upsetting those in authority over him. 'Having given his complete verbal support to Khrushchev's reformism, Brezhnev turned out to be its very antithesis.'[1]

(b) Economic policies

The new leadership soon dropped many of what they considered to be Khrushchev's 'hare-brained schemes;' the division of the party into agricultural and industrial wings was abandoned, and the Ministry of Agriculture was brought back with all its former powers restored. The controversial regional economic councils (*sovnarkhozy*) were abolished and the original industrial ministries were brought back. The leaders had to face up to the problem which was to exercise them throughout the Brezhnev years – the question of how to allocate limited economic resources among all the vital areas of the economy. Brezhnev, with his special interest in agriculture, was keen to invest more in that area; Kosygin wanted to place the emphasis on producing more consumer goods; the military wanted to increase the defence budget to enable the USSR to catch up with the USA in armaments. Brezhnev hoped to reduce defence expenditure and international tension, making more cash available to finance his plans for agriculture. He recognized that Khrushchev had been right to aim for increased production of chemical fertilizers and weed-killers. However, he abandoned the idea of growing maize in every available area and concentrated on increasing output in

Figure 9.1   Brezhnev speaking at a public meeting during a visit to Bulgaria, September 1973.

central Russia. He relied on the conventional methods: the central fixing of quotas, central instructions on what to sow and when, and increases in procurement prices in order to give farmers more incentive. There was a massive increase in state investment in agriculture, which more than doubled in the decade 1965–75; by 1980 no less than 27 per cent of all capital investment was going into agriculture. Statistically the results seemed reasonable: by 1980 gross agricultural output was 21 per cent higher than the average for 1966–70; grain output – always taken as the main indicator for the success of Soviet agriculture – averaged 205 million tons a year during 1976–80 as against only 130.3 million tons in 1961–65.[2]

However, this was insufficient to meet the rapidly growing demand for food from a population which was now much better paid. The government kept food prices low – meat prices, for example, had not increased since 1962, and since average wages had doubled, people could afford to eat more. Some years suffered bad harvests; during the Brezhnev era there were five poor years, mainly because of bad weather; so, for example, although the average grain harvest for 1971–75 was 181.6 million tons, the total for 1972 was only 156 million tons, and the shortfall had to be made up by imports from the USA. Nor did the situation improve: the average annual grain harvest for 1981–85 fell from 205 million tons to 181 million tons, and consequently the USSR had to import some 40 million tons of grain each year. What was wrong with Soviet agriculture? The list of weaknesses is a long one. It was too centralized – farmers were given their orders from Moscow and there was very little room for local discretion and initiative;

many of the collective farms were too big and it was difficult to organize the labourers, who were largely unskilled. Labourers were paid for the length of time worked rather than for the amount produced; nor was any account taken of the quality of what was produced. Although subsidized, many kolkhozy still operated at a loss, mainly because prices for machinery and fuel continued to rise. There was a severe shortage of skilled workers – machine operators and mechanics – which meant that equipment was poorly maintained and continually breaking down. Storage facilities were poor and so were the roads. On top of all that, there was the basic problem which had hampered collective farming from the beginning – lack of motivation – kolkhozniks would put more effort into working their private plots than into the collective. Brezhnev recognized this and allowed labourers to have larger plots – up to a maximum of half a hectare each. In the final years of the Brezhnev regime the private plots were yielding a staggering 30 per cent of total agricultural output, although they made up only four per cent of the USSR's cultivated area.[3] This clearly suggested that the solution to the problem was to de-collectivize agriculture, but of course, ideologically, that was out of the question.

Soviet industry suffered from similar problems to those of agriculture: it was an overcentralized, command economy in which compulsory orders were passed down from the centre, local managers had too little power, the price system did not correspond to supply and demand, and was dictated from Moscow by often ill-informed planners; this made it difficult to calculate the actual costs of production. As industry became more advanced and sophisticated, the centralized system simply could not cope with the new complexities of the situation. Kosygin was one of the few leaders to favour less state control of the economy; in September 1965 he was able to persuade the Politburo to introduce important changes: more powers were to be given to local managers, there would be fewer 'commands' from Moscow, and prices were to be recalculated on the basis of costs of production; enterprises were encouraged to make a profit, which would enable bonuses to be paid for outstanding performance and the development of new technology. The results of the Eighth Five-Year Plan (1966–70) suggested that the Kosygin reforms were having a beneficial effect; official Soviet statistics claimed that industrial output increased by 50 per cent and national income by 41 per cent, both slightly exceeding their targets. However, the Ninth and Tenth Plans were much less successful; production of almost all commodities failed to achieve their targets, and this trend was continued during the period 1981–85.

The seriousness of the situation was partly concealed by the rapid escalation of world oil prices in 1973 and the equally rapid increase in the price of gold in 1979, both of which were produced in large quantities in the USSR. There was a roughly five-fold increase in the prices of both oil and gold; the extra income from gold sales alone was enough to pay for all the grain imports in 1979. The USSR also benefited from an increase in the world prices of raw materials, of which she was a great exporter. Superficially, this surge of new income gave the impression that no economic reform was necessary; but the fact remained that in the early 1980s Soviet industry was on the verge of a crisis. What had gone wrong? Kosygin's reforms turned out to be a great disappointment; the new freedom for managers did not include the right to set prices, which were still decided centrally, and their 'powers' were insufficient to make any real difference. Their one important prerogative – the right to fix their own targets – proved to be counter-productive; it was in their interests to keep the planned targets down, so that they could achieve or even surpass them. As in the days of Stalin, it was still common for managers to send in false results in order to keep their superiors happy. By 1970 Kosygin's reforms were being quietly abandoned and industrial organization had slipped back into its traditional Stalinist mode. There were other contributory factors pushing industry towards crisis-point: a great proportion of industrial plant and machinery was becoming obsolete and needed replacing; but the slow-down in investment meant that the obsolete machinery and equipment continued in use and was continually having to be repaired. This required heavy expenditure which should have been used on improved technology. Another problem was the low birth-rate, which meant that the working population had almost stopped increasing, and there were serious labour shortages in some sectors. The one area of the economy which was unquestionably successful was the production of military hardware. By the early 1970s the USSR had caught up with the USA in numbers of inter-continental missiles, and had developed a new weapon, the anti-ballistic missile (ABM). Unfortunately, the arms race did not stop there – the Americans continued to produce even more deadly missiles, and at each step the USSR strained to draw level again. This was the real problem of the Soviet economy – defence spending was so vast that the civilian areas of the economy were deprived of the necessary investment to keep them up-to-date.

(c) The constitution of 1977

Khrushchev had first announced in 1961 that a new constitution was imminent, to update Stalin's 1936 constitution. When it eventually appeared, many of its clauses formalized what was actually happening in Soviet government and society; the rest were features which ordinary citizens would like to see happening in a 'people's state', but which so far had not materialized. The role of the Communist Party, which had occupied a relatively minor place in Stalin's constitution (article 126), was now given a much higher profile, as early as article 6: 'the leading and guiding force of Soviet society and the nucleus of its political system, its state organizations and public organizations is the Communist Party of the Soviet Union.' Of course, everybody knew that it was a one-party state, but this was the most formal statement of reality so far in Soviet history. Article 1 stated that the USSR was a socialist state of 'the whole people' rather than just 'workers and peasants,' and the intelligentsia for the first time were given equal standing with workers and peasants; thus the Soviets of working people's deputies became Soviets of people's deputies. 'Democratic centralism', which had always been the guiding principle of the party, was now extended to the whole state. Elections to the Supreme Soviet of the USSR and the Supreme Soviets of the republics were to take place every five years instead of every four. The right of the republics to secede from the USSR was retained and the clause which talked of merging the different nationalities into one great Soviet nation was dropped. Other new clauses guaranteed free health services, cheap housing and the right of the individual to take part in decision-making. There was even a clause about protecting the environment, although clearly not much notice was taken of that. With *détente* in mind, article 29 read: 'Relations between the USSR and other states are founded on the basis of observing the principles of sovereign equality; mutual rejection of the use of force and the threat of force; inviolability of frontiers; the peaceful settlement of disputes; non-interference in internal affairs; respect for human rights and the basic liberties; equality and the rights of people to manage their own affairs ...'

Brezhnev was extremely proud of his constitution and claimed that it would last for many decades. Some of the clauses were obviously no more than window-dressing; for example, the idea that ordinary people could play a part in making important decisions was laughable; it was the Politburo which decided things, and the Politburo was still not even mentioned in the constitution.[4] Nevertheless, Brezhnev apparently took it all seriously; he was determined to maintain the supremacy of the party and described the stage which Soviet society had reached as 'developed socialism.' In 1977 party membership was around 16 million, and 17.4 million by 1981. This meant that about one in ten adults were party members. In the words of Robert Service, 'their assigned duty was to inspire and mobilize the rest of society. The idea was that the more members, the better the chance to secure universal acquiescence in the status quo.' But this was not necessarily the case; not all party members were in sympathy with the Politburo, which was frightened to death of any radical change. 'The contemplation of change would have required a concentration of intellectual faculties that hardly any of them any longer possessed.'[5] However, there was probably a large minority of officials within the party apparatus who favoured some kind of reform.

9.2 Everyday life, dissent and opposition

(a) Social changes

Great changes took place during the Brezhnev years; the process of urbanization continued and the USSR moved from being a mainly agricultural country to being mainly industrial and urban. As late as 1926 only 18 per cent of the population lived in towns, but by 1980, out of a total population of 265 million, 63 per cent lived in towns.[6] On the whole life was better in the cities and large towns than in the countryside; there were more goods and services available, and this attracted people to move from rural areas. During the early 1970s the influx was so great that it put a strain on the available resources and accommodation, and the government placed restrictions on further migration. The housing shortage remained a serious problem; in the mid-1970s about 40 per cent of Soviet families still shared flats, and newly married couples almost always had to live with in-laws. Not surprisingly, there was a fall in the birth-rate in urban areas of the Russian Republic and to some extent in the European republics, where an increasing number of couples were happy to have just one child. The most disturbing aspect of this was that since all forms of contraceptives were in short supply, abortion was common practice among women in the European part of Russia. One calculation showed that in the late 1960s, there was an average of six legal abortions per woman over the whole of the USSR, which meant that the average for Russian women was much higher than that. At the same time the Muslim population, especially Tadzhiks, Uzbeks and Kirghiz, was growing rapidly – by 25 per cent between 1970 and 1979; by 1980 the Great Russians made up only 52 per cent of the total population of the USSR, and if the state had survived beyond 1991, they would have been increasingly in a minority.[7]

Brezhnev genuinely wanted the workers to be better-off and more comfortable, and there is no doubt that life did improve for most people. In 1967 the five-day working week was introduced, together with fifteen working days' holiday. Soviet citizens were not as well off as those in Western countries, but at least Soviet society was more egalitarian. In the period 1965 to 1977 real wages increased by almost 50 per cent, and the differentials between urban and rural workers narrowed. Many industrial and blue-collar workers were better paid than some professional groups; for example, in the 1970s a bus driver earned 230 roubles a month, but a secondary school teacher was only paid 150 roubles. Consumer goods may well have been in short supply, but they *were* obtainable in increasing numbers; in 1965, for instance, only 24 per cent of Soviet households owned a television set, but in 1974 the percentage had risen to 71 and by 1986 it had reached 96; similarly between 1965 and 1974 the percentage of those owning a refrigerator rose from 11 to 56, and households owning a washing-machine went up from 21 per cent to 62 per cent. Education was arguably the greatest success story of the Soviet system; illiteracy had almost been eliminated by 1982 and the state was working towards free secondary education for the whole population. The system was strong in science and mathematics, though critics complained that there was too much learning by rote, and that creative and critical thinking were not encouraged. There were sixty universities and eight hundred higher technical schools for the brightest students; the number of Soviet citizens with higher education increased from 8.3 million in 1959 to 18.5 million in 1984.[8]

Other positive aspects of Soviet life were the near elimination of unemployment, and the full programme of social security – pensions, free health care, holidays with pay, child benefits, pregnancy and maternity leave, and free nursery care for children of working parents. On the other hand, the pensions were barely enough to provide for a comfortable retirement and the health care provided seems to have been below the standard of that in the developed capitalist states. There was a marked improvement in diet during the Brezhnev era, though even in 1985 it had not quite reached the levels recommended by dieticians. One trend which gave cause for concern was rising death rates; these had been falling steadily since the Second World War, so that, for example, by the mid-1960s life expectancy for men had risen to 66, and infant mortality had fallen to 22.9 per thousand babies dying before the age of one. However, by the mid-1970s life expectancy for Soviet men had fallen to 63 (it was 69 in the USA) and the child mortality rate had risen to 36 per thousand live births (10.6 per thousand in the USA). Various explanations have been offered for what seems to be a surprising trend in a time of improving diet; these include rapidly worsening environmental pollution, alcoholism, which was becoming a major problem, especially among pregnant women, influenza and pneumonia epidemics in the child day-care centres, and an increasing number of suicides.

One very significant trend was the growth of privacy and the development of free discussion in small, informal groups. In the words of Archie Brown: 'Over drinks and around kitchen tables the most diverse array of political views could be heard, ones which hardly anyone would have dared utter aloud in Stalin's time. The growth of freedom of expression in private circles preceded by two to three decades the achievement in the Gorbachev era of freedom of expression in public.' The increasing amount of accommodation was important in this respect, since it enabled millions of people to move from communal apartments to single-family flats where they were able 'to shut their own front door.'[9] It was a kind of private *glasnost* which helped the formation of small groups of like-minded people, ranging from genuinely progressive reformers to backward-looking nationalists who talked with nostalgia about tsarist days. None of these groups organized any sort of formal campaign, but they did help to prepare the way for the much greater element of *glasnost* under Gorbachev.

(b) Culture, dissent and opposition

Informal groups also discussed literature, art, music and science, and Brezhnev's regime was reasonably tolerant at first, provided that any material which they might circulate did not threaten to turn people against the government's policies. In the early years after Khrushchev's downfall there was a struggle between the conservatives who wanted to ban writings with the slightest whiff of the avant-garde about them, and the more adventurous who wanted to continue the rather more relaxed trend of the early 1960s. The leading literary journals took sides: *Novy Mir*, under its editor Alexander Tvardovsky, took the liberal view that literature should come out with the truth; *Octyabr* took the traditionalist view – its editor, Vsevolod Kochetov, disapproved of de-Stalinization and wanted to see Stalin rehabilitated. Before long it became clear that the conservatives were winning the struggle; in February 1966 two writers, Andrei Sinyavski and Yuli Daniel, were sentenced to seven and five years respectively in a labour camp for spreading 'anti-Soviet propaganda'; Sinyavski had written *On Socialist Realism*, a devastating criticism about life in the Soviet state. Daniel had produced a satirical story meant as a warning against a return to Stalinism; it told the tale of a national holiday on which the state allowed everybody to murder anyone they chose, without punishment. By about 1970 the progressives had been stifled, and although Brezhnev would not go so far as to officially rehabilitate Stalin, it became almost impossible to get anything published which was critical of him. Historian Alexander Nekrich's book about Stalin's mishandling of the German invasion in 1941 was published in 1965, but later withdrawn (see section 7.2(a)). Nekrich could get nothing else published in the USSR; he was expelled from the party in 1967 and eventually left the country. Other historians who encountered problems were Roy Medvedev and Viktor Danilov; Medvedev wrote a book about the Great Terror in which he revealed yet more horrifying details of Stalin's activities; Danilov wrote about collectivization, but both books were banned. Alexander Solzhenitsyn, whose novel *One Day in the Life of Ivan Denisovich* had been permitted by Khrushchev, found that his next two novels, *The First Circle* and *Cancer Ward*, were rejected. The Czechoslovak crisis affected all aspects of

Soviet life; dissidents were outraged at Soviet intervention, while the Soviet authorities became increasingly nervous about the potential evils of liberal attitudes. Tvardovsky was forced to leave *Novy Mir* in 1970, and many writers, including Solzhenitsyn, were expelled from the Writers' Union, which meant that it was impossible for them to publish in the USSR.

This sort of treatment only served to make reform-minded intellectuals even more determined to persevere. More and more writers began to circulate works in typescript, which they knew had no chance of being published, around their little groups; this was known as *samizdat* – self-publishing. In 1970 a Human Rights Committee was formed by the physicists Andrei Sakharov and Valeri Chalidze to protest, among other things, about the dreadful conditions which still existed in labour camps, and to demand freedom of speech and the full implementation of the constitution of the USSR. The KGB was also using a new technique – confining dissidents in psychiatric hospitals or mental asylums, where some were kept for many years. In May 1970 the biologist and writer Zhores Medvedev, Roy's twin brother, was arrested and locked up in a mental hospital in Kaluga. He was diagnosed as having 'creeping schizophrenia', but the real reason for his arrest was that his writings were considered to be anti-Soviet. According to Andrei Sakharov, 'Zhores Medvedev's work in two disparate fields – biology and political science – was regarded as evidence of a split personality, and his conduct allegedly exhibited evidence of social maladjustment.' Sakharov, Roy Medvedev and Solzhenitsyn immediately launched a protest campaign which attracted so much support that the authorities became alarmed and released Zhores after only just over two weeks, which was unheard of; most people were not so lucky.[10] In 1973 the KGB mounted a campaign against Solzhenitsyn and Sakharov which ended with Solzhenitsyn being deported from the country in February 1974. The authorities would have liked to get rid of Sakharov too, but he was such an eminent scientist with an international reputation that they dare not put Soviet scientific links with American scientists at risk (Documents B and D).

The Human Rights Committee was given a new stick with which to beat the government when the USSR, along with the USA and other nations, signed the Helsinki Final Treaty in 1975. One of the terms of this agreement provided for economic and scientific co-operation, and the free exchange of information between East and West; it meant that dissidents were now able to attract world-wide publicity for the fact that their government was reneging on its promises. By the end of 1975 there were some 10,000 political and religious prisoners in labour camps, as well as innumerable dissidents in psychiatric institutions. And yet the Brezhnev regime stopped short of all-out suppression and terror; the Politburo members could not forget that Stalin's purges had got out of hand, and to their credit, they could not bring themselves to have the leading dissidents executed. They accepted that the ideas of the dissidents could not be stifled entirely, but at least they could be dampened down. In 1980 for example, when the Olympic Games were held in Moscow, it was decided to move Sakharov to Gorky (formerly Nizhny Novgorod), a town on the Volga to which foreigners were forbidden to go. He remained there until 1986 when Gorbachev invited him to return to Moscow. The dissident movement was weakened by divisions between the various groups; the Medvedevs were Leninists who wanted to bring socialism back to its pre-Stalin state; liberals like Sakharov came to believe that Western-style democracy was the only way to safeguard the freedom of the individual; Solzhenitsyn criticized almost every known form of government and ended up extolling the virtues of two arguably contradictory positions – Christianity and pre-revolutionary Tsarism. Although the dissident movement gained publicity, its membership was small and the vast majority of ordinary people took no interest in their activities. The public regarded the state with suspicion, but there was a general apathy about politics; they knew that they were powerless to bring about any general change. Most people spent their energies trying to make the best of a bad situation and were more interested in the entertainment programmes on television – sport, thrillers and variety shows – than in politics.[11]

9.3   Brezhnev and eastern Europe

(a) The crisis in Czechoslovakia, 1968

During the early 1960s Czechoslovakia began to experience economic difficulties, and a rift developed between reformers and conservatives. The reformers objected to the over-centralized Soviet control of their economy; for instance, it seemed ludicrous that they should be forced to use poor-quality iron ore from Siberia when they could have been importing high-grade ore from Sweden. Brezhnev paid a visit to Prague in December 1967, but made no attempt to adjudicate between the rival groups. In January 1968 the pro-Moscow leader, Antonin Novotny, was forced to resign, and a reformer, Alexander Dubcek, was chosen as the new party leader. Things began to change rapidly: censorship was removed, and a programme of reforms was announced which included the setting-up of retail markets; the de-centralization of industry, which meant that factories would be run by works councils instead of being controlled from Prague by party officials; the de-collectivization of farms, which would become independent co-operatives; more powers for trade unions; more trade with the West; and freedom to travel abroad. The frontier with West Germany, which had been closed since 1948, was immediately opened. There was even talk of allowing the formation of non-communist political parties. Dubcek still regarded himself as a Leninist but believed that there should be freedom of speech and freedom of the press, so that the communist party could be made aware of the wishes of the people. His intention was that the country would remain communist, but he felt that the party should earn the right to be in power by responding to public opinion. He was also careful to assure Moscow that Czechoslovakia would stay in the Warsaw Pact and would continue to be a reliable ally of the USSR. He called this version of communism 'socialism with a human face,' and as the programme began to be introduced in the early months of 1968, it became known as the Prague Spring.[12]

Dubcek's reforms were extremely popular with the Czech people and led to a great ferment of political discussions and public meetings; the media, especially television, played a vital part in the debate. However, some of the Czech party leaders felt that things were going too far. As for Brezhnev and the Politburo, they watched developments anxiously; most of them had no desire to interfere, and in fact at first some of them actually encouraged the Czechs in their reforms. It was the formation of non-communist political parties and the criticisms of the USSR which began to appear in the Czech press that convinced them that it was time to put an end to the experiment. Leaders of some of the other satellite states, particularly East Germany and Hungary, were also becoming nervous in case Czech reformist ideas spread into their territories. After an 'appeal for help' had been received in Moscow from some of the Czech conservatives (a document which remained locked in the archives until 1992), during the night of 20–21 August, about half a million Soviet and Warsaw Pact troops with tanks crossed the border into Czechoslovakia. There was virtually no resistance from the Czech army, although hundreds of thousands of the public came out on the streets to protest against the invading troops. Dubcek and other leaders were arrested and taken to Moscow where they were forced to agree to drop the reform programme. The reformers were gradually manoeuvred out and Dubcek was replaced as leader by the conservative Gustav Husak, who would do as he was told by the USSR. Not all the states of eastern Europe approved of the Soviet intervention; Yugoslavia and Romania objected, and Tito paid a visit to Prague to encourage Dubcek, shortly before the invasion.

Some historians see the Czech experiment as the way out of the dead-end of Stalinism; it suggested that it *was* possible to reform the mess which communism had got itself into, thanks to Stalin, and that 'socialism with a human face' could win popular support. If Dubcek had stopped short of multi-party politics and overt criticism of Moscow, it could have been a turning-point for the whole communist bloc. But the Soviet Politburo lacked the vision and the courage to take the opportunity. The Soviet handling of the crisis had disastrous results: Czechoslovakia had been probably the most pro-Soviet of all the satellite states, but military intervention only succeeded in embittering the Czechs, and put a stop to any further official moves towards reform in the eastern bloc. Soon afterwards Brezhnev issued a statement which became known as the Brezhnev Doctrine, to the effect that the Warsaw Pact countries were not allowed to follow policies involving any departure from a one-party state; if any developments took place in any member country which seemed to be a threat to socialism, it was the right and the duty of the other member states of the Pact to intervene militarily in order to bring such dangerous developments to an end (Document A).[13] The reform movement in Czechoslovakia had not been entirely subdued. In 1977 a human rights group known as Charter 77 was formed and it soon became increasingly outspoken in its criticisms of the Husak government.

(b) Trouble in Poland

The Communist government in Poland was also getting itself into difficulties; with amazingly insensitive timing, it announced substantial increases in food prices just before Christmas 1970. Such was the public outrage that riots broke out; the Polish leader, Wladyslaw Gomulka, resigned and was replaced by Edward Gierek. The new government did not follow the example of Dubcek in Czechoslovakia and throughout the 1970s its handling of the economy was not especially successful. During the summer of 1980 there were serious food shortages, industrial unrest and strikes in the port of Gdansk and other cities. The strikes were organized by an independent trade union movement led by Lech Walesa; calling itself Solidarity, it began to challenge the communist party for the leadership of the country. By the summer of 1981 the party seemed to have lost control and the country was in chaos. But the communists, now led by General Wojciech Jaruzelski, were determined to hold on to power. There were two alternatives: either the communists regained control of the country, or Warsaw Pact forces would invade, as they had in Czechoslovakia. In December 1981 Jaruzelski, with the approval of Moscow, carried out a well-organized *coup*: order was restored, Solidarity was banned, thousands of its members were arrested, and the government began to introduce some mild reforms in order to 'normalize' the situation. However, there was such enormous support for Solidarity that it simply could not be eliminated. It was the beginning of the end for communism in the satellite states. Unless the economic situation improved there was bound to be more trouble; in 1988 there were more strikes and the process began in which Poland became the first of the states of eastern Europe to reject communism.

9.4 Foreign affairs and détente

(a) The USSR, the USA and détente

Both states remained suspicious of each other; the increasing American involvement in the war in Vietnam, especially the continued bombing of communist North Vietnam in the mid-1960s ordered by President Johnson, seemed to be evidence of the dangers of capitalist aggression. Kosygin was actually on a visit to Hanoi, the capital of North Vietnam, in February 1965 when the American bombing began. It was then that the USSR decided to provide Ho Chi Minh, the communist leader of North Vietnam, with financial aid and ground-to-air missiles. No sooner had Johnson suspended the bombing for a time (March 1968) when the Soviet intervention in Czechoslovakia took place (August 1968); for many Westerners this was evidence of continuing communist expansionism. Probably the most disturbing situation for Moscow was the deterioration of relations with China. In March 1969 fighting broke out along their joint frontier in Siberia; full-scale war seemed a distinct possibility for a time, but fortunately common sense prevailed and a compromise settlement was reached. Given the uncertainty of the situation with China in the Far East, Brezhnev and Gromyko, the Soviet Foreign Minister, tried to improve relations with the West. When Willy Brandt became West German Chancellor in 1969, he brought with him a new policy – *Ostpolitik* – to aim for better relations with East Germany and eastern Europe. He quickly suggested talks and in August 1970 the USSR and the Federal Republic of Germany signed a Renunciation of Force Treaty, accepting the 1945 frontiers of Germany and its division into two states. In September 1971 a four-power agreement was reached (USSR, USA, Britain and France) over West Berlin, which was to be 'an independent political entity' under the sovereignty of neither East nor West Germany. These agreements were a remarkable step forward, removing one of the greatest obstacles to the improvement of East–West relations; they can be seen as the beginning of *détente*. Andrei Gromyko was full of praise for Brandt's courage and determination to move forward. On the German side the general mood was so upbeat that the Federal Republic's Foreign Minister, Walter Scheel, told Gromyko, much to the latter's embarrassment, that he and his wife had decided to call their newly-born daughter Andrea, in his honour.[14]

At the same time the arms race was continuing. The Soviet aim was to draw level with the USA so that they could negotiate a reduction of tension – and of armaments – from a position of strength. The more deeply the Americans became involved in the Vietnam War (between 1961 and 1973), the less they spent on nuclear weapons. By the early 1970s the Soviets had probably overtaken them in numbers of inter-continental ballistic missiles (ICBMs) and submarine-launched ballistic missiles (SLBMs); the Soviets had also developed the anti-ballistic missile (ABM) which could destroy enemy missiles before they reached their targets. The Soviet navy had been transformed to make the USSR into a great sea power. However, in 1970 the Americans introduced the multiple independently targetable re-entry vehicle (MIRV); this was a missile that could carry as many as fourteen separate warheads, each one of which could be programmed to hit a different target. The cost of all this nuclear stockpiling was astronomical for both sides, and so in November 1969 talks began between the USSR and the USA to try and agree on some limits. In May 1972 Brezhnev and President Nixon signed a Strategic Arms Limitation Treaty (known as SALT I) in Moscow. It put numerical limits on each side's ICBMs and SLBMs, although nothing was decided about MIRVs. But the important thing was that the agreement slowed down the arms race, and the term '*détente*' began to be used to signify that East–West relations had progressed beyond mere co-existence into a new phase of considerably reduced tensions. The USA promised to carry out more trade with the USSR, and both sides agreed to continue arms limitation talks and to consult regularly about world affairs (Document C). Brezhnev went to New York in 1973, and Nixon came to Moscow again in 1974; his successor, Gerald Ford, also visited the USSR, meeting Brezhnev in Vladivostock in November 1974. One practical outcome of *détente* was an increase in scientific and technological exchange between East and West.

The USA suffered a number of serious setbacks in the first half of the 1970s which worked to the advantage of the USSR. In 1970 a Marxist, Salvador Allende, was elected President of Chile. American public opinion turned against the Vietnam War, since it was now clear that the communists could not be defeated. In 1973 Nixon admitted failure by withdrawing American troops from Vietnam. In August 1974 Nixon himself was forced to resign in disgrace following the Watergate scandal, and in April 1975 the North Vietnamese overran South Vietnam, making the whole country communist. Vietnam soon made it clear that it supported the USSR's version of communism rather than China's. In the same year, pro-communist governments were established in Laos and Cambodia, and the American attempt to prevent the spread of communism in south-east Asia had ended in complete failure. When both Nixon and Ford persevered in their attempts to bring about closer relations between the USA and China, the Politburo took it as a sign that the USA was feeling fragile and needed Chinese support. Many Americans looked with suspicion on Soviet activities in Africa; they transported Cuban forces to Angola to help Marxist guerrillas, and supported the new left-wing government in Ethiopia. In January 1979 the USA lost a valuable ally when fundamentalist Muslims drove out the pro-American shah of Iran. There was a growing feeling in the USA that the USSR was gaining ground; Zbigniew Brzezinski, the national security adviser to President Jimmy Carter, had been consistently hostile to the Soviet state, and he believed that the Americans had to win back the strategic advantage over the USSR. *Détente* began to falter and the arms race continued. In 1977 the Russians brought out their version of the MIRV, known as the SS-20, which they targeted on western Europe. The USA responded by basing Cruise missiles in Britain and West Germany and Pershing II missiles in West Germany. Yet at the same time talks were being held on limiting nuclear weapons; Carter and Brezhnev met in Vienna in June 1979 and signed a SALT II agreement.

Meanwhile Soviet relations with China had become more complicated; although Mao Zedong, a difficult man to deal with, had died in 1976, his successors seemed no more amenable. In February 1979 the Chinese invaded Vietnam, which was now a strong ally of the USSR. The attack was partly in retaliation for the Vietnamese invasion of Kampuchea (formerly Cambodia) in December 1978, in which the Vietnamese, with the full backing of the USSR, had overthrown the vicious Khmer Rouge regime of Pol Pot, a *protégé* of China. The Chinese attack turned out to be a short, sharp exercise; their troops withdrew from Vietnam after three weeks; according to Beijing, they had 'taught the Vietnamese a lesson.' The communist world was in disarray, and both the USSR and China seemed to be vying for the support of the USA against each other. But relations between the USSR and the USA took a decisive turn for the worse when Soviet troops entered Afghanistan at the end of December 1979; the Cold War reached a new crisis, and unfortunately the United States Senate refused to ratify SALT II.[15]

(b) The USSR and Afghanistan

There was a long history of good relations between the USSR and Afghanistan, with its population of some 20 million Muslims. Its long northern frontier bordered on the Soviet republics of Turkmenistan, Uzbekistan and Tajikistan. In April 1978 a group of left-wing army officers seized power in the name of the Democratic People's Party. There seems to be no definite evidence that the USSR had actually organized the *coup*, but they certainly gave 'advice' and promised to back the new regime if the *coup* was successful. The new government of Nur Muhammad Taraki planned to modernize the country, introducing land reform, bringing an end to the ancient feudal practices, and setting up a socialist system. However, in a country where Islamic authority was strong, changes such as equal status for men and women and the secularization of society were seen as an affront to the Islamic religion. The reforms aroused great opposition and civil war developed. Several thousand Soviet troops were sent to help Taraki, but the fighting intensified. To complicate matters, Taraki fell out with his Foreign Minister, Hafizullah Amin, who wanted power for himself. In September 1979 Taraki tried to have Amin murdered, but the attempt was bungled, and Amin had enough support to turn the tables and have Taraki arrested. After Taraki was strangled in prison, on Amin's orders, Amin became President. Brezhnev was shocked at all this treachery and the Politburo decided that the militant Amin must be removed and replaced by a more moderate Marxist. A special military unit was sent to 'defend Amin's residence and protect Amin,' but it stormed his palace in Kabul and Amin and his family were killed (December 1979). The following day more Soviet troops crossed the border from Tajikistan; by the beginning of January 1980 there were 50,000 of them in Afghanistan, and a new Marxist leader, Babrak Karmal, was installed in Kabul. It was expected that the Soviet troops would remain for a year or perhaps eighteen months 'until full stabilization is achieved.'[16]

Soviet motives for intervention were quite clear: they were reluctant to allow the overthrow of a pro-Soviet Marxist regime once it had been established; it was their 'international duty' to support struggling fellow communists (Document E). There was also the very real fear that the regime would be overthrown by an Islamic fundamentalist revolution like the one which had seized power in Iran in January 1979. This might stir up the millions of Muslims who were Soviet citizens and so destabilize those republics with substantial Muslim populations. The Politburo was probably encouraged by the fact that the USA was still suffering from the 'post-Vietnam syndrome', which meant that they were reluctant to commit troops abroad, and by the fact that the new radical Muslim regime of the Ayatollah Khomeini in Iran, the neighbouring state to Afghanistan, was strongly anti-American. But it turned out to be a disastrous decision: instead of being there for eighteen months, it was almost ten years – February 1989 – before Soviet troops were withdrawn from Afghanistan. Although at the peak there were 109,000 Soviet troops involved, they failed to defeat the Muslim opposition (see section 10.2(b)), and at least 15,000 Soviet troops were killed. In the short term the USSR's action put an end to *détente*; unlike Czechoslovakia, Afghanistan was not a country which was regarded internationally as part of the Soviet sphere of influence. President Carter was outraged; he ordered an increase in the defence budget, stopped the export of grain from the USA to the USSR and withdrew the American team from the Olympic Games held in Moscow in the summer of 1980. The US Senate refused to ratify SALT II. The American Central Intelligence Agency (CIA) did its best to help the Afghan Muslims, as did China, and this placed another obstacle in the way of Soviet–Chinese reconciliation. Afghanistan turned out to be the USSR's Vietnam; in the words of Volkogonov: 'the country was in a trap from which it could escape only by frankly admitting that the whole idea of a mission to Afghanistan had been a mistake, and by withdrawing its troops.'[17]

9.5 The end of an era

(a) Brezhnev departs

By the end of the 1970s Brezhnev's health was in serious decline; he had already suffered several strokes and two mild heart attacks. He ought to have retired, but he enjoyed the trappings of power and was easily persuaded to stay on by some of his colleagues in the Politburo who seemed anxious to postpone the time when a decision would have to be made about the succession. In reality the Politburo – especially Suslov, Gromyko, Ustinov, Andropov and Chernenko – were taking most of the important decisions. Brezhnev's last two years in office were unhappy and humiliating for him; there were a number of embarrassing public appearances when he had extreme difficulty simply reading out the speeches written for him. On one occasion when he was visiting the Transcaucasian republics, he read out in Georgia the speech which had been written for Armenia, without noticing the difference. Since it was televised live, the whole country realized just how senile their leader was; it later emerged that one of his aides had switched the speeches deliberately in order to discredit Brezhnev. It was common knowledge in Moscow that whenever Brezhnev came into the capital, the last limousine in his motorcade was always a resuscitation vehicle. Another painful experience for him was that during the KGB's anti-corruption drive, information came out about unsavoury activities among his own family and supporters. His daughter Galina, who was married to General Yuri Churbanov, a deputy Minister of Internal Affairs, was having an affair with the director of the Moscow State Circus, and they were involved in a huge network of jewel and gold bullion smuggling, bribery and currency speculation. It was a sad end to Brezhnev's career that he should have become an object of pity and the butt of cruel jokes. There was a popular story about his speech-writer being chastized for making one of his speeches too long; 'I said that I wanted a speech which lasted ten minutes,' complained Brezhnev; 'this one lasted for twenty.' 'But Comrade Brezhnev,' replied the unfortunate assistant, 'I told you I was giving you two copies.' His love of medals was well known – he had awarded himself quite a few; a rumour went round that he was about to have surgery on his chest so that there would be room for more medals. Another anecdote told of a visit to Brezhnev by his mother who was worried about his luxurious lifestyle, especially his collection of Western motor cars, said to number at least 50; 'but Lyonya,' she asked, 'what will you do if the Bolsheviks come back?' On 7 November 1982 Brezhnev attended the annual parade to celebrate the October revolution; it was bitterly cold, but he stood throughout the whole ceremony and took the salute. It all proved too much for him and he died three days later.

Brezhnev has not had a good press among historians; there seems to be general agreement that he allowed stability to degenerate into stagnation. He lacked the vision to see what needed to be done to modernize the state, or even to recognize fully what the problems were. According to Robert Service, 'policy was so motionless that it was rarely a topic for glancing comment in *Pravda* or even in the scholarly economic journals ... Only very dimly were Brezhnev and his colleagues aware that doing nothing was a recipe for political disaster.'[18] All through his long period in power Brezhnev's main concern seemed to be to keep the 'nomenklatura' – the ruling elite – happy. They were the holders of important posts who were chosen first and foremost because of their political reliability and devotion to the party, rather than technical or administrative abilities. At the lowest level of the nomenklatura were the administrators of town or city party committees, and the next level was the regional (oblast) committee; there were posts in the secretariat of the Central Committee and in the parties and committees of the republics; the highest posts were in the secretariat of the Politburo. Then there were the posts which the party considered most important in the various organizations like Komsomol, the academic institutions, the ministries, the economic bodies, the police and the KGB. They also included managers of factories and collective farms and some of the leading research experts in universities. The system had taken shape under Stalin and people had come into it from a variety of backgrounds – including peasants and industrial workers; they had been promoted because they were party members and because they were totally loyal to the party. They were rewarded with privileges and power; these were the people who became alarmed at Khrushchev's reforms, and who in the end did all they could to slow them down and sabotage them. Brezhnev gave them what they most wanted – stability and security of tenure – and he did not trouble them with radical changes. Unlike Khrushchev, he did not sack them for their failures, but told them that he trusted them and understood the difficulties under which they were working. Many of these people were extremely powerful locally and were able to get away with ignoring any orders from Moscow which did not appeal to them. The longer this went on, the more powerful and corrupt the elite became, and the more difficult it would be for Brezhnev's successors to reform the system. In the words of Dmitri Volkogonov, who experienced this at first hand as a member of the nomenklatura: 'The Communist ship of state was becalmed, its sails sagging. Party rule in the centre and the periphery was characterized by the outward appearance of activity concealing internal passivity... Corruption flourished at every level, the higher, the worse. Deceit and lies became the rule... to which Brezhnev, being a mild soul, tended to turn a blind eye, even when his own relations were involved in unseemly operations.'[19]

Yet there were some positive aspects of the Brezhnev era; the man himself, in spite of his vanity, had many good qualities. Volkogonov recalled that, unlike Stalin, he actually liked people, he was approachable and would often help somebody outside his immediate circle 'who had touched his heart with a sad story or a request.' Even when he criticized somebody he did it in such a way that he never left them feeling offended. 'In some ways Brezhnev was a kind of good tsar, a Communist tsar, and if it had not been for Czechoslovakia, Afghanistan and Poland, history's view of him might be very different.'[20] J.N. Westwood points out that 'on the whole, his regime was benevolent, with a perceptible attitude of live-and-let-live.' Although he was criticized for allowing stagnation to develop, this at least gave the people something they had lacked for four decades: stability. In some ways the Brezhnev regime actually did better than the West: 'after all, although the claim that there was no unemployment and no inflation in the USSR was exaggerated, these two scourges were unobtrusive minor irritants rather than the large-scale demoralizing phenomena of the Western world of the 1970s.'[21] The unfortunate thing, from the point of view of the survival of Communism, was that Brezhnev, the Politburo and the ruling elite all grew old together. In 1980 the majority of members of the Politburo were well over 70 and had been reluctant to prepare a younger generation of politicians to take over from them. Similarly in the elite, the nomenklatura, the next generation of officials were now middle-aged and were still being denied promotion. They felt restless and resentful, and yet given the Soviet system, there was no way for them to express their dissatisfaction. They felt that Brezhnev and his ageing cronies should go, but there was no mechanism to bring this about, except to try and embarrass them into retirement. In the end 'his General Secretaryship had turned into a ceremonial reign that had brought Communism into its deepest contempt since 1917.'[22]

(b) Interlude: Andropov and Chernenko (November 1982–March 1985)

Brezhnev wanted his favourite crony, Konstantin Chernenko, to succeed him; but Yuri Andropov had other ideas. He had been head of the KGB for 15 years, and as part of his anti-corruption drive he had been doing his best to discredit Brezhnev, his family and his close associates, hoping to spoil Chernenko's chances of coming to power. His plans were successful and the Politburo chose him as the next General Secretary. Born in Stavropol (Northern Caucasus) in 1914 into a Cossack family, he was highly intelligent and progressed quickly through Komsomol and party ranks, becoming Soviet ambassador to Hungary in 1954. It was Brezhnev who appointed him as KGB leader. He was a serious and austere character, and a passionately convinced Marxist–Leninist who strongly disapproved of Brezhnev's apparent lack of commitment to the cause. He recognized that changes were essential, but he felt he had to be cautious so that he could carry the Politburo with him. One of his first measures was a drive for greater efficiency and tighter discipline in all spheres of activity, with a campaign against poor workmanship, absenteeism, alcoholism, corruption and the black market. He started to replace members of the nomenklatura, a reform which was long overdue, and by the time of his death in February 1984, he had already replaced about a fifth of party secretaries and ministers, and about a third of department heads on the secretariat of the Central Committee. He intended, he said, to talk to as many different people as possible in order to pick up new ideas, and he began by visiting a Moscow factory and talking to workers. But tragically Andropov's health soon deteriorated; for some years he had been suffering kidney trouble, and this suddenly became worse, forcing him to spend hours wired up to a dialysis machine.

Andropov's short reign was clouded by failures in foreign affairs. He invited US President Reagan to a summit meeting to discuss arms reduction and a ban on further nuclear tests. Reagan's reply was a complete rebuff; he said that the USSR was an 'evil empire' and in March 1983 announced a new project – a Strategic Defence Initiative (known as 'Star Wars') which would use weapons based in space to destroy ballistic missiles. Then in September 1983 there was an international incident when Soviet forces shot down a South Korean airliner which had strayed into Soviet airspace; all 269 passengers and crew were killed. Tension between the USSR and the USA and NATO reached new heights (Document F). By this time Andropov was seriously ill and on 9 February 1984 he died after only 15 months in office. It is hardly possible to say what the results would have been if he could have lived another five or six years, as he had hoped. Roy Medvedev feels that he could have achieved great things, but others believe that his reforms were not radical enough to save the system.

Andropov had encouraged and promoted reform-minded people – Mikhail Gorbachev, Yegor Ligachev and Nikolai Ryzhkov were all appointed as Central Committee Secretaries. When Andropov realized that he probably had only a short time to live, he tried to make sure that Gorbachev would succeed him. He sent written instructions to this effect to the Central Committee, but Chernenko's supporters intercepted them and Andropov died before he could take any further action. The Politburo chose Konstantin Chernenko as next Secretary-General, although he was 72 years old and already terminally ill with emphysema and hepatitis. He had had an undistinguished career in the party and owed his rise to the fact that for many years he had been a personal assistant to Brezhnev. It seems incredible that the Politburo should have chosen such a man, who was intellectually limited, and so weak that he could hardly speak coherently, to be leader of their state. One suggested explanation is that the majority wanted somebody who would abandon the anti-corruption campaign and leave them in peace and quiet. Chernenko was just the man; he had no ideas of changing anything or even much awareness that things needed to change. As Dmitri Volkogonov puts it: 'Chernenko was not capable of leading the country or the Party into the future. His rise to power symbolized the deepening of the crisis in society, the total lack of positive ideas in the Party, and the inevitability of the convulsions to come.'[23] After only 13 months in office, much of the time too ill to attend Politburo meetings, he died in March 1985.

Documents

(A) An article in *Pravda*, 26 September 1968, explaining the Brezhnev Doctrine.

There is no doubt that the peoples of the socialist countries and the Communist parties have and must have freedom to determine their country's path to development. However, any decision of theirs must damage neither socialism in their own country nor the fundamental interests of other socialist countries... This means that every Communist party is responsible not only to its own people but also to all the socialist countries and the entire Communist movement. Whoever forgets this is placing sole emphasis on the autonomy and independence of Communist Parties, lapses into one-sidedness, shirking his internationalist obligations... Just as, in V.I. Lenin's words, someone living in a system of other states constituting a socialist commonwealth cannot be free of the common interests of that commonwealth.

Source: quoted in John Laver, *The USSR 1945–90*, p. 38.

(B) Andrei Sakharov writes in his memoirs about an essay he had written in 1968.

I gave my essay the title *Reflections on Progress, Peaceful Coexistence, and Intellectual Freedom*...I wanted to alert my readers to the grave perils threatening the human race – thermonuclear extinction, ecological catastrophe, famine, an uncontrolled population explosion, alienation... I argued for a rapprochement of the socialist and capitalist systems that could eliminate or substantially reduce these dangers which had been increased many times over by the division of the world into opposing camps. Economic, social and ideological convergence should bring about a scientifically governed, democratic, pluralist society free of intolerance and dogmatism, a humanitarian society which would care for the Earth and its future, and would embody the positive features of both systems... I sent a copy to Brezhnev... on July 22 it was published in the *New York Times*... It circulated widely in the USSR as well – samizdat was flourishing – and the response was encouraging.

Source: Andrei Sakharov, *Memoirs*, pp. 282–9.

(C) Extracts from the agreement signed by the USSR and the USA, 29 May 1972 – the beginning of *détente*.

1. They will proceed from the common determination that in the nuclear age there is no alternative to conducting their mutual relations on the basis of peaceful co-existence. Differences in ideology and in the social systems of the USSR and the USA are not obstacles to the bilateral development of normal relations based on the principles of sovereignty, equality, non-interference in internal affairs and mutual advantage.
2. The USSR and the USA will do their utmost to avoid military confrontations and to prevent the outbreak of nuclear war. They will always exercise restraint in their mutual relations, and will be prepared to negotiate and settle differences by peaceful means.
3. The USSR and the USA have a special responsibility to do everything in their power so that conflicts or situations will not arise which would serve to increase international tensions. Accordingly they will seek to promote conditions in which all countries will live in peace and security and will not be subject to outside interference in their internal affairs.

Source: quoted in Laver, pp. 38–9.

(D) Sakharov recalls his work with the Human Rights Committee.

The Human Rights Committee met regularly during the winter and spring of 1971, the heyday of its activity. Igor Shafarevich, a mathematician and a member of the Academy of Sciences, volunteered to take part in the Committee's work. He was particularly disturbed by the misuse of psychiatry, by religious persecution and by other actions which violate the victims' spiritual integrity. The Committee's report, which denounced the misuse of psychiatry, was adopted

(continued)

in July 1971. But still earlier I had followed the case of Viktor Fainberg, one of the participants in the Red Square demonstration of August 25, 1968. 'Volunteer policemen' (in fact, KGB agents) knocked out some of his teeth in the course of arresting him, which would have made it embarrassing to try him in open court. Fainberg, who had received psychiatric care as a child, was thereupon ruled mentally incompetent and sent to the Leningrad special psychiatric hospital... Special psychiatric hospitals are operated by the Ministry of Internal Affairs and they have harsh regimens. Convicts are employed as orderlies. Beatings are frequent. Painful proceedings and drugs which have no therapeutic value are used to pacify the inmates and punish them... Fainberg and his friend Vladimir Borisov smuggled notes out of the hospital describing merciless beatings, the wrapping of unruly patients in wet canvas, which causes excruciating pain as it dries and shrinks, and other horrors. When they declared a hunger strike, they were beaten and subjected to daily forced feeding.

Source: A. Sakharov, *Memoirs*, pp. 327–8.

(E) Alexander Bovin, editor of *Izvestiya* and former Central Committee member, defends the Soviet invasion of Afghanistan, in an article in *Izvestiya*, April, 1980.

Developments forced us to make a choice: we had either to bring in troops or let the Afghan revolution be defeated and the country turned into a kind of Shah's Iran. We decided to bring in the troops. It was not a simple decision to take... We knew that the victory of counter-revolution would pave the way for massive American military presence in a country which borders on the Soviet Union and that this was a challenge to our country's security. We knew that the decision to bring in the troops would not be popular in the modern world even if it was absolutely legal. But we also knew that we would have ceased to be a great power if we refrained from taking extraordinary decisions prompted by extraordinary circumstances... There are situations where non-intervention is a disgrace and a betrayal. Such a situation developed in Afghanistan. And when I hear the voices of protest from people who claim to be democrats, humanists and even revolutionaries, saying they are outraged by Soviet 'intervention', I tell them this: If you are against Soviet military aid to Afghanistan, then you are for the victory of counter-revolution. There is no third way.

Source: quoted in Laver, p. 40.

(F) Soviet Foreign Minister, Andrei Gromyko, defends the shooting down of the South Korean airliner in August 1983.

On the coming to power of the Reagan administration, tension in Soviet–US relations increased, with a resultant cooling in the international climate. The new US government did everything it could to undo the work of its predecessors, striking blows at one agreement after another, either emasculating them or, as in the case of SALT-II, declaring them defunct.

Then came a certain night in August 1983 when a South Korean airliner that had blatantly violated the Soviet state border was shot down ... This was only a few days before the final stage of the Foreign Ministers' meeting on European security which was taking place in Madrid, and the response from Washington was a wave of insinuations against the USSR, brazenly exploiting the incident for propaganda purposes ...

[In conversation with American Secretary of State George Shultz] I set out the Soviet point of view: 'We accuse the American side of carrying out a serious and premeditated action against the Soviet Union. How could the plane accidentally divert from the established corridor of five hundred kilometres, not towards international waters but towards the Soviet border, over vitally important military territory in the Soviet Far East, and penetrate and fly in Soviet airspace for more than two hours? Why did this plane not obey warning signals and the order to land which were given in strict accordance with international law and Soviet law?'

Shultz made no reply to any of my questions. I concluded: 'That is why we accuse the US administration of organizing a criminal act against the USSR, only one of many such attacks on us.' That was virtually the end of my talk with Shultz. It was probably the sharpest exchange I ever had with an American Secretary of State, and I have had talks with fourteen of them.

Source: Andrei Gromyko, *Memories*, pp. 296–300.

Notes

1. Dmitri Volkogonov, *The Rise and Fall of the Soviet Empire*, pp. 264, 266.
2. Alec Nove, 'Agriculture', in A. Brown and M. Kaser (editors), *Soviet Policies for the 1980s*, pp. 170–1; Alec Nove, *An Economic History of the USSR, 1917–1991*, p. 379; and pp. 378–93 for more details of economic policies under Brezhnev.
3. Robert Service, *A History of Twentieth Century Russia*, p. 402.
4. J.N. Westwood, *Endurance and Endeavour. Russian History 1812–1992*, p. 431.
5. Service, p. 410.
6. Westwood, p. 600.
7. Martin McCauley, *The Soviet Union 1917–1991*, p. 306.
8. Statistics in this section are from Archie Brown, *The Gorbachev Factor*, p. 18; Westwood, pp. 456–7; Service, p. 409; and McCauley, pp. 297–302.
9. Brown, p. 18.
10. Andrei Sakharov, *Memoirs*, pp. 310–12.
11. Service, pp. 416–420.
12. For full coverage, see K. Dawisha, *The Kremlin and the Prague Spring*.
13. There is a good general survey in R.L. Hutchings, *Soviet–East European Relations: Consolidation and Conflict 1968–1980*.
14. Andrei Gromyko, *Memories*, pp. 197–201.
15. Adam Ulam, *Dangerous Relations: The Soviet Union in World Politics 1970–1982* is highly recommended. Also Richard D. Anderson, *Public Politics in an Authoritarian State:*

Making Foreign Policy During the Brezhnev Years; and R. Edmonds, *Soviet Foreign Policy: the Brezhnev Years.*

16. Volkogonov, pp. 293–300.
17. *Ibid.*, p. 462.
18. Service, pp. 408–9.
19. Volkogonov, p. 278.
20. *Ibid.*, pp. 306–7.
21. Westwood, pp. 460, 466.
22. Service, p. 427.
23. Volkogonov, p. 388.

▪ ⊻ 10 Gorbachev and the end of the Soviet Union, 1985–1991

Summary of events

Mikhail Gorbachev was the last Soviet leader, the man who presided over the end of communist rule in eastern Europe and the Soviet Union, and the collapse of the USSR at the end of 1991. When he came to power in March 1985 at the comparatively young age of 54, he was determined to modernize the Soviet system, which had been stagnating for the previous 20 years. However, at the beginning he had no clear idea of exactly what needed to be done, and he knew that whatever changes he tried to introduce would be opposed by members of the party and the government bureaucracy, if their privileged positions were threatened. He began cautiously, building up a team of like-minded reformers; but progress was slow, and he eventually decided that economic reforms could only be achieved if political reform accompanied them. The communist party began to divide itself into those, like Gorbachev, who thought that the party must modernize to survive, and those who were afraid that reform would weaken the control of the party and threaten their elite positions. **Gorbachev's new thinking included:**

- *uskorenie*   acceleration, particularly in the economy;
- *glasnost*   openness or frankness;
- *perestroika*   restructuring – of the party, the economy and the government;
- **democratization**   which began early in 1989 with elections for local Soviets and the creation of **an elected Congress of People's Deputies**.
- **changes in foreign policy**: he hoped to bring an end to the arms race and the threat of nuclear confrontation, both for economic and moral reasons;
- **a new approach to the satellite states of eastern Europe** – they should be free to choose their own political systems.

The West found such ideas startling, to say the least, coming from a Soviet leader, and at first Western leaders tended to be sceptical of his intentions. British Prime Minister Margaret Thatcher was one of the first international leaders to comment favourably. After their first meeting, shortly before he became General-Secretary, she remarked, 'I like Mr Gorbachev. We can do business together.' In the end he won them all over, even US Presidents Reagan and Bush, the arch-enemies of communism. Some of his policies were brilliantly successful, especially **the development of the USSR's closer relationship with the West**. The USA responded positively to his initiatives, and **the Soviet decision to withdraw from Afghanistan**

in April 1989 helped to bring an end to the Cold War. During 1989–90 when the states of eastern Europe dropped their communist governments, Gorbachev refused to intervene; he even went along with **the reunification of Germany in October 1990**. It was at this point that he was awarded the Nobel Peace Prize.

Although Gorbachev was extremely popular abroad, he was having increasing problems at home, and by the autumn of 1989 his popularity had collapsed dramatically. At the usual May Day celebrations in Moscow in 1990, he was booed off the rostrum. **Criticism came from all sides**:

- The army and the traditionalists (conservatives or hard-liners) in the communist party were outraged that Gorbachev had 'lost' eastern Europe without putting up a fight, and worst of all that he had allowed Germany to be reunited.
- The traditionalists were appalled at the way the party was being deprived of its power; they thought Gorbachev's political changes were going too far, especially on 6 March 1990 when he persuaded the Congress of People's Deputies to amend Article 6 of the Soviet Constitution; the changes meant that **the communist party had lost its monopoly of power in the USSR**.
- The more radical reformers, like **Boris Yeltsin**, thought that Gorbachev was moving too slowly and wanted more decisive action.
- **Gorbachev's economic reforms were a failure**; an economic crisis had been gathering momentum since 1987 and had reached disastrous proportions by 1989. Everything was in short supply, the shops were empty, and everybody blamed Gorbachev.
- **Increasing nationalism became a serious problem** for Gorbachev, as many of the 15 republics making up the USSR began to demand independence. These developments were encouraged by Yeltsin, who was elected president of the Russian republic in June 1991. Gorbachev and Yeltsin were now bitter rivals for power. The three Baltic republics – Latvia, Lithuania and Estonia – declared themselves independent, and the three Transcaucasian republics – Armenia, Azerbaijan and Georgia – were thinking along the same lines. **The USSR was beginning to fall apart**.

Gorbachev meanwhile veered from the left wing of the party towards the right, and back again, trying to muster sufficient support for his policies. His main concern by this time was **to preserve the USSR in some form or other**. In July he reached an agreement with Yeltsin and other republican leaders on the formation of a new USSR – the Union of Sovereign Socialist States – in which the republics had much more power. This new Union Treaty was due to be formally signed on 20 August 1991. However, a group of traditional right-wing Communists decided they had had enough of Gorbachev; they wanted to save the party and the Union and **they planned a *coup* to overthrow him** and prevent the signing of the Treaty. Gorbachev was placed under house arrest in his holiday dacha in the Crimea, but Yeltsin led the opposition to the conspirators, and the attempt failed. Gorbachev was able to return to Moscow, but his days in power were numbered. The communist party had discredited itself by trying to overthrow Gorbachev and put the clock back. **Yeltsin banned the communist party in the Russian republic**, and both Russia and Ukraine decided not to sign the Union

Treaty. In December 1991 Yeltsin and the presidents of Ukraine and Belarus declared that the USSR was dissolved and set up instead a weak association of former Soviet republics, known as the Commonwealth of Independent States (CIS). This new organization was to have no president, and consequently Gorbachev was out of a job. **The USSR formally ceased to exist at midnight on 31 December 1991.**

Main areas of debate:

- What were Gorbachev's intentions? Did he intend to destroy the communist party?
- Why did the Soviet economy prove so difficult to reform?
- Was it a mistake to give the states of eastern Europe 'freedom of choice'?
- Why did Gorbachev and Yeltsin fail to work together successfully?
- Should Gorbachev be regarded as a complete failure?
- Was communism capable of being reformed?
- Why did communism survive in China but not in the USSR?
- Could the USSR have been saved?

10.1 The struggle for reform

(a) Gorbachev gathers his team

Mikhail Gorbachev was born into a peasant family in the Stavropol region of the Northern Caucasus in 1931. His father was a tractor and combine harvester driver; during harvest periods, as a teenager, Mikhail helped his father, and at the age of 17 he was awarded the Order of the Red Banner of Labour. At school he was a bright pupil and was accepted at Moscow State University where he graduated in Law. Returning to Stavropol, he became Komsomol first secretary in 1956, and by 1970 he had risen to become party first secretary for the Stavropol region. After coming to the notice of Andropov, he rose quickly – Central Committee member in 1971 and full member of the Politburo in 1980, at the age of only 49, an unheard-of achievement for those days. During his first few years in the Politburo, Gorbachev managed to give the impression that he was a traditionalist at heart, though he had dropped some hints that he had radical reform in mind. For example, in a speech in December 1984 he used the terms *glasnost* (openness), *perestroika* (restructuring) and *uskorenie* (acceleration); he even talked about 'democratization'. However, he must not have alarmed his elderly colleagues too seriously: after Chernenko's death in March 1985, Gorbachev was the unopposed choice as next General Secretary. Veteran Foreign Minister Gromyko (known as 'Grim Grom') led the way in proposing Gorbachev and was full of praise for his talents. There seemed to be a feeling in the country and in the party Central Committee that it was time for a younger and more energetic leader.

In private, however, Gorbachev had been much more open; on a visit to Canada in 1983 he had told Alexander Yakovlev, the Soviet ambassador in Ottawa, that 'society had to change, it had to be constructed on different principles.' In December 1984, in conversation with Eduard Shevardnadze, who was soon to become Soviet Foreign Minister, Gorbachev had agreed that 'everything's rotten. It has to be changed.' Gorbachev himself remarked to his wife, Raisa, the evening before he was chosen as leader, 'We can't go on living in this way.'[1] He knew that the country needed to be modernized and revitalized; agriculture and industry somehow had to be reformed to make them more productive; in foreign affairs he was anxious to revive *détente* and to extricate the Soviet Union from Afghanistan; and the communist party, which had become set in its ways and attitudes, would also have to be changed. He acknowledged the need for greater social justice, a greater role for the soviets, and more participation by workers at the workplace. At first Gorbachev had no great visionary plan; he knew that he had to tread carefully so as not to antagonize the traditionalists; the changes must be controlled from above. He believed that all these objectives could be achieved within the framework of the Marxist–Leninist one-party state. He apparently could not believe that both the party and the people might not choose to follow him in his modernization of Marxism–Leninism and the Soviet system. But as it turned out, the party apparatus was very slow to respond to the pressure for reform. It was only very late in the day – after the coup of August 1991, when the traditionalists tried to overthrow him – that Gorbachev admitted that the party could not be the vehicle for restructuring the USSR.

His first goal was to build up a team of supporters and get rid of likely opponents. By the end of his first year in office he had manoeuvred a majority for himself in the Politburo, bringing in Yegor Ligachev, Nikolai Ryzkhov, Viktor Chebrikov and Eduard Shevardnadze, and removing several members who were hostile to him, including Viktor Grishin, the Moscow party boss, who was so corrupt that he was known as the Godfather. Shevardnadze was made Foreign Minister in place of the elderly Gromyko, who became Soviet president, and Boris Yeltsin became a candidate member of the Politburo. Gorbachev also replaced 14 out of 23 heads of departments, and 39 out of 101 Soviet ministers; his close ally and adviser, Alexander Yakovlev, was put in charge of culture and propaganda. In the area of personnel changes, Gorbachev had achieved in one year as much as Khrushchev achieved in five. The Secretary-General surrounded himself with reform-minded aides such as Anatoly Chernyaev, who had taught History at Moscow University for a time before joining the party apparatus, and Georgy Shakhnazarov, a man of many talents – poet, writer of science fiction and an expert on political science. Both Chernyaev and Shakhnazarov had worked in Prague on the *World Marxist Review*. Many of these people had been admirers of Khrushchev; and now at last, 20 years later, came Gorbachev, a bright new star, one of whose slogans was 'acceleration'.

(b) First attempts at perestroika

Perestroika – the restructuring of the economy, society and the party – was Gorbachev's answer to the country's problems. However, during his first two years in power, no very dramatic changes took place. The leadership simply did not realize how serious the economic crisis was in 1985; there had been virtually no growth since 1974. It was decided therefore that if more investment was concentrated in the machine-building, electrical engineering and electronics sector, that would effectively modernize the technical base of the economy. In the Twelfth Five-Year Plan (1986–90) investment was set to increase by 23.6 per cent; the targets were a 25 per cent increase in industrial production, a 14.4 per cent increase in agricultural production, and a 14 per cent increase in real incomes per head.[2] The first major agricultural reform was one that Gorbachev had had in mind for some time: he set up one large ministry – the State Committee for the Agro-Industrial Complex (known as Gosagroprom) – to replace the group of ministries which had previously looked after different aspects of agriculture. Its function was to organize the entire business of food cultivation and processing. Unfortunately, Gosagroprom soon developed into yet another large bureaucracy and achieved hardly any of the results which Gorbachev and his advisers had hoped for. Another idea of Gorbachev was to encourage groups of farmers (including family groups) to lease some land from the parent collective which they could farm free of central interference. This too had disappointing results partly because district party secretaries and collective farm managers were reluctant to 'contract-out' any of their land, and because of apathy on the part of peasants themselves.

The most bizarre reform of this early phase was the anti-alcohol campaign, a pet scheme of Ligachev, which involved measures to limit the production and sale of alcohol. The Politburo had apparently not thought through the consequences of its policy: for one thing there was a huge increase in illicit distilling; and as well as being unpopular, it caused a serious loss of revenue, since sales of alcohol brought in more revenue than the state received in income tax. As one observer wrote: 'By giving away its revenue to the bootlegger, the government in the last two years has sharply increased its budgetary imbalace and incurred a deficit which is today being covered in a most dangerous and unhealthy way, by the printing press.'[3] By 1987 all the signs were that the first phase of *perestroika* was not having the desired impact (Document A). Reports were coming in that the reform policies were not being carried into effect on the ground – nothing was actually changing; initial industrial indicators showed that 1987 output was going to be lower than 1986. Another shock for Gorbachev early in 1987 was the revelation that 40 per cent of the entire state budget was being spent on the military and in the attempt to keep up with the USA and Reagan's Star Wars project. It was the military-industrial complex which was doing best out of *perestroika*. This was not what had been intended, and it was clear that much more drastic measures were needed.

(c) *Glasnost* and the Chernobyl disaster

Another strand of Gorbachev's new policies was *glasnost* – meaning 'openness' or 'a making public'. His aim was not that the people should be told everything, or that censorship should be completely abolished, but that there should be a more free exchange of ideas, more debate about current issues and controversies. At the Party Congress in February 1986 he dismissed arguments in favour of caution by insisting that 'There can only be one answer to this, a Leninist answer: under all circumstances, Communists need the truth.' The party should be able to face up to criticism and to indulge in self-criticism. However, the policy was slow to get under way, and the problems of secrecy were demonstrated by the Chernobyl disaster. On 26 April 1986 a terrible accident took place at a nuclear power station near Chernobyl in Ukraine. The core of one of the reactors overheated and the staff, poorly supervised and badly trained, simply tried to cool the reactor instead of shutting it down immediately. There was a huge explosion which released massive radiation; radioactive particles were blown by the wind across Belorussia, Poland and into Scandinavia. Increased radioactivity levels were even reported in western Europe. The leadership in Moscow did not realize how serious the situation was, because the authorities at the power station and in Kiev, the Ukrainian capital, tried to play down the scale of the disaster. It was newspapers in Scandinavia which first revealed that there must have been a nuclear disaster somewhere in the USSR. The news flashed round the rest of the world before Moscow acknowledged that anything untoward had happened. But in fact Gorbachev himself had difficulty getting full information, and he eventually sent an investigation team to find out exactly what had gone wrong.

The investigation into the Chernobyl disaster revealed a sorry tale of carelessness, incompetence and ignorance. Two dozen men were killed almost immediately as they tried to seal off the reactor and prevent a meltdown of its core. The authorities at the power station and the neighouring town of Pripyat were very slow to take action; it was 36 hours before it was decided to evacuate about 50,000 people who were living within a 10-kilometre radius of the blazing reactor; and a whole week passed before a 30-kilometre area was evacuated. During that time, children continued to play outside in radioactive dust, and cattle grazed on contaminated grass. Life went on as normal in most Ukrainian markets long after the authorities in Poland had banned the sale of certain vegetables and warned children not to drink milk. It was eventually revealed in *Pravda* that many of the staff at Chernobyl were unqualified, that drunkenness was rife, and that safety was sacrificed for the sake of higher output.[4] Gorbachev himself later admitted that the whole thing had shaken him deeply, not only because of the human suffering and the devastation that it caused, but because of the realization that a similar network of incompetence, secrecy, misinformation and deliberate deception was operating all over the Soviet Union. Chernobyl was a turning point in his thinking; he now knew that things could not be put right by merely making administrative changes – reform had to be basic and fast.[5]

Gorbachev was full of confidence that the situation could be salvaged; he had no intention of presiding over the dissolution of the USSR or the dismantling of the communist political system. But, as Robert Service points out: 'the irony was that Gorbachev, in trying to prevent the descent of the system into general crisis, proved instrumental in bringing forward that crisis and destroying the USSR.'[6] The first important step was that from June 1986, Glavlit, the body responsible for censoring the press, was told to be more lenient; in July Gorbachev addressed a group of newspaper editors and told them to be more adventurous and to shake up the bureaucracy. In December Gorbachev personally telephoned Andrei Sakharov, who was still living in internal exile in Gorky, and invited him to return to Moscow. This was part of Gorbachev's campaign to get the intelligentsia and some of the dissidents on his side against the bureaucracy and the traditionalists.

In January 1987 the USSR stopped jamming the BBC. The general aim was to use the media to publicize inefficiency and corruption, to educate public opinion and mobilize support for the government's policies. Long-banned anti-Stalin films were shown and novels published, and preparations were made to publish works by the great poet Osip Mandelstam, who had died in a labour camp in 1938.

(d) The second phase of *perestroika*

Gorbachev had reached the conclusion that he must reform the party and its ideas before any radical progress could be made in economic reform. The opposition was gathering itself together, even within the Politburo, where the conservative Ligachev was doing his best to undermine Gorbachev. It was at a Central Committee plenum meeting in January 1987 that Gorbachev gave a clear warning of what could be expected. He attacked Stalin, and although he did not mention Brezhnev by name, he said that the policy of leaving officials undisturbed in posts for so long had been absurd. Democratization was to be the new policy objective: instead of members of local Soviets being appointed by the local party, they were to be elected by the people, and there was to be a choice of candidates (though not of parties). There were to be elections for important party positions, such as committee secretaries, and elections in factories for the workforce to choose their own director. The following November Gorbachev reiterated some of these points in a speech to communist leaders assembled to celebrate the 70th anniversary of the October revolution (Document B). During 1988 dramatic changes were introduced in central government. The old Supreme Soviet of about 1450 members only met for a few weeks each year; it was now replaced by the Congress of People's Deputies of 2250 members, whose main function was to elect a new and much smaller Supreme Soviet of 450 representatives; this was to be a proper working parliament, sitting for eight months a year. The Congress consisted of three chambers of 750 members each; members of two of the chambers were chosen by secret ballot in competitive constituency general elections; the third chamber consisted of representatives of various groups which each had a guaranteed number of seats: the communist party, the trade unions and the co-operative movement had 100 reserved seats each, while the Komsomol, the women's councils, the scientific unions and others had 75 seats each.

The first elections under the new system were held in March 1989; in the Congress as a whole 87 per cent of those elected were communist party members. Well-known figures elected included Roy Medvedev, Andrei Sakharov and Boris Yeltsin. About 20 per cent of the party officials who stood in the elections were defeated. Gorbachev claimed that the results were a victory for *perestroika* and a defeat for conservatism. He pointed out that even though many communists had lost, people had not voted against them because they were communists, but because they were perceived to be bureaucrats and conservatives. A great deal of public interest and even enthusiasm had been generated by the elections, the first semi-free ones for some 70 years. But there were ominous signs for the future of communism, especially when, during its second session, in December 1989, the Congress dropped the system of reserved seats; this meant that at the next election, due in 1994, even Gorbachev would have to stand and put himself

Figure 10.1   The Moscow Summit, May 1988. Gorbachev and his wife, Raisa, greet Reagan and his wife, Nancy, in the Kremlin. From left to right: Mrs Gorbachev, Reagan, Gorbachev, Mrs Reagan.

to the test of a popular vote. As Richard Sakwa puts it, 'the election [of 1989] marked an irreversible step in the evolution of *perestroika* as politics entered the streets and popular consciousness. The various popular fronts and other radical groups, including an increasing number of voters' clubs and associations, represented a growing challenge to the party's comfortable hegemony. The machine politics of bureaucratic socialism, and its attendant empty shelves, mismanagement and corruption, suffered a stinging defeat.'[7] There seemed a strong possibility that the party would split into two sections – reformers and conservatives; many thought this would have been a logical step, but Gorbachev was determined on keeping the party together. The elections had important effects in eastern Europe; the fact that Moscow was willing to allow contested elections, in which communist candidates were defeated, encouraged first Poland and then Hungary to hold multi-party elections, which eventually led to the collapse of communism in the satellite states (see section 10.3).

The economic situation was not entirely forgotten; alongside all the startling political changes, some radical economic reforms were introduced too. The basic principle was the decentralization of state industry, giving more autonomy to individual units. The details were included in the Law on State Enterprises which was to come into operation at the beginning of 1988; 60 per cent of state enterprises moved on to a system of self-management, and the rest were to go over on 1 January 1989. Enterprises were allowed to engage in wholesale trade with each other and set their own prices. Managers were no longer allocated machinery and raw materials by the planners in Moscow, but had to negotiate for themselves. Compulsory targets were no longer imposed from above; once the state had taken its requirements, factories were free to sell the remainder of their products on the open market and make a profit. They were even allowed to deal with foreign firms. A new breed of managers began to develop – some were allowed to train at business schools in the West, others at a new Institute of Management set up in Moscow. Small-scale private enterprises were allowed, ranging from opening restaurants, making clothes and handicrafts, and providing services such as television and motor repairs, painting and decorating, and private tuition. At first businesses were limited to members of the same family, but this was later relaxed, and workers' co-operatives were allowed up to a maximum of 50 workers. One motive for this reform was to provide competition for the slow and inefficient services provided by the state, in the hope of stimulating a rapid improvement. Another was to provide alternative employment in case factories, in the drive for greater efficiency, began to lay off some of their workers. November 1989 saw the introduction of a new law to encourage more leasing in agriculture and other spheres. Workers were allowed to buy out the enterprise which they had leased from the state, though at this point it did not apply to land. However, this was a big step forward towards the creation of a 'commodity market economy' which the leadership had been talking about for some time.[8]

10.2 Foreign affairs – the end of the Cold War

(a) Gorbachev and Reagan

When Gorbachev became leader, US President Reagan was just beginning his second term, and relations between East and West were still strained. Reagan had rejected proposals for arms limitation talks and was pressing ahead with his Star Wars project, forcing the USSR once again to try and match the USA's performance. As Gorbachev became increasingly aware of the seriousness of the Soviet economic crisis, he reached the conclusion that there must be drastic cut-backs in military expenditure; otherwise the USSR would never be able to raise the living standards of its citizens to the levels enjoyed in western Europe. There was only one practical solution – the arms race must be brought to an end. If the Americans insisted on continuing their hard line, then it was up to the Soviets to make the first moves. In the words of Gerald Segal, 'the early initiatives clearly came from the Soviet side, with bold ideas from Gorbachev about INF [Intermediate Nuclear Forces] negotiations and even strategic weapons cuts. It was not so much that the Soviet Union was forced to the bargaining table by the firmness of President Reagan, but more that there was finally a Soviet leader wise enough to take the United States up on an INF deal (zero–zero) that was partly proposed in the expectation that it would never be taken up.'[9]

Gorbachev and Reagan first met in Geneva in November 1985; the two men took to each other, but nothing of importance was agreed. The next meeting, suggested by Gorbachev in order to discuss nuclear disarmament, took place in Reykjavik (Iceland) in October 1986. Reagan and his team went to the summit thinking that Gorbachev wanted to discuss fairly modest reductions in numbers of US missiles in Europe and Soviet SS-20s. They were stunned when the Soviets produced a sweeping set of proposals which included 50 per cent reductions in strategic offensive forces, the complete removal of all INF from Europe, and restrictions on strategic defences, including Reagan's Star Wars. The most breath-taking of all was the proposal for all nuclear weapons to be destroyed within ten years. Gorbachev was extremely persuasive, and it seemed that Reagan was on the point of signing a preliminary agreement when his aides convinced him it was best not to be in too much of a hurry. The stumbling block was Gorbachev's insistence on crippling limits on Reagan's Star Wars programme; Reagan refused to accept this and the summit ended in some disarray.

At first the failure to reach agreement at Reykjavik seemed likely to sour rela-tions between the two states. But Gorbachev would not give up so easily; after the Chernobyl accident he felt very strongly about the need for nuclear disarmament; 'if the peaceful atom is attended by such risk,' he said, 'what does that say about the nuclear weapon?' In another speech he said: 'Our ideal is a world without weapons and violence.' Later he claimed that the fundamental principle of his thinking was that 'nuclear weapons cannot be a means of achieving political, economic, ideological or any other goals...Clausewitz's dictum that war is the continuation of policy only by different means, which was classical in his time, has grown hopelessly out of date.'[10] Other developments helped to keep the atmosphere reasonably friendly; Sakharov's return to Moscow in December 1986, Gorbachev's continued attacks on Stalin and Brezhnev, and the signs that the USSR wanted to withdraw from Afghanistan (see next section). Another summit meeting took place in Washington in December 1987, and this time an important agreement was reached. Gorbachev made a concession to Reagan by not insisting that constraints must be placed on the American Star Wars project; Gorbachev had been impressed by the arguments of his own scientific experts who pointed out that the programme was still only in the early stages of research; the time when it would become reality was so far in the future that it was not worth making a fuss about at this stage. Consequently the two leaders were able to sign the Intermediate Nuclear Forces Treaty, which eliminated intermediate and shorter-range missiles (300 to 3000 miles) from Europe – both the American Pershing and Cruise missiles and the Soviet SS-20s based in East Germany and Czechoslovakia. Strict verification provisions were introduced so that both sides could check that the weapons were actually being destroyed. Although it was Gorbachev who was making the biggest concessions – the USSR had undertaken to destroy about four times as many warheads as the Americans – ironically it was Reagan who was attacked by his own right-wingers who refused to accept that Gorbachev was 'a new kind of Soviet leader', and who described the INF treaty as 'treasonous.'[11] In practice, the treaty meant that only four per cent of the existing stocks of nuclear weapons were to be eliminated; but it was an important turning-point in the nuclear arms race, since it was the first time any weapons had been destroyed.

In April 1988 agreements were signed in Geneva ending the war in Afghanistan. Further summits took place in Moscow in May 1988 and in New York in December 1988, the day before Gorbachev addressed the United Nations General Assembly. Once again he reiterated the Soviet Union's commitment to world peace, and stressed that this had now taken precedence over the class struggle. To prove that he meant what he said, he announced that the USSR intended to reduce its conventional forces by half a million men – ten per cent of the Soviet army. Six divisions, consisting of 10,000 men, were to be withdrawn from eastern Europe; during 1989 these proposals were carried into effect. In the summer of 1988, at the time of Reagan's visit to Moscow, Gorbachev was probably at the height of his popularity, both at home and abroad, and more than anything else, it was his successful foreign policy which was responsible. When Reagan was asked in Moscow whether he still thought the Soviet Union was an 'evil empire', he replied: 'No, I was talking about another time, another era.' In 1989, when the states of eastern Europe one by one rejected communism, the USSR did nothing to prevent it; there was to be no repeat of the earlier Soviet interventions in Hungary and Czechoslovakia. Gorbachev's good relationship continued with the next US President, George Bush. In May and June 1990 Gorbachev was in the USA for a summit with Bush; in August, when Iraqi troops invaded Kuwait, the USSR and the USA issued a joint statement condemning the invasion. Clearly the Cold War was over. But by this time Gorbachev was in severe difficulties; the situation was running out of his control, and he was under attack from the traditionalists who were horrified at the turn of events, and from the more radical reformers who thought that things were not moving fast enough.

(b) Afghanistan and China

When he became leader, Gorbachev had already realized that Soviet intervention in Afghanistan had been a serious mistake. It was an extremely expensive operation, and the quick victory which had been anticipated did not materialize. The Afghan army more or less disintegrated and the Soviet troops were left on their own to prop up the Afghan government. Although there were over 100,000 Soviet troops there at the peak of Soviet involvement, it proved impossible to defeat their opponents – the Mujahadin – who were divided among themselves, but were receiving aid from the USA and China. Continued Soviet involvement was a constant source of tension between East and West, and the USSR was under continuous pressure from the United Nations to withdraw. Gorbachev was determined to extricate the USSR and as early as October 1985 he had secured the Politburo's approval. But the problem was how to achieve it; the main concern of his military leaders was how to effect a withdrawal without it looking like a defeat. And there was the problem of what was to happen to the head of the Afghan government, Mohammad Najibullah. Was he to be left in place? Could he survive? Should he be replaced by a coalition of all the opposition groups? The military did all it could to prolong discussions and delay the inevitable, but in the end Gorbachev had the final say. Talks began, sponsored by the United Nations, and an agreement was signed in Geneva in April 1988: the USSR was to withdraw all its troops over a nine-month period, both super-powers were to stop supplying arms to the combatants and were to cease all interference in Afghan affairs; Afghanistan and Pakistan (to which about five million refugees had fled) agreed not to interfere in each other's affairs. A UN mission was to check that the terms of the agreement were being carried out; many people were sceptical that the USSR would really honour its promises. But they need not have worried: the Soviet troop withdrawal began in May 1988 and was completed on schedule in February 1989. Najibullah's regime survived until 1992; in 1996 he was murdered by the Taliban, a fundamentalist Islamic party. The USSR also co-operated with the United Nations in ending its interventionist role in several other countries – including Angola, Namibia, Cambodia and Nicaragua; Gorbachev's new thinking led him to decide that peace and stability were more desirable than long drawn-out military struggles to establish more socialist states.

Gorbachev and his Foreign Minister, Eduard Shevardnadze, generally put themselves out to improve relations with other states. They were especially anxious to be on better terms with the People's Republic of China; the Soviet withdrawal from Afghanistan removed one obstacle to good relations, and the Chinese were pleased when Gorbachev ordered the removal of 200,000 Soviet troops from Mongolia and Central Asia, along the frontier with China. Relations improved sufficiently for Gorbachev to be invited to visit China, which he did in May 1989. The timing was not good though, since he arrived as protesters were occupying Tiananmen Square in Beijing, demanding political reform and democracy. However, the talks were successful – the USSR and China were officially reconciled, and Gorbachev called for the complete demilitarization of the border, where clashes in 1969 had almost led to war. On 4 June 1989, after Gorbachev's departure, the Chinese army crushed the democracy movement, killing between 1500 and 3000 protesters. Although Gorbachev did not approve of the use of force, the new friendship between the two states continued to flourish, and cross-border trade between them increased. He tried to woo the countries of western Europe by talking of 'the common European home;' he developed a good relationship with British Prime Minister, Margaret Thatcher, and with Felipe Gonzalez, the Prime Minister of Spain. On a visit to Vladivostock he tried to foster better relations with Japan by talking about the Pacific as 'our common home.' As Robert Service puts it: 'if he had gone to the North Pole, he would no doubt have charmed the polar bears with his commitment to "the common Arctic home".'[12] Everywhere he went abroad Gorbachev received a rapturous welcome; in December 1989 he had an audience with Pope John Paul II; in October 1990 he was awarded the Nobel Prize for Peace.

10.3   The end of communism in eastern Europe

(a) Gorbachev's attitude to eastern Europe

It seemed at first as though Gorbachev was so pre-occupied with Soviet domestic and foreign affairs that he had little time to spare for eastern Europe. As soon as he came to power he made it clear to the leaders of the satellite states that the USSR would no longer interfere in their internal affairs. Of course, he wanted communist leaders in power in the Warsaw Pact countries who shared his way of thinking, and he certainly was not thinking in terms of the overthrow of the communist regimes. As late as October 1987 he chastized Todor Zhivkov, the Bulgarian leader, for policies which he thought threatened the communist party's control, and he warned him that there were people around him of 'a pro-Western orientation.'[13] Yet at the same time he continued to talk about 'the freedom to choose.' So what were Gorbachev's intentions for eastern Europe? One theory is that he expected the east European communists to be so impressed with his Soviet model of reformed communism that they would voluntarily imitate it; intervention by force would not be necessary. As the Cold War drew to an end, Gorbachev's ideas gradually changed; the new closer relationship between the USSR and the West meant that they no longer viewed each other as enemies, and consequently Soviet control over eastern Europe was no longer so vital. Provided that there could be a new type of genuinely co-operative relationship between the Soviet Union and the independent states of eastern Europe, it scarcely mattered whether their governments were communist or not. As Archie Brown explains: 'The anti-militarist element in the new thinking, together with accept-ance of the right of sovereign states to choose their own form of government, prevailed mainly because they were values which Gorbachev had come to hold and take seriously ... a Soviet military intervention in Eastern Europe would have involved such a discrepancy between word and deed as to destroy the credibility which Gorbachev had built up in the outside world.' Although the changes which occurred in 1989–90 in eastern Europe obviously went further and faster than Gorbachev and his team had ever bargained for, Brown feels that he deserves great credit for 'the change he introduced in the fundamentals of Soviet foreign policy which made possible the transformation of the East European political landscape.'[14] Robert Service, on the other hand, sees Gorbachev's handling of eastern Europe as rather confusing – certainly for the communist leaders. 'He contented himself with destabilizing the political compounds and standing back to observe the consequences. This was like a trainee chemist running amok in a laboratory. He was dealing with ingredients which, once tampered with, became volatile and unpredictable.'[15] The leaders of eastern Europe felt betrayed; they had known officially since they were told in Moscow in November 1986 that there would be no Soviet military interventions, whatever happened. This information was naturally kept from their citizens for as long as possible, since everybody knew that the communist regimes were only kept in power by the threat of Soviet tanks rolling through their capital cities.

(b) The collapse

To say that the events of 1989–90 in eastern Europe were dramatic is an under-statement. In January 1989 every state east of the River Elbe had a communist government; at the end of 1990 there was only one fully communist, one-party state left in Europe, apart from the USSR itself, and that was Albania; ironically, Albania had been hostile to the USSR ever since Khrushchev had fallen out with China. Why did the political scene change so rapidly? The basic underlying cause was that the communist governments had failed economically; their systems were inefficient, over-centralized and subject to too many restrictions. By the mid-1980s there were problems everywhere; living and working conditions for ordinary people were far below the standard of those in western Europe; the communist record on health, education, housing and social services generally was poor. At the same time, increasing contact with the West showed people how backward their own countries were in comparison and suggested that their living standards were falling even further. How long these regimes might have survived is impossible to say; but the vital change which decided the timing of their collapse was Gorbachev's decision not to intervene. They only existed because the USSR had put them there by force or by the threat of force, and now the prop which sustained them had been removed.

The collapse began in Poland where General Jaruzelski had been leader since 1981. All his attempts to improve the economy had failed; in 1988 he tried to economize by cutting government subsidies, but this drove prices up, and workers responded by coming out on strike. When this had happened in the early 1980s Jaruzelski had used the army to restore order and suppress Solidarity, the trade union movement. But now he decided not to risk using force, since there would be no backing from Moscow; he admitted that he needed the support of the opposition to deal with the economic crisis. Talks began in February 1989 between the communist government, Solidarity and other opposition groups, including the Roman Catholic Church. By April they had produced a new constitution: Solidarity was allowed to become a political party and elections were to be held for a two-chamber parliament. In the lower house the communists were guaranteed 65 per cent of the seats, but the upper house (the Senate) was freely elected. Parliament would elect a President, who would then choose a Prime Minister. In the elections held in June 1989 Solidarity won 92 of the 100 seats in the Senate, and 160 out of the seats which they were allowed to contest in the lower house. A compromise deal was worked out when it came to forming a government: Jaruzelski was narrowly elected President, thanks to the guaranteed communist seats in the lower house, but he chose a Solidarity supporter, Tadeusz Mazowiecki, as Prime Minister. After the collapse of communism in the other east European states, further changes were made in Poland. The guaranteed communist seats were removed, and in December 1990, Lech Walesa, the Solidarity leader, was elected President. The peaceful revolution in Poland was complete.

The Hungarian Communist party had already changed its leadership in May 1988, replacing Kadar with the more radical Karoly Grosz. However, progress was not quick enough for most people; two large opposition parties were formed, the liberal Alliance of Free Democrats, and the Democratic Forum, which represented the interests of farmers. Following the example of the Poles, the Hungarian communists decided to go peacefully. Free elections were held in March 1990; the communists changed their name to the Hungarian Socialist Party, but they still suffered a crushing defeat. The election was won by the Democratic Forum, whose leader, Jozsef Antall, became Prime Minister. The changes in Hungary had spectacular consequences for the German Democratic Republic (GDR) – East Germany. In September 1989, while the communists were still in power in Hungary, Karoly Grosz's government opened Hungary's frontiers with Austria, and allowed thousands of East Germans to pass through Hungary into Austria; from there they could make their way into West Germany. On 6 October Gorbachev visited Berlin for the celebrations marking the fortieth anniversary of the birth of the GDR. Erich Honecker, the East German leader, had been in power since 1971 and had consistently refused all reforms. He organized a grandiose state ceremony with many speeches, a military parade and fireworks. In private Gorbachev hinted broadly that the leadership would soon have to introduce some massive changes or end up in defeat; reportedly at one point he made a remark which became famous: 'Life itself punishes those who delay.'[16] Soon after Gorbachev's departure, opposition quickly gathered momentum in East Germany and there was a wave of demonstrations all over the country demanding freedom and an end to communist rule. Some sources claim that Honecker wanted to use the army to crush the demonstrators, as the Chinese had done in Tiananmen Square in June 1989, although he knew that there would be no backing for this from Gorbachev. There was a huge demonstration in Leipzig on 9 October; special forces had been placed on alert and there were vast numbers of police, and ambulance and hospital services at the ready. Apparently, bloodshed was only averted at the last moment by 'a combination of civic spirit, luck, and the failure of the party chain of command.'[17] The conductor of the Leipzig Gewandhaus Orchestra, Kurt Masur, played an important part in calming down the crowds and preventing violence. Honecker's days as leader were numbered; some of his colleagues were plotting to get rid of him, and on 18 October they forced him to resign. He was replaced by Egon Krenz, who immediately offered concessions. On 9 November 1989 the Berlin Wall was opened; thousands of people flocked out to help break down the wall, demolishing sections of it by hand, and later bringing up heavy equipment. Still the momentum continued; at a crisis meeting early in December, the communist party abdicated its leading role and forced Krenz to resign. Elections were fixed for March 1990.

Although the communist domination of East Germany was now over, very few people were talking publicly about the reunification of Germany. But the economy of the GDR was in serious difficulties; a report published at the end of October showed that productivity was at least 40 per cent below that of West Germany, and that the GDR was on the verge of financial collapse. Krenz appealed to the USSR for aid, but Gorbachev pointed out that the Soviet Union too was in deep economic trouble, and suggested that the GDR should 'foster and constantly strengthen' relations with West Germany; in other words, go begging to Bonn to help them prop up the GDR. Although this advice must have given rise to thoughts of German unification, Gorbachev told Krenz early in November that this was not on the international agenda. Yet there is also evidence that on his earlier visit to Bonn in June 1989, Gorbachev had promised West German Chancellor, Helmut Kohl, that he would help German unification in return for German economic aid for the USSR. Soon after the Berlin Wall came down, Kohl, without consulting anybody, even his own Foreign Minister, published a ten-point programme for reunification. Hans Modrow, the new East German Prime Minister, visited Moscow on 30 January 1990 and told Gorbachev that the majority of East Germans no longer wanted a separate state; it was going to be impossible to preserve the republic. Gorbachev seemed to take this news calmly, and in February he told Kohl that it was up to the Germans to decide things for themselves. In the run-up to the East German elections in March 1990, Kohl staged an election tour in support of the Alliance for Germany, the main opposition party to the communists. The Alliance won an overwhelming victory and in April the new government called for the unification of the two German states.

The USA gave its approval, but there were one or two sticking points before the USSR agreed. Kohl wanted the new Germany to be a member of NATO, but at first this was unacceptable to Gorbachev. He was eventually persuaded to concede this point by US President Bush and his Secretary of State, James Baker, although in his memoirs he claims that the idea to allow the Germans to decide their own security arrangements originated with him and not with Bush. One of the reasons why Gorbachev accepted German membership of NATO was that, after a shaky start, he had developed an excellent relationship with Chancellor Kohl, so that Germany no longer seemed to be a threat to the USSR. Gorbachev's handling of the situation caused some consternation among his colleagues, since he acted very much on his own. 'Without informing Shevardnadze, who had done all the spade work on Soviet–German relations, Gorbachev abandoned all claims as an occupying power and any restrictions on German sovereignty, including the future right to be a member of NATO. Shevardnadze knew that the ire of the military and the conservatives at the "loss" of the GDR would descend on his head. Gorbachev also failed to discuss German unification in the Politburo.'[18] Nevertheless, the decision had been taken: Germany was officially reunited on 3 October 1990.

Meanwhile, events had not been standing still in the rest of eastern Europe. A week after the Berlin Wall came down, Czechoslovakia began what became known as the 'Velvet Revolution'. The first big anti-communist demonstration was held in Prague on 17 November 1989. At first it seemed as though the communists would try to hold on, and some people were injured when police went into action to disperse the crowds. The Civil Rights movement, Charter 77, led by the famous playwright, Vaclav Havel, organized further opposition rallies. After Alexander Dubcek, the hero of the 1968 Prague Spring, had made an emotional speech – his first public appearance since his removal by Soviet troops over 20 years earlier – a national strike was declared. The communists decided it was time to go, and on 29 December 1989 Havel was elected President. In Romania the brutal and repressive regime of Nicolae Ceausescu was also overthrown in December. As unrest mounted across the country, Ceausescu ordered his troops to fire on the crowds of protestors, and many were killed and wounded. This caused outrage, and when Ceausescu and his wife appeared on the balcony of Communist Party Headquarters in Bucharest to address a massed rally, they were greeted with booing, groaning and whistling. He tried to continue his speech, but soon faltered and stopped. The scene was being televised, and at this point the transmission abruptly ceased; nothing like it had ever happened before, but now the whole country could see that at last the hated Ceausescu was being challenged. It seemed as though the entire population of Bucharest streamed out onto the streets. Ceausescu ordered his security forces to shoot to kill. For a time it seemed that order might be restored, but the following day even more people joined in; it was turning into a full-scale rebellion. The turning-point came when the regular army refused to fire on the crowds; the Ceausescus had lost control. They were eventually arrested, tried by an impromptu military tribunal and shot (25 December 1989).

Changes also took place in Bulgaria, although here they were not so clear-cut. In December 1989 the progressive communists in the Bulgarian Politburo voted Todor Zhivkov, who had been leader since 1954, out of office. Free elections were held in June 1990 which were won by the communists, now calling themselves the Bulgarian Socialist Party. Change was a little longer coming in Albania but eventually the communist leadership bowed to the inevitable and allowed free elections; the first non-communist president was elected in 1992. By this time the Soviet Union itself had disintegrated and Gorbachev was out of office.

By the end of 1990 the USSR had not only lost control over the states of eastern Europe, it had also failed to retain much influence in the area. This, according to Archie Brown, was 'a giant failure of Soviet foreign policy over more than forty years,' but not a failure on the part of Gorbachev, although the Soviet military leaders and communist hardliners interpreted it as such, and talked of the 'loss' of eastern Europe. But, asks Brown, 'who actually lost?' He goes on to argue that the only people who actually lost were 'those forces with an interest in con-frontation – ideological, political and military – and who wished to preserve authoritarian regimes.' But everybody else gained: the West gained because it was no longer faced by a hostile Warsaw Pact; the countries of eastern Europe gained because they were now independent; and Russia also gained because it was saved from massive military expenditure and was no longer responsible, and held accountable, for everything which happened in eastern Europe.[19] Gorbachev surely deserves enormous credit for refusing to use force to preserve the com-munist regimes of eastern Europe, even though he must have known that their collapse would make it all the more difficult for him to preserve his own regime in the USSR.

10.4   Gorbachev runs into problems

(a) Opposition from radicals and conservatives

After two years in power, as he moved into the second stage of *perestroika*, Gorbachev was encountering opposition from many quarters. The traditionalists or conservatives, including Ligachev, a man Gorbachev thought was his ally, were alarmed that the changes were much too drastic and that the party was in danger of losing control. The radicals, who included Boris Yeltsin, were impatient and wanted a faster pace of reform. Yeltsin, who was first secretary of the Moscow party, was a controversial politician who had made himself popular with the citizens of Moscow by sacking many corrupt officials, including the mayor. Naturally the bureaucracy, fearful of losing their jobs, detested him. At Politburo meetings he constantly clashed with Ligachev, and although Gorbachev had some sympathy with Yeltsin's views, he could not afford to side with Yeltsin against Ligachev, who controlled the party apparatus. Matters came to a head at a Central Committee plenum on 21 October 1987. Gorbachev made perhaps his most radical statement so far, criticizing his conservative opponents, many of whom were in the audience. 'We must learn to identify, expose and neu-tralise the overt opponents of *perestroika*,' he said, 'those who are holding things up, sticking spokes in the wheels and gloating over the difficulties and failures, those who are trying to push us back into the worst years of the past.' Then Yeltsin spoke: he complained about 'what I can only call the increasing adulation of the general secretary . . . I regard this as intolerable.' He said that the people of the USSR had gained nothing during the past two years, and told the audience that he was handing in his resignation from the Politburo because of lack of support, 'especially from Comrade Ligachev.' As he went to sit down, there was pandemonium in the hall, and a whole string of speakers rushed to defend Ligachev and condemn Yeltsin. The speech was ill-judged and tactless and could hardly fail to embarrass Gorbachev, whose own policies came under attack too; to some extent Gorbachev was forced to retreat from his radical position, which was now discredited, thanks to Yeltsin, and to take up a more central stance, at least for the time being. As Angus Roxburgh points out, 'eventually Gorbachev would persuade the party to reorganize the Secretariat and *apparat*, and give up its privileges, just as Yeltsin had demanded. It might have happened sooner, however, had not Yeltsin provoked the conservatives with his behaviour at the October plenum.'[20]

The conservatives now decided to launch an attack on Yeltsin; on 11 November 1987, even though he was ill in hospital with severe headaches and chest pains, Gorbachev summoned him to attend a meeting of the Moscow party organization. Against his doctors' orders and heavily sedated, he was taken first to a Politburo meeting and then to the Moscow party session. In a state of semi-collapse, he was forced to listen to a series of fierce attacks from party officials whom he had sacked or annoyed. He was dismissed as Moscow first secretary and his resignation as a Politburo candidate member was accepted. Ligachev and the conservatives were triumphant; this was the bureaucracy taking its revenge on the man who had tried to clean them up. After they had all left, it was Gorbachev who went over to Yeltsin, who was still sitting slumped at the table. Taking him sympathetically by the arm, Gorbachev helped him out of the hall, and an ambulance took him back to hospital. Most people thought this was the end of Yeltsin's political career, and for the time being the radical reformers were discredited. Gorbachev and his friend Yakovlev were almost the only reformers left among the leading elite.

Yegor Ligachev was a genuine Marxist, committed to the party's mission, and he agreed with Gorbachev that it was vital to stamp out the corruption, the inefficiency and the indiscipline of the Brezhnev period. He believed it was the party's duty to make the system work, and he disapproved of Gorbachev's talk of the market economy, private enterprise and democratization, because he believed that this would destroy the party's control. When Gorbachev told him that his privatization plans would only involve seven per cent of the total, Ligachev replied: 'That is an illusion. I tasted private property in my childhood [he meant NEP during the 1920s] and I know: they will not be content with seven per cent. Big business and private capital will hog everything.' *Perestroika* was leading to the re-emergence of nationality problems too: in February 1988 trouble broke out in the Caucasus. Encouraged by Gorbachev's calls for a critical look at Soviet history, the council of Nagorno–Karabakh, a region where about 80 per cent of the population was Armenian, voted to take itself out of the republic of Azerbaijan, where Stalin had placed it in 1923, and into the republic of Armenia. Violent clashes broke out between Armenians and Azeris, and the dispute threatened to develop into civil war between the two republics (see section 10.5(a)). The conservatives blamed it all on *perestroika* and in

March 1988 Ligachev and his supporters attacked again. When Gorbachev was about to leave on a visit to Yugoslavia and Yakovlev was in Mongolia, a letter appeared in the newspaper *Sovetskaya Rossiya* from Nina Andreyeva, a Leningrad teacher, defending Stalin and his achievements and condemning recent 'left-wing liberal' developments as alarming and excessive; there were also jibes at Jews, who, it was suggested, were not genuine Russians (Document C). It was, says Martin McCauley, 'a full frontal assault on *perestroika* and it caused the blood of the reformers to run cold.'[21] When Gorbachev returned, he ordered a full enquiry; it emerged that this was no ordinary letter. It had been received some time before, and had been rewritten by Ligachev supporters. Ligachev denied any involvement in the affair but Gorbachev was not entirely convinced. Another conservative attempt to derail his policies had failed, and he tried to make sure that there was no repetition. Ligachev lost his responsibility for the party apparatus and ideology; and it was at the party conference in June 1988 that Gorbachev introduced his plans for the Congress of People's Deputies. This was the beginning of Gorbachev's attempt to transfer the basis of authority within the country from the party to the state. In the existing system, the communist party and the state had fused into the same body. He hoped gradually to shift his power base from the party to the new Congress, elected by the people.

Following the elections for the Congress in March 1989 (see section 10.1(d)) the reformers staged a come-back. The first session, which lasted from 25 May to 9 June, was rumbustious and chaotic, and Gorbachev, who was elected Chairman of the Supreme Soviet, had a difficult job keeping the debates under control. Although the radical deputies were in a minority – no more than about 300 out of 2250 – they were very successful in making themselves heard. The proceedings were televised live, and, in the words of David Remnick, 'no one in the country could tear himself away from these televised sessions. No newspaper, no film, book or play had ever had such an immediate political effect on the people of the Soviet Union ... factories and collective farms reported that no work was getting done. People simply could not believe what they were hearing ... These were days when radical democrats thought that reform of the Party was not only possible, but the only route to change. They were overcome with a sense of triumph and possibility.'[22] The radicals challenged everything: there were criticisms of the KGB, the generals, the party apparatus and the privileges of the elite. Gorbachev allowed all this; it was only during the second session of the Congress in December 1989 when Sakharov proposed that there should be a multi-party system that Gorbachev switched his microphone off and sent him back to his seat. Yeltsin had been elected with a huge majority as a deputy for Moscow, but when the Congress came to its main business of electing the members of the Supreme Soviet, the conservative majority rejected him. After an angry rally of Yeltsin supporters in Moscow, an unknown deputy from Siberia offered to give up his seat in the Supreme Soviet to Yeltsin; Gorbachev went along with this; after his earlier unsympathetic treatment of Yeltsin, he could hardly go against his own call for 'democratization'.

For the first time, there was a recognized opposition to the communist party, both in the Congress, and also in the Supreme Soviet, where there was a vociferous minority of critics, especially from the non-Russian republics – Estonia, Latvia, Lithuania, Georgia and Armenia. Unfortunately for Gorbachev, things were beginning to slip out of control. Thanks to *glasnost* and the extensive television coverage, people knew that communism was being successfully challenged in Poland and Hungary. By the end of 1989 the non-Russians, seeing communism on the run in eastern Europe, were thinking in terms of independence from the USSR. In November 1989 the Georgian Supreme Soviet declared sovereignty, and the following month the communist party of Lithuania declared itself independent of the communist party of the USSR (see section 10.5(a)). At the same time the economy was in crisis; ordinary citizens were affected when consumer and household goods such as soap, toothpaste, cups and saucers, washing-powder and razor-blades simply disappeared from the shops. People's patience began to run out; shortages and poor conditions led to the first serious strikes since the 1920s. In July 1989 the coal-miners of the Kuznetzk region (Kuzbass) went on strike when they found that there was no soap to wash themselves with at the end of their shift. 'What kind of regime is this,' they asked, 'when we can't even get washed?' After staging a sit-in, they decided on an all-out strike; in a matter of days the strike had spread to all the main coal-mining areas including the Donbass in Ukraine. Eventually some half a million miners were on strike, supported by around 160,000 workers in other industries who came out in sympathy. They had many grievances – the lack of soap was just the final straw; they demanded improvements in pay and conditions, pensions, safety, pollution control and management. There were startling political demands too – more power to the Soviets, an independent trade union like Solidarity in Poland, and the cancellation of Article 6 of the constitution, which gave the communist party its dominant role in the political system. The strikers displayed a high level of discipline and organization, holding mass meetings, forming committees and patrols, and working with the police to maintain order. For the first time since the Civil War force was not used against the protesters, and no sanctions were imposed on them after the strike ended. Gorbachev sympathized with many of their demands, and enough concessions were made to persuade them to return to work. The strike was effectively over by the end of July. Gorbachev claimed that the strikes were a statement of support for *perestroika*. In reality, the workers' movement was another emerging independent force pushing *perestroika* in new directions; since the communist party claimed to represent the interests of the working class, it could not afford to ignore their views. In the autumn of 1989 the miners of Vorkuta in the Komi Autonomous Republic went on strike again, with yet more overt political demands – again, the abolition of Article 6, plus direct elections for the presidency, and a rule preventing the head of the party from being President as well.[23]

It was inevitable that sooner or later a major challenge would be mounted to the Communist Party of the Soviet Union. At the second session of the Congress of People's Deputies which began on 12 December 1989, Sakharov tried to call for the abolition of Article 6 of the constitution. This was the occasion on which Gorbachev switched off Sakharov's microphone and refused to allow the proposal to be discussed. According to Archie Brown, Gorbachev had accepted, in private, at least since the summer of 1988, that Article 6 would have to go and that the party would have to give up its leading role and take its place within a multi-party system. 'But he wanted to do this at a time of his own choosing when executive power could be transferred from the Communist Party to elected state executive organs...He wanted to choose the right time...The problem was, however, that when the time was as yet scarcely ripe for the Communist Party establishment – in early 1990 – it was already overripe for a society which had seen Communist Parties removed not only from their constitutionally decreed "leading role" but from actual power in Eastern Europe in the course of 1989.'[24] Nevertheless Gorbachev pushed ahead with his plans. He prepared a new set of proposals to carry the transfer of power from party to state a further important step; two of the main points were the introduction of a presidential system, and the amendment of Article 6 so that the party abandoned its leading role, accepted a multi-party system and adopted 'humane, democratic socialism.' In February 1990 the proposals were put to a Central Committee plenum. Predictably there was a stormy debate; the conservatives did all they could to wreck the amendments to Article 6; both conservatives and radicals objected to the new role of president, which, they said, would carry too much power. Vladimir Brovikov, the Soviet ambassador to Poland, put the conservative case forcibly: 'The general secretary and his closest colleagues are trying to shove the Party onto the sidelines of political life, to turn it from a ruling party into a discussion club, or at best into a pawn in a parliamentary game. To let this happen would be a catastrophe for the country...our leaders are trying to cross out the Party as the leading force in society and to transfer the functions of the Politburo to the President.'[25] However, Gorbachev got his way: the Plenum and the Congress eventually approved the proposals, and in March Gorbachev was elected President of the Soviet Union for a term of five years. Two new bodies came into existence to help the President to function: a Federation Council which consisted of the parliamentary leaders of all 15 republics, and a Presidential Council, which consisted of senior ministers and any other advisers whom the President cared to chose. He could, he hoped, now function increasingly independently of the party.

Gorbachev was soon disappointed once again. The presidency did not give him the power he had hoped for, partly because he had decided to opt for an election by the Congress of People's Deputies instead of by the whole population. His caution was understandable – there must have been considerable doubt as to whether he could have won an election across the entire Soviet Union, given that his popularity was dwindling rapidly, while Boris Yeltsin's was increasing. This meant that Gorbachev's presidency, unlike the Presidency of the United States, somehow lacked legitimacy. Further problems were caused for the new President by the results of the republican and regional elections held in February and March 1990. In the three Baltic republics the elections were won by pro-independence candidates, many of whom were communists; on 11 March Lithuania formally declared itself independent of the USSR, the first of the republics to do so. In elections for the parliament of the Russian Soviet Federated Socialist Republic (RSFSR or simply Russia), the official party candidates did badly; worst of all for Gorbachev, on 29 May Yeltsin completed his dramatic comeback when he was elected Chairman of the Russian Supreme Soviet. Yeltsin now became the focus of attention for all the radical reformers. Although he had no power in the other 14 republics outside the RSFSR, in the political centres of Moscow and Leningrad, where it really mattered, Yeltsin now had an enormous advantage over Gorbachev: he was, in effect, the President of a democratically elected parliament which would become more powerful than the communist party. There were now two presidents, two parliaments and two governments in one country, and even in one capital city – Moscow. On 8 June 1990 the Russian republic announced its sovereignty, which meant, as far as anybody could be certain, that Russian laws took precedence over Soviet ones. Yeltsin's parliament and government would be able to prevent Gorbachev's policies being implemented in Russia; or alternatively, it could implement them in a more radical way than Gorbachev intended. Yeltsin was formally elected president of the Russian Federation on 12 June 1991.

(b) Economic failures

Economic reform turned out to be one of Gorbachev's two major failures; the other was his failure to cope with the problem of the non-Russian nationalities. His economic reforms seemed to have very little overall effect; after four years of *perestroika*, Soviet gross national product (GNP) was more or less static; in 1990 industrial production actually fell by 1.2 per cent and agricultural production by 2.3 per cent, according to official figures, but most experts think the true figures were more serious.[26] Gorbachev had promised that at last life really would improve: there would be goods in plenty in the shops and everybody would be able to afford to buy them. If he could only have delivered on the food and consumer goods front and kept people materially happy, both he and the Soviet system might well have survived. Instead things got worse; during the summer of 1986 there was a cotton wool shortage; in a country which produced completely inadequate amounts of tampons and sanitary towels for its one hundred million women of childbearing age, this was an insult and a disaster.[27] In 1989 the shortages became more widespread, the queues longer and more impatient, and food rationing was introduced. By the end of 1988, meat was rationed in 26 out of the 55 regions of the RSFSR; sugar was even more scarce, and was rationed in all but two of the regions. Even the hospitals were reporting shortages of medicines.[28] One of the reasons for the shortages was that no really dramatic changes occurred either in agriculture or industry. This was because officials in every republic and region only carried out parts of legislation which could be done easily, without damaging their own interests too much. In some areas they actively sabotaged Gorbachev's policies; it scarcely seems believable, but it happened, that in Leningrad the hard-line communist authorities ordered the supply of sausages to be taken from the storage fridges and buried in a trench outside the city. Such were the depths to which they were prepared to sink to discredit Gorbachev. By the closing months of 1989, basic items like tea, coffee, milk and soap were nowhere to be seen in the state shops. Often the quality of the goods available was poor; John Simpson, the BBC's Foreign Affairs editor, was in Moscow for a time, and experienced the awfulness of that most popular of Russian foods – the sausage. 'Have you tasted the sausage?' his friends asked him. 'It's filthy – quite inedible.' He felt obliged to taste it himself, and was forced to agree: 'It was indeed filthy, packed out with gristle and with some strange tasteless white filler. A thin colourless juice leaked from it as I bit into it. Its flavour was indescribably bad. I had once caught worms by eating Soviet sausage, but this was worse. There had been bad sausage in the past, and shortages of food too. What was different now was that people were freer than at any time since the 1920s to discuss the difficulties they were experiencing and to complain about them.'[29] The shortage of soap, among other grievances, led to a serious miners' strike in the summer of 1989 which involved over half a million in the major coal-fields of the USSR (see previous section).

Two aspects of the government's policies which *were* effective unfortunately did not have quite the desired results. One was the increasing number of private family businesses and co-operatives encouraged by the government. This made the shortage situation worse. Instead of starting up small manufacturing industries, as the government had hoped, most of them went into the retail and supply business. They tended to buy up much of the available stocks of goods which they sold at higher prices than in the state outlets. The co-operatives soon got themselves a bad reputation; poorer people – pensioners and the lowest paid workers – could not afford their high prices, and there was resentment at the fat profits which many of them made. The other measure which had unforeseen results was the Law on State Enterprises which came into effect in January 1988. It allowed managers to fix wages depending on availability of labour and levels of production. Output was measured by its value in roubles, which tempted managers not to increase overall output, but to concentrate on more expensive goods and reduce output of cheaper goods. The general trend of wages was upwards, whereas productivity remained static or even declined. The government printed more money to meet its requirements; inflation rose and the budget deficit threatened to get out of control.

The economy was adversely affected by the decline in output of oil and coal, the latter to some extent caused by the strikes. Between 1989 and 1991 oil exports fell by almost 50 per cent, and the fact that world oil prices fell did not help the situation. Another blow came from the events in eastern Europe during 1989–90. Comecon was dissolved and it was decided that trade with the former satellite states would be conducted in hard currency rather than on an exchange of commodity basis. Since hard currency was in short supply, this caused a catastrophic decline in trade with eastern Europe, and a consequent shortage of equipment and consumer goods previously imported from these countries. Nationalist problems within the USSR, as republics began to declare themselves independent, led to a fragmentation of the economy (see next section). When the USSR Congress of People's Deputies voted to increase social benefits, particularly pensions, the expense could only be met by printing more money; this accelerated inflation still further. The State Bank had lost control of monetary growth, and by 1990 there was a current account deficit of the equivalent of roughly 15 billion dollars.[30] Ordinary people could not understand why things had suddenly become so much worse. Not realizing that this was the culmination of 20 years of economic stagnation, they blamed Gorbachev for everything.

10.5 The USSR disintegrates

(a) The republics break away

The nationalist problem was Gorbachev's second greatest failure, and like the economic crisis, it contributed significantly to the break-up of the Soviet Union.[31] The Russian republic (RSFSR), with a population of around 145 million ethnic Russians in 1986, was just one of fifteen republics which made up the Union of Soviet Socialist Republics. It was the largest of the republics, having about 52 per cent of the total population of the USSR. The other 14 republics were: the three Baltic states of Latvia (1.5 million), Estonia (1.1 million) and Lithuania (3 million); the three other western Slavic nationalities of Ukraine (44 million), Belorussia (10 million) and Moldavia (3 million); the three Transcaucasian republics of Armenia (4.5 million), Azerbaijan (5.9 million) and Georgia (3.9 million); and the Central Asian republics of Uzbekistan (16.5 million), Turkmenistan (2.7 million), Kirgizstan (2.6 million), Tajikistan (3.9 million) and Kazakhstan (8.7 million). The communist party elites in many of the non-Russian republics had become entrenched in power during the Brezhnev years, and were corrupt and resistant to change. This was especially true in Transcaucasia and Central Asia; although Gorbachev was able to replace the leadership in some of the republics, he was unable to do much about the local *nomenklatura* in the party and the government.

In December 1986 there were the first disturbing signs that Gorbachev did not understand the strength of nationalist feelings or the delicacy of the relationship between Moscow and some of the republics (Document D). He decided to get rid of the 74-year old Dinmukhamad Kunayev, who had been leader of Kazakhstan since 1954, who had a reputation for spectacular corruption and ran his republic, with the help of his numerous family and friends, like a mafia boss. An article in *Izvestiya* claimed that among his other considerable assets, he had control of 247 hotels, 414 guest flats, 84 cottages, 22 hunting lodges and 350 hospital beds.[32] Certainly Kunayev deserved to go, but Gorbachev made the mistake of replacing him with a Russian, Gennady Kolbin, who had just distinguished himself by cleaning up the corruption in Georgia, and who, it was hoped, would repeat the exercise in Kazakhstan. This was insensitive to say the least; Kazakh nationalist feelings were outraged that a Russian should be foisted on them as their next leader. There was a huge protest demonstration in front of communist party headquarters in Alma Ata, the capital, although it was not entirely spontaneous – Kunayev's family and friends had a hand in its organization. Moscow decided that the Kazakhs needed a sharp lesson: troops were brought in to disperse the demonstrators, who seemed to be mostly students. Some were killed, hundreds injured and thousands were arrested. Gorbachev was shocked by the reaction and by the bloodshed, but he did not back down, at least not immediately; it was only in 1989 that he replaced Kolbin with a native Kazakh.

The problem for Gorbachev was that as *glasnost* and *perestroika* came on full stream, with freedom of expression and democratization, further tensions were inevitable. The various nationalities began to demand greater local control and self-determination. Nor was it just a simple case of non-Russians resisting control from Moscow; in each of the republics there were conflicts between ethnic minorities and the dominant nationality group. In Georgia, for example, there were two minority groups – the Abkhaz who were Muslims, and the Osetins – who each had small autonomous regions of their own within Georgia. There were constant clashes between the Abkhaz and Osetins on the one hand, who protested that the Georgians were trying to interfere excessively in their regions, and the Georgians on the other hand, who complained that the non-Georgians were expecting too much. The most disturbing development was the emergence of a Russian nationalist movement under the leadership of Boris Yeltsin which aimed to use the Russian republic as an alternative power base from which to challenge the hard-line communists and Gorbachev as well. So although Gorbachev had no intention of causing the break-up of the USSR, it seems that this outcome was almost inevitable if he continued with the democratizing element of *perestroika*. However, Gorbachev believed that it ought to be possible to work out a middle way between the existing Soviet system and a total break-down, in which every national group, not just the fifteen republics, became completely independent. He hoped, by persuasion and negotiation, to arrive at a system which still preserved a high level of integration and co-operation.

The first major nationalist test for Gorbachev was a conflict between the republics of Armenia and Azerbaijan over possession of the Nagorno–Karabakh region. The population of this area was 80 per cent Armenian but it had been placed under the jurisdiction of Azerbaijan by Stalin in 1923. Armenian resent-ment had smouldered on and off since then. They had many grievances: they were Christians, whereas the Azeris were mainly Shiite Muslims; they felt that their culture was suppressed and that they were exploited economically by the Azeri authorities in Baku. The new atmosphere in the USSR encouraged the Soviet of Nagorno–Karabakh to request a transfer to the jurisdiction of Armenia (February 1988). Demonstrations were held in Yerevan, the Armenian capital, in support of this demand, and clashes developed between Azeris and Armenians in other parts of Azerbaijan. The worst violence occurred in the city of Sumgait on the Caspian Sea near Baku: 26 Armenians and 6 Azeris were killed. Moscow's official line was that the request could not be granted, since it would encourage scores of similar demands and clashes; however, Gorbachev did promise a just solution. In June 1988 the Armenian Supreme Soviet voted to incorporate Nagorno–Karabakh into Armenia, but this was rejected by the Supreme Soviet of Azerbaijan. The Supreme Soviet of the USSR voted against the incorporation into Armenia. As disorders continued, the Supreme Soviet decided to place Nagorno–Karabakh under direct rule from Moscow (January 1989). This did nothing to solve the problem; ominous border clashes occurred, and the two republics were on the brink of civil war.

In April 1989 a new crisis suddenly erupted in Georgia, where there was a rap-idly growing nationalist movement. Its aims were to press for autonomy from the USSR, but at the same time to deny the Abkhaz people their independence from Georgia. Huge demonstrations were organized, stretching over several days, in the capital, Tbilisi, and although they were almost entirely peaceful, the local communist party leaders decided to use troops to disperse the crowds. Twenty of the demonstrators were killed, including several policemen who tried to protect women in the crowd from assault by the troops, and hundreds were injured;

but the violence was counter-productive: public opinion in Georgia was outraged and quickly turned against the Georgian Communist Party. There was a rush of support for the nationalists and for complete independence from the USSR. In November the Georgian Supreme Soviet declared sovereignty and decided that the Soviet occupation of Georgia in 1921 violated the treaty signed in 1920 between Georgia and Russia. There was great controversy about who should be held responsible for the Tbilisi tragedy, and for a time there was a tendency to blame Gorbachev. But in fact there is plenty of evidence that he did his best to prevent violence. He stated categorically that the situation must be resolved by political means and through dialogue. A commission of enquiry later put the blame on the local party leadership, who were sacked, and on the general in charge of the troops, who was moved elsewhere.[33]

The three Baltic republics had been incorporated into the USSR in 1940 under the terms of the secret agreement between Germany and the USSR, shortly after the signing of the Nazi–Soviet Pact in August 1939. Moscow insisted that they had joined voluntarily and denied any secret agreement. They were occupied by the Germans in 1941 and retaken by Soviet forces in 1944. Nationalist resistance movements waged guerrilla warfare against the occupying forces, and Stalin dealt with them ruthlessly: there were hundreds of executions, and in total, from the three states, some 700,000 people were deported to Siberia. Local cultures were undermined and suppressed; another source of grievance, especially in Latvia and Estonia, was the arrival of large numbers of Russian immigrants attracted by the growing industrialization. By 1989 only half the population of Latvia were native Latvians, while 33 per cent were Russian; in Estonia 28 per cent were Russian. In January 1988 the Estonian People's Front announced their programme. It included the restoration of Estonian instead of Russian as the official first language, the appointment of Estonians to the leading positions in the state, and the replacement of the command economy by a market economy. Independence was not an immediate aim, but clearly that would be the ultimate objective. The Front did not call itself a political party, since the communist party was the only one allowed; in fact many communists were also members of the Front, which did its best to give the impression that it was actually supporting Gorbachev and *perestroika*. Latvia and Lithuania soon followed Estonia's example; the Lithuanian group was known as Sajudis (which simply means 'movement'). Gorbachev seemed sympathetic; the hard-line party elites in all three republics were replaced by more progressive leaders with orders to work with the growing nationalist movements.

However, Gorbachev was worried that the Baltic nationalist movements were becoming too extreme. Although he welcomed their support for *perestroika*, he was against complete independence and even opposed the idea of more autonomy for the republics within the USSR. He was having problems with the Politburo, where Ligachev and the conservatives feared that the situation was on the brink of disaster. The big protest demonstrations in all three capitals on 23 August 1988, to mark the anniversary of the Nazi–Soviet Pact, did nothing to calm them. According to Ligachev, it was time for some sort of crack-down. Gorbachev and his closest ally, Alexander Yakovlev, realizing that the conservatives would have to be appeased, authorized the use of troops; for the first time force was used to break up a rally in Vilnius, the Lithuanian capital, organized by Vytautas Landsbergis (28 September 1988). It was also announced that the new USSR Supreme Soviet would have the power to overrule any laws passed by the republics, including, of course, any attempts to secede from the USSR. The announcement only inflamed the situation further, and even the Supreme Soviets of the three Baltic republics rejected this claim by the Moscow government. The rejection shocked Gorbachev because it showed that a majority of the members of the Baltic Communist Parties were supporting the nationalists. The Estonian Supreme Soviet went further – on 16 November a declaration was passed to the effect that Estonian legislation took precedence over USSR legislation. This was a step too far, and Moscow responded by annulling the Estonian declaration. In January 1989 the Estonians passed a new law, directed at the Russians, requiring all citizens to learn the Estonian language within four years; Lithuania and Latvia followed almost immediately with similar language laws.

The elections for the new USSR Congress of People's Deputies in March 1989 came at the right time for the Baltic nationalists because it enabled them to publish their election manifestos. That of Estonia consisted of all the recent resolutions passed by their Supreme Soviet, which had been annulled by Moscow – the sovereignty of their parliament, a free market economy and the existence of private property. The People's Fronts won the elections to the Congress in the Baltic states. In August Moscow responded to the growing pressures with some concessions: all the national areas were to have more rights, all were to be treated as equals, and national cultures and languages were to be given free rein. But this was not nearly enough to satisfy the Baltic peoples; events were moving rapidly on. Later in the same month of August 1989, the Lithuanian Supreme Soviet voted that the incorporation of Lithuania into the USSR in 1940 was illegal; on the 50th anniversary of the Nazi–Soviet Pact, two million people took part in forming a human chain which stretched from Vilnius in Lithuania to Tallinn, the capital of Estonia. In December the Lithuanian Communist Party, in a desperate attempt to keep the support of the people, declared itself independent of the Communist Party of the Soviet Union. Gorbachev condemned all these events in the strongest possible terms, although he was reluctant to use force. In January 1990 he went to Lithuania himself to talk to the leaders; he mingled with the crowds in Vilnius and talked to ordinary workers. He was taken aback by the strength of their desire for independence, and tried to persuade them that once his planned political and economic reforms were completed, they would be much better off staying in the USSR. He failed; he still could not understand how strongly the Lithuanians, Latvians and Estonians felt. Landsbergis, one of the leaders of Sajudis, and later president of Lithuania, explained it very clearly and simply: 'We are an occupied country. To pretend we are grateful for a little democracy, to go through some sort of referendum to prove our commitment to independence, to talk with Mr Gorbachev as anything other than a foreign leader, is to live a lie ... We have never considered ourselves a genuine part of the Soviet Union. That is something that Gorbachev does not quite understand. We wish his *perestroika* well, but the time has come for us to go our own way.'[34] The Baltic peoples, and indeed all the non-Russians, were greatly encouraged by events in eastern Europe, where, by early 1990, most of the

Soviet satellites had rejected communism and control from Moscow. On 11 March Lithuania duly declared itself independent and Landsbergis, a non-communist, was elected President.

Meanwhile in January 1990, the Armenian–Azerbaijani conflict had erupted again. After at least 60 Armenians had been murdered by Azeris in Baku, Moscow declared a state of emergency. Soviet troops retaliated, killing at least 83 Azeris (some sources put the dead at over 200). Gorbachev defended this action, claiming that it was necessary to bring an end to the atrocities. Probably the real reason for the intervention was to restore communist control and suppress the Azerbaijani National Front, whose members had seized the Communist Party buildings in Baku and had effectively taken control of the capital. This demonstrated that Gorbachev was prepared to use force to keep the USSR together, but it only made the Azeris more determined than ever to break away. He now attempted to deal with the growing demands for independence by the Law of Secession, passed in April 1990. This made secession theoretically possible, but the process was so slow and complex that it seemed deliberately designed to dissuade national groups from attempting it. Firstly, two-thirds of the population of the republic were required to vote for independence in a referendum; this would be followed by a five-year transition period, and then the Soviet legislature was required to give its final endorsement. Smaller national groups within the large republics could opt out of secession and remain in the USSR. This meant that a republic might lose territory on becoming independent. When Lithuania declared itself independent, neighbouring Belorussia demanded the return of the territory of Klaipida which had formerly been part of Belorussia. In the end everybody simply ignored the Law of Secession, but it was an attempt by Gorbachev to gain time for his reforms to work, so that the USSR could become the kind of organization that nobody wanted to leave.[35] He saw this as absolutely vital, since by this time the Soviet Union had lost control of eastern Europe. And yet although he was desperate to preserve the Union, he wanted to avoid the use of force.

After Lithuania declared independence in March 1990, Gorbachev continued his tough line by imposing an economic blockade on Lithuania beginning on 18 April. In June a moratorium was agreed: Lithuania would suspend (but not cancel) its declaration of independence and in return Gorbachev called off the blockade. But this could only be a temporary solution, and tension remained high. By this time the USSR was beginning to disintegrate. Yeltsin had just been elected Chairman of the Russian Supreme Soviet, which on 8 June, on Yeltsin's initiative, declared sovereignty and announced that its laws would take precedence over laws passed by the USSR. At the Twenty-Eighth Party Congress, Yeltsin dramatically resigned from the party and walked out of the Congress. The Soviet system was now being undermined not only by non-Russian nationalists, but by leading Russian politicians in Moscow. Speaking as leader of the Russian republic, Yeltsin told the governments of Estonia, Latvia and Lithuania that he would not support any action to keep them in the USSR by force. Uzbekistan also declared its sovereignty in June, and in July both Ukraine and Belorussia followed suit. In August it was the turn of Turkmenistan, Armenia and Tajikistan.

(b) Gorbachev veers left, then right, and left again

For a long time Gorbachev's reaction to these developments in the nationality problem was to continue with his policy, avoiding violence and trying to slow down the process of disintegration by using the Law of Secession. The trouble with this policy was that it satisfied nobody: it was much too slow for the nationalities who were impatient for independence, while on the other hand the conservatives wanted him to crack down and use as much force as was necessary to preserve the Union. Other pressures on Gorbachev were growing too, particularly in the economic sphere. The whole economy was on the point of collapse; the government was forced to take massive loans from Western banks to pay for the growing imports of grain and consumer goods. Drastic action was needed, and Gorbachev listened to advice from all sides. Most of the economic experts seemed to agree that the USSR would have to change from a command economy to a market economy; the big question was: what was the best way to go over to the market? Nikolai Ryzhkov, the Chairman of the USSR Council of Ministers, was in favour of a gradual move towards what he vaguely called a 'regulated market,' but he was so cautious that his method seemed likely to take years. Gorbachev was put off by Ryzhkov's insistence that food prices would have to rise in order to balance the budget. His most radical advisers told Gorbachev that there was no time to wait; action needed to be quick and decisive.

Gorbachev was attracted by the radical ideas of Grigory Yavlinsky, a young economist working for Yeltsin and the Russian government. He saw this as a chance to improve relations with Yeltsin; in August 1990 he persuaded Yeltsin to support the idea of a joint Soviet–Russian team of radical economists to draw up a plan for rapid marketization. The group produced what became known as the '500 Days Programme', an extremely impressive (at least on paper) 240-page document composed mainly by Stanislav Shatalin with help from Yavlinsky. It was a crash programme involving large-scale privatization, devolution of power to the republics and the setting-up of market institutions. There was no mention of socialism, and there was no way that any country with such an economic system could still be considered communist. Gorbachev signalled his approval of the documents publicly. And yet, as Archie Brown points out, 'they spelled the end of state socialism and were utterly inconsistent with the idea that Gorbachev was still a Communist in any meaningful sense of the term, even though he was still General Secretary of the Communist Party of the Soviet Union!'[36] There was pandemonium when the details of the programme became known. Ryzhkov and his supporters felt that it was unworkable, and he threatened to resign and take the entire government with him if Gorbachev tried to adopt it. The economic ministries and most of the party apparatus were opposed to it, and so were the KGB and the army which would both have their funding substantially reduced if the programme was carried out. One of the main points made by the critics was that since the republics would be in control of their own economies, that would deprive the central union authorities of most of their revenue-collecting powers; this would threaten the survival of the Soviet Union or indeed any other kind of union. Ryzkhov argued that it would cause mass unemployment and the closure of thousands of factories. Gorbachev himself began to have second thoughts, and invited another economist to prepare a compromise document combining the best aspects of the 500 Days Programme and Ryzhkov's more cautious plan. It was this compromise – known as 'Basic Guidelines' – which in October 1990 was accepted by the Supreme Soviet. However, it was an unsatisfactory crossbreed sort of plan, described by Yeltsin as like 'trying to mate a hedgehog with a snake.' What it meant in effect was that the conservatives had destroyed any possibility of a swift changeover to a market economy. Should Gorbachev have gambled and pressed ahead with the programme? The majority of economists now seem to think that, leaving aside the fierce opposition, the plan was unrealistic and the targets impossible; one economist said that it was the equivalent of Stalin's attempts to complete a Five-Year Plan in three years, and that if it had been implemented, the results 'would probably have been worse than today.'[37]

Gorbachev's retreat over the 500 Days Programme offended Yeltsin and the radical reformers and ruined the prospect of any further co-operation. Over the next few months – from October 1990 until March 1991 – he took a distinct move towards the right. He was obviously worried by the strength of the right-wing opposition and saw this move as a kind of tactical retreat, or, as he said later, 'an attempt to steer a middle course'. On 7 November 1990, during the usual celebrations to mark the Bolshevik revolution, a man tried to assassinate Gorbachev with a shot-gun. Fortunately, the guards were alert and he was unharmed. But he was deeply shocked by the incident, and it may have helped to convince him that law and order needed to be tightened up. On 18 November his move to the right became unmistakable; he abolished the Presidential Council, the body which included his most radical advisers like his close colleague Yakovlev; he gave himself as President greatly increased powers; and a new Security Council was set up, with seats for the KGB, army and police. Although Gorbachev repeated that he was still in favour of reform, it looked as though he was more interested in strengthening the traditional pillars of the communist state – the KGB, the *nomenklatura* and the threat of force. Yeltsin and the radicals were horrified. On 24 November the first draft appeared of a new Union Treaty, but it was unacceptable to the republics which felt that it was deliberately vague; it mentioned 'joint control' in many areas of policy, but the republics felt that in practice the centre would continue to dominate.

Gorbachev's problem was that as his relations with the republics and the radicals deteriorated, he found himself pushed more closely towards the conservatives. Having already sidelined Yakovlev, early in December he sacked his liberal Minister of the Interior, Vadim Bakatin, and replaced him with Boris Pugo, a hard-liner and former head of the KGB in Latvia. One of Pugo's first actions was to confer with the defence minister, Dmitri Yazov, and the head of the KGB, Vladimir Khryuchkov, both hard-liners; it was arranged that the army would set up military patrols on the streets of major cities. Gennady Yanayev was appointed Vice-President; he was another conservative, dedicated to preserving the Union, and he was a man whom Gorbachev mistakenly felt he could trust. When Ryzhkov suffered a serious heart-attack in December, he too was replaced by the more conservative Valentin Pavlov. The hard-liners were becoming more vociferous in the Congress of People's Deputies; in October 1990 they formed a group called *Soyuz* (Union) which, by the end of the year, numbered about 600 deputies. They were not all communist party members; what united them was the belief that the Soviet Union was worth preserving, that people should be proud of its industrial and cultural achievements, and especially proud of the fact that the USSR had defeated Nazi Germany. They saw Gorbachev as a wrecker who was out to destroy the greatest state in the world. During the session of the Congress which met in December 1990, *Soyuz* speakers called for strong measures to restore order and maintain the unity of the USSR. Gorbachev replied that he would use all his new presidential powers and if necessary would declare a state of emergency in any republic which tried to break away illegally.

This was the final straw for Foreign Minister Eduard Shevardnadze, the last liberal member of the government. On 20 December, in a dramatic and emotional speech to the Congress, he announced his resignation. For months he had been subjected to criticism from the army and the armaments industry, but since October, when the move to the right began, Gorbachev had ceased to support him, and he felt isolated. The army blamed him as the man who had 'lost' eastern Europe and allowed German reunification, although they knew perfectly well that these had been Gorbachev's decisions. Now his message to the Congress was that the reforming zeal of the liberals and radicals had been betrayed – by some of the reformers themselves: 'Comrade democrats, you have run away,' he told them; 'Reformers have taken cover. A dictatorship is coming. I am being completely responsible in stating this. No one knows what kind of dictatorship it will be or who will come or what the regime will be like. I want to make the following statement: I am resigning... Let this be my contribution, if you like, against the onset of dictatorship.'[38] Shevardnadze's speech caused a sensation; he had not discussed it beforehand with Gorbachev, who was hurt and embarrassed, but most importantly it gave notice, both to the people of the USSR and the rest of the world, of the strong possibility that the conservative backlash would reverse all the changes of the previous few years. Shevardnadze had no concrete evidence of an impending *coup* at this point, but he sensed, correctly, that sooner or later the conservatives would try to remove Gorbachev.

Events in the Baltic republics soon suggested that there might be something in Shevardnadze's warning. On 7 January 1991 Soviet paratroops entered all three republics with the excuse that they were searching for deserters. The situation in the republics had become more complicated, since the Russian inhabitants had organized themselves into pro-Moscow, anti-independence parties, opposed to the democratically elected governments of the republics. In Vilnius, the capital of Lithuania, supporters of the pro-Russian party (*Edinstvo*) stormed the parliament building and called on the Lithuanian government to resign. President Landsbergis issued an appeal to all Lithuanians to rally to the support of the republic; a Lithuanian counter-demonstration responded by chasing the Russians out of the parliament. Russian officials on the spot exaggerated the situation, telling Gorbachev that Lithuania was on the verge of civil war, and calling for the imposition of presidential rule. Gorbachev accused the Lithuanian government of trying to 'restore the bourgeois order' and demanded that they reinstate the Soviet constitution. Without waiting for a response from the Lithuanian government, Soviet tanks and troops went into action in Vilnius, occupying key buildings and seizing the radio and television stations and the television tower, which was surrounded by some 5000 demonstrators; 14 people were killed and 165 injured, some seriously. Everybody expected an attack on parliament, where the deputies were in session. However, the attack did not take place; the presence of many foreign journalists and the television cameras, which had recorded the bloodshed for all the world to see, no doubt made the military think twice before repeating the operation. However, a week later in Riga (Latvia) Soviet troops attacked the Latvian Ministry of Internal Affairs building, killing four people; but again they stopped short of trying to seize parliament.

The whole Baltic policy was a shambles: it had failed to get rid of the republic governments or to impose presidential rule. Gorbachev insisted that he had not given orders for the troops to use force, and the blame was placed on the local commanders. But although he apologized for the deaths in Riga and reiterated that the republics did have the right to secede from the USSR, he emphasized that it must be done on the basis of a referendum and following the rule of law. 'We cannot permit either unruliness or arbitrariness in this matter, even on the part of elected bodies.' Yeltsin made the most of the situation, flying to Tallinn (Estonia) and signing an agreement in which the Russian republic recognized Lithuania, Latvia and Estonia as independent sovereign states, not as Soviet republics. To be fair to him, he was no doubt afraid that the forces of conservatism might try to overthrow his Russian government in the same way. Gorbachev's popularity plummeted alarmingly as a result of the violence in Vilnius and Riga and he came under severe criticism in the media. There was a massive protest demonstration in the centre of Moscow in support of the democracy movements. The Lithuanians decided to start jumping through the required hoops: in February a referendum was held in which over 90 per cent of those who voted were in favour of independence. In March, Estonia and Latvia followed suit with votes of 78 per cent and 74 per cent respectively in favour of independence from the USSR.

Gorbachev continued with his efforts to reach some sort of consensus on the new union treaty; on 17 March 1991 a referendum was held throughout the USSR on the question: 'Do you consider necessary the preservation of the USSR as a renewed federation of equal sovereign republics, in which the rights and freedoms of an individual of any nationality will be fully guaranteed?' Although six republics (the three Baltic states, together with Armenia, Georgia and Moldavia) refused to take part, their share of the total population was relatively small, and in fact, over 80 per cent of the Soviet adult population voted; 76.4 per cent were in favour of the Union. The Russian republic added another question to its referendum: 'Are you in favour of an elected president for Russia?' Seventy per cent voted 'yes'. Now both Gorbachev and Yeltsin could claim that they had mandates – Gorbachev to reconstitute the USSR as a free association of sovereign republics; and Yeltsin to hold elections for the president of the Russian republic.

In spite of Gorbachev's attempts at compromise during the previous six months, the conservatives were not happy with him; how could they be when he was clearly bent on breaking up their multi-national state? He was becoming more impatient with their stubbornness and resistance to reform, and it was obvious to him that the majority of ordinary people were in favour of Yeltsin and reform. Gradually, from March onwards, he began to move away from the hard-liners and turn back to the advisers with whom he felt most comfortable – especially Yakovlev, Shakhnazarov, Chernyaev and Primakov. A meeting was arranged between Gorbachev, Yeltsin, and the leaders of the other eight republics which had taken part in the referendum; it was held in a dacha at Novo-Ogarevo in April 1991, and was the first of a series aimed at producing a constitution for a new federation. The final version was arrived at in August, but it was clear long before then that in the new union, the republics would have sovereign power and the centre would be reduced to dependency on the goodwill of the republics for its revenue. The new union would still be known as the USSR, but now the letters stood for 'Union of Soviet Sovereign States'. Gorbachev came under severe attack in the Congress and at one point he even handed in his resignation. However, the radicals persuaded him to stay on and the conservatives at this point lacked the nerve to give him the final push. On 11 July the Congress approved the general principle of the new union. 'What have you done, boys?' a member of the Politburo was reported to have asked the Novo-Ogarevo team. 'You have thrown away power, and with it the Union.' The date fixed for the formal signing of the Union Treaty was 20 August.

Meanwhile on 12 June elections to choose a president were held in the Russian republic. Yeltsin won a comfortable victory over his five rivals. Significantly, the man who came bottom of the poll with only just over three per cent of the vote, was Vadim Bakatin; although he was a liberal reformer, he was still a member of the communist party, and that was enough to ruin his chances in the eyes of any voter interested in reform. Yeltsin himself had left the communist party in 1990. Soon after his election Yeltsin issued a decree banning political activity by any party, including the communist party, in administrative institutions and economic enterprises in the Russian republic. However, Gorbachev was determined to stick with the party for the time being, but it was to be a drastically changed party. He told a Central Committee meeting in July that 'our party indisputably bears responsibility for the fact that it was not able to erect a barrier to despotism and allowed itself to be used as an instrument of totalitarianism.' He put forward a new draft programme based on 'humane, democratic, market socialism,' pointing out that the term 'communism' was mentioned only in passing. This was because, he said, 'our experience provides no grounds for thinking that this aim is realistically attainable in the foreseeable future.' The Central Committee reluctantly adopted the draft programme in July, probably because the conservatives, who were in a majority, intended to elect a new General Secretary and drop the draft programme, at the next party congress, which was due to be held in November. Most people, including Gorbachev, seemed to think that a split in the communist party between the reformers and the conservatives was now inevitable, and he too planned to bring this about at the next party congress. The difference was, of course, that Gorbachev expected to be on the winning side.[39] In a final meeting with Yeltsin at Novo-Ogorevo shortly before he left Moscow for the family summer holiday at Foros in the Crimea, they discussed the changes that would be made in the government after the signing of the Union Treaty on 20 August. Prime Minister Pavlov, KGB chief Kryuchkov and Defence Minister Yazov were all likely to be replaced by more liberal comrades, once the historic signing had taken place. It later emerged that the dacha had been bugged by the KGB and the conversations recorded. The discussions must have revealed the urgency of the need to get rid of Gorbachev, and certainly Yeltsin believes that this is what decided the timing of the August *coup*.[40]

(c) The August *coup*

It was KGB chief Vladimir Kryuchkov who was the main instigator of the attempted *coup* to overthrow Gorbachev. Other members of the plot – all men appointed and trusted by Gorbachev – included Yanayev, Pavlov, Yazov, Pugo, and even Valery Boldin, Gorbachev's own chief of staff. The plan was to set up a 'state committee' which would declare a state of emergency and introduce the necessary measures to restore order. Yanayev was to take over as acting president, while Gorbachev was to be placed under house arrest in the Crimea, cut off from the outside world. Gorbachev had refused to take any notice of warnings from Shevardnadze and Yakovlev that he should be on his guard; he simply could not believe that these people, who owed their positions to him, would turn against him. On 18 August a small group of the conspirators flew to Foros; they announced that Yeltsin had been arrested (which was untrue) and demanded that Gorbachev should hand over his powers 'temporarily' to Yanayev while the state committee restored order and brought the rebellious republics under control. If the conspirators had expected Gorbachev to cave in without resistance they were very much mistaken. He refused point blank to sign anything, swore at them, called them criminals and then sent them packing. Meanwhile in Moscow the *coup* leaders went on television to announce that Gorbachev had been taken ill and that a state of emergency was in operation to save the country from disorders (Document E). The new Union Treaty, which was due to be signed in a couple of days' time, was cancelled.

At this point things began to go wrong for the conspirators. They had expected that a show of force – some troops and tanks on the streets of Moscow – would be enough to clinch the operation; very little resistance was anticipated from the ordinary citizens of Moscow. But they had made several vital blunders: they had omitted to arrest Yeltsin and other leaders of the Russian republic. They had failed to understand the extent to which things had changed in the country, that people were no longer willing to allow themselves to be browbeaten by the KGB and the party – at least not without putting up a fight. And they had put the wrong man in charge of military operations in Moscow; this was General Pavel Grachev, who in the last resort, could not bring himself to desert Gorbachev and Yeltsin. As soon as Yeltsin heard about the *coup* he acted swiftly and decisively. He rushed to the Russian parliament building, known as the White House, alerted all his colleagues and officials of the Russian government, and broadcast several appeals denouncing the *coup* and urging the people of Moscow to come out and defend the White House and their government (Document F). Shortly after midday, wearing a bullet-proof jacket under his suit, he strode down the front steps of the White House and climbed onto a tank to address the demonstrators and the soldiers. 'Citizens of Russia,' his voice boomed out, 'the legally elected president of this country has been removed from power...We are dealing with a right-wing, reactionary, anti-constitutional *coup d'état* ... Accordingly we proclaim all decisions and decrees of this committee to be illegal ... We appeal to citizens of Russia to give an appropriate rebuff to the putschists and demand a return of the country to normal constitutional development.' For the rest of the day the crowds grew until there were at least 25,000, forming a human chain around the White House (Document G). They passed the time building barricades and talking to the tank crews, urging them not to fire at their own people. At the end of the day there were 50,000 troops in the city, and Red Square and other important points were crammed with tanks.

This was not what the state committee had expected; if the *coup* was to be successful they had to take the White House and arrest Yeltsin and his colleagues. The military commanders were ordered to draw up a plan to storm the building. Next day more troops and tanks were brought into the city; in one incident three young protesters were run over by a tank and killed. By this time the White House was full of deputies and sympathizers who had come in to lend support to Yeltsin and democracy. The cellist Mstislav Rostropovich was there, standing guard with an assault rifle outside Yeltsin's office; so was the poet Yevgeni Yevtushenko (Document H); Shevardnadze and Yakovlev arrived to offer encouragement. The atmosphere was tense, and it was by no means certain that they would emerge alive. Orders were actually given to storm the White House, but one by one the commanders found excuses to delay action. In the end the members of the state committee lost their nerve; by midday on 21 August they had decided to terminate their *coup* attempt, and Yazov called off the military action. One of the commanders later said that it would have been a simple matter to take the White House; the barricades were flimsy and the tanks could have made short work of them. But he admitted that although it could all have been over in 15 minutes, the casualties would have been heavy. 'It was all up to me,' he said. 'Thank God I couldn't bring myself to do it. It would have been a bloodbath. I refused.' The *coup* was over, and the main leaders were eventually arrested, except Pugo, who committed suicide. Yeltsin was the hero of the hour, and Gorbachev and his family, who had been under house arrest in their holiday dacha in the Crimea, were able to return to Moscow.[41]

Some historians have argued that the *coup* was not all that it seemed. For example, Amy Knight has pointed out that during Gorbachev's so-called isolation under house arrest, telephones were working in other buildings inside the compound and in the president's cars. Some members of his personal guards telephoned home; and how was it that his 32 guards, who were still armed, offered no resistance to the five officials who were supposed to be holding him under arrest? The suggestion is that Gorbachev could actually have left Foros at any time, that he had deliberately isolated himself in the dacha, perhaps in some sort of collusion with the conspirators, and was waiting to join whichever side won. Knight also argues that the army never had any intention of storming the White House and that Kryuchkov had telephoned Yeltsin to tell him so.[42] Yeltsin confirms this in his memoirs, but claims, with some justification, that he had not felt able to trust Kryuchkov. In his memoirs Gorbachev angrily denied any suggestions of collusion or that it was a self-imposed house-arrest. On the tenth anniversary of the *coup* attempt he still appeared outraged that anybody could take the suggestion seriously: 'I still had my armed bodyguards. But the place was surrounded by rings of troops and there were helicopters overhead. I kept walking around the compound so I could be seen and they'd realise that I was not ill. Was I supposed to climb over the fence in secret, like a partisan? It's nonsense.'[43] Most historians would probably go along with this sentiment; if the whole thing was a sham, why was it that Gorbachev's wife, Raisa, was so traumatized by her experiences? Archie Brown points out that Gorbachev was utterly devoted to his wife, and that he always discussed *everything* with her. In addition, there is the fact that the conspirators were hoping to reverse all the policies he had pursued since 1988 – including his Union Treaty, which had become almost an obsession with him. Most importantly though, 'it is unthinkable that for the sake of some illusory political gain Gorbachev would have subjected his wife to the uncertainty, stress and suffering which she endured between 18 and 21 August 1991, after which her health was never to be as strong again.'[44]

(d) The collapse of the Soviet Union

Gorbachev seemed to think that he could continue as though nothing had happened. He expected the Union Treaty to be formally approved within a few days and continued to talk about his new programme for the party: 'We must do everything to ensure that the party is reformed and becomes the living force of *perestroika*.' He had not understood the extent to which the communist party was now discredited because of the actions of the hard-liners; it seemed quite bizarre that he could still talk about reforming the party that had just totally rejected and betrayed him. Yakovlev told him in private that to talk of the 'renewal' of the party was like offering first aid to a corpse. However, Yeltsin soon left him in no doubt that the situation had changed dramatically; at a meeting of the Russian Supreme Soviet on 23 August he publicly humiliated Gorbachev, forcing him to read out the list of conspirators and all the people who had collaborated with them; it included every member of Gorbachev's cabinet except one, and numerous other people whom he had promoted and trusted, some of whom had been his friends from student days. It was a heartbreaking tale of desertion and betrayal. Yeltsin proceeded to suspend the activities of the Communist Party of the Soviet Union on Russian territory along with *Pravda* and its other newspapers, and to ban the Russian Communist Party. In the words of Martin McCauley, 'The Party had attempted to drum Yeltsin out of political life in October 1987. Now he drummed the Party out of political life. Revenge was sweet.'[45] On 25 August Gorbachev resigned as General Secretary of the Communist Party; on 5 September the Congress of People's Deputies was dissolved, pending new elections. Gorbechev had lost two of his vital power bases, and the old Soviet Union was on its last legs.

His main hope now lay in the Union Treaty which would bring into existence the Union of Sovereign States. This would operate as a single economic unit, there would be a common foreign and military policy, and there would be regular meetings between the presidents of the states. There would be a president of the Union – Gorbachev – but he would not take precedence over the others. However, Yeltsin was not enthusiastic; he was more interested in the internal politics of the Russian republic where he was planning to introduce a democratic political system and a market economy. Yeltsin claimed that he had no desire to break up the Union, yet he seemed to take every opportunity of weakening its chances of survival. Complications arose for Gorbachev when the Ukrainian President, Leonid Kravchuk, refused to take part in discussions or send representatives. On 1 December a referendum was held in Ukraine, showing a large majority – over 90 per cent – in favour of complete independence from the USSR; a large majority of the Russian inhabitants of Ukraine had voted for independence. Soon afterwards Kravchuk was elected president with over 60 per cent of the vote; it was announced that Ukraine would not sign a Union Treaty which had a central governing body, and would set up its own armed forces. This was the death blow for the Union Treaty and the Union of Sovereign States; the three Baltic states had already declared independence; without Ukraine, the state with the second largest population after Russia itself, the new union was a non-starter.

Yeltsin now took the initiative and had a meeting with Kravchuk and Stanislav Shushkevich, the leader of Belarus (as Belorussia was now known), near the Belarusian capital of Minsk. On 8 December it was announced that since the USSR was in the process of dying, the three of them had agreed to the formation of a much weaker union than the one proposed in the Union Treaty; it was to be known as the Commonwealth of Independent States (CIS). It was to be a purely voluntary association; any decisions it reached were not binding, and it had no powers to collect taxes. However, there would be a joint unified military command, a unified economic area and central offices; these were to be in Minsk, not Moscow. Most significant of all – there would be no president. All this was decided without consulting Gorbachev, although Yeltsin met him on 9 December and gave him the details. Gorbachev was furious; apart from the fact that he was soon likely to be out of a job, Yeltsin's action was, arguably, unconstitutional; US President Bush had even been told about the plans before Gorbachev himself. The other republics were invited to join the CIS, and eventually, at a ceremony in Alma-Ata (the capital of Kazakhstan) on 21 December, eleven of the former Soviet republics signed the agreement. The USSR and the position of President of the USSR would cease to exist at midnight on 31 December 1991. Gorbachev had not been invited to Alma-Ata. The four states which declined the invitation were the three Baltic republics and Georgia. It must have been a bitter experience for Gorbachev; when he introduced his policies of *glasnost* and *perestroika*, he could surely never have imagined that they would lead to the destruction of the vast union of which he was the leader. Now, that union had disappeared, and it only remained for him to resign with as much dignity as he could muster. He resigned formally on 25 December, making a short and dignified speech on television. He acknowledged that mistakes had been made and that many things could have been done better. He listed what he considered to be some of the achievements of his period in office, mentioning the end of the Cold War, the move away from a totalitarian system and towards democratic reforms, the recognition of human rights, and the beginnings of a move towards a market economy. 'Sadly,' he concluded, 'the old system tumbled down before the new one could begin functioning.'

10.6 Assessments of Gorbachev

(a) Was Gorbachev a failure?

How does the historian begin to assess a figure of such immense importance as Gorbachev, whose actions had such sensational results for the USSR and for the rest of the world? At the time of his downfall, and for some years afterwards, a majority of people in Russia dismissed him as a failure, though for different reasons. The old communists, who believed that the Soviet Union and the party still had a lot to offer and were worth preserving, saw him as a traitor. Viktor Alksnis, who was a member of the Soyuz group in the Supreme Soviet, is contemptuous of Gorbachev's refusal to use force. Mark Galeotti, who quotes Alksnis, goes on to note, disturbingly, that: 'Past Russian and Soviet leaders have rarely shied away from the use of violence. It may have made Gorbachev a better human being, but it also made him a failure as a politician.'[46] The more radical of the reformers, like the free marketeers, felt that he stayed with the communist party for too long, trying to reform the unreformable. The great mass of ordinary people, who just wanted an efficient and decisive government which could provide them with a decent standard of living, thought that he was weak and incompetent, a leader who foolishly set the country on the road to chaos, who talked too much and did not act enough. A woman in the street in Moscow told BBC correspondent John Simpson: 'There's no food, no cars, nothing in the shops. What's the point of having money when there's nothing to buy? I tell you honestly, I've come to hate Gorbachev...And I'll tell you something else, I hate the bloody communists as well. They've wrecked this country and don't have the faintest idea how to put things right.'[47] An American observer of Soviet society, John Bushnell, wrote: Few national leaders have failed so spectacularly as Mikhail Gorbachev: in 1985 he set out to reanimate Soviet society and economy, by the end of 1991 he had managed without benefit of war to destroy the Soviet state and lose for Russia the territorial gains of more than three centuries.'[48]

This is surely far too simplistic a conclusion. In fact, his career was a mixture of brilliant successes and disappointing failures. Gorbachev had a whole range of aims and goals; although it may be true that in 1985 he was thinking primarily in terms of reforming the communist system, it is important to recognize that his aims changed as time passed. In 1985 he genuinely believed that the communist party could be reformed and modernized, and that once this was achieved, there could be no better system. The party would be a force for stability (not stagnation) and progress. However, Gorbachev discovered that the majority of the party – the elite and the bureaucracy – was resisting change for their own selfish reasons; by the end of 1987 he was becoming increasingly impatient with the party and its corruption. Throughout the Brezhnev era the leaders had turned a blind eye to the corruption which was rife at all levels of activity. One Soviet academic noted in 1988 that the system was riddled with racketeers and black-market operators; anybody who was an official of any sort was directly connected to public property at some level, and people did not hesitate to lay hands on it for themselves. 'To refrain, to be disgusted, was self-injuring and finally stupid, a gesture which might appease the conscience but actually made no practical difference ... Those who are intelligent, energetic and callous enough will end up managing the most crucial sectors of government administration: first the economy and then politics.' It was Marxism inverted: each was receiving not according to his needs but according to his ability to take.[49] As the enormity of the problem became clear to Gorbachev, he changed his goals: if the party refused to reform itself, then the party would have to lose its dominant role. He reached the conclusion that he would have to reduce the role of the party in the economy, introduce elections for the Soviets, and give them a greater part to play. There can be no doubt that by the summer of 1988 he had dropped much of his Marxist–Leninist thinking; the more he saw of the political and economic systems in western Europe, the more he liked them, although he recognized that they were far from perfect. What appealed to him most was the social democrat model of socialism within a multi-party system. As for the ultimate goal of achieving a Communist Society, he had decided that this was illusory. Gorbachev's new thinking also extended to foreign affairs: he wanted a new relationship with the rest of the world; confrontation and the prospect of nuclear war were unacceptable to him; what he called 'universal human values' were more important to him than class interests.

By the end of 1990 Gorbachev could claim considerable success in achieving these goals. The political scene had changed dramatically since 1985: the highly repressive communist system had gone and there were now strong elements of democratization to be seen. Archie Brown is convinced that, at least from the summer of 1988, it was a *conscious* aim on Gorbachev's part to transform the political system. 'From the spring of 1989 it is scarcely meaningful to describe the Soviet Union as a Communist system ... The greatest part of Marxist–Leninist dogma had been abandoned by then – and by the party leader himself – and so had the most important defining characteristics of a Communist system.' He goes on to explain that, as he sees it, there are five defining features of a Communist system: the supreme authority of the party; a highly centralized, strictly disciplined party; state ownership of the means of production; the aim of building Communism as the ultimate goal; a sense of belonging to an international Communist movement. By March 1990, when the famous Article 6 of the Soviet Constitution was dropped, much of this had disappeared.[50] Gorbachev's other great achievement was to bring an end to the Cold War. And again, although the West responded sympathetically to Gorbachev's new thinking, it was Gorbachev who took the initiative. However, events in eastern Europe were not seen as an achievement by the army and the traditionalists; the 'loss' of the satellite states and above all the reunification of Germany were regarded as the nullification of everything that the USSR had achieved in the Second World War. Many critics say that he should have bargained with the West and got something in return; since the Warsaw Pact had been dissolved, perhaps Gorbachev could have tried to persuade the West to phase out NATO, since both were relics of the Cold War.

Gorbachev's great failures were in the economy and in his nationalities policy, leading to the ultimate tragedy – for him – of the collapse of the Soviet Union. One of the criticisms most often made of Gorbachev is that he did not think his ideas on economic reform through carefully enough. According to economist

Nodari Simonia, he did not have a detailed economic programme, and neither did any of his advisers; he just told people to show initiative and start a revolution from below; unfortunately, the Soviet citizens were not very good at showing initiative. Simonia believes that Gorbachev should have started his economic reforms by privatizing agriculture and small businesses; although private co-operatives were allowed later, he failed to give them sufficient support when they ran into resistance from party conservatives.[51] Gorbachev certainly did not want to destroy the USSR, and right to the end he fought tooth and nail to preserve some sort of Union. But unfortunately he failed to understand the strength of nationalist feeling, especially in the three Baltic states. If he could have brought himself to acknowledge that the Baltic states had a genuine case for independence (the fact that in August 1939 Molotov and Ribbentrop had signed secret protocols allowing the USSR to occupy the republics, which was illegal in international law – see section 7.1(d)) and permitted them to leave the Union, this would have avoided the violence in Vilnius and Riga. Yet he violated his own policy of *glasnost* by claiming that the original documents, which proved that the agreement had actually taken place, were 'not available.' In fact the documents were in the party archives and Gorbachev himself had seen them as early as July 1987.[52]

Even without the Baltic states it should have been possible to construct a viable new federation along the lines of Gorbachev's Union Treaty, which was on the verge of being signed before the August *coup*. It is difficult to resist the conclusion that Yeltsin bears more of the responsibility than Gorbachev for the failure to get the new federation off the ground. Although in public Yeltsin repeatedly denied any desire to break up the Union, his advisers had been working on plans for Russia's complete secession long before the August *coup*. And Yeltsin himself seemed to be seizing every chance to weaken the proposed Union, until in the end it was to be a Union without a president. It looks very much as though Yeltsin wanted to get rid of Gorbachev, so that he would be supreme in Moscow, and would be able to press ahead with his radical policies of democracy and the market economy without interference from the USSR or Gorbachev. The hostility between Yeltsin and Gorbachev was one of saddest features of the situation. On the surface it looked as though they ought to have been close allies; some of the radicals thought that Gorbachev as president and Yeltsin as vice-president would make the perfect team. But Yeltsin wanted to go further and faster than Gorbachev; and apart from that, there seems to have been a basic clash of personalities: Yeltsin was extrovert, ebullient, charismatic and populist; 'it is tempting,' suggests Martin McCauley, 'to regard Gorbachev's jealousy of Yeltsin's charismatic populism as the root of the problem.' Certainly Gorbachev was not the easiest person to work with; by December 1990 he had fallen out with nearly all his team. 'He appeared to be jealous of his primacy. He wanted the limelight for himself. He could not tolerate someone else as an equal . . . By banishing Yeltsin, [in November 1987] Gorbachev was turning him into a political enemy at a time when the political battle for *perestroika* was just beginning. It was a fateful mistake.'[53] Another fatal mistake was that Gorbachev failed to realize the extent to which *glasnost* and *perestroika* were undermining the political and economic foundations of the Soviet system and actually making the situation worse. As Robert Service puts it: 'Localism, nationalism, corruption, illegal private profiteering and distrust of official authority: all these phenomena, which had grown unchecked under the rule of Brezhnev, had been reinforced by the dismantlement of central controls undertaken by Gorbachev. He was Russia's "holy fool", and like the "holy fool" he did not know it.'[54]

In spite of all his mistakes and failures, Gorbachev's unquestionable achievements entitle him to be regarded as one of the greatest reformers in Russian history, and perhaps the individual who made the most profound impact on world history in the second half of the twentieth century. Archie Brown sums up his achievements: 'He played the decisive part in allowing the countries of Eastern Europe to become free and independent. He did more than anyone else to end the Cold War between East and West. He went along with, encouraged, and (in important respects) initiated fundamental rethinking about politics – radically new thinking in the Soviet context about the political and economic systems he inherited and about better alternatives. He presided over, and facilitated, the introduction of freedom of speech, freedom of the press, freedom of association, religious freedom, and freedom of movement, and left Russia a *freer country* than it had been in its long history.'[55] One of the most remarkable things about these changes is that they were achieved peacefully; it is very much to Gorbachev's credit that he always did his best to avoid using force; many of his close associates testified to this and make the point that if bloodshed did take place, as in Vilnius, Riga and Baku, then this was seen by Gorbachev as a failure of politics. Dmitri Volkogonov, not noted for his admiration of Soviet leaders, nevertheless finds some praise for Gorbachev: 'he launched the most fundamental and irreversible changes in Soviet history since Lenin . . . He does not deserve blame, nor does he need vindication. I believe that the historic outcome of those unforgettable years of *perestroika* outweigh all of Gorbachev's mistakes and miscalculations. The invaluable fruit of his reformation was the liberty which has given the former Soviet society a chance to attain a prosperous and democratic way of life . . . If he does not evoke sympathy among his contemporaries, he has certainly earned the gratitude of future generations.'[56]

(b) Was the communist system reformable?

It would be good to be able to report that there is a viable alternative system to the present all-pervading capitalism, with its many imperfections and its grotesque inequalities. In his early days as an active party member, and even when he became General Secretary, Gorbachev believed that Lenin and Bukharin were laying the foundations for such a system. The tragedy was firstly that Lenin died so early before people had had a chance to find out what he really did intend; and secondly that Stalin hi-jacked the fledgling system and turned into a monstrous horror-story far worse than anything that even the Russians, with their long history of repressive regimes, had experienced before. Stalinism was a viable system, but one that was only sustainable by violence and terror. Gorbachev knew that well; like most families, his had suffered under Stalin: both his grandfathers had spent time in labour camps, and three of his uncles had died during the famine of 1932. Yet Gorbachev was convinced at first that the situation *was* retrievable. The party must be open and frank about its faults: Stalin had gone off the rails. Khrushchev had taken the first step towards normality by putting an end to the purges and killings, but then Brezhnev had let things stagnate. Now Gorbachev was ready to take the next major step towards normality: he would shake up and modernize the party apparatus and get things back on track.

But was the communist system capable of being reformed? Could it have survived if Gorbachev had followed different policies? Many Russians would answer emphatically 'yes' to both questions. Andranik Migranyan, a political analyst who for a time was a member of Gorbachev's presidential council, argues that the USSR should have followed the example of China, where priority was given to economic reform in a gradual programme stretching over several years. He believes that the USSR should have put into operation a carefully worked out programme lasting ten years. Instead, they attempted to rush reform through in several areas at once – in politics, in the economy, in foreign affairs and in the nationalities problem, and the strain proved too great for the system. Others believe that the system was beyond reform; it has often been noted that any political system or party which enjoys a long, uninterrupted period in power becomes arrogant, complacent and corrupt. Examples cited include the Indian Congress Party which ruled continuously for 30 years after India gained its independence; and the Christian Democrat Party in Italy after 1945. In the case of the communist party, critics argue that, after 70 years in power, Marxism–Leninism was incapable of responding positively to changing circumstances, and claim that by 1991 the vast majority – perhaps as many as 80 per cent – of party members did not really believe the basic tenets of the ideology; they were only in the party to further their careers. Volkogonov talks about the total bankruptcy of Marxism–Leninism by the late 1980s; 'the Communist system was not reformable,' he states categorically. 'Either it exists, or it does not.'[57]

And yet, Migranyan's arguments are persuasive; given the USSR's material advantages, it should have been possible, with a planned economy, to mobilize all that enormous potential so that its citizens enjoyed a life of reasonable comfort and prosperity. Admittedly the climate is a problem, but it had the great, fertile 'Black Earth' agricultural belt and vast resources, including plenty of water, oil and coal, almost half of the world's natural gas reserves, massive timber forests, and gold and diamonds. Yet living standards were falling, the majority of people were impoverished and Soviet women spent a large proportion of their time queuing for non-existent goods in the shops.

Why was the economic system failing so badly? The main problem was that the system was over-centralized and extremely complex. As industry expanded rapidly under Stalin, a great army of bureaucrats and managers was created to run the state and the economy; eventually the whole system became so huge and so complex that it was almost impossible for the planners at the centre to collect the information they needed. Their function was to gather information about the production potential of every factory and enterprise throughout the Soviet Union, and then to hand out the targets to each one. Under Stalin, when the penalty for failure to meet targets could be execution or a long spell in a labour camp, managers got into the habit of sending in low estimates of their potential output so that they would be given easy targets. After Stalin's death, when the threat of severe punishments was removed, the bureaucrats became entrenched and began to run the country and the economy in their own interests. This system reached its peak under Brezhnev; as Martin McCauley explains, 'so intricate did the system become that it had, naturally, a strong bias against innovation. This was because innovation involved remaking the web of contacts necessary to make the new product . . . The uncertainty of the supply system led to enterprises getting larger and integrating production. Kamaz, the largest truck plant in the USSR, produced 150,000 lorries annually at Naberezhny Chelny in Tatarstan. It had its own foundry, tyre plant and so on. The natural trend towards monopoly meant that a particular product could often only be obtained from one factory in the USSR.'[58]

This system gave rise to all kinds of incredibly inefficient and wasteful practices. There was the example of a cement-making plant and the factory which made plastic bags for cement. The two had been built side by side in a small town about 500 miles from Moscow. There was only a fence between them, but the two were not allowed to trade together. The central planners required the plastic bags to be sent to Moscow – over bad roads and with inadequate transport. The cement factory, while it waited for its share of the bags to be sent all the way back, carried on with production in order to fulfil its targets. Often there was nowhere to store the newly-made cement, so it had to be dumped out in the factory yard. The rain quickly turned it into small hills as hard as rock. As far as the managers of the two factories were concerned, they had met their production targets, and it was somebody else's job to get the cement and the bags to the customers.[59] This sort of example, bizarre as it seems, was repeated in similar ways throughout the whole economy, which consequently was also inefficient and wasteful. The fact that there was no competition of any sort, or any element of the market, removed incentives to increase productivity or to improve quality.

Another key reason for the economic crisis was the massive burden of defence spending. The military–industrial complex accounted for about one-third of the entire economy, and it had first choice of resources. When President Reagan embarked on his Star Wars project, he knew perfectly well that the USSR would have to try to keep up, and in doing so, would, he hoped, irreparably damage their economy. In this way, the USA and the West could claim that they had played a vital part in the destruction of communism and the USSR (Document I). In theory, with the ending of the Cold War, defence spending should have been reduced to more manageable proportions. Given time, with the reallocation of resources, the crisis would have passed and the economy, arguably, would have recovered. However, there was no time; the economic collapse, together with all the other problems, was enough to finish off the communist system and the USSR.

Much has been written about the Chinese communists and how they reformed their economic system.[60] Why did Communism survive in China but not in the USSR? By the early 1970s it was clear that the Chinese command economy, like that in the USSR, was failing to improve living standards for the rapidly expanding population. Almost in desperation, in the late 1970s, the Chinese embarked on a gradual reform of the economy, starting with agriculture. The state sector in industry remained, but its monopoly was relaxed and so competition was introduced. The state sold shares and bonds to workers. The results were impressive: there was a dramatic and sustained growth in the economy, and although there were some problems – inflation, with wages lagging behind prices – the Chinese had proved that it is possible to reform a command economy by gradual change. The ultimate Chinese goal is to achieve a full 'socialist market economy.' The problem for the Chinese government was that the successful economic reforms gave rise to demands for political reform, but from the beginning, the Chinese leader, Deng Xiaoping, had rejected the idea of economic and political reform being introduced *at the same time*. In June 1989, as the tensions and the demonstrations built up in Tiananmen Square in Beijing, the leadership turned to repression. The army cleared the square, killing between 1500 and 3000 of the demonstrators, and they clamped down on the democracy movement in other parts of the country. For about 18 months after the Tiananmen Square massacre, the Chinese leadership, now dominated by its more conservative members, abandoned its economic reforms and returned to central control. But the results were so disastrous in 1989 and 1990 that the government resumed its previous reform policies and headed towards a market economy again. No doubt political reform will have to come sooner or later, but for the time being communism is surviving – along with a reasonably efficient economy.

Why did Gorbachev not follow the Chinese model? Alexander Yakovlev, among others, strongly advised him to try the Chinese way, but Gorbachev believed that the situation was so different in the USSR that the Chinese model would not work there. For example, the Chinese economy was still about 80 per cent agricultural, and neither industry nor agriculture had ever been as centralized as they were in the USSR. The Soviet economy was overburdened by the military–industrial complex, whereas the Chinese spent a much smaller proportion of their budget on armaments. There seemed to be more urgency in the Soviet situation; the Chinese programme worked gradually, and in 1987, when the Soviet leadership first realized the gravity of the economic crisis, Chinese reforms had been under way for almost ten years. This was when the Soviet leadership took the fateful decision that *political reform* was necessary to weaken the obstructive powers of the bureaucracy and so enable economic reform to be pushed through. Unfortunately, they seemed to concentrate on the political reforms and were uncertain which course of economic reform to follow. By 1989 the economic crisis was worse, and decisive action was needed. However, this was the time when the Chinese government had dropped its market reform policies for the time being, suggesting that they were not a success. This convinced Gorbachev that the USSR should also reject any moves towards the market; in October 1990 the decision was taken to stick with central control. But it wasn't long before the Chinese realized their mistake and in 1991 returned to those policies leading ultimately to a market economy. In the words of Martin McCauley: 'The flexible and pragmatic Chinese leadership chose to return to the market while holding the fort against political reform ... Gorbachev was unfortunate that he had to make his decision – that the economy had to be managed from the centre – in 1990. That decision precipitated the collapse of the Soviet Union.'[61]

In theory then, it should have been possible to effect an economic transformation in the USSR without precipitating a crisis, and thereby enabling the Union to continue for many more years. But it may have been necessary to use force, as the Chinese government did. In that case, given Gorbachev's reluctance to cause bloodshed, the prospects for success would not seem promising. Dmitri Furman, a former Gorbachev colleague, believes that 'the fall of Soviet power and the fall of the Communist party were inevitable. But they could have happened in various ways and at various times, like a death. If a different person had become general secretary, the Soviet system could have lasted another 20 years.'[62] The real key to the regime's chances of survival was: could it 'get the economy right'? It would have been extremely difficult, given all the resistance and obstructionism of the bureaucracy and the party apparatus. This of course is why Gorbachev thought it was vital to dismantle the apparatus and bring new personnel in – the political changes *at the same time* as the economic changes. This was the big difference between the Chinese and Soviet reforms. But although the logic seems clear, it turned out to be Gorbachev's most serious mistake: he had weakened the apparatus, but at the same time he had undermined his own power to implement policy. Vladimir Bukovsky, a reformer and social democrat who, from 1980 lived in exile in England, confirms this view: 'His only instrument of power was the Communist Party, but his reforms weakened precisely that instrument. He was like the proverbial man sawing off the branch on which he was sitting. There could be no other outcome except what happened.'[63] By the time the leadership had eventually settled on what they thought was the correct economic programme, in the words of Alec Nove, 'the means to enforce it no longer existed. This, as well as doubts and hesitations about how far and how fast the reform programme should go, plus the disastrous monetary and fiscal policy (or lack of policy), led to failure. Add the centrifugal forces of nationalism and regionalism, and one had collapse. What was there that could hold it all together?'[64]

(c) The legacy of communism

Any country ruled by the same regime for over 70 years is bound to bear the marks of the system, for good or ill. Communism in Russia left plenty of both, though most historians feel that the achievements of communism are outweighed by its ill-effects. But no system could have survived for so long by force alone; one important achievement was that the Soviet system brought benefits in the form of promotion and reasonably well-paid jobs with privileges to large numbers of people from 'lower class' backgrounds who had been excluded from such things under the tsarist regime. Education and literacy became more widespread; even under Stalin, Soviet 'culture' was encouraged, and so was sport; the performing arts, particularly music, were subsidized by the state. Science was given special prominence and funding. Although the methods left much to be desired, another major achievement of the Soviet state was to modernize a country which was still in many ways backward. Perhaps its greatest achievement was that it defeated the evil regime of Hitler and the Nazis, for which the whole world should be eternally grateful. After Stalin's death, although in one sense the system stagnated, it brought a certain stability and an improved standard of living for the majority of its people. As will be seen in the next chapter, during the 1990s there was a good deal of support, especially among older people, for the reformed Communist Party of the Russian Federation, and even for the USSR.

On the other hand the Soviet system left behind a whole range of problems which would make it extremely difficult for any succeeding regime to transform. The economic system was rigid, over-centralized and in need of a complete overhaul. Individual initiative and entrepreneurial spirit had been stifled for generations.The one-party political system, the impossibility of public debate and criticism, and the close control of the media meant that most people knew little about democracy and party politics. The enormous class of privileged bureaucrats and administrators opposed any radical changes. The country was overburdened with its vast military expenditure. Boris Yeltsin had been highly critical of all these aspects of the Soviet system, and had played a vital role in bringing about its demise. Would he be able to do any better?

Documents

(A) Nikolai Shmelev, a radical economist, complains about the state of the economy, in an article in *Novy Mir* in June 1987, an article which could not have appeared openly before the introduction of *glasnost*.

At present our economy is characterized by shortages, imbalances, [it is] unmanageable and almost unplannable... Industry now rejects up to 80 per cent of technical decisions and inventions... The working masses have reached a state of almost total lack of interest in honest labour... Apathy, indifference, thieving have become mass phenomena, with simultaneous aggressive envy towards those who are capable of earning. There have appeared signs of physical degradation of a large part of our population, through drunkenness and idleness. Finally there is disbelief in the officially announced objectives and purposes, in the very possibility of a more rational economic and social organization of life. Clearly all this cannot be quickly overcome – years, perhaps generations, will be needed.

Source: quoted in Martin McCauley, *Gorbachev*, p. 68.

(B) Extracts from Gorbachev's speech to a gathering of communist leaders in the Kremlin, 2 November 1987, during the 70th anniversary celebrations.

Dear Comrades! Esteemed foreign guests! Seven decades separate us from the unforgettable days of October 1917, from those legendary days that became the starting point of a new epoch of human progress... If today we look into our history with an occasionally critical gaze, it is only because we want to get a better, fuller idea of our path into the future.

It is perfectly obvious that the lack of the proper level of democratization of Soviet society was precisely what made possible both the cult of personality and the violations of the law, arbitrariness and repressions of the thirties – to be blunt, real crimes based on the abuse of power. Many thousands of members of the party and non-members were subjected to mass repressions. That, comrades, is the bitter truth. Serious damage was done to the cause of socialism and the authority of the party, and we must speak bluntly about it. This is essential for the final and irreversible assertion of Lenin's ideal of socialism.

The guilt of Stalin and those close to him is immense and unforgivable ... even now we still encounter those who try to ignore and hush up these sensitive questions, and to pretend that nothing special happened. We cannot agree with this. It would be a neglect of historical truth ... Neither the grossest errors nor the deviations from the principles of socialism could turn our people from the path they embarked upon in 1917 ... We are travelling to a new world, the world of Communism. We shall never deviate from this path. [Prolonged and stormy applause.]

Source: quoted in David Remnick, *Lenin's Tomb: The Last Days of the Soviet Empire*, pp. 49–51.

(C) Extracts from Nina Andreyeva's letter in *Sovetskaya Rossiya*, 13 March 1988, and from her conversations with David Remnick, an American journalist.

From the letter: The subject of repressions has been blown out of all proportion in some young people's imagination and overshadows any objective interpretation of the past. Stalin may have made some 'mistakes' but who else could have built the country up so quickly, prepared it for the great victory against the Nazis? They try to make us believe that the country's past was nothing but mistakes and crimes, keeping silent about the great achievements of the past and present. There is no question that [the Stalin era] was extremely harsh. But we prepared people for labour and defence without destroying their spiritual worlds with masterpieces imported from abroad or with home-grown imitations of mass culture.

From her conversation with David Remnick: The thing is, we may not need an iron hand, but in any state there must be order. This is not a state we have now, it is like some anarchistic gathering ... An anti-socialist movement is taking shape in the form of democratic unions and popular fronts. The number of ecological disasters is growing. There is a decline in the level of morality. There is a cult of money. The prestige of honest, productive labour has been undermined ... In the four years of *perestroika* they have undermined the trust of working people – because they have spit on our past ... An unpredictable future cannot be a basis for a normal working existence of the current generation. In the past, a person going to bed at night knew that in the morning he'd go to work and have free medical care – not very skilled care, but free nonetheless. And now we don't even have these guarantees.

Source: quoted in Remnick, pp. 78–82.

(D) David Remnick gathers local opinion on the reasons for the collapse of the USSR.

As I traveled around the Union, opinions varied on when and where the old regime died. Uzbeks in Tashkent and Samarkand told me that the exposure in around 1988 and 1989 of the callous way Moscow had turned all of Central Asia into a vast cotton plantation – in the process destroying the Aral Sea and nearly every other area of the economy – was the turning point. In the Baltic states, the official 'discovery' of the secret protocols to the Nazi–Soviet pact were the key moment... On a trip to the western Ukrainian city of Lvov in 1989, I met with small groups of nationalists who promised that 'one day' their republic of over fifty million people, the biggest after Russia, would strike out for independence and do far more damage to the union than the tiny Baltic states ever could... The old regime collapsed metaphorically on April 26, 1986, at the moment of the nuclear accident at Chernobyl... Within weeks of the accident, people realized that 'Chernobyl' meant 'wormwood', and then pointed to *Revelation* 8.10–11: 'A great star shot from the sky, flaming like a torch; and it fell on a third of the rivers and springs; and a third of the water turned to wormwood, and men in great numbers died of the water because it was poisoned.'

The accident at Chernobyl embodied every curse of the Soviet system, the decay and arrogance, the wilful ignorance and self-deception. Yuri Shcherbak was a physician and journalist who led the fight in Ukraine to publicize the medical and ecological hazards of the accident. 'If it weren't for the danger,' [he said] 'they should leave the Chernobyl plant standing. It could be the great monument to the Soviet empire.'

Source: Remnick, pp. 243–7.

(E) The radio broadcast announcing the *coup* of August 1991 against Gorbachev.

We are addressing you at a grave, critical hour for the future of the Mother-land and of our peoples. A moral danger has come to loom large over our great Motherland. The policy of reforms, launched at Mikhail Gorbachev's initiative and designed as a means to ensure the country's dynamic develop-ment and the democratization of social life, have entered for several reasons into a blind alley. All democratic institutions created by the popular will are losing weight and effectiveness right in front of our eyes. This is the result of purposeful actions by those who, grossly violating the fundamental law of the USSR, are in fact staging an unconstitutional *coup* and striving for unbridled personal dictatorial powers...

The country is sinking into a quagmire of violence and lawlessness. Never before in national history has the propaganda of sex and violence assumed such a scale, threatening the health and lives of future generations. Millions of people are demanding measures against the octopus of crime and glaring immorality.

Source: quoted in Remnick, pp. 461–2.

(F) Broadcast by Boris Yeltsin during the August *coup* attempt.

Soldiers and officers of the army, the KGB, and the troops of the Interior Ministry! Countrymen! The country is faced with the threat of terror. At this difficult hour of decision remember that you have taken an oath to your people, and your weapons cannot be turned against the people. You can erect a throne of bayonets but you cannot sit on it for long. The days of the conspirators are numbered . . . Clouds of terror and dictatorship are gathering over Russia, but this night will not be eternal and our long-suffering people will find freedom once again, and for good. Soldiers, I believe at this tragic hour you will make the right decision. The honour of Russian arms will not be covered with the blood of the people.

[Later, standing on the White House balcony, he spoke to the crowds] The junta used no restraint in grabbing power, and the junta feels itself under no restraint in keeping it . . . Doesn't Yazov have his hands covered in blood from other republics? Hasn't Pugo bloodied his hands in the Baltics and the Caucasus? Whoever fulfils the commands of this illegal committee will be prosecuted! . . . I am convinced that here, in democratic Moscow, aggression of the conservative forces will not win out. Democracy will. And we will stay here as long as it takes for the junta to be brought to justice!

Source: quoted in Remnick, pp. 467, 476.

(G) David Remnick describes the scene outside the White House during the *coup*.

On the barricades outside, as people milled around, their feet sloshing in the puddles, there were new rumours every minute, and every rumour went out over the radio. I saw one man, a vet in his old jungle fatigues, holding a stick in one hand for protection and a bottle of vodka in the other for bravery. The most reassuring sight was the way the soldiers in their tanks welcomed kids aboard and flirted with the girls. There was hope in that.

And there was real hope in the grit of these people. I talked with a middle-aged woman, Regina Bogachova, who said she would sooner be crushed by a tank than move. 'I am ready to die right here, on this spot. I will not move. I am 55 years old and for years nothing but obedience was pounded into my brain. The Young Pioneers, the Young Communist League, the Communist Party, all of them taught me not to answer back. To be a good Soviet, a screw in the machine . . . I heard a rumbling and I went out on to my balcony and

(continued)

saw the tanks rumbling down below. These monsters! They have always thought they could do anything to us. They have thrown Gorbachev out and now they are threatening a government I helped elect. I will ignore the curfew and I'll die right here if I have to!'

Source: Remnick, p. 478.

(H) Verse by the poet Yevgeny Yevtushenko; he wrote it during the *coup* and read it out from the balcony of the White House.

> *No! Russia will not fall again on her knees for interminable years,*
> *With us are Pushkin, Tolstoy.*
> *With us stands the whole awakened people.*
> *And the Russian parliament, like a wounded marble swan of freedom,*
> *defended by the people, swims into immortality.*

Source: quoted in Remnick, p. 476.

(I) General Leonid Shebarshin, a KGB director, reveals his thoughts about Gorbachev, foreign affairs and the collapse of the USSR.

It should have been possible to jettison totalitarianism over a period of time through careful consideration of ways and means. I do not believe that Gorbachev thought his reforms were going to destroy communism. I accept that he was trying to resurrect it ... Anyone could see things were not moving in the right direction. I was presiding over the disintegration of the empire.

Receiving the vital information from the KGB, Gorbachev did not study it and draw conclusions. I don't think he took an overview, or that he cared very much. He was a party man, a functionary. Nationalism was the danger in 1989, and I warned him. The formation of popular fronts in all the republics was definitely no coincidence. The KGB was trying to find out if there were any organizers. Some of the popular front people obtained the posts and jobs they wanted, but you cannot satisfy entire groups of educated people. Our society was never a very happy one, there were shortcomings in the Soviet Union and through nationalism you had a natural sounding board for them.

There are many things I do not like about the United States and Europe. It confirms my suspicions when I hear Americans say that without their efforts the Soviet Union would still be a superpower. I have grounds for knowing that they did everything possible to destroy the Soviet Union economically and politically ... they did what was in their national interest. The country's [USSR] foundations were badly shaken, the economy was sliding downhill, the party had lost authority. By way of rescuing himself Gorbachev and his team forfeited their independence in international affairs; they did not try to hold any position, squandering whatever had been accumulated in order to

> appease their Western partners. The decisive factor was the lack of political will at the centre.

Source: quoted in David Pryce-Jones, *The War That Never Was: The Fall of the Soviet Empire 1985–1991*, pp. 363–5.

Notes

1. Archie Brown, *The Gorbachev Factor*, p. 81.
2. Alec Nove, *An Economic History of the USSR 1917–1991*, p. 399.
3. Brown, pp. 141–4.
4. Angus Roxburgh, *The Second Russian Revolution*, pp. 40–3.
5. Brown, p. 163.
6. Robert Service, *A History of Twentieth Century Russia*, p. 447.
7. Richard Sakwa, *Gorbachev and his Reforms, 1985–1990*, pp. 134–9.
8. *Ibid.*, pp. 279–81.
9. Gerald Segal, 'Ending the Cold War', in David Armstrong and Erik Goldstein (editors), *The End of the Cold War*, p. 42.
10. Sakwa, pp. 324–5.
11. Brown, p. 236.
12. Service, p. 465.
13. Brown, p. 248.
14. *Ibid.*, pp. 250–1.
15. Service, p. 464.
16. David Remnick, *Lenin's Tomb: The Last Days of the Soviet Empire*, p. 240.
17. David Pryce-Jones, *The War That Never Was. The Fall of the Soviet Empire, 1985–1991*, p. 242.
18. Martin McCauley, *Gorbachev*, p. 197.
19. Brown, pp. 250–1.
20. See Roxburgh, pp, 70–8 for a detailed account of this incident and the subsequent sacking of Yeltsin.
21. McCauley, *Gorbachev*, p. 93. See also Roxburgh pp. 83–7 for more details of the letter and its aftermath.
22. Remnick, pp. 220–2.
23. Donald Filtzer, *Soviet Workers and the Collapse of Perestroika*, pp. 94–101.
24. Brown, pp. 193–4.
25. Roxburgh, pp. 172–3.
26. Nove, p. 412.
27. Martin Walker, *Dispatches from the Guardian's Correspondent in Moscow*, p. 4.
28. S. White, *After Gorbachev*, p. 127.
29. John Simpson, *Despatches from the Barricades*, p. 293.
30. Nove, p. 413.
31. See Ronald G. Suny, *The Revenge of the Past*, for a full examination of the nationalities problem.
32. Pryce-Jones, p. 138.
33. Brown, pp. 264–7.
34. Remnick, pp. 238–9.
35. Jonathan Steele, *Eternal Russia: Yeltsin, Gorbachev and the Mirage of Democracy*, pp. 206–9.
36. Brown, p. 152.
37. *Ibid.*, p. 274.
38. Quoted in McCauley, pp. 193–4.
39. Brown, p. 292.
40. Boris Yeltsin, *The View from the Kremlin*, pp. 38–9.

41. Details in this section are taken mainly from the excellent account of the attempted *coup* in Remnick, *Lenin's Tomb*, pp. 435–90. See also Jack F. Matlock, *Autopsy on an Empire: The American Ambassador's Account of the Collapse of the Soviet Union*, New York, 1995, pp. 578–602.
42. Amy Knight, *Spies Without Cloaks: The KGB's Successors*, pp. 17–28.
43. Quoted by Jonathan Steele, 'Mikhail Gorbachev: The Russian revolutionary', *The Guardian*, 18 August 2001.
44. Brown, p. 388.
45. McCauley, p. 248.
46. Mark Galeotti, *The Age of Anxiety: Security and Politics in Soviet and Post-Soviet Russia*, p. 192.
47. Simpson, p. 294.
48. John Bushnell, 'Making History out of Current Events: The Gorbachev Era', *Slavic Review*, 51/3 (1992), p. 557; quoted in Brown, p. 389.
49. Pryce-Jones, p. 381.
50. Brown, p. 310.
51. Steele, *The Guardian*, 18 August 2001.
52. Dmitri Volkogonov, *The Rise and Fall of the Soviet Empire*, p. 528.
53. McCauley, pp. 72, 272.
54. Service, p. 466.
55. Brown, pp. 317–18.
56. Volkogonov, pp. 516–29.
57. *Ibid.*, p. 434.
58. Martin McCauley, *The Soviet Union 1917–1991*, p. 373.
59. Simpson, p. 292.
60. See especially Barry Naughton, *Growing Out of the Plan: Chinese Economic Reform 1978–1993*, pp. 309–26.
61. Martin McCauley, *Gorbachev*, pp. 283–4.
62. Steele, *The Guardian*, 18 August 2001.
63. Pryce-Jones, p. 40.
64. Nove, p. 419.

◪ 11   Russia under Yeltsin, 1991–99

Summary of events

Boris Yeltsin had been elected president of the Russian Federation in June 1991. When the USSR broke up at the end of 1991, Russia became a separate state; **Yeltsin remained president until he retired at the end of 1999.** The problems facing him were complicated in the extreme, since the country needed both a new economic system and a new political system.

Immediately, at the beginning of 1992, Russia was plunged into **'shock therapy'**, the policy of prime minister **Yegor Gaidar**. It was designed to transform the country rapidly into a market economy, and included privatization of all state-owned enterprises, and the end of price controls and government subsidies. **The policy was not a great success, causing inflation, unemployment and poverty.**

Confrontation with parliament – the Supreme Soviet, led by **Alexander Rutskoi and Ruslan Khasbulatov**, two former allies of Yeltsin, was bitterly critical of the 'shock therapy' policies, and tried to reduce the powers of the president. A long power struggle developed:

- December 1992 – Yeltsin was forced to sack Gaidar, who was replaced by **Viktor Chernomyrdin.**
- April 1993 – in a referendum 58.5 per cent of the voters expressed confidence in Yeltsin.
- September 1993 – Yeltsin dismissed the Congress of People's Deputies and the Supreme Soviet and **introduced a new constitution,** giving the presidency more powers.
- September to October – the members of parliament resisted Yeltsin and occupied the parliament building, the White House. Yeltsin called in the army and blasted parliament into submission. Rutskoi and Khasbulatov were arrested.
- December 1993 – the new constitution was approved in a referendum, but in the following elections for the Duma, the new lower house of parliament, the party endorsed by Yeltsin came only a poor second to the communists.

After the confrontation, Yeltsin and Chernomyrdin introduced more moderate economic policies, but there was still little improvement in living standards for the vast majority of the population. A small number of people, mainly former communist party apparatchiks, made huge profits from privatization. **The war in**

Chechnya (1994–96) brought Yeltsin's popularity ratings to a low point; although a ceasefire was arranged, the Chechen separatists were not defeated.

July 1996 – Yeltsin was elected for a second term as president. Although opinion polls were not promising for Yeltsin to begin with, he fought a good campaign and narrowly beat his nearest rival, the communist leader **Gennady Zyuganov**.

August 1998 – Financial collapse – continuing economic problems, together with a world-wide financial crisis and a collapse in the world price of oil, led to a devaluation of the rouble. Yeltsin appointed **Yevgeny Primakov** as prime minister, and the situation slowly began to stabilize. However, in March 1999 Yeltsin dismissed Primakov, and with an eye to his successor as the next president, he eventually appointed **Vladimir Putin** as prime minister. **Yeltsin resigned on 31 December 1999 and in March 2000 Putin was elected president**.

Main areas of debate:

- Why was the transition to a market economy so difficult?
- Was it inevitable that the confrontation between Yeltsin and parliament would end in violence?
- How did Yeltsin succeed in staying in power for so long, given generally low popularity ratings?
- Why was Primakov dismissed when his policies were beginning to improve the economic situation?

11.1   Economic catastrophe and political crisis, 1992–93

(a) Yeltsin, Gaidar and 'shock therapy'

The USSR ceased to exist at midnight on 31 December 1991. Mikhail Gorbachev was out of a job and Boris Yeltsin was left as the most powerful figure in Russia. It was the most amazing come-back in Russian history; in November 1987 everybody thought his political career was over (see section 10.4(a)), but the tables had been turned emphatically and now it was Gorbachev who was finished. Boris Yeltsin was born in 1931 in the Sverdlovsk district of the Urals. His family were peasants; his father, hard-working and successful, was arrested as a kulak in 1934 and sentenced to three years' forced labour. As a boy, the young Boris was daring, adventurous and always in trouble; he never seemed to worry about keeping to the rules; and he carried these qualities forward into his political career. As a young man, he was tall and athletic, and a first-rate volley-ball player. He trained as a civil engineer and worked in the building industry; after a few years he tired of this and in 1968 he joined the party apparatus. By 1976 he had risen to become first secretary of the Sverdlovsk Province Committee and in 1981 he became a member of the Central Committee. His reputation for energy, enthusiasm and the ability to get things done soon became widely known, and Gorbachev brought him to Moscow as first secretary of the city committee. His brief was to clean up the corrupt city administration.

In January 1992 his challenge as president of the Russian republic was even more daunting: it was to clean up the mess left behind by the sudden collapse of the USSR. There were both political and economic decisions to be made. Given that this was a completely new political situation, should fresh elections be held so that Yeltsin could claim a mandate for whatever policies he decided to introduce? Or should the government press ahead with economic reforms and seek the electorate's approval later? Predictably he chose the second option; an election would cause several weeks' delay, and he was impatient to make a start on economic reform, which would best be handled, he had decided, by presidential decree. The disadvantage of this choice was that the Russian Congress of People's Deputies and the Supreme Soviet, alongside which he would have to work, had been elected in 1990; a large proportion of the members were likely to oppose his policies. The second question to be decided was exactly what economic policies should be introduced. The experts agreed that Russia should change to a full, market economy, with 'liberalization of prices' and privatization; but they disagreed as to whether this should be done gradually over a period of some years, or whether it should be attempted rapidly – the 'big bang', the 'cavalry charge' and 'shock therapy' were some of the phrases used to describe this method.

Yegor Gaidar was a young economist who, since 1990, had been head of the economics section of *Pravda* and who was influenced by the theories of the Western monetarists. Yeltsin was attracted by Gaidar's insistence that the necessary changes could be achieved in one year, whereas the other economists varied in their predictions from three years to ten. The key, according to Gaidar, was 'price liberalization', which would set the scene for the privatization of almost the whole economy. Yeltsin made Gaidar a vice-president and gave him the job of carrying through the economic changes (Document A). They gathered around them a small team of relatively young economists (in their late thirties and forties) who shared Gaidar's views; the older politicians looked on them with contempt, considering them to be still wet behind the ears. Vice-president Rutskoi (aged 55) dismissed them as 'young boys in pink shorts and yellow boots' (Gaidar was 46 in 1992!). They admitted that things would be difficult at first, since they were about to administer 'shock therapy'. Yeltsin himself said: 'Things will get worse for everyone for about half a year, then there will come a lowering of prices, and the filling up of the consumer market with goods. By the autumn of 1992 there will be stabilization of the economy, and a gradual improvement in people's lives.' They had a political motive too – they hoped their policies would destroy the old communist bureaucracy or at least weaken it so much that there could never be a return to the old system.

The therapy began on 2 January 1992 when price controls were removed on about 90 per cent of goods, though excluding bread, vodka, public transport and energy. Government subsidies to industry were ended, and enterprises were expected to compete in the marketplace and make a profit. This, it was confidently expected, would help to reduce Russia's huge budget deficit. Freed from restrictions and allowed to 'float freely', prices rose quickly. By the end of January they had shot up by 250 per cent; by the end of March 1992 they had increased by as much as 900 per cent for most goods and services, although average wages only doubled during that period.[1] Something like this had been predicted, but unfortunately it went on for longer than half a year; prices kept on rising throughout 1992, so that by the end of the year even the lowest estimate was that prices were, on average, 30 times higher than on 1 January (Document B). There were plenty of goods in the shops, but most people could not afford to buy them. For the vast majority, the situation was catastrophic: pensioners were worst affected and had difficulty surviving; even those in jobs were not always paid their wages, since factories were selling less and producing less; over a million people lost their jobs. Some enterprises began paying wages in goods – crockery, vodka, sweets and chocolate, coal, and even refrigerators. For months, streets and squares in central Moscow were blocked with crowds of people selling off their possession to make ends meet. From July onwards the situation worsened because the government, itself short of money, was forced to spend less on social services; health care and education suffered worst. People living on accumulated savings were badly hit, since the headlong inflation wiped out their value. Hundreds were made homeless; railway stations became favourite places for the homeless to use as hostels; villages of tents sprang up outside most towns. Collective farmers and workers were able to cope better than most, thanks to their private plots.

The removal of price controls was only the first step in the transition to a market economy. The next phase was the privatization of state property – factories, mines and collective farms were all to be turned into independent joint-stock companies, and the process was to be directed by Anatoly Chubais. There was opposition from the Supreme Soviet, some of whose members had been lobbied and pressurized by the directors and managers of some of the big state industries, who wanted state subsidies to be resumed. It was only when Chubais compromised by allowing state subsidies to continue, that the Supreme Soviet approved his programme in June 1992. At first it seemed as though the intention was for all these concerns to be turned over to the joint ownership of all the people. Chubais introduced a system of vouchers which were supposed to give every citizen an equal share of state property – each worth 10,000 roubles (about £35 at the time they were issued). There were also plans for workers to be able to buy shares in their enterprise. If the intention was to create a sort of capitalism of the people, it failed; 10,000 roubles was a minute amount at a time of rapid inflation; what happened was that in most cases the managers were able to accumulate enough vouchers and shares to take over the ownership of their plant (Document C). This was a great disappointment for the workers, who had even less influence than before on what happened in their workplace. Yet surprisingly, there were very few strikes; perhaps workers were too stunned by the difficulties they had experienced over the previous year to organize protests.[2]

The Supreme Soviet, however, had no intention of letting Gaidar and Chubais continue without opposition. The government's popularity had dwindled steadily, and although most people seemed to blame Gaidar for the chaos, even Yeltsin's massive support was wearing thin. People were disillusioned with politics and politicians. Two of Yeltsin's former supporters became leaders of the opposition in the Supreme Soviet: Alexander Rutskoi, the Vice-president, who had stood by

Yeltsin during the August coup, and Ruslan Khasbulatov, whom Yeltsin had chosen as speaker of the Supreme Soviet. They demanded price controls, more gradual progress towards privatization and more protection for ordinary citizens. Already in the summer of 1992 their protests had forced Yeltsin to make a concession by bringing into the government Viktor Chernomyrdin, an expert on the energy industry. In December there was a great showdown when the Supreme Soviet tried to reduce Yeltsin's powers, but in the end, a compromise was reached: Yeltsin agreed to replace Gaidar with Chernomyrdin; in return the Supreme Soviet agreed to a referendum to test the popularity of Yeltsin's policies. In January 1993 Chernomyrdin introduced controls on prices and on the profits that could be made on certain goods. The opposition seemed to think this was a great victory; however, the situation continued to deteriorate throughout 1993. Industrial production fell by a further 25 per cent during the year, and the rate of exchange worsened: at the end of 1992 it had been 450 roubles to the dollar; at the end of 1993 it was 1250 to the dollar. A report published by the economics division of the Russian Academy of Sciences at the end of 1993, summing up the first two years of 'shock therapy', revealed that no less than one-third of the entire population had incomes so pathetically small that they were below the official subsistence level. Ten per cent of the population, which amounted to about 15 million people, were below the level considered necessary for physical survival. The report came to the grim conclusion that 'a process of marginalization is going on in the population. The number of beggars, homeless people, alcoholics, drug addicts and prostitutes is growing... Our country has been thrown back two centuries to the "savage era" of capitalism.'[3]

(b) Why did 'shock therapy' not work?

One of the main problems was that the privatization programme did not work out as intended. The fact that government subsidies continued to be paid to big enterprises meant that they were not really responding to market forces; the government continued to pay out huge sums of money, whereas one of the aims of the programme had been to reduce the budget deficit. Instead of being jointly owned by the people, by the end of 1995, most of the former state industry had found its way into the hands of a relatively small group of financiers, who became known as the 'oligarchs'; even Yeltsin admits in his memoirs that they had been acquired at 'bargain-basement prices.' They made enormous profits, but from the government subsidies rather than from the market. Instead of reinvesting their profits in Russian industry, which was the government's intention, they transferred them to Swiss bank accounts and foreign investments; total investment in Russia fell by two-thirds. Chernomyrdin, who was in effect the head of Russia's energy industry, resisted the shift to energy prices on the world market, and supplied gas and oil to Russian industry at a fraction of the world price. But industry did not always benefit from this advantage: middlemen bought up much of the oil at the knock-down domestic price, and sold it abroad at the world price, which was often up to 100 times more than they had paid for it. A similar thing happened with subsidized grain. At every level of economic activity there were people willing to take advantage of the fact that the move to the market economy was a 'leap in the dark', that there were no politicians or economists in Russia who were experienced in this sort of manoeuvre, and that there would be mistakes and loopholes to be exploited. Sadly, corruption, fraud, bribery and criminal activity became part of everyday life in Russia. A report given to Yeltsin in January 1994 claimed that criminal mafias had gained control in some form or other over between 70 and 80 per cent of all business and banking. The man who had cleaned up Moscow in 1985–87 now presided over the largest corruption scandal ever seen in Russia.

To be fair to Yeltsin and his government, the unfortunate legacy of communism made their task extremely difficult (see section 10.6(c)). There had been no capitalism and no market in Russia for over 70 years. The Russians had no experience of a competitive environment; no legal standards for market relations had been adopted, and even after the first two years of 'shock treatment', very few market institutions had been created. In this situation, it was extremely rash to attempt a 'cavalry charge' into a full market economy. Other options were available and several were suggested to Yeltsin; these included a programme of privatizing some large state-owned enterprises, the gradual creation of a competitive environment, and a return to private ownership in small and medium-sized workshops and factories, in trade and in service industries. A determined campaign to encourage Western investment in Russia was vital. And according to Roy Medvedev, 'partial liberalization of foreign trade, joint ventures and jointly owned companies, banks and stock markets, and other elements of a market-oriented infrastructure would all be steps in the right direction.'[4] Another weakness which helped to spoil Gaidar's chances of success was the fact that he was trying to introduce fundamental changes into an economy which was already in serious crisis. For over 40 years the USSR had strained every sinew to maintain military parity with an economically more powerful opponent, and this was bound to lead to disaster in the end. It was no coincidence that the world's two most successful economies after 1945 were those of Germany and Japan, the two states which, following their defeat in the Second World War, were restricted from having large armies and major armaments. In Russia the shift from a massive defence industry to a civilian programme could not be carried out in just a few months; it needed continued government planning and guidance.

The reformers were trying to switch Russia over, in a few months, to a system of advanced capitalism which had taken centuries to develop naturally in the West. Western capitalism is based on massive accumulations of capital which Russia does not have. Gaidar and his associates expected financial help from the West, but none was forthcoming; the West even refused to drop the trade barriers put in place during the 1970s because of human rights violations by the Soviet government. However, Russia removed virtually all its trade barriers against Western imports, with the result that Western companies were able to establish themselves in Russia and could undersell many of Russia's own manufactured goods. Russian industry was so inefficient that it could not compete when it was exposed to market conditions. In a sense there was a vicious circle; after the first weeks of 'shock therapy', as soon as people began to feel its bad effects on themselves, they stopped supporting and co-operating with the government. Most people had been attracted to the movement for democracy by considerations of social justice, freedom and civil rights, not by a burning desire for market reform and capitalism. Chubais did not endear himself to the general public when he declared that social inequality was inevitable in any society, and even desirable; 'you cannot expect everyone to live a comfortable, pleasant life' (Document D).

(c) The political crisis and 'civil war' in Moscow

The sudden collapse of the Soviet Union had left the political scene in the Russian republic in a state of flux. The leading politicians talked about democracy, but in the same way that they lacked experience of the market economy, they also had very little idea of how to operate a democratic system. There were no properly organized political parties on the Western model. The constitution was a leftover from the Soviet era; it had been changed so many times that nobody seemed entirely sure what state it had reached. Its main weakness was that it was unclear about the division of powers between the president and the parliament – the Congress of People's Deputies and the Supreme Soviet. According to Ronald Suny, 'Yeltsin neglected to form his own political party, which might have given his government an institutional base of support ... Though embryonic parties had emerged in the last years of the Soviet Union, they were largely elite organizations, often clustered around particular leaders, with unreliable popular support. Without elections they withered away in the first years of the independent Russian republic. Instead of popular parties, powerful interest groups imbedded in the new economy made their own *ad hoc* arrangements with state authorities to their own mutual benefit. Politics moved from the street and the electoral arena into the hallways of the bureaucracy and the backrooms of the presidential apparatus.'[5]

Yeltsin himself came under heavy criticism from some sections of the press which accused him of behaving like the very type of communist party boss which he had criticized so bitterly before 1991, appointing his friends and supporters to all the top positions and operating a kind of 'Sverdlovsk Mafia'. He admits in his memoirs that he had his own chauffeur-driven limousine, he founded his own select tennis club, and hardly ever mixed with other politicians.[6] But although his position seemed to be under threat, he was more secure than he seemed. Political parties were beginning to take shape by the end of 1992, but there were too many of them and they were too loosely organized to present a serious threat. At that point the two most important ones seemed to be the Liberal-Democratic Party led by Vladimir Zhirinovski, which was, in fact, a radical Russian nationalist party; and the Communist Party of the Russian Federation (legalized again since November 1992) under the leadership of Gennady Zyuganov. Parliament presented the most serious challenge to Yeltsin, but it was no more popular with the general public than the president himself. By March 1993 it was three years since the Congress of People's Deputies had been elected, when about 80 per cent of the deputies were communist party members; although they now presented themselves under different labels, many people still saw them as the relics of the corrupt *nomenklatura* of the Soviet period. In fact there was a wide range of opinion in the Supreme Soviet chosen by the Congress, right through from conservative hard-line communists to those who wanted Western-style democracy.

There seemed a chance that the power struggle between Yeltsin and parliament might be resolved in April 1993, when the referendum agreed the previous December was due to be held. Fearing that the referendum would result in an endorsement of Yeltsin's policies and a defeat for themselves, Khasbulatov and Rutskoi, the leaders of the Supreme Soviet, announced that it had been cancelled. Yeltsin responded on 20 March by going on television and declaring that he had placed Russia under 'special administrative rule;' parliament was subordinate to the rule of the president, and would not have the power to cancel his decrees. The Constitutional Court ruled that Yeltsin's action was unconstitutional, and parliament began to discuss the impeachment of the president. Tensions were high: on 28 March there was a huge demonstration of 100,000 Yeltsin supporters on Red Square. The following day the Congress voted on impeachment; the result was 617 for Yeltsin's dismissal, and 268 against. It was a huge defeat for the president, but not quite enough to secure his dismissal; the constitution demanded that three-quarters of the members needed to vote for dismissal – that is, 780 votes. Yeltsin proclaimed victory, but was shrewd enough to compromise: he agreed to drop his 'special rule' decree and parliament promised to allow the referendum to go ahead. Yeltsin had got his way – again.

The referendum was held on 25 April 1993. The two main questions were: do you have confidence in the president, Boris Yeltsin? and do you approve of the social and economic policies carried out by the president since 1992? The results were a victory for Yeltsin who gained 'yes' votes of 58.5 per cent and 53 per cent. Some observers expressed surprise at Yeltsin's success, given the hardships his policies were causing to so many people; but clearly they had even less confidence in the alternatives to Yeltsin. A closer analysis of the voting suggested that Yeltsin had no cause for complacency; although he had massive support in Moscow, St Petersburg, the Urals region and the east, parliament was more popular in the Volga region, in central Russia and in the non-Russian autonomous republics. The political situation had reached stalemate: Yeltsin was determined to press ahead with further measures leading to a market economy, and parliament was equally determined to prevent him.

Predictably, it was Yeltsin who made the most decisive moves to break out of the impasse. He began planning a campaign to get rid of parliament; he had a new constitution drawn up which would make parliament and the bureaucracy subordinate to the president; and he had talks with army leaders. On 18 September 1993 he brought back Gaidar as first deputy prime minister, a sure sign that he intended to go all-out towards a market economy. Moscow was rife with rumours that he was planning to occupy the White House, the Supreme Soviet building, with troops, thus locking out the members. His actions at this time were so blatant that he may have been deliberately trying to provoke parliament into making the first hostile move, so that he would have an excuse to crush them.[7]

On 21 September at 8 pm Yeltsin appeared on all television channels to announce his Decree No. 1400. This stated that the powers of the Congress of People's Deputies and the Supreme Soviet were annulled, and a new dual-chambered assembly would take their place. A new constitution would be presented on 12 December, and elections held for the new assembly. Until then the country was to be governed by decrees of the president. Parliament had no intention of allowing itself to be killed off in this peremptory way; the showdown was about to begin.[8] Khasbulatov and Rutskoi rushed to the White House where they were joined by hundreds of deputies, journalists and supporters, including General Makashov and a group of other generals who wanted to bring Yeltsin down. They barricaded themselves in and announced that Yeltsin's action was a breach of the constitution; they cited a clause which stated that in the event of an attempt by the president to disperse a legally elected body, his powers would automatically cease to exist. Yeltsin's actions were to be regarded as a *coup d'état*, and therefore vice-president Rutskoi was now acting president. In a strange reversal of the situation in August 1991, Yeltsin ordered the army to surround the White House. Although they complied, the generals made it clear to Yeltsin that they were not happy about attacking the White House and dispersing the deputies; they were reluctant to shed Russian blood. The television system sided with Yeltsin, which was a great advantage, but the press was either neutral or supported the Supreme Soviet. The ordinary people of Moscow showed much less interest than in 1991; a poll showed that 75 per cent sympathized with neither side, and there was no large-scale street support for the parliament.

The stand-off lasted from 21 September until 3 October. For the first few days it was relatively easy to enter and leave the White House, but gradually Yeltsin turned up the pressure; more troops were moved in, and late in the evening of 24 September, the electricity was turned off; by the 28th the water supply and telephones were cut off, and police and troops sealed the building off completely. On Sunday 3 October, events took a strange turn: a large demonstration of Supreme Soviet supporters pushed their way through the cordon of troops surrounding the White House and broke the blockade. The soldiers made only half-hearted attempts to prevent them; in fact most of the troops and police seemed to have disappeared. Encouraged by this into believing that the troops had come over to the side of parliament, General Makashov and Rutskoi led a group of some two thousand supporters out of the White House and stormed the headquarters of the Mayor of Moscow. This was occupied without any resistance, and the force moved on to their next target – the Ostankino television centre. However, as the demonstrators tried to force a way in, troops opened fire, and dozens of people fell dead and wounded. The attack was beaten off with heavy casualties. This was the signal for Yeltsin to take the White House by force; it was announced that an armed insurrection was taking place against the government; early the following morning, 4 October, armoured units opened fire on the defenders of the parliament building. Although there was hardly any return fire, the attack continued until about 9 am, when Rutskoi signalled that they were ready to surrender. The offer was ignored and firing was directed at the building itself until it began to burn. At about 11 am the first troops entered the White House and soon people began to stream out with their hands up. Khasbulatov and Rutskoi were arrested, along with other leading deputies; none of them was shot but many were severely beaten up by police.

Official estimates put the death toll at about 200, with between 700 and 800 wounded. Why the situation suddenly exploded on 3 October remains something of a mystery; Roy Medvedev argues that the leaders of parliament fell into a trap prepared for them by Yeltsin. It was important for him to be able to claim that he was acting in self-defence. 'As long as the supporters of parliament were only defending the building and upholding the constitution, Yeltsin had no valid justification for storming the Supreme Soviet building. To have a parliament that defended itself and perished under a hail of bullets was not to his advantage. On the other hand, an armed uprising, a putsch by the opposition forces benefited him politically.' The police and troops were ordered to withdraw so as to lure the defenders of parliament into making 'an insane show of force.' They had given Yeltsin his excuse to attack the White House.[9] The violent action of the 'October Events' divided Russian opinion sharply; Yeltsin supporters claimed that it had been necessary to crush once and for all the remnants of Soviet Communism which wanted to take Russia back to the bad old Stalinist days. But many of Yeltsin's genuinely democratic supporters were appalled by the attack on the White House; some of them abandoned him and some joined the opposition. The supporters of parliament regarded Yeltsin's actions as a criminal breach of the constitution and accused him of establishing an authoritarian dictatorship instead of the democratic system he had promised.

The promised referendum on the new draft constitution was due to take place on 12 December and the elections for the new Federal Assembly on 15 December. This was to consist of two chambers: the first was the State Duma, of which half the 450 members were elected in constituencies and half by proportional representation from national party lists. The second chamber, the Council of the Federation, was to consist of two representatives from each of the various autonomous republics and provinces within the Russian republic. The president was to have considerable say in who was appointed to the second chamber. In the referendum the voters approved Yeltsin's new constitution, though only by a narrow majority. There was still a large number of political parties, and during the campaign for the State Duma elections they formed blocs. Yeltsin, still without a specific party of his own, endorsed Gaidar's party, 'Russia's Choice', which formed a pact with Sergei Shakhrai's Party of Russian Unity and Concord. They favoured a continuation of drastic economic reforms and the rapid move towards a market economy, and expected to win, so they claimed, around 50 per cent of the seats between them. On the left was a bloc consisting of Zyuganov's Communist Party, the Agrarian Party and the Women of Russia. On the right was a bloc calling itself *Yabloko* (Apple) headed by Grigory Yavlinsky, which wanted a more cautious economic policy and the continuation of subsidies for state-owned industries. The only party not to join a bloc was Zhirinovski's Liberal-Democrat Party. The election results were a surprise to everybody and were a clear rebuff to Yeltsin. Gaidar's party won only 14 per cent of the popular vote, and even with their allies they could muster barely 25 per cent, giving them less than half the number of seats they had hoped for. The Communists and their allies won about 25 per cent, and Zhirinovsky's Liberal-Democrats received 22 per cent of the votes. The final results in terms of seats gave Gaidar's party only 70 seats, whereas the Communist bloc had 103 and the Liberal-Democrats 64.

Zhirinovsky's success disgusted most of the other political leaders, since he was seen as the worst type of vulgar, nationalist demagogue; in his television appearances he had talked about restoring the Russian empire, expanding to the Indian Ocean and taking Alaska back from the USA. But he touched a chord with ordinary people when he promised to do something about poverty and the collapse of the social service safety net. Yeltsin had clearly failed to deliver on his promises; prices for basic consumer goods were five times higher in December 1993 than they had been in April, and although wages and pensions increased too, they only rose by about three per cent. The results of the election were a great disappointment for Yeltsin and his supporters, but in practice, his power was not affected; the new constitution allowed him to appoint his own prime minister, to conduct foreign policy, and to dismiss parliament and rule by decree if he felt like it. Such was Russian democracy at the end of 1993.

11.2   The end of 'market romanticism'

(a) Yeltsin attempts to govern by consent

Soon after the elections of December 1993, prime minister Chernomyrdin announced: 'the period of "market romanticism" has ended for us today.' He meant, apparently, that since the 'cavalry charge' towards a market economy had been something of a senseless dream, more moderate policies would be followed. The goal was the same, but the approach was to be more gradual. Gaidar and several other ministers resigned, and eventually only one person remained in the cabinet from Gaidar's team – Anatoly Chubais, who was still in charge of the privatization process. As for the president himself, although the new constitution gave him great power, he wanted to avoid confrontation with the new Duma and he knew that he could not afford to ignore public opinion completely. The next presidential election was due in the summer of 1996; and apart from that, given that Russian politics were still in a state of flux, there was always the danger that he might be overthrown by an insurrection. The new leaders in the Duma seemed much less confrontational than his previous opponents, Khasbulatov and Rutskoi. When Yeltsin proposed that they should sign an agreement to abide by the constitution and not resort to violence, almost all the leaders complied. In July 1994 the Duma approved Chernomyrdin's new budget designed to stop the decline of production and move into a period of growth. Yeltsin seemed to be keeping a low profile and trying to remain above party squabbles.

Now that Gaidar and the radical reformers had been discredited, the two most vociferous parties were Zyuganov's Communists and Zhirinovsky's Nationalists. Surprisingly perhaps, they agreed on several important points: they were both anti-Western and believed that Russia had been taken advantage of by the USA since Gorbachev came to power in 1985. They disapproved strongly of Yeltsin's pro-Western Foreign Minister, Andrei Kozyrev, who wanted Russia to work closely with Europe and NATO. They both advocated the reuniting of the former republics of the USSR into a new multi-national state. They wanted to stop privatization and return to state control of the economy, with government subsidies for the main industries. They wanted more emphasis on law and order and felt it was time to restore national pride. Although Zyuganov was a communist and claimed to hold Lenin sacred, unlike Lenin and Stalin he was not an atheist; he believed that socialist ideas and values are very close to Christian values and he has great respect for the Orthodox Church. Yeltsin listened to what they were saying, and as far as possible, he took on board their ideas. For instance, he began to echo their anti-Western sentiments, criticizing NATO and expressing support for the Serbs during the civil war in Yugoslavia.

However, on economic matters Yeltsin remained committed to Chernomyrdin's policies and to continuing privatization. By the end of 1995 the government had sold or otherwise transferred into private hands about 80 per cent of all enterprises previously owned by the state. Yet the treasury seemed to benefit very little from these sales; most of the enterprises, even those that were profitable and valuable, were sold off at well below what they were worth. In spite of constant protests, this process continued through 1995; the feeling among ordinary Russians was that shady deals were being done, and many officials were pocketing considerable amounts of money. A new wealthy property-owning class was being created which included the former managers of state-owned industries, politicians, government officials, entrepreneurs and bankers. Many officials took advantage of their positions and inside knowledge to make lucrative 'arrangements', and it was difficult to know where the line came between legitimate and criminal activities (Document E). Strangely, Yeltsin, who had once been the scourge of corrupt officials in Moscow, seemed to do very little to restrain or discipline his underlings, nor did he appear especially worried by the generally increasing crime rate.[10] Observers noted that in the countryside just outside Moscow, hundreds of luxurious houses, even small palaces, were being built. But for most people there was no obvious sign of improvement; prices continued to rise throughout 1995, and by the end of the year they had more or less doubled since January. The number of people living in poverty continued to grow, unemployment increased, the death rate increased, and the birth rate declined. Nor had the situation been helped by the outbreak of war with the Chechen republic in December 1994.

(b) Conflict in Chechnya, 1994–96

The Chechens are an Islamic people numbering about one million, who live in the Northern Caucasus to the north of Georgia, inside the borders of the Russian republic. They were never happy under Russian rule, and resistance movements were active from the mid-nineteenth century. They resisted communist rule during the early years and the civil war, and they resisted Stalin's collectivization drive. During the Second World War Stalin accused them of collaborating with the Germans, and the entire nation was brutally deported to Central Asia; thousands died on the journey. In 1956 Khrushchev allowed the Chechens to return to their homeland, and their autonomous republic was restored. In the late 1980s Yeltsin, on the look-out for ways of attracting the support of non-Russian peoples in his struggle with Gorbachev, began to encourage their leaders to assert their sovereignty. In a policy which he bitterly regretted later, he seemed to be inciting all non-Russians to declare independence from the USSR and gave the impression that the Russian republic would support such moves. The Chechens needed little encouragement; according to Ronald Suny: 'at the time of the 1991 *coup* against Gorbachev, a flamboyant officer, Jokhar

Dudaev, was elected by a council of elders as leader of Chechnya, and with a small band of armed men, he took power from the local party boss... After being elected President of the Chechen Republic, in dubious elections, Dudaev defied Russian authority and allowed his republic to become a centre for free-wheeling economic and criminal activity.'[11]

When the USSR broke up, Chechnya proclaimed itself an independent republic, as did four other states – Dniester, Abkhazia, Karabakh, and Southern Ossetia. However, none of them received international recognition. Yeltsin managed to persuade the other four states, along with the rest of the autonomous republics, to remain in the Russian Federation; in 1992 they all signed a new Federation Treaty. This was a considerable achievement for Yeltsin, but the Russian nationalists were not impressed – they wanted a unitary state in which all parts were completely under the authority of Moscow. Only Chechnya refused to sign. Having failed to persuade Dudaev to co-operate, Yeltsin tried to engineer his overthrow from within, using agents to stir Dudaev's enemies into action. When that ploy failed, Yeltsin and his advisers decided to use military force to bring the Chechens back into the fold. The reasons given were that their illegal separatism must be brought to an end, and that Chechnya was being used as a base from which criminal gangs were operating throughout Russia. The decision to attack Chechnya was taken without consulting the Federal Assembly or testing public opinion. When the news came out, the Duma voted overwhelmingly against military action; even some senior army leaders like General Lebed expressed serious doubts about the wisdom of such a policy. There were rumours that the real reason for the invasion was that some ministers had been involved in deals with criminal gangs in Chechnya; the deals had not been honoured by the Chechens, and the Russian attack was therefore a revenge operation.

Whatever the truth behind the rumours, on 11 December 1994, forty thousand Russian troops invaded Chechnya. The government did not expect much resistance, but there was fierce fighting before the Chechen capital, Grozny, was captured in February 1995. All round the world television viewers saw shocking images of Russian tanks rolling through the ruined city. But the Chechens would not surrender. Thousands of refugees fled into the hills; guerrilla forces were organized which continually harassed the Russians, who were not trained to deal with such tactics. Guerrillas attacked Russian troops over the border in southern Russia and threatened to start a terrorist bombing campaign in Moscow. The Russian soldiers grew discouraged; they knew that the general public did not support the war and that even their own commanders were less than enthusiastic; casualty figures grew alarmingly. In the summer of 1996 the Chechens succeeded in recapturing Grozny from the demoralized Russians, who by this time had lost almost twenty thousand of their troops killed. Yeltsin was preoccupied by the presidential election campaign; realizing that the fiasco in Chechnya was ruining his reputation, he promised to end the war and he appointed General Lebed with full powers to open peace negotiations. Lebed was a popular figure who somehow persuaded the Chechens to compromise, though it took some time: eventually the Russians agreed to withdraw their troops and the Chechens agreed to set up a coalition government acceptable to Moscow; they did not drop their demands for complete independence, but there was to be a cooling-off period of five years, after which the status of Chechnya would be considered again. Sadly, the fighting started again long before that.

(c) More elections, December 1995–July 1996

The strains of office were beginning to tell on Yeltsin; he was especially stressed by the conflict in Chechnya, and in June 1995 he suffered a heart-attack. Yet he seemed to have no thoughts of retirement; he simply left the day-to-day running of affairs to prime minister Chernomyrdin. The government was so unpopular that many people thought the Duma elections due in December might be cancelled. Nevertheless, it was announced that they would go ahead as provided for in the new constitution – Duma elections in December 1995 and presidential elections in June 1996. From the early summer of 1995 the political parties and groupings began preparing and lining themselves up for the December elections, which were seen as a dress-rehearsal for the following June. His advisers persuaded Yeltsin that he ought to have a political party to back him – a 'party of power'. Obligingly, Chernomyrdin founded a party which took the name 'Our Home is Russia' (*Nash Dom Rossiya*, or NDR for short); it had a three-point programme: 'a strong state, liberal foundations for the economic life of Russia, and appreciable social measures'. The new party tried to convince the electorate that the government's economic policies were beginning to work, and there is some evidence of truth in this; at least the inflation rate was falling and so was the budget deficit.

The election results were disappointing for the government; they had run a lavish campaign for the new NDR, buying over seven hours of advertising time on television; but they won only 65 out of the 450 seats in the Duma. Yet they ought not to have been surprised; opinion polls had not been promising and there was a general air of discontent in the country. Gennady Zyuganov's Communist Party did best, even though they only bought six minutes of television advertising time! They won 157 seats, and together with their allies, they could muster 186 seats in the Duma, by far the largest grouping. Clearly there was a great deal of residual support and nostalgia for the old days of the USSR and strong communist government. Zhirinovsky's Liberal-Democrats did less well than in 1993, winning only 52 seats. In terms of percentages, the votes of the groups that supported Yeltsin and the government added up to about 25 per cent, the communists and allies had 32 per cent, and the rest were divided among a variety of groups. Although the communists lacked the controlling vote, they were obviously the preponderant party; a communist was elected chairman of the Duma, and many of the committees were headed by communists.[12] The government party had come a very poor second. In a genuinely democratic system the communists would have taken a leading role in the next administration; in Russia, nothing much changed – Yeltsin remained president, at least until the following June, and Chernomyrdin was still prime minister. However, Yeltsin did replace his pro-Western Foreign Minister, Andrei Kozyrev, with Yevgeny Primakov, who was much more of a nationalist.

Almost immediately the politicians began to prepare for the presidential elections; Yeltsin was determined to stand, in spite of his heart problems and the

Figure 11.1   Yeltsin meets the public during the June 1996 election campaign.

fact that opinion polls gave him a popularity rating of less than five per cent. It seemed inconceivable that Yeltsin could win; some of his advisers wanted him to cancel the elections, and even resort to force if necessary to stay in power. To his credit Yeltsin allowed the election to go ahead and over 20 candidates registered to run in the first round, which was to take place on 16 June 1996. It was soon clear that the communist leader, Zyuganov, would be his greatest rival, although the candidates also included Lebed, Zhirinovsky, Yavlinsky and Gorbachev. Early opinion polls put Zyuganov as the likely winner; this caused consternation in the West at the prospect of a return to communism and the Cold War. However, Yeltsin's supporters rallied well, and he threw himself enthusiastically into the campaign. He seemed to have gained new energy; he toured the country, visiting 24 different regions and cities, promising everything to everybody. Wage arrears would be paid to workers, pensions were to be raised, there were to be scholarships for students and compensation payments for savings wiped out by inflation. It was announced that hundreds of millions of extra roubles were to be spent on science, education, hospitals and theatres. The unpopular privatization programme was stopped, and its mastermind, the now universally detested Anatoly Chubais, resigned. In April an agreement was signed for the formation of a union between Belarus and Russia. Yeltsin promised peace in Chechnya and met Chechen leaders in the Kremlin, where a cease-fire was signed. Zyuganov protested: 'Look at Yeltsin's decrees. Why, he is carrying out 80 per cent of our programme.'

The communists had some distinctive policies: Zyuganov continued his anti-Western stance, and laid great emphasis on the communists' concern with social welfare. He advocated policies like those followed by the Chinese, encouraging the manufacture of consumer goods and keeping fuel prices low. Like Yeltsin, he too campaigned vigorously, travelling around the country and drawing large audiences. But he had one big disadvantage: apart from the fact that he lacked any sort of charisma, he failed to distance himself sufficiently from Stalin, whom he often referred to and quoted. This was a great mistake; one Moscow university professor who was sympathetic to the new communist party was reported as saying: 'How could I vote for Zyuganov? I was at one of his demonstrations, and there were thousands of people marching along and carrying portraits of Zyuganov and *Stalin*.' In the first round of voting Yeltsin won a narrow victory with 35 per cent of the votes against 32 per cent for Zyuganov and 15 per cent for Lebed, whose slogan was 'justice and order'. All the other candidates performed disappointingly, and none more so than Gorbachev who received barely one per cent of the votes. Only the first two candidates went forward to the second ballot on 3 July. Yeltsin's health was giving cause for concern again, and at some point during the campaign he suffered another heart-attack. He admits in his memoirs that his advisers decided to deal with this by holding back information, and no details of the illness appeared until after he had been re-elected. His team used all their massive political experience in the intervening couple of weeks to win over the votes from the other candidates. They especially targeted the people who had voted for Lebed; on 18 June Yeltsin appointed Lebed as secretary of the Russian Security Council, and he dropped several hints that he was beginning to look on Lebed as his chosen successor. The ploy was successful: in the second ballot Yeltsin won a comfortable victory with 54 per cent of the votes against 40 per cent for Zyuganov. About 75 per cent of Lebed's supporters had switched their votes to Yeltsin.

It was a remarkable victory, given the low ebb of his popularity at the beginning of the campaign and the disastrous nature of most of his government's policies. The reason for his victory was not that people liked him, but that they liked the alternative even less. In Poland, communist candidates with social democratic programmes actually won elections when the voters got sick of 'shock therapy'. The same could have happened in Russia if the communist party had put forward genuine social democrat policies. But Zyuganov was not a social democrat; he made no secret of his admiration for Stalin, and this showed at the very least, insensitivity to public opinion. When it came to the push, a majority of Russians could not bring themselves to vote a Stalinist-type communist back into power. They gritted their teeth and voted for the lesser of two evils.

11.3   Yeltsin's second term, 1996–99

(a) Economic crisis continues

As Yeltsin began his second term as president, the government put out lots of encouraging announcements about the economy entering a period of growth and the situation becoming normalized. Inflation was reduced to less than two per cent per month and this strengthened confidence in the rouble. However, life was still difficult for tens of millions of ordinary people because of late payment of their wages and pensions. Yeltsin cancelled some of the decrees which he had announced during the election campaign; the reason given was that the money simply was not available. It was claimed at the end of 1996 that the government had only received one-twelfth of the cash from privatization that it had budgeted for. Chernomyrdin, who had earned more respect than most of the government politicians, remained prime minister. But surprisingly Yeltsin brought back Chubais to run the economy, which meant a return to the rapid drive for capitalism. Lebed did not survive long in his new post; Yeltsin found him difficult to work with, and in October he was dismissed from the Security Council. The president had a heart by-pass operation in the autumn of 1996 and was out of action for several months. Early indications were that 1997 would be the turning point for post-Soviet Russia; inflation was kept down to only one per cent per month, and for the first time since 1990, production ceased to fall. Chubais was positively euphoric: 'it seems to me,' he wrote in February 1997, 'that nothing can stop Russia from a long, steep, powerful upward trajectory of growth, constantly gaining in strength.'[13]

The promise was not fulfilled; one of the great weaknesses of the economy was the lack of investment, without which no significant expansion could take place. In the autumn of 1997 external events took their toll; there was a series of crises and financial disasters in the Asian 'tiger' economies – Thailand, Singapore, and South Korea – which affected stock markets all over the world. There was a fall in the world price of oil, because of over-production; the price per barrel, which had stood at $40 in 1980, had dropped to as low as $10 in January 1998. This was a disaster for the Russians, since oil was their greatest export earner; projected profits from oil exports for 1998 were wiped out. Foreign investors withdrew their funds, and the Central Bank found itself struggling to avoid devaluing the rouble. Yeltsin responded to the crisis in March 1998 by sacking his prime minister Chernomyrdin, who had been in office since 1992, and his economics minister Chubais. The new prime minister was Sergei Kiriyenko, a 35-year old businessman from Nizhny Novgorod, who had been minister for fuel and energy for only a few months. He could do very little to improve the situation, and wage arrears mounted in all sections of the labour force. In May there were widespread protests from striking miners demanding Yeltsin's resignation (Document G). They expressed their feelings by blocking railway tracks, thus preventing the movement of goods. As the protest movement spread, the government seemed on the verge of panic; the economic crisis in Indonesia brought down the Suharto regime, and there were serious doubts about the stability of the Yeltsin government. The flight of capital from Russia continued. Even the 'oligarchs' were disgruntled and blamed Yeltsin; Vladimir Gusinsky, the head of a bank and a media-company, stated publicly that the newspapers and television companies that he controlled would no longer support the president.

The International Monetary Fund (IMF) helped by providing massive loans, but the budget deficit was so large that these were used up within a couple of months; the government had to spend much of its gold and foreign currency reserves trying to maintain the value of the rouble at six to the dollar. By early August this could continue no longer, or else the government would be left with no foreign currency at all; and that would mean bankruptcy. Although Yeltsin had promised that there would be no devaluation, it had become unavoidable. On 17 August it was announced that a new 'floating exchange rate' had been introduced. The government did not use the word 'devaluation', but in fact it developed into something even worse – an uncontrolled free fall of the rouble. By the first week in September the rouble had slumped to 20 to the dollar; it was another financial disaster in which millions of people and institutions had their savings and capital rendered worthless.

(b) Primakov to the rescue

As the government floundered, out of its depth in this crisis, the Duma suggested a new prime minister, Evgeny Primakov, who had been Foreign Minister since 1996. To the surprise of most people, including Primakov himself, Yeltsin agreed. A veteran communist – he was almost 70 – Primakov had had a distinguished career; he was a member of the Academy of Sciences, with a doctoral degree in economic sciences, he had been Director of the Russian Institute of World Economy and International Relations (1985–89), and was a member of the USSR Supreme Soviet. He had been highly critical of the entire economic reform programme, and believed that the state should continue to play a considerable role in organizing the economy, especially industry. Western economists were alarmed by his appointment, and the 'oligarchs' were outraged. Although Primakov was not a member of the new communist party, one newspaper owned by Boris Berezovsky lamented: 'The threat of a Communist comeback once again hangs over a Russia which has been lacerated by the economic crisis. Once again, as in 1917, intelligent, well-spoken, and educated parliamentary representatives are leading the country towards a dictatorship.' On the other hand, the ordinary Russian public liked the appointment; even Roy Medvedev, who hardly ever approved of anything that Yeltsin did, was almost enthusiastic about this: 'As I survey all the political leaders of today's Russia, there is not a single person I could name who would be more suitable for the job of prime minister than Primakov.'[14]

Primakov had a clear programme: to make Russian industry competitive on the world market, with support from the government; to reduce imports; to prevent Russian capital from leaving the country, and to attract foreign investment. Soon after his appointment, the economic situation began to improve itself almost before his policies had time to take effect. The devaluation of the rouble made foreign imports more expensive; people were forced to buy Russian goods, and this provided a boost for Russian industry. The world oil price recovered, making Russia's oil exports more profitable. The government was able to repay six billion dollars to Western creditors, wage and pensions arrears were paid, and salaries and pensions were increased. The crisis was passing and opinion polls suggested that 70 per cent of the voters approved of Primakov's policies. Even the Western press was enthusiastic; the French newspaper *Le Figaro* reported on 28 February 1999: 'The situation in Russia is stable, and the author of this surprising stability is Primakov. His public image is of one who rejects confrontation and works quietly. This has calmed and reassured his compatriots. Russian society has begun to dream of wisdom like Primakov's becoming dominant in the government.' However, in Russia most of the press and two private television channels did their utmost to discredit him. Ludicrously, they blamed him for the collapse of the economy and accused him of preparing to organize a *coup*. Suddenly on 12 May 1999 Yeltsin sacked Primakov and the team of advisers which he had gathered round him, and replaced him with the Minister of Internal Affairs, the 47-year old Sergei Stepashin.

Yeltsin gave as his reason for this 'difficult but necessary decision' the need to appoint a younger and more energetic man as prime minister. This was viewed with some scepticism by most observers: Primakov was only eight months older than when he was appointed, and nobody could have shown more energy in working to end the crisis. It was widely rumoured that the real reason for his dismissal was his determination to root out corruption. He began a campaign to find out how the vast amounts of cash were disappearing from Russia. He had a list drawn up of the richest families in Russia and was in touch with the Swiss attorney-general's office to find out who was responsible for the huge deposits of cash in Swiss banks. He encouraged the honest members of the Federal Security Service to pursue shady bankers, importers and exporters, and government bureaucrats and bring them to court. Literally thousands of criminal cases were started. Many people with media connections found themselves under threat, and they had no hesitation in using their influence to get rid of Primakov. When his dismissal was announced, there was consternation and mystification among ordinary Russians. Yeltsin's popularity rate fell to only two per cent.

(c) Enter Putin

Yeltsin was already thinking about the Duma elections which were due in December 1999 and the next presidential election due in June 2000. The constitution prevented him from standing for a third term, and so he wanted to make sure that the candidate of his choice became the next president. In his memoirs he argues that Primakov would not be right for president; he was too old and 'he had too much red in his political palette.' For a time it seemed that Stepashin might be the favourite to succeed. But he lacked experience and charisma; at one point he declared: 'Fighting against corruption and gangsterism – those are our priorities.' Perhaps that was enough to put paid to his chances of being elected. On 9 August Yeltsin dismissed him and appointed Vladimir Putin, the director of the security police, as prime minister, at the same time making it clear that Putin would be his favoured candidate for the presidency. Under the terms of the constitution, if Yeltsin were to retire before the end of his term, the prime minister would automatically become acting president for three months, during which time elections for the presidency must be held. Putin was not very well known to the general public; he was born in Leningrad in 1952 and took a law degree at Leningrad State University in 1975. He worked for the KGB in Leningrad for nine years and then moved to East Germany where he served as a KGB officer from 1984 until 1990. Returning to St Petersburg, he worked for the city administration, and in 1994 became deputy head of the city government. He moved to

Moscow in 1996 and Yeltsin appointed him head of the security services in 1998. He gives the impression of being rather quiet, calm, serious and intelligent. An article in *Izvestiya* described him thus: 'Putin's rare television appearances are striking for their extremely laconic quality. His rather acerbic manner, the toughness of an organization man, is rather pleasing in its own way, although this is overriden by the coldly intelligent, impenetrable look in his eyes. He abides strictly by the wise old rule – that language exists to conceal one's thoughts, and facial expressions, to hide one's feelings.'

At first very few people took Putin seriously as a contender for the presidency; the fact that he was Yeltsin's choice did not seem especially designed to enhance his chances of success. Primakov came out of retirement, announcing that he was called to 'save the fatherland.' He became leader of the Fatherland–All Russia bloc, and the mayor of Moscow, Yuri Luzhkov, agreed to be his prime minister. It seemed like the perfect 'dream-team', and Primakov began to be seen as the most likely next president. But the situation soon changed dramatically; in September 1999 there was a series of bomb explosions in Moscow. Two large apartment blocks were blown up and over two hundred people were killed. Putin claimed that the Chechen rebels were responsible and took the decision for an all-out attack on the Chechen separatists. This time public opinion, outraged by the bomb attacks, was all in favour of the war. Putin impressed everybody by his decisive handling of the situation and his determination to wipe out the warlords and their gangs of bandits. Once again, however, this proved difficult; two years later they had still not been subdued, in spite of the increasing ruthlessness of the Russian troops; tragically, it was the ordinary, innocent people of Chechnya who were suffering most[15] (Document F).

In the Duma elections of 19 December 1999 the war did nothing but good for Putin and the new political group that was backing him – the Unity bloc. The media continued their anti-Primakov campaign and trumpeted Putin's success in teaching the Chechen terrorists a lesson. Primakov's Fatherland–All Russia bloc won only 12 per cent of the votes, while Putin's Unity bloc took 24 per cent, and the Communists 25 per cent. On 31 December Yeltsin resigned as president (Document H), evidently feeling confident that Putin would be his successor. Putin was now acting-president, and he immediately pulled off a master-stroke: his Unity bloc formed an alliance in the Duma with the Communists; together with other small groups of allies, this created a pro-Putin bloc with a majority of votes in parliament, something which Yeltsin had never achieved. The presidential elections were brought forward with the first round held on 26 March 2000. The main candidates were Putin, Zyuganov, Yavlinsky and Zhirinovski; Primakov decided not to stand. It was no surprise when Putin won outright on the first ballot, taking 53 per cent of the votes; once again Zyuganov came second. The Chechen war played an important part in his decisive victory, but there was probably more to it than that. Most people were tired of the years of economic hardship and dismayed at the decline of their country, which had once been a superpower, and was now struggling to maintain its position as a world power. There was a feeling that Putin had the intelligence, the political acumen, the determination and the energy to bring some stability to the country.

(d) Past and future

Since the collapse of the Soviet Union at the end of 1991, the Russian people have experienced what can only be described, for most of them, as a nightmare. In their attempt to push the country headlong into a fully-fledged market economy, Yeltsin's governments made almost every conceivable mistake. Admittedly, the communists had left a disastrous situation; probably no government in the world has ever had to deal with such a daunting compound of problems all at once; it was necessary to make the transition from a centralized command economy to a capitalist market economy, and at the same time to create a democratic political system. Their major mistake, in the view of many observers, was to base their programme on advice from Western economists, who recommended a system based completely on market forces, underpinned by credits and loans from Western governments, banks and the IMF. These Western economists did not fully understand the system they were trying to reform or how difficult it would be for the Russians to carry through those changes. One Western economist who spent some time in Russia was Jeffrey Sachs. When questioned about the reasons for the difficulties, he gave this reply: 'When we undertook the reforms we felt ourselves to be doctors who had been called to someone's sickbed. But when we placed the patient on the operating table and opened him up, we found that his anatomical structure and internal organs were completely different, of a kind we never encountered in medical school.'[16] Sachs left Russia, but Yeltsin persisted with a scheme which was inappropriate for Russia's situation. The result was bound to be chaos. The most distressing aspects were, first of all, the way in which so many people took advantage of the situation to get rich quick; many of the ex-Soviet *nomenklatura*, who had resisted change for so long, decided that if reform had to come, they might as well exploit it and make as much profit from it as they could. When a friend of mine, who was visiting St Petersburg in 1997, asked who owned all the big black Mercedes limousines with darkened windows, he was told: 'The former Communist bosses – they know the ropes!' The amount of blatant corruption and criminality was astonishing; vast sums of money which should have been invested in industry were salted away in foreign bank accounts. When the financial catastrophe came in August 1998, one of the 'oligarchs' was reporting as saying: 'Well, we've made enough money for ourselves now; perhaps it's time to do something for our country.' And secondly there were the social problems which the reforms caused, and the poverty, which by all accounts was more intense and widespread than under the final years of communism.

There were some positive aspects to the Yeltsin era; in the political sphere progress was made towards democracy. If the system is not yet as 'democratic' as that in the USA or Europe, again it has to remembered that it was not a question of restoring democracy; there *was* no tradition of Western or any other type of democracy in Russia. The fact that Duma and presidential elections have taken place at all is a considerable achievement. Political parties are developing, and as more time passes, it seems less and less likely that the country will succumb to a dictatorship. The press and the other media have enjoyed greater freedom than ever before. In the summer of 2001 the situation was looking stable and promising. The economy at last seemed to have turned the corner, and during 2000 the average national income increased by around seven per cent. Thanks partly to the high world price of oil and the continuing effects of the rouble devaluation, Russia had a large balance of payments surplus. Putin has made a good beginning; public opinion is firmly behind his policies and he has earned respect among other world leaders. Like Primakov, he believes that the country needs a strong government, with the state playing an important role in planning within a mixed economy. The country has plentiful natural resources, the people are well educated, there has been a promising expansion of small and medium-sized businesses, and the number of large businesses owned by Russian firms is growing. But there is still a long way to go, and there are many questions which cannot be answered at the moment. For example, can the developing economic success be sustained? Will it benefit the great majority of the Russian people or just the 'oligarchs' and their associates? And will president Putin turn out to be a democrat or an autocrat?

Documents

(A) Yegor Gaidar writes about Boris Yeltsin's qualities (1996).

His is a complex and contradictory character. In my view, his greatest strength is his ability to intuitively sense the public mood, and to take that into account before making decisions full of the greatest consequence. In matters of fundamental importance he trusts his own political instinct far more than any advisers. Sometimes in this way he makes the absolutely right decision, but sometimes he is seriously mistaken. As a rule, what is to blame in such cases is his mood, which changes fairly often and leads him astray. One of his great strengths is his ability to listen. A personal appeal to him can influence him more than the finest, most carefully written document. But a danger is concealed here: whoever gains his confidence and manages to persuade him also has a chance to abuse this confidence, something that has happened more than once, including in the making of very important decisions.

Source: quoted in Roy A. Medvedev, *Post-Soviet Russia: A Journey Through the Yeltsin Era*, pp. 16–17.

(B) Academician Oleg Bogomolov assesses the results of the first phase of 'shock therapy', in an article in *Moskovskie Novosti*, 6 September 1992.

Falling living standards are outpacing the decline in production. Commodity circulation is half what it was; the real income of the population is even less. In comparison to January 1991, the cost of living has risen twenty time over, while wages for those employed in the national economy are only seven or eight times higher... People are trying to adapt to the changing circumstances in order to survive... cultivating vegetable gardens and going into business for themselves, mainly in commerce and services.... The attempt to apply shock therapy in Russia following the Polish model and the advice of a group of Western experts has turned out to be very painful. Will this attempt have a curative effect? Doubts about that are prevalent. But hope remains.

Source: quoted in Medvedev, p. 24.

(C) Viktor Danilenko writes in support of the 'Westernizers' in an *Izvestiya* article, 18 August 1992.

Power today should be organized today in such a way that there would be a government of property owners, controlled by property owners, oriented towards the interests of property owners, and in all ways effectively open to their influence. The most important government decisions should be made directly by people who have shouldered the burden of property.

Source: quoted in Medvedev, pp. 24–5.

(D) Aleksei Ulyukaev also defends 'shock therapy', 20 September 1996.

When people perform a vitally necessary operation (in the absence of anti-biotics, sterile instruments, bandages and dressings, or even electricity) – what they do is painful, and rarely does anyone express gratitude or have anything good to say about them. On the contrary, harsh, sometimes furious, criticism is their lot... But what does that matter? Let out common monument be the capitalism we have built through struggle. Amen.

Source: quoted in Medvedev, p. 85.

(E) Vadim Kortunov, of the State Academy of Management, gives this devastating assessment of the new class of businessmen, 5 December 1996.

The new generation of Russian 'businessmen' has been formed... They are either former members of the *nomenklatura* who were in the right place at the right time when their enterprises were privatized, people who found it easy to change their 'Communist convictions' for the psychology of monetarism. Or else they are openly criminal elements... or else they were youthful new-comers who had not absorbed what they were taught in school but, to make up for it, were not burdened with any symptoms of the thinking process. This

(continued)

generation of 'new Russians' is united by such characteristics as moral nihilism, a total inability to engage in spiritual or intellectual activity, a monetarist psychology, and consequently a parasitic mode of existence displaying the flag of 'free enterprise'. It is therefore quite logical that the growing prosperity of today's Russian businessmen takes place against a backdrop of overall decline in production, impoverishment of the population, inflation, and the ruination of our country's economy as a whole.

Source: quoted in Medvedev, p. 180.

(F) Boris Yeltsin justifies the Russian military actions in Chechnya.

These were military struggles against terrorists, not a war against a people. I think it is high time everyone in the world understood that. International public opinion would like to nail Russia to the wall of shame for its 'war crimes'. But the international community does not know, and does not want to know the main reason for the death of civilians. We have never committed mass executions of unarmed people in Chechnya. There have been no ethnic cleansing or concentration camps. The main reason for the missile strikes and bombs that have brought pain and grief to ordinary citizens is the war unleashed by the terrorist against the Russian people. When I hear about the 'war crimes' of the Russian army, I would like to ask about other 'war crimes'. Isn't it a 'war crime' that the bandits' main source of subsistence is the income from ransoms and the sale of people into slavery. In Chechnya there are at least 2000 slave hostages, and the number is constantly growing.

Source: Boris Yeltsin, *Midnight Diaries*, p. 340.

(G) Boris Yeltsin's account of the 1998 miners' strike.

In 1998 the miners' protest banners included more than the usual economic calls for back wages and so on. For the first time in recent years, the miners co-ordinated a large-scale political platform and took to shouting, 'Down with the government! Dump Yeltsin!' This troublesome resistance continued for more than three months. The miners set up a picket line in Moscow, right outside the House of Government, on Gorbaty Bridge, where they would bang their miners' helmets on the pavement, declare hunger strikes and attract reporters. News stories attacked the government. Celebrities and members of parliament came to visit them ... The scandal was growing.

Vice Premier Oleg Sysuyev, responsible for social issues, raced from one coal district to another, signing agreements almost without looking at them – anything to come to terms. In one of these signed documents I noted a point conceding that the government agreed that Yeltsin must be dismissed. Of course this agreement didn't have a legal leg to stand on . . . But it stood as clear evidence that the government was nearly incapacitated.

Source: Yeltsin, pp. 171–2.

(H) Extracts from Boris Yeltsin's resignation speech, 31 December 1999.

There is just a little time left before a magic date in our history. The year 2000 is approaching, a new century and a new millennium . . . My dear friends! My dear ones! Today I am speaking to you for the last time as president of Russia. Today, on the last day of the outgoing century, I am stepping down from office . . .

I want to ask your forgiveness. I want to apologize for not making many of our dreams come true. What had seemed easy turned out to be extremely difficult. I apologize for not justifying some of the expectations of people who believed that we could jump in one swoop from the gray, stagnant, totalitarian past to the bright, prosperous, civilized future. I believed in it myself. But the one jump didn't work. I was too naive about some things . . . the problems turned out to be far too complicated. Many people experienced upheavals during this difficult time.

But I want you all to know something that I have never said and that is important for me to say today: the pain each of you experienced was reflected by pain in my own heart – sleepless nights, tortuous suffering over what must be done so that people's lives would be just a bit easier and better. I did everything I could. A new generation is coming to take my place, a generation that will do it bigger and better . . . In wishing you farewell, I would like to say to each of you, be happy. You deserve happiness. You deserve happiness and peace.

Happy New Year! Happy new century, by dear Russians!

Source: Yeltsin, pp. 386–7.

Notes

1. Anders Aslund, *How Russia Became a Market Economy*, p. 188.
2. *Ibid.*, pp. 235–6, 251–6.
3. Roy Medvedev, *Post-Soviet Russia*, pp. 43–4.
4. *Ibid.*, pp. 48–9.
5. Ronald G. Suny, *The Soviet Experiment*, p. 489.
6. Boris Yeltsin, *The View From the Kremlin*, p. 236.
7. B. Clarke, *An Empire's New Clothes*, pp. 234, 240.
8. The following is based on the graphic account in Medvedev, pp. 103–130.
9. Medvedev, pp. 121–2.
10. See J. Kampfner, *Inside Yeltsin's Russia*.
11. Suny, p. 501.

12. Medvedev, pp. 204–13.
13. *Ibid.*, p. 282.
14. *Ibid.*, p. 325.
15. Anna Politkovskaya, *A Dirty War*.
16. Quoted in Medvedev, p. 84.

■ ⓥ Suggestions for further reading

There is a huge bibliography on Russian history. This list contains all the books and articles which I have found useful, and which are mentioned in the endnotes to each chapter.

Abraham, R., *Alexander Kerensky: The First Love of the Revolution*, London, 1987.

Acton, Edward, *Rethinking the Russian Revolution*, London, 1990.

Acton, E., Cherniaev, V. and Rosenberg, W.G. (editors), *Critical Companion to the Russian Revolution 1914–1921*, Bloomington and Indianapolis, Indiana, 1997.

Aldridge, R., *The Hidden Hand*, London, 2001.

Anderson, R.D., *Public Politics in an Authoritarian State: Making Foreign Policy During the Brezhnev Years*, Ithaca, NY, 1993.

Andreyev, C., *Vlasov and the Russian Liberation Movement: Soviet Reality and Emigre Theories*, Cambridge, 1987.

Armstrong, D. and Goldstein, E. (editors), *The End of the Cold War*, London and Portland, Oregon, 1990.

Ascher, A., *The Revolution of 1905: Russia in Disarray*, 2 vols, Stanford, California, 1988–93.

Aslund, A., *How Russia Became a Market Economy*, London, 1995.

Bacon, E.T., *The Gulag at War: Stalin's Forced Labour System in the Light of the Archives*, London, 1994.

Barber, John and Harrison, Mark, *The Soviet Home Front, 1941–1945: A Social and Economic History of the USSR in World War II*, London and New York, 1991.

Barmine, A., *One Who Survived: The Life Story of a Russian under the Soviets*, New York, 1945.

Beevor, Antony, *Stalingrad*, London, 1998.

Berkman, Alexander, *The Russian Tragedy*, London, 1989.

Berry, M.J., 'Science, Technology and Innovation', in M. McCauley (editor), *Khrushchev and Khrushchevism*, London, 1987.

Beschloss, M.R., *Mayday: Eisenhower, Khrushchev and the U-2 Affair*, London, 1986.

Bethell, N., *The Last Secret: Forcible Repatriation to Russia, 1944–47*, London, 1974.

Bordyugov, G.A. (editor), *Gotovil li Stalin nastupatel'nuyu voinu protiv Gitlera? [Was Stalin planning a military offensive against Hitler?]*, Moscow, 1995.

Brown, A., *The Gorbachev Factor*, Oxford and New York, 1996.

Brzezinski, Z., *The Permanent Purge*, Cambridge, Massachusetts, 1956.

Bullock, Alan, *Hitler and Stalin – Parallel Lives*, London, 1991.

Bushnell, J., *Mutiny Amid Repression: Russian Soldiers in the Revolution of 1905–1906*, Bloomington, Indiana, 1985.

Carr, E.H., *The Russian Revolution from Lenin to Stalin 1917–1929*, London, 1980 edition.

Carrère d'Encausse, H., *The Great Challenge: Nationalities and the Bolshevik State, 1917–30*, New York, 1991.

Chamberlin, W.H., *The Russian Revolution*, 2 vols, London, 1935; this edition, 1965.

Channon, John (editor), *Politics, Society and Stalinism in the USSR*, London and New York, 1998.

Clark, R.W., *Lenin, the Man behind the Mask*, London, 1988.

Clarke, B., *An Empire's New Clothes. The End of Russia's Liberal Dream*, London, 1995.

Cohen, S.F., *Bukharin and the Bolshevik Revolution*, New York, 1973.

Cohen, S.F., 'Bolshevism and Stalinism', in Tucker, R.C. (editor), *Stalinism: Essays in Historical Interpretation*, New Brunswick, New Jersey and London, second edition, 1999.

Conquest, Robert, *Harvest of Sorrow, Soviet Collectivization and the Terror-Famine*, London, 1986.

Conquest, Robert, *Stalin and the Kirov Murder*, New York, 1989.

Conquest, Robert, *The Great Terror: A Reassessment*, London, 1990.

Davies, R.W., *The Socialist Offensive: The Collectivisation of Soviet Agriculture, 1929–1930*, Cambridge, Massachusetts and London, 1980.

Davies, R.W., Harrison, Mark and Wheatcroft, S.G. (editors), *The Economic Transformation of the Soviet Union*, Cambridge, 1994.

Davies, S., ' "Us against them": social identity in Soviet Russia, 1934–41', in S. Fitzpatrick (editor), *Stalinism: New Directions*, London and New York, 2000.

Dawisha, K., *The Kremlin and Prague Spring*, London, 1985.

Deutscher, I., *The Prophet Armed: Trotsky 1879–1921*, Oxford, 1954.

Deutscher, I., *The Prophet Unarmed: Trotsky 1921–1929*, Oxford, 1959.

Deutscher, I., *The Prophet Outcast: Trotsky 1929–1940*, Oxford, 1963.

Deutscher, I., *Stalin*, London, revised edition, 1966.

Dukes, P., 'From Soviet to Russian History', in *History Today*, vol. 43, August 1993.

Edmonds, R., *Soviet Foreign Policy: The Brezhnev Years*, London, 1983.

Edwards, O., *The USA and the Cold War*, London, 1997.

Erickson, J., *The Road to Stalingrad*, London, 1975.

Erickson, J., *The Road to Berlin*, London, 1983.

Erickson, J., 'Barbarossa – June 1941; Who Attacked Whom?', in *History Today*, July, 2001.

Erickson, J. and Dilks, D. (editors), *Barbarossa: the Axis and the Allies*, Edinburgh, 1994.

Ferro, M., *Nicholas II, the Last of the Tsars*, London, 1991.

Figes, O., *Peasant Russia, Civil War: The Volga Countryside in Revolution, 1917–21*, Oxford, 1989.

Figes, O., *A People's Tragedy: The Russian Revolution 1891–1924*, London, 1996.

Filtzer, D., 'Labour', in M. McCauley (editor), *Khrushchev and Khrushchevism*, London, 1987.

Filtzer, D., *Soviet Workers and the Collapse of Perestroika*, Cambridge, 1994.

Filtzer, D., 'Stalinism and the Working Class in the 1930s', in J. Channon (editor), *Politics, Society and Stalinism*, London and New York, 1998.

Fischer, Fritz, *Germany's Aims in the First World War*, London, 1967.

Fitzpatrick, S., *The Commissariat of Enlightenment: Soviet Organization of Education and the Arts under Lunacharsky*, Cambridge, 1970.

Fitzpatrick, S., 'The Great Departure. Rural–Urban Migration in the Soviet Union, 1929–33', in W.R. Rosenberg and L.S. Siegelbaum (editors), *Social Dimensions of Soviet Industrialization*, Bloomington, Indiana, 1993.

Fitzpatrick, S., *The Russian Revolution*, Oxford, second edition, 1994.

Fitzpatrick, S., *Stalin's Peasants. Resistance and Survival in the Russian Village after Collectivization*, New York, 1994.

Fitzpatrick, S., *Everyday Stalinism. Ordinary Life in Extraordinary Times: Soviet Russia in the 1930s*, Oxford and New York, 1999.

Fitzpatrick, S. (editor), *Stalinism: New Directions*, London and New York, 2000.

Gaddis, John L., *The United States and the Origins of the Cold War, 1941–1947*, New York, 1972.

Galeotti, M., *The Age of Anxiety: Security and Politics in Soviet and Post-Soviet Russia*, London, 1995.

Gatrell, P., *The Tsarist Economy 1850–1917*, London, 1986.

Gatrell, P., 'Peasants and Politics', in *Modern History Review*, April 1995.

Gatrell, P., 'Russian Industrialists and Revolution', in Acton, Cherniaev and Rosenberg (editors), *Critical Companion to the Russian Revolution*.

Gershenkron, A., 'Agrarian Policies and Industrialization in Russia, 1861–1917', in *The Cambridge Economic History of Europe*, vol. 6, part 2, Cambridge, 1965.

Gershenkron, A., *Economic Backwardness in Historical Perspective: A Book of Essays*, New York, 1965.

Gerson, L.D., *The Secret Police in Lenin's Russia*, Philadelphia, 1976.

Getty, J.A., *Origins of the Great Purges: The Soviet Communist Party Reconsidered, 1933–1938*, New York, 1985.

Getty, J.A., *The Road to Terror: Stalin and the Self-Destruction of the Bolsheviks, 1932–39*, New Haven, Connecticut, 1999.

Getzler, I., *Kronstadt, 1917–1921: the Fate of a Soviet Democracy*, Cambridge, 1983.

Gide, A., *Back from the USSR*, London, 1937.

Gilbert, Martin, *Second World War*, London, 1995 edition.

Glantz, D. and House, J., *When Titans Clashed: How the Red Army Stopped Hitler*, Kansas, 1995.

Gleason, A., Kenez, P. and Stites, R. (editors), *Bolshevik Culture: Experiment and Order in the Russian Revolution*, Bloomington, Indiana, 1985.

Gorbachev, M., *Memoirs*, London, 1996.

Gorodetzsky, *Grand Delusion: Stalin and the German Invasion of Russia*, Yale, Connecticut, 1999.

Gromyko, A., *Memories*, London, 1989.

Hagenloh, P.M., ' "Socially harmful elements" and the Great Terror', in S. Fitzpatrick (editor), *Stalinism: New Directions*, London and New York, 2000.

Haimson, L.H., 'The Problem of Social Stability in Urban Russia, 1905–1917', in *Slavic Review*, No. 5, Columbus, Ohio, 1964.

Hanak, H., 'Foreign Policy', in Martin McCauley (editor), *Khrushchev and Khrushchevism*, London, 1987.

Harris, J.R., *The Great Urals: Regionalism and the Evolution of the Soviet System*, Ithaca, NY, 1999.

Harris, J.R., 'The purging of local cliques in the Urals region, 1936–7', in S. Fitzpatrick (editor), *Stalinism: New Directions*, London and New York, 2000.

Hasegawa, T., *The February Revolution: Petrograd, 1917*, Seattle, Washington, 1981.

Hasegawa, T., 'The February Revolution', in Acton, Cherniaev and Rosenberg (editors), *Critical Companion to the Russian Revolution*.

Haslam, Jonathan, *The Soviet Union and the Struggle for Collective Security in Europe, 1933–39*, London, 1984.

Heenan, L.C., *Russian Democracy's Fateful Blunder: The Summer Offensive of 1917*, New York, 1987.

Hellbeck, J., 'Fashioning the Stalinist Soul. The diary of Stepan Podlubnyi, 1931–9', in S. Fitzpatrick (editor), *Stalinism: New Directions*, London and New York, 2000.

Hill, C., *Lenin and the Russian Revolution*, London, 1947; this edition 1971.

Hoch, S.L., 'Malthus, population trends and peasant standard of living in late imperial Russia, in *Slavic Review*, Vol. 53, No. 1, Columbus, Ohio, 1994.

Holloway, D., *Stalin and the Bomb. The Soviet Union and Atomic Energy*, Yale, Connecticut, 1994.

Hosking, G.A., *The Russian Constitutional Experiment. Government and Duma, 1907–1914*, Cambridge, 1973.

Hough, J., *How the Soviet Union is Governed*, London, 1979.

Hughes, J., *Stalin, Siberia and the Crisis of the New Economic Policy*, Cambridge, 1991.

Hunter, H. 'The Overambitious First Soviet Five-Year Plan', *Slavic Review*, Vol. 32, No. 2, Columbus, Ohio, 1973.

Hunter, H., and Szyrmer, J.M., *Faulty Foundations. Soviet Economic Policies, 1928–1940*, Cambridge, 1994.

Hutchings, R.L., *Soviet–East European Relations: Consolidation and Conflict 1968–1980*, London, 1983.

Hyde, H.M., *Stalin: The History of a Dictator*, London, 1971.

Kampfner, J., *Inside Yeltsin's Russia*, London, 1994.

Katkov, G., *Russia, 1917: the February Revolution*, London, 1967.

Katkov, G., *The Kornilov Affair: Kerensky and the Break-up of the Russian Army*, London, 1980.

Kenez, P., *Cinema and Soviet Society, 1917–1953*, Cambridge, 1992.

Khrushchev, N., *Khrushchev Remembers*, New York and London, 1971.

Khrushchev, N., *Khrushchev Remembers. The Glasnost Tapes*, New York, 1990.

Knight, A., *Spies Without Cloaks: The KGB's Successors*, Princeton, New Jersey, 1996.

Kochan, L., *Russia in Revolution, 1890–1918*, London, 1966.

Koenker, Diane, *Moscow Workers and the 1917 Revolution*, Princeton, New Jersey, 1981.

Kotkin, S., *Magnetic Mountain. Stalinism as a Civilization*, Berkeley, California, 1995.

Kuromiya, H., *Stalin's Industrial Revolution: Politics and Workers, 1928–32*, Cambridge, 1988.

Leffler, M.P., *A Preponderance of Power: National Security, the Truman Administration and the Cold War*, Stanford, California, 1992.

Leffler, M.P., *The Spectre of Communism, the United States and the Origins of the Cold War*, New York, 1994.

Levin, N., *Paradox of Survival: The Jews of the Soviet Union since 1917*, London, 1990.

Lewin, M., *The Making of the Soviet System*, New York and London, 1985.

Lieven, D.C.B., *Russia and the Origins of the First World War*, London, 1983.

Lieven, D.C.B, *Nicholas II: Emperor of All the Russias*, London, 1993.

Lieven, D.C.B., 'The Aristocracy and the Gentry', in Acton, Cherniaev and Rosenberg (editors), *Critical Companion to the Russian Revolution*.

Lincoln, W.B., *Red Victory: A History of the Russian Civil War*, London, 1991.

Luxmore, J. and Babiuch, J., *The Vatican and the Red Flag. The Struggle for the Soul of Eastern Europe*, London and New York, 1999.

Malia, M., *The Soviet Tragedy: A History of Socialism in Russia, 1917–1991*, New York and London, 1994.

Malia, M., 'Revolution fulfilled. How the revisionists are still trying to take the ideology out of Stalinism'; review article in the *Times Literary Supplement*, 15 June 2001.

Mandel, D., *The Petrograd Workers and the Soviet Seizure of Power*, New York, 1984.

Martin, T., 'Modernization or neo-traditionalism? Ascribed nationality and Soviet primordialism', in S. Fitzpatrick (editor), *Stalinism: New Directions*, London and New York, 2000.

Massie, R.K., *The Romanovs: the Final Chapter*, London, 1995.

Mastny, V., *Russia's Road to the Cold War: Diplomacy, Warfare, and the Politics of Communism, 1941–1945*, New York, 1979.

Matlock, J.F., *Autopsy on an Empire: The American Ambassador's Account of the Collapse of the Soviet Union*, New York, 1995.

Mawdsley, E., *The Russian Civil War*, London, 1987.

McCauley, Alistair, 'Social Policy', in Martin McCauley, (editor), *Khrushchev and Khrushchevism*, London, 1987.

McCauley, Martin (editor), *Khrushchev and Khrushchevism*, London, 1987.

McCauley, Martin, *The Soviet Union 1917–1991*, London, second edition, 1993.

McCauley, Martin, *Stalin and Stalinism*, London, second edition, 1995.

McCauley, Martin, *The Origins of the Cold War, 1941–1949*, London, second edition, 1995.

McCauley, Martin, *Gorbachev*, London, 1998.

McCauley, Mary, *Bread and Justice: state and society in Petrograd, 1917–22*, Oxford, 1991.

McDonald, D.M., *United Government and Foreign Policy in Russia, 1900–1914*, Cambridge, 1992.

McNeal, S., *The Plots to Rescue the Tsar: The Truth behind the Disappearance of the Romanovs*, London, 2000.

Medvedev, R.A., *Let History Judge: The Origins and Consequences of Stalinism*, New York, second edition, 1989.

Medvedev, R.A., 'New Pages from the Political Biography of Stalin', in Robert C. Tucker (editor), *Stalinism: Essays in Historical Interpretation*, New Brunswick, New Jersey, second edition, 1999.

Medvedev, R.A., *Post-Soviet Russia. A Journey Through the Yeltsin Era*, New York, 2000.

Merridale, C., *Moscow Politics and the Rise of Stalin*, London, 1990.

Millar, J.R., 'Mass Collectivization and the Contribution of Soviet Agriculture to the First Five-Year Plan: A Review Article', in *Slavic Review*, December, 1974.

Nove, A., 'Industry', in M. McCauley (editor), *Khrushchev and Khrushchevism*, London, 1987.

Nove, A., *An Economic History of the USSR, 1917–1991*, London, third edition, 1992.

O'Connor, T.E., *The Politics of Soviet Culture*, London, 1983.

Overy, Richard, *Russia's War*, London, 1998.

Pethybridge, R., *Witnesses to the Russian Revolution*, London, 1964.

Pethybridge, R., *The Spread of the Russian Revolution. Essays on 1917*, London, 1972.

Pipes, R., *Russia under the Bolshevik Regime, 1919–1924*, London, 1993.

Pipes, R., *The Russian Revolution, 1899–1919*, London, 1997 edition.

Politkovskaya, A., *A Dirty War*, London and New York, 2001.

Pryce-Jones, D., *The War That Never Was. The Fall of the Soviet Empire, 1985–1991*, London, 1995.

Rabinowitch, A., *Prelude to Bolshevism: the Petrograd Bolsheviks and the July 1917 Uprising*, Bloomington, Indiana, 1968.

Radkey, O.H., *Russia Goes to the Polls: the Election to the Russian Constituent Assembly, 1917*, Ithaca, NY, second edition, 1989.

Radzinsky, E., *The Last Tsar: The Life and Death of Nicholas II*, London, 1992.

Radzinsky, E., *Stalin*, London, 1996.

Radzinsky, E., *Rasputin*, London, 2000.

Read, C., *From Tsar to Soviets: The Russian People and their Revolution, 1917–21*, London and New York, 1996.

Rees, E.A., 'The Primacy of Politics', in J. Channon (editor), *Politics, Society and Stalinism in the USSR*, London and New York, 1998.

Remnick, D., *Lenin's Tomb: The Last Days of the Soviet Empire*, New York and London, 1993.

Rigby, T.H., *Political Elites in the USSR: central leaders and local cadres from Lenin to Gorbachev*, London, 1990.

Rittersporn, G., *Stalinist Simplifications and Soviet Complications: Social Tensions and Political Conflicts in the USSR 1933–1953*, Harwood, Chur, Switzerland, 1991.

Roberts, G., *The Soviet Union and the Origins of the Second World War 1933–1941*, London, 1995.

Rosenberg, W.G., 'The Constitutional Democrat Party (Kadets)', in Acton, Cherniaev and Rosenberg (editors), *Critical Companion to the Russian Revolution*.

Roxburgh, *The Second Russian Revolution. The Struggle for Power in the Kremlin*, London, 1991.

Sakharov, A., *Memoirs*, New York and London, 1990.

Sakwa, R., *Gorbachev and his Reforms 1985–1990*, London, 1990.

Salisbury, Harrison E., *The 900 Days: The Siege of Leningrad*, London, 1969.

Schapiro, L., *The Origin of the Communist Autocracy*, London, second edition, 1977.

Scott, John, *Behind the Urals: An American Worker in Russia's City of Steel*, Bloomington, Indiana, 1973 edition.

Segal, G., 'Ending the Cold War', in D. Armstrong and E. Goldstein, *The End of the Cold War*, London and Portland, Oregon, 1990.

Serge, V., *Memoirs of a Revolutionary*, Paris, 1951; this edition, London and New York, 1984.

Service, R., *Lenin: A Political Life*, vol. 3, *The Iron Ring*, London, 1995.

Service, R., *A History of Twentieth Century Russia*, London, 1998 edition.

Service, R., *The Russian Revolution 1900–1927*, London and New York, third edition, 1999.

Service, R., 'Joseph Stalin: The Making of a Stalinist', in John Channon (editor), *Politics, Society and Stalinism in the USSR*, London and New York, 1998.

Service, R., *Lenin: A Biography*, London, 2000.

Shanin, T., *The Roots of Otherness: Russia's Turn of Century*, vol. 1 *Russia as a 'Developing Society'*, London, 1985; vol. 2. *Russia, 1905–7: Revolution as a Moment of Truth*, London, 1986.

Siegelbaum, L.H., 'Social Paternalism and Soviet Rural "Notables" in the mid-1930s', in S. Fitzpatrick (editor), *Stalinism: New Directions*, London and New York, 2000.

Simms, J.Y., 'The Crisis in Russian Agriculture at the End of the Nineteenth Century: A Different View', *Slavic Review*, vol. 36, Columbus, Ohio, 1977.

Simpson, J., *Despatches from the Barricades*, London, 1990.

Slezkine, Y., 'The Soviet Union as a communal apartment, or how a socialist state promoted ethnic particularism', in S. Fitzpatrick (editor), *Stalinism: New Directions*, London and New York, 2000.

Smith, G.A.E., 'Agriculture', in M. McCauley (editor), *Khrushchev and Khrushchevism*, London, 1987.

Smith, S.A., *Red Petrograd: Revolution in the Factories, 1917–1918*, Cambridge, 1983.

Smith, S.A., 'Factory Committees', in Acton, Cherniaev and Rosenberg (editors), *Critical Companion to the Russian Revolution*.

Steele, J., *Eternal Russia: Yeltsin, Gorbachev and the Mirage of Democracy*, London, 1994.

Steele, J., 'Mikhail Gorbachev: The Russian Revolutionary', in *The Guardian*, 18 August, 2001.

Stites, R., *Russian Popular Culture: Entertainment and Society since 1900*, Cambridge, 1992.

Stone, N., *The Eastern Front*, London, 1998 edition.

Suny, R.G., *The Revenge of the Past*, New York, 1993.

Suny, R.G., *The Soviet Experiment*, New York, 1998.

Taylor, R., 'Soviet Cinema – The Path to Stalin', in *History Today*, vol. 40, July, 1990.

Tolstoy, Nikolai, *Stalin's Secret War*, London, 1981.

Tompson, W.J., *Khrushchev: A Political Life*, London, 1995.

Trotsky, L., *The History of the Russian Revolution*, London, 1932–33, this edition 1977.

Trotsky, L., *Diary in Exile*, 1935; this edition London, 1959.

Tucker, R.C. (editor), *The Lenin Anthology*, New York and London, 1975.

Tucker, R.C., *Stalin in Power: The Revolution from Above 1929–1941*, New York, 1990.

Tucker, R.C., 'Stalinism as Revolution from Above', in Tucker, R.C. (editor), *Stalinism: Essays in Historical Interpretation*, New Brunswick, New Jersey, and London, second edition, 1999.

Ulam, A.B., *Lenin and the Bolsheviks*, New York and London, 1965.

Ulam, A.B., *Dangerous Relations: The Soviet Union in World Politics 1970–1982*, London, 1983.

Viola, L., *The Best Sons of the Fatherland. Workers in the Vanguard of Soviet Collectivization*, New York and Oxford, 1987.

Volkogonov, D., *Lenin: Life and Legend*, London, 1994.

Volkogonov, D., *The Rise and Fall of the Soviet Empire*, London, 1998.

Volkogonov, D., *Stalin: Triumph and Tragedy*, London, 2000 edition.

Volkov, V., 'The concept of *kul'turnost'*: notes on the Stalinist civilizing process', in S. Fitzpatrick (editor), *Stalinism: New Directions*, London and New York, 2000.

Waldron, P., *The End of Imperial Russia, 1855–1917*, London, 1997.

Walker, M., *Martin Walker's Russia: Dispatches from the Guardian Correspondent in Moscow*, London, 1989.

Watt, D.C., *How War Came: The immediate origins of the Second World War 1938–1939*, London, 1989.

Westwood, J.N., *Russia against Japan*, London, 1986.

Westwood, J.N., *Endurance and Endeavour. Russian History 1812–1992*, fourth edition, London and New York, 1993.

White, S., *After Gorbachev*, Cambridge, fourth edition, 1994.

Wildman, A.H., *The End of the Russian Imperial Army*, 2 vols, Princeton, New Jersey, 1980 and 1987.

Wildman, A.H., 'The Breakdown of the Imperial Army in 1917', in Acton, Cherniaev and Rosenberg (editors), *Critical Companion to the Russian Revolution*.

Williams, W.A., *The Tragedy of American Diplomacy*, New York, revised edition, 1962.

Wilson, E., *Shostakovich, A Life Remembered*, Princeton, New Jersey, 1994.

Yeltsin, B., *The View from the Kremlin*, London, 1994.

Yeltsin, B., *Midnight Diaries*, London, 2000.

■ ⩔ Index

Berlin   xxviii, 26, 164, 344, 363
  Congress of (1878)   xviii, 69, 72
  Treaty of (1926)   270
  Red Army capture of (1945)   xxv, 268
  blockade and airlift (1948–49)   xxvi, 328
  Wall   xxvii, xxx, 364–5, 415
  1971 agreement on   389–90
Bessarabia   281, 292
Black Hundreds   50, 140
blat   xiv, 247
Blok, Alexander   23, 176
Bloody Sunday (1905)   32–3, 55–7
Bolshevik Party (later known as the Communist
    Party)   xiv, xx, 1, 3, 4–8, 30–1, 34, 36, 45,
    50, 51, 52, 53–4, 75
  and the 1917 revolutions   83–5, 92–4,
    96–114, 115
  in power   see Communist Party of the
    Soviet Union
Bosnia   62, 70–2, 74
bourgeois, bourgeoisie   27–8, 101, 105–6,
    139–40, 157, 175–6, 181, 230–1, 251
Brandt, Willy   389
Brest–Litovsk, Treaty of (1918)   xx, 120,
    135–6, 137
Brezhnev, Leonid   xxvii, xxix, 3, 351, 369,
    372, 377–95, 410, 443
  rise to power   377, 378–9
  economic policies   379–82
  and eastern Europe   377–9, 387–9
  Doctrine   xxviii, 377, 388, 396
  foreign policies   xxviii, 378, 389–92
  and the 1977 Constitution   382–3
  assessments of   393–5
Britain   xix, 62, 270
  relations with Tsarist Russia   65, 69–70
  intervention in Russian civil war   121, 142–3
  Soviet relations with   165–6, 267–77, 283–5,
    320, 328
  during World War II   268, 281, 304–6,
    309, 317
Brown, Archie   385, 413, 417, 420–1, 429,
    436, 441
Brusilov, General Alexei   xix, 63, 76–7, 78,
    99, 115
Bukharin, Nikolai   xxii, 124, 133–4, 154,
    167, 195, 198, 230, 241, 251, 441
  attacks Trotsky   198
  supports NEP   158, 160–1, 200
  opposes Stalin   201–2, 206–7, 209
  his decline and fall   xxiv, 235, 237, 261–2
Bukovina   281
Bulgakov, Mikhail   252–3, 359
Bulganin, Nikolai   241, 332, 344–6, 350–2, 362
Bulgaria   72–3, 269, 321–2, 326, 412, 416
bureaucracy   170, 172–4, 242–3, 371–2,
    379, 383, 393–4, 404, 406–7, 417–18,
    424, 443–4, 455
Bush, George   401, 411

cannibalism   217, 301
capitalists, capitalism   27–9, 101, 131, 159–61,
    181, 222, 316–17, 458, 475
Carr, E.H.   6, 83
Carter, Jimmy   xxviii, 391
Castro, Fidel   365

Caucasus   121, 208, 216, 256, 296
Ceausescu, Nicolae   416
Chagall, Marc   177
Chalidze, Valeri   xxviii, 386
'Charter 77'   377, 388, 416
Chechnya, Chechens   xxv, xxxi, xxxii, 20, 166,
    291, 332, 454, 464–6, 472, 476
Cheka (secret police)   xiv, 120, 125–6, 130, 137,
    139, 148, 155, 157, 174, 176, 185, 199
Chekhov, Anton   23
Chelyabinsk   294
Chernenko, Konstantin   xxix, 378, 393, 395–6
Chernobyl – nuclear accident   xxix, 406,
    410, 448
Chernomyrdin, Viktor   xxxi, 453, 457, 463–4,
    466, 469
Chernov, Viktor   26, 96, 99, 120, 126–8
Chernyaev, Anatoly   404
Chernyshevsky, Nikolai   25, 29
Chiang Kai-shek   xxii, 205, 270, 328
Chicherin, Georgi   165, 205, 270
Chile   390
China   xxx, 267
  and Russia before the revolution   67–9
  relations with the USSR   xxvii, xxviii, xxx, 205,
    270–2, 328, 342, 367–9, 389, 391–2, 412
  communist victory in   xxvi, 328
  and war in Korea   329
  economic reforms in   442, 443–4
Chubais, Anatoly   456, 459, 463, 467, 469
Chuikov, General Vassily   297, 306
Church, Russian Orthodox   see Orthodox
    Church, Russian
Churchill, Sir Winston   xxv, 283, 285, 321–2,
    339–40
Civil War   1, 3, 120–1, 141–54, 187–90
  causes of   120, 141–5
  events in   xx–xxi, 120–1, 145–8
  reasons for communist victory in   148–51
  effects of   151–4, 170
class divisions and conflict   4–5, 11, 12,
    27–8, 139–40, 374, 410
Cold War   4, 268, 312, 316–29
  responsibility for   316–20
  events during   321–9, 391–2
  'thaw' in   362, 389–90
  end of   409–12, 413, 437, 439
collective farms (kolkhozy)   149, 204, 207–13,
    263, 352–3, 377, 381, 456
collective security   xxii, 267, 272–8
collectivization   xxi, 3, 185, 193, 207–18,
    251, 256, 258
  introduction of   207–14
  results of   214–18, 331–2, 352
Comecon (Council for Mutual Economic
    Assistance)   xiv, 328, 423
Cominform   xiv, xxv, xxvi, 326
Comintern (Communist International)   xiv,
    xxi, xxiii, xxiv, 123, 146, 164–5, 195, 267,
    269, 271–4
'command economy'   4, 221, 381, 429
commissars   xiv, 119
committees of village poor   see kombedy
Commonwealth of Independent States
    (CIS)   xxx, 403, 437
communes   see mir

Communist International *see* Comintern
Communist Party of the Russian
Federation 459, 462–4, 466
Communist Party of the Soviet Union
early reforms after October 1917 119
and Constituent Assembly elections 120,
126–8
wins the Civil War 3, 141–51
and treatment of nationalities 147–8,
166–9
political structure of 169–70
and foreign affairs 164–6, 269–82
and culture 174–80
purged by Stalin 185, 230–41
totalitarianism and the 1936
Constitution 241–4
and World War II 307–8
under Khrushchev 345–6, 351, 358–9,
361, 369–73
and the missed opportunity of 1968
(Czechoslovakia) 388
and the 1977 Constitution 382–3
stagnates under Brezhnev 392–5
Gorbachev's attempts to reform 401–2,
406–8, 418–19, 421–2, 433
faces challenges 419–21, 439
and the *coup* of August 1991 434–6
dissolution of 436–7
assessments of 438–9, 441–6
Congress of People's Deputies xxx, 401,
407–8, 419, 423, 427, 430–1, 436
Congress of the Russian Federation 453,
455, 459–63
Conquest, Robert 185, 217, 232–3, 235,
240, 242
Constituent Assembly xx, 92, 116, 119,
155, 185–6
elections to 95, 99–100, 105, 108, 120,
126–7
closure and dismissal of 109, 120, 127–8
Constitutional Democratic Party *see* Kadets
constitutions
1918 169–70
1922 xxi, 170–4
1936 xxiii, 194, 241–2, 257
1977 xxviii, 372, 382–3
1993 453, 460–1
consumer goods 225–6, 312, 345, 357,
363, 384, 420
corruption and criminality 244, 246–7, 393,
395, 457–8, 464, 465, 471, 473, 476
Cossacks xxv, 141, 149, 312
Council of People's Commissars *see*
Sovnarkom
Crimea xxv, 147, 150, 291, 295, 332
Crimean War (1854–56) xviii, 22, 69, 70
Cuba 374
missiles crisis 3, 342, 365–7, 374
Cultural Revolution xxii–xxiii, 251–8
culture
before the revolution 18, 23–4
under Lenin 174–9, 190
repressive attitude of Stalin towards 244–58,
313–14
under Khrushchev 358–61
under Brezhnev 385–7

Curzon Line 147–8
Czechoslovak Legion xx, 143–6
Czechoslovakia 270, 410
Soviet treaty with (1935) 273
occupied by Nazis 276–7, 285
after World War II xxv, 269, 326
Warsaw Pact invasion of (1968) xxviii, 377,
379, 385–6, 387–8
collapse of communism in xxx, 416

Dagestan 166, 174
Daniel, Yuli 385
Danilov, Viktor 385
Dardanelles 65, 69, 72, 78
Dawes Plan (1924) 270
de Gaulle, Charles 364
Decembrists 24
dekulakization xiv, 209–14
democratic centralism 158–9
democratization 401, 407, 418–19
Deng Xiaoping 444
Denikin, General Anton xxi, 141, 143–7,
149–50
deportations xxv, 240, 256, 281, 291, 304,
311, 332, 426
de-Stalinization xxvi, 331, 342,
346–8, 385
détente 368, 378, 383, 389–92, 397, 404
Deutscher, Isaac 5, 197, 208, 236
Diaghilev, Sergei 23–4
dictatorship of the proletariat 28, 31,
120, 124, 164, 170, 181, 184, 361
Dimitrov, Georgi 273
dissent, dissidents 385–7, 407
Djilas, Milovan 327, 338–9
Dnieper Dam 220
Doctor Zhivago xxvii, 252, 359
Doctors' Plot (1952) xxvi, 316
Don region 157
Donbass 42
Dostoevsky, Fedor 23, 359
Dubcek, Alexander 387–8, 416
Dudaev, Jokhar 464–5
Dudintsev, Vladimir 359
Dukes, Paul 7
Duma xiv, xviii–xix, xxxi, 6, 11, 36,
38, 44–9, 53, 57–9, 74, 75
during World War I 76, 80, 82, 86–90
from 1993 453, 462–3, 465–6
Durnovo, P.N. 74
Dzerzhinsky, Felix 125, 137, 199

East Berlin xxvi, 363, 364–5
East Germany *see* German Democratic
Republic
Eastern Europe 269, 317–28, 348–50, 368,
377, 387–9, 401, 408, 412–17
Eastern Question 70–4
Economists 29
education 125, 175, 190, 225, 247, 249–50,
355, 358, 384, 445
Ehrenburg, Ilya 335, 359
Eisenhower, Dwight D. xxvi, xxvii,
362–4
Eisenstein, Sergei 107, 178, 256, 310
Ekaterinodar 141

Nicholas II, Tsar   xviii–xix, 1, 4, 10, 41
  ideas and policies   50–1, 68
  and 1905 revolution   11, 32–7
  and the Dumas   44–9, 53, 59
  growing unpopularity of   53–4
  and outbreak of World War I   74
  during World War I   63, 75–7, 87–8, 90
  and February 1917 revolution   79–83, 85
  abdicates   1, 64, 83
  death   140–1
  assessment   53–4, 85
Nihilists   24
Nixon, Richard   xxviii, 390
NKVD (People's Commissariat of Internal
  Affairs)   234–5, 238–9, 281, 291–2, 332, 344
nobility   13–17, 22, 80, 83, 234
nomenklatura   393–5, 424, 430, 459, 473, 475
Novaya Zhizn (New Life)(Gorky's
  newspaper)   106, 136
Nove, Alec   40, 43, 149, 152, 154, 220, 222,
  227, 313, 355, 357, 371, 445
Novocherkassk   xxvii, 141, 361
Novotny, Antonin   387
Novy Mir (New World)   xv, 359, 385–6, 446
nuclear accidents   xxix, 406
nuclear weapons, development and build-up
  of   xxvi, 312, 314, 319, 329, 362–3, 365–7,
  390–1, 409–10

October (Eisenstein's film)   107, 178, 256
October Manifesto (1905)   xviii, 11, 32, 36
October Revolution (1917)   see
  revolutionaries and revolutions
Octobrists   xv, 17, 36, 37, 45–6, 47, 48, 60, 76
Oder–Neisse Line   317, 321–2
Odessa   36, 50, 282, 292
OGPU   xv, 174
oil   42, 227, 356, 381, 423, 454, 457, 469–70
Okhrana   xv, 12, 16, 32, 49
Order Number One (Soviet)   95, 114–15
Ordzhonikidze, Sergo   xxii, xxiii, 168, 172,
  231–2, 236, 247
Orel   146, 150
Orthodox Church, Russian   20, 21, 23,
  179–80, 189–90, 250–1, 308, 360, 464
Osetins   425
Overy, Richard   305, 307

Pakistan   411
Panslav movement   71–2
Paris, Treaty of (1856)   70
Paris Summit (1960)   363–4, 374
partisans, during World War II   288, 290, 293–5
Pasternak, Boris   xxvii, 252, 359–60
Paulus, Field Marshal von   297–9
peaceful co-existence   361–2, 367, 372, 397
peasants   6, 119–20, 181, 310
  before World War I   19–20, 25–7, 34, 35,
    38–42, 50, 51
  and 1917 revolutions   97, 98–100, 102,
    105, 108, 110–13
  and communist land policies   128–30,
    142, 155
  during Civil War   149–50
  and NEP   158–63, 190, 200–1, 203–4
  and forced collectivization   193, 207–18, 222

after World War II   311, 313, 345
  under Khrushchev   352–3, 357–8, 371
  under Gorbachev   405
Peking   see Beijing
People's Will (political party)   xviii, 26
perestroika (restructuring)   xv, xxix, 3, 370,
  401, 403, 404–5, 417–20, 440–1
'permanent revolution'   164, 199
Persia (see also Iran)   69–70
Petliura, Simon   167
Petrograd   6, 63, 81–5, 89–90, 92–7, 98–115,
  116–17, 132, 133–4, 147, 151, 155, 176–7,
  187–8
  Soviet   xviii–xix, 6, 63, 82, 84, 92–6, 98–114,
    116–17, 137
  becomes Leningrad   182
Pilsudski, Marshal Josef   53, 271
Pipes, Richard   7–8, 45, 50, 85, 96–7, 104,
  109–10, 139, 184
Platform of the Forty-Six   197
Plekhanov, Georgi   28–9, 30, 127, 183
Pobedonostsev, Konstantin   13
Podgorny, Nikolai   369, 378
Podlubnyi, Stepan   214, 217
Poland, Poles   xix, 125, 133, 135, 166, 256,
  268, 270, 278–80
  before World War I   20, 36, 42, 52–3, 59
  during World War I   63
  war with Russia in 1920   xxi, 122, 147–8, 164
  during World War II   xxv, 279–80, 303–5
  after World War II   xxvi, xxviii–xxix,
    269, 311, 321–2, 326, 342, 348, 377–8
    388–9, 406
  end of communism in (1989)   xxx, 389, 408,
    414
Politburo   xv, 169–71, 172–4, 182, 189, 198–9,
  200–2, 231, 234, 242, 312, 378, 383, 386,
  393, 394, 396, 411, 418
pollution   229, 384, 407, 448
Poltava   34
Popular Front   274
population   10, 13, 20, 37–8, 78, 218,
  224–5, 245, 382, 384
Populists   25–6, 28
Port Arthur   35, 67
Portsmouth, Treaty of (1906)   36, 69
Potemkin (battleship)   xviii, 36
Potresov, Alexander   183
Potsdam Conference (1945)   xxv, 268, 322
Prague Spring (1968)   xxviii, 387–8, 416
Pravda (Truth) newspaper   xv, 52, 101,
  102, 196, 202, 211, 214, 226, 236, 254,
  346, 370, 396, 406
Presidium   xv, 170, 242, 344–5, 350–1,
  369–70, 378
Primakov, Yevgeny   xxxi, 433, 454, 466,
  470–1, 472
privatization   418, 429, 453, 455–9, 464, 473
procurements   see grain
Progressive Bloc (1915)   76, 80, 83, 92
Prokofiev, Sergei   24, 175, 254, 256, 314
Provisional Government (1917)   1, 4, 6,
  17, 64, 83, 92–117, 136–7
  rivalry with Petrograd Soviet   94–105
  overthrow of   106–8
Pskov   64, 82, 107, 246

socialist realism   194, 245, 251–6, 359
Socialist Revolutionaries (SRs)   xx, 84, 92, 95–6,
    101–2, 104–5, 112, 115, 119–20, 143, 155, 169
  early history of   26–7, 34, 36
  and the Dumas   45, 47
  relations with Lenin and the Bolsheviks   105,
    106, 124–5, 135–8
  Left   96, 97, 102, 119–20, 124–5, 126, 135–6,
    142, 155
  Right   96, 106, 112, 126, 135, 186
  and Constituent Assembly election   120,
    126–8
  repression and purges of   120, 138, 157
Solidarity movement (Poland)   xxviii–xxix,
    378, 389, 414
Solzhenitsyn, Alexander   xxviii, 360, 377, 385–7
Sorge, Richard   283, 294
South Korean airliner shot down (1983)   395,
    398–9
Soviets of Workers' and Soldiers' Deputies   27,
    36, 57, 101–2, 103–14, 128, 131, 142, 156,
    169–70, 186–7, 191
  become Soviets of People's Deputies
    (1977)   382
  democratization of   407
sovkhozy   see state collective farms
sovnarkhozy (regional economic councils)   xvi,
    355, 357, 379
Sovnarkom   xvi, xx, 119–20, 125–6, 128, 169,
    172, 242
Soyuz (Union)   431
space programme   356, 363
Spanish Civil War (1936–39)   xxiii, 275–6, 288
Spiridonova, Maria   96, 142
Sputnik   xxvii, 356, 363, 372
spy planes   see U2 spy planes
Stakhanov, Alexei, and Stakhanovites   xxiii,
    225–6
Stalin, Josef   xxi–xxvi, 3, 5–8, 78, 119, 146,
    166, 182, 343, 360, 367, 369, 372, 385,
    410, 419, 441, 463, 468
  background and early career   195
  and the nationalities   166–9, 170–4, 256–8
  relations with Lenin   123, 170
  relations with Trotsky   148, 199, 258
  and the power struggle after Lenin's
    death   193, 195–203
  gets to supreme power   202–3
  abandons NEP   201–2, 203–7
  and the Five-Year Plans   218–30, 312
  and collectivization   207–18, 251, 256, 258,
    331–2
  foreign policy under   267–8, 269–82
  introduces the purges and the Great
    Terror   230–41, 386
  and totalitarianism   242–4
  and cultural policies   175, 244–56
  relations with Nazi Germany   267–8, 274–9
  unprepared for German invasion   268,
    282–9, 331
  during World War II   268, 289–310, 335–7
  meetings with Allied war leaders   321–2
  repressive policies after World War II   269,
    311–16
  and the Cold War   268, 316–29, 339–40
  relations with Eastern Europe   269, 317–28

  death of   193, 316, 329
  assessment   185, 227–30, 329–33, 336–9, 447
  compared with Lenin   184–6, 333
  denounced by Khrushchev at 20th Party
    Congress   330, 342, 346
Stalingrad (Tsaritsyn)   220, 223
  during World War II   xxiv, 268, 295–9, 311
Stanislavsky, Stanislas   23, 176, 179
'Star Wars'   see Strategic Defence Initiative
state, meant to wither away under
    communism   131, 142, 169, 181–2, 331, 361
state capitalism   131
state collective farms (sovkhozy)   204, 207, 262,
    352–3
state economic ownership   119–20, 149–50,
    152–4, 159, 206–7, 215, 463
State Enterprises, Law on (1988)   408–9, 423
Stavropol   403
Stepashin, Sergei   xxxi–xxxii, 471
Stolypin, Petr   xviii, 11, 17, 38–9, 46–7, 49, 51,
    53, 57
Stone, Norman   78–9, 100
Strategic Arms Limitation Treaties (SALT I
    and SALT II)   xxviii, 378, 390–1, 399
Strategic Defence Initiative (Star Wars)   xxix,
    395, 405, 409–10
Stravinsky, Igor   24, 178
strikes   xix, xxx, xxxi, 18–19, 29, 33–7, 44,
    51–2, 54, 60, 78, 79, 81–5, 112, 125,
    155–7, 223–4, 361, 420, 469, 477
Struve, Petr   32
Sukhanov, Nikolai   195
Suny, Ronald Grigor   179, 185–6, 203, 459, 464
Supreme Council of the National Economy
    (VSNKh)   xvi, 131, 153–4
Supreme Soviet   241–2, 382, 407, 419, 453
  of the Russian Federation   453, 455–7, 459–63
Suvorov, Viktor   287
Sverdlovsk (Yekaterinburg)   294, 454

Tadjikistan   20, 166, 168, 241, 384, 424, 428
Taliban   412
Tallinn   427, 432
Tambov   113, 157, 189
Tannenberg, Battle of (1914)   63, 75
Tatars   xxv, 20, 168, 174, 260, 291, 332
Tatlin, Vladimir   177
Taylor, F.W., and Taylorism   131, 220
Tbilisi   xxx, 347, 425
Tchaikovsky, Peter   178
Teheran Conference (1943)   xxv
terror and violence, drift towards
    under Lenin   136–41
Thatcher, Margaret   401, 412
Tiananmen Square   412, 415, 444
Tikhon, Patriarch   250
Timoshenko, Marshal S.K.   280
Tito, Josep Broz   326–7, 348, 349, 375
Tkachev, Petr   25, 30
Tobolsk   102
Tolstoy, Count Leo   23
Tomsk   238
Tomsky, Mikhail   202, 207, 235
totalitarianism   242–4, 437, 450
trade unions   18, 29, 36, 49, 50, 52, 84, 101,
    111, 120, 155–6, 158, 223, 355, 407